Disability is Natural

Revolutionary Common Sense for Raising Successful Children with Disabilities

Kathie Snow

BraveHeart Press
Woodland Park, Colorado

Disability is Natural
Revolutionary Common Sense for Raising Successful Children with Disabilities
By Kathie Snow

Library of Congress Card Number: 00-193464
Snow, Kathie
    Disability is natural: Revolutionary common sense for raising successful children with disabilities / Kathie Snow
    Includes bibliography and index.
    1. Parenting. 2. Disability - Social Policies 3. Child care

    ISBN Number 0-9707636-5-4 : $26.95

First Printing March, 2001

Published by:
BraveHeart Press
P. O. Box 7245
Woodland Park, CO 80863-7245 U.S.A.
1-866-948-2222, 1-719-687-0735
www.disabilityisnatural.com

Logo and cover designed by Kathie Snow.
Logo polished by Ken Keegan.

For each child with a disability living today,
and for those not yet born:
may you live the life of your dreams,
for your disability is irrelevant.

THERE IS ONE THING STRONGER THAN ALL THE ARMIES IN THE WORLD,
AND THAT IS AN IDEA WHOSE TIME HAS COME.
Victor Hugo

Disability is Natural

"What do apples have to do with disability?" my son asked when I showed him the logo on the cover of the book. It's a question you might be wondering about, too.

There have always been people with disabilities in the world and there always will be. Disability, along with gender, ethnicity, age, and other traits, is simply one natural characteristic of being human. This principle is embodied in at least two different federal laws. It's an idea whose time has come.

Disability is natural. An individual with a disability is a person, first and foremost, and is more *like* people without disabilities than he is different.

Apples are natural; they come in different sizes and different colors. A green apple is more like red apples than different.

On the cover, five apples are nestled in a bowl; one of the five is green. The sun's rays touch them all equally. In our society, twenty percent of the population—one in five—are individuals with disabilities. And if you use your imagination as you view the symbolic image, can you see that the "is" on the bowl could look almost like a "1" and a "5" (as in one in five)?

CONTENTS

1 Good News! 9

THE WAY THINGS WERE

2 Our History: Out of the Shadows and Into the Light 17

THE WAY THINGS ARE

3 The Medical Model and the Genesis of Grief 47
4 Labels and Attitudes 65
5 Multitudes of Myths 81
6 The Errors of Conventional Wisdom 103
7 Special Education Isn't So Special 133
8 Services for Young Children: Help or Hindrance? 163
9 Therapy: Beneficial Remedy or Toxic Antidote? 193

THE WAY THINGS CAN BE

10 A New Paradigm 219
11 People First Language 233
12 Transformation 267
13 Self-Determination 293
14 Tools for Success: Meeting Needs and More 315
15 Natural Lives in Community 389
16 The Early Years 435
17 Inclusive Education: Blueprint for Success 451
18 Homeschooling, Unschooling, Alternative Education 519
19 Bright Futures for Teens and Young Adults 531
20 Promoting Positive Images 555
21 Leadership and Influence 577

Afterword 605
References and Bibliography 607
Appendix 609
Index 629

Cautious, careful people,
always casting about to
preserve their reputation
and social standing,
never can bring about a reform.

Those who are really in earnest
must be willing to be anything
or nothing in the world's estimation,
and publicly and privately
in season and out,
avow their sympathies with
despised and persecuted ideas
and their advocates,
and bear the consequences.

Susan B. Anthony

Good News!

COMMON SENSE IS VERY UNCOMMON.
Horace Greeley

Disability is a natural condition. Children with disabilities are more like children without disabilities than different. These two facts, in combination, create the good news that children with disabilities—including your child—can enjoy successful, natural lives.

The second piece of good news is that for this to happen, you don't need to change the system—to get more supports, better services, and such—and you don't need to change your child, through therapies and interventions. You'll simply need to change the way you see your child, and then change the way you've been doing some things.

Many of the suggestions I'll share with you have been shared with thousands of parents across the country, during workshops I've presented in dozens of states. And the suggestions work. I know, because they've worked in our family's life. More importantly, they're working for parents who have attended my workshops.

The philosophies, principles, and ideas in this book are considered revolutionary by some, but they're really common sense—the common sense many parents have lost during the years they've been at the mercy of the service system. The ideas on the pages that follow are revolutionary simply because they go against the conventional wisdom about children and adults with disabilities.

The premise upon which this book is built—that disability is natural—may be considered a radical principle, but it, too, is common sense. How can disability *not* be natural? People with disabilities have been in the world since the beginning of time, and will be until the end of time. Disability is so natural and common, in fact, that it doesn't leave anyone out: it touches people of all ages, races, religions, and socioeconomic groups. Disability does not discriminate! Furthermore, the concept that "disability is a natural part of the human condition" has been in at least two federal laws for a number of years. It's just that few people have actively and publicly promoted the concept until now.

When professionals have heard my message, some have called it "unrealistic." (Most of us know we're on the right track when professionals tell us that.) Adults with developmental disabilities—the real experts—have called it "the truth," and asked, "Why isn't anyone else spreading the news?" I don't know the answer to that question, but I hope you'll begin spreading the good news, too.

After my son, Benjamin, was diagnosed with cerebral palsy at the tender age of four months, our family woke up in Disability World. We entered the Service System after getting his Passport to Services (his label) from the professional Gatekeepers. We hopped (or were pushed—it was a little disorienting, as I recall) on the roller coaster ride of early intervention, alternately flying high and dipping low. The merry-go-round of therapies kept us going in circles; we couldn't seem to get off since it never slowed down. We were occasionally battered and bruised while making our way through the maze of services, programs, and entitlements. It was a crowded place, with lots of other families trying to find their way. And a variety of Gatekeepers were responsible for keeping us in orderly lines and making sure we followed all the rules.

I spent the first three years of Benjamin's life wondering when things would "get back to normal." Then one day the sobering realization hit: this *was* normal, for our family. In my head, I reluctantly accepted the facts of life in Disability World. But in my heart, I resisted, believing this wasn't where our family belonged.

Then two things happened over the next few years that confirmed my intuition was correct. We began our journey back to the real world, eventually leaving the world of services and systems behind. Entering Disability World had taken only an instant: the moment when my son was given his label. It took a little longer to leave it—three years. As Mark Twain once said, "It's easier to stay out than to get out."

The first event that put us on the path away from Disability World was my participation in a leadership development program for parents of children with disabilities and adults with disabilities—Partners in Policymaking—sponsored by the Texas Council for Developmental Disabilities. The intense training validated my heart's desires: that my son *could* have the same kind of life we wanted for our daughter—a normal life.

This was in stark contrast to the lessons I was learning from professionals in the system. I was told how "needy" my son was, but therapies would help "fix his problems" and interventions would "get him ready." Learned experts advised me to be "realistic" about my son's future. The professionals were doing their jobs, and trying to be helpful, but their messages and assistance intensified my frustration, fear, and confusion. Our lives were not our own; our daily activities revolved around services. My son's future seemed cloudy.

The Partners training was life-changing, and it put me on a course to take our family's life back. I learned state-of-the-art practices from experienced trainers. And listening to the wisdom of many of my classmates—adults with developmental disabilities—taught me what was really important. I soon realized the original dreams I had for Benjamin *were* realistic. The immediate result of my newly-acquired knowledge was our decision to turn down a special ed preschool placement for three-year-old Benj. Instead, he went to a church preschool two mornings a week, just like other children his age.

The second event that led us out of Disability World once and for all didn't occur for three more years (I was a slow learner back then). It also involved heeding the wisdom of a person with a disability: my six-year-old son. Benjamin tearfully and angrily told me he didn't want to go to physical and occupational therapy anymore. He told me many times, but I didn't listen. Then one day he said, "I don't want to go anymore—I just want to be a regular kid!" I heard him—finally—and on that day, we were set free.

Contrary to the dire predictions of professionals, the sky didn't fall when we said no to special ed preschool, and then no to therapy. In fact, just the opposite happened: Benjamin (and our family) thrived. Along the way, I regained the common sense I had lost in the jungle of professional jargon, expert opinions, conventional wisdom, and intrusive interventions. Our lives were once again our own. We were back to living normal, natural lives. We left clienthood behind and rejoined our community as citizens. Your child and your family can do the same. And you can begin dreaming for your child again.

This is not like any other book written for parents of children with disabilities. It's not about learning more about your child's specific condition, how to get more services, dealing with the grief process, or anything else about your child's "problems." As you'll see, the problem isn't your child's disability at all; the problem is how disability is perceived.

The current practices in Disability World—early intervention, early childhood education, therapies, special education, vocational-rehabilitation, and other programs—aren't working. Our children are not getting what they really need. They're isolated and undereducated in public schools and excluded from community activities. And their futures are uncertain, considering the unemployment rate for adults with developmental disabilities continually hovers around 75 percent.

Many of us recognize flaws in the disability service system, so we work to change it, by trying to get more services, more funding for programs, and more laws. But we have more of these things than at any other time in history, and our children are *still* excluded and marginalized. The solution is not "more," but "different"—if we think differently and act differently, we will get different results.

I mentioned that my Partners training was a life-changing experience. But it did more than teach me state-of-the-art practices in disability issues. As a result of my participation in Partners—and quite by accident—I became a public speaker and trainer in disability issues. After I graduated from Partners in 1991, our family moved to Colorado. The Texas Partners coordinator invited me to return to Texas and do a presentation for the next class of Partners. The topic of my presentation was the use of People First Language. Every Partners graduate was required to complete a project within six months of graduation. I had chosen to write an article about People First Language and disseminate it to the general public, the media, and organizations serving people with disabilities. The Partners coordinator thought it was valuable information that should be shared with the thirty-five parents and people with disabilities in the second year's class of Texas Partners. I was nervous about speaking before a group, but I was passionate about the topic. Speaking from the heart is far easier than "giving a lecture."

At the last minute, the coordinator informed me the speaker who was scheduled to present the history of the Parent Movement would not be able to attend. She wondered if I could deliver that presentation, too, if the original speaker shared her information with me. On a wing and a prayer, I agreed. The rest, as they say, is history.

Partners coordinators around the country network with one another (over 40 states have Partners programs), and before long, several invited me to present to their classes.

Over time, I expanded the number of topics I presented, adding history of disabilities, special education and inclusion, community inclusion, and more. Invitations to present at state and national disability conferences followed. And while I've been labeled a "trainer," I'm also a student, learning from the thousands of parents and people with disabilities I've met at trainings and conferences. The genesis of this book was born from these relationships and experiences.

This is not a scholarly manual, with hundreds of citations from research papers and professional studies. Except for the chapter on history, it's a collection of stories about real people and their experiences. Many are from my family's life. Others are from parents and people with disabilities I've met during the past ten years. We can learn so much from one another, about what's working and what's not. None of us need to struggle so much—we can benefit from the experiences of others. Some of the stories you'll read are composites, for the same things are happening to parents in small towns and big cities, regardless of what disabilities their children have. Others stories represent the specific details one family or one individual experienced. In general, I've used pseudonyms to protect people's privacy.

Woven throughout are critical commentaries of today's conventional wisdom and the service system it spawned. Special education, therapies, services for young children, vocational-rehabilitation, respite, and other assistance are examined. I propose that not only is the service system not working, but it's also harmful to our children and families for a variety of reasons that are thoroughly detailed.

When I've presented this information at workshops, some of it angers parents. I tread on the hallowed ground of programs and services that parents have fought hard to get. And some parents are both surprised and horrified that I don't support the notion that we should all be clamoring to get every service our children are "entitled" to. I *could* support today's programs and services if they were the best we could do for our children—if they presented positive images of our children; if they promoted inclusion, participation, and contribution in all areas of life; and if they significantly improved the lives of our children and our families. But they don't do any of these things.

Children with disabilities are diagnosed, labeled, and then whisked into one set of services or another. In general, these services remove children from the natural environments of childhood to segregated settings, where experts work on their bodies and brains, to the detriment of their hearts and souls. Interventions and treatments to "help children reach their full potential" are provided and, in the process, our children are dehumanized, reduced to defective body parts. They're known more by their labels than their names.

Segregated preschools and segregated public school classrooms isolate children from the time they're tiny three-year-olds until young adulthood. Along the way, programs and treatments for children lay waste to families. The natural lives and activities of family members become subservient to the schedule of services. Moms and dads, following the expert advice provided by doctors, therapists, and other professionals, shuttle their children with disabilities to and from therapies and other services, while trying to remain active in the lives of their other children. Families become fractured while being "helped" by the system.

The experiences of the majority of parents I've met are similar to mine when my son was young: we enter Disability World and promptly lose our common sense. It's replaced by the conventional wisdom of the service system, which we learn from experts in the field.

Arriving in Disability World, our reality changes and we begin living unnatural lives. This book can change all that.

We'll start by reviewing the history of people with disabilities. Confucius said, "Study the past if you would divine the future." Where we've been will show us how we got to where we are today, and give us a glimpse of where we may be going. Chapters 3 thru 9 will examine today's conventional wisdom and the services most of us are familiar with. I'll present a variety of critical perspectives that may be unfamiliar to many parents. These perspectives detail the problems in the system, but they're not the problems we usually associate with the system: low funding, poor services, and so forth. Instead, they're the problems the system inflicts on children with disabilities and their families: segregation, isolation, exclusion, and other negative outcomes.

In the second half of the book, I'll follow my own advice, which is: never complain about a problem unless you already have a solution. Beginning with Chapter 10, I'll provide solutions to the problems outlined in the first half of the book. And there are many solutions to choose from that—starting right now—can make an incredibly positive difference for your child and your family.

I hope you'll read the chapters in order; they build on one another. In addition, some of the solutions I propose in the second half of the book may not make as much sense unless you clearly understand the problems I lay out in the first half. But if you're a "skipper" and can't resist going on to the second half first, know that the book is constructed in such a way that chapters in the two halves roughly correspond to each other. For example, Chapter 7 details the problems of today's special ed system; Chapter 17 provides information on how to make inclusive education a reality for your child. I hope, however, that the logical order of the chapters—a beginning, middle, and end—will appeal to your sense of adventure as you travel down a new path toward natural lives for your child and family.

As I mentioned earlier, the solutions I propose are working for families all across America. Many parents embrace these new ideas right away. Others are skeptical at first, but after taking a little time to let the ideas gel, they try new ways of doing things and are pleased with the results. These solutions can work for you. And when they do, I'd love to hear about them. So please share your good news with me!

Some parents, however, are resistant to new ways of thinking because it's too painful. In the traditional ways of helping our children, we've pretty much looked to the system for help—we've looked outside ourselves. We have, in essence, depended on experts to help us "solve the problems" of our children's disabilities. When I lay out the dilemmas of today's conventional wisdom—the wisdom most of us have followed to the letter—some parents feel I'm personally criticizing their actions or saying what they've done for their children is wrong. Thus, they feel that acknowledging better ways of doing things equals an admission of wrong-doing in the past. But this just isn't so! Personally, I've made many, many mistakes because I didn't know any better—I was doing what I thought was right, because that's what I learned from the experts! But learning new attitudes and perspectives, and discovering new ways of doing things, had nothing to do with what I did in the past. It was no reflection on my intentions or my abilities. I was simply doing the best I knew to do *at the time*. Think of it this way: for years many of us cooked with conventional ovens. Then one day, the microwave oven appeared. It's a better way to cook many things. This doesn't mean, however, that using a conventional oven in the past was wrong—it was the only oven we had! The ways we've traditionally done things for our children are the only ways we knew to do things, until now. With the new knowledge in this book, you'll simply be discovering new ways of doing things that can replace the old ones.

Because this book is different from most books on the subject, I'm taking the liberty of making it different in another way. Instead of a formal acknowledgments page that readers often skip, I'm including my acknowledgments right here, so everyone will know who helped me along the way, for none of us are successful on our own.

On June 1, 1999, I began writing this book. It was a dream that is now a reality. This book is the product of the life experiences of many parents and people with disabilities I've met at Partners programs across the country and at conferences in the United States and Canada. I thank everyone who has been in the audience for my presentations. Each and every person who shared a life story, asked questions, and challenged my thinking, has contributed to my learning.

The ideas in this book are also the result of the expertise I gained from professionals who have positive visions for people with disabilities—professionals who started as my mentors, and who are now mentors and friends. I thank them all for their wisdom and their willingness to share. It would be impossible to list all the names without inadvertently leaving someone out, so I won't make the attempt. You know who you are. I would, however, like to acknowledge and honor those who have, too soon—way too soon—passed on to the heavens: Jerry Kiracofe, Ed Roberts, Herb Lovett, and Tom Tyree. Their wisdom and goodness live on in me and others whose lives they changed.

I thank and honor Colleen Wieck, executive director of the Minnesota Governor's Council on Developmental Disabilities and creator of Partners in Policymaking, and Jopie Smith, coordinator of the Texas Partners program. Colleen and Jopie provided the leadership and vision that started me on this path back in 1990. I want to be just like them when I grow up!

Thanks to those who read the initial draft of this manuscript and shared their valued opinions with me: Colleen and Jopie; Laura Buckner, coordinator of Texas Partners; Vicky Davis, coordinator of Missouri Partners; Christine Pisani, coordinator of Idaho Partners; Joyce Smith, coordinator of North Dakota Partners; and Charmaine Thaner, my dear friend. Laura and Joyce are also parents of children with disabilities and graduates of Partners. These seven friends helped make the manuscript better, but any errors are mine alone.

To my mother and stepfather, Iris and Robby Robinson; my father and stepmother, Felix and Thelma Stoker (This is like accepting an award! I'm almost through, so hang in there.); my brother, Steve Stoker; my sister, Sandi St. Claire, and her family; and Charmaine and her family; thank you for believing in me.

And to my husband, Mark, and my children, Emily and Benjamin, thank you for allowing me to desert you for hours at a time while I cozied up to the computer. Thanks for believing me all the times I said, "I'm almost through!" Thanks for the meals you cooked, the clothes you washed, and the cleaning you did. And thank you for the hugs, kisses, and love that sustained me. I am who I am because of you.

Now, dear reader, on to the next chapter. We'll go back in time to the way things were; it's our first stop on the journey to natural lives for our children and families.

The Way
Things Were

FELLOW CITIZENS,
WE CANNOT ESCAPE HISTORY.

Abraham Lincoln

Our History
Out of the Shadows and Into the Light

2

> THE HISTORY OF AN OPPRESSED PEOPLE IS HIDDEN
> IN THE LIES AND THE AGREED-UPON MYTHS
> OF ITS CONQUERORS.
> *Meridel LeSueur*

People with developmental disabilities have always been part of the world and they always will be. But from the beginning of recorded history, they have, for the most part, existed in the dark shadows of society. Only during the last fifty years of the twentieth century did they begin to emerge into the light. The history of people with disabilities is as old as the world and it's still being written. You, your family, and your child are now part of this history.

This chapter will present a broad perspective of Euro-American disability history to provide a basic understanding of developments over time. In no way is this a complete history of people with disabilities. Perhaps when I'm very old I'll have time to write that, and when you're very old, you'll have time to read it. I've tried to include those parts of history that are specifically relevant to parents.

This overview is not pretty. Much of it is hard to take. Cruelty, paternalism, segregation, prejudice, and gross misunderstanding are intermixed with bits of understanding and a little benevolence here and there. Learning about the past will help you understand what's happening in your child's life, and the lives of others with disabilities, today.

History does repeat itself. Many old attitudes and actions are being recycled and repackaged into twenty-first century rhetoric. If we're ready to put a stop to the cycle, we must change the present (for our children) and the future (for children not yet born).

To convey the mood of previous eras, I sometimes use language common to the time. This is not the language we want to use today. In later chapters, we'll explore new attitudes and ways of speaking that are more dignified and respectful.

You'll see a recurring practice throughout this chapter: infanticide (the killing of babies). Unfortunately, it continues today in one form or another, a result of society's pervasive marginalization of children.

In ancient times, newborns with visible disabilities or differences were killed shortly after birth for a variety of reasons. It was believed the displeasure of the gods was manifested in a "sick" newborn; the baby was filled with evil; or the mother had mated with an animal or had seen something horrible that imprinted itself on the baby.

Children who would not grow up to contribute to the family's economic well-being were burdens and, therefore, expendable. Those who brought shame on a family were eliminated. Poverty, hunger, and the low economic status of "common" people, as well as religious or cultural prejudices, all contributed to this state of affairs.

Many congenital disabilities were not apparent until later in life, so not every baby with a disability was murdered at birth. But when children's disabilities or differences *were* discovered, many were abandoned. Some learned to fend for themselves; others were taken in by strangers where they often ended up as slaves, prostitutes, or beggars.

ANCIENT GRECO-ROMAN SOCIETIES

Ancient Greek and Roman cultures profoundly influenced the United States and other Western nations. Today's democracy, law, philosophy, and medicine can trace their origins to these early societies. Unfortunately, their views on people with disabilities, women, children, and slavery also influenced modern cultures.

Divine Intervention

Many ancient societies believed a variety of gods controlled the universe. Priests, who were both religious and political figures, exerted powerful influence over the general populace: they claimed they were in direct communication with the gods and could interpret the gods' actions. Things that could not be explained rationally were attributed to divine intervention. Disability, illness, and other human conditions were thought to be caused by the gods' displeasure. To please the gods and protect themselves from the wrath of the gods, people shunned—and sometimes killed—individuals with disabilities.

Hippocrates: Natural Causes of Disability

Hippocrates (c. 460–c. 377 B.C.), the Greek physician known as the "father of medicine," disputed the conventional wisdom of his time. He proposed natural causes, not the fickle fingers of the gods, produced different physical conditions. These new ideas, however, were not integrated into the cultural beliefs that influenced people's daily lives.

Aristotle and Perfection

The Greek philosopher and scientist Aristotle (384–322 B.C.) also made great contributions to his society and to our modern world. Today, though, we know some of theories contained significant errors. He concluded, for example, that the brain cooled the blood.

Aristotle promoted a social hierarchy that profoundly influenced hundreds of generations to follow. Men (upper class males) represented perfection and women represented the first level of deformity within mankind. Below women were children, slaves, and, of course, people with differences or disabilities.

The quest for human perfection resulted in the murder of children with disabilities. To rid Grecian and Roman societies of imperfection and to please the gods, parents abandoned babies with disabilities and left them outside to die ("exposure"), threw them over cliffs, starved them to death, or smothered them. In many communities, laws *mandated* the abandonment and/or death of sick or "deformed" infants. Some children were "rescued" by strangers, and were then raised to be slaves, prostitutes, or entertainers. Some were purposefully maimed to increase their value as beggars.

It wasn't just "imperfect" babies who were killed; parents who were considered inferior were also slaughtered. Ancient societies wanted to ensure that imperfect individuals wouldn't create any more of their kind. (This notion reared its ugly head again, most notably in the United States, and then in Nazi Germany, in the twentieth century. If we're not careful, it might return once again.)

Court Jesters: Slave Entertainers

Many children and adults with disabilities were sold or given to royals, the nobility, and the wealthy, where some were forced to become performers. Young men with cognitive disabilities were often castrated; this prevented them from achieving sexual maturity. As eunuchs, they seemed to be neither male nor female. They remained boyish, with high voices, and little or no body hair or muscular development, regardless of age. Known as jesters or fools, they dressed in silly costumes and entertained the rich. But their entertainment value was not limited to skillful performances. Audiences were also entertained by their disabilities: how the performers did or did not talk, walk, eat, and so forth. Court jesters were following in the footsteps of the "stupidus" performer of ancient Roman theater. (Think about this in October when you see court jester Halloween costumes in stores.)

THE INFLUENCE OF CHRISTIANITY

With the advent and spread of Christianity, the lives of people with disabilities improved somewhat. Because Jesus was kind to people who were perceived to be different, more humane practices evolved. However, Christian beliefs about extending charity to people with disabilities or differences also led to stereotypical and negative attitudes (which we still have today) reflecting the belief that people with disabilities are to be pitied and taken care of because they cannot care for themselves.

Many stories in the Bible illustrate the perceptions about people with disabilities during early Christianity. In Matthew 11:5 of the King James version of the Holy Bible, Jesus describes some of his acts to his followers: "The blind receive their sight, and the lame walk, the lepers are cleansed, and the deaf hear, the dead are raised up, and the poor have the gospel preached to them." Thus, faithful and/or repentant people are cured by Jesus, while those without enough faith or who do not repent their sins can not (or will not) be cured.

Other verses include references to demons being cast out. A story in chapter five of the book of John describes how Jesus commanded a lame man to walk: "Behold, thou art made whole; sin no more, lest a worse thing come unto thee." If a person had a disability, the condition was thought to have been caused by moral imperfection (sin). Thus, imperfection of the soul leads to imperfection of the body. Furthermore, the person wasn't seen as "whole," creating the myth that people with disabilities were less than human. This validated the notion that they should be cured so they would once again be "whole." (This belief lives on in the twenty-first century.)

Overall, Christian beliefs resulted in people with disabilities being treated with kindness and mercy. However, these attitudes also led to pity, segregation, and exclusion since people with disabilities were considered unworthy, evil, or sinful.

During the early years of the Christian era, the public killing of children with disabilities lessened as compassion became a sign of strength. But abandonment and starvation behind closed doors continued.

EARLY ASSISTANCE AND INCARCERATION

The fall of the Roman Empire in the fifth century created hardship throughout Western Europe. Disorganization reigned. But the Roman Catholic Church continued to grow, opening the first hospitals, orphanages, and facilities for older people. Church leaders provided help in the belief that good works would earn them a place in heaven.

In the eighth century, Roman Catholic doctrines prohibited the abandonment of babies, but the practice continued. In response, the Church opened foundling hospitals where parents could leave their unwanted babies. But only the basics of food and shelter were provided, so many children did not survive beyond their early years.

From Biblical times, leprosy (an infectious bacterial disease) was a dreaded condition. People with leprosy were incarcerated in leper colonies. In the thirteenth century, however, leprosy was on the wane. Public officials decided to put the empty leprosariums to good use. At the time, Europe was dealing with increased population, families had been torn apart by two hundred years of holy wars (the Crusades), and there were legions of poor people. One solution to this mess was to put "undesirables" in the former leprosariums, the "cities of the damned." A new form of "care" emerged, and institutional life for people with disabilities and differences was beginning.

Who were the undesirables? Orphans, vagabonds, prostitutes, widows, criminals, adults and children with disabilities, and others who were perceived to be worthless. Stakes and irons helped the authorities maintain total control in the asylums.

Another new method of social control was the "idiot cage." In many communities, leaders wanted to ensure that undesirables didn't cause problems for the community. People with disabilities and differences were put inside wooden cages which were located in the town center. Not only were they "kept out of trouble," but townspeople were provided with free entertainment as they gawked at the "creatures."

(Are there any similarities in today's world? What about the observation cubicles adjacent to treatment rooms? Certainly the *intent* of watching children being assessed or treated isn't the same intent as the isolation of the idiot cages. However, a person in an idiot cage *knew* he was being observed. The same is not true for children or adults who may be watched without their knowledge, by physicians, therapists, trainees, and others. People who do not have disabilities would probably never tolerate this invasion of privacy.)

The "ship of fools" was used to maintain order along the coastline. Undesirables, including people with disabilities, were rounded up and put on a ship which sailed from port to port. Residents of the cities where the ship landed could buy tickets to board the ship to stare, ogle, and delight in the antics of the "fools" on board. Later, the ship's crew would unload the passengers at the last port, leaving them to fend for themselves in a strange community.

THE RENAISSANCE: HOPE FOR ALL

The Renaissance, from the mid-fourteenth century to the mid-sixteenth century, once again brought hope that conditions for people with disabilities would improve. The revival of classical learning, the concept of the dignity of the individual, and greater interest in the arts and sciences were hallmarks of the Renaissance. Humanists promoted ideas that led to better health care overall, and a better understanding of disabilities.

THE REFORMATION BRINGS DEATH AND DAMNATION

During the sixteenth century, religious leaders in Western Europe protested many of the tenets of the Roman Catholic Church. Amid political, moral, and social chaos, the Protestant Reformation was born, as new Christian sects split from the Mother Church. Religion, politics, and lawmaking were intertwined, and the lives of people with disabilities were negatively affected by religious dogma.

Martin Luther (1483–1546), John Calvin (1509–64), and other Protestant leaders believed people with disabilities and differences were possessed by the devil. Religious authorities—Roman Catholic and Protestant—used a variety of methods to drive Satan out: priests spat on people, took them to holy places, or performed exorcisms. If parents suspected their child with a disability or difference was filled with evil, they often attempted to "beat the Devil" out of her. If the child happened to die, the death was considered an unfortunate consequence of a responsible act.

Some authorities took a less accusing position: healing hands could cure the sickness if the victim had faith and was deserving of a cure. However, an unsuccessful healing was taken as proof the person truly was filled with Satan.

Foundling hospitals for abandoned babies exceeded capacity even though infanticide continued behind closed doors. European countries were beginning to create and enforce laws that prohibited the killing of young children. But the crime was not considered murder, since babies were not considered as valuable as adults. The punishment for killing a "normal" unwanted child was often a mild penance meted out by the church.

The murders of babies with disabilities, however, often went unpunished altogether. Society accepted insanity pleas or the church politely looked the other way since the parents had done a "good deed" by eliminating a Satanic force from the community.

ELIZABETHAN POOR LAWS AND COMMUNITY RESPONSIBILITY

The pendulum swung the other way under England's Queen Elizabeth I (1533–1603) when she began a revolutionary policy of government-sanctioned welfare that included people with disabilities. Under the famous Poor Laws of 1601, churches continued to be responsible for taking care of their own, but with added regulations imposed by Parliamentary law. The laws weren't purely benevolent, however. They were also a means of social control. By mandating that needy and deviant people be served, the government could control those who "polluted good society."

Poor children were taught trades; honest, unemployed men were given work; sick and aged persons (including people with disabilities) were taken care of; and vagrants were punished. Residents within the church parish jurisdiction were taxed to pay for this care, and church leaders administered the programs. The welfare state was born. (This was the beginning of the road we're still on in most modern societies: people with disabilities and differences are recipients of services, a bureaucracy manages the services, and public tax dollars fund the services.)

Revisions to the law moved local control to a central authority: the bureaucratic universe expanded. Church parishes built workhouses and any needy person who refused to work was denied any and all assistance. Conditions in the workhouses became so harsh that life on the street was preferable to charitable assistance.

Two new philosophies were emerging. The first reflected the belief that poverty, regardless of its origins, equaled moral delinquency. The second promoted the notion that people with disabilities should be taken care of by bureaucrats and professionals who know what's best. These erroneous beliefs became entrenched in most Westernized societies, and we're still living with them today.

RADICAL THINKING

In the late 1600s the English philosopher and physician John Locke (1632–1704) proposed new theories that have had a long-lasting and profound influence on society and education. He theorized that all minds were "blank slates." Proponents of Locke's ideas interpreted them to mean *all* people could develop intelligence and capacities through experiences. Prior to this, the conventional wisdom was that people with cognitive disabilities were unable to learn.

Across the English Channel, the French moralist, Jean Jacques Rousseau (1712–78), influenced generations of philosophers and educators. He believed all people (not just the nobility) had worth and value, and all were basically good and highly sensitive to their surroundings. Rousseau promoted the idea that all humans achieved goodness through the inspiration of nature, but this goodness could be betrayed by a corrupt society. He recommended a simple life in the country or in small towns instead of big cities. Later, this specific idea influenced social reformers in America: many institutions for people with disabilities were built in the countryside.

Philippe Pinel (1745–1826), a French psychiatrist, made significant reforms in the area of mental illness. He personally removed the chains from patients in French mental hospitals, where many had been chained for over thirty years. The conventional wisdom of the time was that a person's sinfulness and immorality led to dementia and madness. (Here's the connection between sin or immorality and disability again.)

But Pinel proposed these conditions were caused by brain dysfunction. His theories created a shift from physical abuse to humane treatment and moral management, and he emphasized vocational and work experiences for patients in mental hospitals as a form of therapeutic treatment.

AMERICAN COLONIES AND COMMUNITY RESPONSIBILITY

Colonists who crossed the Atlantic for freedom in the land called America brought many customs from the Old World, but they also created new customs and laws that reflected their new communities. Information from the Veteran's Administration web site details the spirit of community within the colonies. A 1636 declaration agreed upon by

Pilgrims stated, "If any person shall be sent forth as a soldier and shall return maimed, he shall be maintained completely by the Colony during his life." Since there was no central government in charge, residents of the colonies worked together to care for their own.

Many of the colonists emigrated from England and other countries in pursuit of religious freedom, and they took their faith and its responsibilities seriously. According to their Christian beliefs, the poor would always be a part of society. The "deserving poor" (those whose poverty was beyond their control, such as widows, orphans, and some people with disabilities) weren't seen as a threat to the community; they were just part of life. They were often cared for in the local almshouse.

Over time, some almshouses evolved into infirmaries for people with a variety of health needs. As the population in the colonies increased, however, residents found it harder to care for certain people. So in the mid-1700s, a Virginia statute was enacted to create the first hospital for people with mental disabilities.

THE REVOLUTIONARY WAR AND DISABILITY COMPENSATION

In the early part of the Revolutionary War, and for the first time ever, cash from the government supplemented (and in some cases, replaced) care from the community. The Continental Congress allocated a benefits package for soldiers who acquired disabilities in battle and for dependents of soldiers killed in battle. While these pensions weren't considered "welfare" in the way we use the term today, this was certainly the beginning of the U.S. government's assistance to people considered needy, and veterans and their families were perceived to be the "deserving" needy.

INDUSTRIAL REVOLUTION: NEW TECHNOLOGY, NEW PROBLEMS

Across the Atlantic, incredible inventions of manufacturing equipment created the first factory jobs in Europe in the mid-1700s, and the Industrial Revolution was born. New jobs and new products radically changed and enhanced European economies. But people with disabilities did not share in the benefits.

Prior to industrialization, most people were self-employed in farming or skilled trades, such as blacksmithing, carpentry, masonry, and other occupations. At a time when everyone in the family played an important role on the family farm, we can assume some individuals with disabilities successfully contributed to their family's economic well-being. But the factory jobs—which required workers to produce mass quantities as quickly as possible—were not available to people with disabilities. Workers who couldn't keep up the grueling pace were excluded.

As more and more people left the farm for factory jobs, the population of urban areas increased dramatically. Residents of cities and towns exerted control over who could live in their communities; unwanted newcomers were run out of town. No one wanted the undesirables: people with disabilities, criminals, orphans, prostitutes, widows, poor people, and anyone else considered deviant or economically dependent.

In the early 1800s, European cities saw extreme wealth and extreme poverty, and infanticide continued. By the 1850s, hundreds of dead babies floated on the Thames river in London, filled up ditches, and littered parks. In France, the sewers were full of tiny corpses.

POPULATION CONCERNS: RESTRICT BIRTHS, ELIMINATE DEFECTIVES

The grim predictions of Thomas Malthus (1766–1834) reflected and reinforced societal concerns about population growth. Malthus, an English clergyman, economist, and social philosopher, wrote his *Essay on the Principle of Population* in 1798 and revised it in 1803. His message supported and expanded the existing theory that population growth would outstrip the food supply.

Malthus noted that natural controls of disease, war, and famine might keep the population size in balance. But voluntary reproductive restraints, such as delaying marriage and sexual abstinence within marriages, would enhance society's economic well-being. Additional reductions in population could be achieved by eliminating the so-called defectives in society: only those who contributed to society should receive its benefits. (This antiquated philosophy is still with us. Many educators and professionals demonstrate a reluctance to invest in our children's education, believing children with disabilities will never contribute to society.)

THE WILD BOY AND NEW METHODS OF TEACHING

In 1799, a ten or eleven-year-old boy who had been found in the woods was brought to Jean-Marc Gaspard Itard, a French physician and scholar. His work with the boy (whom he named Victor) led to advanced thinking about people with developmental disabilities.

Apparently, Victor had been abandoned in the forest when he was three or four and had survived by learning from animals (wolves, it was supposed). Victor did not use human speech and his behavior was more animal-like than human. Philippe Pinel, Itard's mentor, believed Victor was an "incurable idiot." But Itard felt Victor's "retarded" condition was due to the lack of typical childhood learning experiences. Itard asked for and received permission to teach Victor.

Itard took Victor into his home, and he and his female housekeeper used experiential and sensory training to help Victor acquire new skills. After four years, Victor demonstrated impressive strides in his learning, but he never reached the level Itard hoped for. The doctor eventually abandoned his dream of making Victor "above normal," but the experiment positively influenced educators throughout the following century. The experiences of the "Wild Boy of Aveyron" reinforced the belief that children with cognitive disabilities could learn.

DOROTHEA DIX AND THE RISE OF ASYLUMS

Back in America, social reformer Dorothea Dix (1802–87) was shocked by the deplorable conditions in prisons, jails, and poorhouses, where many people with disabilities were warehoused alongside criminals. She campaigned for better treatment of persons with mental illness, as recommended by Phillippe Pinel.

Due to her influence, more than thirty asylums for people with mental illness were established across the United States to ensure patients were treated humanely instead of being abused in jails and prisons. (At the time, mental illness was a broad category that probably included people with cognitive, learning, or sensory disabilities.) Dix's efforts to improve conditions were laudable, but the success of asylums accelerated the institutional segregation and isolation of people with disabilities.

A new philosophy was emerging: deviancy could be linked to problems in the home and community. If people were taken out of these troubling environments, deviancy could be cured. Asylums were built with the best of intentions: to provide a more home-like environment than prisons where patients could "get well," away from the chaos and confusion of their families and communities. They would reap the benefits of a simple life in the country. In addition, conventional wisdom dictated that patients not have *any* contact with their families until they were cured of their deviancies. By building institutions out in the country, away from communities, administrators could prevent families from trying to visit their relatives. In the middle of the 1800s, the number of institutions was on the rise.

SUCCESS IN SENSORY TRAINING GROWS, CROSSES THE ATLANTIC

Itard's progress with Victor, the Wild Boy of Aveyron, influenced one of his students in France, Edouard Seguin (1812–1880). Seguin's book, *Idiocy, Its Treatment by the Physiological Method,* was radical for its time, focusing on expert diagnosis, recognition of individual differences, and an emphasis on sensory and motor coordination training. He believed children with cognitive disabilities could achieve higher levels of thinking through these new methods. In 1844, the Paris Academy of Science honored Seguin for solving the problem of "idiot education."

While the language used in Seguin's time is offensive to us today, his theories were valuable, effective, and long-lasting. His work influenced many physicians and educators who followed him, including Maria Montessori, a pioneer in the education of young children with and without disabilities. In 1850, Seguin moved to the United States and began working with American leaders in the training school movement.

TRAINING SCHOOLS FOCUS ON EDUCATION

In 1817, Thomas H. Gallaudet opened the American Asylum for the Deaf in Connecticut. The success of this school was followed by the opening of similar schools in several states. In 1864, Gallaudet College in Washington, D.C. became the first institution of higher learning for people with disabilities.

Samuel Gridley Howe (1801–1876), an American humanitarian and physician who was involved in many social issues of his time, directed the Perkins Institute for the Blind, where he pioneered new training techniques. In 1832, he established the Massachusetts School for Idiotic and Feeble-Minded Youth, an experimental boarding school.

Howe and Edouard Seguin both stressed that, after intensive training, children with disabilities would be able to lead productive lives in their own communities. Students in the training schools received academic education, instruction in self-help skills, and physical training to improve their sensory abilities. Word of the school's success spread rapidly and many parents clamored to have their children enrolled.

A new hope for children with disabilities was evolving. The humanitarian plan to "cure deviancy" seemed to be working. To meet the demand, more schools were built to house and train greater numbers of children and young adults.

At first, Howe believed in the value of residential training schools. But he later recognized the dangers of segregation and bravely began to speak out against facilities that isolated and excluded people with disabilities from the mainstream of society.

FROM TRAINING TO INCARCERATION

The initial success of the training school movement didn't last long. In pre-Civil War America, economic woes affected thousands. High unemployment was worsened by the influx of immigrants who were willing to work for very low wages. Young people with disabilities from the training schools could not compete in this job market. When they could not find work, they often ended up in poorhouses or jails.

Nevertheless, reformers continued to promote their schools. More and more parents wanted their children to receive the benefits of training, and enrollment swelled. But the schools were not prepared for the flood of students. The original focus of the schools—training and education—was soon lost in the attempt to accommodate large numbers of new residents. The training schools quickly became custodial care facilities. Students became inmates. People with disabilities were viewed as economic burdens. The growth of these institutions exceeded the administrators' wildest dreams.

Administrators recognized their custodial facilities could serve a wider population. Every community still had its share of so-called deviants who were incarcerated in local poorhouses. But if the institutions took charge of these misfits, administrators could get state funding to pay for their care, relieving cities and towns of the financial burden. This action, of course, made citizens feel safer. Protecting communities from deviants became an additional function of institutions.

As the population of institutions swelled, administrators grew concerned about operating costs. They devised quite a solution: use the residents as a source of free labor. "Higher-functioning" inmates were forced to do tasks which were crucial to the daily operation of the institutions, including the supervision of "lower-functioning" inmates. Some institutions began growing their own food, with inmates providing the free labor. Administrators promoted manual labor as "therapy." Superintendents were able to kill two birds with one stone: they could keep the institutions financially solvent and provide "training" at the same time.

A VOICE IN THE WILDERNESS CRIES FOR REASON

Samuel Gridley Howe and Edouard Seguin were dismayed at the turn of events. But it was too late to stop the burgeoning new industry. In 1866, Howe was asked to give the keynote address at the opening of a new institution. But he shocked the audience when he criticized institutions and warned about the dangers of segregation. He did, in fact, tell the stunned audience that children and adults with disabilities should be included in their communities and surrounded by people who didn't have disabilities. In this way, children who did not have speech would learn to speak, those with troublesome behavior would learn about acceptable behavior, and so forth. Few heeded Howe's wisdom. (Nor is his wisdom heeded today: special ed preschools routinely congregate children with disabilities. How do we expect a young child to learn to speak when he is surrounded by other young children who also don't speak?)

THE CIVIL WAR: INCREASED AWARENESS OF DISABILITY

Americans became more familiar with disabilities during the Civil War, as veterans returned home with permanent disabilities acquired in battle. Just like after the Revolutionary War, these individuals were valued and honored for their contributions to national service. They received pensions as compensation for their "losses" (permanent disabilities).

In 1866, the National Home for Union Veterans was opened. The care provided was vastly better than the care for people with developmental disabilities in public institutions. Attitudes about soldiers who acquired disabilities were very different from attitudes about people who were born with disabilities. Veterans were men with personal histories of past successes, and society felt they had contributed to the betterment of society. Children and adults with developmental disabilities were not seen in the same light.

DOOMED TO BE CURED: THE MEDICALIZATION OF DISABILITY

While previous reformers had been concerned about social and educational issues regarding people with disabilities, new leaders in the field were physicians interested in the medical aspects of disability. In 1876, superintendents of institutions created the (take a deep breath before going further) Association of Medical Officers of American Institutions for Idiotic and Feebleminded Persons. It later became the American Association on Mental Deficiency (AAMD), and today it's called the American Association on Mental Retardation (AAMR).

The organization's purpose was to study the causes of, and treatment for, idiocy and feeblemindedness (mental retardation, in today's vernacular). Residents of institutions were viewed as patients who needed to be cured. Despite Samuel Gridley Howe's warning, residents were categorized and segregated by disability.

The population of institutions continued to grow. Many parents truly believed the institutions could help their children; others simply wanted relief from the financial and emotional burdens of caring for their children at home. Institutional care was thought to be economical and fiscally conservative. By the turn of the century, conditions in institutions worsened. Overpopulation and understaffing, along with low budgets, contributed to harsh conditions at many facilities.

THE IQ TEST: FIRST HELPFUL, THEN HARMFUL

The IQ test had benevolent beginnings, but it quickly became a dangerous tool. In 1905, Dr. Alfred Binet (1857–1911), a French psychologist, was asked by his government to create a way of identifying "retarded" children who might need extra help in school.

Binet's test went against the conventional thinking of his time. Many professionals accepted the theory that intelligence was hereditary and unchangeable. Educators routinely made assumptions about children based on their *parents'* achievements or lack thereof. Binet was reportedly concerned about the widespread belief that some children could never improve their learning abilities, so he dictated three principles for the appropriate use of his test: (1) the test score does not define anything innate or permanent about the child and what is measured cannot be designated as "intelligence" or any other abstract element; (2) the scale is a rough guide for the purpose of identifying children who need extra help, not a device for ranking children; and (3) low scores do not mean a child is innately incapable.

Today, according to several books on the subject, there is a great deal of controversy about Binet's motivations. Some researchers believe Binet's test was benevolent and helpful: it could identify children who needed extra help. They note that Binet tried to preserve the integrity of the test with his three principles. They're dismayed, however, by the later misuse of this type of testing, which will be described shortly.

Others who are critical of intelligence tests (and other forms of professional measurements) question Binet's intent and the rationale for testing children, in general. Why, for example, did a child need to be professionally tested when his abilities were easily observed by the classroom teacher? Was it possible Binet *did* have a hidden agenda to identify children with "sub-normal intelligence" for the purpose of classification and exclusion? There's a great deal of speculation with no definitive answers.

At any rate, Binet's test became known as the IQ test. Professionals imported the test to the United States, modified it, and began using it to identify and rank persons they believed to be defective. Ignoring Binet's three principles, professionals set in motion a gross misuse of testing that, as you'll see, has irreparably harmed, and continues to harm, children and adults with disabilities.

Causes of Mental Deficiency: The Parents—Who Else?

In the early 1900s, H.H. Goddard, the director of research at the Vineland Training School for Feebleminded Girls and Boys in New Jersey, was studying the causes of mental deficiency. He gathered information about the families of residents in an attempt to prove that mental deficiency was hereditary. His most famous study was of the Kallikak family. One member of the family—young Deborah Kallikak—was a resident at Vineland. The name Kallikak was a pseudonym, the combination of the Greek words for good and evil.

Goddard reportedly traced Deborah's heritage through interviews and other methods. He "learned" that during the Revolutionary War, a man he called Martin Kallikak had a romantic evening with a tavern maid. The brief relationship resulted in pregnancy and the unwed mother gave birth to a son. In the meantime, Kallikak returned home, married a "well-bred" young woman, and they began a family.

Goddard's research into the family tree supposedly demonstrated that Kallikak and his wife produced intelligent and upstanding citizens. But descendents of the child produced by Kallikak and the tavern maid, according to that family tree, all had mental deficiency, low morals, and a variety of social ills. Along with other respected professionals of the time, Goddard believed single genes controlled complex human traits, such as temperament, behavior, and intelligence, and these genes were passed from parents to their children.

Goddard and his peers accepted as *fact* the theory that intelligence was a measurable entity that was fixed and unchangeable. He promoted the idea that levels of intelligence could be charted along one straight line, from primitive to advanced.

In addition, Goddard believed people in the institutions who had been categorized as idiots and imbeciles had a certain "look" about them. Taking this theory a giant step further, he deduced that feeblemindedness could be diagnosed by observing a person's *physical appearance*. (Don't laugh; this is still happening today!)

In Goddard's day, an idiot was a person who had the mental functioning of a three-year-old or less. An imbecile was defined as a person with the mental function of a three to seven-year-old. Within both classifications were degrees of deficiency: high, middle, and low-grade. But Goddard believed there was another class of mental defectives composed of adults who functioned within the eight to twelve-year-old mental level. He called this category "morons," from a Greek word meaning foolish.

Goddard and his peers believed that since idiots and imbeciles were so easily diagnosed (they had the "look"), most had been identified and locked up in institutions. Because they were incarcerated and unable to marry or have sex, they couldn't make any more idiot or imbecile babies. This was good, Goddard believed, because once all the idiots and imbeciles died off, these forms of mental deficiency would die with them. America would never again be threatened by the "moral menace" of idiots and imbeciles. In institutional settings, the inmates were safe from society and, more importantly, society was safe from them.

But the new class—morons—was a different story. They weren't as easily identified as idiots and imbeciles; they didn't have the "look." This was a serious problem: because morons "looked" normal, they could "pass" for normal human beings. Thus, they were running loose in society, wreaking havoc by having moronic children. For the safety of America's present and future, Goddard believed, morons should be identified and then incarcerated in institutions to prevent them from reproducing. The threat to America was grave: morons were reproducing themselves in record numbers.

Goddard and his peers also decided a person's employment status and innate intelligence were connected. In the institutions, administrators had developed tests to correlate "mental age" with what they called "industrial ability." Once again, they took things a step further, using what disability historians have called circular logic. They promoted the idea that experts could classify typical adults based on the type of work they did. For example, if an adult held a job that a child could do (simple cleaning, for instance), the adult must have the simple mind of a child (feeblemindedness). While Goddard's theories seem ridiculous today, he was a well-respected professional whose views influenced other professionals, government policies, and societal attitudes. (Today, we're still living with the remnants of these philosophies: professionals routinely assign a "developmental age"—Goddard's "mental age"—to many children with diabilities.)

As America was opening its arms to immigrants in the early years of the twentieth century, Goddard convinced government officials that his version of the Binet test should be used to screen immigrants arriving at Ellis Island. Anyone found to be feebleminded would not be allowed into the United States. In 1913, the U.S. Public Health Service reported (based on Goddard's test results) that 79 percent of Italians, 80 percent of Hungarians, 83 percent of Jews, and 87 percent of Russians tested were feebleminded.

Even Goddard was surprised and disturbed by the results of his tests. But his "proof" was accepted. Later, his research profoundly influenced the U.S. Congress: it passed legislation that severely limited immigration from countries where "low intelligence" was observed. This was a devastating policy. Years later, when Jewish people were fleeing Nazi Germany, the once-friendly borders of the United States were closed.

More IQ Test Aberrations

Psychologist Lewis M. Terman of Stanford University also modified Binet's test, creating the Stanford-Binet test. While Binet's original test featured open-ended questions, Terman's version included questions that allowed for only one right answer. People who (1) did not have experience or familiarity with the subject of Terman's questions, (2) used a different way of thinking, and/or (3) had a non-English speaking background, did not perform well on the test.

Terman expanded the use of the IQ test, moving it beyond institutional use. He began testing average Americans to see if the tool could be used for ranking people into a variety of classifications. Through widespread testing of typical adults, Terman concluded the average mental age of adults in the United States was sixteen, just four "intelligence" years above the moron level described by Goddard. His shocking results also "proved" that intelligence was hereditary and unchangeable, and that lighter-skinned people were inherently more intelligent than darker-skinned people. Terman, of course, was "white."

Terman's "success" sparked the beginning of the standardized test industry. Norms, mental age, and standard deviations could all be decoded by the Stanford-Binet written test. Professionals accepted it as an accurate measuring device of intelligence and developed other tests using the Stanford-Binet as a model.

(Critics of IQ testing—both then and now—note that no one has proved the Stanford-Binet or any other test can measure intelligence, for intelligence is not a "thing" that can be measured. Still, the multi-million dollar test industry continues to crank out standardized tests. Professionals continue to value them. Educational funding is often based on test scores. The public still believes in their validity and accuracy. And people with disabilities continue to be harmed by them. Today, people with low IQ scores are still believed to be inherently incapable, so they're shuffled into segregrated settings and they remain at the bottom of our social hierarchy.)

In 1917, Robert M. Yerkes, a psychologist and professor at Harvard University (and colleague of Goddard and Terman), tested almost two million Army recruits at the time of World War I. After compiling data from thousands of the tests, Yerkes concluded the average mental age of "white" American adults was just thirteen, only *one year* above Goddard's moron status. His study also correlated intelligence to ethnicity: "white" people were smarter than "dark" people. His suppositions were accepted as fact, becoming part of the conventional wisdom of the time.

The research of Goddard, Terman, and Yerkes, combined with U.S. census figures, showed a dramatic increase in the number of feebleminded Americans. Hysteria was growing. Psychologists, institution administrators, and politicians fueled the fire which was reported by the media. According to the experts, America was in danger of ruination because of the increased number of morons.

The declaration that feeblemindedness was hereditary was devastating to families of children with disabilities. Parents were at fault: they were responsible for bringing imbeciles, idiots, and morons into the world. The shame was almost unbearable. For people with disabilities, a new era of cruelty—the eugenics movement—was beginning.

EUGENICS: THE ULTIMATE CURE

As originally described in 1883 in Europe, eugenics is the study of scientific methods to strengthen the human race by controlling the mating, and thus the hereditary worth, of groups in our society. The word is from the ancient Greeks and means "well-born."

In the early part of the twentieth century, not only was feeblemindedness believed to be hereditary, but people with so-called low intelligence were said to have low *moral values*. Therefore, if society controlled who had children and who didn't, Americans could be assured future generations of mental defectives would no longer weaken society. A new method of social control was initiated.

Legislation was passed in twenty-five states mandating the sterilization of people with disabilities. Young women were given tubal ligations, often without their (or their parents') knowledge or permission. Many were told they were having appendectomies. Doctors castrated young men or performed vasectomies. (The vasectomy was specifically developed for the purpose of sterilizing men with developmental disabilities.)

As a way of relieving the overcrowding in institutions, administrators began discharging some people with disabilities, but only after they had been sterilized. Many states enacted laws banning the marriage of feebleminded persons. Laws prohibiting "mixed-race" marriages were also enacted.

Lawsuits were filed to stop sterilization practices, but the Supreme Court upheld the state mandates. In the 1927 *Buck v. Bell* case, Chief Justice Oliver Wendell Holmes, writing the majority opinion, declared that "three generations of imbeciles are enough."

Over time, the eugenics movement in the United States ran out of steam as the research of Goddard and others was eventually discounted. And little by little, many state laws were rescinded, but not before thousands of people with disabilities were involuntarily sterilized.

SPECIAL EDUCATION STARTS, STALLS: EDUCATORS NOT READY

While many people with disabilities were incarcerated in institutions, the majority were living at home with their families. Some benefited from the work of educators who believed children with disabilities could successfully remain in their communities if they were educated. Rhode Island opened the first special education class in the United States in 1896. By 1923, 34,000 students with disabilities were enrolled in special education classes in several states. However, many educators indicated they were not ready to handle these students, so they turned to the experts in the institutions for help. In response, many institutions incorporated "schools" in their facilities.

Unfortunately, staff members in many institutions clung to the belief that cognitive disabilities were hereditary and could not be improved by education. *The Almosts: A Study of the Feeble-Minded* was a widely-used textbook which demonstrated that people labeled feebleminded were "almost," but not quite, human.

WORLD WAR I AND VOCATIONAL REHABILITATION

In World War I, thousands of American soldiers went to war and returned with acquired disabilities. The federal government's response to this calamity was different from its responses after previous wars.

In 1917, Congress passed the Vocational Rehabilitation Act to provide training and education to "restore" veterans with acquired disabilities to employable, productive status. The Act was not passed out of national sympathy for veterans with disabilities, nor because of a moral obligation to veterans who had given their all in defense of their country. It was an economic decision, based on the belief that supporting industry was in the best interest of government and society. Veterans were seen as economic assets: they had been successfully employed before their military service. With retraining and education, they could once again become valuable employees and contribute to the nation's economy.

The purpose of educational restoration and training (rehabilitation) was to retrain individuals so their disabilities were not barriers to employment. Job accommodations and modifications weren't part of the employment landscape. A veteran who had lost an arm, for instance, would be retrained for a job he could do with one arm. Physical and occupational therapists were called in to help. (This was essentially the beginning of these two disciplines.) But people with developmental disabilities remained at the mercy of institutions or were hidden away at home. There was no reason to invest in *them*. What could they contribute to American society?

INVISIBLE CITIZENS

From the 1920s to the 1950s, most adults and children with developmental disabilities were invisible. At least one public institution was operating in every state, and the population of institutions increased from 25,000 to over 100,000. At their peak, public institutions housed only about four percent of people with developmental disabilities, but the majority of public funds were allocated for institutional services.

Even children and adults who lived at home were, for the most part, invisible. The shame of having a child with a disability, the prejudice directed toward the family and the individual, and the lack of community supports and acceptance kept most children and adults with developmental disabilities hidden behind the walls of their own homes. It was not unusual for children with disabilities to be sent off to the back bedroom when company came for a visit.

NAZI EXTERMINATION: INSPIRED BY AMERICAN SUCCESSES

In 1933, Adolph Hitler made the forced sterilization of "undesirables" one of his first priorities. Eugenics was the focus of Nazi Germany: the "superior" Aryan Nation was to be preserved and cleansed of all "inferior" persons. Influenced by the theory of inherited feeble-mindedness and the success of sterilization—both from the United States—Nazi doctors began sterilizing adults with mental illnesses and developmental disabilities, people who were Jewish, and other "inferiors."

But Hitler's desire to maintain the strength and purity of the so-called Aryan race led him to move beyond sterilization. His next efforts were directed at eliminating children with disabilities to purify the future gene pool, as well as to free up funding for the war effort.

On the recommendation of Nazi doctors, children with disabilities were admitted to hospitals and other medical facilities. Their parents willingly brought them, based on the promise of new treatments and cures for their conditions. But death was the only "treatment" provided. Nazi physicians methodically poisoned many children with drug injections. Other doctors starved the children to death, proud that they saved money: no funds were spent on food *or* poisons. Parents were told their children died during treatment. The bodies were then cremated.

Next, adults with disabilities were targeted for death. Once again, the ploy of "improved treatment" was used to entice them into medical facilities. Once there, all pretense was dropped, and instead of using **drugs** or starvation, the Nazis gassed and then cremated them. Efficient killing methods **were** perfected using people with disabilities; six million Jews and others who were considered inferior were next.

INSTITUTIONAL HORRORS EXPOSED

The induction of young men into the military during World War II caused a shortage of staff members in many institutions. Conscientious objectors filled many of these positions, in lieu of joining the service. While long-term staffers were accustomed to the conditions inside institutions, the newcomers were not. Shocked at the injustices and cruelty they saw, they raised public awareness of the horrific conditions in most public institutions. In 1948, Albert Deutsch published *Shame of the States,* a photographic scrapbook of one of the better institutions. But America wasn't quite ready to face one of its ugliest secrets.

FDR: A GREAT LEADER, BUT WHAT IF?

In 1933, Franklin D. Roosevelt took office as the thirty-second president of the United States. Americans remember Roosevelt as an outstanding and well-loved leader who helped the country recover from the Great Depression, created Social Security, and ensured the success of the Allies in World War II.

Roosevelt had a significant physical disability, the result of contracting polio as an adult. This respected leader could have raised society's awareness of people with disabilities, demonstrating that disability is nothing to be ashamed of and is not a barrier to success. Instead, with the full cooperation of the news media, he successfully hid his disability from the public.

Americans knew Roosevelt had polio, but most did not know how it affected him. In private, he used a wheelchair. In public, however, he skillfully disguised his condition by wearing leg braces to help him "walk" as he was supported (shoulder-to-shoulder) by the arms of a son and Secret Service men.

FDR's interest in disability issues was basically limited to research about polio. He lent his support to a fund raising campaign; children were used to collect donations. The Roosevelt dime was created in his honor, and the campaign became the "Mothers March of Dimes."

People who had acquired orthopedic disabilities from the polio virus—at least those who weren't rich, famous, or politicans—were not immune from the prejudicial practices usually reserved for people with congenital disabilities. The conventional wisdom of the day was that people "crippled" by polio needed *moral training* to ensure they would not develop immoral characteristics which would lead them into the underbelly of society— the lower class or the criminal class. A crippled body was indicative of a crippled mind.

WORLD WAR II AND MEDICAL REHABILITATION

During and after World War I, as you'll recall, the government instituted vocational rehabilitation to get soldiers with acquired disabilities back into the work force. But by the time of World War II, not only could veterans with acquired disabilities be retrained for new jobs, their bodies could be restored to "normalcy" or "near-normalcy" by physicians using the latest medical techniques. As a result, medical rehabilitation was born as a distinct specialty: the American Board of Physical Medicine was created in 1947.

After the war, medical rehabilitation expanded from the military community to general society: first to civilians with acquired disabilities and then eventually to people with developmental disabilities. It's a relatively new entry in society's approach to the "problem" of disability.

PRECIOUS BABIES OR BURDENS?

In the 1940s and early 1950s, the stigma and shame of disability continued to be an invisible wall that separated families from mainstream society. And the labeling and medicalization of disability often made it feel like a fate worse than death.

From about the 1940s and continuing into the mid-1960s, some institutions began serving people with disabilities from the cradle to the grave. When a developmental disability was diagnosed at birth, many physicians urged parents to institutionalize the baby immediately. Parents were assured this would be best for everyone: the child could get the proper care and parents would be relieved of the overwhelming responsibility. While a new mother was still in the hospital after giving birth, she was advised to go home, tell everyone the baby died, and forget about the child who would be a financial and emotional burden to the family. Some parents followed this advice; most did not. The majority of children with disabilities grew up in their family homes, not in institutions.

While many parents did not abandon their newborn babies to institutions, some reversed their positions later. When parents sought help for their growing children, they were told services were only available in an institution. There were no community-based services. The majority of children with disabilities were legally excluded from public schools. Some parents did eventually place their children in institutions in order to get the help their children needed. Others did so because they were unable or unwilling to care for their children at home any longer.

THE PARENT MOVEMENT

The end of World War II brought peace and prosperity to the United States, and Americans were free to focus on their families and their society. Parents of children with disabilities turned their energies to creating better lives for their children. For many, this meant trying to improve the conditions in the institutions where their children lived. Others wanted their children to be able to attend public school. But how could they make these changes? It was hard to go it alone. Parents realized there was strength in numbers, so they banded together and things began to happen. They were giving birth to the disability rights movement, but no one—including them—knew it at the time.

In the 1930s, a few local support groups were started in the states of Ohio and Washington. Later, the Welfare League for Retarded Children was started in New York. By the early 1950s, over eighty parent groups in nineteen states had been established. The first national conference for parents was held in Minneapolis in 1950. The ninety persons in attendance created the National Association of Parents and Friends of Retarded Children, which later became The Association for Retarded Citizens, known today as The Arc. Similar organizations, representing different disabilities, were soon formed.

Today, we look back and call this part of our history the Parent Movement. The actions of small groups of parents, working together to improve the lives of their children, started us on the course we're on today. But remember, they didn't know they were planting the seeds for the development of the disability rights movement. Keep this in mind throughout this book; I hope we're planting seeds for a movement toward natural lives in community for children and adults with disabilities.

Home-Grown Help

In homes across the country, a variety of forces collided, igniting fires of creativity that burned for the next twenty years. Tired of their children being excluded, parents took things into their own hands.

Their first goal was education. Public schools weren't required to accept children with disabilities, especially children with significant disabilities. Homeschooling, as we know it today, was not part of the culture of the 1950s. Private schools for children with disabilities existed, but most were expensive residential facilities. So, between the efforts of individual parents and the disability organizations they founded, a small percentage of children with disabilities were educated. Using the borrowed locations of churches, basements in public school buildings, and other settings, including their own homes, parents found ways to educate their children. There was no set formula on how to do this; groups and individuals decided what they needed and made it happen. Many children were not educated in traditional academics. There was no automatic presumption they would be capable of having real jobs in the community. In many cases, life skills were seen as more important than academics.

Education was important, and so were every day childhood experiences. Parents began involving their children with disabilities in bowling and other sports, scouting, field trips, and other enjoyable pursuits. In general, these activities were segregated since children with disabilities were usually excluded from opportunities offered to typical children.

More time passed and the children of these enterprising parents were becoming young adults. What next? Employment, of course. Jobs in the community were not an option for most young people with disabilities at this time, but many parents still wanted their children to have the typical adult experiences of work. Again, they looked to themselves and the groups they were affiliated with for the answer. Sheltered work environments were created in garages, borrowed facilities, and other locations where young adult children could learn skills or engage in work-like activities for part of the day.

In hindsight, these efforts could be viewed as the beginnings of segregation in the community, a practice many of today's parents don't embrace. Still, what these dedicated parents achieved was nothing short of incredible. While some children and young adults languished in institutions or in the back bedrooms of their parents' homes, others were learning in home-grown schools, having fun in community activities, and participating in work-like environments.

In the context of society's expectations and beliefs about people with disabilities at the time, these children and young adults were living the good life. Their parents were motivated, caring, and unstoppable. Much of the success of these courageous moms and dads can be attributed to the support they received from one another. Parent-to-parent support proved to be a tremendous resource then; it's just as valuable today.

INSTITUTIONS GROW; THE MEDICAL MODEL FIRMLY ENTRENCHED

As more attention was paid to the dire conditions of the institutions in the 1950s, funding was increased to meet the demand for better care. Conventional wisdom dictated that *medical research* would provide answers to the so-called problem of mental retardation and other disabilities. The medicalization of disability became more firmly entrenched.

Under the medical model, disability was seen as an illness, a disease, an abnormality—a *problem within the person*. Soon, money for research took priority over money for services.

The populations of institutions continued to increase. Most began to look like hospitals, with large sterile rooms for "patients." Little education and few meaningful activities took place behind the beautiful facades of the buildings. The barren environments inside included huge wards, with cribs and beds lined up end to end; tile floors and walls; toilets with no stalls; and white-coated staff members who were more like guards than caregivers. Residents—inmates—were segregated by sex, age group, and disability. Day rooms were bleak and uninviting places where adults and children were left to entertain themselves. Many prisons and jails had better living conditions than institutions.

A FEDERAL FOCUS ON DISABILITY

For the first time ever, the federal government—led by President John F. Kennedy—took an interest in *developmental* disabilities, perhaps because disability touched the life of the President's family.

A variety of Kennedy family biographies detail that Rosemary, the President's older sister, had mental retardation. Some biographers, however, suggest she actually had a mental illness. Evidently, the family chose to portray her as having mental retardation because they believed it wasn't as stigmatizing as mental illness. When Rosemary was a young woman, physicians performed a lobotomy, removing the front part of her brain. The procedure was requested by her father, in the hope it would provide a cure. Afterwards, Rosemary could no longer care for herself and she was institutionalized. (If she didn't have a cognitive disability before the surgery, she most likely had one afterward.)

President Kennedy recognized mental retardation as an issue of national significance. He created the President's Panel on Mental Retardation, which recommended that local communities work with federal and state agencies to provide community-based services. In 1963, The Mental Retardation Facilities Construction Act authorized funds for community-based facilities for people with mental retardation, university affiliated training facilities, and mental retardation research centers.

INHUMANITY OF INSTITUTIONS EXPOSED

In 1965, Senator Robert Kennedy toured the Willowbrook State School in his home state of New York. He was dismayed by the deplorable conditions. Some children and adults were naked, sitting in their own excrement. There was nothing to do and little, if any, treatment or care. Residents were abused by staff as well as other residents.

In 1965, Burton Blatt, a professor at Syracuse University, and Fred Kaplan, a professional photographer, used a hidden camera to expose the miserable conditions in institutions. Their book, *Christmas in Purgatory*, documented the overcrowding, filth, hopelessness, and inhumanity of institutions. When excerpts were reprinted in "Look" magazine, Americans finally saw the horror of institutions.

"NORMALIZATION"

The "principles of normalization" made their way to the United States from Denmark in 1969. "Normalization" did not refer to making people with disabilities "normal." The concept focused on the importance of normal routines (the kind most people experience) for people with disabilities whose lives were controlled within the abnormal settings of congregate living facilities. For example, people should experience normal rhythms of the day (going to work or school) and the year (enjoying holidays and vacations); normal developmental experiences; the freedom to make choices; and so forth. This philosophy positively influenced many professionals, as well as people with disabilities and their families.

"DEVELOPMENTAL DISABILITY:" A NATURAL PART OF LIFE

The 1970s saw the passage of Public Law 91-517, the Developmental Disabilities Services and Facilities Construction Amendments, which authorized creation of a Developmental Disabilities Council in each state. DD Councils work toward systems change on behalf of people with developmental disabilities. The term "developmental disability" was coined to describe a significant, permanent disability that manifests itself before a person reaches the age of twenty-two. (See the current definition in the appendix.)

The DD Act includes a philosophy that I've woven throughout this book. (It's also now included in special education law.) Here it is:

> Disability is a natural part of the human experience that does not diminish the right
> of individuals with developmental disabilities to enjoy the opportunity to live
> independently, enjoy self-determination, make choices, contribute to society, and
> experience full integration and inclusion in the economic, political, social, cultural,
> and educational mainstream of American society.

Read it again, especially the first nine words. Internalize this philosophy. Live it, breathe it, and spread it to everyone you know.

INSTITUTIONS CONTINUE

Even with federal attention focused on developmental disabilities, the horrific conditions in the institutions worsened. In 1972, television reporter Geraldo Rivera and a film photographer secretly entered a children's unit at the Willowbrook institution in New York (the same one Senator Kennedy visited). His television report documented the deplorable conditions. Children were naked or only partially clothed. They were screaming, crying, silently staring, or sleeping on the bare floor. Some were tied to their beds. While the film recorded the horrible sights and sounds, Rivera told his television audience the camera could not reproduce the overwhelming stench in the building.

Children who had difficulty feeding themselves were fed by staff members. Mush was forced down their throats so fast that some choked to death. Speed was necessary to ensure everyone got *something* to eat. Others died of pneumonia after food went into their lungs, and hepatitis (caused by people being exposed to human excrement) took the lives of many. Physical and emotional abuse by staff members (and other residents) was not uncommon. Days were endless and seasons unchanging. The children had nothing to do, no one to talk to. It was a warehouse of human cargo.

Under pressure and facing lawsuits, institutions slowly began to change. Overcrowding was the most critical issue. In 1974, President Nixon issued Executive Order 11776, which reaffirmed President Kennedy's goal of returning one-third of the 200,000 people with developmental disabilities in institutions to community residential placements. The Justice Department was ordered to strengthen the legal rights of people covered by the order.

Amendments to Social Security regulations authorized payments for residential care in Intermediate Care Facilities for the Mentally Retarded (ICF-MR) in the community, and the Supplemental Security Income (SSI) program was established. Other laws and amendments relating to the deinstitutionalization of people with disabilities were enacted at both the state and federal levels, resulting in reductions of the number of people living at state institutions. (But there are still thousands of people with disabilities, including children, living in institutions, congregate facilities, and nursing homes today.)

NEONATALOGY AND INFANTICIDE IN THE MODERN ERA

The 1960s and 1970s saw the development of a variety of services, techniques, and technology that radically improved the the survival of newborns with significant medical needs. The field of neonatalogy was new and exciting. In spite of the incredible improvements in neonatal care, however, many babies still did not survive. Infanticide was being practiced under the bright lights of modern hospital nurseries.

Many obstetricians and pediatricians shared the beliefs held by society: children with disabilities lived pathetic lives; they were financial and emotional burdens to their families; their lives were so hopeless that most would be better off dead; and so on. These physicians (like most Americans at the time) could not imagine *wanting* a child who had a disability, especially when the parents could replace the "defective" child with a "healthy" child by getting pregnant again, as soon as possible. When a baby with a disability was born, doctors passed their own personal beliefs to the parents: it would be best to let the baby die.

We'll never know how often this happened. It was only when several of these cases were reported in the news that Americans learned newborn babies with disabilities were being denied life-saving medical treatment. In some cases, babies shared the fate of young children with disabilities during the Nazi regime: they were starved to death in the NICU.

In several highly-publicized cases, raging battles were fought in hospitals and in the courts. Parents and their doctors were generally on the side of no treatment. Neonatalogists and hospital administrators insisted treatment be provided. Sanctity of life vs. quality of life was argued. Legal, moral, ethical, and medical issues were jumbled together.

The situation did not go unnoticed by the federal government; lack of treatment was viewed as a form of discrimination based on disability. As a result, hospitals were put on notice: failure to provide medical care because a patient has a disability was a violation of Section 504 of the Rehabilitation Act of 1973 (described below). Additional federal mandates were issued, but some were later declared illegal.

DISCRIMINATION BASED ON DISABILITY PROHIBITED

In 1973, people with disabilities were afforded legal protection at the federal level—for the first time—with the passage of the Vocational Rehabilitation Act. The law also expanded rehab services and directed states to give priority to individuals with the most significant disabilities.

While many aspects of the Act were good for people with disabilities, Section 504 was great. It prohibited discrimination based on disability in any programs or services receiving federal funds. Thus, colleges and universities, hospitals, state and local governments, public schools, transportation systems, and any other entities that received federal funds could not discriminate against people with disabilities. It was a watershed event.

For several years, however, Section 504 was unenforceable because the regulations weren't written. Bureaucrats had not recognized its powerful implications until after it was passed, and they began stalling for time. Disability activists agitated for the regulations to be issued. A stand-off between activists and bureaucrats began. The will of people with disabilities eventually prevailed when the regulations were issued in 1977. Section 504 is one of the cornerstones of equal rights for people with disabilities.

PARENTS WIN EDUCATIONAL VICTORY

In the early 1970s, parent groups in several states were advocating for public education for children with disabilities. When their efforts failed, they filed right-to-education lawsuits on behalf of their children.

One of these was *PARC v. the Commonwealth of Pennsylvania*. The Pennsylvania Association for Retarded Citizens (PARC) sued Pennsylvania for denying children with disabilities access to public schools. After one day of testimony, in which the state did not deny the allegations by PARC, the court directed the two sides to agree on a settlement. The result? Pennsylvania must educate children with disabilities in settings similar to other children and include parents in the planning process.

In his argument before the court, the attorney for the parents, Thomas Gilhool, referenced the 1954 Supreme Court ruling in *Brown v. Board of Education of Topeka*. Remember the lesson from civics class? The parents of a young African-American girl in Kansas tried to enroll their daughter in the neighborhood school, which happened to be a "white school." The school denied her admission, saying she had to go to the "Negro school" several miles away. (Today, this routinely occurs to children with disabilities: they're denied admission to their neighborhood schools and sent to schools where "special ed programs" are housed.) While the *Brown* case was about racial segregation, the same issues were applicable to the segregation of children with disabilities. The landmark Supreme Court decision in the *Brown* case held that "separate educational facilities are inherently unequal."

At the federal level, the 1974 Amendments to the Elementary and Secondary Education Act addressed provisions related to the education of students with disabilities. In 1975, a combination of forces (the 1974 Amendments, state right-to-education cases, and parental advocacy) merged, leading Congress to enact the Education for All Handicapped Children Act, Public Law 94-142. The basic tenet of the law is a free, appropriate public education in the least restrictive environment for children with disabilities. In 1986, it was amended to include services for infants and toddlers. The 1990 amendments included a significant change: the law was renamed the Individuals with Disabilities Education Act (IDEA). When, as parents, we feel we have little or no power, we must remember that the actions of parents helped ensure the passage of special education law.

INDEPENDENT LIVING: BEING IN CONTROL OF YOUR LIFE

In the 1960s, during one of our nation's most tumultuous decades, civil rights, war protests, flower power, and free speech issues were all front page news. A quieter revolution was also underway—as evidenced by a California newspaper headline about the "helpless cripple" who was attending college—and it had profound and long-lasting implications for people with disabilities.

In 1962, Ed Roberts was attending the University of California at Berkeley along with thousands of other students. But Ed was the only one required to live in the university's Cowell Hospital. Why? Because the school believed the campus infirmary was the only suitable place for the "cripple." As a result of contracting polio when he was fourteen, Ed had quadriplegia and needed assistance with breathing. He used a wheelchair and slept in an iron lung at night. He could only move a couple of fingers on his left hand. After successfully fighting for admission to the university, he was an eager student by day and an unwilling "patient" by night.

Ed's determination motivated others with significant physical disabilities to enroll at UC-Berkeley. Soon, the "rolling quads," as they called themselves, began breaking down barriers. Ed believed old attitudes and paternalistic authority—not disability—were the greatest barriers facing people with disabilities. The physical barriers on campus were the product of these old attitudes.

Ed and his buddies combined good old-fashioned American ingenuity with a little help from their friends to achieve independence. They poured cement (under the cover of darkness) to create the first curb cuts in the nation; set up a twenty-four hour wheelchair repair clinic to ensure round-the-clock mobility; ramped campus housing; hired people to provide personal assistance services; and trained each other in ways to live as independently as possible. Ed and his cohorts now had the freedom and independence to run their own lives. The Independent Living Movement was born.

After college, Ed went to a state voc-rehab counselor for help getting a job. The counselor took one look at Ed and told him he was "too handicapped" to work. He told Ed to go home and collect his disability benefits. Ed didn't follow this advice and, several years later, California Governor Jerry Brown appointed Ed the director of the state voc-rehab system!

According to Ed, independent living is more a psychological idea than a physical concept. In hundreds of presentations across the United States, he taught thousands of people (including me) that being independent is not about being able to walk, talk, or perform functional skills. It's about being in control of your life and making your own decisions.

Under Ed's hands-on leadership, the world's first Center for Independent Living (CIL) was opened in Berkeley in 1972, based on the model Ed and others created at the university. Ten CILs in California followed. Soon, thanks to Ed's magnetic leadership and unwavering determination, dozens of CILs sprouted from coast to coast.

Ed believed the primary role of independent living centers was advocacy: doing it (targeting the human services industry) and teaching it (helping people with disabilities acquire the skills to live independently and advocate for themselves). He wanted CILs to serve people of all ages and with all disabilities. In addition, Ed strongly believed CILs should be run *by people with disabilities*. Who knows better how to help people with disabilities than other people with disabilities? Ed's personal experiences had demonstrated that the paternalistic attitudes of most "helping" professionals actually *prevented* success and independence for people with disabilities.

Today, hundreds of CILs are in operation all over the world, a moving testimony to the man known as the Father of the Independent Living Movement. Ed's unexpected death from a heart attack on March 14, 1995, was an incomparable loss. Also lost is the purity of Ed's dream. For several years before he died, Ed was disappointed and concerned that many CILs were moving away from the original independent living mission. Instead of staying focused on advocacy (and being the watch-dogs of service providers) many had *become* (and continue to be) service providers themselves.

CILs are usually funded through federal rehabilitation services monies, and the original goal was for CILs to become self-sufficient. Apparently, some have found it easier to continue receiving government funding and provide something tangible (services) instead of the intangible (advocacy and training). Ed believed CILs had a responsibility to advocate for better voc-rehab services. With an unemployment rate for people with developmental disabilities that continually remains around 75 percent, someone needed to be bird-dogging voc-rehab and other service providers on a regular basis. That's hard to do if you're a provider yourself! Still, the legacy of Ed Roberts and his independent living philosophy continues to grow as new generations of people with disabilities and their families embrace the original independent living philosophy of being in control of your own life.

SELF-ADVOCACY: SPEAKING FOR OURSELVES

In Sweden in the 1960s, a few professionals, advocates, and young adults with cognitive disabilities recognized that people with disabilities didn't always need their parents or other adults speaking for them. They were capable of self-advocacy—of speaking for themselves. For the first time, professionals and parents began listening to the young people whose lives they controlled. One of the more important philosophies generated by the young adults was: we are *not* our disabilities, we are "people, first." And with that, the People First Movement (also known as the Self-Advocacy Movement) was born.

Like the Parent Movement and the Independent Living Movement, the People First Movement was another bolt of lightning in the thundering skies of disability rights and advocacy. The first self-advocacy conference was held in Sweden in the 1960s. This landmark event was followed by similar conferences in England (1972) and Canada (1973).

The trailblazing movement spread to the United States when several people with disabilities from Oregon attended the Canadian conference. Inspired, motivated, and determined, they spearheaded the first U.S. conference in Oregon in 1974. Expecting a few hundred attendees, conference organizers were delightfully shocked when more than 500 individuals from across the United States showed up.

The People First Movement grew and evolved, just as the Independent Living Movement did. Today, over 600 self-advocacy chapters in the United States include people with all types of disabilities.

The local and state organizations are often known as People First or Speaking for Ourselves chapters. Unlike Centers for Independent Living, which are essentially business-like entities, People First chapters are similar to support groups (but they're far more than that). At regularly scheduled meetings, individuals with disabilities meet for friendship, to learn and share advocacy skills, and to discuss other issues of importance. For many, especially people who grew up in institutions, speaking up at their initial People First meeting is often the first time they've ever spoken for themselves and been listened to!

People First meetings, including the international conferences held every two years, are planned *by* people with disabilities, *for* people with disabilities. The only people *without* disabilities who attend regular meetings are the chapter advisors. The advisor role is clearly defined: provide direction when asked, but don't try to run the meetings, thank you.

The People First Movement spawned a new organization, Self-Advocates Becoming Empowered (SABE), in the early 1990s. SABE was created to (1) help people with diabilities move from institutions into communities and (2) close down public institutions.

THE AMERICANS WITH DISABILITIES ACT

The Parent, Independent Living, and Self-Advocacy Movements, along with a patchwork of federal laws, helped move people with disabilities from the shadows to the light. With the passage of the Americans with Disabilities Act (ADA) on July 26, 1990, people with disabilities were finally afforded full legal equality. Unlike previous laws that focused on specific entities—programs receiving federal funds (Section 504) and education (IDEA)—the ADA addressed civil rights in all areas of American society.

The ADA prohibits discrimination on the basis of disability in employment practices, in the public services of state and local governments, in public accommodations (theaters, restaurants, child care facilities, and so forth), and in telecommunications. While the law is not perfect, most agree it has allowed people with disabilities—and our society—to make significant progress toward inclusion and the elimination of discriminatory practices.

The ADA has become a model for similar laws in other countries. The United Nations, the European Union, and the Organization of American States have created resolutions calling for the elimination of all forms of discrimination against people with disabilities, particularly in employment.

MORE CHANGES NEEDED

More progress has been made in disability issues in the United States during the last fifty years than in hundreds of previous years. We have more laws (state and federal), programs, entitlements, and services than ever before. However, individuals with disabilities are still excluded, isolated, segregated, ignored, marginalized, and devalued. How can this be? Why is this still happening, in spite of the incredible progress that's been made? Because we can't legislate attitudes, perceptions, and morality.

Many people in American society still do not believe children and adults with developmental disabilities are equal or able in body, mind, or spirit. Too many people still accept the old misconceptions (myths) as truths. There is no doubt that—as Ed Roberts believed—*old attitudes and paternalistic authority constitute the greatest barriers facing people with disabilities*, including your child and mine.

If educators and society *believed* that children with disabilities are more similar to children without disabilities than different, and that they're competent learners and belong with their typical peers in public schools, we would have never needed special education law (P.L. 94-142) back in 1975. Even with the law, however, the beliefs of many educators have not changed: the majority of children with disabilities are undereducated, placed in segregated settings, and/or devalued by an educational system that doesn't believe in our children's abilities to learn, or their right to belong.

If employers and our society *believed* adults with disabilities are more like adults without disabilities than different, and that they could be productive employees, contributing their skills to their employers' businesses, we wouldn't need vocational-rehabilitation laws, nor would we need the Americans with Disabilities Act to prohibit job discrimination based on disability. But even with these laws, the majority of employers' opinions have not changed. The unemployment rate for adults with developmental disabilities remains perpetually high in the neighborhood of 75 percent.

If business owners and our society *believed* that adults and children with disabilities like to browse at malls, attend symphony performances, eat out once a week, use typical child care facilities, and do the same things most Americans take for granted, more stores and restaurants would be ramped, more restrooms would be accessible, TTY units would be more widely available on public telephones, day care and preschool facilities would not deny admission to children with disabilities, and on, and on, and on. And we wouldn't need the Americans with Disabilities Act to prohibit discrimination based on disability in the areas of public accommodations and telecommunications.

Yet even with the law, the attitudes of many in society have not changed: children with disabilities are still excluded from typical day care and preschool settings; many restaurants, stores, and theaters remain inaccessible; and many doctors and hospitals do not provide sign language interpreters to people who need them. The list is endless.

If local and state government officials *believed* people with disabilities want to vote in elections, participate in park and rec activities, and experience the same benefits and responsibilities of citizenship most Americans take for granted, we wouldn't need Section 504 and the Americans with Disabilities Act to prohibit discrimination based on disability in the areas of public services (state and local governments). Yet these two laws haven't changed the attitudes of most public officials: numerous polling places are still inaccessible; many park and rec activities are either inaccessible or segregated; most communities still don't have enough curb cuts; and the full benefits of citizenship are unavailable to many.

Until *attitudes and perceptions change*, no law can ensure that children and adults with disabilities will experience inclusion in education, employment, or community activities, or enjoy the precious, but common, rights and responsibilities of American citizenship.

WHERE IS THE PROBLEM?

Since the beginning of recorded history, one group or another (ancient priests, social reformers, educators, physicians, bureaucrats, and others) has taken charge of the "problem" of people with disabilities. And up to this point in time, every authoritarian group has found people with disabilities unacceptable the way they are.

At one time, African-American people were found unacceptable by the Euro-American majority in the United States. In essence, African-Americans were told, "You cannot ride in the front of the bus, drink from this water fountain, work for this company, vote, or come through the front door because of your skin color." Society saw the problem as being within people whose skin was "black."

Then African-American people began to change things. They knew the "problem" was not inside of them, and they stopped waiting for the majority to change. If change was going to happen, they knew they would have to make it happen. As a result of the Civil Rights Movement, laws were passed, but language and attitudes changed, too. And society began to realize the problem wasn't within people who had "black" skin; the problem was in society's attitudes. African-American people didn't need to change; they didn't need to become "white-skinned" like the majority. Society needed to change and it did.

A similar situation was repeated in the Women's Movement. In essence, women were told, "You can't be a soldier, run a company, fly an airplane, or be paid the same as a man.

You can't do any of those things because you aren't a man." The dominant male power structure in society saw the "problem" as being within people who were female.

Then women began to change things. They stopped waiting for the dominant power structure to change. They knew if change was going to happen, they would have to make it happen. While the Equal Rights Amendment was never passed, policies, language, and attitudes changed. And society realized the problem wasn't within people who were females; they didn't need to change. The problem was in society's attitudes. Society needed to change and it did.

Things still aren't perfect regarding the human rights of various groups in our society and their inclusion into the mainstream, but we've come a long way. Now it's our turn to move society in a new direction. Can we learn from those who have gone before us? Others have had to destroy the myths that surrounded them and free themselves from the shackles of prejudice. We can, too.

People with developmental disabilities are told, "You can't be in a regular ed class, go to college, live where and how you want, have a good job, be included in society, get married, have kids, or control your own life. You can't do these things because you have a disability." Thus, people with developmental disabilities are considered unacceptable *the way they are*. The dominant majority in society—people without disabilities—sees the "problem" as being within people who have disabilities.

African-American people didn't need to change, women didn't need to change, and people with disabilities don't need to change. The problem is not within people with disabilities; the problem is society's attitude toward people with disabilities. African-American people and women are fine just the way they are. *People with disabilities are fine just the way they are, too.* Society—not people with disabilities—needs to change. But we must stop waiting for society to change. If change is going to happen, we must make it happen.

The concept that disability (like ethnicity and gender) is a natural part of the human experience has been a part of the Developmental Disabilities Act for many years. It is also included in IDEA. It's time for all of us to recognize the validity of the philosophy. There have always been people with disabilities in the world (just as there have always been women and people from various ethnic backgrounds) and there always will be.

We can no longer depend on professionals or the government to pave the way. In the past, authorities have led people with disabilities down paths that resulted in death, isolation, segregation, sterilization, exclusion, dependency, and second-class citizenship. We can no longer let any group—professionals, bureaucrats, educators, physicians, lawmakers, or any other authorities—be in charge of people with disabilities. We cannot let others decide the fates of our children and families. We must not continue making our children and others with disabilities wait for change (more money, more programs, more laws, or more anything). We must lead the way toward a more inclusive society—now, today, this minute! We can't wait for others to do it for us.

We've examined our history. But the past continues to shape the present. In the next section, we'll look at the different pieces of the puzzle that constitute today's Disability World. We'll begin with the moment in time when history imprinted itself on the lives of children with disabilities and their families: D-Day—the day of diagnosis.

The Way
Things Are

DOUBT IS THE BEGINNING,
NOT THE END,
OF WISDOM.

George Iles

The Medical Model and the Genesis of Grief

NEVER DENY THE DIAGNOSIS, BUT DO DENY THE
NEGATIVE VERDICT THAT MAY GO WITH IT.
Norman Cousins

Disability has historically been viewed as a "problem" of one sort or another: spiritual, social, educational, or something else. Mythological gods, civil authorities, churches, educators, psychologists, social reformers, and bureaucrats, among others, have all taken turns at solving the perceived dilemma. But when physicians took greater interest in—and control over—people with disabilities, disability became entrenched within the medical model, joining the assortment of illnesses and diseases that physicians (and our society) make war on every day. And within this paradigm, the grief process has been firmly established as an appropriate response for parents when their children are diagnosed with developmental disabilities.

There's a curious and significant connection between the grief process and the medical model. The same diagnosis that enables a child to be eligible for services (help) can also plunge parents into the grief process (harm). The fear that results from the stigma of the label is the initial consequence. But there are other harmful consequences that affect not only the parents, but also the child and the entire family, in very insidious ways.

The medical model and the grief process are inextricably linked. And a closer look at the medical model forces us to confront some of the larger issues facing our society. It will also cause us to question the concept of what a disability really is. This will lead us to question the need for grief.

WHAT IS THE MEDICAL MODEL?

The medical model is one we're all familiar with. It represents the conventional response to illness or discomfort. You feel bad, you go to the doctor, and he prescribes the cure. Day in and day out, the medical model works, and it's appropriate for the majority of illnesses, injuries, infections, and other conditions. Most of us recognize the benefits of an antibiotic for an infection or having a broken bone set in a cast. Under the medical model, physicians recognize deficits in the body and attempt to provide remedies.

THE QUEST FOR PERFECTION

In today's highly medicalized society, most Americans expect (and some actually demand) a solution from doctors for every complaint. In general, we like the medical model. We're a society that seeks perfection, just like the ancient Greeks. They pleaded with their heavenly gods for help, we plead with the gods of medicine and they oblige.

Twenty-first century medicine is big business. We want to believe—and sometimes we're told—that for every problem, there's a solution. Any condition that interferes with society's notion of human perfection or normalcy is an enemy to be defeated. We fight cancer, make war on the common cold, and battle birth defects. We combat indigestion with chewables, attack gray hair with loving care, and fight plaque with mouthwash. A visitor from outer space watching our television or reading our magazines and newspapers might believe us to be dangerous society: one at war with itself. At the societal level, we fight poverty, make war on drugs, battle teen pregnancies, and more. No one is immune from the onslaught of messages that we must, at all costs, continue the quest for individual and societal perfection.

Do we seek perfection because of our own personal desires? Do we crave perfection because of societal pressures? Do we demand perfection because the providers of goods and services (including the government) tell us they can provide it?

Can we not recognize that perfection, like beauty, is in the eyes of the beholder? In seeking perfection, we demonstrate that we have no respect for natural differences in humanity. By demanding perfection, we demonstrate our fear of the natural human condition.

We once viewed childbirth, menopause, aging, and other conditions as natural occurrences. But in today's world, they have become medical "problems" that require the intervention of physicians.

The relationship between humans' quest for perfection and medicine is circular. Because we don't want to suffer, we seek medical solutions to every problem. And then because medicine promises solutions—if not right now, then in the future—we expect an end to suffering. And, for some, if suffering cannot be alleviated, death is the answer. We seek perfect health: the end of all pain and suffering. Over the years, medicine has promised and delivered many solutions. Society continues to push for more.

These are complex issues that cannot be adequately covered in this book. Other authors have written about them in great depth. As the parent of a child with a disability and a supporter of the inclusion of all people with disabilities and differences, I question the benefits of our continual quest for perfection, no matter the cost. And I don't mean the financial cost. What is the *emotional* cost to ourselves, when we cannot accept our own humanity, nor the humanity of our children? If we cannot accept anything less than perfect in ourselves, how can we accept imperfections in others? *Just how good do we have to be?* Is there a *societal* solution that can move us beyond the quest for perfection so that natural differences among us can be accepted, or can the answers be found only in the depths of our own souls?

WHAT IS A DISABILITY?

Before going further into the issues of the medical model we must consider the concept and definition of disability. To begin with, there is no definition of "able-bodied." A person is considered able-bodied not because she meets a particular standard of physical or intellectual ability, but only because she doesn't have a disability!

So what is a disability? It's whatever the government (or any organization that provides services) *says it is*. A disability is a condition or state of being to which a label is attached. The label is an administrative term for the purpose of identifying and categorizing individuals who may be eligible for entitlements and services, or who may be protected by certain laws. Ultimately, disability labels are simply *sociopolitical passports* to gain entrance into the Disability World of services, programs, entitlements, and laws. There are probably as many definitions of disability as there are programs, services, and regulations.

Picture a dart board. Now imagine that all the little colored targets represent the numerous programs and laws for people with disabilities. To discover a definition of disability, throw the dart and see where it lands. What did you hit? Special education? Supplemental Security Income (SSI)? The ADA? Worker's Compensation? Medicaid? Early childhood services? Section 504? Veterans' Affairs? Other? The definition of disability can change depending where your dart lands.

The definition parents are most familiar with is "developmental disability." This federal definition (in the appendix) is used to determine if our children qualify for services and entitlements mandated at the federal level. But just about the time you think you know what a disability is, you might learn it's something else. It happened to me.

"100 Percent Disabled"

During a summer garage sale at our home, Benjamin set up a lemonade stand to earn a few bucks. "Lemonade! Get your ice cold lemonade!" he called out every time new browsers emerged from their cars.

I noticed a couple walking up our street and recognized them as neighbors who lived in a home near the bottom of the hill. We had never officially met these folks, but we regularly waved when we saw them in the neighborhood. When they reached our house, I expected them to pause to catch their breaths; we live at 8,600 feet elevation and it's easy to get out of breath very quickly. Instead, they energetically checked out the merchandise and stopped by Benj's lemonade stand for a moment.

The fiftyish-year-old man then approached me, motioned to Benj in his power wheelchair, and said, "I see your son is uh, uh, uh—" "Yes," I said, helping him out, "my son has cerebral palsy."

"Oh, yeah," he replied, relieved that I had given him the words. Then he continued with, "Has he been like that all his life?" I gave him the short version of how Benj came to have cerebral palsy via prematurity and an intraventricular brain hemorrhage. He beamed then and proudly said, "Well, I'm 100 percent disabled, too!" "Oh, I see," I said, but I didn't see at all. His wife joined us, we chatted about the garage sale, and then they left, briskly walking down the hill.

Later, I found out he had been injured on the job, resulting in some government agency (probably Worker's Compensation) categorizing him as "100 percent disabled," which meant he was never expected to work again. Evidently, he received enough cash benefits and entitlements to continue the lifestyle he enjoyed when he was employed.

What a paradox. Many adults with significant developmental disabilities are labeled unemployable, but don't want to be. My neighbor, who was considered able-bodied most of his life, who had spent years as a successful businessman, and who had acquired a disability as a mature adult, "couldn't" work and was satisfied. I don't doubt he had some sort of disability. But I have never known any adults who have lived with a developmental disability since childhood, proudly announce what percentage of disability they have. Instead, they choose to *minimize* the effect of disability on their lives.

I wondered: if my neighbor was considered "100 percent disabled," yet he could walk up our steep hill without being short of breath, what percentage of disability did Benjamin have—200, 500, or 1,000 percent?

Remember: a disability is whatever the system says it is, and a disability label is simply an administrative term—a sociopolitical passport—for services and entitlements. That's all it is. Think about it.

When is a Disability Not a Disability?

Before moving back to the issue of the medical model and the grief process, there's one more thing to consider. Because my son doesn't receive any services—by choice—I could say my son does not have a disability. Yes, he has cerebral palsy, but technically I don't need to invoke his disability status unless he enters the service system or his rights under various disability-related laws are violated.

Now, think about your own child. Does he have a disability all the time? No, not really. Keep this in the back of your mind for now.

THE MEDICAL MODEL AND DISABILITY

From our history, we know that various methods have been used to try to cure people with disabilities. The conventional wisdom of the various eras dictated the cure. The holy spit of priests was used. Parents tried to beat the Devil out. Isolation from the community and training were tried. Today, swimming with dolphins is supposed to work for some. Surgery, drugs, and other interventions are routine.

Some medical conditions that often resulted in disabilities (like polio) have been eliminated by vaccine. Individuals who were infected by the polio virus have never been "cured," but the virus is no longer a threat in most Western societies. However, even as some conditions are eliminated, more crop up when new conditions are identified, and then classified, as disabilities.

With all the attempts at cure and with all the efforts toward prevention, there are more conditions classified as disabilities today than ever before. Thus, there are more people with disabilities than ever before. And the incidence of disability continues to rise because of improvements in medical care. Premature babies who once died now live, but they may have congenital disabilities; people survive life-threatening injuries but may acquire disabilities; and because we're all living longer, we acquire disabilities as we age.

The dilemma of disability being viewed through the medical model lens is that most disabilities are not illnesses. People with disabilities do get sick, but a disability—in and of itself—is not usually an illness. And the majority of developmental disabilities do not cause death. A person with Down syndrome, for instance, may die prematurely because of heart failure, but the disability itself didn't cause death.

With disability under the medical umbrella, however, society perceives disability as an illness and people with disabilities are viewed as unhealthy. Thus, disabilities are treated like other ailments (deficits): identify the condition, provide a remedy, and try to restore the patient to "good health."

In addition—and perhaps more importantly—because developmental disabilities are permanent conditions (unlike the flu, a broken leg, or other temporary conditions) which may affect a person's lifestyle and/or abilities over time, the condition of the body and the person as a whole *are seen as one,* so the person—not just the body—has a deficit.

Our society, with doctors leading the charge, has determined that disability is abnormal (even though we don't have a definition of normal). Because there is no cure—no way to make the disability go away—society (including physicians, parents, educators, and others) sees a developmental disability diagnosis as a tragedy, a huge problem to be solved, and/or a life sentence of disappointment. And here we find the genesis of grief: the diagnosis brings a sense of loss, and grief is seen as a necessary and appropriate response. The disability diagnosis is a double-edged sword: one edge cuts a path to services while the other edge wounds hearts and contributes to the grief process.

Reductionism is another practice within the medical community that contributes to the so-called grief process. In the eyes of doctors, nurses, therapists, and other health care professionals, people are often reduced to malfunctioning organs which are in need of repair. Listen to the conversations in a hospital, doctor's office, or therapy center:

> The ruptured spleen in 610 needs to go to the lab.

> We've got a by-pass coming in at 11:00.

> I've got a spina bifida assessment next.

Professionals who talk this way say it's simply a shorthand method of speaking; a fast, efficient way of communicating with one another. But it's more than that. It proves the reductionist mode of thinking. We think in words; what we think comes out of our mouths.

If I have strep throat, I might not mind being referred to as my body part because it's a temporary condition and it doesn't really impact my entire life. But for children and adults with disabilities, the reductionist practice can be devastating. The status of their body parts take precedence over who they are as human beings. Parents often adopt this practice and focus on "deficient" body parts instead of the whole child.

We usually accept the conventional wisdom of doctors in our heads, while in our hearts we try to reject it. (We should listen to our hearts!) Unfortunately, and without any malicious intent, we spread the news about our children—using the medical (deficit) model—to family, friends, educators, and others. Then *they* become focused on a child's body parts instead of the whole child.

THE DAY OF DIAGNOSIS

Let's look at a routine doctor's visit for a moment. I tell the doctor my symptoms. He examines me, gives my condition a name (diagnosis), prescribes a treatment, and tells me what to expect (prognosis). He's familiar with my condition; he's seen it many times before and he might have experienced it himself. He knows, with some certainty, that whatever treatment he's recommending will be successful.

But a dilemma arises when the diagnosis is a developmental disability. There is no prescription to be given, no injection to administer, no way to quickly remedy the condition or "restore the patient to good health." There is no cure for a developmental disability and the condition is permanent. What's a doctor to do? *Something* must be done. He feels obligated to provide a solution to the "problem." And we expect him to do something; we practically demand it.

Because a doctor's prognosis for a developmental disability cannot address "recovery," the focus is on achieving a level of "normalcy" via medical intervention, and even social and educational services. The prognosis becomes a prophecy of doom, as the physician peers into his crystal ball and sees mostly darkness, with a few points of light here and there.

Most diagnoses of developmental disabilities are made by specialists, rather than a family doctor or general practitioner. Pediatricians and pediatric specialists such as neurologists, orthopedists, ophthalmologists, physiatrists, psychologists, and psychiatrists see only children. They don't have adult patients. Thus, most have little or no knowledge about people with disabilities who may be very successful. And most doctors probably don't have adults with disabilities as friends or coworkers. If physicians don't *know* about successful women and men with developmental disabilities, they cannot know what possibilities exist for our children. They might not even be aware that adults with developmental disabilities *can* be successful.

If physicians know only that many adults with developmental disabilities are in sheltered group homes, adult day care centers, or similar programs (because that's what they learned in medical school or from society) they might believe such a future is not only the norm, but also the best that can be expected. The prognoses and treatment recommendations physicians give us are not based on their personal knowledge about long-term outcomes, but on conventional medical wisdom. (Next time you see the physician who diagnosed your child, ask if he personally knows any adults who have the same disability as your child.)

Doctors are human. Regardless of their medical training, most physicians and health care professionals view disability not only through the medical model, but also through their own personal lens: it's a tragedy and they wouldn't want it to happen to them. A report in the June 2, 1999 issue of the "Journal of the American Medical Association" detailed a study showing that doctors and nurses were more likely than family members to consider severe disabilities in a premature infant as a "fate worse than death."

When my son was born seven weeks prematurely, he spent three weeks in the NICU before coming home. I heard many conversations between doctors and nurses about the babies in the unit. Much of the language included derogatory descriptions that were commonly used in that setting. My least favorite was their referral to premature babies, in general, as "bad babies." I'm sure they meant it in a medical way, but it still reflected their attitudes. What we think comes out of our mouths. This type of language represents gross unawareness and unfamiliarity with the stark reality that people with disabilities *can and do live highly successful, happy, and fulfilled lives.*

But negative attitudes about babies with disabilities aren't new. The study of "congenital defects" is called teratology. The ancient Greek root is "teratos," which means monster.

The Latin word "monstrum," as in a divine portent, has been used to describe newborns with disabilities.

The lack of knowledge about successful adults with developmental disabilities, coupled with the physician's dependence on conventional wisdom, weighs heavily on the doctor's prognosis about your child. Whether your child was two months old, two years old, or twelve years old, the physician formed an opinion about your child's future without really knowing your child, your family, or the environment he'll grow up in, and with little or no consideration of your child's current abilities.

Now let's examine the diagnostic scenario of a child with a developmental disability, a permanent condition for which there is no cure. The initial meeting with a physician can come about in a variety of ways. Some babies are diagnosed at birth or in early childhood, a situation which may come as a surprise to many parents. In other cases, parents suspect "something wrong" in an older child and see a physician to confirm a suspected condition. Regardless of when the diagnosis is made, similarities in the outcome exist. We'll look at both situations. In all cases, the doctor gives the name of the condition (diagnosis), pre-scribes treatment, and tells parents what to expect (prognosis). (When they don't know what to call something, they use the generic "developmental delay" or something similar.)

Two life-altering situations arise from this scenario: parents enter the grief process and the child enters the service system. Both profoundly affect the family and the child in a variety of ways.

The Diagnosis of Babies

When a woman is pregnant, she's often asked, "What do you want, a boy or a girl?" Almost invariably, the answer is something like, "Oh, it really doesn't matter, as long as it's healthy." Translation: as long as the baby doesn't have a disability. What's the message here? That babies and children with disabilities are sick or unhealthy, which makes them (pick one or more): abnormal, invaluable, pitiful, sad, tragic, or unwanted.

When a baby or very young child is diagnosed with a congenital disability, parents are given the name of the condition and the doctor reviews what he knows about the condition. Sounds pretty cut and dried, but we know it's not. Upon hearing the name of the condition and/or the prognosis, parents are plunged into the grief process. We have been programmed to grieve:

- We grew up with the notion that people with disabilities deserve our pity. *Now we have a child who will be pitied.*

- Organizations raise money to "fight birth defects" or to cure the "victims." *Now we have a "defective" child.*

- Through prenatal testing, other parents are making sure they have "healthy" babies by aborting fetuses with disabilities. *But we didn't (or couldn't) do that.*

- News reports detail the high cost of premature and other newborns who require "expensive, life-long medical care." *And those are our children.*

- We seldom hear about, nor do we know, any successful people with disabilities. *So what kind of future can we expect for our children when they're adults?*

The deck is stacked against us. Upon hearing the diagnosis, we feel there's more bad than good. The office visit becomes something other than just a visit to the doctor: it's like we're in a courtroom and the judge is passing sentence. We're not just told about our child's *condition*. Many of us are told of the negative consequences the disability will have on our child's development and his social and educational experiences. We may even be told about the negative effect on the family.

Our doctors are kind and patient, empathetic and sympathetic, but the bottom line (we feel at the time) is that our children's deficits far exceed their capabilities. We begin grieving; we're saddened and angry over the loss of the the baby we expected, the baby we dreamed about.

The Diagnosis of Older Children

If your child was diagnosed as a preschooler or later, your experiences were probably different from those of parents whose children were diagnosed at birth or in infancy.

For years, perhaps, you suspected something was "wrong." Maybe you sought help, but your concerns were dismissed before you finally found a physician or an educator who listened to you. Discovering that your child's condition had a name might have been a great comfort. Until the time of diagnosis, you may have felt you were somehow responsible for your child's behavior or learning difficulties. When a professional finally acknowledged what you suspected all along and prescribed treatment, you received a mixed blessing: your child would finally start getting the help she needed, but you also learned of the potential life-long difficulties she might have.

At the other extreme, you may have thought your child was a little behind or a little different, and you weren't too concerned about it. But when the diagnosis was made, you experienced the same shock felt by parents of babies and toddlers.

In either case, parents often experience the same grief reactions previously described. In some situations, parents of older children may feel a greater "loss" than parents of newborns and very young children. For example, if Martha's child is not diagnosed until he's seven or eight, she's had all those years to get to know her son, to dream for him, to visualize him as an adult. All those dreams may be stripped from her the instant the diagnosis is made. In addition, she may feel she no longer knows her son; the person inside her son's body isn't who she thought he was!

Not only are Martha's dreams disturbed, so are her son's. The effect of the diagnosis on him can't even be imagined. He's had years to define himself, to see himself as a typical rough and tumble boy who has lots of energy. He knows he has difficulty reading and following directions, but he's trying his hardest to improve. On the day of diagnosis—in one instant—he's gone from being Seth to an "ADD kid."

While Martha might be concerned and relieved at the same time, Seth is devastated. Even though Martha presents the information to him in a loving way—telling him he'll now get the help he needs—and even though Seth might act relieved and grateful on the outside, Martha has no way of knowing how this is affecting him on the inside.

Does Seth need to "grieve" over the loss of his so-called normalcy? He's still the same great kid, but his world has been turned upside down. When he starts "acting out," is this his personal angst coming out or is he rebelling against being labeled and treated differently?

Many parents have told me stories that are strikingly similar. Here's a composite. A fifth grade boy receives a diagnosis of attention deficit disorder. He begins to receive special education services in public school. Things should be going well since he's getting the help he needs. Instead, he begins acting out because the special help makes him feel stupid or different. He hates going to the special ed room. Kids call him "retard." His acting out increases. Now he acquires an additional disability label: an emotional or behavioral disorder. Things go downhill from here.

THE DEATH OF DREAMS

Initially, all parents have dreams for their children. We have pictures in our heads of what a child will look like, what type of family we'll have, and so forth. Fathers dream of playing ball with a son or protecting their little princess from high school Romeos. Mothers dream of sweet kisses and hugs, and fulfilling the girlhood dream of being a mother. Many parents dream big, long dreams about their children: college graduation, a wedding twenty years down the road, and grandchildren. In the time it takes the doctor to tell us our child's diagnosis, however, those dreams evaporate before our eyes. Our world is shaken to the core. Some of us become numb, some of us try to be brave, and some of us become angry. The hope, the dreams, and the bright future we pictured for our child is gone, replaced by a very scary unknown world.

In describing the prognosis, the physician gives parents many different bits of information, depending on the disability. But almost all predictions have one thing in common: we're told far more about what our children will not accomplish, than what they will. We're given the "bad" news: our children's perceived deficits far exceed their abilities.

In medical vernacular, our children are brain-damaged, have a birth defect, or are abnormal. We're told about a course of treatment, which—according to the doctor—must be carried out if we want our children to reach their maximum potential. The doctor's message is intended to be a realistic and honest appraisal of a child's condition and what it will take to make things "better." But the unspoken message is a life sentence of disappointment.

This practice has become more pronounced in recent years. Today, doctors frequently diagnosis children as early as possible, providing detailed descriptions of the child's "problems." These early diagnoses are intended to help the child by enabling parents to get the greatest amount of services as soon as possible. Early intervention—and the earlier the better, according to experts—is seen as extremely valuable.

In other cases, physicians may give dire pronouncements about a child's condition and his future to protect themselves from lawsuits. If, for example, a physician gives a rosy prognosis which the parents later believe was inaccurate, the parents may decide to sue.

Because society has elevated doctors to god-like status—in general, we trust them, and don't question their wisdom—many parents accept the pessimistic appraisal of their child. We buy it hook, line, and sinker.

The power of physicians is so great that we take the prognosis about our child's condition and future as an *accurate statement of fact*. But the prognosis is really only a *prediction!* And typically, it's not a very accurate prediction, for it's based on disability myths and guesswork. Again, the prognosis is not based on personal knowledge the physician has about people with disabilities.

Parents who accept the doctor's prediction pass it on to their families and friends, and then to professionals in the child's life: therapists, health care providers, educators, service coordinators, and others. Soon, everyone knows the so-called facts about this child and the disability. Again, these "facts" are based on myths derived from the disability label; they're not based on the real child. Still, everyone believes them to be true.

Before any of our precious children have had an opportunity to define themselves, they've been defined by their disability labels. There is no greater loss.

CORRUPTION OF THE GRIEF PROCESS

When Elisabeth Kubler-Ross wrote her book, *On Death and Dying*, she identified five sequential responses observed in people who were dealing with the death of a loved one: denial and isolation, anger, bargaining, depression, and acceptance. Much has been made of her work by professionals in the fields of medicine, sociology, and mental health. And the general public has embraced the concepts of the grief process.

Our society, it seems, has taken her *observations* and turned them into *requirements:* to successfully deal with the loss of a loved one, you must go through all the steps in the proper order. Grievers are expected to proceed through a crisis in the orderly manner described above.

But it hasn't stopped there. Today, almost any event that's perceived as a "loss" falls under the category of grief. People diagnosed with cancer or other conditions, workers who have lost their jobs, men and women who divorce, as well as others who face some change in their lives, are frequently seen as people in crisis, victims of tragedies, or survivors of catastrophes. They are *expected* to grieve over a perceived loss. There is no end to the categorization of victims, or to the responses our society creates to the routine circumstances of being human. We often believe "suffering" through any number of natural occurrences elevates us to victim status. Have we become victims of our own beliefs in victimization?

Do not underestimate the power of these developments, for their effects are pervasive and long-lasting on parents of children with disabilities. Professionals and others (including family members and friends) often assume an expertise that is non-existent. Psycho-babble results:

- Parents who are seen as not doing enough for their children, as well as those who refuse to accept professional help, are accused of being "in denial."

- Parents who are perceived to be doing too much for their children are said to be overcompensating because they feel "guilt" or are "depressed."

- Parents who disagree with experts (physicians, educators or other professionals) are said to have "displaced anger."

People who surround us, from friends and family to professionals who barely know us, become armchair psychiatrists. Everyone "knows" that whatever difficulties we face are caused by the child, his disability, and the accompanying grief. We even analyze ourselves.

GRIEF: A SET-UP FOR PARENTS

The grief process is unnecessary. It's a crock! We're set up for it by a society that views the birth of a child with a disability as a tragic loss.

Why do we grieve? Our children didn't die. *They're alive!* Put this book down and go look. We can't be grieving over the actual death of a child, so we must be grieving over the death of an *image:* the perfect child. We're back to that perfection stuff, again.

We have not produced the child of our dreams. Sadness results. We have produced a "defective" child. Guilt and shame result. We're entering uncharted waters. Fear results. But we're comforted when we're told that our grief is natural. Our feelings and reactions are based upon society's "beliefs" (myths) about people with disabilities.

When our children are diagnosed at birth or shortly thereafter, most of us must fight to maintain the joy of giving birth to a new baby. When Shana's third child, Michaela, was born with Down syndrome, doctors and nurses in the hospital didn't help her celebrate Michaela's birth. The atmosphere was totally different than when her other two children were born. When the nurses brought Michaela to Shana's room, there were no happy smiles on their faces. They moved slowly—with grim expressions of sympathetic sadness and pity—as they handed Shana her "burden." Some parents have said no one gave them a baby shower after the births of their children with disabilities; family members and friends felt "there was nothing to celebrate."

When we tell family members and friends about a child's diagnosis for the first time, most people respond with empathy, sympathy, or pity. We hear responses like, "Oh, I'm so sorry." or "Oh, no!" or "How sad." or "What are you going to do?"

It's no wonder parents feel the need to grieve. Our hearts tell us to and those around us expect it. Grief may be considered a natural reaction to the loss of a loved one, but we didn't lose a loved one. *We only lost an image!* And images are figments of our imaginations. If we can *create* images, we can also *change* them. We can create new ones; we can do anything we want with them. Our minds are very powerful!

So much attention has been paid to parents' grief that a virtual industry has been created to address the issue. Professional manuals—from a basic physician's desk reference to specialized books on pediatric rehabilitation—discuss it in depth. These manuals warn that telling parents about a child's disability should be viewed as a crisis intervention. Some recommend advising parents to seek psychological counseling to deal with their grief. And if parents are so inclined, they can buy their own books on the subject and attend grief counseling workshops.

How can we *not* grieve, when everyone expects us to? Indeed, we would probably be considered abnormal if we *didn't* grieve. But who has put us into the mindset to grieve? In general, society; specifically, physicians who provide the diagnosis, prognosis, and recommended treatment.

It doesn't seem to matter to us that doctors aren't absolutely sure the prescribed treatment is appropriate. We expect doctors to give us some remedy and they oblige. They're doing the "something" I mentioned earlier. This is an important action for both the doctor and the parents. The doctor feels good that he can recommend some form of treatment, and his recommendations may actually restore some of the hope the diagnosis stripped away. It's a neat solution, but it may not be the right solution.

Doing Something Makes Us Feel Better

Based on the recommendations of a physician, parents dive into the world of the service system. It feels good to be doing *something* to help our children. If the diagnosis breeds grief, then treatment—therapy, interventions, or special programs—seems to be the antidote to grief.

Treatment for the child is almost a form of psychological treatment for the parents. For example, taking a child to physical therapy twice a week—"I'm doing all I can for my child"—makes us feel better about the situation. The treatment, of course, is based on the medical (deficit) model: fix the problem, the defect, the child.

A benevolent scheme emerges. Professionals and parents jointly plot the best methods to ensure the doctor's recommendations are carried out. Initially, everyone agrees to the scheme, for it represents taking action "for the good of the child." Parents and professionals labor feverishly on the child, then watch (and wait) for improvement. Family and friends support the efforts. This conspiracy of hope and help succeeds for awhile.

But in the vast majority of families, the promise of treatment wanes when the child doesn't "get better" to the degree, or at the speed, hoped for. A variety of forces collide and the parents are left wondering what hit them. For some, it takes only months, for others it's years. The ongoing doctor visits, therapies, dealing with the system, and other intrusions in our lives take their toll. Frustration, anger, and impotency pervade our spirits, overwhelming the tiny bit of hope that was inspired by the doctor's treatment plan.

Over time, the grief subsides, or we push it out of the way. But for many, grief rears its ugly head again and again. It's never far from the surface. Birthdays and other milestones, observing the progress of other children, watching younger children "pass up" the child with a disability, and other events are constant reminders of the death of the dream.

GRIEF IS UNNECESSARY

The whirlwind of grief that follows the disability diagnosis and the labeling of our children is unnecessary. If you're still dealing with this grief mumbo-jumbo, stop it now! Snap out of it! Wake up and smell the coffee! You've been programmed to grieve and I'm the deprogrammer.

We've felt sad for ourselves because there's something "wrong" with our children, but have we ever considered what this does to our children? What does it feel like to be told (or to overhear) that there's something "wrong" with you—and to hear it over and over and over again? If you've said these words about your child, resolve to never say them or think them again. Recognize and believe that disability is a natural part of the human experience, which means *there is nothing "wrong" with your child*. There is something wrong with society, but not your child. So your child has Down syndrome or cerebral palsy or autism or whatever. So what? That's life. Get over it! Let go of "Why me (or my child)?" and adopt "Why not me (or my child)?" instead.

If one of your other children wears glasses, do you grieve over that? No, because you saw it as a natural part of life, and no physician told you horrible things about your child when he gave her the vision exam. Know that your child's disability—regardless of the type or severity—is as natural a condition as children having pimples or needing glasses or wearing braces on their teeth. It is our society that has drawn the line separating natural conditions into categories of disability.

Reject the doctor's prognostications. No one can say what your child is capable of or what her future can be. No one has the right to steal your dreams. *No one has the right to define your child's potential—no one, not even you.* Refuse to let anyone define your child by his disability.

Recognize the label that's been attached to your child for what it really is: a medical diagnosis. The medical diagnosis is then transformed into an administrative term that becomes a sociopolitical passport to services. *That's all a label is: a passport to services!* It must never be used to predict a child's potential or limit a child's opportunities to have a real childhood and a successful life. A disability label is a life sentence of hopelessness only if we choose to see it that way.

It's time to restructure our own thinking and separate the child from the label. (More about this in a later chapter.) Your child's disability is not a condition that she needs to "overcome." *A disability simply means part of his body works differently.* Discard society's perception that your child has a "problem." The disability is simply a condition for which your child may need specific tools, assistance, and accommodations to enable him to succeed. *You* need certain tools, assistance, and accommodations to succeed; so does your child.

THE IMPACT OF TECHNOLOGY ON THE GRIEF PROCESS

What if doctors and parents focused on identifying and providing technology, tools, accommodations, and/or modifications for a child as early as possible? If this happened at the time of diagnosis or soon after, I propose the grief process would be interrupted or would not occur at all.

Physicians assume responsibility for recommending the appropriate solutions to the so-called problems of disability. A wide menu is available, including long-term therapies, drugs, and other interventions. As this menu has grown, so has the medical community's influence over the lives of people with disabilities. But it's not just medical professionals who exert power. Insurance companies, HMOs, Medicaid, and other gatekeepers of health care services exert as much (and sometimes more) power as physicians.

But does power equal expertise? In the disability field, it does not. Every day, children and adults with developmental disabilities are forced to live with the consequences of the lack of expertise—the ignorance—of those in the health care industry who exert powerful influence over their lives.

During the past thirty or forty years, great advances have been made in technology. Cellular telephones, home computers, and other high-tech devices are just a few of the items that make our lives easier, more productive, and so forth. And the impact of technology on people with disabilities is nothing short of miraculous. Power wheelchairs, screen readers, speech synthesizers, and a variety of high and low-tech assistive devices have enabled people with disabilities to achieve a level of independence once thought impossible.

For people who need assistive technology devices and other equipment, doctors hold the key—the prescription pad. They, along with insurance providers, have the power to provide or deny the tools needed by people with disabilities.

We know the circumstances that have led us to this point: doctors have expanded their sphere of influence, and Medicaid, insurance companies, and other providers will pay for devices only if they're "medically necessary." Sometimes physicians are our allies and go to battle with us against the insurance companies. Other times, it's the doctor we fight with.

So unless we're wealthy, we're dependent on physicians and insurance providers when it comes to many items our children need. But there are crucial issues we must consider about doctors having the power to control access to assistive technology.

What do most physicians really know about the assistive technology and accommodations needed by people with disabilities? Little or nothing. Many physicians rely on the recommendations of therapists and other professionals when prescribing a wheelchair or communication device, for example. Some rehabilitation physicians *do* have more experience than the diagnosing or primary physician, especially those rehab specialists who treat adults with acquired spinal cord injuries. But in general, pediatric specialists may not have the expertise parents assume they have.

When physicians have little experience with equipment, they're often reticent to prescribe it. Or if a doctor has a particular bias for or against a product, his feelings impact his decision to prescribe or not.

Prior to getting Benjamin's power wheelchair, I researched them high and low. During an annual check up with the pediatric orthopedist, I enthusiastically described the power wheelchair we wanted for Benjamin. It would stand him up, and the seat would rise to enable him to reach things or be at eye level with others. The doctor wrinkled up his nose and said, "Oh, I don't think you'll like that chair. It's too big." "Do you know any other children who have this chair," I asked. "No," he replied, "but I've seen the literature on them and they just look too big."

Luckily for us, he wasn't the doctor who would be writing the prescription. If he had been, we'd probably still be fighting him over it. Our family physician, who knew little about disabilities and assistive technology, willingly wrote the prescription. He trusted our expertise.

The rapidly changing technology world pumps out new products faster than any of us can keep track of. Doctors (or therapists) don't usually keep up on the latest, nor do they always know how beneficial a device might be. The best sources of information about equipment are other people with disabilities who use the same or similar devices and, to a lesser degree, the manufacturers of the devices. After all, what can a physician (or a therapist) really know about wheelchairs, communication devices, and other equipment unless he uses them himself or is very close to someone who does?

When parents ask for a prescription for an assistive device, some physicians or therapists may be reluctant to endorse the device if they feel parents are not being "realistic" about how it could help a child. Moms and dads *do* know what's best for their children (or they have the ability to learn), but they must often spend a great deal of time and energy trying to convince a physician, therapist, educator, or some other professional that an assistive device is necessary.

Parents who have the greatest luck getting equipment use a physician who readily admits he doesn't know much about assistive technology. Often, these are family doctors—non-specialists—who depend on the expertise of parents. They trust parents to do the research on what their child needs. When parents advise the doctor exactly what they want, the good doctor writes the prescription without hesitation.

But the greater issue facing children with disabilities is when medical professionals or parents are unable—or refuse—to see assistive technology devices and accommodations as tools for success. For example, a child who does not have intelligible speech would be able to express herself with a communication device. But the parents, therapist, and/or the doctor may resist getting such a device. "If we get her this, she'll never learn to talk," they say. Their focus is on one characteristic of the child—the perceived deficit—instead of the child as a whole.

In the case of children who do not have independent mobility, parents or professionals may resist getting a very young child a wheelchair, feeling it's an admission they're giving up on the child ever walking, or fearing the child will never learn to walk if the child uses a chair. Walking is seen as more important than independent mobility.

In both of these examples, parents and professionals focus on restoring the child to normalcy through endless and grueling hours of therapy, surgeries, and other medical interventions. The goal is to achieve an able-bodied standard. In too many cases, assistive devices and accommodations are considered only as a last resort, and only after years of therapy have failed to normalize or near-normalize the child. When parents and professionals isolate a particular characteristic of the disability to fix, they frequently ignore the overall needs of the child, such as independence, social opportunities, and more.

Assistive devices are simply tools to make life better. You and I use them every day. The lights in our homes and offices let us see when it's dark outside. Hammers let us build things. With computers we can do more. Look around your home right now. It's filled with equipment and devices to make your life better. Would you deny yourself those things? Most of us would not. We say things like, "I couldn't live without my microwave oven," or "How did we ever get along without computers?" Yet parents and professionals frequently deny children with disabilities the devices they need to be successful.

Now, back to the connection of the grief process and assistive technology. What would happen if physicians knew the value of and promoted the use of assistive technology and accommodations as early as possible? What would happen if they focused on the child as a whole and helped parents do the same? What would this do to the grief process?

In my own case, for example, what would have happened if the doctor had said, "Benjamin has cerebral palsy. I'm not sure how that's going to affect his ability to walk. He may never walk independently. He may be able to walk one day, but with great difficulty. Or he may be able to walk just fine. I just don't know. But what's most important is Benjamin's overall development. We don't want him missing out on opportunities to learn, to develop social skills and feelings of self-worth, and all the other components of a typical childhood. So if he's not walking by eighteen months or age two—the time when typical kids are upright and mobile—let's get him a wheelchair he can control so he can learn independence like other two-year-olds. We can still work on helping him walk, but let's stay focused on his overall development."

If this had happened, would I have initially felt differently about my son's disability? Would I have taken a different approach to his needs? I think so. As it was, the doctor's prognosis was that with a lot of therapy, Benjamin would probably walk unassisted one day. Like other parents, I took my cues from him. I based my feelings and actions on the "expert's" recommendations because I didn't know any better at the time!

This doctor, who was a very nice man, did not talk to me about assistive devices and accommodations. He did not give me a variety of potential scenarios. His focus was on one part of Benjamin's body—making his legs normal through therapy—not on Benjamin as a whole child.

I realize now the doctor was doing his best to give me hope: hope that if we did enough, everything would be "all right" (Benjamin would walk). He may have thought the mere mention of a wheelchair would have devastated me more than the diagnosis. Perhaps his own personal bias—that *he* would be devastated to have a child who needed a wheelchair—influenced his attitudes. His words and attitudes shaped my attitude, and it was years before I was able to see things differently. In fact, it wasn't until I met and learned from adults with disabilities that my attitude began to change.

Let's look at some other scenarios. When a physician talked to the parents about the prognosis for a child with Down syndrome, what if he said, "Some children with this condition have difficulty developing intelligible speech. If Margi is not talking by age two or before, let's look at lots of options: communication devices, sign language, communication cards, or other things. All young children need to be able to express themselves and be understood, and we don't want Margi to miss out on the experiences that come with communication. Oh, and by the way, make sure to surround Margi with others who talk and who do the things you want her to do: she'll learn best by being around typical children."

With some conditions, physicians and parents might not know the specific issues ahead of time. But when a particular issue does arise, what if the physician recommended assistive technology and/or accommodations instead of focusing on how to remedy the perceived deficit? Let's assume a child experiences "behavior differences." This characteristic could fall under a variety of disability categories: autism, sensory integration, attention deficit/hyperactivity disorder, and others. Instead of focusing on and prescribing "behavior management" or drugs, what if the physician said, "Let's not make a hard and fast decision about Johnny. Part of this could be his personality and part of it could be the way his brain is wired. Let's make sure Johnny has lots of opportunities to succeed. Let his teachers know that just because Johnny likes to move at warp speed in the classroom doesn't mean he's not learning. Perhaps Johnny learns best when he's moving. Let's figure out some strategies to make sure Johnny has the accommodations and the tools he needs for success."

During the time of diagnosis and prognosis, when parents are very vulnerable, the attitudes and recommendations of physicians profoundly influence parents' attitudes and actions forever (or until they acquire new attitudes). When physicians focus on restoring body parts to normalcy, ignoring the importance of assistive technology and accommodations, parents are unable to see the many possibilities for a child's success. By sharing information with parents about assistive technology and accommodations (tools for successful living) physicians have the power to lessen or even end the grief parents feel.

Unfortunately, however, many physicians continue to see a disability as a deficit to be fixed. But we can help them learn. (More about how to impact this sort of change in Chapter 21.) In the meantime, think about the day the doctor told you about your child's "problems." What could he have said about assistive technology or accommodations that would have made you feel differently about your child's condition and his future?

If, at the time of diagnosis, we were given options about devices and accommodations that would enable our children to lead more natural and successful lives, we could hold on to the dreams we had for our children; the diagnosis would not have the power to strip them away. We would have no need to grieve over the loss of child we dreamed of.

But it's never too late. Regardless of what's happened in the past or where your child is today, you can make positive changes in your child's life. In the second half of this book, I'll share strategies that can restore your dreams for your child, and help your child dream for himself.

REJECT THE MEDICAL MODEL; LET GO OF THE GRIEF

As parents who love and support our children, we must reject the medical (deficit) model of disability. Do not let a disability label or a doctor's prognosis convince you that your child needs to be changed. She doesn't need to change or be changed; society needs to change. Your child is fine just the way she is. *Your child is perfect.* If you don't believe that, change the way you think! Change your definition of perfect, don't try to change your child. Either all of us are perfect or none of us are.

If you're unable to believe what I'm telling you at this very moment, *pretend* to believe it for now. By the time you finish this book, you'll have new skills and a new understanding, and you will believe.

Let go of the grief society tells us we should feel. You don't need to "work through it;" *just let it go.* It's a waste of time; it saps our energy; it perpetuates pity toward our children. It sends a devastating message to our sons and daughters. We must celebrate the births and lives of our children instead of mourning for the "dream child" we think we've lost. Our children deserve nothing less.

Eliminate any pity you feel for yourself, your family members, and especially your child. He doesn't need your pity, he needs you to believe in the wonderful possibilities for his life.

Rise above the extreme bias and the profound lack of understanding most physicians and society in general have about disability. As a society, we've come a long way, but we're still in the Dark Ages when it comes to understanding the basics about people with disabilities. We continue to view disability as a problem within the person who has the disability. But the problem is not within the person. As you'll see throughout this book, the problem is society's attitudes and perceptions.

WHAT IF?

What will it take to ensure that no parents are ever again asked to bear the burden of society's prejudices? For that's what parental grief really is: a reaction to societal attitudes about people with disabilities.

What if, when you were growing up, society viewed disability as a natural condition? Imagine if you had gone to school with children with disabilities, if one of your best friends had a disability, if everywhere you went, children and adults with disabilities were a part of the community where you lived. What if you knew adults with disabilities who were successful in business, were married with children, and were valued members of their communities? Imagine that when you were pregnant, the possibility of giving birth to a child with a disability was discussed casually, like a discussion of what your baby's eye or hair color might be.

Considering all these imaginary scenarios, would you have experienced the sadness, grief, and confusion we take for granted today? Don't we want a world where all parents can celebrate the births of all their children, regardless of their perceived differences?

In today's neonatal intensive care units (NICUs), physicians, nurses, social workers, and others stand ready to counsel grieving parents, and direct them to other professional helpers. What if these experts held different attitudes about babies and children with disabilities which allowed them to help parents celebrate their children's births instead of setting the stage for mourning a perceived loss?

One of my greatest hopes is that starting now, no parent ever feels the need to grieve or feel sad about having a child with a disability. This hope can only be realized when society, in general, and physicians, nurses, and personnel in hospital nurseries, in particular, adopt the belief that disability is a natural part of the human condition. But it has to start with us. When we adopt this belief and when our actions are driven by this belief, we can help others see it, too. Change is inevitable.

Always remember that fifty percent of all "experts" (physicians, educators, and other trained professionals) graduated in the lower half of their classes! They don't know everything. They can learn a lot from us. And we can learn a great deal from our children.

FROM DARK GRIEF TO BRIGHT REALITY

The medical model is the genesis of parental grief. Diagnoses, prognoses, and labels attached to our children plunge us into a dark world. Then the promise of services and treatments temporarily lifts us from the darkness. But when we reject the medical model and the negative stereotypes presented by doctors and accepted by society, we can anchor ourselves to the reality that our children have bright futures and unlimited potential, as you'll see in the second half of this book. And this belief has a greater influence over your child's success than any disability label. This is so important, I'm going to say it again, a little differently this time. *Your belief in your child and his potential has a greater influence over his success than his disability.*

When we accept the fact that there have always been people with disabilities in the world and there always will be, we can more easily internalize the belief that disability is just one of many natural characteristics of humanity. It's how we've *perceived* disability that's made it abnormal, and our perceptions can change. When our perceptions change, our actions will change.

In the meantime, our children are forced to live with the labels doctors have assigned to them. Labels are very powerful words. Where did they come from and what do they mean? Are labels relevant? Do we really need them? We'll find out, next.

Labels and Attitudes

THE NAME WE GIVE TO SOMETHING
SHAPES OUR ATTITUDE TOWARD IT.
Katherine Paterson

Labels: we can't live with 'em; we can't live without 'em. The same labels that entitle our children to services also relegate our children to second-class citizenship and exclusion. Attitudes about children with disabilities and labels are intertwined. The labels professionals assign to children, and society's attitudes about children with disabilities, deeply impact our children's lives. It's a mighty mess.

THE ORIGINS AND EVOLUTION OF DISABILITY LABELS

In the past, disability diagnoses and their accompanying labels were not as specific as they are today. A very few labels covered many different disabilities. There were probably just as many different types of disabilities as there are today, but they weren't all recognized or categorized, so they were lumped in with other conditions. But even though we had fewer disability categories in the past, labels caused just as many problems as they do today.

The ancient Greeks referred to people with intellectual disabilities as idiots. The original word, "idios," referred to anyone who was not a public official. The meaning changed over time. Next, it described a person who lacked professional knowledge, and later it meant one who was ignorant. Originally, the label didn't entitle anyone to services, but it did serve to identify people for the purpose of relegating them to the bottom of the class structure. Centuries later, imbecile and moron came into use as additional descriptors of "mental deficiency," and they *were* used to categorize people and decide services.

Modern definitions of these terms can be found in any current dictionary:

- Moron: A mental deficient who may take a normal place in society, but needs constant supervision.

- Imbecile: A mental deficient who may learn to communicate with others, but is incapable of earning his own living.
- Idiot: A mental deficient who is incapable of learning and understanding, is completely helpless, and requires constant care.

For many years, these labels were medical descriptors of different levels of mental retardation. Today, the words are used as slurs and insults. What does it say about our society that disability labels have become derogatory slang? (Vow not to use these words anymore.) The ways our language evolves provides insight into how our society thinks.

Language is never static, it's always evolving. New words are added to our vocabulary all the time; old words become obsolete; and the original meanings of words change.

While the exact origins of some disability names and labels may be obscure, many originated in the medical community. The naming of some disabilities occurred when a physician observed a set of conditions that affected certain parts of the body. Since medicine has its roots in ancient Greece and Rome, many medical terms are derived from Greek and Latin, as seen in the following examples:

- Spina bifida, both Latin words, translates literally as a forked spine.
- Cerebral palsy comes from several words. Cerebral is a Latin variation of the word brain. Palsy (tremor) is a variation of paralysis, which is a compound of two Latin words: "para" means at the side and "lyein" means to loosen. It literally means the brain sends tremors that loosen a side or part of the body.
- Epilepsy is from two Greek words: "epi" means upon and "lambanein" means to seize. In ancient Greece, epilepsy described a person who was "seized upon" by some force.
- Crippled comes from the Latin root word "claudus." The Roman Emperor Claudius was said to be crippled. The origin of the word is fuzzy: was Claudius given his name because he was crippled or did cripple come into use because of Claudius' condition?
- Autism is from the Greek word "autos," which means self.

In 1866 in London, Dr. John Langdon Haydon Down used the term "mongoloid" to describe children who (he thought) resembled descendants of Ghengis Khan from Mongolia. At the time, there was speculation genealogy could leap across ethnic lines. Later, mongoloid was discarded in favor of the term we're familiar with today, Down syndrome. Many disabilities—especially some syndromes—have been named after the physicians who first identified or studied them.

Labels for Levels of Disability

While labels have been used throughout history, they took on a greater significance with the growth of institutions and the medicalization of disability during the twentieth century. Physicians began using more specialized labels to identify different disabilities, and attached adjectives to categorize the level of disability.

In the institutions, they began making distinctions between "high-grade imbeciles," "low-functioning morons," and so on. Such descriptions became more important as time went on. If doctors could classify people in distinct and narrow categories, they could effectively design a treatment program based on the disability. It was assumed (erroneously) that persons with the same disability also had the same needs!

This practice continues in the medical field and it's been adopted by many special education departments: identify the disability, design and standardize a treatment or educational program for that disability label, and fit the child into the treatment or the program. Seldom, either in medicine or education, do medical professionals or educators truly take the specific and unique needs of a child and her family into consideration when designing treatment or educational services. Instead, services, programs, and treatments are dictated by the disability label.

While we don't use idiot, imbecile, and moron as disability labels anymore, many professionals (physicians and educators) still label a child "low-functioning," and the child is doomed to live with that label forever. What does this type of descriptor really mean? "Low-functioning" as compared to what or whom? Is the child "low-functioning" all the time, in every area? Probably not. But the label sticks anyway. If a child was "low-functioning" in some areas, but "high-functioning" in other areas, why don't we average the two to arrive at "normal"?

"Educable mentally retarded" (EMR) and "trainable mentally retarded" (TMR) were originally used in the institutions. Medical books define "educable" as having an IQ score of between 50 and 70, with an expectation that children with an IQ in the upper range may achieve reading skills at the fourth to sixth grade level. "Trainable" is defined as having an IQ of between 20 and 49 and no capabilities are described. Thus, are no capabilities expected? If not, then what *are* the expectations for children in a TMR class? If they can only be "trained," why don't we train them for the cheerleader or football squads?

What *does* go on in a TMR classroom? Is it a training class? What are we training the students for? To perform in a circus? To fold sheets and towels? To be good little kiddies?

EMR and TMR are horribly demeaning descriptions. How can any adult (professional, educator, or parent) believe that a living, breathing human being cannot learn, that he can only be trained? And what happens when a child proves he can be trained? Does he get bumped up to "educable"? Of course not. Too often, these descriptors are used throughout a person's life, regardless of the individual's achievements, knowledge, or experiences.

During the 1950s, feeblemindedness and other labels indicating "mental deficiency" were replaced by the generic mental retardation label. Later, the three levels of mental retardation (idiot, imbecile, and moron) were replaced with four descriptors: mild, moderate, severe, and profound. Returning to medical books again, mild MR represents an IQ of 50 to 70, moderate means a score of 35 to 49, severe equals an IQ of 20 to 34, and profound represents a score of 19 and below. People who have an IQ between 71 and 84 are said to be in the "borderline" category.

While the four new descriptors were originally used to specify levels of severity of mental retardation, they were soon being applied to other disabilities as well, as in "severe autism" or "moderate cerebral palsy." These descriptors are used in the same way "high-grade imbeciles" or "low-functioning morons" were used in the institutions: for standardizing treatment regimens. But these routine attachments to disability labels further stigmatize our children.

As an example, a regular education teacher might not object to including a child with "mild mental retardation" in her class. But she might automatically reject a child with a label of "severe mental retardation." In either case, the teacher has never even met the child. Her decision is based solely on the disability descriptor, which both precedes and defines the child.

Another problem with disability descriptors is they mean different things to different people. One person's "mild" autism is another person's "moderate." When my son was diagnosed at four months of age, the doctor said Benjamin had "moderate cerebral palsy." A couple of years later, the physical and occupational therapists sat me down for an official meeting. Gravely, they said Benjamin probably had "severe cerebral palsy." By that time my attitude was, "So what? Should I 'grieve' all over again?" What difference did it really make?

When Benj was in third grade, a new student moved into the district: another third-grade boy who also had a label of moderate cerebral palsy. Because they shared the same label and descriptor, some people thought they were practically twins! But they were two different kids, with unique and individual needs.

What truths do mild, moderate, severe, and profound really tell us about a person? None! But they do incite emotions in people who believe the labels are accurate: "Oh, he's severe!" and "Well, she's just mild." But what if the IQ score is wrong? What if an assessment was given incorrectly? In far too many cases, labels and their descriptors are assigned as permanent levels of "deficiences."

Level of Disability vs. Level of Need

In the early 1990s, a representative from the AAMR (American Association on Mental Retardation) presented information at a national conference about changes in terminology the association was considering. Mild, moderate, severe, and profound would be eliminated, in favor of the following descriptions of a person's level of need:

- Intermittent: Does not require constant support.
- Limited: Requires ongoing support of varying intensity.
- Extensive: Requires daily and ongoing consistent levels of support.
- Pervasive: Requires an ongoing high level of support for all activities of daily living.

These seem to be a step in the right direction: identifying a person's needs tells us more than a level of disability. But even these descriptors leave much to be desired. If a person's needs are categorized as "pervasive," are we really to believe there's nothing the person can do without support? Does this mean an individual would never be in a situation where he could do some things with no support or less support than usual? If we return to a previous example, which child would a teacher feel most comfortable including in her classroom: one with intermittent needs or one with pervasive needs?

Instead of using one word adjectives, detailing the *specific and unique needs* of an individual is not only far more accurate, but it's also more dignified and respectful: Yolanda needs help going to the bathroom; Shawn needs help at mealtime. People that don't have disabilities also have needs that vary from day to day, from situation to situation. Yet because there's no service system to help them, no one attempts to define categories of needs or levels of competence to men, women, and children who don't have disabilities.

When my husband and I installed a new metal roof on our home, we both worked hard to do it right. We didn't know how to install a roof, but we learned by doing. There were many different tasks: cleaning the old roof, nailing down new tar paper, cutting the metal roof to fit the joints, and so forth. In disability jargon, my husband had an "intermittent" level of need, while I had a "limited" level of need. However, when I was trying to carefully cross the highest part of the roof and feeling great fear, I had a "pervasive" level of need. I needed lots of support from my husband so I wouldn't fall off the roof!

If categorizing the level of need isn't appropriate for people without disabilities, why is it appropriate for people with disabilities? Who does this really benefit and what good does it really do? Again, it's more for the benefit of professionals in the service system than for individuals who must carry the designations. When decisions are being made about providing help to a person with a disability, professionals think it's easier to identify a category than to detail the unique and specific needs of an individual. But assigning arbitrary and inaccurate descriptors to a disability label causes more harm than good.

Mental Retardation

In addition to discussing new terminology for levels of need, the AAMR representative at the conference was drawn in to a mini-debate about the term mental retardation (MR). Many in the audience said it was an antiquated term that's rife with negative inferences, so it should be changed. Others (mostly parents of adult children) were adamant that it was an accurate description. "Let's call a spade a spade," one said. "Our kids are retarded. Changing what we call them won't change that!"

But it *is* time for this term to become obsolete. For too many years, people who are said to have this condition have been the most ostracized individuals in our society, simply because of the label that's been assigned to them. In Chapter 11, I'll review terminology that is more respectful toward individuals with disabilities.

The word "retarded" provides another example of how the original meaning of a disability label has been corrupted and turned into a slur. What is the absolutely worst insult one child can hurl at another on the school playground? "Retard!" When typical children use that word on one another, what does it tell us about their feelings toward people with disabilities? And adults routinely use the word as an insult, as well.

One group of experts has shared the belief that retardation is actually caused by the environment. When people with an MR label are forced into segregated settings, treated like children, and prevented from living the lives of their choice, they are in "retarding environments." They're prevented from learning and growing because of the restrictive settings they inhabit. To which group can we attribute this profound wisdom? The top experts in the disability field: young men and women who have been told they have mental retardation. What does mental retardation really mean? It simply means a person's cognitive abilities may develop differently than the so-called norm.

Invented Conditions

The late Burton Blatt, the professor at Syracuse University in New York who helped expose the horrible conditions in institutions, described mental retardation as an "invented disease." In his book, *In and Out of Mental Retardation,* he warned of the dangers of "telling stories" about people with disabilities.

Stories that are believed to be factual lead to the creation of invented conditions. Long ago, for example, doctors in charge of institutions and others involved in research told each other stories about people: "Joe has an IQ of 55 and he behaves this way . . ." and "Susan can't do this and that . . ." and so forth. Then they said, in essence, "So when we see [such-and-such] characteristics in a person, we'll call it 'mental retardation'."

We could apply Blatt's theory to other disabilities. Cerebral palsy manifests itself in so many different ways, it could also be called an invented condition. The same is true for autism, attention deficit disorder, hyperactivity, and other disabilities that have no biological markers. Think about it: at one time or another, physicians and other experts got together and talked about people who had specific characteristics. The experts then decided to call those characteristics by a specific name. There are no biological markers for most developmental disabilities; no concrete tests that can "prove" a child has a certain condition. In general, children are diagnosed with a developmental disability based on a set of characteristics that have been named something, and the diagnosis is made by observing these characteristics. Spina bifida, some syndromes, and certain other conditions *do* present specific biological markers. Even so, stories that have been told about these conditions have created the illusion that people who have the same disability are all alike.

Physicians and other medical professionals may readily acknowledge there are many individual differences among children who have the same disability. But when it comes to services, educational placements, participation in typical community activities, and other needs and wants of families and children, these distinctions just don't seem to count. All the school hears is "mental retardation" when it comes to placement. All a therapist may hear is "cerebral palsy." All a park and rec program hears is "epilepsy." Too many people see the disability before they see the child. And people (including some parents) make judgments about the child based on the "stories" they believe are true about a particular disability.

The majority of parents I've asked have told me their children have surpassed the expectations predicted by doctors and other professionals. Is it possible that the only stories physicians know about people with disabilities are negative ones?

MORE CORRUPTION OF MEANINGS

The evolution of language is ongoing. Today's vocabulary includes many disability-related terms whose original meanings have been corrupted; the words are now disparaging adjectives. What does this say about society's perceptions of people with disabilities? Without being aware of it, many people use disability terminology in ways that marginalize people with disabilities, even though they're not talking about people with disabilities:

"How lame!"

"What a spastic!"

"Don't be a retard!"

"He turned a deaf ear."

"What are you? Blind?"

"The economy was crippled by the strike."

"The company is handicapped by its old equipment."

And don't forget the previously mentioned, idiot, imbecile, moron, and retard, which are now derogatory terms. I'm sure you can think of more examples. We must watch our own language—we must stop using these terms—and then we must educate others on the misuse of disability descriptors.

PURPOSE OF LABELS

Why do we have disability labels? When I've asked this question at trainings, someone almost always yells out with a mixture of anger and pain, "To separate us!" Yes, labels do separate us, but that's a consequence of labeling, not the purpose.

Disability labels have only one purpose: to get services. As I described in Chapter 2, labels are administrative terms that are used as sociopolitical passports to services.

Who uses labels to determine eligibility for services? Anyone who provides services: early intervention services, early childhood programs, special education, vocational rehabilitation, disability organizations, Medicaid, private insurance and health care providers, and others.

In one very narrow sense, disability labels are beneficial: they provide our children with a passport to services. Some of us try to get as many labels as we can for our children in order to get as many services and supports as possible.

Labels are like double-edged swords, however. They cut both ways. The same labels that enable our children to receive services also lead our children down the path to segregation and exclusion. Our children are routinely judged (usually negatively) based solely on their labels.

HOW LABELS INFLUENCE PROFESSIONALS

Educators, service providers, and other professionals have great power over the lives of children with disabilities. And the attitudes of professionals—how they see and behave toward our children—are profoundly influenced by labels.

In this chapter, I'm going to expand the definition of professionals to include people who are not traditionally associated with disability issues, but who are in a position of influence or power: typical preschool staff members, park and rec employees, and others who may make decisions that affect our children. Any of these professionals can be gatekeepers: they can open the gates to our children or keep them closed.

It's easy and pleasant to work with folks who have positive attitudes about our kids. And it's dreadfully difficult to deal with people who have negative attitudes. We're often shocked and amazed by the negative attitudes of people who are supposed to be our allies: professionals who work with our children. Where do these negative attitudes come from?

Like everyone else, professionals learn their initial attitudes from their parents. Those who specialize in disability-related fields acquire additional attitudes and beliefs from their university training or at professional seminars where, in general, old ways of thinking about people with disabilities are still being taught. Some professionals probably subscribe to the long-held perceptions that disability means a negative deviance from the norm.

Many, if not most, professionals do not have personal relationships with people with disabilities, just as most physicians don't, as I mentioned in the previous chapter. Unless people have positive, personal experiences, they're stuck with stereotypical attitudes and perceptions from a variety of sources: their training, their professional experiences, their upbringing, the media, and societal views.

Professionals and parents often have great difficulties with one another because their attitudes are poles apart. If, for example, we see many positive characteristics in our children, or if we espouse great possibilities for them, professionals tell us we're "not being realistic." We feel they're being negative, while they feel they're simply being honest and helpful by bringing us down to reality (their reality).

When Benjamin was three, he had spinal cord surgery which resulted in us spending a great deal of time with a pediatric orthopedic surgeon. Like any young child, when Benjamin learned a new word or phrase, he delighted in saying it over and over. He loved the rhythm of "pediatric orthopedic surgeon." Say it again and again to see what I mean.

A few weeks after his surgery, during an occupational therapy session, he said, "Mommy, when I grow up, I want to be a pediatric orthopedic surgeon!" I gushed, "That's great, Honey! They make a lot of money so you can take care of Daddy and me when we're old."

The therapist looked at me with downcast eyes and said, "Excuse me, Kathie, could I see you out in the hall a moment?" You know what happened next, right? When we were in the hallway, she said, "You really shouldn't tell Benjamin things like that." "Things like what?" I asked. I knew what she was talking about, but sometimes it's good to play dumb and make people say what they mean.

"You shouldn't let him believe he could be a doctor," she replied. "What do you mean?" I asked, again knowing exactly what she meant. "You're not being realistic about things, Kathie," she patiently explained. "He'll never be a doctor!"

"Why not?" I asked. With a big sigh and her patience running out, she said, "Because he has cerebral palsy!"

"Well, if he wants to be a doctor, I'm sure he'll figure out a way to do it," I replied. "Besides, with the way technology is changing, by the time he's old enough to be a doctor, he could be a surgeon who uses computers and lasers instead of a scalpel." With another exasperated sigh, she led me back into the therapy room, shaking her head in disbelief.

I felt her attitude was negative; she felt it was realistic. She believed my attitude was unrealistic; I felt it was positive support for my son. She wasn't a mean person; this was simply what she believed. In her college training and in her professional experience she probably acquired the notion that children with labels were unfit for certain professions.

We changed therapists after this episode. I didn't want Benjamin to be around people who didn't believe in him. Later, I often wondered if it was threatening to her, that a young child who needed her help could one day grow up to achieve as much or more than her. Or perhaps she was bothered by a mother who believed anything was possible for her child, a mother who wouldn't accept her version of reality.

When we're dealing with professionals who are negative or hard to get along with, we need to consider what may be behind their behaviors. It's important to remember that attitudes are learned: old attitudes can be unlearned and new ones learned.

WHEN LABELS CREATE FEAR

We all use labels, all the time. Things that we drive are labeled cars, places we buy things are labeled stores, people who have jobs are called employees, and so on. A literate society couldn't exist without words that have the same meaning for everyone.

Some words, used alone, are harmless. But in context, they may be loaded with emotion. Hearing the word tornado makes us think of whirling winds. But if I hear that my community is under a tornado watch or warning, I begin to feel strong emotions of apprehension, fear, and worry.

In society's current way of thinking, the words we use as disability labels are—in any context—loaded with powerful emotions and negative perceptions. Consider these scenarios:

- When a regular education teacher hears that a child with cerebral palsy will be in her class, what will she feel?

- If you call a day care center director and ask if she takes children with autism, what will she feel?

- If the T-ball coach learns that a child with Down syndrome has signed up for the team, what will he feel?

Unless these folks have already had positive experiences in similar situations, each will probably feel some level of fear, nervousness, or apprehension. The labels they hear have such a great impact on them they can't see beyond the label to the real child.

Fear has been called a primary emotion, one that's basic to all living creatures. Most of us know about the "fight or flight" reactions to fear. In our cavemen days, fear enabled us to survive by allowing us to choose to stay and fight or flee for our lives.

In the twenty-first century, we don't often encounter a sabre-tooth tiger who wants to make a meal of us! Most of today's fears are more psychological than physical, and the fight or flight reactions aren't really appropriate. But our human physiology still utilizes this primitive (and important) reflex. If we don't need to physically fight or run for our lives when we're scared, our fears will come out one way or another, usually as anger, sadness, guilt, confusion, or some other feeling.

Think for a moment of the fear you might experience while waiting anxiously for your teenaged daughter to return home on a Friday night. She's an hour late. Where could she be? Was she in a car accident? Did some other bad thing happen to her? Your mind is wild with fear. But this is not a tangible enemy; you can't fight it and you can't run from it.

The primary emotion of fear expands to encompass other emotions. You move from worry to frustration to anger and then the sequence repeats itself. You begin praying for her safe return. You're on the verge of tears and your heart is pounding when she casually walks through the front door. Do you rush to her, hug her, and tell her how very, very glad you are to see her home safely? Even though that's what you *feel,* that's probably not how you react.

Instead, you would probably yell, "Where have you been? That's it! You're grounded!" In the course of your yelling or perhaps later, you *would* tell her how frightened you were and how relieved you are that she's safe. But your primary emotion—fear—was replaced by worry, concern, nervousness, sadness, and finally, anger.

When we feel fear and we can't fight or flee, our reactions come out in one way or another. So let's look at the teacher, day care director, and T-ball coach to see how their fears come out as something different.

The teacher may feel she doesn't have enough knowledge or training to teach a child with cerebral palsy. She's fearful because she's supposed to be an expert teacher and for the first time in her career, she feels she might fail. She's never been around a person with a physical disability; she feels it would be an uncomfortable situation. She fears the unknown.

The day care director doesn't know a thing about autism except what she's seen in the movies. She's afraid she wouldn't know what to do with a kid like the *Rainman* character. What if he scares the other children and their parents? She's heard that "autistics" don't talk and can be violent. What if this made her lose customers? She doesn't feel she can take the chance. She fears the unknown.

The only thing the coach knows about people with Down syndrome is that they're "retarded." He's scared he wouldn't know how to handle the situation, and he can't see a kid like that on his team. Besides, what could a "retarded" kid learn from team sports? He fears the unknown.

Underneath it all, people are primarily afraid of failing. Professionals are not so different from you and me. We're all afraid of the unknown; we're all afraid of failing. Most of us try to avoid situations in which we might be uncomfortable or unsuccessful. We have pictures in our heads of the way we want things to be, and our three professionals can't picture kids with disabilities being part of their environments. They're afraid.

But we don't always *see* their fear. They may not even recognize what they're feeling as fear. If they *do* recognize it, they may not be able to admit it to themselves, and they surely can't admit it to us. Their fears are hidden behind professional wisdom, organizational regulations, or outright falsehoods. Their fears come out as something else. Their actual responses might be:

- Teacher: "I really think your child could learn better in the special ed room; my classroom doesn't have what he needs," or "I don't think he's ready for a regular class."

- Day care center director: "We're not trained to handle special needs children," or "I'm afraid we're full and we have a long waiting list. Why don't you try another center?"

- T-ball Coach: "The other kids are so much bigger. We wouldn't want your son to get hurt, so maybe you ought to wait a couple of years," or "Isn't there a special program for kids like yours?"

Instead of fear, we see, hear, and feel rejection, discrimination, prejudice, and maybe even downright cruelty and meanness.

When people give us reasons for not including our children—like the ones above—how do we usually react? Some of may have a keen insight; we recognize what's really happening and we handle it successfully. But most of us wear our hearts on our sleeves. If we feel our children are being excluded because of their disabilities, we're ready to fight. We react with anger, threats, tears, and more. At that point, we've lost the opportunity to make allies. Instead, we've just created adversaries.

If you *do* encounter a professional who honestly admits to being afraid or scared, don't ridicule her. Respect her and thank her for her honesty, and help her learn what she needs to know to feel confident. Be aware that even when acknowledging fear, few people will actually say, "I'm afraid." Instead, they might say: "Well, I'm not sure I know how to do this," or "I've never done anything like this before."

Listen not just to a person's words, but also to her body language. Communication experts say that ninety percent of our communication is non-verbal. We use our eyes, bodies, tone of voice, and more. If you're not already, be more sensitive and aware of non-verbal communication.

Never take personally any negative attitudes or actions directed to you or your child. Recognize these behaviors as signs of fear, ignorance, or unawareness. While there *are* some mean people in the world, most are either afraid or just don't know any better. If we always react to negative encounters with anger, we miss opportunities to impact peoples' attitudes. Worse, we've added fuel to the fire. Instead of taking things personally and responding in kind, call up your courage and patience and view these situations as wonderful teaching moments!

"WE'LL LEARN TOGETHER!"

When Benjamin was in kindergarten, he came home one day with a notice about the community park and recreation T-ball league. He wanted to sign up, so I filled out the form and he took it back to school the next day. The T-ball coaches would take all the forms and divide the players into teams. Each coach would then call his players and give them the schedule of practices and games. I was told this would occur in about two or three weeks. On the form, I did not mention that Benj used a wheelchair; I would discuss the issue with the coach when he called.

Living in a small town has its advantages and disadvantages. Somehow, one of the T-ball coaches heard about Benj signing up and called me immediately. (It's possible the school secretary—she collected the forms—called the coach when she saw Benj had signed up. She was, coincidentally, the volunteer secretary of the T-ball league!) It's also possible the coach's son, who was in Benj's kindergarten class, told the coach.

At any rate, I was somewhat prepared for his call. I anticipated there might be some resistance to Benj playing on a regular T-ball. I was ready: I could use the fact that Benj was included in public school as an argument as to why he should be included on the T-ball team. I could cite the ADA and talk about non-discrimination. I could, if it came down to it, scream and/or cry. As it turned out, none of this was necessary.

When the call came, the coach identified himself in a friendly way and said, "I haven't met your son, but I understand he's in a wheelchair." "That's correct," I replied, and said no more. There was a long silence on the other end. I waited. Finally, he said, "Well, uh, uh, you know, we've never done anything like this before and, uh, well—"

At that point, I could have angrily started ticking off all my arguments. Instead, something came over me. Before the coach could say another word, and with a big smile on my face (telegraphing my positive attitude), I said, "You know, *we've* never done anything like this before, either! We'll learn together!" And with that, the tension was broken and we began discussing the accommodations Benj would need to be a successful team member.

When the coach called, his concern—his fear—was based on a disability label. He didn't know Benjamin's exact disability, but he had an image of a "handicapped wheelchair-bound kid." His concern was understandable: he was being asked to do something he had never done before and was fearful. Was he a mean person? No. Was he prejudiced? Yes, but it was a prejudice born out of ignorance, not malice. Once he was educated about Benjamin (first by me, on the phone, and then later by Benjamin, in person) the label became irrelevant. Benjamin's T-ball season turned out to be a wonderful experience.

WHEN LABELS DEFINE HUMAN POTENTIAL

Remember Lewis Terman, the Stanford psychologist who modified the Binet test in the early 1900s? He theorized his new Stanford-Binet test could be used on the masses, so people could be slotted into accurate classifications that could potentially dictate their status as citizens. Today, disability labels are often used in the same way.

Flip through the pages of almost any physician's desk manual, look up a disability label, and you can find not only a description of the condition, but also predictions about the life of an individual with that disability. Potential IQ scores are bandied about, as are details about the need for long-term care, the likelihood of the person achieving a "near-normal" life, recommendations for sheltered work environments, and more. For many experts, a developmental disability diagnosis is often more than a medical condition: it also defines a child's human potential.

Routinely, physicians predict children's futures based on their labels; educators shuttle children off to segregated classrooms because of their labels; community activities exclude them because of their labels; and we—society in general and parents in particular—have lower expectations for children because of their labels. We say children *without* disabilities have unlimited potential, and we should say the same about children with disabilities. But when we allow labels to define a child's potential, we inadvertently put up obstacles and barriers which a child may find insurmountable. It's these barriers, not the disability, that will get in the way of his success.

We do things to children and adults, based on the myths and labels attached to them, that we would never do to children and adults without disabilities. I know adult women with disabilities who have voluntarily had their tubes tied when they were in their early twenties. When I've asked these ladies why they did this, their answers were all similar: "Well, I knew I wouldn't be able to be a good mother because of my disability." Upon further questioning, they revealed their parents and the professionals in their lives repeatedly sent this message to them from the time they were old enough to understand it. When they were in their early twenties (or younger), being sterilized was considered a "realistic" and appropriate course of action. And yet, these young women wistfully state they always had dreams of getting married and having children.

Many—if not most—adults with developmental disabilities have dreams of employment. But they remain unskilled and/or unemployed, because they have been given the message that they're unemployable because of their disabilities. Others desperately want a home of their own, but gatekeepers in the system (and sometimes their parents) hold them prisoners in institutions, group homes, and adult foster care.

Why do these spirit-killing actions occur? Because parents and/or professionals let a child's disability define the child's potential.

When Johnny, who doesn't have a disability, tells his parents he wants to be an astronaut when he grows up, they respond, "Go for it!" But when Mary, his sister with a disability, says she wants to be an astronaut, mom and dad gulp, hem and haw, and then finally say, "Well, we'll see," or something worse: "Mary, people with disabilities can't be astronauts."

When Johnny shares his dream, his parents know he'll probably change his mind a zillion times before he's actually old enough to choose a career. They don't make judgments about Johnny's potential to become an astronaut. They know how important it is to let Johnny dream. But with Mary, they're trying to be realistic (a skill they've learned from professionals). They don't want Mary to be disappointed when she can't be an astronaut. But they don't worry about this with Johnny. Why do they with Mary? Only because she has a disability.

Can't Mary's parents let her dream, like they let Johnny? Don't they know that Mary, just like her brother, will change her mind many times before she's an adult?

How can we do this? As parents, we know what it feels like when others destroy the dream we had for our children. How can we, in turn, do the same thing to our children?

Parents of typical children trust their children. They know their children will figure out what to do with their lives as they grow and mature. We must learn to trust children with disabilities the same way. We cannot risk their futures by stealing their hopes and dreams.

Our children see themselves through our eyes. If we don't believe in them, how can they believe in themselves? If we don't see them as capable, how can they see themselves as capable? If we don't dream big dreams with them, how can they dream for themselves? Their disabilities won't prevent them from being successful, but our lack of belief in them will. Can there be anything more unfair to children?

Remember, a disability label is simply a sociopolitical passport that opens the door to services. That's all it is. It is not a definer of our children's potential or humanity. Later on, I'll show you how we can prevent labels from defining our children, as well as ways to revive our dreams.

WHEN LABELS JUSTIFY EXCLUSION

Labels are used to identify a child's disability for the purposes of getting services and treatments. And the ultimate goal of these services and treatments—whether it's stated or not—is to make the child "as normal as possible." Many professionals and parents often feel that until the child reaches a certain level of normalcy, he can not or should not be included in regular education classes, community activities, or other typical childhood experiences. As a result, children are excluded. A variety of explanations are used to justify this exclusion.

Physical Appearance Factor

"If a child doesn't look normal (uses a mobility device, has Down syndrome, doesn't look or act her age, or whatever), she must not be normal. She can only be included if and when she looks more normal. She might be uncomfortable around normal people and they would certainly be uncomfortable around her."

Some people claim to be "uncomfortable" around people who look different. Is this because they're reminded that "this" could happen to them? Shall we make our children wait and wait until they meet society's artificial standards? What about children who will never look "normal"? And how can anyone make the absurd assumption that a child with a disability would be "uncomfortable" around so-called normal people? This is a remnant of the conventional wisdom of the institutional era when it was believed the "feebleminded" didn't belong in society.

Functional Abilities Factor

"If a child can't do what other people do, he's not normal. Therefore, he can not or should not participate in normal activities. If and when he can (take your pick): walk, talk, feed himself, behave appropriately, add, subtract, multiply, divide, write, or act like normal people, then he can participate in normal activities."

If accommodations are made or supports provided, a child can successfully participate regardless of his functional abilities. None of us do things exactly the same. Should a child be penalized because of his differences?

Contribution/Participation Factor

"If a child cannot contribute to and/or participate in typical childhood activities like other children, there is no reason for her to be included in these activities. If and when she can contribute and/or participate like normal children, she can be included."

We all contribute and participate in our own ways. There's no standard to measure the contributions or participation of typical children. Why should one be imposed on children with disabilities?

Disruption Factor

"A child who is disruptive cannot be allowed to ruin things for other children. When he can learn not to disrupt, he can be included—maybe."

If we take the time to learn what a child really needs, and if we provide him with the appropriate supports and modify the environment, the disruptions would probably subside and/or they would no longer be perceived as problematic. Children without disabilities don't have perfect behavior; why should we impose a standard on children with disabilities?

Benefit Factor

"If a child doesn't learn normally and can't do things normally, he will not benefit from being in a regular classroom or any other typical environment. If and when he can learn normally, do things the right way, and benefit from the activity, he can be included."

None of us can know all the benefits a child may be receiving from his environment and the people in it. If a child is participating in something he enjoys or is with people he likes, we must assume he's benefiting from the experience. We don't try to measure the benefits typical children receive, why should we do it to children with disabilities?

There are other, more specific, rationales used to justify exclusion, but most would fall under the general categories described above. Many decisions are made about our children before anyone has even met them. Labels define and limit our children.

EUPHEMISTIC LABELS

While professionals seem to have no compunction about assigning derogatory labels to human beings, the same is not true for places in "Disability World." For some reason, the powers-that-be want to put a good image on the places where people with disabilities are forced to spend a great deal of their lives. Look around your own community and you'll see what I mean.

When I first met twenty-year-old Daniel, he described a variety of terrible things he routinely experienced while living in a group home for people with cognitive disabilities. It was a private residential "school" that cost his parents a bundle, and it was known as one of the finest in the state. When I asked him the name of the place, his reply was refreshingly honest, "The real name was Hope House, but it should have been called Hopeless House!"

At developmental centers for infants, special ed preschools, sheltered workshops, adult day care facilities, developmental centers for adults (they've probably got an eye on your child as a future client), and everything in between, we find names like: New Hope, Opportunity Center, New Beginnings, Special Touch, Freedom Center, Sunshine Home, New Horizons, Opportunities Unlimited, New Directions, and others.

The vast majority of these programs and services segregate, isolate, and exclude people with disabilities from the mainstream. What's going on here? Are benevolent names bestowed on these entities as a joke? Are the names for the benefit of professionals or clients? Perhaps both. A professional would probably enjoying working at The Opportunity Center more than The Non-Opportunity Center. And clients probably wouldn't get within a mile of the place if it was called Hopeless House. Ditto for parents, if they were encouraged to take their children to The Segregated Center. Ponder the irony of using euphemistic names for places where opportunity, freedom, hope, and sunshine don't exist.

ENOUGH IS ENOUGH

The classification of people with disabilities has been with us forever. From ancient times through today, those "in charge"—priests, physicians, social reformers, educators, and others—told stories about people with disabilities. Out of the stories grew myths and labels, from the ancient "idios" to today's multitude of disability categories. Today, a label is attached and the myth follows. These myths continue to have a life of their own. These myths can destroy lives.

Disability labels have changed over time. Definitions and meanings have evolved. The number of settings where labels are used has grown. Labels are being used as classifiers and identifiers in medical, educational, and social arenas. And our children's humanity and potential are bruised, battered, and defined by the labels they carry. Far too often, a child's label is more of a disability than the actual condition. Like the numbers tattooed on the bodies of Jewish people and others in Nazi Germany, labels separate children with disabilities from the rest of humanity. Like a jail cell that restricts freedom, labels prevent children from experiencing life to the fullest.

On behalf of our children, we must actively refute the myths that surround our children and others. We must refuse to accept the traditional and inaccurate meanings of disability labels. We must not believe them. *We dare not let our children believe them.*

We have an obligation to teach others that our children will not be defined by disability labels. Our children are children, first. They are human beings with unlimited potential. We cannot allow this potential to be denied by the prognoses and "realistic" pronouncements of physicians, professionals, and educators.

Regardless of the notion that we're all created equal, a class system *does* exist in this country, fueled by prejudice and discrimination. Women, people of color, and others continue to dismantle this class system and the social apartheid that goes with it. People with disabilities must do the same, by first removing the language barriers, especially labels, that keep them on the fringe of society.

Individually and collectively, we can start a gentle—but revolutionary—campaign with our words and our actions which will destroy the traditional views of disability and create new perceptions based on the paradigm that disability is natural. We can change things for our children and other people with disabilities. I'll show you how in later chapters. In the meantime, let's take a look at how disability myths are perpetuated throughout our society.

IF THOUGHT CORRUPTS LANGUAGE,
LANGUAGE CAN ALSO CORRUPT THOUGHT.
George Orwell

Multitudes of Myths

In 1999, Abby was excited about attending her state senator's monthly town meeting. The legislator spent the first part of the meeting discussing the next legislative session and then took questions from the audience. Abby asked the senator—who was also a mother—about supporting a bill that would provide services for babies with developmental disabilities. Without missing a beat, the senator replied, "No, I can't support that bill. Government money shouldn't be spent on freaks of nature." She turned to the next questioner as Abby, the mother of a child with Down syndrome, sat frozen in shock.

People with disabilities continue striving for equality—not just legal equality, we have that in a variety of federal laws—but for social and moral equality. So far, many have not been successful, because they can't get past the greatest barrier facing people with disabilities today: myths that generate negative attitudes and perceptions.

The status of people with disabilities is not related to facts or truths, but to theories, myths, and outright falsehoods that are perpetuated in many ways. These perceptions influence actions, such as social policies intended to "help," laws designed to reverse discrimination, and today's conventional wisdom (described in Chapter 6). In this chapter, we'll look at how myths are sustained and spread through literature, movies, television, and the news media, as well as by disability organizations. When we understand the how and why of myths, we're in a better position to end them once and for all.

People from diverse ethnic backgrounds, women, and other groups have been invisible (ignored), marginalized, and set apart because of myths. People with disabilities are no different. But many of these groups have unshackled themselves from the chains of exclusion and destroyed the myths that surrounded them. People with disabilities must learn from them; if others have done it, we can do it.

In the twenty-first century, people with developmental disabilities are not as invisible as they once were. Individually, many are very visible: they're included in public schools, in jobs, and in their communities. Laws, social policies, and the actions of children and adults with disabilities and their families have all made a difference in this regard. In the big scheme of things, the progress of the last fifty years is nothing short of phenomenal.

There is, however, at least one area where people with disabilities as a group are invisible. Specifically—and ironically—it's in the area of diversity. Today, there is a groundswell of individuals and organizations furiously promoting the recognition of, and respect for, differences. Books, magazine articles, employee manuals, conferences, news reports, television programs, and other sources urge us to embrace and celebrate the diversity of religious, cultural, ethnic, age, sexual orientation, and gender differences. And this is a wonderful, long-overdue concept.

But in all the mainstream books, articles, and reports I've seen, seldom are people with disabilities included as one of the "groups" whose differences should be embraced and celebrated. Why does this happen? Is it because people with disabilities are still invisible; that diversity experts simply don't recognize people with disabilities as a group? Could it be that promoters don't *know* that people with disabilities have been ostracized as much as—or more than—other groups? Or is it possible the disability community is excluded from mainstream diversity campaigns because of the pervasiveness of disability myths—myths that portray people with disabilities as second-class citizens, existing in the shadows of society? Is the disability community not equal to other groups, in the minds of diversity promoters? I don't know the answer; if you do, clue me in.

THE POWER OF PERCEPTION

Growing up, all of us developed attitudes and perceptions based on what we learned from our parents and other people in our lives. Our parents learned from their parents, who learned from their parents, and so on. The beliefs and opinions passed down to us were (and are) very powerful. Some of these views stay with us forever; many change once we have personal experiences that shape new attitudes.

Books, movies, and the news media also have an extremely powerful impact on us: they reflect, as well as reinforce, public opinion. They can also be persuasive forces in creating new attitudes.

We all learn new things from a variety of sources, and in the process, we determine what is accurate and truthful. Those of us with intimate and personal experience with disability are able to sort out truths, half-truths, and outright falsehoods in depictions of individuals with disabilities. But people who have little or no experience with real people with disabilities may accept what they learn from books, television shows, movies, and the news media, as factual information.

Other perspectives about people with disabilities are disseminated to the general public by disability-related organizations. But these well-meaning organizations may often do people with disabilities more harm than good, as I'll demonstrate later in this chapter.

You know the saying, "Perception is greater than reality." Never has this been more true than for people with disabilities. As I was writing this chapter, two chance meetings with strangers occurred, almost as if they were preordained to be in this book.

"Touched by an Angel"

My children and I were in a gate area at the Colorado Springs airport, waiting for my mother's flight to arrive from Texas. Emily and I sat at the end of a row of seats, and Benj was in his wheelchair, facing us.

A man who appeared to be in his sixties or seventies was sitting close by. He walked over to us, leaned toward me, pointed at Benjamin and, in a conspiratorial whisper said, "If I try to tell him something, will he understand me?" (For a fleeting moment, I considered answering sweetly, "Actually, no. He's from Mars. Do you speak Martian?")

"Why don't you ask him?" I replied in a friendly voice. The man leaned down toward Benjamin and gently said, "Did you know you're special?" (I'm groaning inside.) Benjamin just looked at him. The man continued, "On the day you were born, an angel touched you right here," and he put his forefinger on Benjamin's upper lip where we all have a little cleft between our nose and mouth. Benjamin pulled his head back slightly at the man's touch.

I jumped in with, "I think an angel touched all of us, don't you?" (I felt like we were in a commercial for the television show, *Touched by an Angel*.) The man looked at me, then back at Benjamin and said, "Do you understand what I mean? That you're special?" Benjamin cocked his head, "Well—" he started and then paused, unsure of what to say next. "You're very kind," I interrupted, "But I think we're all special, don't you?" "Well, yes, I guess so," he replied. Then he returned to his seat.

A few moments later, we moved closer to the window for a better view of the runway. When we were out of earshot, we all giggled. Benjamin confessed he didn't quite understand what the man meant (even though we've had many family talks about perceptions of people with disabilities). Benjamin doesn't see himself as special or different because we've never treated him as special or different!

We talked about why the man said what he did and discussed how many people feel sorry for people with disabilities, feel they're special, and so on. I asked Benjamin how he might respond the next time something like that happened. He thought for a moment and said, "I'll tell 'em to 'Put a sock in it!' " I told Benj that, as much as that's exactly what I felt like doing, it would be rude and wouldn't give us a chance to educate people.

"I Feel Sorry For Your Son"

A couple of weeks later, Benj and I were at the Colorado Springs public library. While I went down a stack, he stayed in an open space, reading his library book about Stephen Hawking. This British scientist, famous for his work on black holes and the Big Bang theory, has Lou Gehrig's disease (ALS), and uses a power wheelchair and a speech synthesizer. Every child needs heroes and Stephen Hawking is one of Benjamin's.

As I was searching for a book on the shelves, a boy about ten approached me. He looked toward Benjamin and said, "I feel sorry for your son." "Oh, really?" I asked. "Why?" This was obviously not the reply he expected, for he became embarrassed and stammered, "Well, uh, you know, uh, uh—"

I took his hand and led him toward my son. "Come on, I want you to meet my son. What's your name?" I asked. "Julian," he answered. When we reached Benjamin, I said, "Benjamin, this is Julian. He said he felt sorry for you and I wanted him to meet you so he would know there's nothing to feel sorry about!" Benj extended his hand in welcome, shook Julian's hand, and said, "Nice to meet you, Julian."

"Julian," I asked, "Why do you feel sorry for Benjamin?" "Well," he replied, "You know, um, uh—because he can't walk and stuff." I looked at Julian and explained, "We don't feel sorry for Benjamin and other people don't need to feel sorry for him. That's probably something you learned from your parents, but no one needs to feel sorry for people with disabilities. In his wheelchair, he can go where he wants to go and do what he wants to do. See Benjamin's chair, Julian?" He nodded. "Benjamin," I said, "tell Julian what these wheels are like." Benjamin started to speak, when Julian burst in, "Oh, I know! The wheels are just like my shoes! I walk in my shoes and he goes on his wheels!"

In that instant, he got it! He had a big grin on his face—disability and differences were forgotten—and he and Benj began talking about their books. Later, Benj said at first he really wanted to tell Julian to "put a sock in it" but he knew that wouldn't be nice. Julian's attitude was forever changed because of his chance encounter with Benjamin. The "Angel Man" from the airport didn't get it right away, but maybe after some reflection he will.

LITERATURE AND MOVIES

A review of many popular books, television shows, and movies, including classic stories, reveals that distorted portrayals of people with disabilities are the norm.

Villains and Bad Guys

Many famous villains have disabilities or physical differences. They're often the personification of evil. Some may show a softer side, but the evil image remains dominant. A partial listing includes:

- Captain Hook in *Peter Pan*
- Quasimodo in *The Hunchback of Notre Dame*
- Captain Ahab in *Moby Dick*
- Mr. Potter, the mean banker in *It's a Wonderful Life*
- *Frankenstein*
- *Dr. Jekyll and Mr. Hyde*
- The "one-armed man" in *The Fugitive*
- *Phantom of the Opera*

We're also familiar with "generic" bad guys who have eye patches, missing arms or legs, prosthetic arms or legs, or other visible "abnormalities:" pirates on the high seas, gunslingers in the Old West, and evil-doers in today's action-adventure movies. These characters fill the bill nicely as frightening villains who have disabilities or physical differences.

Heroes and Brave Souls

When people with disabilities aren't being depicted as villains, they're at the other end of the spectrum: extremely good individuals who are simultaneously pitiful and heroic.

Children's literature often includes tragic characters who are portrayed as overcoming giant obstacles, struggling against overwhelming odds, or achieving stupendous feats. People with disabilities may also be depicted as emotionally unstable, eccentric, or both. This category includes:

- Tiny Tim in *A Christmas Carol*
- Sleepy, Grumpy, Sneezy, Happy, Dopey, Doc, and Bashful in *Snow White and the Seven Dwarfs*
- Young children who used wheelchairs in the classics, *Heidi* and *The Secret Garden*
- The "blind lady" in the suspense film, *Wait Until Dark*
- The Vietnam vet in the movie, *Coming Home*
- *Rainman*
- The "blind man" in the film, *The Scent of a Woman*
- *Forrest Gump*

Comic Figures

Let's not forget portrayals that are supposed to make us laugh. They rely not on clever humor, but on the characteristics of certain disabilities. A short list includes:

- *Dumb and Dumber*
- The man who stuttered in *A Fish Called Wanda*
- Cartoons that feature Mr. Magoo, Elmer Fudd, Porky Pig, and other animated characters with obvious disabilities or differences

We may be fond of some of the shows and books in the lists above. At the same time, we're able to recognize that some portrayals are so mythical they border on the absurd. But many typical moviegoers or book readers may not always separate myths from realities.

How Images Affect Our Children

If you're a parent of a child with autism, you've probably heard, "Oh, you have a kid just like Dustin Hoffman in *Rainman!*" How many fans of this movie have assumed that everybody with autism has "idiot savant" numerical abilities the way "Raymond" did?

If your child has a physical disability and uses a wheelchair, some children may be afraid of your child. Why? Because people with physical disabilities in movies are often seen as frightening. At the other end of the spectrum is pity. The emotions generated by characters who appear pathetic influence people's actions: absolute strangers have approached Benjamin in public and patted him on the head, prayed over him, hugged and kissed him, and pressed money in his hand!

Unrealistic, mythical depictions of individuals with disabilities reinforce existing beliefs that people with disabilities are (take your pick): incapable, sick, different, pitiful, scary, not whole, super-human, tragically heroic, and on and on. The truth is that people with disabilities are more similar to people without disabilities than different. For example, an accountant who uses a wheelchair probably has more in common with other accountants than with other people who use wheelchairs!

In general, the entertainment industry cranks out many images that are never wholly truthful. Embellishments and creative license are the the norm. In action-adventure movies, virtually impossible feats are common. In this case, exaggerations enhance the entertainment value—the excitement—of a film. Embellished portrayals of people with disabilities, however, enhance the already exaggerated stereotypical perceptions of pity, ultra-heroism, or some other unfounded characteristic.

A Few Good Movies

Only a very few movies focused specifically on people with disabilities have depicted them as sharing the common experiences of all humans: love, hate, joy, sadness, success, failure, and every other human characteristic. *My Left Foot,* the autobiography of Christy Brown, an Irish man with cerebral palsy, was very good. Daniel Day-Lewis, who starred as the main character, did an admirable job in a physically difficult role.

One Flew Over the Cuckoo's Nest, the engrossing tale of life in a "mental institution" starred Jack Nicholson. It demonstrated the "normalcy" of men who are diagnosed with a variety of psychiatric labels. *Born on the 4th of July,* starring Tom Cruise, was a film based on the true story of a Vietnam veteran (Ron Kovic) whose legs were blown off by a land mine. In addition to depicting Kovic's experiences, the movie also demonstrated the power of advocacy. But why didn't actors with disabilities star in these roles?

At least two performers with disabilities have successfully entered the professional acting field. Marlee Matlin, an actress who is deaf, starred in *Children of a Lesser God.* (I hate that title, though!) In the now-defunct television series, *Life Goes On,* the character of Corky, a teenager with Down syndrome, was played by Chris Burke, who has Down syndrome.

Steel, an action adventure movie featuring basketball star Shaquille O'Neal had a deep impact on my son. A young woman in the movie who was on the police force used a power wheelchair that was just like my son's. But hers was equipped with weaponry and other high-tech devices. After seeing the film, my son bugged me to outfit his chair like hers. I told him his power chair was already a weapon (my toes regularly get in the way of his wheels), and that he didn't need anymore defensive or offensive artillery! With a big sigh, he reluctantly accepted my decision, but then added that if he couldn't have weapons, he at least wanted some of the tools on James Bond's cars: smoke screen, bullet proof tires, oil slick thingamajig, and other goodies. Ahhh, the power of movies.

A few portrayals on network television show people with disabilities as real people. A physician on *ER* uses one crutch, the dad on *Frasier* uses a cane, and a character on *Becker* is blind. Some progress is being made. But do these actors really have disabilities?

When will the creative forces behind television shows and movies begin using people with disabilities as consultants, as actors, or in other roles that will enable them to contribute to the accurate portrayal of people with disabilities When will people with more significant disabilities be part of the story line? When will *actors with disabilities* portray *characters with disabilities?* Is this any different than when Euro-American actors painted their faces black to portray "darkies," because African-Americans weren't allowed in the entertainment industry?

Will any of this happen without our influence? We can't wait to be asked; we must make inroads on our own. Are there any budding consultants, writers, producers, directors, or actors out there? There's one in my house and he's raring to go.

THE NEWS MEDIA

When we look at the news media, we see an uneven pattern. Many newspapers and television news stories are beginning to use more appropriate language, thanks to advocates who have taken the time to educate writers and reporters. However, we still see too many "pity" stories in which persons with disabilities are portrayed as the struggling heroes, or their families are portrayed as saints.

Journalists often repeatedly refer to a person's disability, when one reference is all that's necessary. Similar situations occur when reporters write about "the first African-American" or "the first woman" to do this or that: the person's "difference" is repeated again and again.

Responsible journalism requires truthful, unbiased, factual reporting. But truth can be elusive. If a reporter doesn't *know* all sides of the story, doesn't know where to look to find the whole story, or doesn't take the time to determine if there's more to the story, the truth has not been told. When we see biased writing about people with disabilities, we know the truth—the whole truth—has not been written.

When Is News Not News?

The news media is supposed to report the news, not create it. But the power of the media is so great today that a story which doesn't include "new" information becomes news just because it's reported.

Over several consecutive days in August of 1997, *USA Today* featured a series of articles about prenatal testing and congenital disabilities. Included were articles about families who had children with disabilities: one couple aborted a fetus who was diagnosed with Down syndrome, another family took their child with Down syndrome home to raise and love, and a mother bemoaned the terribly cruel burden of raising a child with multiple disabilities. (The score: Against Children with Disabilities - 2; For Children with Disabilities - 1.)

One article in the series was entitled, "Is the Disabled Life Worth Living?" I was astounded! Would a reporter do a story on, "Is the African-American Life Worth Living?" or "Is the Jewish Life Worth Living?"

The mere *existence* of the question insinuated that people with disabilities don't have lives that are worth living! If there was *no doubt* about the issue in the minds of the newspaper folks, they would have never posed the question! The headline itself—whether one read the article or not—marginalized and dehumanized people with disabilities. Included in the article were interviews with experts about the value of prenatal testing, aborting fetuses with disabilities, and whether the lives of premature babies and infants with disabilities should be saved.

What does this article say about our society? Was this real or created news? Why did the reporter and the publisher feel compelled to insult the estimated 54 million Americans with disabilities?

In August of 2000, ABC's *Nightline* aired a program about "saving premature babies." The issues discussed by the three panel members were: how to decide which babies should be saved, the cost of their care, and the quality of life of infants with "birth defects."

One of the panel members was a woman who had given birth to premature twins several years before; one of the babies died at or near birth, while the other survived, apparently with no disabilities. (I never learned if the baby who died was "allowed" to die or if he died following aggressive medical intervention.) A physician and a nun/medical ethicist rounded out the panel. With one exception, the entire program was biased against saving premature babies who may have developmental disabilities. Only during the very end of the program was there a hint of fairness: the physician noted that not all parents thought having a child with a disability was a terrible thing.

Why didn't *Nightline* have a panel member with a disability, or a parent of a child with a disability? Why did the show's producers choose three panelists who, in the main, shared similar opinions?

After reading the *USA Today* articles or watching the *Nightline* broadcast, it's highly possible people who don't know any better might ponder the following:

- Children with "birth defects" are expensive. Since parents can find out about a "defective" fetus before it's born, if they choose to have it, they're on their own! No government funds or insurance ought to be spent on the child's care.

- If parents don't know the child is "defective" before birth, they ought to let nature take its course once the baby is born. If the baby can't survive on its own, without medical intervention, the baby should be allowed to die.

- If the lives of children and adults with disabilities aren't worth much, why should we bother educating them or hiring them?

- Maybe we ought to rethink this assisted-suicide stuff. If the lives of people with disabilities aren't worth living, maybe we should help them kill themselves.

In the *Nightline* program, what if the focus wasn't premature babies but people of other ages? If they had been talking about a ten-year-old or a forty-year-old who had the same medical conditions a premature baby might have (jaundice, breathing or eating difficulties, and so forth), few would question whether aggressive measures should be taken to save the person's life. I seriously doubt if anyone would even consider "letting the patient die" by withholding food and water and/or medical care. I doubt if a physician or a medical ethicist would approach the parents or family members with, "Well, we don't know what kind of quality of life John will have. He may not be able to walk or learn the same way as before. He might need a feeding tube. So should we let him live or die?"

A ten-year-old or a forty-year-old who *acquires* a disability is perceived to have a track record of success, and value as a human being. But babies born with disabilities are seen as less valuable than other human beings. Their value is further diminished when the discussion turns to the cost of care. No one would question the dollars spent to save the life of our imaginary ten-year-old or forty-year-old. But many think it's a waste of money to save newborns with disabilities.

You and I would not develop negative attitudes about people with disabilities from negative media coverage. We know better. But the odds are good that many Americans *do* learn negative and prejudicial attitudes about babies and others with disabilities from the media.

Let's assume a hypothetical scenario. You want your child included in a regular education classroom and you've identified a potential teacher. What happens if the classroom teacher read the articles or saw the program I've described, and believed your child's life wasn't worth living? Would she want your child in her class? If she did, would she invest much in your child's education? We must never underestimate the power of the media in shaping attitudes and perceptions.

What Does God Have to Do With It?

In 1997, Dr. James Dobson of the Focus on the Family religious organization wrote a book entitled, *When God Doesn't Make Sense.* The book was promoted on the cover of the organization's monthly magazine. "When God Doesn't Make Sense" was emblazoned across the top. A lot of white space was in the middle of the cover, and at the bottom was a small photographic image of a young boy wearing plastic leg braces and using old-fashioned wooden crutches. If you're familiar with children with physical disabilities, you know the plastic leg braces were appropriate in the 1990s, but the wooden crutches were not. The only places to find those anymore are in hospitals (for use by people who have a broken leg) or in someone's dusty attic. Today's pediatric crutches are made of high-tech metals in bright colors. I don't know if the little boy in the picture really had a disability or if he was a model.

The imagery was disturbing: a child with a disability representing the concept of "when God doesn't make sense." The layout—very large type dominating the very small image of the young boy—was designed to evoke an emotional response. But in the long excerpts of the book inside the covers of the magazine, there was no mention of disability. So what did disability have to do with God not making sense? If the article (and the book) demonstrated no connection to disability and God, why was this image chosen? Was it simply sensational journalism—an emotionally provocative cover to sell the magazine and the book—or *was* the intent to show that when God doesn't make sense, the result is children with disabilities? What effect might this image have on how people see our children? Worse, what effect might it have on a child who uses crutches and leg braces? Is he to believe he's the result of God not making sense?

A Snotty-Nosed Kid Makes News

When Benjamin was in third grade, a newspaper reporter visited our home to do a story about how Benj was a typical kid in the neighborhood inclusive school. The reporter from the small weekly newspaper was a nice lady who spent some time with me alone and then interviewed Benjamin. I stayed close by in case Benj needed me, and in the event the reporter didn't understand his answers or his speech.

The story that appeared in the paper was, overall, a positive portrayal. However, the reporter made a point of describing how eight-year-old Benjamin still needed help blowing his nose. This fact wasn't part of the interview process. It just so happened that during the reporter's visit, I saw Benjamin about to sneeze. Like any other eight-year-old, he often forgot to cover his mouth. When I saw the sneeze coming, I ran to cover his mouth with a tissue before he sprayed the interviewer. With the tissue still covering his nose and mouth, he blew his nose. Imagine my surprise when this innocuous event became part of the story. Worse, it seemed it was included to evoke pity: an eight-year-old with a disability still couldn't blow his nose by himself.

Would the reporter have included this bit of trivia if the story had been about an eight-year-old master chess player or an eight-year-old fashion model? Were the positive images in the story negated by this one specific incident? Perhaps I should have let Benjamin spray the reporter that day. I wonder if she would have included a tantalizing tidbit about being on the receiving end of a face full of snot.

THE POWER OF MEDIA IMAGES

Volumes could be written about the media and negative images of people with disabilities. The few examples I've shared are representative of media reports we see and hear every day. Stories like these reinforce and revitalize prejudicial attitudes about people with disabilities: inaccurate theories that—in the past—led to segregation, incarceration, sterilization, and, ultimately, death. Today, these stories fuel the beliefs that people with disabilities are heroic and angelic at one extreme or pitiful and needy at the other. In between are questions about whether the lives of people with disabilities are worth living, or if the lives of babies with disabilities are worth saving.

How does all this affect our children? It's like being charged with a crime and presumed guilty instead of innocent. Our children are forced to defend themselves against collective prejudices and inaccurate portrayals.

Stereotypical images diminish the opportunities for our children to define themselves, for they've already been defined. Matt can't be defined by his love of books, for he's already known by his label. Kaitlyn can't be known for her desire to be a ballerina: this is not a "realistic" dream since she has a disability. She's known by her label, too. In schools and community settings, our children are often marginalized, excluded, ignored, or discriminated against because their disabilities have defined them as incapable, unworthy, incompetent, or some other unfavorable characteristic.

People who have no other images of, or experiences with, people with disabilities often internalize inaccurate, harmful perceptions and believe them to be true. Is it any wonder, then, that typical children are often frightened of people with disabilities? That adults may feel both sorrow and revulsion for children and adults with disabilities? That society focuses on the differences and not the similarities between people with and without disabilities?

How do detrimental media images affect professionals, friends, and other family members who are in our lives? If educators believe the lives of children with disabilities are worthless—if they see no future for our children—how much time, energy, and resources are they willing to invest in our children? If an employer doesn't feel a young person with a disability will be a valuable employee, will he even offer an interview?

If members of our extended families feel children with disabilities cause us "pain and suffering" or are "burdens," how do they feel about a grandchild or a niece or nephew who has a disability? Our own parents want to protect *us*—after all, we're still *their* babies. Under these circumstances, how do they feel about our sons and daughters with disabilities? Perhaps they feel anger toward the child for causing us pain. Maybe our parents feel we've brought shame on the family, or they're disappointed we didn't abort a "defective" fetus. And if our sons and daughters who *don't* have disabilities believe their brothers or sisters with disabilities are "special" because they get more of our attention, what does that do to our families? We can influence how our children are perceived by others. I'll show you how in later chapters.

DISABILITY ORGANIZATIONS, FUND RAISING, AND STEREOTYPES

Children with disabilities and their families have numerous allies in the many disability advocacy organizations who speak on our behalf, help influence legislation, and provide supports and assistance. These organizations also promote images of people with disabilities. And therein lies a problem.

The fund raising and public relations efforts of disability organizations create a paradox: in order to raise money, they portray people with disabilities as different, pitiful, and/or needy. Even though these groups are working on our behalf, their messages reinforce negative stereotypical images. If they promoted the ideas that disability is a natural condition, and people with disabilities can and do live happy, positive, productive lives, who would give them money?

The very *existence* of organizations that raise funds on behalf of people with disabilities is proof (to society) that people with disabilities are different and needy. Certainly, the original goal of the early parent organizations (mutual support and advocacy) was good. And the current power of these groups directed toward influencing legislation and public policies is beneficial. But have some disability organizations moved too far from their roots?

It's one thing when people gather to share concerns and interests. It's great when members of grassroots associations are able to influence public policy. But can many of the larger disability associations still be considered grassroots organizations? With large budgets, paid lobbyists, and professional staffs, they're more like big corporations than grassroots organizations. Does true citizen advocacy still have a place here?

The *great number* of disability-specific organizations sends the message that the "problem" of disability is extremely large, otherwise there wouldn't be so many groups, right? When it comes to fund raising, all of these groups must compete against one another for charitable donations. Raising money is hard work; creative methods to reach potential donors are critical.

In marketing vernacular, how do each of these groups "position" themselves to ensure their organization gets the donations they need? Must they demonstrate that *their* constituents are more needy than the constituents of other groups? Or that the disability they represent is more serious or problematic than others?

When we consider the messages disability organizations convey to the general public, it's easy to understand why we have difficulty getting our children included in public schools and community settings. Many of us are trying to ensure our children are seen as children, not their disability labels. But society is unable to see our children that way. The primary image is the disability and its so-called problems, and this notion is—intentionally or not—promoted by many disability groups.

Organizations representing the interests of other minority groups exist, but their number is small in comparison to disability organizations. The NAACP represents African-American people. NOW represents women. Both are very large, well-known groups, but they don't have to compete for donations against organizations representing similar constituencies. They don't have to emphasize how bad things are for their particular group as compared to a similar group, the way disability organizations do. They don't use pity to garner donations. The focus is aimed at justice or civil rights.

Do some disability organizations do more harm than good? This is an issue of importance for all of us.

The Terrible Telethons

Of all the fund raising activities generated by disability organizations, telethons probably inflict the most harm to positive images of people with disabilities. Yet telethons are also one of the most successful activities in terms of dollars raised. Ironic? No, it's to be expected.

Telethons have a singular purpose: to raise money—lots of it—most of which does not go to people with disabilities. During a telethon, people with disabilities—in essence—enter the homes of the viewers via the television set. Real live people with disabilities being interviewed on stage, coupled with the running commentary about the great needs of these "victims," are designed to tug at the heart strings of viewers and entice them to help, by giving cold, hard cash.

The "Jerry's Kids" slogan of the Muscular Dystrophy Association (MDA) telethon is used as a descriptor of people who have muscular dystrophy regardless of their ages. This paternalistic approach reinforces the stereotype that people with disabilities never grow up and are, therefore, never competent. Again, if fund raising activities such as telethons spent hours focused on positive images of people with disabilities, no one would give them a penny. "Incompetent" works to bring in the bucks!

It's no wonder telethons pull in millions of dollars every year. On the MDA telethon, Jerry Lewis and his entertainment buddies do a super job pleading for dollars to "fight" muscular dystrophy. And the so-called fight is legitimized by the appearance of well-known corporate sponsors. However, these giants of business appear to be in competition with one another to see who can get the most air time, as they present their checks and review all they've done to raise money. Are these appearances anything less than free advertising? Would these businesses give less money if they didn't get to appear on national television?

Do we really need money jars on the counters of convenience stores, which scream pity as they gobble up customers' spare change? Or would we rather the owners and managers of these stores create truly accessible environments for customers, and employ qualified people with disabilities in their businesses?

Do we really need Hollywood performers to plead for the cause? What if, instead, they simply changed their own personal perceptions and behaviors, and used their influence to employ qualified people with disabilities in the entertainment industry?

Telethons promote the "plight" of people with disabilities, along with the solution: more money. Viewers are led to believe that more money will solve the problems facing people with disabilities. But the problems described on telethons are not the most significant problems people with disabilities face every day: exclusion, segregation, devaluation, poor education, unemployment, and more. Money cannot buy equality or inclusion; money cannot change people's hearts and minds. Telethons don't address the fact that equality, justice, opportunity, and inclusion are the real needs of people with disabilities.

If a telethon host was really truthful, he would announce that the issues facing people with disabilities can only be solved when personal attitudes and social policies change. Unfortunately, it's easier for fund raisers (as well as individuals, organizations, and government) to throw money at the "problem" than to make significant, long-term changes in personal beliefs and social policies.

Several disability organizations no longer sponsor telethons, and others have modified their format, perhaps to distance themselves from the MDA telethon. Still, the very nature of any telethon—asking for donations to help find cures, to fund research, to help provide more services, or whatever—is demeaning. Furthermore, the messages of a telethon perpetuate disability myths.

Behind the Scenes at a Telethon

In the late 1970s, before becoming a wife and mother, I worked at a television station in a big city in Texas that carried the MDA telethon every year. As a camera operator, I ran a studio camera during the telethon two years in a row. After I became a broadcast director, I was in charge of getting the show on the air. It was an enlightening experience.

Prior to directing the telethon, I thought it was great that our station helped MDA: the telethon was a worthy event put on by an honorable group. (I didn't know anything about disabilities at the time.) Not until I was in charge of directing the telethon did I discover my beliefs were erroneous.

I learned the station did not *donate* the air time to MDA, they sold it, just as they sold air time for thirty second commercials. As a result, a great deal of the money raised in this Texas city didn't go to MDA; it went to pay the television bill. Included in the bill were several thousand dollars to pay the wages of numerous staff people (including myself) working on the telethon.

Now, there's nothing wrong with a local television station charging MDA for the air time and the staff expenses. But it was disconcerting that viewers were *led to believe* MDA had a great civic partner (the TV station) that was generously sharing its assets in "the cause." Pshaw! It was strictly a business deal!

The fantasy of goodwill didn't end there, however. The telethon hosts at the local station (high-profile news anchors) didn't donate their time, nor did they have any personal interest in MDA. They put on a great act of sincerity and compassion for which they were paid! I'm not criticizing the hosts; they were just doing a job. But it was shocking to realize the *image* of all these good people pulling together for a great cause was false. People at the television station were working on the telethon because they were getting paid, not because they were part of MDA's cause.

In addition to the funds expended for the local broadcast, MDA also spent a ton of money at the annual telethon planning meeting. The chief engineer and myself, along with hundreds of other local television employees from across the country, were wined and dined in Las Vegas for three or four days several months before the telethon. Of course, during the telethon, no hosts ever reveal what percentage of the money raised goes to people with disabilities, research, or operating costs. I'm not sure how many viewers would give money if they knew it was going to pay for high-dollar Las Vegas conventions!

Another shocking realization occurred during the many planning meetings I had with local MDA executives. We spent hours discussing the set, the telephone banks, the placement of the tote board, how and when the hosts would "go to the tote board," and other aspects of the local cut-ins. It was then I learned the tote board amounts we would show were not exactly truthful. The local MDA executives *would decide* what amount to reveal on the tote board throughout the broadcast. They would never put the actual amount up; it would always be an amount much lower than what had really been pledged at the time.

This was a ploy to increase donations. Telethon executives felt that revealing the actual amount of pledges received at any given point might have a negative effect. Viewers might think, "They've got enough, I don't need to pledge," or "They've passed last year's total; they don't need my money." It was an eye-opening experience, one that's probably common at every local station across the country, as well as at the national level.

Anything for Money, Money, Money

Telethons aren't the only fund raising strategies used by disability organizations. Direct mail campaigns, community activities ("walks," "runs," and more), door-to-door and telephone solicitations, thrift stores, using poster children, and a variety of other methods focus the public's attention on the disability represented by the organization. But is this really the kind of attention we need or want?

There's a public relations maxim that bad publicity is better than no publicity. But this doesn't always hold true, especially when pitiful, needy, or other unfavorable images of people with disabilities are used to generate publicity and attention. While these images practically guarantee donations, they're also extremely harmful to people with disabilities.

Many organizations, sensitive to criticism by people with disabilities, are trying to clean up their acts. For example, some claim they no longer have a poster child. Lest we be fooled, however, it's important to know some have simply changed the name. Children are still being used as valuable commodities, but now they're called "ambassadors" or some other euphemistic term. Some groups no longer choose a child who looks the "most pitiful" to demonstrate the consequences if people don't donate. Instead, they choose a "healthy-looking" child to prove to donors what good things their donations can achieve. (Have you ever noticed that no matter which type of child they choose, it's always a "cute" kid? Somehow, it's "sadder" when something "terrible" happens to a "cute" kid, so people give more money. They probably think if they used an "ugly" child, no one would give a penny!)

We should not be surprised when perfect strangers approach people with disabilities in malls, airports, and other public places and give them money. If they give money to people with disabilities indirectly (via telethons, direct mail, and so forth) why not do it in real life?

One day, while Benjamin was minding his own business, rolling up and down the aisles in the grocery store, a lady approached him, mumbled something about his condition, and thrust a dollar bill in his hand. I jokingly told him he should have demanded at least a ten!

Mary Alice, a high-powered executive, travels a great deal. She has cerebral palsy and frequently uses a cane. While waiting to board a plane, she was sitting in a gate area, holding a newspaper in one hand, and reading it intently like half the other people who were waiting. Her other arm was nonchalantly resting on the armrest of the chair and in that hand was an empty coffee cup she hadn't yet thrown away.

Another professional-looking female traveler hurried by Mary Alice. She paused long enough to drop some coins in Mary Alice's empty coffee cup. The donor evidently felt she had done her good deed for the day. Mary Alice was so astounded, all she could do was laugh out loud (and she laughed even harder after she counted the meager donation)!

We must laugh at some of these outrageous situations in order to keep from crying. But these examples of the pity felt toward people with disabilities is a serious issue we must address.

Healthy Babies; Pain and Suffering

The efforts of some disability organizations focus on "healthy babies." The implication is obvious: babies with disabilities are (perceived to be) unhealthy, and unhealthy babies are (perceived to be) unwanted, pitiful, and costly babies.

We're told that, with enough contributions, the organization will help stop the "pain and suffering" of newborns with disabilities. Certainly, some babies may have pain, but how often is pain the result of the actual disability? In far too many cases, physical pain felt by a newborn is induced by hospital personnel during the many procedures they routinely perform (without anesthesia) on preemies and other babies with congenital disabilities!

(Health care professionals don't intentionally inflict pain, but tiny babies still feel the pain of needle sticks, tubes, and other invasive measures. It's unfortunate that many believe newborns aren't entitled to the same pain relief measures adults count on. Interestingly, a newspaper article in June of 2000 reported the medical community is finally recognizing that newborns do feel pain! Will wonders never cease? Further, the article noted that procedures such as repeated heel sticks, for instance, cause a child's body to develop more pain receptors, resulting in permanent ultra-sensitivity to pain in that area. I could have told them that! My son's feet are extremely sensitive, no doubt caused by the numerous heel sticks—the repetitive taking of small amounts of blood with a sharp needle—he received during his first three weeks of life. His feet were black and blue for weeks.)

Is it possible the pain and suffering described by disability organizations is really the perceived pain and suffering that supposedly descends on parents? Or is it the pain and suffering society must endure to put up with "the needy" or "the pitiful" or "the sick" in its midst—people who may never reach their full potential, and so on, and so on, and so on?

The Prevention Theme

A quick check of the web sites of major disability organizations representing mental retardation, cerebral palsy, Down syndrome, spina bifida, autism, muscular dystrophy, and others conditions, confirms that their goals are to provide assistance and advocacy, to improve the quality of life for people with disabilities, and to work toward prevention and/or cure. If enough money is donated, organizations can find ways to prevent the disability via research into cures, prenatal testing, and so forth.

Prevention is not a new theme. During the eugenics movement in the early 1900s, institution superintendents, policy makers, and dominant forces in American society agreed that the so-called feebleminded should be forcibly sterilized so they wouldn't give birth to any more "defectives." That was *their* method to prevent developmental disabilities. Later, that particular method fell out of favor, but the prevention theme did not. It just took on a new suit of clothes.

"Prevent pain and suffering" and/or "prevent the condition" have become the new mantras of prevention. Today, it's a philosophy that's accepted by most Americans, especially since it's been adopted by organizations representing virtually every medical condition of today's world. Organizations that represent heart disease, cancer, AIDS, arthritis, and other conditions also promote the dual message: support and help the "victims" and prevent (or cure) the condition.

Prevention is promoted as part of an organization's mission because the theme increases donations. In addition, the prevention theme is perceived to be commercially effective, economically fashionable, and morally responsible:

> If we can prevent people with disabilities from being born, and cure the ones now
> living, no one will have to suffer from the dread conditions. Think how much
> money could be saved if society didn't have to spend tax, research, or medical dollars
> on the unfortunate! Think what a better world we would all live in! Just imagine

how good we'll feel about ourselves if we've given money to eradicate these horrible conditions off the face of the earth!

Much good has been done in the name of prevention. Researchers have discovered vaccines, medicines, and other treatments for many conditions. A few diseases *have* been totally eliminated by prevention methods. In spite of years of research, however, people still have heart disease, cancer, arthritis, and countless other conditions, including developmental disabilities. Common sense seems to tell us that the quest for curing all conditions is fruitless: for every condition that's cured, new ones will pop us. Still, few would argue that preventing "pain and suffering" isn't a noble and worthwhile cause.

The Dangers of Prevention Mentality

When people watch a telethon, open a direct mail solicitation, or take a telemarketing call and are hit with the prevention angle, it's often a short mental leap from acknowledging that the disability should be prevented to wondering whether or not *people who have the particular disability should also be prevented.* Under these circumstances, it's easy to understand how society continues to hold unfavorable perceptions about people with disabilities.

But the greatest harm of the prevention mentality is to people with disabilities themselves. Disability organizations are sending the message, "We're here to help you, but we're also working to make sure there aren't any more like you." They might add, "We don't want anyone else to suffer like you have." Or even, "We don't want anyone else to be a burden to their families or society, like you've been." Of course, no disability organization *overtly* sends these negative messages. But their unspoken messages, via the prevention theme, are abundantly clear.

What must this feel like to adults with disabilities? What does it do to their hearts and their minds? What might it do to your child right now, if he knew the disability organization which helps him is trying to prevent the births of other children like him? It's too painful to even think about, but we must.

Surely there are people within disability organizations who don't accept the prevention/cure mentality, yet the practice continues. Why? Perhaps organizations think if they *did not* promote prevention, they would be accused—by default—of condoning the acceptance of "deviance" (the disability). In this position, they would probably feel awkward seeking donations for assistance if they're not trying to prevent the condition that caused people to need help in the first place.

It's important to realize that all organizations who promote prevention can do so only because their members support or allow this activity. Parents are active members of these groups; we're on the governing boards as well. Thus, we're partially responsible for the mixed messages transmitted by the disability organizations we associate with. As board members and constituents, we can refuse to sanction messages that demean and degrade children and adults with developmental disabilities. If we don't, the myths surrounding people with disabilities will continue and worsen, as in the following two examples.

Babies With Disabilities: OK to Terminate

In 1999, a great controversy erupted when Peter Singer of Australia was named to the DeCamp Professorship of Bioethics at Princeton University's Center for Human Values.

According to various news reports, Singer holds the position that killing a "defective" infant is not morally equivalent to killing a person.

He proposed that parents should have the right to kill certain newborns up to twenty-eight days after they're born, because at that stage they are non-persons. He specifically mentioned babies with Down syndrome, spina bifida, and hemophilia. His professed logic is that these babies will endure a life of pain and suffering, so their lives aren't worth living, especially when parents can immediately conceive a "normal" child as a replacement.

Singer is guilty of perpetuating a variety of myths which may influence the general public's attitudes about people with developmental disabilities. After all, as a respected professor at a distinguished Ivy League university, he must know what he's talking about, right?

Disability advocates responded to Singer's appointment by writing letters to Princeton and protesting on the campus, demanding the removal of Singer from his exalted position. As of this writing, however, he's still in place.

His views are seen as amoral and dangerous. In the final analysis, however, isn't he simply promoting prevention? It's just that his method of prevention is abhorrent to us. How far apart, though, is his message of prevention from the prevention theme promoted by disability organizations? It's only a matter of degrees. Think about it.

Sin and Disability, Again

Across the Atlantic, in the *London Sunday-Times* edition of July 4, 1999, a front page story took the prevention issue a step further. The article was about Dr. Bob Edwards, a pioneer embryologist in England who helped develop in-vitro fertilization in the 1970s.

At an international fertility conference in the summer of 1999, Edwards told his audience it would soon be a sin for parents to have a child that carries a genetic disease, and that parents have a moral responsibility not to give birth to children with disabilities. He noted that society must become concerned with the "quality" of children.

What are we to make of this? What does the "quality of children" mean? That children with disabilities are of low "quality," or that children with disabilities lower the "quality" of society? Edwards is taking us backward to a time when parents were blamed for inflicting imperfection (a child with a disability) on the world. And once again, a connection is made between sin and disability.

But on the grand scale, how different is Edwards' point of view from the prevention mentality of most disability organizations? If we think about it carefully, isn't it also only a matter of degrees?

Advocates for Exclusion or Inclusion?

There are other harmful myths perpetuated by disability organizations. Some groups continue to provide segregated services and facilities—therapies and services for children; sheltered workshops, day programs, and group homes for adults; and other special programs—even though most people with disabilities want to be included in their communities. These organizations send the clear message that their "clients" are (pick one): incompetent, needy, dependent, or "not ready" for real life in the community. And there are some organizations that provide segregated services while simultaneously advocating for inclusion. What do these actions communicate to the public? "We support and advocate for inclusion and equality, but we really want your money to help pay for segregation," or "Inclusion is fine for some people, but not for these people." Under these circumstances, are disability organizations truly our allies?

Measuring Good Works

Many disability organizations do a variety of good works on behalf of people with disabilities. They influence legislation, provide support groups for families and individuals, and sponsor other activities that enhance the lives of people with disabilities. But we must measure these good works against the harm done by the pity approach in fund raising activities. In which direction does the scale tip?

When my son was diagnosed with cerebral palsy at the age of four months, I became involved with a disability organization in my city, where I started a parent support group, wrote a newsletter, spearheaded an equipment fair, and became a board member. One of the responsibilities of board members was fund raising, so several of us attended a United Way seminar to learn the best techniques.

We were taught the basics and then we began brainstorming specific ideas for our organization. The United Way staffer asked if any of us had a child with cerebral palsy. I raised my hand in reply. "How old?" she asked. "A year," I answered. "Boy or girl?" she asked. "Boy," I replied. "Cute?" she asked. With a big smile, I proudly answered, "Yes!"

She pointed her finger at me and said, "There's your answer, ladies and gentlemen. Use her kid and any others you can find. They're gold mines!" Never, my mind screamed. At the time, I didn't have the backbone to express my outrage; I just directed the talk away from using children as pawns in the begging scheme.

When Benjamin was very young, my focus was on young children with cerebral palsy. I didn't pay any attention to issues facing adults with developmental disabilities until I was in the Partners in Policymaking leadership development program. Then I began to care about them, after realizing my son would grow up to be an adult with a disability!

A week or so after our Partners class had learned about supported and competitive employment and independent living, I attended the disability association's monthly board meeting. At this particular meeting, one of the staff members gave his report about the difficulty he had getting adult clients to the weekly bowling game. Every Wednesday evening, the association's bus made stops at several nursing homes and picked up fifteen or twenty young adults with cerebral palsy to take them bowling. This was all new to me; my mind was reeling. Why were young people living in nursing homes? I snapped out of my fog and continued listening.

On the previous Wednesday, several residents at one of the nursing homes weren't able to go bowling because they weren't ready on time. The aides in the nursing home failed to get them dressed. I was the only board member who hadn't heard all this before. Evidently, it was a recurring situation. I asked a few questions and learned the following: these particular individuals were men and women in their late twenties and early thirties who lived in nursing homes because they could not get the physical assistance they needed to live in their own homes. Further, the aides often left them in their beds all day, in their pajamas or totally naked, because there was no reason to get them up and dressed. Most of these individuals had no opportunities to do anything except go bowling on Wednesday nights (in a "special" league, of course).

Board members began discussing the issue: what should be done to ensure the nurses' aides got these people dressed on time? I sat with my mouth agape as they haggled over strategies to motivate the nurses' aides.

Finally, I interrupted with, "Why aren't we helping these 'clients' find ways to get personal assistance in their own homes? What are we doing to help them get out of the nursing home and into their own homes? Are we doing anything to help them get jobs?"

I thought my questions were relevant and intelligent. But now it was the board members' turn to stare with mouths agape. They looked at me as if I had just arrived from outer space. After a long moment of dead silence, the discussion continued as if my questions had never been asked.

The people on this board were nice people. But they were stuck in the traditional paradigm of "helping the needy." And, unfortunately, the type of help provided to most people with disabilities is not really the help they want and need.

"Guilt by Association"

There is still another issue to consider about the influence of disability organizations. Many of our friends, neighbors, and acquaintances believe the attitudes and activities of these groups are universally supported by people with disabilities (you and me). People with disabilities are sometimes seen as one huge group—"the handicapped"—who think as one. Many Americans assume you and I are part of these organizations and that we share their views. Thus, people we come in contact with may incorrectly assume we feel sorry for our own children and we want others to do the same, so the myths continue.

Disability is Not the Problem

Requests for charitable donations to help people with disabilities, regardless of the fund raising methods used, reinforce the pervasive myth that the "problem" of disability originates within people who have disabilities. But disability never has been—and never will be—the problem. The real problem is, and always has been, society's attitude toward people with disabilities.

Even those organizations who have moved beyond the old ways of thinking are often unable to let go of their traditional methods of fund raising, public relations, and promotion. Internally, they recognize that societal barriers create the real problems facing people with disabilities, and they're working to help remove those barriers through legislation and other means. But externally, they still use the pity approach to raise money. Why? Because it works. What if an organization tried to raise funds with this approach:

> Let's create inclusive communities! A contribution of only $25.00 will enable us to help our community include all people with disabilities and differences. Your donation will be used for training and technical assistance in schools, businesses, and other organizations. With your help, our community will be a place where everyone is included and everyone belongs!

If disability organizations took this approach, they would be signaling a recognition that society, not people with disabilities, needs to change. And such an effort would advance the inclusion of people with disabilities in schools, employment, and communities more rapidly than traditional approaches. But would this request generate as much income as the pity approach? No, not at the present time. In the future, perhaps it could . . .

Finding a Balance

Parents who are active supporters of disability organizations may feel my observations are unjust criticisms. Many parents and their children have received personal benefits from disability organizations and, therefore, feel very protective. People who serve on boards or committees and those who volunteer are good people who have the best of intentions.

But if our children are to achieve success in the real world, if we want society to move beyond pity and stigmatizing myths, then the organizations that purport to represent people with disabilities must change. We know they have the power to shape attitudes, influence legislation, and more. We can help these organizations use their power in ways that will create a more inclusive society. To truly represent the best interests of people with disabilities, organizations can't have it both ways: they cannot advocate for better lives with one hand, while promoting prevention and asking for hand-outs with the other. In Chapter 21, I'll detail how we can positively influence disability organizations.

MYTHS AND REALITIES: HOW AMERICANS FEEL

A 1991 Louis Harris poll, "Public Attitudes Toward People with Disabilities," commissioned by the National Organization on Disability, revealed the mixed feelings held by Americans:

- 92% felt admiration because people with disabilities overcome so much
- 74% felt pity for people with disabilities because of their situation
- 58% felt awkward or embarrassed, because they don't know how to behave around people with disabilities
- 51% felt lack of concern, because people with disabilities can manage okay
- 47% felt fear, because what happened to people with disabilities might happen to them
- 16% felt anger, because people with disabilities cause inconvenience
- 9% felt resentment, because people with disabilities get special privileges

At first glance, it may seem good that more people feel admiration (92 percent) than pity (74 percent). But these two feelings are, perhaps, flip sides of the same coin. Many Americans may admire astronauts because they're brave explorers; we admire entertainers because they're talented. But people with disabilities aren't admired because of their talents or abilities. They're admired because they've had to "overcome" so much: the burden of a horrible fate (the disability). Society doesn't realize, however, that it's not the disability that needs to be overcome. It is, instead, the attitudinal barriers perpetuated by the same people who feel admiration and pity. I don't want anyone "admiring" my son because he has cerebral palsy, for crying out loud!

The survey also showed that 92 percent believed "society will benefit from having people with disabilities become more productive and contribute to the economy rather than receiving welfare benefits." Ninety-five percent felt that, "given how many difficulties people with disabilities face in their daily lives, the least society can do is to make an extra effort to improve things for them." And of those people surveyed who are involved with a person with a disability on a regular basis, "more than four out of five said their relationships are pleasant and easy."

The survey also revealed that:

- 30% would be concerned if a co-worker had a serious disability
- 23% would be concerned if they had a supervisor with a disability
- 25% would be uncomfortable if their child brought a child with a disability home
- 50% would be uncomfortable with their child dating a person with a disability

The myths about people with disabilities are deeply imbedded in our culture. Once in his life—only once—Benjamin was taken in by a myth. After I asked him to do something, he said, "I can't because I have a disability." I almost went ballistic! He had not learned this from me. In fact, when either of my children say they can't do something, I encourage them to try it. If, after they've given it a good shot, they still can't do it, then I lend a hand. When Benjamin gave me that excuse, I told him to never, ever say that again. I can only surmise that he was simply repeating what he had heard someone say to him or about him. When we don't challenge the myths, we allow them to become truths.

TIME FOR AN ATTITUDE ADJUSTMENT

As individuals, we each have our own distinct perceptions and attitudes, and we recognize them for what they are: our personal opinions. However, when the same perceptions and attitudes are shared *by a group*—policy makers, doctors, or others—they take on the appearance of fact. Facts are then translated into social policies which shape and reinforce attitudes, which go around full circle and influence personal and societal behaviors.

On our journey to creating more natural and successful lives for children with disabilities, we need to understand society's perceptions and attitudes about disability. There's no doubt our society needs an attitude adjustment. Some parents might argue this point, saying they don't care what society thinks—society's opinions are unimportant. I would like to agree. But we cannot ignore the reality that every single day, our children and families deal with policies, systems, and people that are influenced by society's negative impressions of people with disabilities. With that in mind, it's critical we understand—and then work to change—the myths that surround our children and others with disabilities.

REMEMBER WHERE WE ONCE WERE

Your child and your family have probably been on the receiving end of negative societal attitudes about disability, just as my son and my family have. You could probably write a book about the insulting, outrageous, hurtful, stupid, unbelievable, silly, and downright cruel behavior and language that's been directed your way.

But the majority of people we deal with are not cruel or malicious, regardless of how they appear. Most people who act in a prejudicial or discriminatory manner do so out of ignorance. They're not stupid; they're simply uneducated about people with disabilities. They've learned their attitudes, based on erroneous information—disability myths.

With this in mind, think about what you knew about disabilities before your child was diagnosed. If you're like me, the answer is nothing! Before we had our children, most of us were ignorant about people with disabilities. Isn't it possible *we* might have entertained thoughts such as:

- I don't think someone like that should be in my child's school.

- Kids like that take all the teacher's time, and the other kids in the class will suffer. Isn't there a special school for those kids?
- What a cute little girl—how sad she's in that wheelchair. Her parents must really be angels.
- Wow! I thought we had problems, but look at him! What if we had to put up with a kid like that?
- Geez! If I ever end up like that, just shoot me and put me out of my misery!

Some of us may have had experiences with disability prior to our children's diagnoses. Perhaps we knew a family member or friend with a disability, or maybe we worked in careers that were connected to people with disabilities. In those cases, we learned attitudes about disability specific to our personal or professional experiences. But as parents, we've learned different attitudes because disability directly touches our lives through our children. And once we've personally recognized that our original perceptions were not accurate, we reject the stereotypical views that others assume to be true. *We should consider ourselves fortunate to have the opportunities to learn from our children.*

As we attempt to educate people about inaccurate or prejudicial attitudes and perceptions, we must be patient. Even though we often feel hurt or angry by others' attitudes or actions, we must understand that most people have simply not had the opportunity to learn what we know. They haven't had the enlightening, life-changing experiences we've had! Being angry at people because they speak or behave in ways that are hurtful is counterproductive. If we want people to learn from us, we must have their respect. To earn their respect, we must first respect them.

Think about what happens within our own families: when our children don't know something, we don't get angry at them, we help them learn. Remember this when you encounter people who don't know how to behave or speak respectfully toward people with disabilities.

DESTROYING THE MYTHS

Society's myths prevent people from seeing who our children really are; the myths obscure the view. Pathetic portrayals and unflattering images from literature, entertainment, news, and disability organizations have powerfully influenced society's perceptions and attitudes about men, women, boys, and girls with disabilities.

We must not believe the myths about our children. Our children are children first. No one, including parents, should make assumptions about a child with a disability based on the disability label. We can help destroy the myths about our children. The starting point is within our own hearts.

We must not believe the tales we've been told about our children's potential, abilities, or futures. When people in our children's lives perpetuate the myths, we must take a stand and gently, but firmly, correct the error.

And never can we let our children accept the myths as truths. The destruction of a soul is far more debilitating than any disability.

Unfortunately, not only do myths have power over the way individuals think, they're also powerful enough to justify the policies and procedures of today's conventional wisdom. That's where we'll go next.

The Errors of
Conventional Wisdom

> THE WHOLE HISTORY OF CIVILIZATION IS
> STREWN WITH CREEDS AND INSTITUTIONS
> WHICH WERE INVALUABLE AT FIRST,
> AND DEADLY AFTERWARD.
> *Walter Bagehot*

Conventional wisdom—the "way we do things"—represents the collection of accepted customs, actions, and beliefs of a given society. In the past, conventional wisdom about the treatment of, and services for, people with disabilities has resulted in:

- the abandonment and death of babies with disabilities
- exorcisms and "beating the Devil out"
- incarceration in "idiot cages"
- forced sterilization
- confinement in cruel and inhumane institutions
- exclusion from public education, employment, and community activities

We look back at history and shake our heads in horror and disbelief. How was it possible for these things to happen? What kind of people perpetrated these acts on people with disabilities? What kind, indeed. Leading minds of the times. Experts. Professionals. Caring people. Even loving parents. (Ouch!)

The conventional wisdom of the past represents institutionalized cruelty, sanctioned and approved by the dominant majority. But with few exceptions, there has seldom been any sustained outcry against the propaganda and persecution that have enveloped people with disabilities, all of it benevolently done "for their own good." And in every era, questioning the wisdom and power of the experts and authorities wasn't a common practice.

Since the 1950s, however, parents *have* questioned conventional wisdom, and as a result, have brought about significant and positive changes for children with disabilities. Parents, in concert with people in the medical, educational, and legislative arenas, have helped create the conventional wisdom of today. But we need to be careful what we ask for; we just might get it.

We wanted our children to receive a public education.
We didn't get just public education, we got special (segregated) education.

We wanted our children to receive the help they need.
We didn't get just the needed help, we got special (segregated) programs and services.

QUESTIONING CONVENTIONAL WISDOM

Hindsight tells us the conventional wisdom of the past was wrong. How do we know today's conventional wisdom isn't also wrong? Shouldn't we question it—sooner rather than later?

Ten, twenty, or fifty years from today, how will parents and adults with disabilities (including our own children) look back on the beginning of the twenty-first century? Will they look at early intervention, early childhood education, special education, vocational-rehabilitation, and other services and wince? Will they ask, "If parents wanted their children included in society, why did they embrace special, segregated services?" Will they wonder how we could be unaware of the ramifications of today's conventional wisdom?

I urge you to keep these thoughts in the back of your mind. There's no way to know how many people in the past questioned the conventional wisdom of their time. But I hope you'll take a hard look at today's accepted customs. I hope you'll question *everything*, because the conventional wisdom in Disability World does *more* than create a system of services. It also erases our common sense and causes great harm to children with disabilities and their families, as I'll demonstrate throughout this, and succeeding, chapters.

While doing presentations, I've asked parents, "Which is the bigger issue you're facing: having a child with a disability or dealing with the system?" A chorus of voices blend frustration, confusion, and despair into a symphony of anger, with the reply "The system!"

But why are we so frustrated and angry? There are more laws and more services and more funding for people with disabilities than ever before in history. Today, we have more specialized forms of therapy than ever before. Billions—yes, billions—of dollars from state and federal coffers are spent on people with disabilities every year in the United States.

Maybe we're angry because our children with disabilities still don't have what they really need. They still face exclusion, segregation, and isolation because laws, programs, and services can't ensure inclusion, community, friendships, and other precious elements of life.

THE FOUNDATION

In a nutshell, the foundation of today's conventional wisdom is two-pronged. First, it reflects the belief that because people with disabilities are so different or needy, they require specialized services. Second, it presumes these services are beneficial for, and can meet the needs of, people with disabilities.

Your personal experiences might prove that one or both of these statements are untrue. Many parents have realized (with anger and dismay) that the service system cannot meet the needs of their children. Others are questioning the assumption that special services are necessary or beneficial. Even as—or because—we doubt the effectiveness or appropriateness of the system, we work diligently to change it. Parents and other advocates agitate for increased funding of programs, more appropriate services, and smoother access to the system, in an effort to improve the system and its services.

A System Based on Flawed Logic

We try to change things without realizing we're attempting to modify a system that's based on flawed logic: the age-old assumption that the "problem" of disability is within people with disabilities. Until the underlying philosophy of the system is changed, it will continue to be ineffective, at best, and inappropriate, at worst.

For centuries, professionals and authorities have looked at people with disabilities and asked, "What should we do *to* them? What should we do *for* them? What should be done *about* them?" And today's system continues this practice.

Services as a Moral Obligation

Our culture feels a moral responsibility to help the ever-broadening category of "the unfortunate." Many of today's supports and services for people with disabilities reflect the ancient philosophy of "giving alms to the needy." Providing help is typically a benevolent action, but systemic assistance from the government breeds a patronizing and paternalistic attitude towards people with disabilities. It's the experts helping the inept; the haves helping the have-nots; the wealthy system giving to the poor masses; the powerful controlling the powerless.

Parents view services and supports as entitlements or rights guaranteed to their children by law. But the "entitlement mentality" many of us adopt can cause real problems: we lose our common sense and become dependent on the human services system and its professionals to meet the needs of our children and families.

When Ideas Become Realities

Conventional wisdom creates new realities. Many of these realities are grounded in illusions and myths. Nevertheless, they appear as reality, truths, or facts. These realities, however, first started as an idea in someone's head. And the idea becomes a reality only when a need for it is created; it cannot spring up on its own.

As an example, institutions for people with disabilities did not just appear one day. They became a reality only after authorities had an idea about what to do for (or to) people with disabilities. Based on their ideas or theories, authorities then created a *need* for institutions. (Notice that people with disabilities did not create the need for institutions, authorities did. It wasn't as if a bunch of people with disabilities got together and said, "Hey! We don't know each other and we're not at all alike, but let's leave our homes and our communities and move into a prison-like building and live miserable lives.") Until authorities *said* there was a need for institutions, they did not exist. Once authorities "proved" institutions were both necessary and beneficial, the reality of institutions became entrenched and fixed, and the idea was validated.

While an idea becomes a reality based on a particular set of circumstances, the reality can continue indefinitely even though the circumstances change, so long as a need continues. At one point, for example, the reality—and the validity—of institutions was based on what they could do for people with disabilities (fix or cure them). When this idea ran out of steam, however, institutions didn't die a natural death. Instead, the need was shifted from what institutions could do for people with disabilities to what they could do for society: protect good citizens from deviants.

In a few states today, the "need" for institutions has been disproved and invalidated. People with disabilities are successfully living in their communities; they don't need (never did, actually) the specialized care of institutions. This has resulted in those states closing institutions for people with disabilities.

Today's conventional wisdom has created many new realities. For example, professional expertise and parental advocacy have decreed that infants and young children with disabilities need specialized services. The need was created, resulting in the reality of early intervention and early childhood education programs. But the *idea* that created the reality is an illusion; it's another myth. Babies and young children with disabilities can achieve success the same way typical children achieve success: through the loving support of their families and their communities. (I'll show you how in later chapters.)

In every era, the development of conventional wisdom began with attitudes and perceptions about people with disabilities. Then services and treatments were designed, based on the "facts" (myths) about people with developmental disabilities. And society concurred, even if—or when—people with disabilities did not. They were, in fact, never consulted!

In our era, this trend continues, with one major difference. In the last fifty years, people with disabilities and their families have had a greater influence over conventional wisdom than they did in the past. Knowing this should give us pause: we bear some responsibility for the current system. At the same time, we should recognize that, as successful advocates, we can use our influence to move the current system, and our society, in a new direction.

In this chapter, I propose that today's conventional wisdom is not only erroneous, but also dangerous, because it's founded on myths, theories, and assumptions. If we look at today's service system with a critical eye, many of us will regain our common sense. In turn, we can create a new conventional wisdom based on truths.

THE CAUSE AND "PROBLEM" OF DISABILITY

As I've previously mentioned, conventional wisdom sees the "problem" of disability as being within the person with a disability. This premise will be disputed throughout this book, but first I want to focus on where disability actually originates.

In general, today's conventional wisdom addresses the *symptoms* of disability, not the *cause*. I'm not talking about the physical causes of cerebral palsy or Down syndrome or any other condition. I'm talking about the causes of disability within our society. In addition, I'm not talking about disability as it's legally defined, but in how it's perceived.

For example, one symptom of my son's cerebral palsy is the inability to walk. But with his power wheelchair, he has independent mobility. Thus, not being able to walk isn't a problem. Instead, the problems Benjamin experiences are environmental barriers: stairs instead of ramps, curbs instead of curb cuts, narrow doorways instead of wide ones, doors that are too heavy, and so forth.

In my son's case, environmental obstacles and barriers are the *cause* of his disability. If there were no barriers or obstacles that prevented my son from going where he wanted, would he (or others who use wheelchairs) still have a disability? In the broadest sense, the answer is no.

Our home is extremely accessible. It wasn't always that way, but we widened doors, poured a ramp, lowered counters, and so forth. We removed the obstacles that prevented Benjamin from going where he wants, doing what he wants, when he wants. We focused on changing the environment, not Benjamin. In this environment—his home—Benjamin doesn't have a disability; he doesn't have "problems."

The Focus on the Person vs. the Environment

Parents and professionals—individually and when working together—typically focus on what a child is unable to do (the "deficits"), placing the "problem" of disability within the child. But the focus should be on environmental barriers. As an example, if a child is unable to speak or has speech that is unintelligible, the problem is not lack of speech, it's the lack of others being able to understand her. The problem is really ours, not hers. Using today's conventional wisdom, however, we see the problem as being within the child: because she can't speak, she has a problem.

In this case, the focus should be on the larger issue of communication, not just on speaking. This doesn't mean her parents "give up" on her ever speaking, nor does it mean her parents shouldn't help her learn to talk. It simply means the first priority should be providing the child with an effective means to communicate. She can still be helped and encouraged to learn to talk, but while she's doing that, she needs to be able to communicate in whatever way is best for her.

A *symptom* of her disability is the lack of oral speech. The actual *cause* of disability is environmental: others cannot understand her speech patterns. But if she's provided with an effective method of communicating, her disability is no longer problematic. In fact, her disability label could become irrelevant.

Children and adults with disabilities are often "blamed" for their problems. We say, "She can't walk," yet we haven't given her the tools for independent mobility. We say, "He can't control his behavior," when we haven't taken the time, made the effort, and/or been successful in identifying his needs, providing support, or modifying the environment.

If we look at the causes of disability as being within the environment, we're not shifting "blame" to society. Instead, we're acknowledging the reality that disability is more a product of the environment than the human body. In other words, conditions in the environment cause more difficulties and problems than conditions of the human body!

"Who Has the Disability?"

A variety of hypothetical stories have been circulated that illustrate the issue of environmental barriers creating what we call dissability. Here's one to consider.

Barry, a sighted person, visited a town where everyone is blind. When he dined at the hotel restaurant, he was unable to read the Brailled menu. But the waiter modified the environment: he read the menu to Barry.

While he waited for his dinner to arrive, the sun went down and the room became pitch dark. There were no lights in the restaurant (the employees and local customers didn't need them) and Barry was unable to see the meal the waiter set before him. He accidentally knocked over his water glass and unintentionally pushed much of his food off the side of the plate. He complained to the waiter, who responded by bringing Barry a flashlight. The restaurant was proud of how well it treated its "special" customers, but Barry was outraged and embarrassed. He needed both hands to cut his meat, so he couldn't hold the flashlight. By placing the flashlight in various positions on the table, he tried to find a way to aim the beam at his plate, but was unsuccessful. He gave up after eating only a few bites. Barry was beginning to feel like an alien.

Tired, hungry, and frustrated, he began his trek through the darkened restaurant, on his way to the hotel lobby to check in. After only a few steps, he crashed into a group of diners, almost knocking over a baby in a high chair. The waiter came to his rescue, grabbed his arm, and led him out of the restaurant to the front desk in the hotel lobby. On the way, Barry heard whispers, although he couldn't see who was doing the talking. "Poor thing," a woman's voice said. "Hush!" exclaimed a man to his giggling children, "It's not nice to laugh at people like that." Barry was mortified.

Once they reached the lobby, the waiter placed Barry's hand on a pillar close to the hotel registration counter. Afraid Barry might offend hotel customers if he ran into them or the furniture, the waiter wanted Barry to stay in one place. "Sir," he began, "I need to get back to the restaurant, but I don't want you to get hurt or lost. So please stay right here. Someone will be with you in a moment." Barry couldn't see the waiter's face, but he heard both pity and anger in the man's voice.

Barry could hear other people checking in. He assumed there must have been several ahead of him. After ten or fifteen minutes had passed, things quieted down and Barry could hear the two desk clerks whispering. He couldn't hear the entire conversation, but he did catch an exasperated, "I don't know!" followed by, "I've never had one either."

"I'd like to check in please," Barry interrupted. "I don't have a reservation, but I need a room just for tonight. Do you have any rooms that have lights in them?"

"Well, uh, no, we don't. Sorry," the clerk replied. Barry's discomfort increased as he gingerly made his way toward the sound of the clerk's voice and said, "But I need a room with lights. I can't see in the dark. Don't you have at least one room with lights?"

"No, sir, I'm afraid not," came the reply. "We've never needed to have a room with lights—I mean, we just don't have people like you here very often."

Who has the disability in this scenario? The environment was perfect for the majority, but it created many barriers for Barry and he experienced great difficulties. In this environment, Barry—not the people who were blind— had a "disability."

Let's take the story further and say Barry falls in love with a woman who is blind. She wants to move to this community and Barry wants to be with her. He takes a new job as a salesman; he'll need to call on businesses in the community on a regular basis. What might happen next?

Under conventional wisdom, Barry is thought to have many needs and problems, so professionals will enter Barry's life to meet his needs and remedy the problems. First, they'll assess Barry and identify all his deficits. To make him "OK" (like the majority), they'll give him Braille Therapy. This skill will be necessary in his new job. In addition, Barry will be provided with twice-weekly Cane Therapy. He'll need lots of practice with a cane before he'll be "ready" to get around at night and in darkened rooms during the day (there are no lights in any buildings since no one needs them). During Cane Therapy, professionals will teach Barry the right way to hold a cane, the right way to sweep it in front of him, and so forth. He'll also receive Orientation Therapy so he can learn how to be successful in any environment. They'll start with his home, teaching him which room is which, and they'll move on to teaching Barry things like knowing how to distinguish between a bottle of shampoo and a bottle of rat poison. The long-term goal is for Barry to become as much like a "normal" (blind) person as possible. There's no prediction on how long this might take, nor any guarantees the goals will be reached. Still, from a professional standpoint, therapy is the only avenue to take.

To the chagrin of the experts, Barry turned down all the therapy. He's found an alternate solution to this dilemma. Experts and other professionals consider it "radical," but to Barry, it's just common sense. He'll identify and use the tools he needs for success.

Instead of going to Cane or Orientation Therapy, he'll purchase several different types of flashlights, with lots of extra batteries. These tools will be helpful at night and in darkened rooms during the day; he won't ever mistake the rat poison for the shampoo with his trusty flashlight and long-lasting batteries. Instead of going to Braille Therapy, he'll use various pieces of assistive technology, including a computer and a scanner that can be modified to translate Braille into written English and vice-versa. As much as possible, he'll ask for help from Braille-users. He knows the best way to learn Braille is not through endless hours of practice, but by actually doing it in real life.

Now, take a moment and think up your own scenario, one where everyone has a disability similar to your child's, and the environment they're in meets their needs. Then someone without that particular disability enters the scene. What would happen? Can you see how the environment produces what we label "disability"?

THE PARADOX

Today's system doesn't recognize the paradigm that disability is more a product of the environment than the body. Instead, conventional wisdom puts the problem of disability within the person. In turn, this leads to presumptions that (1) special services are required to solve the problems of people with disabilities and (2) the problems of people with disabilities can be lessened if they're made more like "normal" people. Add these two fundamentals together and you have a third (faulty) assumption: special services can make people with disabilities more like normal people.

Therein lies a paradox. Several disability-related laws (the ADA, IDEA, and Section 504) promote equal rights. By outlawing discrimination based on disability, these laws are attempting to right the wrongs of the past. They say, in essence, the "problem" of disability is a societal problem; that the barriers faced by people with disabilities are attitudinal and environmental. But the majority of programs and services and/or the way they're implemented (including early intervention, early childhood education, special education, and voc-rehab) send the opposite message: the "problem" is in children and adults with disabilities, so we will focus on them and not society.

Shall We Change People with Disabilities or Society?

Disability is not the problem. Never has been, never will be. There have always been people with disabilities in the world and there always will be. Today, people with disabilities constitute the largest minority group (an estimated 54 million people) in the United States. But, like other minorities, now and in the past, people with disabilities are adversely affected by the negative, stereotypical opinions of the dominant majority. The situation facing people with disabilities today is no different than what African-Americans, women, and other groups have faced in the past. What we can learn from these other groups is crucial: they didn't need to change, society needed to change, and it did.

So shall we continue trying to change our children or shall we work on changing society? It's a tough question for many parents. Some say, "I'm *not* trying to change my child. I'm just trying to get him the help he needs to walk [or talk or whatever]." Parents often view treatments, programs, and services in a very positive light, believing they provide help and hope to their children. But underneath the help and hope are unintended messages and consequences that are destructive and harmful. As you'll discover in the remainder of this chapter, all is not always what it seems.

Furthermore, when we focus on addressing the child's so-called problems, we pin our hopes on treatments and interventions. But what happens when these don't succeed in "normalizing" the child—helping him walk, talk, or whatever? Will we blame the failure on the child or the professionals providing the treatment? Or will we recognize that the premise (and the promise) of interventions was faulty to begin with?

THE GET-READY PHILOSOPHY

The get-ready philosophy is one of the cornerstones of today's conventional wisdom. It's a simple paradigm: this child is not ready for [whatever] but [this service or intervention] will get him ready. The get-ready model dovetails nicely with the medical (deficit) model. These two don't just dovetail, though. They often overlap and are sometimes indistinguishable from one another. The get-ready model is a tool used by educators, therapists, voc-rehab counselors, other professionals, and even parents, as a way of addressing "problems" which need to be remedied.

Most programs and services for children and young adults with disabilities are based on the get-ready or deficit models. And these programs, based on age groups, are stepping stones in the ladder of the readiness paradigm. But, again, we have a paradox.

Special Programs Get People Ready for More Special Programs

Instead of preparing children with disabilities ("getting them ready") for real life, special programs actually just prepare kids for the next level of special programs! "Prepare" is probably the wrong word; once in the system, children are simply propelled along the path of special services.

I have not met one parent whose child has been judged "ready" to leave the world of special programs for life in the real world. There are probably a few out there somewhere, but I've never met a mom who was told, "Well, little Mary did so great in early intervention, she doesn't need early childhood education services." I've never met a parent who was told, "Johnny has successfully graduated from two years in the early childhood class. He won't need special ed in public school. Just send him on to regular kindergarten!" And, of course, I've never met a parent who, at some point during a child's twelve to fifteen year public school career, was told, "Jill doesn't need special ed services anymore. She can take regular classes from now on."

Children are automatically shuttled from one program to the next. Early intervention propels babies and toddlers into early childhood education; early childhood education launches preschoolers into special education; and special education thrusts students into voc-rehab and the adult service system. At that time, many will join the estimated 75 percent of people with developmental disabilities who are unemployed.

Children with disabilities who were deemed "not ready" become adults who are still "not ready." The last stop may be the dead-end of a sheltered workshop, the mind-numbing boredom of an adult day program, endless hours of repetitive skills training which will never be put to use, or years of waiting for voc-rehab to come through with a "job placement." Many adults will be expected to stay home and collect "disability welfare" (Supplemental Security Income or some other government check) which will earn them the dubious privilege of living below the poverty line for the rest of their lives.

We must ask: why aren't children with disabilities "OK" the way they are? Why do they have to get ready for anything? Because they don't meet the artificial standards for readiness or normalcy set by experts, professionals, parents, and society, in general.

One of our first tasks in helping our children lead successful lives is to disregard artificial standards of normalcy and readiness. Parents and families—not professionals—must be the definers of what's normal. Readiness is not a relevant or meaningful concept.

Many people might look at my son and say he's not ready for this or that or the other. There are some things Benjamin will never be able to do. But guess what? There are some things *I* will never be able to do! Yet no one looks at me and says I'm not ready for something. Why? Because I don't carry a disability label (yet).

For a moment, let's accept the readiness model to further explore the rationale of special services. Let's assume children with disabilities aren't ready for whatever. If this is so, why can't parents or friends or family members help children with disabilities get ready? Why can't children with disabilities get ready like other children do? Why do children with disabilities need special government-funded programs?

Why? Because conventional wisdom dictates that parents, friends, family members, and people in our communities are not competent to meet all the so-called special needs of children with disabilities because they are not the experts, the professionals, or the anointed ones. Perhaps parents are not considered "ready" to take responsibility for their children. For some reason, on-the-job-training and living with one's child for twenty-four hours a day, seven days a week doesn't count!

This is nothing new, however. Public education is another example of professionalism usurping the responsibilities of families and communities. Public schools exist only because years ago, policy makers, bureaucrats, and social reformers convinced society that parents and other "ordinary" people were not competent to educate children; only trained teachers could do this. For most of recorded history, of course, children *have* been taught by their parents and others in the community: there *were* no "professional" teachers (unless you were wealthy and hired a private tutor). Everyone was a "teacher" and all contributions to a child's upbringing were valuable.

In the broadest sense, however, there's light at the end of the tunnel. In certain circumstances, parents *are* seen as competent instructors of their children. The most significant testimonial of this paradigm is the increased number of parents who are successfully homeschooling their children. State legislatures are acknowledging, via homeschooling laws, that parents are competent to educate their own children. Another example is occurring in Colorado and other states, where, under state law, parents can now be their children's "official" driver's education instructors. Could we use these examples to open our minds to the reality that parents are the experts on their children and they—not bureaucracies or professionals—are responsible for their sons and daughters?

The Myth of Measuring for Readiness

The belief that children with disabilities aren't ready is a myth, grounded in the bigger myth that our society has a universal code of readiness. Professionals use a variety of developmental tests and scales to "objectively" measure readiness. But the use of these tests has been corrupted on a scale equal to the corruption of the "grief process."

The *only* thing we can learn from measuring a child with a developmental test is *what a child can or cannot do at that moment in time.* But professionals (and parents, sometimes) hold test results up as the Holy Grail. Based on the results of tests, children are pushed into more interventions and treatments, held back in preschools, excluded from participating in typical community activities, and more. We believe children will not or can not be successful until they meet the levels on developmental scales. This is hogwash!

At age three, Benjamin got a big zero on a question of a standardized developmental test because he couldn't tell the professional tester what was on the flash card. It was a picture of an iron and an ironing board. Guess what? He had never seen me iron! The contraptions collected dust in the utility room closet. But the *reason* Benjamin didn't know the answer wasn't relevant to the tester. She only cared whether he knew it or not. Based on this lack of knowledge, she might have hypothesized that Benjamin had "sub-normal mental functioning" and/or lived in a deprived environment.

It's also a myth that parents, relatives, friends, and people in our communities are not competent to help children with disabilities. Parents are *the best people* to help their children. Friends and family members who know and love a child are also far better at helping a child than professionals. When we accept the premise that professionals can help our children better than we can, we've sold ourselves short. And we make our children pay the price by subjecting them to the segregation and isolation inherent in most special programs and services.

There's one more absurdity about the get-ready model, and it involves the transfer of knowledge. Professionals spend hours, days, and years attempting to teach children skills in artificial and segregated settings. At some point, professionals may say a child is finally "ready." But is he really?

Let's look at what often happens. The child goes out in the real world (a general education classroom, a community activity, a job, living on his own, or whatever), but he's unsuccessful, even though everyone agreed he had mastered the appropriate skills. What went wrong? Skills learned in isolation, in counterfeit environments, in settings that have been manipulated for the purpose of teaching the skill, are often not transferable to real life settings!

The Cardboard Bus

A classic example that illustrates this point is the story of the cardboard bus. I've heard variations of this true story from several professionals who have, thankfully, learned from their mistakes and are now teaching others. Following is a composite of the tales I've heard.

A group of young adults with developmental disabilities needed to learn how to ride the city bus. In a large training room, professionals created an artificial environment that included an almost life-sized cardboard bus, a bench on which to wait for the bus, a sign that identified the bus route, bus tokens, and more.

After weeks of instruction, the small group of students had successfully learned about riding the bus. In the training room, they could wait patiently on the sidewalk bench; when the bus "arrived," they were able to ask the bus driver if this was the right bus for them; they knew which bus tokens to use; and so on. By the standards set in the artificial environment, they were ready. But when the day came for them ride on a real city bus, they failed. Why? Because at the intersection, there were four corners and four bus stops and they didn't know which one to use!

The professionals learned a priceless lesson: the only way for people to learn how to ride a bus is for them to actually ride a bus! Further, they realized they couldn't teach this skill to a *group*, because that's not how individuals would really behave in real life: they wouldn't always travel around with eight or ten other adults with disabilities. The solution was for the instructors, with help from volunteers, to provide individual lessons by really doing it. When one of the students needed to go somewhere, an instructor or volunteer accompanied him on the bus and helped him learn the skill through experience.

Because children with disabilities are not considered ready for real life, we take them *out* of their natural environments (where they learn naturally, without having to be "taught" everything) and put them in artificial, segregated environments to teach them what *we* think they need—to help them get ready. Whew! When/if they *do* move into natural settings—the real world—they often fail. In the worst case scenario, they're jerked back into the special setting for remedial training. In the best case scenario, we recognize our mistake, put children in their natural environments for real learning, and help them forget what they learned in the counterfeit setting!

We can take this example and apply it to many, many situations facing children with disabilities. Can you think of examples in your own child's life? Wouldn't it be wiser, not to mention more respectful, to simply let children learn in the real world to begin with?

"Not Ready" Really Means "Never"

Special programs and services *may* help some children. But the "not ready" message— whether it's spoken or unspoken—can be extremely harmful, because it often really means "never."

Most of us are "not ready" for certain things at certain times in our lives. For example, fourteen-year-old Sam is not legally ready to drive until he's sixteen. Faith, a college junior, decides she's not ready to get married until she graduates. Adam, a sixty-year-old electrician, is not ready to retire until he's saved enough for his dream vacation. But at some point, all of these people *are* ready: at sixteen, Sam is of legal age to drive; after she graduates from college and is successfully employed, Faith decides she's ready to marry; and when Adam has saved enough for the cruise he's always wanted to take, he's ready to retire.

These examples are representative of the readiness issues that face people without disabilities. Readiness may be determined objectively, by laws that prescribe when one can drive, vote, and so forth. It may be determined subjectively, by the personal choice of the individual (when to marry, retire, take a vacation, or change jobs).

But readiness for children and young adults with disabilities is determined by the professionals in the system—the gatekeepers of advancement—who send the message that most people with disabilities are never ready. We're told:

- A six-year-old is still not ready for kindergarten (much less first grade) because he still doesn't "act" like a six-year-old.

  But he's already spent two years in the special ed preschool. If two years there didn't get him ready, how will a third?

- A thirteen-year-old is still in the elementary school resource room because she's not ready for eighth grade in the middle school. She can't do *sixth-grade* math, much less seventh-grade language arts or eighth-grade history.

  But how will staying in the resource room another year get her ready for an age-appropriate inclusive classroom?

- A nineteen-year-old is not ready for anything. He's not ready to go to college because he wasn't appropriately educated, and he's not employable because he's not acting mature enough.

  But will another year in a special ed room or a special training program help him get on with a real life?

In the earlier examples of the teen driver, the college student, and the retiree, the concept of readiness focused on one specific area of each person's life. But for children and adults with disabilities, being "not ready" is often generalized to include almost all areas of development or achievement. A concrete improvement in one specific area, for example, isn't interpreted as a sign that readiness has been achieved. Global improvements—in cognition, behavior, physical abilities, and/or other areas—must be attained before children with disabilities are deemed "ready." Let's revisit the examples of children with disabilities:

- The six-year-old may finally achieve "behavioral readiness," but then professionals (and maybe even his parents) decide that since he's not "academically" ready, he still can't move on to kindergarten. First it's one thing, then another. This child can't win!

- The thirteen-year-old is treading water in the sea of special education. Because she's never been in any regular classrooms, she's had no opportunity to learn math, language arts, or history. Who has prevented her from learning? The same educators who say she's not ready. Since they didn't believe she was ready in first, second, third, fourth, and fifth grades, they know she's still not ready. At this rate, she'll never be ready.

- The nineteen-year-old should be entering the typical adult world, but he's stuck in the system and carrying lots of baggage. There are probably a variety of jobs he could do right now, and he may even dream of going to college, but he doesn't meet the standards of the special ed and voc-rehab experts. If he's not acting "responsibly enough," perhaps it's because he hasn't been *expected* to become responsible. It's hard to mature and learn to be responsible in segregated settings where low expectations are the norm.

Children *without* disabilities don't usually experience these barriers. In most states, children enter kindergarten at different levels of development. Some are considered mature for their ages; others are immature. Some enter the public school system reading; others don't. In general, there is no kindergarten "entrance criteria" for typical children. Why, then, do we impose an artificial criteria on children with disabilities?

Most students without disabilities are in age-appropriate classrooms, even if they're not at "grade level" in every subject. That's because they start out in an age-appropriate classroom in kindergarten and continue to move up with their peers. Yes, some children are held back (although many schools are rejecting this antiquated practice), but seldom would a thirteen-year-old without disabilities be in a fifth grade classroom. If children with disabilities are continually held back or kept in ungraded classrooms, how can they ever progress socially or educationally?

High school students who don't have disabilities are expected to beat the bushes to find their first job. Working in fast food, retail, or some other entry level position is the norm. Some do well; others don't. It's part of growing up and learning. Those that don't do well learn from their mistakes: they learn not to pick their noses when they're flipping burgers or how not to get caught when they flip off the manager behind his back! But high school students with disabilities don't even get the *chance* to experiment and learn and make mistakes! The special ed teacher and voc-rehab counselor assume the responsibility for directing the student's employment future.

Sequential Isn't Always Sensible

The readiness model also focuses on people being ready based on their acquisition of skills in a sequential order. For example, if a child needs to achieve a skill we'll call "C," we say she must first achieve skills "A" and "B." Sometimes this is logical. Other times it's totally illogical.

It's logical that I must know the difference between the brake and the gas pedals before I learn to drive. It's illogical to assume that before I open a checking account, I must know how to balance a bank statement. For too many people with disabilities, illogical and unnatural sequences of achievement are demanded in a variety of areas.

When an individual with a disability does not learn the sequential steps in order, he's often prevented from making *any* progress until he *does* master the sequence. Proponents of the sequential model seldom examine the global harm it can cause. They also fail to recognize that the only way to learn some things is by doing them; no preparation and no sequential instruction is necessary or even desirable.

"Write Your Name in the Top Right Hand Corner"

About two months into his kindergarten year, Benjamin had homework. In his backpack was a project that was started at school which he had not finished. The teacher sent a note with instructions on what needed to be done. The homework was an art-like project, the same things kindergartners have been doing forever: cutting on the lines stamped on construction paper to get the shape of an animal, the eyes, nose, tail, etc., and then gluing them in the right places.

Because it took Benjamin longer to do this type of activity, I assumed he had simply run out of time during class. I helped him finish and didn't think too much about it. But he started bringing unfinished work home every day. After talking with other parents, I discovered their children didn't have this homework. I decided to talk to the teacher to find out why Benjamin wasn't getting his work done during class.

"Well, Kathie," she explained, "the first thing the children have to learn is how to write their names on their papers. Since Benjamin can't write yet, the teacher's aide is trying to help him learn to do that. She's doing hand-over-hand, but he's just having a really hard time doing it. By the time the other children have finished the lesson, Benjamin still hasn't gotten his name on his paper, so I send it home for him to finish."

I knew the objective of the work wasn't "art," although that's what it usually looks like to parents. There were actually many things children were supposed to learn from this activity: writing their names on their papers, learning colors, cutting, gluing, following directions, knowing where body parts are, and much more. I was concerned Benjamin was being left out of the different learning activities. As the teacher talked the children through the lesson, reviewing colors and body parts, Benjamin wasn't participating. He was still working on writing his name.

I hated that he was missing out. Because he couldn't do step "A" to the teacher's satisfaction (writing his name), he was not allowed to learn the other steps in the lesson ("B" and "C" and more). When I expressed my concerns, the teacher was sympathetic but insisted it was critically important for Benj to learn to write his name in the top right hand corner of the page. "After all," she added, " he'll need to do this for the next twelve years in public school!"

I put on my thinking cap. The next day I ran an errand and had the solution: a name stamp with one inch letters that spelled out Benjamin's name. It had a fat handle Benj could grip easily. I purchased a stamp pad with washable ink. Benj practiced with it at home that afternoon. What fun! He loved doing it: loved seeing his name on paper, on his hand, on the table, and on me—which is why I bought washable ink.

When I took Benj to school the next day, I took the stamp and stamp pad in and showed them to the teacher. With great excitement, I asked Benjamin to demonstrate how well he could stamp his name. With him sitting there listening, I enthusiastically explained what a great solution this was: Benj could get his name on his paper lickity-split and then get on with the project during class, just like his classmates. He wouldn't need to bring work home to finish. I told his teacher it didn't matter whether Benjamin stamped his name on the top right hand corner, the bottom left hand corner, or on the back of the paper!

The teacher wasn't enthusiastic about my idea, but she accepted it. She still hung onto the sequential model. But once *Benjamin* knew I expected him to stamp his name on the paper and get on with his work, he had the power to make it happen.

At age thirteen, Benjamin writes plays, stories, and letters on the computer. But he still does not write his name the way the kindergarten teacher would have liked. When absolutely necessary, he can scribble a signature that resembles the handwriting of a physician on a prescription pad: a "B" with a squiggly line that follows. If doctors can write illegibly, so can Benj!

He still uses a stamp, but now it's self-inking (which is what I should have bought in the first place). When he's older and has a checking account, he'll let the store clerk write out the check and he'll use his signature stamp to sign his name.

If I had allowed the teacher to continue inflicting the sequential model on Benjamin, the outcome would have been predictable. At some point during the year, she would have gravely said something like, "Benjamin doesn't know the shapes of animals or where body parts go. He's so far behind the other kids—after all, he does have a significant disability. Perhaps he has a mental disability, too." Benjamin's lack of progress would have been attributed to his disability. Never would the teacher acknowledge that his lack of progress was a direct result of her withholding opportunities for him to learn since she focused on one isolated skill.

The sequential model is used by educators and other professionals all the time. Unfortunately, many parents buy into this way of thinking, too. The effect on our children is disastrous. Let's look an example involving reading, a skill that's perceived to be the foundation of learning in a general education classroom.

If Anna cannot read at grade level, she's excluded from a regular ed classroom because she's "not ready." As a result, she's denied the opportunity to learn geography, social studies, history, and other subjects that are taught in the regular ed environment. Anna falls further and further behind on the readiness ladder. Yet Anna could have been learning these subjects in ways that don't involve reading: by having someone read the books to her, listening to the books on tape, through hands-on experiential activities, by watching videos on the subject, using academic computer software, or through other ways that are right for her.

The readiness model and the sequential model are two of the gods of today's conventional wisdom. They're routinely used on children with disabilities, yet they're often inappropriate and harmful.

In Anna's case, teachers make global assumptions about her ability to learn because she is "behind" in one specific area (reading). These assumptions will doom Anna: educators will give her fewer and fewer opportunities to learn, her "not ready" circle will expand, and by the time she should be graduating from high school, she'll be seen as hopeless. Few will look back and see that her lack of ability and progress were *induced* by the school system. Her failure to learn will be attributed to her disability. It happens all the time.

Our Children Wait and Wait and . . .

One of the most serious outcomes of the readiness and sequential models is that they make children wait, and all the while, their lives are passing them by. They're told "You can't do this, you're not ready. We'll tell you when you're ready." Children with disabilities must be the most patient group of people in the world (whether they like it or not) because "wait" is both a word and an unspoken message they hear so often.

Who are we—parents or educators—to interfere with a child's love of learning and curiousity? How dare we "retard" a child's progress simply because he doesn't meet *our* definition of readiness? We must not make children wait—not one more minute—to live life! Children with disabilities don't need to get ready. They're ready just the way they are!

The Devastating Message of Readiness

What happens to a child when he's told, "You're not ready," over and over and over again? When educators tell him that, he can probably ignore it the first few times, chalking it up to a "dumb" teacher. But if told enough times, he'll begin to believe it.

When he hears this message from his parents, he may also reject it initially, believing his parents are just being "mean" by not letting him do something. But when told over and over again by his parents, he'll internalize the belief and accept it as truth. Children see themselves through our eyes.

If—in his mind—he'll never be ready, why should he even try anymore? Under these circumstances, how can he believe in himself? How can he dream anymore? How can he achieve success when his parents don't believe in him? Does he wonder why he's not good enough the way he is? Does he wonder just how good he has to be? The greatest barrier to his success is not his disability, but the crushing and pervasive belief that he's not-OK the way he is and never will be.

HIGH STANDARDS DEMANDED; YET HIGH STANDARDS DEMEAN

Under today's conventional wisdom, professionals measure children with disabilities against standards that are both artificial and subjective, and these standards are applied very unevenly. In many cases, higher standards are demanded of children with disabilities—higher standards that ultimately demean our sons and daughters.

When babies without disabilities are "late" reaching developmental milestones, we chalk it up to individual differences. But almost all perceived differences in babies with disabilities are attributed to the disability, with no consideration of individual differences.

Two-year-olds demonstrate their emerging independence by repeatedly saying their favorite word ("No!") and by rebelling against their parents. Even though this is thought to be a difficult time for parents, it's welcomed as a natural part of development. Young children with disabilities typically go through this same stage of development, but many do it *in their own time and in their own way*. If a child with a disability doesn't demonstrate this emerging ability (asserting his independence) until he's five, however, no one celebrates this development: it's not "normal" behavior for a five-year-old. Because this stage of development didn't occur at the "right" time—according to developmental scales—the child's behavior is perceived as aberrant or manipulative. The child may acquire another label at this point—a "behavior" label. This is patently unfair to children!

As I mentioned earlier, most kindergartners without disabilities begin school with varying levels of abilities, but students moving from special ed preschools are often prevented from attending typical kindergarten classes at age five until they've achieved proficiencies dictated by the early childhood authorities. Unfortunately, parents who believe in and accept the readiness and sequential models often behave like professionals and hold their children back until they're "ready." What standards must typical children meet to enter kindergarten? In general, none. But children with disabilities are held to a higher standard.

(With all the hubbub these days about "standards," however, a few states *are* implementing entrance criteria for all kindergartners. If a typical child doesn't meet the criteria, he's put in a special class—remedial kindergarten?—where he'll spend the year "getting ready" for "real" kindergarten. Some of the inappropriate practices in special education are now influencing general education, and I hope all parents actively advocate against this ridiculous practice.)

In a class of twenty-five typical fourth-graders without disabilities, there are twenty-five students with twenty-five different learning styles, whose levels of social and academic skills may or may not be "at grade level." Some fourth-graders read at a sixth grade level but behave like second graders; others read at a second grade level but behave like sixth graders. In public schools (even with all the rabble about academic standards), allowances are made for individual differences. Children who are nine or ten, depending on their birthday, are in fourth grade, even if they perform math at a sixth grade level and read at a third grade level.

But the same is not true for most children with disabilities. They're often held to a much stricter standard. Parents are told their children with disabilities cannot be included in an age-appropriate general ed classroom, even with supports, services, and curriculum modifications, because their children don't "function" at the proper level in academics, in social skills, or in some other area. Why are children with disabilities penalized and excluded when they're not at grade level and other students are not?

When young adults *without* disabilities move out on their own, they do it whether they're "ready" or not. They learn from their mistakes. There are no readiness standards for young adults without disabilities. I recall moving away from home and routinely calling my mother long distance to ask her how to cook a roast, unstop the toilet, and for many other things! If readiness standards had been applied to me, I'd probably still be living in my parents' home!

But standards *are* applied to young adults with disabilities, especially to those who receive services from the system. They aren't expected to simply move out on their own. Instead, they're transferred from the care of the parents in the family home to the care of staff at a group home. Here, they're supposed to learn how to be responsible adults.

How can this possibly happen in a "home" ruled by house parents who enforce strict rules; where you live with five other people you don't know and may not like; and where bedtime, meal times, free time, and work time are prescribed by rules and regulations? Who made the determination that young people with disabilities automatically need such places, when no such automatic assumptions are made for young people without disabilities? The determination is made solely because an individual has a disability and is presumed to be incompetent.

Once they're in a group home, the high standards continue. Staff at group homes routinely write "habilitation plans" for young men and women that mandate what skills must be attained before they are deemed capable of living on their own. For example, John must make up his bed every morning within thirty minutes of waking up. Mary must wash, dry, and put her dishes away within thirty minutes of every meal. Immediately after showering, Tom must hang his towels to dry, instead of leaving them on the floor. Do professionals who write these plans live according to the standards they set for others? And would they enjoy living with five strangers, according to the rules and regulations of others?

"I Failed"

Twenty-two-year-old Dan was "educated" in special ed segregated classrooms for most of his school years. His label was "severe" learning disabilities. When I met him at a conference, I asked him to tell me about himself: did he have a job, where did he live, what did he like to do? Shyly, Dan said he lived at home with his parents. "Do you want to live on your own?" I asked. He brightened for a second, before becoming embarrassed. "Oh, I did live in a group home for awhile," he said, "but I failed, so I had to move back with my parents."

"What do you mean 'you failed'?" I asked. "Well," he explained, "the staff said there were three things I didn't do right. I didn't balance my checkbook every month, I made too many long distance phone calls, and I didn't know how to pick the right kind of friends." (If your mouth is hanging open like mine was, you can close it now.)

For these "infractions," Dan was kicked out of the group home and sent back to his parents' home. He was not considered "ready" for life in a group home, and if he couldn't make it there, he surely couldn't make it on his own, right? Are we to believe that the staff people at the group home always lived up to the same standards they imposed on Dan? Do we mandate that young adults without disabilities who don't meet a specific criteria move back home with mom and dad?

Why do we demand more from children and adults with disabilities than we do from those without disabilities? Who, among us, has the right to impose our standards of behavior and abilities on others? And how many of us would allow this practice to be imposed on us or on our children who don't have disabilities?

When professionals (and sometimes parents) don't know how to help a child learn, don't know how to provide accommodations, don't see how a child could possibly succeed, or simply don't believe a child belongs, the get-ready model provides an instant solution. "Sorry, he's not ready," puts the problem back on the child, lays it in someone else's lap, or simply prolongs actually dealing with the child and/or his needs. In any event, it ensures the child will remain not only segregated and excluded, but also prevented from experiencing opportunities to learn and grow.

There is no global eligibility criteria adults and children without disabilities must meet before they're allowed to participate in the everyday activities of school, work, recreation, friendship, and the like. But today's conventional wisdom *does* mandate the use of eligibility criteria—based on artificial standards of readiness—on people with disabilities. In the process, opportunities for growth and learning are delayed and sometimes snuffed out altogether.

RESPITE CARE

Respite care is becoming a standard component of today's conventional wisdom. In some states, respite might fall under "family support" or "in-home support" programs.

Respite care programs are the result of legislative advocacy by parents and other disability advocates.(Dictionaries define respite as an "interval of rest or relief.") Originally, respite care services were created to prevent out-of-home placements of children with disabilities. The concept was grounded in the belief that a child with significant needs was at great risk of being institutionalized if the parents didn't have in-home help and/or temporary breaks from the daily care of the child. For example, a respite care provider could take care of the child in the home, when the parents needed a night out, when the rest of the family took a vacation, and so forth. Alternatively, the child might be taken to a care facility for an evening, a weekend, or longer, so the family could have "rest or relief."

Respite care services were intended to keep families intact, and the cost was less expensive than institutional care. The original concept—to prevent the institutionalization of children with disabilities—was a worthy goal. But for the majority of children with disabilities today, the odds of being placed in an institution or other congregate setting are extremely low. In many states, respite care has gone from being an emergency service provided to a few parents who are in dire straits, to a benefit or entitlement for every family that qualifies.

Parents have organized and successfully advocated for respite, resulting in state legislators allocating funding for the services. But few programs are as good as parents wish. Still, parents proclaim respite is a good thing. However, there are real problems with respite care, and I'm not talking about lack of funding or poor service delivery. The problems are rooted in the very principle of present day respite care.

Respite care programs come in all shapes and sizes, and each has its own eligibility criteria. Typically, parents who qualify are entitled to a certain number of respite hours or dollar amount for the year. In some programs, parents must demonstrate a great need in order to qualify. They must, in essence, compete against other parents for the available slots, and "the neediest" win. We're in a race to see if we can make our child look worse off than the next, our families more needy than others. (The things we do to our families and children—in the name of getting services—is demeaning at best and shameful at worst.)

In many programs, once a family is deemed eligible, the respite care agency matches the family with one or more "trained" respite care workers. When respite is needed, the agency sends out one of the identified caregivers. However, there are no guarantees a family will always get the same caregiver. They may get whoever is available, whether or not the family knows the person. Some programs allow families to choose their own respite care providers; Grandma can be put on the state payroll.

Some state regulations mandate that the respite provider can only take care of the child with the disability. In this situation, parents must split their children up when they go out for an evening: the child with the disability and the professional caregiver stay home together, while the other children are sent to the regular babysitter's home or wherever!

A minority of parents have learned an ugly truth: children with disabilities have been abused by respite care workers. The majority of respite care workers are probably good people. But like other low paying jobs, being a respite care worker is usually not someone's choice for a long-term career. More often, it's either part-time employment or a temporary position for people in between jobs.

Respite is another one of those good ideas gone bad. I'm treading on hallowed ground here, I know. But what is respite care, really? It's babysitting. Why do state governments pay babysitting fees for parents of children with disabilities, but not for other parents? And how would those parents feel about us if they discovered their tax dollars were paying for our babysitters?

Yes, many parents of kids with disabilities are stressed out and/or need extra help. But guess what? The same is true for parents whose children do not have disabilities. I know many families who don't have kids with disabilities that have more stress and greater needs than our family. And, yes, parents do need a break sometimes, whether their kids have disabilities or not. But when parents of typical kids need a break, they don't say they need "respite;" they simply hire a babysitter or drop their kids off at a friend's house! Why do we demand respite care?

The Messages of Respite Care

A variety of powerful, unspoken messages are transmitted by the premise of respite care services:

- A family cannot meet all the needs of a child with a disability without the help of "professional caregivers."

- Because raising a child with a disability is so stressful, parents are entitled to professional services (or state reimbursement for hand-picked babysitters) so they can take a break from the child.

- Because a child with a disability is so disruptive or troublesome to normal family life, he needs to be taken care of by someone else so the family can do what it wants or needs to do.

- Respite care professionals are more qualified to care for children with disabilities than typical child care providers or babysitters.

Many of us believe these myths. Do we really want to see ourselves and our children this way? Shouldn't we be insulted and outraged by these assumptions about our children and families? How do these messages make our children feel about themselves?

What does it say about us, as parents, when we say we need respite because our children have disabilities? Are we giving credence to the myth about the "tragedy" of children with disabilities? Are we admitting that our children are "problems"? Are we conceding our own incompetence? Is it possible we believe society "owes us" something because of the "burdens" we face?

Why would parents want a respite care worker—a stranger—taking care of their children? Yes, the person might be very nice, but wouldn't we rather have family, friends, the teenager next door, or the nice widowed grandma at church take care of our children? How can we believe that a professional respite care worker is better able to take care of our children than someone—a friend or relative—who already knows and loves our children?

You might feel like screaming that a regular babysitter wouldn't work, that you *must* have respite because the workers are trained in how to tube feed your child, monitor the oxygen or the trach, or do something similar. But consider this: are you a registered nurse or a registered dietitian or a registered respiratory therapist? Probably not. But you learned how to do all these things; you do them every day. Even if a respite care provider has been trained how to use medical equipment, you still have to train her about the specifics of your child. And what if you don't get the same one twice in a row? If you can train a "professional" about how to meet your child's needs, you can also train the teenager next door, your best friend, or other people who could be excellent babysitters.

Parents of children with autism and similar disabilities often say they cannot use typical babysitters because of their children's behavior. After one experience with their child, they say, a babysitter refuses to come again. But it doesn't have to be this way. As you'll see in later chapters, we can make significant changes to ensure our children and families lead more natural lives.

Even if we *can* designate someone we know as a respite care provider, why would we want to make the loving, generous act of a family member or friend into a fee-for-service? What happens if the program's payment isn't made on time, and a grandmother or friend who now depends on the money gets mad at the family? We all know how dangerous it is to mix money and family members or friends. It's fraught with potential disaster. And personally, I'd be offended if my mother or sister consented to take care of my children only if they were paid!

When my children were younger and I needed a babysitter, I wanted someone who knew and cared about my children, not a stranger who was there just because she was getting paid. My children are too valuable to leave them in the care of someone like that, even if the person *has* been trained as a professional caregiver.

Dependence and Frustration

Many parents feel eternally grateful for respite care services. At the same time, they may also feel pain and anger. While their friends use babysitters on a regular basis so they can go to the movies or to the mall, parents of children with disabilities feel left out because they can't do these things as easily. They may not be able to call the respite agency on short notice, or they may need to reserve their allotment of hours for really important things. The fact that friends are able to casually leave their children with teenagers or other babysitters, while we must use a professional, only serves to make us feel more different and isolated from the mainstream.

Parents may blame marital or family difficulties on the lack of respite care: "Our family life would be better if we didn't have so much stress because of John!" When we do this, we're covertly laying the blame on our children. We're implying the child with the disability is the cause of the stress or problems we're facing. Our lives, we feel, are somehow better when the respite care provider can take the "problem" away for a short time. We're not so callous that we openly blame the child, though. We blame the lack of respite services.

When we rely on respite care services, we cut ourselves off from other people who could help us with child care. We stop looking for natural supports, like the teenager next door or the grandmother at church. We don't spend a lot of time working with those who could be good babysitters. Why bother when we can count on the system, right?

Yes, we can count on the system until our hours or the dollars run out. But what happens when we use up the allotment in the first half of the fiscal year? Just because the entitlement ends, does our need for child care end as well? Of course not. Our reliance on the system leaves us vulnerable, for we have no where to turn for help when the system lets us down. But if we believe people in our community are capable of helping us, we always have somewhere to turn for help. A babysitting co-op, the girl next door, other families, relatives, and many other options are available. You'll learn how to make this a reality in Chapter 15.

HOW CONVENTIONAL WISDOM IMPACTS FAMILIES

In addition to the specifics mentioned regarding respite, today's conventional wisdom, overall, can be harmful because of the messages it sends. The spoken and unspoken messages of the service system are pervasive and destructive.

Messages of Incompetence

One of the foundations of conventional wisdom is that children with disabilities need specialized help, provided by specialized professionals. The overall *spoken* message to parents is, "Because of your child's disability, your child (and/or your family) is now entitled to certain services and, in some cases, cold hard cash." The *unspoken* message is, "You are not competent to handle this situation, so we'll step in and do what's necessary." And we, the wise parents, believe the lie.

In early intervention, the *spoken* message is: "Your baby is at such risk, he is entitled to the special help of professionals and services in order to minimize the effect of developmental delays and help your baby reach his potential." The *unspoken* message is, "Loving your baby, playing with him, helping him learn, just like all parents do is not enough. You're just a parent and your child needs more than you can give him. And even if you have successfully raised other children, you still don't have the knowledge or skills to handle this situation." And we, the people who know our children best, believe the lies.

In early childhood education, the *spoken* message is, "Your three, four, or five-year-old child with a disability is so far behind and so unprepared, she is entitled to special ed preschool where trained professionals will help her get ready for public school. Further, with enough help, the child's disability can be ameliorated in special ed preschool and maybe she won't need special ed services by the time she reaches kindergarten."

The *unspoken* message for stay-at-home moms is, "Keeping your child at home is not an appropriate option. You don't have the skills to maximize your child's development, nor are you competent to meet your child's special educational needs. Sending your son or daughter to the neighborhood preschool two or three days a week is also not appropriate. Regular preschools are not competent to handle your child's needs; only we have the skills to meet the needs of children with disabilities."

The *unspoken* message for working moms is, "The day care center cannot provide all the special care and education your child needs, even if it is the place where your other children have been (or are being cared for), and even if the center's employees know your child because they've been caring for him for a long time. The day care staffers have not been trained in how to help children with developmental disabilities. Your child needs to attend the special ed preschool for part of the day, and then we can bus your young child to the day care center." And parents, along with experienced day care and preschool staffers, believe the lies.

In special education, the *spoken* message is, "Because children with disabilities have so many problems and special needs, and because they are so different from typical children, they need specialized help from specially trained teachers in special settings. The *unspoken* message is, "Children with disabilities are not competent to be in regular classes. Furthermore, regular education teachers are not competent to teach children with disabilities, the regular educational environment is not appropriate, and even the combined wisdom of parents and educators is not enough to meet the child's unique needs." And experienced parents, along with regular educators, believe the lies.

In the lives of young adults, the *spoken* message is, "Because of their disabilities, teenagers are entitled to receive help from the special ed system and the voc-rehab agency. These experts will determine what kind of careers are appropriate and will place students with disabilities in part-time jobs in the hope they'll be successful in an entry-level job. Students who are not employable at the present time will attend special programs to help them get ready for a real job (one of these days)."

The *unspoken* message is, "Your teenager is not competent to find a job or determine her future on her own. Even if she has the support of her family and even if she has dreams, she needs the expertise of professionals who will determine what she's capable of doing." And parents, along with their budding young adult children, believe the lies.

Conventional wisdom sends the message that parents and their children are incompetent and need specialized help before they can be successful. In addition, according to conventional wisdom, friends, neighbors, and others who are not "experts" are not capable of helping children with disabilities. Balderdash!

Messages of Self-Doubt and Dependency

Self-doubt and dependency are other harmful side effects of disability-related service systems. When the mother of a baby with a disability is first told of the supports available, she's comforted. "Thank goodness there are professionals to help us through this difficult time," she thinks. After the initial diagnosis (regardless of the age of the child) we often feel relief and gratitude that help is at hand.

But underneath the relief are frightening and confusing pangs:

- This situation must be worse than I thought, otherwise why would I need all this help?

- I know I just couldn't handle things alone.

- Maybe I'm not smart enough, good enough, competent enough, loving enough, maybe that's why I need all this help.

- I must not be as good a parent as I thought.

Some parents bury these thoughts and pretend they don't exist; others are aware of them, but choose to ignore them; and some let them simmer for awhile until an event or a comment brings them to the surface in an explosion of anger, tears, or both.

The confidence and common sense of parents are undermined and eroded by all the help provided. Physicians, social workers, therapists, psychologists, educators, service coordinators, and others surround the family with professional wisdom and advice. These experts send an unspoken message to parents: "We know best, do as we say." The power of paternalism brings seemingly welcome relief: someone else can take over or assume some responsibility. As a result, experienced, loving, competent parents begin to doubt their abilities to successfully raise their children.

Some parents accept the premise that they need expert help without question. They may be too frightened and confused to do otherwise. For the good of their child, they let the professionals take over. The experts know them as "great parents."

Other parents accept the services and supports, but they don't necessarily accept the premise that experts know best. They want more than what the professionals recommend or they may want things in a different way. To get what they want, they argue, cajole, and threaten. They become known as "uncooperative parents."

Some parents question the appropriateness of the services offered and they reject the notion that experts know best. They find other ways to help their children. They're known as "noncompliant parents."

Of course, I'm generalizing to a great extent to paint composite pictures of the many hundreds of parents I've talked with during the last ten years. During the thirteen years of my son's life, I've been in all three positions at one time or another. Some parents may stay in one position, while others may move back and forth between two or three positions.

What the first two positions have in common, however, is dependency. Parents become dependent on services and the professionals who provide them. Some parents choose dependency because it feels safe. Others choose it because they don't know there are other options. Many parents don't like feeling dependent, but they put up with it in order to get what their children need. In almost all instances, self-doubt creeps in and begins to grow.

We don't get what we need; we get what's offered. As a result, our children are often denied opportunities for success because we're unwilling or unable to move outside the service system for solutions. Who says experts know what's best for our children and our families? Why do we believe they have all the answers? Why do we feel their solutions are more valuable than ours? There are many possibilities out there, but we limit ourselves to the services offered by the system.

We lose our our dignity, autonomy, and self-direction when we let the service system assume responsibility. When strangers interfere in our families, even strangers we might like, we allow our family's self-worth to be impoverished. We allow ourselves to be defined as unable, weak, or unworthy for the task. We're being rescued, but underneath we're uncomfortable with our inability to save ourselves and we often begin to dislike the rescuer. The cycle of self-doubt, dependency, and anger keeps us in an unremitting state of stress.

The basic foundation of parents knowing what's best for their children is eroded. When the service system intrudes into the daily lives of our families, we lose the self-confidence that's absolutely necessary for a healthy family life. If the interference and intrusion that are routine and common to *our* families happened to the majority of families in the United States, a social revolt would erupt. Why do we sit back and take it, when others wouldn't?

Dependence on the service system tells our children we don't believe in the strength of the family and our own resources (friends, relatives, community, etc.) to handle the family's needs. We send a very clear message to our children: our families are weak and dependent on paternalistic forces. Thus, the victim mentality is born: whatever our problems are, they're not our fault; it's someone else's responsibility to help us.

The demand for the security of the service system creates disincentives for us to take personal responsibility for ourselves and our successes and failures. Why should we go out and find what we need in our communities when we can just go to the service system for help? And when the help from the service system doesn't work out, it's easy to blame the system instead of ourselves. We lose the ability to dig deep within ourselves to find personal resources and solutions. We are then unable to teach our children that *they* have untapped capabilities within themselves.

We lose our sense of reality and become out of touch with our communities. The service system creates a false reality. We no longer see the real world the way it is. When we depend on professionals for support, we cut ourselves off from the naturally-occurring supports that surrounded us before the diagnosis of our child. We inadvertently push friends and family members away by thinking only professionals can help.

We have no more time for living normally. Therapies, special services, and medical appointments fill our days. Therapists, service coordinators, and others we see on a regular basis become our new friends. They know what we're going through (we think), while others don't. Perhaps we've just never given others a chance. We learn to speak the same language as the experts, the professional jargon others don't understand. We reject the natural supports of our communities and become dependent on the artificial supports of paid professionals.

Dependence on the service system reduces our children and our families to the status of clients who must be served. Our humanity is ignored. We are no longer permitted to be spiritual creations who have the same inner needs common to all human beings. The focus is on rehabilitation and restoration, regardless of the cost to our souls.

The "entitlement mentality" we learn from the service system brings out the worst in most of us. Many of us will go to the ends of the earth to get what our children are entitled to. Notice I did not say what our children "need;" I said "entitled to."

I have met many, many parents whose lives are in turmoil, who are full of anger, and who spend huge amounts of time fighting with the system over entitlements. Because their children are entitled to something, parents are determined to get it, whether their children really need it, whether it's truly appropriate for the child and the family, and/or whether or not there's a better way to get it. We'll do whatever it takes, regardless of the stress it and tension involved. When we subscribe to the entitlement mentality, our view of the big picture and what's really important becomes murky.

One way society deals with the discomfort of people with disabilities being in its midst is to "do something"—provide services—for or to them so they'll be more "normal." When we participate in the service system, we unknowingly reinforce that this discomfort is justified. Some of us are embarrassed by our children and their disabilities. Some of us feel we must apologize for our children's conditions. Some of us work overtime to make our children "normal." And we often want so much from the service system that our advocacy roles become full-time positions.

What messages do all these issues send our children? What messages are communicated to our families, friends, and neighbors about how we feel about our children and others with disabilities? Are we willing to let this continue?

By following the conventional wisdom of the service system, children with disabilities and their families live their lives by the dictates of the gatekeepers. Choice, free will, and self-determination are frequently replaced by dependency, intimidation, and victimization.

We recognize that the conventional wisdom of the past was wrong. How do we know today's conventional wisdom isn't also wrong?

Standing on Principle is Often Illogical

Nancy was a wonderful advocate and stay-at-home mom to three children. Brandon, the youngest, was born with a cognitive disability. Nancy never put Brandon in any type of special programs, even though many professionals urged her to do so. She wanted him home with her, the way her older children had been, playing with kids in the neighborhood, and learning from her and his surroundings—living a typical life.

When Brandon was four, professionals once again recommended enrolling him in the early childhood education program (which happened to be located in the neighborhood school her other children currently attended). Nancy declined the ECE program, but indicated she wanted the speech therapy that was a service of the preschool. The ECE staff said therapy could only be provided if Brandon was enrolled in the special ed preschool classes. Nancy knew this wasn't right: even though Brandon didn't attend the preschool, he was still entitled to speech services through the ECE program.

As it turned out, Sally, the speech therapist—on her own—told Nancy she would be happy to provide speech therapy (informally) without Brandon being enrolled in the preschool. Nancy could bring Brandon to the school two or three days a week, in the mornings before the school day started. Nancy was excited about this turn of events.

But when the ECE professionals heard about this, there was an immediate snag: nothing like this had ever been done before, and they weren't about to set a precedent. They were quite aggravated the speech therapist had even proposed such a solution. Sally's idea was quite simple (and brave), but the ECE director wouldn't allow it.

When I met Nancy, she described this situation to me, finishing with the announcement that she was preparing to initiate a due process hearing with the school over the issue. She was very angry and had spent many hours arguing with the ECE staff, sharing her story with other parent-advocates, and gathering ammunition for the hearing.

After she gave me all the details, I asked her several questions and learned she had a good relationship with the school (except for the ECE people). She frequently volunteered in her other children's classrooms, and she was friendly with the principal and many teachers. Brandon would be attending this school when it was time for kindergarten and Nancy expected him to be included in a regular class at that time. She had already been scoping out which teachers would be good for Brandon, based on her knowledge of her other children's teachers.

I asked Nancy if she and her husband had good health insurance. After she indicated they did, I said, "Nancy, let's think about this. Do you really want to sue the school and turn your current allies into life-long enemies? After all, you've already got two kids there and Brandon will spend six years there. Whether you win or lose the due process hearing, do you want to send your kids to a school where they hate your guts? Why don't you just get Brandon private speech therapy through your health insurance, instead of setting your family up for a lot of problems?"

Dumbfounded by my comments, her face contorted by anger, she yelled, "Because he's entitled! It's the law!"

"So what?" I asked. "Is making sure he gets everything he's 'entitled to' worth all this when there's another way to get what he needs? Is standing on principle worth the chaos? Worth making enemies? Worth wrecking your emotional life in the turmoil of a due process hearing?" She thought for awhile, sighed deeply a couple of times, and finally said, "No, of course not. What was I thinking?"

Nancy, like so many of us, had bought into the entitlement mentality and was willing to lose much in order to gain little. Other parents of children with disabilities had encouraged Nancy to challenge school district personnel. Like many of us, Nancy was ready to use her son's rights as a baseball bat, beating people over the head to force the issue. In the meantime, she was shooting herself in the foot!

Should we expect schools to obey the law? Of course we should. At the same time, we must anticipate the outcomes—intended and unintended—of our actions. Standing on principle is sometimes a shaky proposition. When our actions do more harm than good, the principle needs to be replaced by common sense.

Zealously following a principle, a law, or a practice, with little or no thought to the outcome of our actions, is both irresponsible and illogical. The foolishness of conventional wisdom can make fools of us all.

AN ARTIFICIAL WORLD

Did you see the movie, *The Truman Show?* If you haven't seen it, rush right out and rent it for tonight. If you have seen it, it's worth a second look. The film has nothing to do with people with disabilities, but it has everything to do with an artificial world versus the real world. The story line provides an excellent metaphor for disability issues.

Truman, the main character, lives in a world that was created just for him. But he doesn't realize he's living in a counterfeit world. Everything seems normal and natural because this is all he's ever known. But a few things happen that make him question the world he lives in. Curiousity, anger, and fear lead him to discover the truth at the end of the movie. Truman confronts Christof, the man who created this artificial world. (I've wondered if the character's name is a play on the words "of Christ," as if he's the creator and savior of Truman.) Christof tells Truman something like, "But Truman, I created you. I know what's best for you."

When the movie ended, I was reeling. The scenarios in the movie paralleled what happens to people with disabilities in the service system.

Christof and his staff had created an artificial world around Truman, and Truman believed it was real. In this counterfeit world, he was safe and protected. His needs were provided for; he was given everything Christof and others thought he needed. And for a long time, this was fine with Truman; he didn't know anything else. He never had real choices or freedom, even though he thought he did. Again, he didn't know any different.

But Truman had had a taste of something he needed that wasn't in his world (you'll learn what this is when you watch the movie), and he wanted more. Even though he was absolutely terrified to leave the safety of his world, he started trying to go outside his environment to find it. In response, those who felt they "knew what was best" for him continually set up barriers. But Truman bravely challenged these obstacles. In the process, he began questioning everything. Finally, he discovered he was surrounded by a counterfeit world. His life had been defined by myths and programmed by others. His was a difficult and soul-wrenching journey, but in the end, he was both powerful and free.

The service system has created an artificial world around people with disabilities, based on myths, and we think it's real. The service system provides us with what it thinks our children and families need. We're safe and protected in this world. But we're like Truman: we really don't have our freedom; we really don't have many choices. We realize the system can't provide what we or our children really need, but we're stuck in a belief system that tells us this is the only way.

When we realize what we need is outside of the artificial world of the service system, we're often scared to leave its safety. If and when we do escape, however, we discover inner strength and conviction that were there all along. The ability to succeed on our own was always there. It was simply lying dormant until a spark lit the fuse.

Christof told Truman, "I created you. I know what's best for you." The service system creates clients out of our children and tells us, "We know what's best." Some of us stay in this artificial world forever. Some of us, like Truman, successfully fight to get out of it and discover a whole new world of freedom and choices and community support—a world we had forgotten existed. (In later chapters, I'll detail how we can make a successful getaway like Truman did.)

THE IDEAL VS. THE REALITY

From a distance, life in the United States is good for people with disabilities. We're the first nation to pass a comprehensive civil rights act to protect people with disabilities from discrimination. Federal law mandates the education of children with disabilities. Other federal and state laws and regulations impact the lives of children and adults with disabilities in a variety of ways. And we have more services and supports than ever before—more than any other nation in the world.

But when we examine the situation up close, we see a very different picture. A paradox exists—a real conundrum—that may be easily explained, but hard to correct systemically. (There is, however, much we can do as individuals to eliminate the paradox from our lives, as I'll demonstrate in the second half of this book.)

If the Americans with Disabilities Act (ADA) prohibits discrimination based on disability, why do we still have programs and services that segregate people with disabilities from the mainstream of society? If the Individuals with Disabilities Education Act (IDEA) mandates a free and appropriate education in the least restrictive environment, why are so many students with disabilities segregated and uneducated? If vocational rehabilitation programs are intended to help individuals with disabilities acquire job skills and find work, why does the unemployment rate for adults with disabilities continue to hover around 75 percent? We could ask similar questions about all federal and state laws covering people with disabilities.

How can the same federal government that passed the ADA continue to provide support for segregated programs that defy the spirit, if not the actual intent, of the ADA? Federal dollars are funneled into state programs that are still isolating people with disabilities in sheltered workshops and segregated living arrangements. How can the federal government that guarantees the right of children with disabilities to a free and appropriate public education continue providing special education funding to states that blatantly disregard the sprit and intent of the law? Think about other laws and policies at the state and federal levels and ask similar questions. Why does all this happen?

I believe it's because we (everyone in society) say one thing, but do another. We talk the talk, but don't walk the walk.

The ideal doesn't mesh with society's version of reality. The ideal: people with disabilities should enjoy all the rights and responsibilities inherent in American citizenship. The reality: because people with developmental disabilities—according to societal perceptions and conventional wisdom—are so different, needy, inept, incompetent, and/or worthless as they are, they must get ready for full citizenship. And the programs and services available today are intended to do just that.

It's unfair to wag our collective fingers at society and the system unless we're willing to point those fingers at ourselves, too. We—parents of children with disabilities—are part of the society that talks the talk, but doesn't walk the walk.

We have advocated for special services, we've rallied for more funding for specialized programs, and we beat our breasts about all the things our children (and families) need that the system should provide. And then we rant and rave because our children aren't included. But how *can* they be when they're in special programs—the special programs we've demanded? We must be careful what we ask for; we may just get it.

VALUABLE COMMODITIES

Today's conventional wisdom and the service system need to change. Most people who are recipients of services, and a number of those who work within the system, agree on this point. But the system is resistant to change, for a variety of reasons. Maintaining the status quo is always easier. Slogging through legislation and bureaucratic policies takes time. Funding issues are always problematic. Shifting from one paradigm to another is difficult. All of these contribute to the barriers we face in effecting systems change.

Underneath the surface resistance, however, lies a solid economic fact: people with disabilities are valuable commodities. Hundreds of agencies exist and thousands—maybe millions—of Americans have jobs today, thanks to children and adults with disabilities who use the service system!

I doubt if employees of a human services agency gather around the water cooler and say, "Thank goodness for people with disabilities. If it wasn't for them, we wouldn't have jobs." But if they did say this, it would be a true statement. Thousands of workers are dependent on people with disabilities for their livelihoods! Remember this when you're dealing with the bureaucratic system that doles out services to the "deserving needy;" *they work for you and are dependent on you for their livelihoods!*

Many in the system—individual employees, heads of agencies, and others—will be resistant to any change that could impact their salaries, power, or positions. Any attempt to streamline the system or downsize large, inefficient bureaucracies would be rebuffed if it meant people would lose their jobs.

IS THERE A SOLUTION?

Will the system—can it—change? Certainly it can. But can it improve to a degree that would suit most people with disabilities and their families? Probably not.

All human services systems are paternalistic. It's the nature of the beast. The haves provide for the have-nots. The givers give to the takers. The fortunate professionals help the unfortunate victims. The learned experts guide the helpless.

In addition, all human services systems are behind the times. Their behemoth-like size prevents them from moving quickly and responding to the ever-changing needs of its clientele.

If we choose to be recipients and accept help from the system, we must play by the system's rules. And, yes, the rules can change—they can become fairer, more user-friendly, and so forth—but they're still the system's rules.

The solution is to get out of the system and into your community, as I'll describe in later chapters. Children and adults with disabilities need to move from clienthood to citizenship. What we and our children need can be found in our communities. Before you begin shaking your head in disbelief, wondering what planet I'm from, stay with me. The journey to a more natural life—a successful life—for your child and your family is just beginning.

Too many of us (including me, at times) have accepted conventional wisdom—without question—to the detriment of our children and families. We absolutely must carefully question and thoughtfully consider today's conventional wisdom. If we don't like what we see, we must challenge it, and create a new vision and a new reality for our children. Our vision must be based on our own real-life knowledge and experiences, not on the artificial intelligence supplied by the service system.

Change is inevitable. We can sit back and hope. We can choose to do nothing. Or we can instigate a peaceful revolution. We each have a choice to make.

One of the most problematic cornerstones of conventional wisdom for children with disabilities and their families is special education. That's where we'll go next. Following that, we'll look at the current situation regarding services for young children and pediatric therapies.

A GOVERNMENT THAT IS BIG ENOUGH
TO GIVE YOU ALL YOU WANT
IS BIG ENOUGH TO TAKE IT ALL AWAY.
Barry Goldwater

Special Education Isn't So Special

THE WORLD OF EDUCATION IS
LIKE AN ISLAND WHERE PEOPLE,
CUT OFF FROM THE WORLD,
ARE PREPARED FOR LIFE
BY EXCLUSION FROM IT.
Maria Montessori

In 1997, in an elementary school resource room, a seven-year-old girl who has cerebral palsy is being taught to fold towels. No attempts are being made to teach her reading, writing, and arithmetic. Her disability has defined her destiny. The most this child will ever achieve, the educators believe, is the mastery of a few basic functional skills.

In 1998, in a middle school resource room, two thirteen-year-old boys are playing with baby toys. One has a cognitive disability and no oral communication. The other has physical and cognitive disabilities. Their school records indicate they have "profound" intellectual disabilities. Educators (and their parents) don't believe they're capable of real learning, so school personnel just try to keep them happy and occupied.

In 1999, in a high school cafeteria, a young man with a cognitive disability spends most of his school day mopping the cafeteria floor before and after the other students have eaten. No one believes he has the capacity to learn academic skills, so why waste the time? Educators have decided he might be able to find a job cleaning floors, so that's the focus of his "education."

The federal law mandating a free and appropriate public education for children with disabilities has been with us now for a quarter of a century. Incredible changes have taken place during the past twenty-five years. Who knew, in 1975, that home computers, microwave ovens, and cell phones would become common appliances? Who could have predicted that technology would bring us routine space shuttle flights, heart transplants, and the cloning of sheep?

With all these amazing changes, who would believe that during the last twenty-five years, the education of children with disabilities has changed so very little?

In thousands of schools across the country, special education looks like it did twenty-five years ago. Segregation, exclusion, and specialized services have been the cornerstones of conventional wisdom about special education. Concerned and dedicated parents were instrumental in ensuring the original passage of special education law, P.L. 94-142 (now IDEA) in 1975. Today, however, a new generation of parents is questioning the way the law is implemented. They've learned that special education is not always special and it's not always an education.

In this chapter, we'll review the origins of special education, examine the barriers in implementing the spirit and intent of special ed law, and look at key players in the special ed process: educators and parents.

THE CRISIS IN PUBLIC EDUCATION

One of the biggest issues facing many—if not most—parents of children with disabilities is the poor quality of education their children are receiving. But this is not just a special education issue. Parents of children *without* disabilities feel schools are doing a poor to mediocre job, so it's not just students with disabilities who may be getting short shrift.

Critics of today's schools are many, and their opinions on how to improve schools are varied. The loudest voice is coming from politicians. Unfortunately, parents and educators have ceded their power to elected officials, and their voices are no longer heard. And children—whose every day experiences are impacted by the authority of government—well, we've never listened to them in the past, so why start now? The solution proposed by politicians (state and federal) is to toughen standards: to ensure every child is proficient in every subject.

We like to think this is altruism at it's highest: ensuring all children are educated equally is right, just, and fair. But any politicial speech on the subject exposes the real purpose: economics. Governors, senators, and representatives, as well as those campaigning for public office, issue dire warnings about the threat to our nation's economic standing if children aren't educated to a higher standard. "We won't be able to compete in the global economy," they lament, "if we don't improve education in public schools."

The principle that society should provide the same education to all students is longstanding; it's been with us since the earliest days of public education. But is it a valid—or valuable—principle?

Two hundred years ago, the first schools in our country were operated by churches, and attendance was voluntary. The primary goal was to teach all students to read so they could study the Bible. These early efforts were, at the core, a form of social control: if children could study the Bible, they would grow into responsible adults.

What started as a service of the church eventually moved under the umbrella of state government. Education as a method of social control became entrenched: students were to receive a moral education so they would be good citizens. Parents, it was believed, did not have the ability to do this. The state must intervene to make sure it was done, and done properly.

With the influx of immigrants in the late 1800s and early 1900s, leaders in government and industry were worried that the social fabric of America was in danger of being torn apart. Immigrants, with their own customs and languages, were suspect. It was believed they did not have the same moral code as Americans.

At the same time, industrialists knew the children of immigrants (and Americans in the middle and lower classes) would become the factory workers of tomorrow, and politicians knew they (the immigrants) would become United States citizens. A public education, designed and decreed by state government, would ensure these children would one day be honest factory workers and law-abiding citizens of good character. In the minds of social reformers, politicians, and business leaders, only the wisdom, power, and coercion of the state could ensure children would be raised up to be good Americans; parents could not be trusted with the responsibility.

In order to accomplish their lofty goals, reformers believed a standardized curriculum would bring all students to an accepted level of achievement. Ultimately, students (then and now) were not given opportunities to learn what *they* wanted or needed to know; students—and their parents—were not competent to make these decision. The state mandated what students should be taught. (At the core, we should question whether or not education should be in the hands of government, but that's another story.)

As society has changed, schools have failed to keep up with societal changes. Today's school day looks about the same as it did a century ago. It was modeled after the factory day of the Industrial Revolution: everyone should be in place when the whistle blows (the bell rings); morning break is morning recess; lunch is lunch (eat when you're told, even if you're not hungry); afternoon break is afternoon recess; and everyone goes home when the whistle sounds (the bell rings). This schedule was one way to train children how to become dependable factory workers.

Today, our economy is service-based, not factory-based, and the workplace is very different. But in most communities, the school day still follows the original factory model. In most places, even today's school *year* conforms to the bygone days when children were let out of school to help plant crops on the family farm (spring break). During summer, children needed to be home to help cultivate and harvest crops (today's summer vacation).

In the past, students were taught history, government, grammar, and other basics by a teacher giving oral instruction; common people didn't have access to many books or other written materials. Thus, students were expected to memorize everything since written references weren't readily available. Today, however, books, videos, radio, television, and the Internet can provide anyone with information on just about any subject—including what's taught in public schools—and this information doesn't need to be memorized because it can be accessed in an instant. (Should we still be expecting children to memorize facts or should we be helping them learn how to find what they want and need to know?)

One inherent flaw in our educational system is this: the focus is on how teachers teach instead of how children learn. Historically, students have been perceived as empty vessels into which teachers pour knowledge. But most of us can recall our own years in the public school system and easily refute the validity of this perception. How much do you remember of what you were "taught" by a teacher?

Children and adults learn best by doing. We could define education (which may have little or nothing to do with public school) as being able to put into practice—being able to use—what we know. To that end, memorizing facts isn't learning unless we can use what we've memorized. Further, we only learn what's relevant to us.

Take this book, for example. The words you're reading cannot *teach* you anything. They can only give you information. You'll *learn* from this book only if you're interested in the topics, the information is relevant and valuable to you, and you can make use of it.

Whether we realize it or not, most of us are self-taught. Over the years, we've acquired *information* from a variety of sources. But all of us have *learned* the most by experience. Learning is a life-long participatory endeavor.

In its highest form, "teaching" is the art of helping a person learn what's important to him. But in the past and today, teaching continues to be viewed as the act of one person (the teacher) giving information to another person (the student). Within this paradigm, if the student doesn't "learn" what the teacher "taught," the student is viewed as a failure. We say he can't learn, he's lazy or unwilling, or we attach some other descriptor that lays the problem in the student's lap. (My high school geometry teacher told my mother I could get better grades if I would just "apply myself." But I wasn't interested in geometry! It had absolutely no relevance to my life.)

Many Americans still accept the notion that public schools can and should teach all things to all students. But this makes no sense. All children are not interested in the same things, at the same time, and in the same way. And what students say they want or need to learn is ignored; politicians, educators, and even most parents disregard the opinions of children.

Public education is paternalism at its highest. State governments, with or without input from educators, parents, or children, decide what students need to learn. This demonstrates a profound disregard and disrespect for children as human beings and natural learners, as well as a disregard and disrespect for parents' abilities to make important decisions about their children's education. (But we can't hold others wholly responsible; since the beginning of public education, parents have trusted—or at least accepted—the wisdom of the state.)

Not only do most educators focus on teaching instead of learning, they also teach to the norm: the idealized (but unrealistic) "average" student. In overcrowded classrooms, teachers don't feel they have the time or the energy to focus on individual learners or individual learning styles (in general, they're right). There are, of course, exceptions: teachers who use a variety of unconventional strategies to ensure their classrooms are places of real learning.

The dilemmas in public education can't be blamed on any particular group—educators, politicians, or parents—we all share in the responsibility. But politicians are expecting teachers to get us out of this mess via educational reforms focused on "standards." In many states today, if educators don't elevate the learning of all students, schools will be penalized. At the same time, however, politicians aren't addressing the needs of teachers, such as smaller class sizes and other issues.

I find it curious there's been no public outcry from teachers' unions (National Education Association and American Federation of Teachers). At the highest levels, and behind the scenes, I'm sure union leaders are working with politicians to address the issues important to teachers. But in the larger public arena, educators appear to be standing helplessly by as they're scapegoated for all the problems in public education. Individually, many chafe against unfair accusations. So why aren't they publicly and collectively agitating against public opinion, not to mention regulations, that indict them as guilty? I don't know the answer. Perhaps it's because, as civil servants, they're unwilling—or feel unable—to oppose the authority of those who pay their salaries (local, state, and federal governments). Or maybe they're afraid public opinion against them will increase if they publicly defend themselves. I just don't know.

Furthermore, why haven't parents risen up against regulations that penalize children? The political solution to poor education is to "hold schools accountable." And many state governments are creating recommendations and/or policies which forbid "social promotion:" if a student cannot meet the educational standards of his grade level, he'll be held back (flunked!). The politician rhetoric of the 2000 presidential campaign included the mantra, "leave no child behind." Hmmmm, we won't leave a child behind, but it's all right to hold him back in school. Does this make sense?

The real losers in educational reform are, as always, the children. We say we'll hold educators accountable and even punish schools, but who is really punished? Children who are held back and made to feel stupid. When a child is held back, does anyone say to him, "It was your teacher's fault, not yours."? I don't think so. Why aren't parents, alone, or in collaboration with educators, wresting power over their children's lives away from politicians and bureaucrats?

Since its inception, education has been (and continues to be) a pervasive form of social control. Thoughtful critics have recognized that public education is essentially an unproven theory that has never been tested. (We test children, but not the theory of public education.) Society accepts public education, but never fully endorses it, as evidenced by the many "reform movements" that have tried to influence and change how our society educates and treats children.

Many students who don't have disabilities may be able to get as much as possible out of their school experience, and many supplement formal instruction with their own learning activities. But children with disabilities—especially those in segregated settings—often suffer great consequences when schools are unable to meet their basic needs, much less their specific needs.

Global improvements in special education will come about only when we see global improvements in the whole of public education. To that end, we need to move beyond our interest in special education and work with parents of typical children, as well as with legislators, educators, and other policy makers to improve education for all children.

A LITTLE SPECIAL ED HISTORY

When P.L. 94-142, the Education of All Handicapped Children Act (reauthorized in 1990 as IDEA, the Individuals with Disabilities Education Act), became a federal law in 1975, the U.S. Congress promised to help states pay for the additional costs of educating children with disabilities if the states would follow the provisions of the law. The law is, in essence, a funding stream for those states who wish to receive federal dollars for special education. During the nine years following the law's passage, state education departments submitted their plans for implementing the federal law. New Mexico was the last state to submit a plan in 1984; by then all fifty states were participating.

Congress pledged funding to states, some of which would be passed on to school districts. A gradual increase in federal support was promised, from the original 5 percent to 40 percent by 1982. At the present time, however, the federal contribution has never exceeded 8.5 percent of the costs. When schools tell parents they don't have adequate funds for special education, they're partially right. Congress has never allocated the 40 percent originally promised.

The intent of the law was to ensure access to public education for all students with disabilities. Until the federal law was passed, a mishmash of state education laws allowed some students with disabilities to attend public schools, but others were excluded. In passing the federal law, Congress was trying to abolish the practice of states picking and choosing which children with disabilities they would educate. This federal concept is known as "zero rejection."

Congress did not believe the presence of a disability automatically precluded a child from attending regular classes in his neighborhood school. The framers of the law stressed the importance of focusing on the child's individual needs, not on the disability label, which led to the regulation that every child would have an Individual Education Program (IEP). According to the law, special education means "specially designed instruction, at no cost to parents, to meet the unique needs of a child with a disability."

LEAST RESTRICTIVE ENVIRONMENT (LRE)

For the majority of students with disabilities in our country, the promise of the law has never been realized. Before going further, let's look at some specific parts of the law:

Each public agency shall ensure:

(1) That to the maximum extent appropriate, children with disabilities, including children in public or private institutions or other care facilities, are educated with children who are nondisabled; and

(2) That *special classes, separate schooling or other removal of children with disabilities from the regular educational environment* occurs only if the nature or severity of the disability is such that education in regular classes with the use of supplementary aids and services cannot be achieved satisfactorily. [Section 300.550 General LRE Requirements] (italics and underlining added)

In determining the educational placement of a child with a disability, including a preschool child with a disability, each public agency shall ensure that

(b) The child's placement is determined at least annually, is based on the child's IEP, and *is as close as possible to the child's home;*

(c) Unless the IEP of a child with a disability requires some other arrangement, the child is educated in *the school that he or she would attend if nondisabled;*

(d) In selecting the LRE, consideration is given to any harmful effect on the child or on the quality of services that he or she needs; and

(e) A child with a disability is not *removed* from education in age-appropriate regular classrooms solely because of needed modifications in the general curriculum. [Section 300.552 Placements] (italics added)

The law's intent is for children with disabilities to start out in regular education classes in their neighborhood schools, with appropriate supports and services. The language of the law is clear that a child should not be removed from the regular educational environment, put in special classes, or receive separate schooling, unless the child cannot be successfully educated in the regular educational environment with the use of supplementary aids and services. Further, a child should not be removed from the regular classroom environment (to a more restrictive setting) just because he needs curriculum modifications.

But far too many children with disabilities start out in the most restrictive setting (a special ed school or room) and must try to earn their way out by achieving some standard of "readiness." Some never do, and they remain isolated from the mainstream of their school community for twelve or more years of public education.

Parallel systems of education—regular and special—exist in many school districts today. Yet Congress never intended for special education to become an entity of its own. Special education is not a place; it's supposed to be services, supports, modifications, and accommodations provided to a child to meet his or her unique needs.

INCLUSION: A NEW WORD FOR AN EXISTING PHILOSOPHY

The emerging conventional wisdom about the education of children with disabilities is inclusion. What is inclusion? It depends on who you ask. Schools often define it one way, parents another. My definition, based on the experiences of my son and other students with disabilities at our neighborhood inclusive elementary school, is this:

> Inclusion is children with disabilities being educated in the schools they would attend if they didn't have disabilities, in age-appropriate regular education classrooms, where services and supports are provided in those classrooms for both the students and their teachers, and where students with disabilities are fully participating members of their school communities in academic and extra-curricular activities.

Contrary to the beliefs of many educators (and some parents), inclusion is not a new concept. The philosophy—as demonstrated by the language in the law on the previous page—has been in special education law since its inception in 1975. Congress didn't use the word "inclusion," but is there any doubt that what we call "inclusion" reflects the ideals Congress had in mind when it wrote the law?

Inclusion: Every Child's Right

Children *without* disabilities are included simply because they're citizens of their school communities. We don't question the right of typical children to attend their neighborhood schools, in age-appropriate classrooms. Our society presumes that typical children have the capacity to learn, can be successful, and so forth. But when a disability label is attached to a child, these beliefs often fly out the window, replaced by myths that relegate students with disabilities to second-class citizenship, who must somehow *earn* the right to belong—the right automatically bestowed on children who don't have disabilities or differences.

If we want our children to grow up to be successful in the real world, we have to start them out in the real world. In inclusive schools, kids with disabilities learn academics, social skills, responsibility, and more. They learn how to be wonderfully ordinary children who—like millions of others—are our country's future. Segregated education simply teaches children how to survive in segregated settings.

CONVENTIONAL WISDOM OF EDUCATORS

It's difficult to precisely define the conventional wisdom of educators about special education, because school districts interpret IDEA differently. Even within school districts, individual schools may use vastly different special education practices. Parents and other advocates usually see the law in black and white: it means what it says. Educators see shades of gray, depending on how they interpret the law.

A handful of schools have transformed themselves into inclusive schools. Others are "experimenting" with inclusion: they identify one or two regular ed classrooms where more than the natural proportion of children with disabilities attend. (The natural proportion of children with disabilities in public schools is 10 percent; thus, in a class of twenty, there should be no more than two students with disabilities.) If the experiment doesn't work, educators throw up their hands and say, "See we told you it wouldn't work!" and they go back to the old way of doing things.

Some schools say they're inclusive when they're actually practicing "reverse-mainstreaming:" typical children visit the segregated special ed room a couple of times each week. There are schools who claim to be inclusive because children with disabilities are "included" in art, music, PE, gym, and/or lunch. The remainder of the school day, however, the students are in segregated settings. And, believe it or not, some principals claim their schools are inclusive because students with disabilities are in the same *building* with typical students, even though they never set foot in a regular classroom.

Many schools do the exact opposite of what Congress intended. They base a child's placement on his disability label. Schools have made the *services* of special education into a *place* of special education. Instead of providing services to students in the least restrictive environment (regular classroom in the neighborhood school), educators create a place—special ed building or room (most restrictive environment)—where students must go to receive services. A child's placement is supposed to be based on her IEP, but this mandate is seldom followed. Instead, many schools look at what "programs" they already have in place and slot children into these existing programs.

Unfortunately, many parents have accepted a school's interpretation and implementation of special ed law. Countless times, when I've asked parents why their children don't attend the neighborhood school, they answer, "Because there isn't a program there." They have accepted the belief that children should fit into the programs(s) set up by schools.

Based on how educators choose to implement the law, it's apparent that the conventional wisdom of many educators is that children with disabilities simply do not belong in the regular educational environment. Some children, however, appear to belong more than others. Children with the most significant (or the most visible) disabilities are excluded from regular classrooms in greater numbers than are children with less significant conditions. School districts may follow the "zero rejection" concept in the broadest sense, in that they don't totally exclude children from a public education, but many routinely exclude children with disabilities from the regular education environment.

Special education isn't always special and it's not always an education. For too many of our children, it's a one-way ticket to exclusion. In Chapter 17, I'll show you how we can change this.

What Happened to the Law's Good Intentions?

If the framers of federal special education law had such great intentions, why are schools so far from the ideal?

Public education is the responsibility of states, not the federal government: it's a "state's right." That's why schools in California may look different than schools in Tennessee. Prior to the passage of the federal special education law, many states already had their own provisions regarding the education of students with disabilities. Some were good; some were not. Students with "mild" disabilities might have been allowed in public school, while students with more significant disabilities may have been excluded altogether, or they may have been "educated" in a segregated facility. As I mentioned previously, in order to receive the federal dollars promised in P.L. 94-142, states had to agree to educate *all* children with disabilities.

Looking back, it seems Congress and the educational community were not "on the same page." Members of Congress were influenced by the deinstitutionalization mandates initiated by President Kennedy in the early 1960s, which continued under Presidents Johnson, Nixon, and Ford. Congress had a new perception of children with disabilities that included moving away from the medical model of disability. This new perception was to be a new beginning in the education of students with disabilities. It was, however, a very different perception held by educators. This, plus a variety of other forces created the special ed system (separate education) that's common today.

States already had some experience setting up separate programs for "special populations" (bilingual, remedial, reading, and others), which were funded under state and federal regulations. Each of these programs had to follow specific procedures for the delivery of services. The complicated funding streams influenced how the specialized services were organized and delivered. Educators implemented these special programs using special teachers, special teaching methods, and special locations. (Authors of some books on the history of the educational services indicate that educators have frequently misinterpreted the regulations on the implementation of these programs.)

When P.L. 94-142 came along, the new way of doing things proposed by the framers of the law—not basing services on the disability label, educating children in their neighborhood schools, and so forth—didn't automatically change the way educators operated. School administrators and teachers had no model of what this would look like. They were familiar with the models that already existed; models where special populations were apart from the general population via specialized classrooms and/or educators. (I recall, as a first-grader in 1956, being pulled out of class by a speech therapist several days each week. He led me, and several other students, down the hall to a room where we had "group therapy." I couldn't pronouce "R" and a couple of other letters very well, and I have no idea if therapy was beneficial or if my speech simply improved with the passage of time.) Instead of opening the doors to children with disabilities and providing them with needed services within the mainstream of the school community—following the spirit and the intent of the law—educators responded by doing what they already knew how to do: create more special programs.

In addition, the manner in which state legislatures enacted funding provisions for state and local education dollars contributed to the segregation of students with disabilities. In many states, schools received more money for students who were in the most restrictive settings! Thus, there was a great incentive for schools to segregate children with disabilities. As a result of revisions in IDEA '97, this discriminatory practice is now prohibited.

CONVENTIONAL WISDOM OF PARENTS

The conventional wisdom of parents is a mixed bag. Twenty years ago, this might not have been the case.

After the passage of P.L. 94-142, parents reveled in their victory. They had the power to influence federal legislation, but unfortunately, they were unable or unwilling to influence how school districts implemented the law.

Perhaps parents were so glad their children were able to receive a public education, they didn't make too big a fuss if the law wasn't followed exactly. A majority of parents may have shared the belief that special classes and special teachers were appropriate. The conventional wisdom of educators and parents might have once been closely aligned: kids with disabilities will only succeed if they're given special services by special teachers in special (segregated) settings.

Over the years, however, parents have recognized that even with all the special services, their children were leaving school as young adults with no education, no skills, and no way to successfully enter the adult world of work or post-secondary education. Parents began questioning the segregation that had become synonymous with special education, as well as the lack of real learning in segregated environments.

Today, some parents continue to believe that segregation is fine; others are at the opposite end of the spectrum, they want their children included in regular ed classes. In the middle are parents who support a combination of specialized services in the resource room and visitation to regular classrooms for art, PE, or music. Regardless of their positions however, few are totally satisfied with their children's education.

BARRIERS TO INCLUSIVE PRACTICES

If the philosophy of inclusion has been in the law for the past twenty-five years, why is it so hard to make it happen? We may think the problem stems from the school's special ed policies. Other times, we're told the school doesn't have the money to "do inclusion." Some of us may feel our children continue to be excluded because of inaccurate assessments. But these are probably not the real reasons our children are not included.

What happens in most IEP meetings is driven not by the law, funding, or a child's educational plan. Instead, the personal attitudes, beliefs, and values of educators, along with the internal politics of the school or the district, are the dynamics that drive the meeting and its outcome. I estimate about 95 percent of what really goes on in an IEP meeting has little or nothing to do with your child, and everything to do with these other factors.

Some of us may know there's more going on in an IEP meeting than a discussion of our child's education. We feel or see undercurrents that create tensions which lead to disagreements. But because we're so emotionally involved in the situation, we're unable to view the situation with detached coolness. Our hearts rule. We often react with anger, fueling an already volatile situation. We're often unable to let our sensible minds see what's really behind the rationales presented to us.

Many of the barriers to inclusion are rooted in the beliefs and actions of educators. But the actions and beliefs of parents also have a significant effect. Let's look at some of the dynamics that influence IEP meetings.

Dual Systems of Education

In schools that are not practicing inclusion, sharp lines often divide regular and special education. Our children pay a price for the lack of cooperation between these dual systems of education. Classroom teachers, school administrators, and other staff members generally do not see children with disabilities as equal members of the school community: they "belong" to the special ed teachers. It's no wonder regular education teachers are often reluctant to assume any leadership roles in moving schools toward inclusion. They don't see themselves as part of the special education equation.

There are several things at work here. In the majority of colleges and universities, teacher training is, itself, segregated: student teachers going into special education are educated one way and are deemed the "experts" on children with disabilities. Regular education student teachers aren't taught, nor are they expected to know, very much about kids with disabilities. (Teachers and parents with experience in inclusion have learned, however, that a good teacher is a good teacher, who can teach children with disabilities even if she knows nothing about special education!)

Classroom teachers believe they aren't competent to teach kids with disabilities, because they haven't received specialized training. Exceptions to this antiquated method of educating future teachers are being made: Syracuse University in New York changed its programs to ensure all teachers are competent to teach all children.

Overall, the segregation of students with disabilities begins in the minds of teachers. Whether a teacher received her teaching certificate twenty-five years ago or day before yesterday, most educators see themselves as either special educators or regular educators and few are willing to cross the line that divides them.

The manner in which state education departments certify teachers can create artificial barriers. For example, a special ed teacher who is certified to teach students labeled "severe and profound" may not be allowed to teach students labeled "mild." Thus, even within the special ed department, teachers and "their" students are categorized and separated. If teachers are divided into categories, is it any wonder students are, too?

Loss of Identity

Educators share the same feelings common to most of us. They want to protect what's theirs, feel what they do is important, put their training to good use, and be respected for their hard work. When the line between regular and special education becomes blurred—as it does with inclusion—some special educators may feel threatened. The turf they previously owned is no longer exclusively theirs.

Special educators, having invested many years in the specialization paradigm, may be unwilling to let go of the old ways of thinking and doing. Some feel inclusive education means not only the loss of stature for special education teachers, but also the outright loss of their careers: "If all the kids with disabilities are in regular classroom, and there's no longer a special ed room, what will I do?"

Because they haven't taken the time to investigate inclusion (or because they don't want to take the risks of doing something different), they don't realize their expertise is still a vital component in inclusive education. They don't understand they'll be needed more than ever; their roles will simply change. They'll become teachers of teachers, helping classroom teachers learn specific skills and strategies; they'll become co-teachers with regular education teachers in the classroom; they'll be valuable consultants to their entire school communities; and more. The sky's the limit for those willing to brave this new world.

Turf Wars

Turf issues are powerful motivators that help maintain the status quo of exclusion and separation. Classroom teachers feel underpaid and overworked. Their classes are too large. Worries about weapons and drugs adds insult to injury. They want their jobs to be less stressful, not more.

When classroom teachers are having difficulty with typical students, they often call for "back-up" in the form of the special ed teachers. A typical child whose behavior is "disruptive," who doesn't perform "at grade level," or who displays any number of unacceptable characteristics is perceived to need special education services. Classroom teachers may not take the time to figure out what might be causing the "problem." They don't think they can handle the situation alone, they don't feel they have the time, and/or they might feel angry at the student for causing disruptions. It's easier to hand the "problem" off to special ed.

If regular educators don't feel they can handle typical students with "problems," they surely don't believe they can handle the additional work and accompanying stress of a "special ed" student. And some classroom teachers simply don't want the additional responsibilities of the student with a disability, the accompanying paperwork, and all the other details of special education: "That's not my job! That's what the specialists are here for! They don't pay me enough as it is!"

Just like special educators, most classroom teachers have not investigated best practices in inclusion to learn that the addition of a child with a disability also means additional support in the classroom. And this support can help the teacher with her entire class, not just the child with a disability. Teachers who have had success with inclusion often welcome students with disabilities in their classrooms, for they've learned the extra help makes teaching easier and more fun.

In some schools, a classroom teacher may feel competent to assist a student, but decides to call in the specialists for political reasons. If she tries to handle a difficult situation on her own, she may risk starting a turf war if she doesn't call in the special ed troops.

Internal Politics

In addition to the special ed vs. regular ed turf issues, schools—like most other organizations—are rife with internal politics that profoundly influence day-to-day operations. A variety of power struggles and unofficial hierarchies lurk behind the benevolent facade of many schools.

If you've been unsuccessful in advocating for inclusion, there's a good chance the failure occurred because you were caught in the cross-fire of the internal politics within the school building or the district. It's possible the reasons you were given—little Johnny's not ready, the teacher isn't ready, or there's not enough money—are convenient excuses. The real reasons you were unsuccessful might have been because the principal was mad at the special ed director, the special ed teacher doesn't like the classroom teacher, or over-sized egos got in the way of common sense, cooperation, and legal mandates. The power of internal politics should never be underestimated.

In a mid-sized school district, several special and regular educators at one elementary school admired the inclusive practices at another elementary school in the district. They spent a great deal of time talking with the principal and teachers at the inclusive school, learning how they could successfully and quickly implement the same strategies in their school. When they discussed the proposal with their principal, Mr. Jones, he waved them away with, "Oh, we'll eventually do inclusion in our school, but we'll do it our way. There's no need for us to copy someone else's methods. I'm sure we can do it better when the time is right."

The teachers argued there was no reason to reinvent the wheel. Mr. Jones adamantly refused to even consider their request. The educators strongly suspected the principal's ego and professional jealously were standing in the way of progress. The principal at the inclusive school was known for a variety of innovative educational practices. Mr. Jones consistently rejected any and all ideas implemented by the progressive principal.

In this case, general and special educators wanted to do inclusion, but their principal's ego stood in the way. There are as many barriers to inclusion as there are people who don't support it.

Inclusion and Resource Rooms Don't Mix

Many parents and educators are discovering that under the present structure of most schools, it's almost impossible to practice inclusion while simultaneously maintaining a resource room or other special program, for one simple reason: special education teachers can't be in two places at once.

When we're unsuccessful at achieving inclusion for our children, educators give us a variety of rationales to justify their position:

- Your child is not ready.
- The regular ed teachers are not ready.
- Your child's needs are best met in the resource room.
- We don't do that at this school.
- Your child *is* included!

I'm sure you could add to this list. Some educators truly believe these justifications. Others know they're on the edge of deception, but they're unwilling to give the real reasons. You'll see why in a moment.

Successful inclusion requires support in the regular education classroom for students with disabilities and their classroom teachers. And support can mean anything, depending on the individual needs of the student, the abilities and/or needs of the classroom teacher, and the environment of the classroom. Support could mean a special ed teacher is in the classroom for parts of the day. A classroom teacher might need support in modifying the curriculum and adjusting lesson plans. It could also mean teachers integrate new methods of instruction in the classroom via co-teaching, cooperative learning groups, activity centers, and so forth. Support might mean providing a student with small group instruction, adaptive equipment or materials, alternative methods of testing, or something else.

Let's say Beverly and Jim want their son, Jared, included in regular education classes throughout the day. Currently, he "visits" art, PE, and music classes, but he spends most of the day in the resource room. This elementary school has two resource rooms, each staffed by a special ed teacher and a paraprofessional assistant. No students with disabilities are fully included in regular classrooms. Most have schedules similar to Jared's.

For Jared to be successfully included in Mrs. Tanner's regular ed classroom, one of the special ed teachers and/or one of the paraprofessionals will be needed to assist both Jared and Mrs. Tanner in a variety of ways. Seems simple, but it's not. When a special ed teacher or a para is in Mrs. Tanner's room, one of the resource rooms is understaffed.

But what if a special ed teacher or para is not needed *in the classroom?* Mrs. Tanner only needs help modifying the curriculum for Jared and learning some specific strategies to assist him; she could work on this while her students are in art or music. But this won't work either, because the special ed teacher must find time to perform the needed tasks. While she's doing this, the resource room is understaffed.

Because many parents are not well-connected to their children's schools, they often don't know how schools work, what resources and assets are available, and which teachers do what. Like Beverly and Jim, many parents don't know what it would take to make inclusion work, and about the different components that need to be in place to ensure Jared's inclusion is successful. Many educators don't know either unless they're very creative and open minded and/or they've already successfully included other children. And there's no way for Beverly and Jim to brainstorm ideas with other members of the IEP team, for the conversations at the meetings never even get that far.

Educators believe Jared can't be included in Mrs. Tanner's room because there is no one to provide support. A special ed teacher or para can't do it, because they're needed in the resource rooms all day. Under the current operating procedures at this school, no children with disabilities could be included in regular classrooms all day because there are no extra people to provide support. An exception could be made only if neither the child nor the classroom teacher needed support of any kind from the special ed department. Educators believe students cannot be included until additional people are hired, but that won't happen because they "just don't have the money."

The IEP team probably won't reveal all this to Jared's parents. If they did, they would be guilty of deciding placement based on funding. This goes against the spirit and intent of IDEA. Instead, Beverly and Jim will be told an assortment of reasons why the special ed room continues to be appropriate: Jared's not ready, his behavior hasn't improved enough, he can't do the grade level work, and so on, and so on, and so on.

Jared will remain segregated and isolated because educators feel they don't have the staff to support a resource room and inclusion. They're unwilling or unable to see alternatives to their current practices. However, as I'll describe in Chapter 17, inclusion can be implemented without additional funds, if schools creatively reallocate existing resources.

Parent-Educator Tensions

As children, we grew up under the influence and power of the public school system. As adults, the perceptions we have of schools were created and shaped by our experiences as children, by what we learned from our parents' attitudes, and from society in general. If we had positive experiences as students, we probably have positive views of the public school system as adults. And negative experiences would lead to negative perceptions. For purposes of this discussion, I'll assume most parents started out with positive attitudes towards schools.

When our children started school, we trusted teachers and saw them as good people who cared about their students. We saw them as allies who would help our children be successful. But negative experiences during the IEP process shatters our positive attitude and trust is broken. The hope we felt for our children is endangered. We were counting on educators to help our children. The people we thought we could trust are no longer our allies. What will happen to our children? We become fearful, angry, and pessimistic. The stage is set for ongoing parent-educator tensions. We develop an "us vs. them" mentality. We see educators as our enemies.

Most of us don't realize the problems we're facing are only the tip of the iceberg. We can only see what's in front of us, here and now: a troubled realtionship with educators. But there's a long history of relationships between parents and educators that impacts your current situation.

Within a given school community we can find all types of parents of kids with disabilities. Some are happy with the status quo of segregated services. Many are agitating for changes that will lead to inclusion. And others fall somewhere in the middle.

Because all parents are not of one mind, school personnel often feel buffeted to and fro trying to get along with them. Let's say ten parents are happy with the education their children are receiving in the segregated special ed room. If the parents are happy, educators feel they must be doing a good job and that makes them happy.

But there are seven or eight parents who want more services or inclusion or something else the school isn't providing. This diverse group of parents is very unhappy. Educators discover that what worked with the happy group of parents isn't working with the unhappy ones. "What gives?" they think. "What's wrong with the parents who are unhappy? Why are they so hard to get along with? Why aren't they grateful, appreciative, and satisfied with what we're doing for their children?"

All this might be happening to you right now, but similar situations have occurred since the day your child's school opened its doors. Your relationship with educators didn't start from scratch, even though it may feel like it to you. Educators have been dealing with parents who came before you, and those relationships (good and bad) impact you, now.

Parents impact educators, who in turn, impact other parents. If you want an inclusive setting for your child, but all the other parents in the school are pleased as punch with the segregated resource room setting, you're the odd one out. The happy parents have been sending positive spoken and unspoken messages to educators; messages the educators like. Educators perceive that you, on the other hand, are sending negative messages and these messages don't feel good to the educators. Because they're human, they react negatively (just as we might), as demonstrated in the following examples.

The special ed teacher who has proudly spent her life in the resource room feels your wishes for inclusion are a slap in the face. In her mind, your desire to keep your child out of her classroom is insulting: you're saying she doesn't know what she's doing, what she's doing is wrong, that you think you know more than her, and so on.

To the principal who doesn't support inclusion, you're a busybody trying to dictate how the school will be run. If the principal doesn't want inclusion at her school, there's no rationale you can provide that will make it happen. "That mom is just trying to force us to do this to prove she's got power. I don't let my teachers tell me what to do, so I'm sure not going to let a parent do it! I'll show her who's in charge!" she thinks.

The special ed director who has been running the department for years is outraged and disgusted by one more parent who's trying to push this "inclusion stuff" down his throat. He knows the law, this is his department, and the majority of other parents over the years have appreciated his hard work. "Who does this ungrateful upstart think she is, wanting inclusion? Why can't she be happy like all the other parents?" he thinks.

To parents who don't support inclusion, you're a threat. Your desire for inclusion and rejection of segregation suggests what they have been doing is wrong. They can't support your efforts: doing so would discredit their own actions, attitudes, and values.

These examples are, of course, generalizations and oversimplifications. But still, they're representative of the undercurrents that produce tension and prevent inclusion in many schools.

We like to think educators always maintain a professional posture, but they have prejudices, beliefs, and experiences that drive their actions, just as we do. If educators have had negative experiences with parents in the past, they may not come into an IEP meeting with an open mind. They may be prejudging you: "Those Down's kids' parents are the hardest to deal with," an educator thinks. Or you may be prejudged in a more specific way: "There's no way I'll approve that communication device this mom wants. We went through this with that other mom last year and it was a mess," the special ed director thinks.

The negative experiences educators had with parents who came before us can affect how educators see and treat us. The human component is a powerful force, greater than any law and any principle.

MYTHS THAT BLOCK INCLUSIVE EDUCATION

Many educators—teachers, principals, special ed directors—reject inclusion outright. They continue to defy the national movement toward inclusion, based on myths that (pick one or more): inclusion is too costly, it "takes away" from typical kids, regular ed teachers aren't yet "ready," students with disabilities aren't "ready," or any number of the zillions of other misconceptions.

Seldom does the governing body of a school district—the school board—ever get involved in the issue of inclusion. And, typically, it can take as few as one or two people in a district to prevent a school or an entire district from practicing inclusion. Similarly, one or two people can also be responsible for making it happen.

But there are two specific beliefs—myths that parents and educators accept as conventional wisdom—that create barriers to the successful inclusion of children with disabilities. It's time to dispel these myths.

Myth #1: A Student with a Disability Needs an Aide

This myth has caused great problems for a great many people, most especially the student. Sometimes the school demands an aide for a student: "Yes, Tommy can be included in the regular classroom but only if he has a paraprofessional with him at all times."

The parents agree and Tommy is now in a regular classroom. If the parents disagree, however, inclusion is not an option and Tommy stays in a special ed room.

Sometimes the *parents* demand an aide for their child: "Hannah must have an aide in the regular classroom to help her [do this and that and the other]." If the school agrees, everything is hunky-dory. If they disagree, Hannah's placement might be in the special ed room for most of the day, with "visitation" in art, PE, or music.

But students don't need aides, teachers and classrooms do. Many parents, in describing their child's education, have told me about their child needing an aide. When I point out the aide should "belong" to the teacher and not the child, many parents respond with "Yeah, well, whatever—" as if it doesn't matter. But it *does* matter. In both philosophy and in practice, it matters a great deal.

When the philosophy of a school or a classroom is that a student needs an aide, it's assumed the aide is responsible for the student: academically, behaviorally, and in many other ways. The classroom teacher is responsible for the twenty-something other students in the classroom, but not that kid. He belongs to the aide. The message is clear to everyone, including Michael, his teachers, and his classmates: Michael is *in* the classroom, but he's not part of it. This is not inclusion. We could call it integration or mainstreaming, perhaps, since the student is physically in the classroom. But he's not included because he's not really part of the class; he doesn't belong.

In practice, when the aide is assigned to the student instead of the teacher, the aide and the student are often "attached at the hip." In some schools, they call the aide a "shadow," since she shadows the child everywhere he goes and in everything he does.

What child would ever want a grown-up following him around all day? What child *needs* a grown-up with him all day? When we (parents or educators) insist that a student needs an aide, we're presuming the student is incompetent. We're also laying the "problem" of disability in the child's lap. The aide, then, is expected to help solve or manage the child's so-called problems. We might also be saying the classroom teacher is incompetent if we believe she can't "handle" the needs of the child.

If, however, the school's policy is that an aide is assigned to the classroom teacher, it's assumed the teacher takes responsibility for the student with the disability, just as she does with other students. Her behavior toward the child with the disability reflects the attitude that he is an equal member of the class, and he's expected to do well, participate in class activities, and take responsibility for his learning.

In this scenario, the classroom teacher directs the paraprofessional to help the student with a disability as necessary, not all the time. The child receives support and assistance not only from the para, but from the classroom teacher, other professionals, and his classmates. The actions of the classroom teacher and the paraprofessional convey the attitude that she (the para) is there to help the teacher and the classroom (in whatever way the teacher directs), not just the one student with a disability. All of these actions by the teacher are a determining factor in whether or not the child is really included—if he truly belongs.

When the Aide Belongs to the Student

Let's look at an example. If Ms. Aide is assigned to Shawn, what are the ramifications and messages of the situation? Because Ms. Aide "belongs" to Shawn, it means Shawn also "belongs" to Ms. Aide. They quickly become an inseparable pair, with Ms. Aide taking responsibility for Shawn.

Ms. Teacher, the regular ed teacher, doesn't need to concern herself with Shawn since Ms. Aide is there. After all, Ms. Teacher has twenty-something other students to worry about. As a result, Ms. Teacher doesn't get to know Shawn, she probably won't know anything about his learning style or how to help him, and she might not even know what Shawn and Ms. Aide do all day. Because Ms. Teacher has little to do with Shawn, she cannot model appropriate, positive interactions with him.

The other students don't have a clue about how to connect with Shawn. The only interaction they observe is a dependent relationship between Ms. Aide and Shawn. It's very likely Shawn is viewed as an "outsider:" he's physically in the same classroom, but he's not a participant in classroom activities.

There's a good chance Ms. Aide will sit next to Shawn all day, helping him with everything whether he needs it or not. The two of them might even sit in the back of the classroom—away from the other students—so their conversations don't disturb the rest of the class. Again, even though Shawn is in the classroom, he's not part of it. He's not included. Ms. Aide becomes very protective of Shawn. She might even start doing his work for him, instead of helping him do it. Shawn is learning a great deal from Ms. Aide: he's learning all about dependency.

Shawn is probably also learning whatever Ms. Aide decides to teach him, or whatever she thinks he can learn. This may or may not be what's in his IEP, and it may bear no correlation to what his classmates are doing. What does he have in common with them? He's in their presence, but shares nothing.

Because Ms. Aide is always so close to Shawn, the other kids stay away. Shawn has little or no chance of developing friendships, of learning how to ask other kids for help, or of helping other kids, because Ms. Aide is always in the way. Shawn's mother might as well go to school with him every day—that's what it's like when an adult is your "shadow." The other kids don't see Shawn as a regular kid, even though he is in a regular classroom. He's a "special kid in a regular class." He's seen as needy, odd, different, incapable. He's not really a part of this class—he's an outsider. Who wants to be friends with him?

Ms. Teacher is like many teachers: she doesn't really like having other adults in her classroom. Teachers become accustomed to autonomy, to solely controlling what happens in the classroom. In this case, Ms. Teacher tolerates the intrusion of another adult because Ms. Aide and Shawn are pretty much invisible. And since Ms. Aide is there Ms. Teacher doesn't have to take responsibility for Shawn.

When Shawn's mother wants to find out how Shawn's doing, Ms. Teacher directs her to Ms. Aide. And if Ms. Aide is ever out sick, look out! Disaster strikes since Ms. Teacher doesn't know what to do.

When the Aide Belongs to the Teacher

Now let's look at Melissa in an inclusive classroom, where Ms. Para, the teacher's assistant, "belongs" to Mrs. Educator, the classroom teacher. Mrs. Educator is responsible for every student in her class, including Melissa. Mrs. Educator takes the time to get to know Melissa, just as she does the other students. She expects Melissa to participate in class and she models positive interactions with Melissa so the other students will learn that Melissa is an equally valuable member of the class.

Mrs. Educator, Ms. Para, the special ed teacher, and Melissa work together to determine when and how Melissa needs extra assistance. Sometimes Ms. Para provides one-on-one, sometimes Mrs. Educator or the special ed teacher does. Often, Mrs. Educator divides the class and she and Ms. Para or the special ed teacher each work with half the class. In this way, Melissa gets the help she needs and all the students receive the benefits of a smaller student-teacher ratio.

A hallmark of Mrs. Educator's class is cooperative learning groups. Children work in small groups across many subject areas. They're not grouped by ability, but by diversity. They're all expected to help one another, including Melissa. She participates alongside her friends.

Melissa is helped not only by the two adults in the classroom, but also by her classmates. Katie helps Melissa take her coat off and hang it up when she arrives at school. Nicole sits next to Melissa during reading time and helps her learn new words. This is not unusual, though, for everyone in the class is expected to help everyone else. Melissa is not singled out as being the only student who needs assistance. During these times, Ms. Para often helps other children.

Like everyone else in the class, sometimes Melissa struggles when learning new things. That's part of life. No one steps in to do her work for her. She's learning—really learning. Mrs. Educator uses her monthly lesson plans as a guide for modifying Melissa's curriculum. She plans ahead and gets help from Ms. Para and the special education teacher in adapting the curriculum to meet Melissa's needs.

When Melissa needs to go to the restroom, Ms. Para helps out. But Mrs. Educator, as well as one of the school secretaries and a couple of other teachers also know what to do if Ms. Para is not available.

At first, Mrs. Educator didn't know if she'd like having another adult in the classroom most of the day. But she loves it now. Ms. Para helps her not only with Melissa, but with all the kids, especially the two boys who always seem to get into trouble. Not only that, Ms. Para provides assistance to Mrs. Educator in other areas, such as grading papers, taking playground duty, and other routine tasks. What a blessing to have her!

Students, Teachers, and Classrooms Need Support

Inclusion means providing supports for the student, the teacher, and the classroom. Support for the student must be provided in ways that promote equality and participation, not dependency and exclusion. When educators or parents insist on assigning an aide to the student, all bets on real inclusion—and belonging—are off.

Every classroom teacher my son had in elementary school had an assistant. The Melissa scenario was very similar to the real-life situations in several of my son's classes. At the beginning of every school year, I told the teacher and the teacher's aide (TA), "Before you do anything for Benjamin yourself, first see if a classmate can do it." Why should the teacher or the TA always help Benjamin with his coat and other things? His classmates helped. That's what friends are for. At home, I'm not my son's maid. I regularly yell, "Emily, come help your brother!" Likewise, we expect Benjamin to help us.

A teacher's assistant—one that truly supports the classroom teacher in creating an inclusive classroom—can provide great benefits to children with disabilities, the classroom, and the teacher. Everyone wins.

Myth #2: Pull-Out Services are Necessary and Beneficial

When parents want their children included in regular classrooms, the issue of related services (especially therapies) and other pull-out activities often becomes a real dilemma. For purposes of this discussion, let's define pull-out services as physical, occupational, speech, and other therapeutic interventions, as well as specialized help in any subject area (reading, math, etc.). Three different scenarios will be presented, followed by observations about the positive and negative impacts of these interventions.

The experiences of many parents demonstrates a distinct correlation between related services (delivered via the traditional pull-out method) and inclusion. In general, the more related services, the less inclusion; the fewer related services, the more inclusion.

Resource Room Scenario: When children are segregated in a special ed room (resource room or whatever your school calls it) for most of the day, the delivery of related services presents no problems. The therapist or other specialist goes into the room and does "group activities." She may also pull certain kids aside, to a corner of the room for one-on-one.

Pseudo-Inclusive Classroom Scenario: In some so-called inclusive schools or classrooms, children with disabilities stay in the regular classroom most of the day, but get pulled out for therapies or specialized help in academic subjects. They might be taken to the empty gym for physical therapy (PT), out in the hallway for occupational therapy (OT), to a special room for speech therapy (ST), or to the special ed room for help with math. Sometimes they're given one-on-one attention. Often, however, the professional roams the hallways like the Pied Piper, taking one kid out of this room, two out of that one, and so on, and soon a parade is making its way to the special room for group help.

One dilemma in this model of service delivery is that many children are out of the regular ed classroom as much as they're in. Children who receive many different types of specialized help may be pulled out several times a day or many times in a week. This creates several problems. Being pulled out of class has great stigma attached to it. It fairly screams, "Stupid!" Classmates don't have a clue where this kid is going or for what purpose. It often appears to be very secretive. Is he getting punished, rewarded, or what? The whispered "He's going to the 'retard' room," has been heard more than once by students who are being pulled out. Children who are pulled out often lose the status of being "regular kids" in the eyes of their classmates. Opportunities for making friends are diminished, and children are more likely to be excluded and teased.

In my daughter's third grade class, a classmate was pulled out several times a day. (The teachers would have preferred the student receive help in the classroom. But the boy's parents insisted he be pulled out for specialized assistance.) One day I asked Emily how Brian was doing. "Who?" she asked me. "Brian," I repeated, "you know, Brian with the blonde hair and glasses?" "Oh, him," she responded, "I guess he's okay. He's not really in our class, you know, the teachers always take him somewhere else." Emily was not being malicious; she was simply stating her perception, a belief that was held by her classmates. It was hard for Brian to make friends. Being together all day long—during academics, recess, lunch, gym, art, music—facilitates friendships through shared experiences. Everyone belongs. But Brian was perceived as a visitor; he didn't share the familiarity and experiences of belonging.

When a child is pulled out, the classroom teacher has no idea what or how he's doing and learning. This discontinuity becomes pervasive, until the classroom teacher is totally out of touch with the student. Classroom teachers may eventually feel like my daughter did: "He doesn't really belong."

When a child is pulled out for therapy, she's missing whatever is going on in the classroom. While her body parts are being worked on in the gym, is she missing science or math? If so, what provisions are in place to help her keep up with the academics she's missing? What's really more important? A little bit of therapy or continuity in learning?

Another dilemma of pull-out therapy is the question of effectiveness. When children are taught skills in isolated settings, can they generalize these skills into their whole day? For example, an OT might have a child stack blocks or string beads or perform some other activity to build fine motor skills, increase finger and hand dexterity, and the like. Brittany might be expected to perform such activities (in therapy vernacular) with 80 percent accuracy, 90 percent of the time, in the special ed room with the OT present. (Gag!)

But how do these skills actually help Brittany throughout her school day? These are not skills that are useful to the fourth-grader. So why are these activities on Brittany's IEP? Why did the therapist write such goals? Because most therapists use both the medical and the get-ready models, that's why. The therapist may assume that (1) because Brittany is unable to use her hands in a "normal" way, she must ensure that Brittany develops her fine motor skills in a sequential fashion and (2) until Brittany has mastered these activities, she's "not ready" to learn how write with a pencil or do other things that fourth-graders do.

How do stacking blocks and stringing beads help Brittany use a pencil? Therapists assume this treatment is effective because they've been trained that way. What if, instead of stacking blocks and stringing beads, Brittany's therapist helped her parents and the classroom teacher find large pencils, or adapted smaller pencils by using large grips that Brittany could grasp easier? What if they let Brittany hold the pencil any way she could, instead of forcing her to practice fine motor skills in an attempt to teach her to hold the pencil the "right way"? What if, instead of pulling Brittany out, the therapist assisted Brittany during computer lab time or writing and penmanship time? She could help Brittany learn to write using a drawing program on the computer with the mouse as the pencil. In reality, except for signing one's name on a check, how important is handwriting in today's world? With computers, how much handwriting do any of us really do anymore?

If Brittany is unable to write the "correct" way, the therapist may decide Brittany isn't "trying hard enough" or "doesn't have the ability." But does anyone question the methods used to help Brittany, her interest in therapy, or the relevance of therapeautic activities to Brittany? Does anyone use common sense?

When parents closely examine school-related therapies, many realize their children are not transferring skills learned in isolation to the overall school day. Stacking blocks, stringing beads, climbing stairs, rolling on a scooter board, and almost all types of therapeutic activities taught in isolation have little or no relevance to children's education.

The Inclusive Classroom Scenario: In truly inclusive classrooms, students stay in the classroom all day and services are brought to them. If Tom needs extra help in math, the special ed teacher or other specialist comes to the classroom during math time and provides assistance to Tom in the least intrusive method available. Instead of focusing only on Tom, the special ed teacher might have Tom and a few other students who need assistance all work together as a group within the classroom. There's no stigma that's attached to Tom in this instance, and Tom benefits from receiving extra help in the company of his peers. In fact, other students might even ask to join the group when they see the advantages of small-group assistance. Because his curriculum has been modified appropriately, Tom does much of his work independently.

Tom needs PT assistance, so the therapist provides services in the setting that's most appropriate and relevant to Tom: during PE class. Sometimes she collaborates with the gym teacher to modify activities; at other times she physically helps Tom perform various exercises alongside his classmates.

How Valuable is Therapy in School?

In examining the myth that therapy is always necessary and beneficial, I propose that most therapies provided in public school are not worth all the fighting parents must endure to get them. Because parents view therapy as beneficial and because IDEA entitles students to therapies (as decided by the IEP team), they assume therapy in school is valuable.

If our children have been receiving private therapy over the summer, for example, and the amount of this private therapy will be reduced once school starts (because there's not enough hours in the day), parents may try to replace private therapy with therapy at school. Children who are not diagnosed until their elementary school years (those with ADD, LD, or similar conditions) may have never had any type of therapy and all this is new to parents. In any case, parents may gladly accept any help offered by the school district or they may demand every service their child is entitled to, without weighing the pros and cons.

When Congress included related services in IDEA, the intention was good, but the implementation has always been poor. The therapeutic interventions allowed under IDEA are not intended as replacement for private therapy; they're intended to enable the child to benefit from his educational experience. But they often do the opposite. Therapy in school often diminishes a child's learning opportunities, especially if a student is pulled out for therapy and misses academics in the classroom.

In addition, school therapists (like private therapists) usually subscribe to the deficit model. The focus is on fixing the "problem," instead of enhancing the child's education.

Seldom does a child's IEP reflect the amount and/or type of therapy requested by parents. Educators or therapists tell us there are too many children who need services, so everyone is limited in what they get. Parents have learned to ask for more than they really want, knowing the school will offer less. We often spend a great deal of energy arguing with educators about therapy.

Parents may be pleased if their child ends up with two half-hour PT sessions a week, believing these will be similar to the two half-hour sessions with the private PT. Guess what? They aren't.

Many parents have extraordinary misconceptions of what school therapy looks like. Because they're familiar with private therapy, they may believe school therapy is similar.

And because most haven't visited the school while their children are receiving therapy, they never know what's really going on. If they did, many would say, "Thanks, but no thanks" to therapy in school.

Pull-out related services, as described previously, may be one-on-one or group therapy. In either case, what are children missing in the classroom when they're pulled out? How do they make up the academics they miss? Is the amount or the quality of the therapy worth what children are missing academically and socially in the classroom?

If your child is receiving therapy at school, is it group or individual? Have you asked? Have you visited the therapy sessions to see what they're like? At your child's IEP meeting, the therapist probably didn't chime in with, "During the two therapy sessions each week, Kendall will be with four other students. Subtracting the time it takes to round them up and get them back to class, the group will actually get about fifteen minutes of therapy each session, so individually, each child will receive about three minutes of therapy." How much therapy is your child really getting?

In a group therapy setting, are five children doing five different things or are they all doing the same thing? If they're all doing different things, how much attention can the therapist give each of them? If they're all doing the same thing, how individualized can the therapy be?

When you take your child to private therapy, you have an appointment. That time is your child's and the therapist is focused only on her. School therapy is incredibly different. Real-life stories tell the tale: therapists call in sick and no replacement is provided; when a substitute is provided, continuity is lost and children don't respond well to strangers; therapists take maternity leave and no replacement is provided for months, if at all; therapists run late, so they shorten therapy time to get back on schedule; therapists "forget" your child on one or more days; they change the schedule without telling anyone; teachers schedule a class activity during your child's therapy time, so therapy is missed and not made up; teachers and aides tell the therapist what they think she should be working on, so the game plan from the IEP is changed; and on and on and on.

Is Therapy Relevant to Your Child and Her Learning?

The most important issue about therapy is not whether your child is getting the full amount she's entitled to. What's most important is whether therapy is relevant to your child. Is it meaningful to her? Does she feel there's a purpose to it? And can she generalize the skill or activity into other areas of her school day?

Does therapy help a child acquire real skills that are useful to her in the classroom? Does the therapy enable her to learn more, learn more effectively, and/or learn what's important to her? If therapy doesn't enhance a child's success in school, why are we doing it?

If therapy activities are not relevant to the child, therapy will not be effective. In pull-out therapy sessions, students often do purposeless activities in isolation. If a child can stack seven one-inch cubes ten times in a row, how does that skill help her in school? Is therapy actually beneficial? Following is a a composite of several true stories.

Kristin is happily engaged in her regular education class when the therapist pulls her out for therapy. Now Kristin is unhappy; she doesn't want to stop what she's doing in the classroom. She's not a robot that can be turned on and off. Is she motivated to cooperate with the therapist? Probably not. Will she do well in therapy today? Probably not. Does she care about therapy? Probably not.

In this situation—and thousands of other situations repeated daily—therapy is not relevant to the child. Kristin sees no value in it. It's not important. Will therapy prove beneficial to her under these circumstances? Probably not. Finally, are the benefits of this therapy session—if there are any—greater than the benefits Kristin is missing in the classroom?

The System is Flawed

The problem is not that therapists are bad; the problem is in the system. We cannot monitor everything that does or does not happen when our children are at school. And the IEP team is often not really a team at all. As I detailed earlier, there are turf issues that get in the way of teamwork. Maybe the therapist doesn't like the teacher or vice-versa; the principal only wants the therapist there during a certain part of the day; the therapist's case load (our kids) is too large; or—who knows?

During an IEP meeting, we like to believe everyone is working together. In most cases, however, once the meeting is over, everyone goes their separate ways; they may have little or nothing to do with one another until the next IEP meeting or until a crisis occurs. This is a team?

If the therapist doesn't show up for a day, a week, or a month, how do the parents know? They usually don't. In most cases, the teacher doesn't even know when the therapist is supposed to be there, so she has no way of knowing what's going on. Has anyone on the team been given the responsibility for keeping track of related services? If not, how will everyone know what's what?

The therapist often has little contact with the parents to begin with; with her busy schedule, there's no way she can call every parent every time she misses a session or is late for one. Also, if she calls the parents to tell them their child isn't getting the therapy as promised, the parents will probably yell at her; no way is she going to keep the parents posted!

The special ed teacher doesn't call the parents to let them know; she assumes the therapist takes care of that; if not the therapist, then surely the classroom teacher is handling it.

It would be nice if these descriptions were exaggerated, but they're not. While some parents have very positive experiences, the majority of parents experience the scenarios I've described far too often.

From Hands-On to Hands-Off (Consultation)

When Benjamin was in an inclusive first grade classroom, his teacher (Mrs. M) and I both agreed that he would not be pulled out for PT and OT—the therapists would serve him in the classroom—and we wanted the therapy to be relevant and meaningful to Benjamin. I did not want the therapists using the deficit model with Benjamin: identifying the problem and fixing it. Instead, I wanted them to help Benjamin learn to do things that would help him be successful in school.

While this should be the major consideration for every child receiving therapy in school, it's usually not. Because therapists often work from the deficit model, they write therapy goals that have little or no impact on the child's overall success at school. The focus is on body parts.

Mrs. M and I wanted the OT to help Benjamin improve his keyboarding and hand-writing skills. We already knew a computer keyboard would be Benjamin's pencil and paper. While we wanted him to be able to hand write his name, we recognized that handwriting was not the most effective way for him to do schoolwork.

We wanted the PT to focus on things like helping Benjamin learn to transfer from his walker to a desk chair. In addition, we wanted the PT to help with environmental issues of the classroom, such as identifying the best placement for furniture to accommodate Benjamin's movement through the room using his walker and wheelchair, as well as other issues pertaining to Benjamin's independent mobility at school.

Well! This was not at all what the therapists had in mind. The PT wanted to pull Benjamin out and have him walk up and down the stairs to strengthen his legs so he could learn to walk without his walker. The OT simply wanted to help Benjamin "improve his fine motor control." (What exactly does that mean, anyway?)

I told the PT that going up and down the stairs would not be relevant to Benjamin. I explained that he would "buy it" the first time, because he would think he was going up-stairs to the library or the cafeteria. But as soon as he realized he was going upstairs only to go right back down again, he'd balk.

I also explained that learning to walk wasn't the most important thing in the world. Her eyes got real big as I said, "If Benjamin walks, that's fine, if he doesn't, that's fine, too. If Benjamin uses a wheelchair all his life, he can still have a great life. But if he's not educated he won't have a great life. I don't want Benjamin pulled out of class to walk up the stairs. While he's doing that, he'll be missing academics. If you believe strengthening his legs is important for him in transferring, you can work on that only if you make it relevant and meaningful to Benjamin. Do therapy during recess time and help him climb the ladder to the slide. You'll get the same effect as having him walk up the stairs in the building. And he'll like doing that, because after he gets to the top of the slide, he'll have fun sliding down." The PT agreed.

The OT then explained how she would like to take Benjamin to another room (a combination office, storeroom, testing room) to work with manipulatives to improve his fine motor skills. I politely reiterated my wishes that he not be pulled out of class and explained that we wanted her to work on keyboarding and handwriting skills. We suggested she help Benj at a time and in a way that was relevant and meaningful to him: when the class was working on writing. She reluctantly agreed.

Okay, it's a done deal. (We thought.) A few weeks of school went by and all was well. Then during the next three or four weeks, things started falling apart. Mrs. M let me know the OT missed a couple of sessions and was late for two more. On one occasion, when the OT arrived late, the class was doing math instead of writing, and she didn't know what to do. The OT walked up to Mrs. M as she was instructing the class, interrupted her, and asked, "Well, I guess we can't do writing since it's math time, so what do you want me to do?" Mrs. M told the OT she couldn't talk to her right at that moment. Later, Mrs. M said she couldn't believe this "professional therapist" didn't know how to adjust to the situation, and she was shocked the OT interrupted the whole class.

About the same time, the teacher's aide told me the PT was working on things we never discussed. In addition, the PT was showing the TA how to help Benjamin transfer using a method that was in direct opposition to the way I had taught the TA—a method Benjamin was accustomed to at home. I called an informal meeting (not an official IEP meeting) with the therapists and the teachers to discuss these issues.

The OT blew up first. She let us know that what we were asking her to do—helping Benj with keyboarding and handwriting skills—was not "therapy." Barely able to contain her anger, she said "Anybody can help him do those things! I'm supposed to do real therapy!"

I held firm and repeated what we wanted her to do. "I'm sorry," she said, "I just can't continue this. I want off the team." Then she stormed out of the room. Mrs. M and I turned to the PT and Mrs. M asked, "Do you want off the team, too?" The PT said no, but admitted she was also having difficulty with our requests. "What you want me to do isn't therapy. I feel like I'm cheating Benjamin by not doing what I think is right," she explained. "I understand your feelings," I replied. "Let Mrs. M and I think all this over for a few days and we'll figure something out."

Without even knowing it, the OT had said the magic words. She was absolutely right: *anyone* could help Benjamin learn keyboarding and handwriting skills. The teacher's aide and Mrs. M were already helping Benjamin with lots of things. And, because they were both with him every day, they knew Benjamin better than the therapists.

Mrs. M and I decided we didn't need either therapist to provide direct services anymore. Their visits to the classroom were often disruptive, Benjamin wasn't crazy about them, we always had to convince them to do what we thought was important, and they didn't have positive attitudes. Why should we continue with this situation?

We told the therapists we wanted their services on a consultation basis only, and asked if they would be willing to meet with the team (Mrs. M, the teacher's aide, the special ed teacher, and myself) once a month to answer questions, provide technical assistance, brainstorm, and so on. They both eagerly agreed. They were relieved we still needed them, but they were also glad to get out of an uncomfortable situation.

The teacher's aide (Ms. K) was already helping Benjamin with the computer throughout the day when he asked for help. It didn't take much for her to learn how to help him with the specifics of keyboarding skills and writing his name using hand-over-hand techniques. Having Mrs. K help him acquire these skills was the most natural thing in the world. Benjamin loved her, he hadn't really liked the therapists coming in anyway, and she was already more of an expert on how Benjamin moved in his walker and his wheelchair than the PT was.

We realized the actual time the therapists were in the classroom assisting Benjamin was a miniscule proportion of his entire school day. How much help was he really getting from them during those few minutes? When Ms. K, Mrs. M, and the special ed teacher learned strategies and techniques from the therapists (and me) at our monthly meetings, they could successfully implement them throughout Benjamin's day.

Even his classmates got into the act, helping in various ways. Several of them took it upon themselves to help Benjamin transfer from his walker to his wheelchair. Their encouraging words, friendship, and no-nonsense approach were just what Benjamin needed. With adults, he would sometimes whine and complain, but his friends would have none of that. He was far more motivated to interact with his friends than with interfering adults. The benefits to Benjamin, his classmates, and teachers were enormous.

From then on, Benjamin had no direct hands-on therapy in school. The therapists became consultants to his teachers; he received the benefits of the therapists' expertise indirectly and with greater effectiveness. The help he received in the classroom—throughout the day—from the teacher and the teacher's aide was relevant and meaningful to him.

Less Direct Services = More Inclusion

Providing related services should not impact a child's inclusion, but it does. IDEA does not mandate that children be removed from the regular educational environment for therapies and other related services. Pull-out services are simply a consequence of how schools implement special ed law in their policies and procedures.

Inclusion can become a reality, with children receiving the related services they need, if parents, educators, therapists, and others carefully consider what a child really needs to be successful and if members of the IEP team work creatively and collaboratively to meet the child's needs. Does a child need direct hands-on therapy to achieve an isolated, functional skill, or does he need assistance in the classroom that will help him throughout the day?

We must also keep the big picture in mind. Ten years from now, what will be more important to a child's success? The little bit of therapy he received in public school or the learning and belonging he experienced in an inclusive classroom?

TRADITIONAL SPECIAL ED ADVOCACY ROLES

In the special ed process, parents play the role of advocate, an incredibly important job. All parents have their own ideas about how best to advocate. Some of us are successful some of the time, others none of the time. The advocate role appears to be relatively simple: represent your child's interests and contribute your knowledge to the IEP process, as an equal member of the IEP team. However, most parents have learned, to their dismay, nothing is simple about the IEP process. And, as we've seen, there are a variety of dynamics that affect the process.

In my travels, hundreds of parents have shared their advocacy stories. Based on these stories, I've identified four primary profiles of the roles assumed by most parents. Many of us have evolved from one role to the next; some of us combine two or more roles into one; and others switch back and forth. The descriptions are not specific to advocacy in the public school domain however; they include behaviors we use in other areas of advocacy. Regardless of the positions we assume, few of us wield as much influence as we'd like.

Just-a-Mom (or Dad)

Most of us routinely start off in this category (I did). When our children are first diagnosed (or enter the special ed arena), everything is new and unfamiliar. We're quickly surrounded by professionals using jargon we don't understand. Initially, we're naive and unsure of ourselves. It's natural to respond with "I'm just a mom" (or something similar) when we're inundated with new information. Further, many professionals tell us (directly or indirectly), "Well, you're just a mom. We don't expect you to understand all this."

As we gain wisdom from personal experience, many of us move on to another role. But some of us choose—either consciously or unconsciously—to stay in this role and we exhibit a variety of traits.

"I'm just a mom," may be a plausible response when we don't understand something. But whiners and/or those of us who feel sorry for ourselves use this role as an excuse. Instead of admitting we don't understand something, asking for clarification, and taking a responsible role, we whine, "I'm just a mom. How did you expect me to understand that?"

Other times, we *choose* not to understand something because we don't agree with it. Instead of being honest and saying, "No," or negotiating an acceptable compromise, we try to weasel out of dealing with the situation by saying, "I'm just a mom, I don't understand."

Some of us stay in the Just-a-Mom role because moving out of it seems too difficult. We may have been told, "You're just a mom," so many times we really believe it. Perhaps we believe we can't handle the overwhelming responsibility.

In any event, our advocacy efforts in this role are usually unsuccessful because we're reactive instead of proactive. We float along reacting to what others are doing, buffeted by the ideas, recommendations, and power of others. We may be very unhappy with the way things are, but we just can't seem to find the means to improve the situation.

Many who stay in this position often end up feeling impotent and weak, then anger sets in when they feel victimized. The anger might be directed at the professionals. It might turn inward, where it rears its ugly head as guilt. It can be misdirected toward family members, including the child with the disability. In the best case scenario, the anger is controlled and it propels parents to move into another position for effective advocacy.

When we're in the Just-a-Mom state, our actions can put our children and our families in precarious positions. Often, a mom or a dad is the only person who is capable of seeing the child as a whole being. But when we let others take charge of our children's lives, and when we don't call on our courage and be proactive, the needs of our children and our families become lost in the shuffle.

Professional-Parent

We often move into this position from the Just-a-Mom stage. Sometimes the two positions overlap. When we're in the Professional-Parent role, we want experts to see us as professional peers. We're comfortable in our positions as advocates, we've learned to speak the jargon, and we form positive relationships with professionals. We respect the wisdom of professionals and work very hard to get all the services, supports, and interventions they recommend. Being an equal partner with professionals is important. Because we see professionals as the experts, we believe everything—or just about everything—we're told about our children and the recommended interventions. Sometimes we accept the conventional wisdom of professionals even when it goes against our intuition and common sense.

Within this position are those of us who are "professional therapy moms." We focus on remedies for our children's disabilities, based on the expertise and guidance of professionals. We often run helter-skelter to a variety of therapies, interventions, and other treatments, even though the schedule is detrimental to ourselves, our children, and our families. We come to believe doing the *most* for our children equals doing the best for them. (I've assumed this role.)

In this position, we often gauge our children's success by the opinions of professionals, instead of what we see with our own eyes and feel with our own hearts. When/if our child is not as successful as everyone believes she can be, therapies are increased, experimental treatments are tried, or other forms of intervention are added in the hope that "something will work, if we do it long enough and hard enough."

The effects on our children are potentially devastating: their childhoods evaporate before our eyes, as most of their days are spent receiving "treatments." Further, we're often not able to see them as our precious children anymore. They're body parts, minds, or behaviors that need improvement. At this point, we've internalized the medical/deficit model of thinking about our children. Our children quickly realize they're not "good enough" just the way they are.

Some of us stay in the Professional-Parent role forever. Some move in and out of it, depending on who the professionals are and what they're recommending. We may begin to reject the presumed expertise of professionals, especially when we're on the losing end and not getting what we believe our children need. At this point, we may move into the Mother- (or Father)-from-Hell position.

Mother-from-Hell

"I'm mad as hell and I'm not going to take it anymore," might be the mantra of parents in this category. (I've been here.) When we've had to argue with professionals about getting what we believe our children need, when we feel experts are treating us (and our children) unfairly, when we feel professionals are being unreasonable, when we realize experts don't know everything, and that they often prevent our children from achieving success, we proudly become Mothers-(or Fathers)-from-Hell.

In this position, we learn the laws, we know our rights, and we loudly invoke them at the appropriate times. We begin to use the laws as baseball bats, beating people over the head with them every chance we get. We may surround ourselves with other Mothers-from-Hell, bringing these big guns with us to IEP meetings, creating World War III. We're proud of the status we've achieved: professionals are scared of us, they'll do what we want. They know we can cause big trouble if they don't, and we may even resort to suing the pants off the school district. We relish the new powers we have. Our anger over injustice has made us strong.

Some of us stay in this position for a long time, developing powerful reputations that precede us. Educators may whisper our names to one another, with appropriate warnings. Mothers-from-Hell come to believe the ends justify the means, and any means is appropriate as long as we get what we want. Unfortunately, our egos often get the best of us. Our perspective gets cloudy and we're unable to accurately discern when other types of advocacy methods might be more effective. We often seek retribution instead of justice.

As time goes by, we make enemies of many of the professionals we come in contact with, even those who were (or are) potential allies. Unfortunately, we don't realize that when people are forced to do things, they'll only do the minimum—grudgingly—and only as long as they're being watched. We can't send a hidden camera to school every day to ensure our demands are being followed. Worse, we don't consider how our actions might affect our child. Why would we want to entrust our children to people who hate our guts?

I-Quit

This is the role most often assumed by parents whose children have reached middle or high school. However, it can happen to parents at any time. In this position, we no longer have any faith our advocacy efforts will work. When we move into the I-Quit role, we're beaten down, worn out, tired through and through, and we're just biding time until our children graduate or age out of school. We no longer exhibit overt anger at the school system or professionals. We just give up.

In most cases, we've spent years advocating for our children, sometimes successfully, sometimes not. We may or may not have used effective advocacy strategies. By this time, that point is irrelevant. Even those of us who have been strong, overcoming negative forces for years, can just run out of steam. In some ways, this position looks similar to the Just-a-Mom role. When we assume the I-Quit position, our children's lives are no longer their own: educators and other professionals make the decisions since we're no longer proactive and have dropped out of the equation.

Parents in this position may have been advocating and dealing with professionals for twelve or more years. We mistakenly assume that once our children are out of high school, all the problems will be over and they can live their lives free of interference. For some, this may be true. More often, however, we don't realize that another set of professionals awaits our young adult children. Vocational-rehabilitation counselors, the Social Security Administration, and others must soon be dealt with if our children get help from the system.

When we've given up advocating, the dangers to our children are great. The middle and high school years are crucially important: they're the springboard for our children entering the adult world of work or post-secondary education. We desperately want out of the system, but since we quit advocating, we must go to the experts for vocational help. At some point, we may no longer have to deal with the system anymore, but our children will. Sadly, if we haven't prepared them for self-advocacy, they'll be at the mercy of experts.

OUR LEADERSHIP IS VITAL

It's easy to be discouraged and angry with the special education system. We may feel the odds are against us and that we'll never be successful. But we will.

Regardless of the age of your child and regardless of your past efforts at advocacy, it is both possible and realistic to take a new direction that will ensure your child's success in the real world. Our leadership is vital—to our children, other parents, and school systems. No one knows our children like we do. When Congress enacted special ed law, and in its subsequent reauthorizations, it specifically recognized the importance of parents in the IEP process. But *how* we provide leadership will make the difference between our success and failure, and in the second half of this book, you'll find a variety of specific strategies you can use immediately to help your child and your family live the lives of your dreams.

In the meantime, let's look at another piece of today's conventional wisdom: services for young children with disabilities.

Services for Young Children: Help or Hindrance?

8

> THE HEARTS OF SMALL CHILDREN
> ARE DELICATE ORGANS.
> A CRUEL BEGINNING IN THIS WORLD
> CAN TWIST THEM INTO CURIOUS SHAPES.
> *Carson McCullers*

Babies and young children are precious gifts. What joy they bring to parents and to our society—we say children are our future. Childhood is traditionally viewed as a carefree time. For children with disabilities, however, childhood isn't always carefree, and society doesn't always include our children in the noble notion that children are our future.

With the enactment of P.L. 92-142 (now IDEA) in 1975, schools were mandated to educate all school-age children with disabilities, and to identify all children with disabilities from birth to age twenty-one. In addition, the law included *options* for states to provide services for children under five. Some states chose to exercise those options, and began to provide services for young children in the late '70s and early '80s. Amendments to the law in 1986 removed the optional provision, and mandated states to provide services for children with disabilities from birth to age five.

Children with disabilities (and at each state's option, those at risk of developing disabilities) from birth to age three are eligible for early intervention (EI, also called ECI-early childhood intervention). A child's eligibility continues until the beginning of the school year during the year she turns three. Children with disabilities who are three, four, or five are eligible for early childhood education (ECE) services, (sometimes referred to as early childhood special education-ECSE).

State departments of education have the overall responsibility for ECE programs, while school districts operate the programs. EI services, however, may be under the state education department, health and human services, or some other agency.

EI and ECE services are both intended to provide assistance to children with disabilities. However, this is another good intention that's often gone awry. Instead of being helpful to children with disabilities and their families, EI and ECE programs can cause harm. The manner in which these programs are implemented frequently segregates children and their families from the mainstream of society, holds children back, focuses on a child's perceived deficits, prohibits the child's future inclusion in regular education, and creates an unhealthy dependency on the system. We'll look at why and how this happens.

EARLY INTERVENTION: ASSISTANCE OR INTERFERENCE?

Do EI services provide appropriate assistance, or do they interfere in the natural lives of babies and toddlers with disabilities and their families? Throughout this chapter, I'm not suggesting we ignore the unique needs of babies and their families; but there are other ways families can get the help they need, as I'll detail in the second half of this book. Also, I'm not implying that people who work for EI programs are bad people; it's the system—not the people who work in the system—that is flawed. Let's look at part of the federal law (IDEA, Part C):

> The Congress finds that there is an urgent and substantial need
>
> (1) to enhance the development of infants and toddlers with disabilities and to minimize their potential for developmental delay;
>
> (2) to reduce the educational costs to our society, including our Nation's schools, by minimizing the need for special education and related services after infants and toddlers with disabilities reach school age;
>
> (3) to minimize the likelihood of institutionalization of individuals with disabilities and maximize the potential for their independently living in society;
>
> (4) to enhance the capacity of families to meet the special needs of their infants and toddlers with disabilities; and
>
> (5) to enhance the capacity of State and local agencies and service providers to identify, evaluate, and meet the needs of historically underrepresented populations, particularly minority, low-income, inner-city, and rural populations.

States are required to make every effort to identify children who may be eligible for services, advise parents of available services and their legal rights, and provide a service coordinator to help write an individualized family service plan (IFSP). The IFSP is similar to an individualized education program for students with disabilities. The IFSP, however, considers the needs of both the child and the family. In general, the purpose of the IFSP is to outline these needs and detail how the needs will be met.

What does EI look like? It's hard to draw a composite picture because there are so many variables. For example, some states offer far more than the federal minimum (providing service coordination). They may provide free or low-cost therapy, infant stimulation classes, play groups, or other activities. In addition, the way professionals implement even the minimum standard often varies from one state to another. Some parents may be receiving EI services, but have never heard the acronym "EI" because their state has a different name for the program.

The Service Coordinator

The service coordinator meets with the family to discuss the strengths and needs of the child and the family, and maintains contact with the family as long as the child receives EI services. She also helps write the IFSP, which includes statements about the expected outcomes (goals) and how these outcomes will be met.

According to the law, "The service coordinator [shall be] from the profession most immediately relevant to the infant's or toddler's or family's needs (or who is otherwise qualified to carry out all applicable responsibilities under this part) who will be responsible for the implementation of the plan and coordination with other agencies and persons." If they wish, parents can assume the role of service coordinator.

Family-Driven, Culturally-Competent

EI provisions include language about family-driven IFSPs and services that are culturally competent. The intent is to ensure that *parents* decide what is appropriate for their families, based on the family's unique needs and cultural background. Unfortunately, these provisions are often meaningless. Instead of helping the family search out possible resources of assistance, service coordinators may describe a menu of state-funded services to select from, which may not provide the individualization mandated in the law.

Natural Environments

EI legislation has been revised over time, but in many areas of the country, the revisions are not being implemented. When the law was reauthorized in 1997, a new provision specifically mandated that EI services be provided to children in their "natural environments." Babies and young children do better—whether they're being assessed for services or receiving services—in their natural environments, instead of the artificial settings of therapy centers, professional offices, or other unfamiliar locations. In essence, this provision requires that services be taken to the child in his natural environment, instead of taking the child to services delivered in an unnatural environment.

However, EI programs in many states continue to operate as if no changes have been made in the federal regulations. In one state, for example, the local director of an EI program in a metropolitan area announced that babies must still be brought to the EI clinic because the EI staff "wasn't sure what 'natural environments' really meant, and, besides, we can't have our therapists driving all over town."

A natural environment is just that: it's the environment that's natural to the child. If a baby stays home with mom, that's his natural environment. If he goes to day care, that's his natural environment. If a toddler goes to mom's day out twice a week and is home with mom the rest of the time, those are her natural environments. But many EI programs plead ignorance or lack of funding, or give some other justification for ignoring this important regulation in order to maintain the status quo.

Questioning the Premise of Early Intervention

The conventional wisdom of EI services reflects the beliefs that:

- Families of babies and toddlers need professional assistance as soon as the child is identified as having (or being at risk for) a developmental disability.

- Professional early intervention (therapy, home visits by experts, and other efforts) can reduce the effects of a child's diagnosed disability and/or reduce the chances of an "at risk infant" developing a disability.

The very premise of early intervention—that families of babies with disabilities need years of ongoing professional assistance—is insulting. It reinforces the perception that there's something so terribly wrong with this baby that Big Brother (state and federal governments) must step in to help make things right. And the notion that we need a formalized plan (the IFSP) to make sure all the needs are met and everything is done correctly is highly paternalistic.

Remember, however, that the government did not enact EI legislation of its own accord. Parents of children with disabilities and their advocates contributed to the current situation. They said, in essence, "Our kids need special help! We can't handle this alone."

Years ago, services for a small percentage of very young children were provided in institutions. No services in the community were available. So, today's EI services are considered better than institutionalized services. But institutional services and EI services in the community both share the same basic premise: parents are unable to successfully raise a baby or young child with a disability without professional intervention.

We must reject the unspoken messages that families are not competent to meet their babies' needs. Every family—whether or not a disability is present—needs a variety of supports and assistance. Families who have typically developing children go to extended family members, friends, neighbors, co-workers, and others in their communities for help. It's assumed, however, these same supports aren't appropriate for our families: the help is not specialized, not provided by professionals, doesn't meet the "special needs," and so forth. We're supposed to go to the system for help!

But perhaps the worst provision of the law is: "to reduce the educational costs to our society." Whoa! What are we to make of the notion that, in the twenty-first century, children with disabilities are viewed as economic burdens? This philosophy has been the basis for inhumane treatment of people with disabilities throughout history.

How did this provision get into the law in the first place? Was it a carrot to entice Congress to fund EI programs? In other words, perhaps the overall justification for funding EI programs was economic. The dollars invested early would reap financial benefits later, based on the theory that it costs less to provide interventions for babies and young children than for special ed services for school-aged children.

How do you feel about your child or other young children with disabilities being perceived this way? If we take this economic line of thinking further, it's easy to see how society continues to discuss the value of allowing newborns with disabilities to live. If they were never born, that would totally eliminate an economic burden, wouldn't it? To take this line of thinking even further, perhaps one day our society will want "prenatal intervention," in which the government will pay for every pregnant woman to be screened. If a developmental disability of the fetus is suspected, the government will pay for an abortion. Not unlike the eugenics period of the past, is it? Let's look at the economic statement again:

> The Congress finds that there is an urgent and substantial need . . . to reduce the educational costs to our society, including our Nation's schools, by minimizing the need for special education and relatedservices after infants and toddlers with disabilities reach school age . . .

According to the majority of parents I've met across the country, this goal is not being reached. I've mentioned it before, and you may know this from your own experience, but special services for young children generally *do not* minimize the need for special education and related services for school-aged children with disabilities. On the contrary, receiving EI services almost guarantees that a child will remain in the special ed system. Two or three years in ECE is the next rung on the ladder, followed by twelve or more years receiving special ed services, where many children are doomed to a life of segregation and a paltry education, unless parents intervene and stop the dismal cycle.

EARLY INTERVENTION: THE IDEAL VS. THE REALITY

Some parents have reported extreme satisfaction with EI services. They like the support they get from their service coordinators and they feel their children and families are receiving the appropriate services.

But more parents have said the way it's supposed to be doesn't mesh with reality. Professionals often "recommend" treatments and services with a heavy hand that borders on coercion. Many parents don't feel they're in charge, nor do they always feel they have real choices. The choice is often between some and none; parents are told, "This is what we have, take it or leave it."

On the surface, EI services appear to be the answer to many parents dreams: babies born with disabilities and their families can begin receiving help from professionals as soon as the diagnosis is made and the IFSP is written. But do we really want our little ones to be clients of the system right out of the womb?

EI services often feel like a life line to parents who may be drowning in confusion and fear following a baby's diagnosis. But few of us—if any—question whether EI is right for our children and families. We don't examine the pros and cons before we jump in with both feet. Most of us don't even consider a downside might exist!

If we do feel uneasy, how many of us feel we can say no, and that will be the end of it? How many of us even know what to say no to? When my son began receiving EI services, I don't recall the professionals giving me the "big picture" of what we were getting into. I don't recall anyone asking, "Do you want our help?" It was just assumed I would go along with the plan. And, initially, I did.

When introduced to EI services, our first impression is of a nice, helpful service coordinator enthusiastically listing all the beneficial services of EI. We feel we're being given this wonderful gift; we wouldn't dare turn down this generous offer or reject the benefits our children are entitled to, would we? What kind of parents wouldn't do *anything* to help their children? The pressure to accept EI services is enormous.

Some parents don't understand they have a *choice* about receiving EI services. They've been told "it's the law" and are fearful they'll get in trouble if they reject EI services! At the other extreme are parents who feel they've been "burdened" with a "special needs child," and feel they're owed everything they can lay their hands on.

"He's at such risk!"

Benjamin was four months old when our family began receiving EI services, as well as PT and OT, all within a few days after he was diagnosed with cerebral palsy. The case manager (this was the term used in 1987), Michelle, was a friendly young lady who came to our house once a month. Like most parents, I didn't really understand what EI was, I just knew we now had people around us—"experts"—who seemed to know more than I did. At first, it was a good feeling. But soon I started questioning the "expertise" of the experts.

During many of her visits, Michelle brought hand outs about how to parent. "What's this?" I wondered. "We've done a pretty good job with two-year-old Emily. Why do I need this stuff?" But I simply took the information and thanked her. (I didn't have the backbone to speak up at this time.) As I got to know Michelle, I learned she was in her early twenties, married, and had no children. As an older mom of thirty-seven, I was almost old enough to be her mother!

When the first August of Benjamin's life rolled around, Michelle excitedly told me about the infant stimulation program at the therapy center where seven-month-old Benj was already getting PT and OT. She informed me the "school" would start in September and I needed to hurry and enroll Benj before all the slots were full. The classes were half-day, Monday through Friday. Michelle said Benjamin would be with ten or so other babies with disabilities in a class with three or four teachers. Since the school was in the same building as therapy, the therapists would pull him out of "class" for PT and OT.

I politely declined, explaining that Benjamin spent most of his day breastfeeding, sleeping in my arms, or playing with Emily, dad, and me. (My backbone was getting a little stronger.) I couldn't imagine dropping him off somewhere for half the day, five days a week! It just didn't feel right. But Michelle wouldn't take no for an answer. She insisted it was critically important for Benjamin to get infant stimulation. I held my ground, telling her that my baby son got all the stimulation he needed at home with his family. Michelle didn't hide her disappointment.

A year passed. Michelle continued to do monthly home visits, and I took Benjamin for PT and OT three or four days each week. During therapy sessions, I occasionally went down the hall to investigate the infant stim classroom. The door was always closed, but I could see the babies and toddlers through a narrow vertical window in the door. Most of the children were often crying, even though several adults were in the room attending to them. I felt sad for the babies.

During her home visit in August, Michelle reminded me that Benjamin was now nineteen months of age and, once again, it was the perfect time to enroll him in the infant stimulation program. Again, I told her thanks, but no thanks. She persisted, "But he really needs this; he's at such risk!" I held my ground, even though I felt a tremendous undercurrent of, "If you're really a good mother, you'll do this for your child." When she left that day, I felt such relief. "Who does she think she is," I thought, "coming in here and telling me how to raise my child? She doesn't even have kids of her own, what does she know?"

But that wasn't the end of it. For the next three weeks at PT and OT, the therapists began asking me if I had considered enrolling Benj in the program. This was all new; they had never done this before. I realized Michelle had asked them to influence me. It was now a conspiracy! No, no, no, I told them over and over again. In the meantime, Michelle was calling me every few days to try to convince me to enroll Benjamin. "Visit the school," she pleaded, "then I know you'll change your mind." I agreed to the visit, hoping that would be the end of it.

It was a large, bright room filled with toys, orthopedic positioning devices, bean bag chairs, and more. I met with the director, a grandmotherly-type with a Ph.D. and impressive professional credentials. She showed me around the room, explaining what they did every day: playing, singing, having snacks, and participating in other learning activities. The routine, however, was strict: all the babies had goals to meet!

I knew I wasn't going to put baby Benj there, but I didn't tell the director this right away because I was curious to learn more. I asked her how they transitioned little babies and toddlers into the program, especially babies who stayed home with their moms and were not accustomed to strangers and strange environments (like my son who was still breast feeding and spending lots of time in my arms). "If I enrolled my son in the program," I asked, "would I come with him the first few days to get him used to things and then gradually fade out of the picture?"

"No, no," she sternly replied, "that doesn't work. On the first day of school, you bring him to the door, one of us will take him from you, and you just turn right around and go back home." "But if I did that," I said, "Benjamin would be terrified. He doesn't know any of you and he'd think I was abandoning him. He would cry and cry." "Well, yes, he probably would. Lots of our babies do that," she patiently explained. "Some even cry the whole three-and-a-half hours they're here each day. But that stops after a few weeks. We're used to it. Benjamin will be fine."

Oh, no he won't, I thought. I thanked her for her time, more sure than ever I was making the right decision. When Michelle and the therapists next talked to me about it, it was my turn to be stern, "I am not putting Benjamin in a place where they think it's okay for babies to cry for weeks!" And to think this program was run by so-called experts in child development!

The interesting end to this little story is that Michelle became pregnant and took six months off for maternity leave. Time passed and Benjamin turned three, so it was time for him to leave the EI program. Michelle came one last time, to give Benjamin an "exit" assessment. He "passed" the so-called intelligence test with flying colors.

As she was preparing to leave for the last time, Michelle turned to me and said, "Kathie, I want to apologize. Since I had my baby, I understand what it feels like to be a parent. I can't believe I tried to tell you and all the other parents in my case load how to be good parents before I knew how to do it myself. But that was my job. I'm sorry for all the dumb things I said and did. And I'm also sorry for badgering you about the infant stim school. I was so worried about Benjamin's development. I kept telling you he really needed it and you kept telling me he was fine—that he needed his family more. You were right. Parents do know best. I'm sorry I didn't respect you more."

Parents all over the country have shared their EI stories with me, and service coordinators can be found at both ends of the spectrum. Some are overbearing and exert too much power over families; others are uncaring and uninformed. In the middle are those who are wonderfully competent. Most professionals have good intentions. They also have our children's best interests at heart. But they operate under their own set of beliefs, which may or may not match ours.

A mom whose twin girls are currently receiving EI services described a recent home visit from EI professionals. During the service coordinator's monthly visit, she brought along a physical therapist for a PT "check-up." Several months earlier, the PT indicated the babies didn't need therapy, but she would visit occasionally to monitor their progress. On this particular visit, the PT and the service coordinator talked with the mom and played with the babies. At one point, the PT noticed a traditional baby walker (the type a baby sits in and scoots around) in the corner of the living room. With the voice of authority, she announced, "We don't like baby walkers for kids with delays."

Who exactly is "we"? And what's wrong with using a baby walker? The therapist gave no explanation; her announcement was a command.

This mom is older and not easily intimidated. Her response to the therapist was a big smile and nothing else. She told me she had no intention of doing what the "experts" say. She and her husband know what's best for their baby girls.

It's not uncommon for parents to believe the IFSP and EI services offer a total solution. But many find the reality is an empty promise. They're frustrated by the lack of services, inappropriate services, and a system that breeds frustration, confusion, and dependency.

The Consequences of EI Services

We owe it to ourselves and our children to carefully consider the consequences of EI. If your child is older than three, I hope you'll help parents of younger children understand the issues.

We're led to believe only professionals have the wisdom to help us. But most EI professionals have little, if any, personal life experiences in raising a child with a disability. (There are exceptions, of course. Many EI programs employ parents of children with disabilities.) What makes us think professionals know more than us? They *do* have professional experience and training, but it's based on the medical/deficit model. Our children's disabilities are seen as "problems" that need to be fixed.

When we buy into the EI paradigm, we unintentionally accept the devastating notion that we can't parent our own children without help from experts. Parents of babies *without* disabilities don't usually have professionals looking over their shoulders. If EI services were ever proposed for every family in America, I hope we would have a social revolt against government intrusion unlike any this country has ever seen.

Too often, EI services interfere in a family's privacy and erode a family's autonomy and self-determination. They also send the clear message that family members and friends are not competent to support us. People who know us and love us, who have common sense and wisdom, are shut out. Let's take a closer look at these issues.

The Stress of Interventions

The lives of most babies with developmental disabilities and their families are aberrant. But this aberrancy is not caused by the child's disability, it's caused by the whirlwind schedule of interventions we embrace. Read that sentence again.

If we're running our babies to play groups and programs all over town, we risk fragmenting our families. Relationships suffer, family unity dissolves, emotions are on the edge, stress builds, and on and on.

Even in the best case scenario, when service providers deliver services in the baby's natural environment, the professional intrusion can create discomfort and tension. If our babies are home with us, we feel the need to clean the house before the professionals arrive. We want our other children to be on their best behavior and/or out of the way. Our days are scheduled around professional visits to our homes. A leisurely trip to the grocery store is a thing of the past; rushing around at warp speed becomes the standard mode of operation. Parents who are employed outside the home must juggle work schedules and try to figure out how to bring order to a chaotic schedule of interventions, while maintaining a reasonable and healthy schedule for other family members.

On top of trying to manage the daily schedule, we also worry about the actual services, and in many cases, about how to pay for the services that are not free. Is our child getting the right services? The right amount of services? Have we met our insurance deductible? How much extra will we owe this month? And on and on. (I remember those days and the memories bring back the stress all over again!) Parenting is a tough job, and EI services should theoretically ease the stress associated with parenting a very young child with a disability. But the intrusion of interventions can actually increase our stress!

And what about the stress on our babies and toddlers with disabilities? Their lives—their natural childhoods—are significantly impacted. Their nap times, play times, and daily routines must be changed to accommodate interventions. The stress adults experience is manifested in a variety of ways, and, hopefully, we can manage the stress to minimize its effect on ourselves and others. But what about babies and young children? How does this stress affect them? Can we always see the stress? Can we measure it and gauge its present and long-term effect?

Learned Dependency

It's difficult, if not impossible, to accurately measure long term outcomes of EI services on children or their families. However, one long-term impact—an unintended outcome—is learned dependency.

When families use EI services, many parents and their family members learn not to trust themselves to know what's best. We're told in subtle and not so subtle ways that we're not competent, that the situation is beyond our expertise, and we should depend on the experts for help. Whatever self-reliance a family already has (or has the capacity to develop) is often stripped away and replaced by dependence on the service system. In too many cases, parents who learn dependency have a difficult time unlearning it. They believe the system will always be there for them.

Dependency learned from EI assistance often leads to parents being dependent on other systems down the road (ECE, special education, voc-rehab, and others). In some cases, close relationships and real caring may develop between parents and EI professionals, and parents often come to expect this in future dealings with professionals. Sadly, many parents are in for a rude awakening when they enter the bureaucracy of the public school system when the child turns three.

Isolation from Natural Supports and Typical Experiences

When we become dependent on the service coordinator and other professionals, we rob ourselves of our common sense. Pretend for a moment there were no EI services. Who would we go to for help? Our extended families? The next door neighbor? The grandma at church? Other parents? A parenting group?

When we have the phone numbers of our friendly service coordinator and all the other professionals who surround us, we call them first. Unintentionally, we cut ourselves off from friends, family members, and resources in the community who could provide much needed and valuable natural supports. We become isolated and often feel we don't "belong." Many parents of school-aged children still experience the pain of this social isolation—an isolation that began with EI services and continues through ECE and special education.

Our children become isolated from the natural experiences of childhood when their time is spent in interventions and therapies. They miss out on many opportunities to experience typical—and important—childhood activities and states of being. And they're no longer babies; they've become clients.

Monthly Disappointments

The constant monitoring of a child's progress in EI programs is enough to cause parents monthly heartaches. Parents have told me stories of watching their babies develop and grow and do new things. The joys of parenthood are great. We're so pleased with every new thing a child learns and accomplishes.

Our pride and pleasure are often diminished, however, when an EI expert arrives with another assessment or developmental chart, or when we realize the baby is not meeting the "goals" in the IFSP. We learn our babies are still "behind," according to the charts. Whatever accomplishments our babies have achieved are good, but not good enough. Our babies are still not-OK as compared to "normal" babies. Just how good do they have to be?

Some of us are able to ignore the disappointment produced by the official tests. We understand the EI professional is just "doing her job." Even so, many of us become beaten down and demoralized by these routine assessments. After awhile, we no longer rejoice at our children's triumphs. Their successes—large and small—are overshadowed by the generalizations made by the professionals. We once believed and celebrated, but now we begin doubting our children and ourselves.

EI professionals don't intentionally try to hurt our feelings and burst our balloons, of course. They're trying to be helpful. But here we are, doing as much as we possibly can to help our precious children, and it's still not enough. How good do *we* have to be? We may become wracked with guilt, embarrassment, and shame. Most of us are working our little tushes off to handle everything coming our way—we're not watching soap operas and eating bonbons all day—but we still doubt our own abilities and actions because our children don't measure up to artificial standards of normalcy, as reflected in developmental charts.

Transition Surprises

Many parents are overjoyed at the EI supports and services their families receive. But joy often turns to shock and dismay when their three-year-old transitions from a family-friendly EI program to the early childhood education (ECE) program operated by the school system.

As clients, we assume the service system is all connected, and that everyone in the system is working together on our children's behalf. In a perfect world, this might be true. In our imperfect world, however, nothing could be further from the truth. Exceptions certainly exist, but in general, EI folks have little or nothing to do with ECE folks. Their programs are usually not operated by the same agency, they serve different populations, and their services focus on completely different issues.

Even though the law mandates that EI service coordinators help with the transition to ECE services, parents often discover their EI service coordinator can't (or won't) answer questions about the ECE program. Maybe she really doesn't have a clue. Maybe it's a turf issue; professional jealously may be rampant. Perhaps the EI professional doesn't like the ECE teacher, or maybe it's the other way around. Either way, parents and children suffer the consequences when the two entities operate on different wave lengths. A process that's supposed to be a smooth ride is actually riddled with pot holes. And that road usually takes families to the next level: early childhood education.

EARLY CHILDHOOD EDUCATION: PREPARATION OR SEGREGATION?

It is immoral to segregate young children with disabilities. But this crucial issue has been buried by all the hoopla about how great early childhood programs are. In an era when—in most quarters—society has recognized the danger and injustice of segregating people with disabilities, we have no compunction about segregating preschoolers with disabilities. We are, in effect, institutionalizing and segregating them under the seemingly benevolent cloak of special ed preschool.

The overall rationale of early childhood education is similar to early intervention: professional intervention during the early years can minimize the effects of the disability and/or may help prevent disabilities in children who are considered at risk of developing disabilities. In addition, it's hoped that providing a child with ECE service will reduce the need for special education services when children are school-aged (ages five to twenty-two), "reducing educational costs to our nation."

It's important for parents to understand that the same special education rules that apply to school-age children apply to preschool-age children (three to five-year-olds). While children receiving EI services have IFSPs, preschoolers receiving ECE services have individual education programs (IEPs), just like school-age students. Regarding placement, the law says a child should be educated in a school "as close as possible to the child's home" and "unless the IEP requires some other arrangement, the child is educated in the school that he or she would attend if nondisabled." [Section 300.522 Placements] These and other provisions are collectively called LRE (least restrictive environment). In addition, a preschooler's IEP must contain a statement detailing how the "disability affects the child's participation in appropriate activities."

Parents are often shocked to learn that LRE regulations apply to special ed preschools, because in most ECE programs, school districts usually offer only *one* environment: the segregated special ed preschool class. This is not the least restrictive environment! The *intent* of early childhood education is routinely corrupted by the actual implementation in schools across the country.

What Does ECE Look Like?

Typically, an ECE program occupies a classroom in an elementary school where children with disabilities, ages three and four,(and sometimes five and six), are congregated together, along with special educators and paraprofessionals (also called teacher's aides, shadows, or some other title). Therapists and other providers visit the room as necessary.

Based on the number of children who are eligible for services, there may be only one ECE program in a small district, but several in large districts. Thus, ECE programs do not always exist in every elementary school. As a result, many preschoolers with disabilities do not attend the public school in their neighborhood. Thousands of preschoolers with disabilities endure long bus rides, four or five days each week.

In some states, a school's ECE program is loosely modeled after the school's kindergarten class: if kindergarten is all day, so is the ECE class. As a result, some very young children spend all day in a public school building. In the afternoons, they're expected to take naps—or try to—on mats on the floor. In some districts, ECE might be a half-day program, for three to five days during the week.

The majority of ECE programs are segregated: only young children with disabilities attend. Some programs, however, claim they're inclusive because children who don't have disabilities also attend. These students are recruited to provide young children with disabilities with "typical role models." In many cases, these students pay tuition, while services for children with disabilities are free, based on IDEA's mandate of a free and appropriate public education. Often, the typical children are the sons and daughters of teachers in the district (it's the easiest way for the school district to recruit typical children).

The number of typical children in an ECE class is usually small. In a class of fifteen, for example, there may be only three or four children without disabilities. Because there's a maximum class size, the number of typical children may fluctuate. If the class is full and a new preschooler with disabilities moves into the district, the district is obligated to serve him. Thus, a typical child may be removed to make room for a child with a disability.

In some school districts, ECE services are merged with Head Start classes. Ironically, some of these blended classes exclude children with significant developmental disabilities. Several years ago, my best friend, Charmaine, and I were asked to present a special education workshop to parents and educators in a blended Head Start program. While discussing the trainings with the Head Start executives, we asked, "What types of disabilities do the children in the Head Start classes have?" "Speech delays and learning disabilities mostly," replied the Head Start director.

"What about other types of disabilities?" we asked. "Are there any children with cerebral palsy, Down syndrome, spina bifida—" The director interrupted before we could continue with our laundry list of developmental disabilities. "No, no," she said. "We don't have kids like that in Head Start." Confused, we pressed on with, "Do you mean there are no children with those disabilities in the district or do you mean they just don't go to the Head Start program?" She stunned us with, "Oh, I'm sure there are kids like that around, but they can't come to our program. There's a special program in the district for them."

The Head Start director had forgotten that the two trainers she was speaking to were parents of "kids like that." A few months later, this Head Start program and the district were punished for excluding children with significant disabilities from Head Start classes.

A very few progressive school districts across the country provide ECE services in the least restrictive environment: preschoolers with disabilities attend typical preschools or day care centers and services are brought to them. They're not congregated in a public school.

Do Parents Actually Choose ECE?

Parents of typical children usually spend a great deal of time and effort investigating preschool and day care settings prior to making a decision about which one to use. They don't entrust the care of their precious children to others until they've found the best place.

But parents of children with disabilities usually don't do this prior to enrolling their kiddos in a special ed preschool. We don't usually drop in for an unannounced visit. (We might not even know where the class is until the IEP meeting!) Nor do we call a child care facility state licensing board for more information. And we probably can't talk to other parents about the place since the confidentialty provisions of IDEA prevent us from finding out which children are enrolled in the class. We simply assume everything is hunky-dory because ECE is a federally-funded program and it's in a public school building.

Many of us don't really *choose* ECE, in that we usually don't compare it to other preschools in our communities and then select it as the best place for our children. Instead, we simply accept ECE for a variety of reasons: it's free, we believe the experts, we're afraid to try typical preschools, or we really do think it's the best place for our children.

But how can an environment that's segregated be the best place for our children? It's critical that we carefully examine any preschool setting before we place our children there. We must not assume ECE programs are always appropriate for our children. Like EI programs, they may provide some benefits, but they can also cause harm.

What Do Children Learn in Segregation?

Our children are learning all the time, everywhere they are. Learning is as natural as breathing. Children learn from touching, seeing, tasting, hearing, smelling, doing, and more. They learn from adults, other children, and their environments.

Three, four, and five-year-olds with and without disabilities are at the stage where they're acquiring valuable social skills. They soak up everything that surrounds them— good and bad. Most of us try to provide opportunities for our children to experience positive interactions and environments, and to prevent (or at least limit) exposure to harmful interactions or environments. We have no guarantee the decisions we make are the right ones. But combining facts, experience, gut instincts, and intuition seems to serve us well. When it comes to enrolling our children in ECE programs, however, we often don't use our parental wisdom.

One of the goals of ECE services is to minimize the effects of the child's disability, so why do we put children with disabilities all together? In special ed preschool, what do children with disabilities learn from one another and from the segregated environment?

Let's shift gears slightly and consider there are many ways to learn a foreign language. If you want to learn French by the "immersion" method, for example, you're immersed in the new language during class time. You learn quickly, because French words are the only words spoken; you're in a totally French-speaking environment and no English is spoken. If you need to go to the bathroom, you have ask permission to leave the room in French. Most of us would learn French pretty fast!

Now back to ECE. Estimates put the number of students with disabilities to be approximately 10 percent of total student enrollment. (In society-at-large, people with disabilities of all ages constitute approximately 20 percent of the American population.) This 10 percent is considered the "natural proportion." Inclusion advocates (educators and parents) have recognized the importance of maintaining the natural proportion in educational settings. So in a class of twenty, there should be no more than two children with disabilities. Higher ratios would represent an unnatural proportion and, thus, an unnatural environment.

Few ECE classes have natural proportions. Some classes are totally segregated: only children with disabilities attend. In other classes, a few typical children are sprinkled in and the natural proportion is actually reversed. Thus, ECE classes are unnatural environments. And the fact that the majority of three and four-year-old children in our society do not attend public schools also makes an ECE classroom an unnatural environment.

Now consider a child with a disability in an ECE classroom in a public school building: he's immersed in an abnormal, unnatural environment. What shall we expect him to learn in this setting? What happens when children with autism, for example, are surrounded by other children who have autism? What do they learn? How to have "more" autism: they learn each other's behaviors.

Our children don't learn only from the teachers and the activities in an ECE class. They learn from each other. If a four-year-old is "delayed"in social development, and she's surrounded by other children who have social, emotional, or language delays, how will she acquire four-year-old social skills? Would she not learn them better by being with her mom (assuming Mom treated her like a four-year-old) and/or around typical four-year-olds?

Let's think about a typical preschool for a moment. Specifically, let's think about a four-year-old class that meets three mornings a week. In the class of fifteen typical children are three boys who, when they're together, are "big trouble." They play too rough, fight among themselves and with other kids, won't listen to the teacher, and so forth. But when the teacher separates them, making sure they play and sit with other children, they're each delightful, well-mannered little boys. In this scenario, would the teacher *ever* intentionally group these three boys together, allowing them to feed off each other, or would she do everything in her power to ensure they were surrounded by other children who brought out the best in them?

Now think about ECE classrooms. Conventional wisdom dictates that children with disabilities need to be in special settings where highly-trained professionals can give them the help they need. Common sense, however, tells us that a child who is non-verbal, for example, should not be in a classroom full of other children who do not speak! That we even *consider* doing this is mind-boggling!

While I never put my son in a special ed preschool, Benjamin did learn unusual things from the segregated—and unnatural and abnormal—settings of private PT and OT. When he was four, he asked me if Colin, his four-year-old cousin who lived in another state, still walked with a walker. I didn't understand what he was talking about. After asking him a couple of questions, it became clear. Benjamin thought *every* child learned to walk with a walker because that's what he saw during the hours he spent at therapy! He had this belief even though he went to a neighborhood church preschool with typical kids two days a week. The long-term experience of regularly seeing other children in walkers at therapy gave Benj a distorted view of the world.

What inaccurate perspectives and inappropriate behaviors are kids with disabilities learning in the unnatural environments of special ed preschools and other segregated settings? What is the long term impact of the segregation of young children? What impressions are they forming about the world? How do they feel about themselves in these settings?

In the landmark Supreme Court decision outlawing racial segregation in public schools, *Brown v. Board of Education of Topeka* in 1954, the Court found that "separate educational facilities were inherently unequal." Chief Justice Earl Warren, writing about keeping African-American children out of "white" schools, said in part:

> To separate them from others of similar age and qualifications solely because of
> their race generates a feeling of inferiority as to their status in the community
> that may affect their hearts and minds in a way unlikely ever to be undone.

By segregating children with disabilities in unnatural environments, isolating them from typical peers and experiences, are we not putting their hearts and minds at risk? Professionals urge us to get specialized treatment because our children are "at risk." But the risk they speak of is focused on a child's functional abilities. Seldom, if ever, do professionals consider the potential life-long risks to our children's hearts and minds. Who will assess the risks to our children's spirits if we don't?

We do whatever it takes to protect our children from physical dangers. We don't let them play with matches, run in the street, or do other things that might cause bodily harm. Why then, don't we do whatever it takes to protect their hearts and minds from harm?

What impressions do others—older students, teachers, parents, and others in the school community—have of children who attend the "special preschool"? And how does it make a child's parents and brothers and sisters feel about the child?

From talking to parents across the country, I know many moms and dads are concerned about the segregation in most special ed preschools. Yet they still send their children to these classrooms, even when their good judgment and intuition tell them it's wrong.

Why do we follow the recommendations of early childhood professionals even when they go against our better judgment? Perhaps because (1) we're made to feel guilty if we don't follow the directives of the experts who purport to know what's best for our children; (2) we're not given a true picture of ECE programs, so we don't even know to question this segregated placement; (3) we may see ECE classes as a child care or preschool setting which gives us a break from our kids at no cost; and (4) we may truly believe the ECE program will better prepare our children for inclusion in elementary school.

If segregation is not good for children with disabilities, why do schools allow it? Schools, as well as other institutions, do what's best and what's easiest for them, whether or not it's good for the people they serve. Congregating young children with disabilities in a special ed preschool class is not done for the benefit of the children; it's for the convenience of the staff. From the school's perspective, it's easier and more cost efficient to keep staff and services in one location rather than spreading them around where they're really needed: in typical preschools, day care centers, or children's homes. But this perspective is usually not shared with parents. In fact, we're not given any rationale for segregation. Parents assume a segregated preschool is an appropriate setting only because they've been told that by the professionals who are employed in the field!

Natural vs. Artificial Environments

Wouldn't all children with disabilities benefit from being in their natural environments instead of the artificial environment of a segregated preschool? Wouldn't they acquire skills faster, easier, and more naturally when they're surrounded by their families, other caring adults, and typical children?

Three and four-year-olds who don't have disabilities are at home with mom and a brother or sister; at a neighborhood preschool with other little friends; in day care, where they're known and loved by ladies who have taken care of them for years; or at grandma's or some other familiar place. Most five-year-olds are in a kindergarten class in the neighborhood elementary school. Typical children live and breathe and learn in their natural environments.

Most children with disabilities start out in their natural environments, but when parents learn about ECE programs, everything changes. We take away familiarity and comfort and replace them with something new and different, at a time when children are very vulnerable and very impressionable.

When children are in ECE programs, what wonderful experiences are they missing in their natural environments? Licking the beaters while helping Mom bake cookies; learning all about shopping during a trip to the grocery store; or having the chance to make new friends at the church preschool. Our children are young for such a very short time. Are we willing to let their childhoods slip through our fingers because someone tells us ECE is so important? What's more important to a child than being in a place that's comfortable and safe, surrounded by people who know and love you? Public school will come soon enough.

We do things to young children with disabilities we would never do to children without disabilities. Most of us would never even consider putting a typical three-year-old on a bus for a forty-five minute bus ride, twice a day, five days a week. But we do it to kids with disabilities without giving it a second thought. How can child development experts condone such practices? How can we?

For children who are in day care or some other child care setting, the situation can be even worse. What are we doing to a three-year-old when a school bus picks him up from home in the morning, takes him to special ed preschool, then another bus picks him up from the preschool and drives him to his day care at noon, and then, finally, he goes home at supper time? Where does he think he "belongs"? Would *you* be stressed out if you had a schedule like that? As adults, most of us are constantly try to reduce the stress in *our* lives, but we don't seem to mind piling it on our children. Can we not see that such a situation is potentially harmful instead of helpful?

Continuity and safety are extremely important to young children. To grow up emotionally healthy, they need to know they're protected, they need to know who they can count on, they need to know where they belong. Who does our imaginary three-year-old count on throughout his long day? How many adults are in his life for brief periods of time? How much stability does he feel? Is it possible his development may be *hindered* by the instability, discontinuity, and confusion that result from the hectic schedule? If his behavior deteriorates, if his learning stagnates, and/or if he's frustrated, angry, scared, and tearful, do we really need to ask why?

Many parents have responded to my criticism of ECE programs by telling me how much their children are learning and how their children love going to school. I have no doubt many children learn in ECE settings and many may really enjoy being there. But these positive outcomes do not negate the risks to our children's spirits. Since it's impossible to compare the long-term benefits to the risks, shouldn't we err on the side of caution? Alternatives to ECE programs are discussed in later chapters—alternatives that do not put our children at risk.

Is ECE a Stepping Stone to Inclusion or Exclusion?

One giant myth about ECE is that it's a stepping stone to an inclusive placement in elementary school. But the transition from ECE to public school kindergarten or first grade often shellshocks parents, leaving them disappointed and angry.

Few educators actually tell parents, "If you put your three-year-old in our ECE program for two years, we'll guarantee he'll be in an inclusive kindergarten program in his neighborhood school when he's five." But many parents get the idea—from someone, somewhere—that their child *will* be included in a regular ed kindergarten class after he "graduates" from the ECE program.

Parents of preschoolers may not be aware that, just as ECE programs may be housed in only one or two schools, elementary special ed "programs" are often located in specific schools. While parents may have tolerated sending their four-year-old to the ECE program that's forty-five minutes from home, they expect their child will attend the neighborhood school for kindergarten. The anticipation turns to bewilderment and anger when they learn the IEP team is *not* considering a regular kindergarten class in the neighborhood school. Instead, the team recommends placement in a special ed room, with visitation to a kindergarten class, *in the same school where the child has been attending ECE.*

Many school districts follow this practice. They locate their early childhood program in an elementary building where they house special ed "programs." The district congregates staff and services; the children are expected to follow.

Many, many parents have shared their stories about absolutely shocking IEP meetings when their children turned five. Some were horrified when the IEP team insisted their child remain in the special ed preschool for yet another year. How can a child "fail" special ed preschool? Of course, educators don't call it "failing," they just say, "He's still not ready." If the ECE program couldn't "get him ready" in two years, what makes them (or us) think they can get the job done in one more year?

Even though parents may be frustrated and disappointed, they often agree to one more year of ECE. Others get mad, threaten to sue, and make enemies. And there are all kinds of situations in between these two extremes. In any case, everyone's unhappy. Even parents who loved their children's ECE programs and who had great relationships with their child's teachers, can quickly turn sour on the whole special ed process. Many feel betrayed and vow to never again trust the school system. This is not an auspicious beginning for what will be a long-term relationship with educators in the district.

While it's often educators who recommend retaining children in a special ed preschool for another year, there are instances when parents insist on holding a child back until "she's ready." Parents provide a variety of justifications for doing this:

> *"Amy is so small for her age. I'm worried about how she'll do with kids that are so much bigger."*

Perhaps Amy will be small for her age all her life. How do we know there won't be a child who is smaller than Amy in the regular ed kindergarten class? And what if she doesn't grow all that much this next year? How many years should she stay in special ed preschool? Until she's how big? Should physical size really be a criteria?

"Max is just not socially mature enough. One more year will make all the difference in the world."

He might be socially immature for several years. So what? Lots of kids without disabilities are socially immature. How do they learn to mature? They surely don't gain maturity by being around kids who are younger! They grow and develop by being around kids who are the same age or older. If Max is held back in preschool and he doesn't mature in the next year, then what? Should he stay in preschool until he's eight or nine? What criteria is used to measure social readiness?

"Krista still doesn't know her ABCs like the other kids. I want her to be ready."

Children enter kindergarten at all different levels. Some kids know their ABCs when they start, others don't. In a class of twenty-five typical kindergartners, there are twenty-five different kids who are at all different stages. If Krista hasn't learned her ABCs by this time, maybe it's because she's not interested in them yet or because she needs to learn other things right now. But this doesn't mean she shouldn't go on to kindergarten. She'll learn her ABCs when the time is right for her. Maybe she hasn't learned them because the special ed preschool teachers don't think she's capable and they haven't tried very hard. Maybe a regular ed kindergarten teacher would see her with different eyes.

Kindergarten Entrance Criteria?

In most schools, there is no kindergarten entrance criteria for children who don't have disabilities. Why should there be criteria for children with disabilities?

Unfortunately, some states have recently instituted kindergarten readiness (and other states are considering this). If children without disabilities do not meet a specific criteria, they're educated in special "developmental" or prekindergarten settings. Those who are still not deemed ready after a year often get shuttled into special education. This is a dangerous idea. More and more children who do not "fit" a school's idea of a typical student are being referred for special ed services. It seems schools across the country will do whatever it takes to weed out students perceived to be different.

In general, however, parents of typical children are usually not told their children aren't ready for kindergarten; in most school districts, there's no place for typical children to "get ready." They're enrolled in kindergarten because they're five, regardless of their academic or social achievements. If an educator *did* tell parents they couldn't enroll their child in kindergarten because the child isn't ready, the parents would be justifiably outraged. But professionals inflict an artificial criteria of "readiness" on preschoolers with disabilities simply because there's a "place" (the special ed preschool) for them to "get ready."

The Harm in Holding Children Back

Parents who hold their children back do so with the best of intentions, but the outcomes of their decisions can be dreadful. Typical children who are held back during the elementary school years tell compelling stories about what it felt to be labeled "dummy" by their friends. In elementary school, age difference isn't always important, but this changes over time. By the time children are in middle or high school, students who are older than their peers are often teased or ostracized.

If you or someone you knew were held back, think about the negative effects it caused. One of my dear friends was held back by his well-meaning parents. For years, he lived with the belief that he was stupid. It wasn't until he finished college and became a teacher that he was able to shed that image of himself. His parents and teachers never verbally said he was stupid, but their actions did.

Now, think about kids with disabilities. They already have enough to deal with. Why would we load one more thing on their already full plates? And consider this: how would most kindergarten teachers feel about including a six-year-old with a disability who has "failed"—or was held back in—the ECE class?

Low Expectations Spell Disaster

Educators in a special ed preschool class may allow children with disabilities to behave in ways that are considered inappropriate in typical settings. "Oh, that Robert—he has [whatever], you know how those kids are. They're just like that," a special educator might think. Thus, many children learn inappropriate behaviors during their years in an early childhood class. When it's time for little Robert to move on to kindergarten, the ECE teacher reluctantly reports that Robert is not ready because of his "behavior problems." Where did he learn these behaviors? From other children with disabilities who have unusual or immature behaviors, in an unnatural and artificial environment, and all of this was sanctioned by teachers who have low expectations.

At the other end of the spectrum are educators who—with or without permission—use behavior modification techniques (including aversive methods) that may hurt children emotionally and physically. Parents of typical children would never allow adults to hurt their children in any setting, but cruel and inhumane treatment of children with disabilities is often tolerated in special education settings.

When children with behavior issues are in neighborhood preschools or other natural environments, they learn what's acceptable and what's not. With support from a caring teacher and typical friends, many inappropriate behaviors subside and new ones never have a chance to take root. In addition, teachers in natural settings would never use aversive methods of behavior control—the other children in the class wouldn't stand for it!

Educators have low expectations not only about children's behavior, but also about children's abilities. They often have stereotypical attitudes about children with disabilities. If they don't think a child with Down syndrome, for instance, is capable of learning his numbers or letters, they often won't even attempt to teach him those skills. A child may demonstrate great capacities at home, but not at school.

If a child can do certain things at home, why isn't she doing them at school? Maybe because the teacher doesn't help her in a way that's comfortable. Or maybe the child cares about pleasing mom, but not the teacher. Who knows? Many children with disabilities in special ed preschools are bored. They're not in an environment that stimulates them; or they're not in an environment that feels good; or they're not in an environment that they enjoy. When they're bored, they usually do one of two things: they shut down completely and zone out ("Clint's just not making the progress we expected."), or they entertain themselves in ways that are unacceptable to the teacher ("Maya's starting to have behavior problems."). From the teacher's perspective, students like Clint and Myra are demonstrating they're "not ready" for a regular kindergarten class.

Special Ed Baggage is a Heavy Load

Often, preschoolers with disabilities are automatically excluded from regular education kindergarten classes *because* they attended the special ed preschool! Our children's labels and special ed baggage precede them. Educators can't see them for who they really are; they only see them in light of their labels and histories. Many teachers are unwilling or unable to believe a "special ed student" could become a "regular ed student." The perception, "Once a special ed student, always a special ed student," is not only pervasive, but it also becomes the reality.

Rare is the kindergarten teacher who says, "Yes! I'll be happy to include a child who has been in the special ed preschool for two years." Instead, she might think, "If Sarah's so needy she had to be in special ed preschool as a three and four-year-old, how am I supposed to handle her when I've got nineteen other five-year-olds in the class? I don't think my room is the right place for her. The special ed folks should continue to handle her."

Would the kindergarten teacher feel differently if Sarah had spent the last two years learning at home with mom, in a neighborhood preschool, or in a regular day care setting? The teacher might think, "If she did well there, she'll probably do well in my class."

ECE EXPERIENCES

Early childhood education has been embraced as a panacea. Many educators and parents feel it's an unqualified success. Parents and other advocates have supported the notion that young children with disabilities need special education preschool services. But the following real-life experiences shed a new light on the conventional wisdom of ECE.

Cassie: Choice or Coercion

Julie's daughter, Cassie, was just about to turn three and Julie was frantic. She had a positive experience with EI services, but she just didn't feel right about sending Cassie off to the special ed preschool. At a parent support group meeting, Julie was in tears, as the first day of school loomed closer and closer. After she described her concerns, another parent (Kate) said, "Look, if you're not comfortable with this—if you don't feel it's right for Cassie—then don't send her."

"What do you mean?" Julie stammered, wiping away her tears. "Just don't send her," Kate repeated. "But what will they do to me if I don't?" she asked. "What are you talking about?" Kate asked. "They won't do anything to you. It's not mandatory, it's your choice. If you don't want to send her, you don't have to." Julie's eyes widened as she said, "You mean it really is my choice? They made me think I *had* to send her. *They said it's the law.*" She then detailed the dire predictions the ECE director made about Cassie's future if Julie didn't send her to the special ed preschool.

Julie had tried to listen to the little voice inside her about what was best for Cassie, but she had been thoroughly intimidated by the ECE director. When Julie learned she could say no, she was relieved Cassie wouldn't be forced to attend the preschool, but she was angry about the coercion used by ECE professionals.

Dustin: Programmed to Fail

In the early childhood preschool program in a rural school district, five-year-old Dustin was held back for a year. Dustin had a syndrome that typically results in cognitive and speech delays, as well as metabolic irregularities. Many people with this syndrome are always hungry. They cannot sense when they're full and easily become overweight.

When Dustin was finally allowed to move on to an inclusive kindergarten at his neighborhood school, his parents were relieved. They didn't know, however, that the actions of the ECE staff had programmed Dustin to fail.

Dustin's neighborhood school was not the same school where he attended the ECE program. As a result, he knew no other children at the neighborhood school. His IEP called for him to be in a regular kindergarten class in a school that claimed to be inclusive. A teacher's assistant (TA) would be in the classroom for support, and Dustin was to receive speech therapy in school. At this time, Dustin talked, but most of his words were unintelligible to everyone but his family.

When he entered kindergarten, Dustin was almost seven. He was already big for his age, partly because of the metabolic irregularities caused by his disability. The almost two year age difference between Dustin and the other kindergartners added to the size difference. He was about the size of a big third or fourth grade boy.

Dustin was a very friendly and sweet boy. Unfortunately, the kindergarten teacher—Ms. Walker—was ambivalent about having Dustin in her class. She was never given much information about who Dustin was as a person. The ECE teachers shared Dustin's thick file with Ms. Walker, but most of what she learned about Dustin were his perceived deficits. Because the kindergarten teacher failed to get to know Dustin, she was unable to model positive interactions with him. Thus, the other children had no way of knowing how to make friends with Dustin. In addition, no one tried to learn his speech patterns. The responsibility for Dustin was relegated to the teacher's aide.

The special ed preschool did a great disservice to Dustin. In the three years he was in their program, they never helped him learn appropriate ways of approaching and interacting with other kids. Because his preschool class was full of other kids with disabilities, many of whom had behavior issues, Dustin's unusual behavior was accepted by his teachers. They didn't think he had the ability to learn more appropriate behaviors.

When Dustin attempted to communicate with other children in the inclusive kindergarten class, he was often ignored because the other kids didn't even realize he was talking to them. They interpreted his speech as a series of grunts and noises. Because he was ignored so often, Dustin had learned (in preschool) other ways of getting the attention of his classmates. In what he thought was a friendly way, he gave a tap on the shoulder, a little punch in the arm, or some other form of touching.

In kindergarten, since no one had taken the time to get to know him and because he was so much bigger than his classmates, this physical contact was perceived as bullying and aggressiveness. The first time this happened, Dustin was reprimanded for "hitting." In his mind he wasn't hitting, so punishment in the time out chair made no sense. The second time it happened—on the first day of school—he was sent to the principal's office. Of course, the principal didn't know Dustin from the next kid. She chewed him out and handed him back to the TA who was now his unofficial guard.

As the weeks went by, a vicious cycle emerged. When Dustin "hit" another kid, the TA took him to an empty classroom where the two stayed for various lengths of time. Dustin saw other kids go by in the hallway and tried to escape his mini-prison. His guard held him back. Eventually, the TA led Dustin back to the classroom. Once there, he was so excited to see the other kids that he once again made physical contact ("hitting," according to educators). So he was taken back to his jail—his personal classroom—again.

Still, no one took the time to figure out Dustin's behavior. When he supposedly "hit" other kids, he was smiling and laughing, attempting to be friendly. Educators interpreted this as a sign of a severely disturbed personality. "What kind of kid laughs as he's hurting another child?" they asked. Soon, Dustin was spending the entire half-day kindergarten in the empty classroom with the TA. Little by little, she moved a few books and toys to the room. Never did the educators talk to Dustin's parents about the situation, and never did his parents visit the classroom to observe Dustin's progress. His parents found out about the situation only after Dustin's older sister—a fourth grader at the same school—heard about his predicament from other kids!

After an emergency IEP was called (half the school year had gone by), the parents tried to work with the school to arrive at a solution. Various things were tried over the next few months, including: putting Dustin in a first grade class, with bigger, older kids and with a wiser teacher; trying the kindergarten class again; staying in his personal classroom and bringing other kids to visit. None of these environmental changes made a difference, because none of the teachers tried to get to know Dustin. "He's a violent child," was the consensus among the teachers. Yet people who knew Dustin at home and at church never saw violence.

With a month or so left of kindergarten, the final blow was struck. Because of all the problems throughout the year, the TA and Dustin had become mortal enemies. She had resorted to physically restraining him for most of the day, while he struggled to free himself from her grip. He spent each day in his personal classroom, alone with the TA. He took every opportunity to look out the small window in the door, his eyes searching for other children going down the hall. When he saw some, he would try to leave the room and join them. The TA kept the door locked, so Dustin's efforts were never successful. When he cried or demonstrated anger at his imprisonment and isolation, the TA made him sit in the time out chair. Things got worse and worse.

At the end of one fateful day, the TA stood with Dustin on the front sidewalk, waiting for the special ed bus to take him home. She squatted down on the ground in front of him to tie his shoelaces. How the next event actually transpired is open to speculation. The TA reported that as her head was bent over while she tied his shoes, Dustin intentionally bent down and "head butted" her, causing extreme pain and almost "knocking her unconscious." As soon as Dustin got on the bus, the TA had someone drive her to a hospital emergency room to see if she had a concussion (she didn't). She filed worker's compensation and was out of school for two weeks because of her "injury."

The principal didn't let Dustin return to school for two weeks since the TA wasn't there to take care of him. When she did come back, the school called an IEP meeting and expelled (yes, expelled) the kindergartner from school for violence. His parents knew Dustin didn't intentionally hurt the teacher's aide. They felt he must have moved his head to look down at the same time the TA's head was coming up, and they bumped heads accidentally. But with Dustin's "violent history," educators assumed it was a purposeful act. Interestingly, none of the educators ever showed any interest in the bump on Dustin's head.

While educators at the neighborhood school (and his parents, to some extent) bear great responsibility for the difficulties Dustin faced, the die was cast during the three years he spent in the ECE program. Dustin's parents were urged to fight the expulsion, but they didn't want their son to ever set foot in that school again. They found a different school—in a different district—where Dustin successfully began first grade the next September (as an eight-year-old).

Benjamin: "Someone to Talk To"

We were still living in Texas when Benjamin turned three and became eligible for preschool services. The ECE program happened to be located in our neighborhood school, where our daughter Emily would be attending kindergarten at the same time Benjamin could go to the ECE preschool. I attended the IEP meeting even though I had no intention of enrolling Benj. I went for the "practice" and to see if the program was any better than what I had heard from other parents. I planned on enrolling Benjamin in a neighborhood church preschool program two mornings a week, but I didn't tell this to the "handicapped preschool" folks.

During the meeting, the special ed preschool teacher asked if Benjamin could talk. When I told her he could, she gleefully exclaimed, "Oh, good! Now I'll have someone to talk to. See, none of the other kids in this year's class can talk!"

I couldn't believe what I heard. Did she not talk to the other students because she didn't think they could understand? I knew I didn't want my son around this educator. She was a polite, friendly person, but her comments demonstrated the negative generalizations she had about children with disabilities.

How did this teacher (who happened to be a speech therapist!) expect the children to learn to talk when they're in a room full of other children who don't talk, and when she had no plans to talk to them? None of those children should have been there. They all needed to be in natural settings where they would be exposed to other children and adults who could model language. I wondered if the other parents were told none of the children in class could speak. If so, would they have felt differently about placing their children in that environment? Did they know their children's speech wouldn't develop in a classroom where no one talked?

We enrolled Benjamin in the church preschool, two mornings a week, where he made lots of typical friends. He was invited to birthday parties and did all the things three-year-olds do in a typical preschool. All the kids quickly became accustomed to playing on the floor with Benj, getting his walker for him, and more. Benjamin's disability and his needs were no big deal to the kids or the teacher. If she ever needed extra help, she just yelled down the hall and the preschool director came to lend a hand.

Emmett: Freed From a Retarding Environment

While Benjamin never went to the ECE program at the neighborhood school, I still had the opportunity to learn more about it. Emily was in kindergarten at the school, in the classroom just across the hall from the ECE classroom. Kindergarten was full day and so was the ECE class. On many mornings and afternoons while taking Emily to class or picking her up, I chatted with one or two parents whose children were in the ECE class. One of the moms was Sandy, the mother of Emmett.

Emmett was almost six, so he should have actually been in a kindergarten class, but the IEP team had convinced Sandy that another year in the ECE class would be good for him.

Emmett had a label of pervasive developmental disorder, and he talked very well when he wanted to. (So much for what the ECE teacher told me about none of the kids in the class being able to speak.)

Even though Sandy took Emmett to school and picked him up every day, she didn't really know what went on in the classroom. I volunteered in Emily's room (often taking Benjamin with me), so I saw the kids in the ECE class when they were allowed out of the room. Sandy wanted to volunteer in Emmett's class, but the ECE teachers didn't allow volunteers in the room. (Red flag!)

On one occasion, I saw the ten students in the ECE class emerge from their room, attended by two teachers and one teacher's aide. They were on their way to the lunchroom, silently walking down the hall in single file. At first glance, this was an unusual sight. Most kids can be rowdy when traveling in a group down the hall, and seldom is the line straight! Upon closer inspection, however, it was easy to see why they stayed in line. The teacher in the front of the line was holding the end of a long nylon strap which was connected to the left wrist of each child. The end of the strap was in the hand of the teacher's aide who brought up the rear. They were all tied together, like miniature prison inmates. And all this to walk forty paces down the hall to the cafeteria!

This school was about two blocks from our home. When I went to the neighborhood grocery store, the route took me within a block of the school. Several times during the school year, I saw bright patches of red ahead of me on the side of the road (there were no sidewalks in the neighborhood). There they were—the very youthful members of the ECE class and their three wardens, all tied together again, and all wearing matching red t-shirts, walking to the grocery store or some other nearby location for a "field trip."

Several times, I saw them in the grocery store, still tied together. The purpose of these trips? To teach the children how to behave in public. Is that not the job of parents and families? And how does going to the store, being tied to other kids, all wearing matching red shirts, being guarded by three adults also in matching red shirts, teach a child how to behave in public?

I shared this information with Sandy every time I saw her. She didn't like it, but she felt powerless to do anything about it. I began urging her to get Emmett out of the ECE class and into Emily's kindergarten class. There was no reason he shouldn't be there. Why should any of those children be in that class? I was so thankful I didn't put Benjamin there.

As the year progressed, Sandy became more and more concerned about Emmett being in the ECE class. When Emmett was frustrated or upset, he sometimes pinched or bit himself. Sandy received reports from the ECE teachers that he was doing more of this at school. One afternoon Sandy noticed both of Emmett's ear lobes were deep purple. She asked the teacher's aide how his ear lobes got bruised. "Oh, he did it to himself," the aide replied, and then she walked off.

That night, Sandy called the ECE teacher at home. Mrs. G sternly and explicitly described what happened. Emmett became frustrated early in the day and began pinching his earlobes. Mrs. G asked him to stop. When he didn't comply, she decided to try out a new aversive behavior management technique. She asked him, a second time, to stop. This time he did. Then she explained to Emmett that he shouldn't do that and to prove her point, she pinched both of his ear lobes ("just a quick pinch"). Emmett began crying ("just a little"). In anger, he pinched his ear lobes again. When he stopped, Mrs. G pinched again ("lightly").

This "technique" went on most of the day. Sandy was furious. She told the teacher (and later the principal) that no one was to ever use aversive behavior techniques on Emmett.

(You do realize this could have never happened in a typical preschool, an inclusive kindergarten class, or any other natural setting. A teacher would know she couldn't get away with this abuse in front of typical kids or adults who may come in and out of the classroom—volunteers and others.)

After this incident, Sandy was *really* ready to get Emmett out of the class. Because I was close to Emily's kindergarten teacher (Mrs. B), I felt comfortable talking to her about Emmett joining her class. Sandy was hopeful. Mrs. B was in her sixties and was a no-nonsense—and very loving—teacher who knew absolutely nothing about kids with disabilities. But she knew about kids. When Benj accompanied me during my volunteer time in the class, Mrs. B was friendly and kind, modeling great behavior for Emily's class-mates. (She once told me she was going to hold off retiring until Benj was kindergarten age, because she wanted him in her class! I kissed her. The next summer, however, we moved to Colorado, so Benj never received the benefits of Mrs. B's love and wisdom.)

Mrs. B said she would love to have Emmett in her class. It was fine with her for him to just transfer in immediately as a full time kindergarten student. Mrs. B didn't think too highly of the ECE teachers to begin with. In her old-world common sense, the three and four-year-olds in the class had no business at a public school anyway. She thought they should be home with their moms or at preschool or wherever they'd naturally be. And she believed the five-year-olds in the ECE class should be in kindergarten, period. It pained her to see how the children were treated. When the afternoon bell rang, many were sound asleep. They would be rudely awakened to get on the bus for the long ride home (this was not the neighborhood school for most).

Sandy, Mrs. B, and I planned a strategy for Sandy and Mrs. B to get Emmett moved into the kindergarten class. I stayed out of it, publicly. I'm sure the school authorities would have accused me of interfering. No IEP meeting would be called; an informal approach would work best. Sandy and Mrs. B wanted Emmett in the kindergarten class full-time, but the ECE teachers agreed only to part-time participation to "see how he would do." Emmett started off visiting the kindergarten class an hour a day for a few days. Mrs. B encouraged the ECE teachers to let him spend the whole morning there. It was wonderful. Both Sandy and Mrs. B were amazed at the progress Emmett was making, academically and socially. In just a few short weeks, he learned more than he had in the two years he'd spent in the ECE room. Emmett positively blossomed. He began talking more, he made friends and was invited to birthday parties, and his life was like other kindergartners.

On a regular basis, the ECE teachers interrogated Mrs. B about Emmett's behavior. They seemed to be looking for any reason to snatch him back and keep him in the ECE room. Emmett did need help in some areas, but Mrs. B simply asked two or three of the more mature kindergartners to give Emmett a hand and things worked out fine. By March, Emmett had been participating in the kindergarten class during the morning for about six weeks. Then Mrs. B convinced the ECE teachers to let Emmett stay in the kindergarten class until after lunch. The ECE teachers reluctantly agreed.

Disaster struck on the first day Emmett went to the cafeteria with the kindergartners. I was volunteering that day and was in the cafeteria with the class. All the kiddos were going through the lunch line. As Emmett neared the cashier, I saw her talking to him, but

I couldn't hear the words. Then Emmett bolted from the cafeteria and the cashier yelled for someone to stop him. A lunchroom monitor took up the chase. Mrs. B was in the teacher's dining room next door and didn't see all this. I ran outside, following the monitor, who was chasing Emmett on the playground. He was running all over the place. There was no way the monitor was going to catch him. I asked a couple of Emmett's friends to bring him to me. I knew he'd come with them, but not with the angry monitor.

In the meantime, the principal and Mrs. B came onto the playground. The cashier had told them the gory details of the incident. According to the cashier, Emmett "stole" a cookie. While going through the lunch line, he saw a basket of cookies and picked one up. He didn't know the cookies were "extra." Like many of the other kids, Emmett had a prepaid lunch pass, so he had no cash. When the cashier told him the cookie was a quarter, Emmett didn't know what she was talking about. Evidently, she repeated herself in a loud voice, scaring Emmett, and he ran off. The principal was enraged: no student was allowed to steal at her school! She ran to the ECE classroom and told the teachers what happened.

The bell rang, signaling the end of lunch recess. I walked back to the classroom with Emmett and Emily and some of the kids who were helping Emmett calm down. As we entered the hallway, Mrs. B and the ECE teacher were talking. The ECE teacher took Emmett by the hand and told him he couldn't be in kindergarten anymore since he didn't know how to behave. Without another word, she led him back to the ECE room and shut the door. I was close to tears, as was Mrs. B. She had argued with the ECE teacher, saying Emmett simply made a mistake and he shouldn't be punished for it. It didn't matter to the ECE teacher. Emmett was hers again.

We found out that Emmett had never been through the lunch line on his own. In the ECE class, the children always had their teachers hovering over them telling them everything to do. Emmett had no real experience in the lunch room. Mrs. B's defense of Emmett was to no avail and the principal backed the ECE teacher all the way.

I drove home lickity-split and called Sandy to tell her what happened. Needless to say, she was very upset. When I saw her that afternoon as we picked up our kids, she said the ECE teacher called her to discuss the "incident." She said the teacher seemed to gloat about it, as she reminded Sandy she had "predicted" Emmett wouldn't be able to handle kindergarten. He was remanded to the ECE class until further notice.

But this story has a happy ending. After a few weeks of wrangling, and with the support of Mrs. B, Sandy was able to get Emmett back into the kindergarten class for the whole day, where he finished out the year.

An interesting side note to this story is how the students in Mrs. B's class viewed the children in the ECE class. All the kids in the special ed preschool looked "typical." There were no kids in wheelchairs, with Down syndrome, or with any other visible disability. Yet the kindergartners saw them as "different." Why? Because the kindergartners knew *they* were supposed to be the youngest kids in school! Some had younger brothers and sisters, and *they* didn't go to public school. Why did *these* kids? Also, Emily and her classmates were very aware of how the kids in the ECE class were treated by their teachers. They watched them troop down the hall chained together. But familiarity breaks down barriers.

Benjamin looked "more different" than the kids in the ECE classroom. And even though he didn't attend the school, Emily's classmates got to know him when he was with me while I volunteered. They became familiar with Benjamin's speech patterns, his walker, and his big orthopedic stroller. Quickly, this "stranger" was welcomed as "Emily's little brother, Benjamin." When Emmett joined the class, he was also quickly accepted as a new friend, even though his speech and some of his behaviors were a little different.

But the kids in the ECE class who, from a distance, looked like typical kids—were perceived as strange and different. Because the kindergartners never got to know the kids in ECE, they judged them from afar. What they saw were kids who were tied together when they left the room, who sat at their own table in the lunchroom, who played apart from the other kids on the playground, and who were surrounded by adults all the time. Even so, a few kindergartners tried to be friendly to the preschoolers several times, but their efforts were rebuffed. When they attempted to speak to the preschoolers in the hallway, the ECE teachers chided them to "Be quiet!" and shooed them away.

I was sad and happy about all this. Sad that the precious children in the ECE class were judged so harshly by other kids. Happy, knowing if the kids in kindergarten got to know the kids in ECE, they would be friends, just as they were friends with Benjamin and Emmett. The structure of ECE programs, putting preschoolers in public schools and then segregating them, breeds prejudice against children with disabilities and differences.

Dylan: Mother and Mother Goose Know Best

Let's look at how things can work differently, as exemplified by the experiences of my friend, Charmaine, and her son, Dylan. Charmaine is a school teacher in the small district where we both live, and her two older children were in home day care when they were younger. When she went back to work after Dylan was born, Charmaine took Dylan to this same day care home. The summer before Dylan was eligible for ECE services, Charmaine decided she did not want him to attend our district's special ed preschool.

Consider this very carefully. For sixteen years, Charmaine was a special ed teacher, then she became a second grade regular ed teacher so she could create an inclusive classroom—one of the few in her school that was truly inclusive. As a classroom teacher, she didn't allow the special ed teachers (her former co-workers) to pull kids out to go to the resource room. The special ed preschool was located in the school where Charmaine taught, and ECE personnel often called on Charmaine for technical expertise. She was very familiar with the ECE program and *she didn't want her son there.* Is it instructive that an experienced special educator, a wise parent, and an expert on her own son, recognized that the district's ECE program was not the most appropriate placement for her son? How many of us know as much about the ECE classrooms we send our kids to as Charmaine did?

Why didn't Charmaine feel the ECE program was appropriate for Dylan? Because she knew he learned best by imitation—he routinely watched other children and copied what they were doing—which is one of the many ways all children learn. Charmaine knew there were a few typical children in the ECE class, but most of the other students had language delays and behavior issues. Dylan, who has Down syndrome, wasn't speaking yet, so how would he learn to speak if he was with children who didn't speak? Also, Charmaine knew she didn't want Dylan learning inappropriate behaviors. (She thought none of the students belonged in the segregated environment either!)

Charmaine felt the neighborhood Mother Goose Preschool was the most appropriate environment for Dylan. She visited it several times with and without Dylan, she knew the owner, and she did her homework. At the IEP meeting, Charmaine made her case. The

IEP team—including the district's special education director—agreed the most appropriate placement for Dylan was the Mother Goose Preschool.

The summer went by and in late August, it was time for Charmaine to register Dylan for Mother Goose. But the special ed director refused to pay the tuition, even though it was "understood" the district would pay since the IEP team agreed on the placement. The private preschool tuition was less than what the school would have allocated for Dylan if he had attended the district's ECE program. Charmaine and the district went through a mediation process to settle the dispute. Charmaine prevailed and the district paid the tuition for the next two years and provided services for Dylan at Mother Goose. When he turned five, Dylan began his elementary career in an inclusive kindergarten class at the neighborhood school, alongside several of his classmates and friends from Mother Goose.

Benjamin: "Does He Like to Be Cuddled?"

Benjamin's experience at the neighborhood church preschool in Texas was wonderfully successful. When he was four, we moved to Colorado at the beginning of a new school year. Emily started first grade in the neighborhood inclusive school; I started checking out preschools for Benjamin.

The school district encouraged me to send Benj to the ECE class, which was not in our neighborhood school. (It was the same ECE program Charmaine didn't want Dylan in, but this was several years before, and Charmaine and I had not yet met.) I made an appointment to visit the program, but I also planned on checking out several of the neighborhood preschools in our small town. Benj and I set off one morning for our visit to the ECE program. We spent a couple of hours there; I observed and asked lots of questions. Benjamin was the only child in the room with a physical disability. At the time, he was using a pediatric walker and an orthopedic stroller.

The class was composed of about three typical kids (the peer role models) and about twelve kids with disabilities, all of whom had language delays or behavior issues. At the end of our visit, the director asked if Benjamin would be joining the class. I told her I hadn't made a decision yet, but would let her know. "Well, please give us several days notice," she instructed. "We'll have to rearrange the furniture in here somehow or another to make room for his stroller. We've never had anyone like Benjamin in the class." I didn't feel good about this place.

After leaving the ECE class, we drove to a neighborhood preschool that intrigued me: it was a huge old log cabin, surrounded by tall pines. Unannounced, I entered the building, pushing Benjamin through the front door. "Hi, can I help you?" asked a friendly, frazzled-looking, middle-aged lady who had kids hanging onto her knees. I told her I wanted to talk to someone about enrolling Benjamin. She introduced herself as the owner, took the kidlets back to their classroom, returned to the "living room" (the old log house had, at one time, been a huge family home), and we sat down to talk.

"What's your name?" she asked Benjamin. He told her. "Well, there's lots of toys for you to play with while your mom and I talk, Benjamin!" she said with a big smile. I took him out of his stroller, laid him down on his tummy on the floor, and put some toys in front of him. To the uninitiated, Benjamin's stroller looked like a very fancy, very expensive stroller. But I'm sure Martha had an idea four-year-old Benjamin had a disability when he didn't just jump out of the stroller and begin running around the room. Very gently and diplomatically she asked, "Does Benjamin not walk yet?" I explained that he had cerebral palsy, and that I was looking for a preschool for him a couple of mornings a week.

Martha told me all about her preschool, which was a day care center as well. "We'd love to have Benjamin in the four-year-old class," she added. "It meets on Tuesdays and Thursdays from 8:30 to 11:30. Now, we don't know anything about cerebral palsy, so can you teach us what we need to know?" "Of course," I replied. "Good, then I think we'll do just fine. By the way, does Benjamin like to be cuddled?" she asked. "You bet he does," I said, grinning. "Oh, good!" Martha exclaimed. "We like to cuddle, too, so he'll fit in perfectly!"

Could there be any doubt which preschool was best for Benjamin? Because he was *entitled* to special education preschool services, I could have sent him to the ECE program for free, five mornings a week. But was that the best environment for him? It might have been the most "appropriate" within the special ed paradigm, but it wasn't what I considered *best* for my son. Do we settle for "appropriate" just because ECE is a free entitlement? Don't we want what's best for our children? I chose to pay tuition for two days a week so my son would be in a place where he would be cuddled and loved.

Benjamin made friends, learned, and had fun at Martha's. When our family visited McDonald's on Saturday mornings for breakfast, we were regularly approached by Benjamin's new friends. "That's Benjamin, he's in preschool with me," they would tell their parents. Our family met other families, thanks to Benj's friendships. Several months later, when he started kindergarten in the inclusive elementary school, he was nervous on the first day, just like lots of others, but the sight of some of his "old" friends from Martha's preschool made the day go a little smoother.

WHAT'S BEST FOR YOUNG CHILDREN AND FAMILIES?

If we want our children to be successful in the real world, they must start out in the real world. Children with disabilities may need more supports than other children; and they may learn things differently, in their own time and in their own way. But young children with disabilities are more like other children than they are different. When we accept the paradigm that disability is natural, we recognize that our children need—and are entitled to experience—the richness of natural childhoods, not artificial ones.

Before parents grab hold of the EI lifeline, we should question if we want and need the help that's offered. Services from the system should be our last resort, not our first option. We need to know we can say no.

In my son's case, I said no to the infant stimulation classes, but in hindsight, I wish I had said no to all EI services, for I allowed myself to be sucked into the black hole of the service system. At the time, it felt natural to gravitate to professionals for support. I didn't know any better. I had bought into the medical model of disability: let's do everything we can for Benjamin to fix him. Of course, I never used those exact words, but that was the intent of services and therapies.

I let the EI case manager, therapists, and other professionals become closer than friends and family. Unknowingly, I was leaving my natural community behind and replacing it with the service system. I liked the case manager most of the time, but I often resented her visits, feeling I had to get my kids, my home, and myself in perfect order before she arrived. All of us, I felt, were on display and being judged. A silly impression? Of course. A realistic observation? Absolutely.

There were times I wanted to yell, "That's it! We don't need you anymore." But I didn't have the courage to do that. And, of course, that would not have been "appropriate" behavior. I could have taken Benjamin out of the EI service system. But I felt pressure to do things "right" and felt guilty when I didn't do what was recommended. Taking Benj out of the program would have probably made me feel even guiltier. I didn't have the backbone I have today.

If I knew then what I know now, I would have done things very differently. In talking to thousands of parents during the last ten years, I've learned many others feel the same. I hope parents of very young children with disabilities can benefit from the experiences of those who have gone before them. I hope the messages in this book, coupled with their own insights and wisdom, will enable them to believe in their abilities to successfully raise their young children without the intrusion of the system.

For too many parents and their children, early intervention services are the beginning of a life-long dependency on the service system. Once you've gotten a taste of all the "help" that's out there (even if it is a bad taste), it can be very difficult to escape from the system. As a result, many of us continue pushing our children down the system's path to early childhood education, then to special education, and then to adult services and vocational-rehabilitation. The payoff our children receive is life-long clienthood instead of citizenship; dependency instead of interdependency; and a lifetime of being told what's "wrong" with them, coupled with efforts to "fix" their problems. Can we allow our children to be infected with feelings of inadequacy and worthlessness?

We dare not see our children as the professionals do: as abnormal children who need to be made normal or as normal as possible, according to traditional standards. It's probably good to measure and grade things like gasoline and beef and restaurants. Those measurements tell us something about what we're buying. But it's not good to grade and measure babies. Regardless of the disability or its severity, they are, first and foremost, babies! And they're perfect just the way they are. I hope parents who want to get out or stay out of the EI system know they can say no to *early interference.*

We can also say no to early childhood education. Segregating and isolating children in special ed preschools—and excluding them from their natural environments—is an unfair and perverse practice that may cause permanent injuries to children's hearts and minds. Are we willing to take the risk?

Some of the services provided to young children with disabilities may be beneficial to children and their families. But there are many ways to find the help and support we need right in our own communities. Because paid professionals step into our lives when we feel very vulnerable, we often see them as saviors and we come to depend on them. In the process, we forget that our communities are rich with natural supports. In later chapters, I'll detail how we can raise children with disabilities in the most natural ways possible.

For now, know that babies and young children with disabilities need the same things other babies and young children need, more than they need professional services. And parents are fully competent to meet their children's needs and start them out on the road to success.

There's one more piece of today's conventional wisdom that needs a closer look: therapy. That's where we'll go next.

Therapy:
Beneficial Remedy or Toxic Antidote?

9

I WISH THEY COULD ONLY TAKE ME AS I AM.
Vincent Van Gogh

When a developmental disability is perceived as a "problem," pediatric rehabilitative therapy is viewed as a beneficial remedy. But for many children with disabilities and their families, we should rework the old axiom, "The cure is worse than the disease," into: "The treatment is worse than the disability." Too many times, therapy is actually a toxic antidote.

When a developmental disability is diagnosed, physicians or other health care professionals usually recommend or prescribe a treatment plan, based on the conventional wisdom of remedying the so-called problem of the disability. This paradigm puts the origin of the problem within the child instead of within the environment. And that's one of the dilemmas of therapy.

When my son was diagnosed with cerebral palsy at the tender age of four months (he was really only two months old, since he was born two months prematurely), the pediatric neurologist said physical therapy and occupational therapy would be helpful. Like many parents of babies with disabilities, I was enthusiastic about therapy.

Even though Benjamin and I spent almost as much time with therapists as we did with friends and relatives, it was years before I thought much about the long-term effect of therapy on my son or our family. Therapy became part of our family's routine, and seemed the normal thing to do. It wasn't until I learned about the consequences of therapy—from adults with disabilities and from my own son—that I began questioning the universal assumption that therapies for children with disabilities are always beneficial.

Many of us are familiar with the three main types of therapy: physical therapy (PT), occupational therapy (OT), and speech and language therapy (ST). To this list, we can add: play, art, music, pet, dance, and gardening therapies, as well as horseback riding, swimming with dolphins, and other activities that are believed to be therapeutic remedies.

But are therapeutic remedies truly beneficial? The life experiences of many families and people with disabilities tell a disturbing story about therapy. When I've presented this information at workshops, some parents rethink therapy and make changes in their lives right away. For others, it takes several months or years of reflection before change feels right. The process of changing our deepest beliefs is often difficult and, for some of us, only happens over time. The ideas in this chapter may feel "wrong" to you right now, but "right" in a month or a year. In my case, I received new insights into therapy when my son was three. But it wasn't until he was six that we finally made a change. There are alternatives to professional therapy (discussed in later chapters) that can help our children. As you think about your child and therapy, listen to your heart, learn from the experiences of others, and let your child lead you.

A caution before going further: some parents misinterpret my message, so I want to make sure that my position is clear. I am not implying we shouldn't help our children. I am saying (1) there are serious consequences for children and families in the therapeutic landscape, and (2) there are other methods we can use to help our children. Furthermore, my observations are not an indictment against therapists. Most are very nice people. I loved some of my son's therapists like family.

I'm on hallowed ground here, I know. Many parents don't want to hear what I'm saying. When my son was a baby and a toddler, I wouldn't have wanted to hear this, either. At that time, I never thought to question conventional wisdom. Most parents don't. But we must.

For the first six years of my son's life, I could have won an award for being the "Therapy Mom of the Year," if there was such a thing. If we weren't going to therapy, we were doing home programs. My living room could have been mistaken for a therapy room. I moved the furniture out and bought a big orange therapy ball (the biggest!). I had to inflate it inside since it wouldn't fit through the front door. We had therapy benches and other therapy equipment in our home.

In one of our photo albums, a snapshot shows my three-year-old daughter sitting one of her dolls on an eighteen-inch ball. She was doing what she saw the therapists and mommy do to her baby brother. I thought it was so cute at the time. (Today, it pains me to look at it.) At the time, I never doubted what I was doing was right, even during the times my son or I felt uncomfortable. I was sleepwalking through a mine field and didn't know it. Finally, my son and other people with disabilities woke me up and gave me a different perspective. I hope their stories will give you a different view of therapy, too.

GOOD INTENTIONS, QUESTIONABLE OUTCOMES

The helping professionals who perform therapy do so with the best of intentions. Each has probably devoted years in college and post-graduate training learning to be the best therapist possible. They truly believe they can help a child reach her maximum potential. And we follow their directions because we agree or don't know any better.

Pediatric therapists have little or no contact with adults with disabilities, and little or no knowledge about the long-term effects of years of therapy on the human spirit. They don't know they're often helping with one hand and hurting with the other.

In this chapter, we'll examine and question the ultimate effects of therapy. What does it do to our children's hearts and souls? In the long run, which is more "disabling:" the body's inability to perform skills or a deep-seated belief of unworthiness?

Your child might not be telling you, right now, that therapy is having a negative effect on his heart and mind, even if it's having a positive effect on his body. On the other hand, he may be telling you and you're not listening: if he's crying or angry or resisting or demonstrating in some other way that he doesn't want to go. In any case, we must recognize that just because we can't "see" something doesn't mean it's not there. We need to really listen to our children, to the spoken and unspoken messages they're sending us. They are far wiser than we know.

I have great respect for the wisdom of adults who have grown up with a disability. They, along with our children, should be our greatest teachers and most well-respected experts. Doctors and therapists don't *know* what it's like to have a disability, and we don't, either. As a parent, I know my son and his body better than anyone else, but in truth, I don't know what it's like to be him. I can only give it my best shot. And I can do better if I listen to him and others with disabilities.

Adults with developmental disabilities have personal experiences parents will never have, experiences similar to the ones our children live with today. Will we continue to accept conventional wisdom or will we heed the voices of real-life experience? Will we listen, with our hearts and our minds, to our children?

During a break in a workshop I was giving, a young mom told me she thought I was all wrong about therapy. She was taking her eighteen-month-old daughter to therapy several times a week and was enthusiastic about the progress her daughter was making. In addition, her daughter attended two different play groups each week. This mother defended her actions, and I understood her feelings. I probably would have responded the same way when Benjamin was younger. I replied that it was important for her to consider the "big picture."

"How do you think your daughter will feel about all this when she's an adult?" I asked. "Well," she replied, "I think she'll be grateful that we spent all this time and money on her." Observing all this was a young lady in her mid-twenties who has cerebral palsy and uses a wheelchair. When she heard the young mom's comment, a big hoot erupted from her mouth, "You think your daughter will *thank you* for putting her through all this?" With a big grin and a friendly chortle, she added, "You'll be lucky if she doesn't curse you!" She then went on to tell us stories of her own years of therapy when she was a child.

We need to stop and think about all the "good" we think we do. Is it possible doing good can actually be bad?

A CLOSER LOOK

Once upon a time, physicians were the only providers of medical care. The doctor did everything: diagnosed illness, performed surgery, concocted medicines, and more. As time passed, these services became specialized and the medical field grew to include pharmacists, therapists, and others.

Therapies were first provided on a large scale for men who had acquired disabilities: veterans of World War I. Ever wonder how occupational therapy got its name? Originally, rehabilitation therapists would use occupational activities—typing, woodworking, basket weaving, and so on—to retrain injured soldiers for an occupation. After World War II, medical care—including therapy—was more sophisticated and *medical* rehabilitation efforts were directed toward "restoring normal functioning" in soldiers with acquired dis-abilities. (Remember that the prefix "re" means to do over again.)

Let's look at an adult therapeutic scenario in today's world. Pretend I'm sixty years old and just had a stroke. I can no longer walk. I'm right handed, but can no longer use my right hand. In the hospital, at the rehabilitation center, and then in my home, the physical thera-pist will try to help me walk again. The occupational therapist will attempt to restore normal functioning in my right hand and arm.

Prior to the stroke, I spent my life walking and using my arms and hands. As therapy begins, even if I've lost part of my memory due to the stroke, there's probably a good chance I still know what it *feels like* to walk and use my arm and hand, and I know what it *looks like* to do the things I once did.

Therapy progresses. Weeks later, I'm beginning to be able to use my hand again. But walking is harder. The PT thinks I should be making better progress. She redoubles her efforts. I'm beginning to not like therapy anymore. Perhaps I may never walk again; so be it. I'm ready to get on with my life. Get me a good wheelchair so I can be as independent as possible and send me on my way. Then I'll say bye-bye to the therapist, bye-bye to rehab!

The therapist is disappointed in my attitude. I'm not being a very "cooperative" patient. She "knows" if I would only try harder, I could walk again. She's told my doctor what she thinks. The doctor is disappointed in me, too. He also "knows" I could walk again if I really wanted to and tried harder. He urges me to continue with the physical therapy. I resist. The therapist and the doctor alternately encourage and berate me to do what they want. They paint a grim picture of what my life will be like if I don't learn to walk again. I'm tired of all this. After a great deal of argument, I convince the doctor to write a prescription for a wheelchair. It's my body, my life, my choice.

This vignette illustrates two points. First, rehabilitation therapy attempts to restore normal functioning in adults who, through injury or illness, "lost" one or more life-long functional abilities. Second, adults can choose whether or not to continue the treatment.

There are huge differences in the therapeutic experiences of children and adults. Chil-dren who are born with developmental disabilities—unlike adults who have *acquired* disabilities—do not have years of experience walking, talking, or whatever. Thus REhabilitation (to do again) is not appropriate for children! They don't need REhabilitation, they need habilitation! (And they really don't need therapy for that!) In addition, children are seldom given the opportunity to *choose* whether or not to continue with therapy.

We need to consider several questions about pediatric therapy. What unspoken mes-sages do our children receive from therapy? Can therapy actually be harmful to children and families? How do we know therapy is always beneficial for our children?

THE UNSPOKEN MESSAGES OF THERAPY

Few of us eagerly anticipate going to the doctor or the dentist. We don't relish the idea of having a medical examination or a tooth filled. Is it because we hate our doctors and other health care providers? No, they're probably very nice human beings who are there to help us. We don't like going for any number of reasons: it's embarrassing, it's uncomfort-able, and/or we don't like admitting we're "not OK" at the moment. When you or I decide to see *any* health care provider, we're essentially saying, "I'm not OK." And the health care provider replies, "That's right, you're not OK, but I can make you OK." So, even though we don't like to go, we do because it will make us OK again. We think, "It will be over soon and then I'm done with it—I won't have to do that again for a long time."

Every time we take our children to therapy, we're sending them this very powerful unspoken message: *"You are not OK."* How can we do this to children we love so very much?

We do it because we've been told therapy will help, that it's "good for them." Therapists identify the "deficits" and therapy attempts to REstore our children to normalcy. If this is not possible, then REmediation of the condition is attempted: make it less troublesome. The "problem" of disability is seen as being within the child, not in the environment. And every single time we take our children to a therapy session, we're agreeing with the deficit model of thinking. So while we're trying to help our children's bodies, have we considered what therapy is doing to their minds?

In the chaos of trying to make sense of our world when our children are newly diagnosed, when we're drowning in disbelief, fear, or confusion, the promise of therapy is like someone throwing us a lifeline to rescue us from the thundering seas. Why would we question something that promises to help?

When presenting this information at workshops, a loving, kind, involved parent (usually a mom) says, "But my child *loves* going to therapy." When my son was a baby and a toddler, I would have said the same thing. In a moment, I'll describe children's experiences in therapy, but first, a closer look at the unspoken message of therapy.

Unspoken messages are like invisible radio waves: we can't see them, but they're there. We send unspoken messages in many ways. Our actions, tone of voice, body language, and facial expression all "say" more than our words. Experts have theorized that 90 percent of communication is non-verbal.

When our children are babies, they probably don't understand the unspoken message of therapy, but this changes quickly as our children grow and develop. We don't verbally tell our two, three, or four-year-olds, "There's something wrong with you and the therapist will fix it." But they get this message anyway. When they see that their brothers and sisters or their little friends don't have to go to therapy all the time, they begin to wonder why they must. Some children rebel against therapy at very young ages, by crying or arguing or acting "stubborn." Older children—perhaps five-year-olds and above—might resist by questioning why they have to go. Even if they "like" therapy, there are times when they'd rather be doing something else.

"Be the Way I Want You To Be"

To more clearly understand what it might feel like when a child gets the "not-OK" message, let's consider this scenario. Meet Susan, a happily married wife and mother. Kind and loving, fun and friendly, Susan is well-loved by her family and friends. She's put on a little weight since her marriage to Dave, sixteen years ago. On her thirty-seventh birthday, her husband hands her a beautiful card. Imagine Sue's surprise when she opens it and discovers a membership certificate to the local fitness center. If Sue had hinted to Dave that she wanted such a gift, she might have been happily surprised. But this wasn't the case.

What's the message Susan is hearing from Dave? "You're not OK, you need to fix yourself, you need to lose weight, you need to get back to normal, you need to be the way I want you to be, and I'm giving you this membership for your own good." If you're Susan, how does it feel to be told you're not OK, especially by someone who loves you?

As an emotionally mature adult, Susan can choose how to accept this unspoken message. In her "hurt" status, she might pout or cry or get mad at the insult. In her "wise" status, she can graciously thank her husband, tell him she'll check it out, and talk to him about this in private at a later time. Dave might respond that he didn't mean to hurt her feelings: "A couple of times you said you wanted to lose weight. I thought I was helping."

We could envision a variety of other scenarios that are similar: a young man only feels valued if he follows in his father's footsteps and takes over the family business; or a daughter hates the piano, but is forced to take lessons because the music teacher told her mother she has a talent for music.

Making our children go to therapy sends the unspoken message, "You are not OK the way you are. Be the way I want you to be." We don't do this because we're selfish or mean. We've been programmed to think this way, by a society that says if a person can't walk, talk, feed himself, or something else, he's not OK. In the deepest recesses of our hearts, we also may be hoping therapy will take the disability away and our dream child will be restored to us. We may also be ashamed or embarrassed by the way our children look or act, and we hope therapy will make our children more normal so we won't feel shame or embarrassment anymore. Regardless why we do this, it's a destructive practice.

"I'm Not Good Enough"

Because therapy is on-going, children receive the same message over and over and over again, like a broken record. And, unlike adults, children with disabilities don't have the experience or the maturity to be able to choose from a variety of responses to the not-OK messages. Nor can they analyze the situation. They only feel one thing: "I'm not OK. If I *was* OK, mom and dad wouldn't make me go to therapy all the time."

I have not yet heard a child *say* she has internalized the not-OK belief. I'm not sure many children would be able to identify, and then explain, that feeling. But I *have* heard from adults with disabilities about this issue. At some point during their lives—sometimes while they were still receiving therapy and sometimes not until years later—they began to recognize feelings of unworthiness and shame. Their stories share a common theme.

Because they were taken to therapy all the time, they felt they were not "good enough" the way they were. They thought they must be sick, bad, or abnormal—otherwise, why would they have to keep going back? They already knew they were different from their brothers and sisters and friends; going to therapy made them feel even more different. They also felt sad: their bodies were not able to do what their parents and the therapist wanted (they didn't meet the therapy goals). They were ashamed of who they were. They could not make the disability go away; they couldn't make their parents happy.

"I Don't Love You Enough to Stop the Hurt"

Adults with disabilities have said that, in addition to the mental pain, therapy also caused physical pain. Tears would flow when arms and legs were being stretched. As children cried and endured the pain, they were often hurt even more by their mothers' passivity. "Why," thought one, "doesn't my mother rescue me from my abuser [the therapist]?"

In other situations, they wondered why their mothers didn't love them enough to stop the emotional pain of therapy. And this pain came from various quarters. Sometimes, therapists were verbally abusive or mean, in the eyes of the child. Thomas noted that his mother was always very protective of him and his two brothers, except when it came to therapy. His strong-willed mother became passive around the therapist; she never stepped in to protect him from the unremitting orders of the "drill sergeant" therapist.

Emotional pain also occurred when children were unable to lead typical lives. While their brothers and sisters and friends could keep playing or watching television or doing something else, they had to stop what they were doing and go to therapy—over and over again. Sylvia always felt her parents loved her siblings more: they let her brother and sister have fun and do things they wanted to do, but they wouldn't let Sylvia.

Adults with developmental disabilities have told stories of other long-lasting effects of therapy: the discomfort of being touched. They learned early on that being touched wasn't a good thing. It hurt. Strangers were allowed to touch you. Their hands made you do things your body couldn't do. As adults, some are still reluctant to be touched. This has caused long-term sadness and discomfort, for which they've sought psychotherapy. They've had to learn how to accept (and give) physical closeness: hugs, kisses, sexual intimacy.

The helping hands of therapists can hurt the bodies and the minds of children who are powerless to stop the pain. And the pain is doubled when children feel their parents don't love them enough to protect them.

Benjamin's Decision

Traveling around the country doing presentations has enabled me to meet the true experts—adults with disabilities. Over the years, their stories have touched me greatly. They also made me very uncomfortable for I was still taking Benjamin to therapy twice a week. After hearing their stories, I would ask myself, "What am I doing to my son? What if he has to spend years on a psychiatrist's couch when he's an adult because of what therapy is doing to him—because of what I'm doing to him by making him go to therapy?" Then I would argue with myself, "But if he doesn't get therapy, he'll never learn to walk or feed himself or transfer or sit up straighter or learn to write. He has to keep going to therapy so he can do all these things." And so it went.

One day, though, I listened to my son. His words were like a magnet, pulling the stories I'd heard from adults from the hidden recesses of my brain, creating a powerful force I could no longer ignore.

He was in first grade, in the inclusive neighborhood school, where he was "just one of the kids." Being a stay-at-home mom except when I'm traveling, I drove my two kids to and from school every day, carting some of their friends along. Twice a week, Benjamin had therapy after school. One of the days was an hour of OT, the other an hour of PT. Every afternoon, when the car was loaded with talkative kids, back packs, and a wheelchair, Benjamin asked, "Mom, do I have therapy today?" On the days when I said, "No, not today," he yelled with joy and told me everything he wanted to do when we got home.

On the two days when I replied, "Yes, as soon as we drop off the other kids, you've got therapy," he would dejectedly respond with an "Oh." After a couple of months of this, his response changed to, "I don't want to go today." "I know," I replied, "but you need to go." End of conversation. This routine continued for a few more weeks, and he became increasingly upset every time I told him it was therapy day. He cried and yelled that he didn't want to go. I assured him I understood how he felt (yeah, right!) and told him he still had to go. I didn't know it at the time, but the end was near.

On a cool and sunny afternoon in late fall, Benjamin asked if it was therapy day. When I said it was, he exploded in tears and rage. I was accustomed to the tears at this point, but the rage was new. Through near-hysterical sobs, tears streaming down his six-year-old face, he shrieked, "I don't want to go anymore, Mom! I've been going all my life and I'm not going anymore! I just want to go home like the other kids. I want to be a regular kid!" And then he melted, crying uncontrollably.

His courage and determination and sadness were overwhelming. How could I not respect his desire to control his own life? It all happened in a split second, but it felt like a lifetime. I took a deep breath, gathered my wits, and said, "Okay, Benj, if you don't want to go anymore, you don't have to go. We'll find some other way for you to get exercise, all right?" Grinning and wiping his snotty nose on his sleeve, he cheered up and said, "All right! Let's go home."

"Well, no Benj," I said, "the therapist is waiting. You have to tell her you're not coming anymore." His joy turned to fear. "No, I can't. Let's go home and call her on the phone," he pleaded, the tears starting to flow again. "Benjamin, this is your decision and I'm backing you up. But it's your responsibility to tell the therapist." On the drive over, we talked about how he should handle the situation once we got there. I was still hoping what I was doing—what I was letting Benjamin do—was right. But by the time we left the therapist's office that day, I knew Benjamin had made the right decision.

We entered the therapy room, and Benjamin said he wanted to sit on my lap. The PT was sitting at a desk doing paperwork. The OT was standing, waiting to take Benj to the OT area. I told them Benj had something to say. The OT stood five or six feet in front of us, looking down at him, waiting. It took a few moments for Benj to gather his courage. He had his arms around my neck, holding on tight.

His tears began again, he cocked his head toward the OT and took a big breath. "I'm not coming to therapy anymore," he squeaked, then continued on quickly before his bravery ran out. "I've been going to therapy all my life and I don't want to come anymore. I just want to go home after school like everyone else. And my mom says it's okay." Big heaving sigh. He did it.

The therapist's response was not unlike my original replies to his pleas. "Oh, Benjamin, I know therapy is hard sometimes, but you're doing so good," she said sweetly. He shook his head "no" at her and strengthened his hold around my neck. To make this long story a little shorter, I won't include all the dialogue that was embedded in my brain that day. The short version is that she repeatedly tried to cajole him to go into the other room for therapy. She tried bribing him with new toys he could play with, and used a variety of other approaches. With each request, she moved a little closer. Benj continued to shake his head at her, maintaining an iron grip around my neck. A stand-off was at hand.

I finally learned what it must feel like to be a child with a disability, to have a powerful adult trying to control you, with no means of escape. She squatted down to be at eye level with Benj, leaned in toward him, and put her hand on his arm. He tried to move away, but had no place to go, so he pushed back against me, and I tried to push back against the chair, which was against the wall, and we went nowhere fast. There was no way out. His hold on my neck was almost lethal—I never knew he had so much strength in his arms.

Exasperated that every method to get him off my lap and into the other room had failed, the therapist tried one last time. With her face inches from Benj's, her hand grasping his arm, she looked him in the eye and asked, "But Benjamin, don't you want to *get well?*"

I was shocked into speechlessness (which seldom happens). *Never had I told Benjamin he was sick!* (Or had I?) Did she really feel Benj was sick? I had no way of knowing. I only knew I had heard enough. I put Benjamin in his chair and told the therapist, "We're going now. You and I can talk about this on the phone." That evening, the therapist read me the riot act. "You're going to ruin his life. You're throwing away the last six years of therapy. He's going to get contractures." And on and on it went.

I got the message that I was an unfit mother who was not looking out for her child's welfare. I repeated my son's desires and my support of his wishes, thanked her for all the good work she had done in the past, and signed off. Our family was finished with therapy.

Benjamin is a young teenager now and neither he, nor I, have ever regretted the decision he made at the tender age of six. When we reminisce about when he was little, he wistfully says, "Going to therapy didn't make me feel like a regular person." And each time he tells me this, I apologize to him for making him go. He always ends our dialogue with, "Well, Mom, I'm glad you finally listened to me, not the therapists and the doctors."

Our lives were irrevocably changed for the better once I stopped taking Benjamin to therapy. Every member of our family felt such freedom! A sense of calmness surrounded us. Tensions we thought were "normal" simply disappeared. No more fretful tears from Benjamin. No more planning a schedule around the therapy sessions. No more telling Emily she couldn't do something because I had to take her brother to therapy. No more worrying about Benjamin's "progress" or dealing with insurance. Our lives were our own.

Even though I often felt frustrated and uncomfortable during the years of therapy, I didn't fully realize—until we got out of it—how intrusive therapy was in our family's life. In hindsight, therapy was like a long-lost aunt who comes for a visit. At first, there's excitement at the newness of it all. Then she decides to stay longer and longer. You don't like it, but routine sets in. When you finally tell her enough's enough, you experience euphoria when she goes back home. And you see life with new eyes.

HOW THERAPY HURTS CHILDREN AND FAMILIES

Taking our children to therapy becomes so routine, and seems so necessary, that we seldom stop to think about its affect on our whole family. Let's look at some of the unfortunate and unintended consequences that cause hurt for children and families.

Fears and Tears

Is the experience of therapy good for our children? How would we know? Is there a way to measure this? Probably not. We can only go with our gut instinct, based on our children's experiences and our interpretation of those experiences. Many parents (including myself, at one time) have stated, "My child loves going to therapy!" But there's no way we can know this with certainty.

For babies and toddlers, therapy is a mixed bag. Can they have fun at therapy? Of course. Most therapists are kind and gentle and try to make therapy enjoyable with toys and other manipulatives. But therapy isn't always pleasant. Many babies and toddlers are distressed and cry. Sometimes the mom will interrupt the session and take the baby in her arms to comfort him. But many times, the session continues with the therapist trying to keep on working in spite of the baby's discomfort. The baby is only there for thirty minutes and every minute counts, right? No one thinks of the baby's immediate needs; at this moment, the long term goals of therapy are paramount. Could the baby be crying because she's hungry, tired, scared, wet, uncomfortable, or what? It doesn't seem to matter for therapy comes first.

Some babies and toddlers can't turn to their moms for help during a therapy session because their moms are not there. Parents may use their child's therapy appointments as a time to run errands or to have a break. They drop their babies off and pick them up at the appointed time. While they're away, they have no idea what's happening to their children.

At some therapy centers, parents are discouraged or prevented from sitting in on the session. Therapists may feel the child will be "distracted" by the mother's presence. This is both ludicrous and cruel. A baby or toddler is more comfortable when mommy is nearby. Our babies need us close to them. How could a parent, in good conscience, sit in a waiting room and listen to her child cry in the other room? How could a therapist, in good conscience, allow this to happen?

Is it possible the real rationale for excluding the parents from a therapy session is to ensure the therapist maintains control? If a young child is not cooperative—for whatever reason—he will resist the therapist and reach out to his mother for comfort. When this happens, the therapy session is interrupted and the therapist feels she is unable to accomplish the goals for that session. If the mom's not there, the therapist can continue her work, even while the child fusses or cries.

What might this feel like to an infant, a young toddler, or even a school-aged child? For a baby or toddler, being left with a stranger can be scary. What does it do to a child to have strange hands touching, pushing, holding, and moving body parts in ways that may not be pleasant? How does a child make sense of the change from the tender loving hands of a parent, to the unfamiliar, manipulating hands of a therapist?

It's understandable we may believe our children "love" therapy. From the age of four months until he was about three years old, I think Benjamin did have fun during many of the therapy sessions. If he began to cry, I tried to comfort him as the therapist continued. If the initial cry erupted into a full-fledged wail, I told the therapist to stop what she was doing and try something else while I continued to comfort Benjamin. If that still didn't work, I simply told her to stop altogether. I held Benjamin for the remainder of the session and the therapist and I talked about how the therapy was going, in general, and discussed specific concerns.

When I think about the years Benjamin spent in therapy, I have memories of stepping in to comfort him when he was upset during a session. How proud I've been of what a great advocate I was for him. And during most of the six years he received therapy, I believe I did intervene appropriately. But I was brought up short recently when Benjamin and Emily were watching some old home movies, which included one of Benjamin's therapy sessions. To my horror, I watched as Benjamin fussed and struggled against the therapist. My voice is on the tape saying things like, "Benjamin, stop fussing and listen to Mary," or "Oh, Benjamin, you don't need to cry." I'm ashamed of what I did. I'm saddened that I let my son down when he needed me to protect him.

I would have never let someone do something to Emily that made her cry. Why did I let it happen to Benjamin? Because everyone told me (and I believed them) that therapy was good for Benjamin. We allow many bad things to happen to our children, all done "for their own good."

During the times I asked the different therapists to stop when Benj was upset, and we spent the remainder of the session talking, I felt they was uncomfortable doing this, not because they weren't caring people, but for a variety of other reasons. Therapists couldn't bill the insurance company for "talking." They were afraid the supervisor might think they weren't doing therapy. The inability to complete the scheduled activities might put a crimp in meeting the long-term goals they had set for Benjamin. Simply talking to me ("consultation") was not the same thing as performing therapy. I found these "talking" sessions beneficial and I often learned a lot. More time should probably be spent simply talking with therapists, but they don't get paid just to talk, they only get paid to perform manipulations on children's bodies.

At one facility where Benjamin received therapy for several years, children were treated in two large rooms, with four or more therapists in each room working on mats in the corners or on big therapy balls in the center of the room. I was often dismayed by the crying of babies and young children. Therapy continued as if nothing was wrong.

One day, I witnessed a therapist working with two-year-old Samantha on the largest therapy ball. With Samantha lying on her back on the ball, the therapist rolled the ball back and forth, putting Samantha upside down with each roll, her head almost touching the floor as the therapist held on to her ankles. Samantha was screaming and crying. The therapist made no effort to stop, slow down, or comfort Samantha in any way, and the little girl had no family member there to protect her. After watching this for several minutes, I walked over to Samantha and began singing to her. She quieted down a little. The therapist's angry glare told me she was not happy with what I was doing.

I mumbled I was just trying to help calm the little girl. The therapist casually responded, "Oh, she always does this. She's from a real dysfunctional family and she cries all the time. You'll get used to it. I did." I retorted, "No one should get used to a little kid crying!" The therapist shrugged, took Samantha off the ball and moved away.

On another day, a little boy about three was on a mat, whimpering and crying as a therapist stretched his legs. His mother sat in a chair next to the mat, ignoring her son's pleas of "Mommy, mommy!" The therapist continued stretching, disregarding the boy's pain and distress. At one point, the mom got mad and told her son he'd get a big spanking right then and there if he didn't start cooperating and stop crying.

In another part of the room, a little boy about four wasn't "cooperating" so his therapist took him behind a partition and put him in "time out." She was trying to use a strategy parents use, but she didn't know how to do it properly. For example, a four-year-old should spend no more than four minutes in time out, and when time out is over, the incident should be forgotten.

The therapist left the little boy behind the partition for about ten minutes. When she went back to get him, I heard her ask him if he was going to do all the bad things he had been doing (not cooperating with her). She verbally berated him for all the "bad" things he had done. At the end of her tirade, she yelled, "Now, you're not going to do that anymore, are you?" He boldly replied, "Yes, I am!" at which point she left him in time out for another ten minutes. I was appalled!

This had obviously become a battle of wills between a powerful adult and a powerless child. I wondered how she would bill this session to an insurance carrier. Did the therapist have the parents' permission to do this? Would they get a report of this session? If so, would they be mad at the therapist or would their anger be directed toward their son? What benefit was this child receiving from therapy? Was it harming him?

The majority of therapists at this center were competent professionals and kind individuals. Not every child I saw there was treated in the ways I've described. And sometimes a therapist who was rough with one child was sweet and tender with the next. But after seeing similar things happen week after week, I approached the head therapist and requested permission to address the therapists at the next inservice training. I explained I wanted to talk to them about the importance of positive relationships between therapists and children. She said she'd get back to me. After reminding her of my request several times, she reluctantly gave her permission, but indicated she wanted a *panel* of parents to share their views. She and the other therapists would select other parents to join me.

At the appointed time, I was one of three parents addressing the assembled therapists. They let me go first, and, as delicately as possible, I shared my belief that the feelings of the child must be paramount during therapy sessions. I went on to detail that therapists should stop therapy or at least change what they're doing and comfort children when they cry or resist.

I also expressed my opinion that any time a child cried, she was trying to communicate and therapists needed to listen. I reminded these professionals (all had specialized in pediatric therapy) that this was especially true for children who had not yet acquired the ability to speak, regardless of their ages: crying might be the only way to communicate.

The other two parents on the panel had obviously been chosen to contradict my perspectives. They both disputed my concerns, saying they didn't mind if their children cried during therapy. They emphatically stated that even though *they* might be uncomfortable when their children cried, therapy was for a child's own good and crying was just the price to be paid for all the improvements therapy would bring about.

After our brief presentations were done, the therapists were given time to ask us questions. You know who got hammered, don't you? Then the therapists shared the following perspectives:

- Children cry just to "get out" of doing therapy, not because they're being hurt or because they're upset.

- Everyone *knows* children with disabilities learn to manipulate other people. Even six month old babies learn to manipulate therapists!

- Since crying is just a manipulation tool used by children to get out of therapy, the therapists have to ignore the crying if they're going to do their jobs.

Are you as shocked as I was? I have no formal training in pediatric therapy or early childhood development, but I knew these "experts" were wrong. They might have known a lot about therapy, but they didn't know much about children and love and tenderness. They knew little about the importance of children feeling secure. They didn't see their "clients" as children first; they saw them as "manipulators." (They were probably taught this in college.) And most felt no responsibility for the children's spirits, only their bodies.

This experience reminded of a line of dialogue in the movie *My Left Foot*, when the mother of the young man with cerebral palsy said, "Better a broken body, than a broken heart." The language is from the 1950s and is outdated, but the sentiment is timeless. The mother understood that a "broken heart" caused far more hurt than a "broken body."

The events I've described are not meant to indict the entire cadre of therapists who work hard to help our children. I'm sure many therapists would be horrified by the behavior of some of their colleagues. The majority of therapists are probably kind and loving and patient. At the same time, we must understand that therapists are not *trained* to be caring and compassionate and thoughtful (although we hope that's part of their make-up). They're trained to restore a body to "normalcy" or help a body achieve its "maximum potential." That's their focus.

Therapists receive the same basic training in college and then some go on to specialize in pediatrics, geriatrics, sports medicine, and the like. But how much training do pediatric therapists receive about children (not just their bodies), about families, and about the emotional trauma therapists have the capacity to inflict?

We do things to children with developmental disabilities we would never, ever do to children that don't have disabilities. Most parents surround their babies and young children with tender loving care, protecting them from all harm. But in our zeal to "help" our children via therapy, we thrust babies and children with disabilities into situations where the potential for physical, mental, or emotional harm is great. In the belief that we're doing what's best, we allow them to suffer physical and emotional pain at the hands of others, we force them to do things they're uncomfortable doing, and we teach them they have no power to protect themselves from harm. How will these lessons affect them as they grow?

Therapy Steals Childhoods

When children are attending therapy—whether at the therapy center or in their own homes—what are they missing? Regardless of where therapy takes place, the time our children spend in therapy means they're missing countless typical childhood experiences. By taking them out of their natural environments and putting them in unnatural ones, or by changing their natural environments into unnatural ones, we often steal their childhoods from them. Therapy address bodily functions, while many other needs are ignored.

Time spent in therapy means children may no longer have enough time to be mommy's baby, play with their friends, sleep, go to big brother's soccer game, or do the many other natural things babies and children want and need to do. And when they miss out on "doing," they also miss out on learning!

How does this theft of childhood manifest itself in our children? Have you ever thought about it? In my own family, I believe my son learned how to interact better with adults (especially females) than other children, simply because he spent so much time with the female therapists and me. He didn't talk until he was close to three, after seven months of speech therapy. Once he began talking, he spoke in paragraphs, not baby talk. Adults were often impressed with his vocabulary and speaking abilities. But his long sentences and speeches sometimes got in the way of his making connections with other children his age.

And by going to therapy so frequently, Benjamin didn't get to spend as much time with his sister or other children just "being a kid." In hindsight, our lives were very unnatural.

In addition, a life spent in medical/therapeutic surroundings creates a skewed sense of the world. As I mentioned in the previous chapter, when my son was four, he asked if his four-year-old cousin still walked in a walker. Benjamin thought every child learned to walk by using a walker, since that's what he saw in therapy two or three days each week.

How do our children learn about rainbows and sunshine and storms if they spend so much time under the umbrella of therapy?

Therapy Disrupts Family Life

How has taking your child to therapy affected your family's life? In general, the activities of the entire family are affected by the therapy routine. You might want to go to your sixth grader's soccer game after school, but you can't because your three-year-old has therapy. Or you can't do your share of the car pooling because of your child's therapy. I'll share some experiences parents have shared with me.

Ellen takes her three-year-old to therapy faithfully. It means, however, that her six-month-old has to be awakened from his nap. She can't change her daughter's appointment; no other times are available. When the baby is awakened from his nap, he's fussy. Ellen is frazzled trying to get her sleepy baby and her three-year-old loaded into the car for the forty-five minute drive to therapy. By the end of the day they're all worn out. This happens three days out of five, fifty-two weeks of the year.

Dennis and his wife, Charlotte, have spent a year planning a family vacation to Disney World. A week or so before the trip, Charlotte tells the therapist their toddler won't be at therapy for two weeks. The therapist is dismayed; little Tyler is "on the verge of walking." She's afraid the two weeks off will really interrupt Tyler's progress. Dennis and Charlotte are torn. If they go ahead with their trip and Tyler "falls behind," guilt will consume them. If they cancel the trip, everyone in the family will be disappointed, and guilt will consume them. They can't win.

Debbie and Steve live in a rural area and had a great family life until their youngest started going to therapy. Steve's job gives him two days off during the week, but he has to work Saturdays and Sundays; Debbie stays home with their three children, ages five, three, and one. The five-year-old attends kindergarten for half a day. Before their one-year-old with a disability began therapy, their "family days" were the two days off during the week when Steve was home. After kindergarten let out, they drove into town for fun, went shopping, had picnics at the park, or just stayed home together.

When therapy was recommended, the only days it could take place were the two weekdays when Steve was off since they only had one car. It would be a one hour drive each way. Their "family days" were over. Debbie and Steve drove the baby to therapy, sometimes taking the three-year-old, sometimes leaving her home with the babysitter who also took care of the kindergartner when school was out. There was no way to schedule the therapy so they could all spend time together on Steve's days off. After looking at the "big picture," Steve and Debbie decided enough was enough. They stopped therapy and discovered other ways to accomplish what the therapists were working on. They regained their family life.

Therapy regimens often cause conflicts and disrupt a family's sense of unity. Today's families already feel fractured through divorce, both parents working, children engaged in activities here and there, and more. Our lives are too complicated. We would all benefit from simplifying our lives and making more time for our families.

Therapy Affects Brothers and Sisters, Too

If you and your child have spent much time in therapy sessions, you know therapeutic interventions can dramatically affect your other children, as well. When Benjamin began therapy at four months of age, two-year-old Emily went with us. But it was hard for her to sit quietly by for thirty minutes, two times a week, while her brother got to play with the therapist and toys. Trying to keep her occupied meant I couldn't pay attention to what Benjamin and the therapist were doing. As a stay-at-home mom, I had planned on keeping both my kids home until time for kindergarten. Reluctantly, I enrolled Emily in a "mom's day out" program at church. On the way to therapy on Tuesdays and Thursdays, I dropped her off at the church. Emily hated it. I hated it. But we did it anyway.

Many parents tell stories about the resentment that builds when mom spends more time with one child than the others. "Yes," we think, "but our other children should be more understanding. Little Johnny's needs are so much greater, so he'll always take more of my time." Depending on their ages and their personalities, brothers and sisters may or may not understand. Other children in the family often feel short-changed. Sometimes, unacceptable behaviors develop, as children try to get "equal time" in any way possible. Negative attention is better than no attention.

Sometimes therapy *should* take a backseat to the needs of the family as a whole. We *should* cancel therapy so the whole family can go to Lizzie's ballet recital or Brandon's karate test. Parents have described how Mom handles the therapy and Dad picks up the slack by making sure the other children's needs are met. But this is unfair to everyone in the family, including the child with the disability. He needs to feel he's part of things, and he doesn't want to feel he's the cause of family disunity. And Brandon and Lizzie need to feel they're as important as their brother who goes to therapy.

When Parents Think and Talk Like Therapists

When we're immersed in therapy, it's as if we've gone to a foreign country: everyone's speaking a language we don't understand. We quickly remedy this situation by learning the lingo of therapists. This can be helpful since sharing a common language makes it easier to converse. But our acquisition of their language can be very detrimental. (My husband once proudly recognized that the Thanksgiving turkey he was about to carve was in the supine position. That should have been a clue that things were out of whack!)

As soon as we start sounding like therapists, we begin portraying our children the way therapists see them: as a collection of deficit-riddled body parts. I know. I've done it. During Benjamin's therapy career, I could talk about his range of motion, navicular bones, hamstrings, heel cords, adductors, abductors, and on and on. I became an expert on AFOs, SMOs, SMAFOs, and all the other "O"s in orthotics.

Speaking professional jargon makes us feel more "equal" to the professionals. Maybe we believe this will increase our chances of getting what our children need. In far too many cases, these efforts backfire.

In an IEP meeting, for example, we point out all of our children's deficits—in the most clinical manner—to illustrate their great needs. About this time, the classroom teacher realizes there's no way a kid that has so many "problems" can be included.

The language of the medical model is the language of deficits, the language of body parts, and the language that demeans and disrespects the very humanity of our children. Why don't we tell therapists to speak our language (plain English)?

We can become so devoted to the promise of therapy that we lose our sense of who we really are—moms and dads. We sometimes mimic the therapists when we're at home with our children, making sure they do everything "right." Not content to let our children play with toys, write with a pencil, or feed themselves in any way they can, we begin doing our own brand of therapy on them. I was brought up short one day when Benjamin pleaded with me, "Mommy, please—you're not the therapist, you're my mom." Our children's lives often become one long therapy session.

ARE THERAPEUTIC INTERVENTIONS BENEFICIAL?

Because many of us trust professionals, we don't ask if therapy will be beneficial to our children; if it will accomplish what the professionals say it will. We take their word that it will. Wait! Did you catch my mistake? What's wrong with the phrase I used, "if it will accomplish what the professionals say it will"? If you answered, "The professionals didn't *say* what therapy is supposed to accomplish," you win the prize!

Doctors and therapists are usually vague about the expected outcomes of therapy, because they don't know what's possible; it's a very inexact science. Therapists talk to parents in very general terms as they tell us what they're working on and for what purpose. (If your child's therapist doesn't volunteer this information, I surely hope you ask.)

A strange thing happens when our children are newly-diagnosed and the doctor recommends therapy. The physician is probably intentionally evasive about what therapy might accomplish, because he truly doesn't know what the outcome of therapy will be. Regardless, because we want answers, we often assume or infer our own meanings of what the physician tells us. When Benjamin was diagnosed with cerebral palsy at four months of age, the physician described, in broad terms, how PT and OT "would help." He made some casual remarks about other aspects of Benjamin's development, one of which was that he thought Benjamin would probably be able to walk, but not before he was at least four years old. I heard what I wanted to hear: Benjamin will walk by the time he's four. I chose not to hear the doctor saying, "I think" and "probably."

Once therapy started, I was told more about cerebral palsy and how therapy would help with the "spastic tone" and all the rest. None of that mattered to me. All I wanted the therapist to tell me was that Benjamin would walk by the time he was four. But she couldn't tell me what I wanted to hear. She wouldn't confirm what the doctor thought. When I asked when she thought he *would* be able to walk, she replied, "Well, we just don't know, Kathie. We'll work on it, but we don't know when."

The odd thing about therapy is that professionals and parents see it very differently. Professionals *know* they can't predict specifics, while most parents are expecting definitive outcomes. Even though we may talk to therapists a great deal, we're usually not on the same wavelength. At the time we start taking our children to therapy (usually just a short time after the diagnosis) we're still in such a state of confusion that we don't even know *how* to talk to therapists and doctors about therapy. As I mentioned previously, the suggestion that our child can be helped by therapy is like a life line being thrown to a drowning swimmer. At that moment, none of us question if the lifeline is appropriate, we grab it and hold on for dear life.

Does Therapy Produce the Intended Results?

How can we know if therapy is successful when we don't really have specific outcomes in mind? For a child with a physical disability, therapists can get out their goniometer (like that jargon?) and measure the amount of flexion in the child's knee to determine the range of motion. If he can extend his knee further this time than he did the last, then we might say therapy is beneficial. (But is it possible an increase in the child's range of motion is due to a variety of circumstances, not just therapy?)

What does increased range of motion, as measured by the therapist, mean in practical terms? That the child will walk? Won't walk? Will walk if he continues to increase his range of motion, and, perhaps, his strength and balance? We really don't know what it means. There is no way to transfer the goniometer measurement into a specific outcome.

A child with low muscle tone may be asked to squeeze a ball X number of times in so many seconds. The therapist then gets a baseline and begins working to improve the child's strength and dexterity. After so many weeks, the child can now squeeze the ball harder and faster. A measurable improvement is noted. It's assumed therapy is beneficial. But let's take it further. Does this mean he can now hold a spoon and feed himself or hold a pencil to learn to write his name? We don't know. There's usually no way to transfer this "improve-ment" into an outcome—the acquisition of a specific skill.

Visit any medical library and look up the research on therapies for children. Half the studies will probably show therapy as beneficial and half will show therapy has no effect. Honest. When I was researching a surgical procedure (selective dorsal rhizotomy) we were considering for Benjamin, I spent a year learning all I could about it. On one visit to a medical library, while searching for literature about the surgical procedure, I came across a research paper on physical therapy for children with cerebral palsy. I was shocked to read that comparisons between two control groups were negligible. One group had been in therapy for a year, the other in a preschool-like setting with no therapy.

Why, I wondered, do physicians recommend therapy if there are no guarantees or no certainty of the outcomes? There are at least three reasons I've considered. You might think of more. Doctors recommend therapy (1) because the medical model of disability man-dates that doctors do *something*; (2) doctors know that parents *expect* them to do something; and (3) physicians believe therapy won't hurt and it might help, so why not try it. Of course, physicians, therapists, or parents have not thoughtfully considered the harm therapy may cause to children's bodies, as well as their spirits.

Many parents have said, "But I *know* therapy has helped my child." No, we don't know that. What some of us do know is that our children may be doing things now they couldn't do before. *But we don't know the new skill is a result of therapy.* How do we know a child wouldn't have acquired the skill, whether or not he went to therapy? Perhaps he would have done new things on his own schedule, instead of the therapist's, and perhaps he would have done them in a different way or in a different sequence. The only way we could say *with certainty* that therapy has been beneficial to a child is if we cloned him, put one in therapy and kept the other one out, then compared the two.

There's another consideration about the effectiveness of therapy. Let's go back to the example from earlier in this chapter, when I had a stroke and was receiving therapy to learn how to walk again. I pointed out that even if I had lost part of my memory, I would probably still know what it felt like and looked like to walk again. But this is not always true for children who are born with developmental disabilities. Take a child with a physical disability who does not have the ability to walk, for example. He has no way of "knowing" what walking feels like. He has no memory of walking, nor does he know what it looks like for him to walk. The methods used on an adult who is "relearning" aren't necessarily appropriate for children who have never learned in the first place!

The concept of "rehabilitation" for children and adults with developmental disabilities is goofy. RE means do again, for a second time, or do over. For adults who acquire a disability, REhab makes sense: they try to relearn the skills they lost through injury or illness. But children who are born with developmental disabilities aren't RElearning skills, they're learning them for the first time. Grammatically speaking, shouldn't their services be called habilitation? How can you be in REhab if you've never had HAB to begin with? Doesn't this tell us that many programs and services for people with developmental disabilities have not been designed specifically for them? That perhaps they are simply deviations of the original programs designed for people with acquired disabilities?

For years, pediatric therapy was simply a modified version of the same treatment methods used on adults. In the 1980s, neuro-developmental therapy (NDT) became the new mantra of many pediatric OTs and PTs. A simplified description of the NDT philosophy provided to me by therapists is this: therapists help babies with developmental disabilities acquire skills by letting the baby *feel* what normal development is, by positioning and helping them move their bodies in ways that mimic the positions and movements of typically-developing babies. This makes a great deal of sense. But does it work? Again, who can say, for sure?

I know in my son's case, the NDT therapists would sometimes spend a great deal of time working on skills in a sequential manner. Some skills he achieved in order, others out of order, and some not at all. Why? Was it because certain body parts just couldn't do it, was it that the therapist wasn't doing something right, or could it have been that Benjamin wasn't interested in achieving that skill?

All children with disabilities have abilities, skills, and talents. Sadly, these are often overlooked by therapists and parents because they're not done the "right" way. For example, a child has learned to hold a pencil and write his name, but because the pencil is not held in the typical fashion or the arm is not positioned in the normal way, this ability is not recognized. He's holding the pencil or his arm the "wrong" way. The goal of writing has been met, but therapy continues in an effort to make the child do it the "right" way. The message to the child is very clear: you're still not good enough.

Continuing with this example, let's weigh the importance of this particular skill within the big picture. How many of us hold our pens and pencils the "right" way? How many of write using the penmanship skills we were taught in school? In fact, how many of us spend much time handwriting anything these days? Think about other skills therapists work on and question their importance. Is it important that our children meet the artificial standards set by professionals or is it more important for our children (1) to learn to do what's meaningful to them and (2) to do these things in ways that are right for them?

In many instances, parents, physicians, and therapists have formed a conspiratorial brain trust to decide what's appropriate, what's best, or what's right for a child. We need to use our common sense about therapy and our children. We also need to listen to our children and take their feelings and needs into consideration.

The Developmental Model

Pediatric therapy follows the developmental model (similar to the sequential model, mentioned in Chapter 6), in which a child is expected to perform step A, followed by step B, step C, and so on. Therapists often insist on following this rigid schedule even when it's inappropriate. When Benjamin was eighteen months old, I discovered, quite by accident, that he wanted to try and walk.

The therapists had been working diligently on getting him to crawl; helping him walk was never attempted. In the developmental sequence, one must crawl before one can walk. I had asked the therapists several times about getting him a pediatric walker, but was told it would be a grave mistake: putting him in a walker before he was "ready" could cause "irreparable damage." One day, I was putting him on the floor to play. When his feet happened to touch the carpet first, as I was still holding him under the arms, he began a walking motion. Excited, I "walked" him around the living room. He couldn't stand up by himself, but his feet were walking!

Coincidentally, he had an appointment with the orthopedist a few days later. I showed the doctor what Benjamin was doing and asked him about a walker. He was also excited and said, "Sure, let's get him one!" I said I was both surprised and pleased by his answer, but still concerned about the "irreparable damage" the therapists warned me about. With a chuckle, he said using a walker would definitely not hurt Benjamin. He continued, "What the therapists don't always think about is that Benjamin might not be where a typical eighteen-month-old is physically, but in his head he wants to be an eighteen-month-old, and eighteen-month-olds don't spend their days on the floor. They're upright, moving around the house. That's what Benjamin wants to do. That's what he needs to do and he knows it."

That doctor's visit made me realize that our therapists were really stuck in the developmental model. In Benjamin's head, he was an eighteen-month-old and he wanted to be upright, not on the floor all the time. Eighteen-month-olds don't spend a lot of time locomoting on hands and knees. But because Benj still wasn't crawling in the typical fashion (he "commando" crawled), the therapists were determined to focus on this particular skill. They didn't focus on the needs Benjamin was communicating; they focused on what *they* thought was right, developmentally and sequentially. All the while, Benjamin was missing out on opportunities to "be" like an eighteen-month-old—to learn and explore—because he wasn't upright and didn't have the mobility of other children his age.

Could it be that many children with disabilities are "behind" not because of their disabilities, but because of the actions of therapists and parents? The developmental model penalizes children. If a child doesn't have the "developmental skills" appropriate to this age (as measured by experts and their charts), we deny him the opportunity to be his age.

When we use the developmental model to the exclusion of a child's unique and personal needs and situation—when we let a child progress only if he follows the designated sequence—we stifle his emotional, social, and cognitive development. I know, from the experiences of my own family and other families, that many children become further delayed because they're denied the opportunity to "be their own age."

Knowing what I know today, I would have insisted on getting my son a power wheelchair when he was two. Two-year-olds are moving toward independence from their parents, exploring their worlds, and learning at every turn. But at age two, Benjamin was dependent on adults to put him in his walker or to push him in an orthopedic stroller, as if he was still a baby. He learned dependence at a time he should have been learning independence. At the time, I was like other parents: I had "bought into" the medical and developmental models, and was in full agreement with the therapists that we should work on his ability to crawl, walk, and all the other developmental skills in sequence.

But the focus should have been on helping Benjamin achieve what other two-year-olds were achieving: the beginnings of independence. He didn't need to walk to do this, but he did need independent mobility. As it turned out, Benjamin didn't have independent mobility until he was six. Before his therapy career was over, we bought him a pediatric three-wheeled motorized scooter, against the advice of the therapist who said he wasn't "ready." She said if we got him the scooter, we were "ensuring that Benjamin would never, ever walk—why would he want to walk when he can ride on that thing?" Indeed.

My husband and I realized no one was looking at Benjamin as a "whole child." Therapists saw him in terms of his body parts that "didn't work right." When he was in first grade, Benjamin could walk to recess in his walker. Everyone was thrilled at the longer and longer distances he could go. Of course, by the time he got out to the playground, his laborious efforts were for naught—recess was over! As he was going out the door, the other kids were running back in. The time-consuming walk back to the classroom meant he missed out on academics. Educators and therapists saw the progress made by body parts and were happy. For awhile, I felt the same way.

Then I realized my son was missing out on the opportunity to play with other kids during recess. What did he need more? To walk or to experience typical activities? Using a wheelchair would not keep him from being successful as an adult; but not knowing how to get along with others, not learning how to play, not understanding how to make friends—all these could get in the way of his success.

The power scooter enabled Benjamin to "be his age." He was able to race out to recess, chase other kids and let them chase him, initiate games, make friends, and do all the fun things kids do at recess.

When we're ruled by the developmental philosophy and its sequence of activities, we keep our children in a perpetual stage of infancy and dependence. In the belief they must follow the developmental sequence, we deny them the tools they need to get on with their lives, such as mobility aids, communication devices, computers, and other devices. How can we continue to subject our children to therapeutic interventions that focus on body parts, while ignoring the needs of the whole child?

If Therapy Works, Why Do Children Still Have Disabilities?

Finally, we must ask this question about the effectiveness of therapy: if it's so effective, why do children and adults still have developmental disabilities? If therapy really worked, wouldn't we see fewer children with disabilities? Wouldn't children who were once labeled become "unlabeled" when their body functions were restored to normalcy?

These questions have no definitive answers. We do know therapy is an inexact science. Physicians and therapists are unable to give us hard facts about the effectiveness of therapy. And of all the children and adults I know who have developmental disabilities, only a miniscule percentage have "finished" therapy in the sense that all the goals were successfully reached and/or the person achieved "normal" or "near-normal" function.

In most cases, therapy is simply stopped at some point. Therapists often recommend ending therapy when the "patient" is no longer "showing improvement." This is especially true as a child moves into the teenage years. While many adults with acquired disabilities (spinal cord injuries, strokes, etc.) may be in long term therapy, seldom do we see adults (including young adults) with developmental disabilities receiving long-term therapy. This is reserved for children with developmental disabilities, for whom there is still "hope of recovery." Young adults who have been released from therapy relate the attitudes of therapists: if therapy hasn't normalized the person by young adulthood, it's time to give up.

WHEN PLEASURE BECOMES WORK (OR WORSE)

In addition to the three biggies of physical, occupational, and speech therapies, other new therapies are regularly added to the mix. Hippo therapy (horseback riding), art, music, horticulture, dance, pet, play, dolphin, and other therapies are all in vogue today. You name it and we'll make it into therapy! We've taken activities that children might find pleasurable and institutionalized them as therapies.

In seeking to help our children, many of us try anything and everything. Some children attend so many different therapies they have no time to be children. Some parents take their children to so many different therapies they have no time to be parents. They are, instead, therapeutic assistants, chauffeurs, time keepers, and consultants.

What are we doing to children when we turn leisure activities into the work of therapy? When a child loves music, for example, what message are we sending when we take her private love of music, her exploration of it, her joy in it, and turn it into a form of treatment? At that point, we no longer let her enjoy music *her* way; she must do it the *right* way. Further, she can no longer do it when she wishes; she must do it during therapy time, whether she wants to or not. And, finally, we'll make sure to measure the outcome of the music therapy. It's not enough that the benefit is sheer enjoyment, calmness, happiness, or something else. We'll attach a goal to the activity and keep working at it until the outcome (whatever it may be) is achieved.

Prior to the end of Benjamin's therapy career, we were told about a therapeutic horseback riding program for children with disabilities during the summer. I had always kept Benjamin out of segregated programs (except private PT, OT, and ST), so I wasn't too excited about this segregated activity. "But it's *not* segregated," I was told. "The brothers and sisters of the kids with disabilities can be in the class, too." (I guess this made it pseudo-inclusive.) Both of my children were present during this discussion and they were both excited (at first) about going horseback riding. With some reservations, I enrolled six-year-old Benjamin and eight-year-old Emily for eight weeks of twice weekly sessions.

At the stables were five or six kids with disabilities and about the same number of brothers and sisters. Picture Emily, not too sure of herself (but enjoying it all the same) riding around the corral at her own pace.

Picture Benjamin, a therapist and three volunteers surrounding him on the moving horse at all times, stabilizing his feet, his ankles, his knees. Shouting commands. Benjamin sitting on the horse the regular way. Benjamin sitting on the horse backwards, having to catch and throw a ball. Benjamin lying across the horse on his stomach, looking down at manure and up to the therapist as he tries to grab the toy she's dangling in front of him.

Now picture Benjamin asking, "Mom, why does Emily get to ride and I have to do all this stuff? Why can't I just ride the horse like she does, Mom?" The unspoken message to Benjamin was, "Because, you're not OK the way the you are, but this will help you be OK. When you're OK, you can ride the regular way, like your sister."

Leisure activities provide many benefits. Music helps me relax. Dancing is fun. Playing with our pets and watching fish in an aquarium are delightful. Riding horses is pleasurable. Do we dare risk teaching our children to hate what they once loved because it was forced on them as therapy? Are we not being selfish and short-sighted when we turn our children's pleasures into work? If a child loves art, for example, what might it feel like to be forced to paint because it's "good for him" instead of painting for the sheer fun of it?

Think of your own personal interests or hobbies. Would you still enjoy them if you had to "perform" them at a scheduled time, in a specific place, and in a certain way under the watchful eyes of a professional who expected you to meet certain criteria?

At the other extreme, what happens to a child who cares nothing about music, for example, but he must go to music therapy because the professionals or his parents believe it will help? If he doesn't enjoy music to begin with, he probably won't enjoy music therapy. He probably will learn, however, to hate music for the rest of his life.

Why can't we simply let our children enjoy pleasurable activities at their own pace and in their own way? Can't we understand they'll still receive benefits from these activities? Do we doubt our own abilities to help our children in the most natural ways possible?

IF THE TRUTH WAS TOLD

Prior to a mother taking her child to therapy for the very first time, what if the pre-scribing physician said, "Mrs. Howard, little Scott is now one and he needs therapy. I can't promise you that it will work, but it's worth a try. The therapists will look at him, tell you everything that's wrong with him, and they'll try to make him normal. If they can't make him completely normal, they'll do their best to make him look as normal as possible.

"Now, here's the deal: you'll need to take Scott to therapy for at least the next seven years—maybe longer, depending on how hard he works. PT, OT, Speech—he'll need to go to each one, at least once a week, for thirty minutes. As soon as he can tolerate it, we'll bump him up to an hour each time. This is minimum. He'll need to go year 'round, but you can take two weeks off for vacation. The therapy sessions cost a minimum of $75.00 an hour—you do have insurance don't you?

"If you follow my instructions and the advice of the therapists, you might see improve-ments. But there are no guarantees. I know you want an accurate picture of all this, so let me do some figuring. I'll base this on a total of three therapy sessions, an hour each, for the next seven years . . . Well, it looks like little Scott will spend a minimum of 1,050 hours in therapy; your family life will be disrupted for at least for 2,100 hours, this number includes the hour spent at therapy and a thirty-minute drive each way.

"I'm sorry I can't give you a better estimate of what other effects this will have on your family and Scottie, but every family is different. Just don't plan on having a normal family life—but you knew that, didn't you? Oh, and this will only cost $78,750.00. This is the cost of the therapy. I didn't factor in gasoline expenses or any other items. And even though I can't promise you any specific outcomes, I know Scottie's future is worth that, right? By the way, you don't have a cap on your insurance do you, Mrs. Howard?"

If this imaginary—but truthful—scenario routinely took place, what percentage of parents would sign their children up for therapy?

IF NOT THERAPY, WHAT?

If we don't take our children to professional therapists, how can they get the assistance they need? In lots of different ways, as I'll specifically describe in Chapters 14 and 15.

But here's an overview to keep in mind until you get to those chapters. When we shift the paradigm and see that the "problem" of disability resides in the environment and not the child, we can easily move in a different direction. Instead of focusing on a child's "deficits" and attempting to "normalize" or change the child, we can focus on strengthening a child's abilities and modifying the environment. We can eliminate the "deficit" paradigm and use the "ability" paradigm, recognizing that every human being has strengths, talents, gifts, and capacities.

Instead of therapeutic interventions, we can use natural ways of assistance—within our own homes and in our communities —that build on a child's strengths and capacities. In addition, our focus will not be on what a child can't do, but on how we can help him do what he needs to do. And in most cases, this means providing the child with tools (for independent mobility, effective communication, and so forth) and accommodations.

To move toward this direction, we'll need to look at our children and presume competence. We'll also need to treat children with disabilities as children, first, not as patients. Doing all of this will allow a child with a disability to achieve the common, but precious, goals of independence and self-determination—the same goals we have for all children.

WHY BENJAMIN CRAWLED

For six years, several different sets of therapists worked zealously to get Benj to crawl. The technical term is actually creeping (locomoting on hands and knees), but in the universal language of parents, crawling is the word we generally use.

When Benjamin was very young, he "commando" crawled: pulling himself along with his forearms, tummy scraping the ground, with his legs dragging behind, just as soldiers do when they're crawling under barbed wire. He was never able to get up on hands and knees and crawl in the typical fashion, even though therapists worked diligently on this skill. Still, he got around the house just fine in his own way. Often, he arrived at his destination with his pants or shorts down around his ankles—the constant rubbing against the floor just pushed them down, down, down. (I was glad his diaper didn't get pushed down, too!)

Remember that Benj resigned from his therapy career during the late fall of first grade. That next January, my husband and I were watching the Super Bowl game on television. Benj was lying on the floor playing. He yelled, "Look at me! Look at me!" To our amazement, he was up on his hands and knees, and he crawled about three or four feet. Then his body relaxed and he was flat on the floor again. My husband and I were stunned. Benjamin had never crawled like this, even when therapists had held up his middle and manipulated his arms and legs. Benjamin was extremely proud of himself. We all laughed and cheered.

A few days later, I had a meeting with all of Benj's teachers to touch base with "the team." I told everyone about Benjamin's four-foot crawl. All the educators around the table oohed and aahed—all except one. Mrs. C, the gym teacher, was a funny, kind, lovable, and loving sixty-something lady who has taught PE for about 150 years! Short, white-grey curly hair. Black sweat pants. White t-shirt. Whistle on a chain around her neck.

After the murmuring subsided, Mrs. C piped up. "I don't understand why this is a big deal. He's been crawling in gym class for the past three weeks." My jaw was hanging on my chest. "What?" I yelled. "How did you get him to crawl?" "Me? I didn't do anything," she replied. "I had all the first-graders playing some games where everyone had to crawl. Benjamin saw his friends do it and he started doing it, too."

At that moment, I realized Benjamin was not motivated to perform for the therapists. He was motivated to be like other kids. When I share this story during a workshop, a parent in the audience often has a similar story of her child doing something unexpected because the child was motivated by his peers. Do you have one? Perhaps you do, but just never thought about it this way.

NO ONE CAN PREDICT THE FUTURE

When Benjamin was very young, the pediatric orthopedist taught me a valuable lesson. On a day when I was wringing my hands over Benjamin's progress and reviewing what the therapists were doing, I asked the doctor, "Do you really think Benjamin will ever walk?" His answer was one that all parents should hear, for his words weren't just about my son, but about all children. He said, "You know, Kathie, I just don't know. I see kids in here all the time that I think should be able to walk and they don't. And I also see kids that I don't know how in the world they could ever walk, and yet they do. If a kid is going to walk, he will and if he's not, he won't."

At the time, I was frustrated by what I saw as a non-answer. But later, I realized the value of his words. This wise man was telling me, in a subtle way, "Don't count on therapy to make everything happen." But he was also trying to tell me something even more important: whether Benjamin walked was up to Benjamin. Not that he would consciously choose whether to walk or not, but that he knew what he was capable of doing and what was best for him (whether we did or not), in spite of everything being done to him.

QUESTION AND LISTEN

If your child is currently receiving therapy, take the time to closely examine the pros and cons. Explore therapy's effect on your child and your family. Talk to your child about therapy. Even if your child is non-verbal, listen to his messages about therapy. Talk to your family. Listen to the little voice inside. What do your instincts tell you?

We've now reviewed various components of today's conventional wisdom—the ways things are. I've laid out many issues we should consider about the service system in Disability World. Now it's time to look at the way things *can* be!

The Way
Things
Can Be

THE SIGNIFICANT PROBLEMS WE FACE
CANNOT BE SOLVED AT THE SAME LEVEL
OF THINKING WE WERE AT
WHEN WE CREATED THEM.

Albert Einstein

A NEW PARADIGM

> THE GREATEST DISCOVERY OF MY GENERATION
> IS THAT HUMAN BEINGS CAN ALTER THEIR LIVES
> BY ALTERING THEIR ATTITUDES OF MIND.
> *William James*

Disability is a natural part of the human experience that does not diminish the right of individuals with developmental disabilities to enjoy the opportunity to live independently, enjoy self-determination, make choices, contribute to society, and experience full integration and inclusion in the economic, political, social, cultural, and educational mainstream of American society.

The Developmental Disabilities Assistance and Bill of Rights Act

Think about it. There have always been people with disabilities in the world and there always will be. Like ethnicity and gender, disability is simply a natural part of humanity.

The following statements might not make sense to you right now. However, I present them at this time so you can keep them in the back of your mind as you read this chapter.

- The inability to walk is not a disability.
- The inability to talk is not a disability.
- The inability to eat unassisted is not a disability.

The list can go on. If you wish, insert what your child is unable to do at this time and say it isn't a disability. Now read on.

How can we internalize the belief that disability is natural? What needs to happen in our heads, our hearts, and our lives to accept this new paradigm? And will changing our attitudes about disability really make a difference? Yes, it will.

DISABILITY IS A SOCIAL CONSTRUCT

Before we look at the paradigm shift we must all make, let's review what a disability is. In Chapter 3, I detailed how a disability is a condition of the body identified by a physician within the medical model. Further, a disability is whatever the government (or a service provider) says it is. A disability label is an administrative term that's used as a sociopolitical passport for entitlements or benefits, or to identify individuals who may be protected by certain laws. Remember, there are probably as many definitions of disability as there are programs, services, and regulations.

Disability is a social construct. That is, it's a concept that was created by our society. There are many conditions of the body that are different from the so-called norm, but not all of them are classified as disabilities. By identifying which conditions of the body entitle a person to services or protections, the concept of disability was constructed.

It's a concept that sends mixed messages. Laws such as the Americans with Disabilities Act (ADA) address the reality that environmental, architectural, and attitudinal barriers prevent people with disabilities from being part of the mainstream. It places the problem of disability within the environment. Yet most services and programs continue to promote the notion that the problem of disability is within the person. Under this paradigm, the person must be fixed, changed, or restored to normalcy so he'll fit in society.

Pondering what disability really means can be a mind-boggling experience. I spend a great deal of time questioning, hypothesizing, and wondering. I've described how, on one hand, developing a concrete, universally-accepted definition of disability is impossible. Yet, there are many specific definitions of disability.

Is the *concept of disability* useful or valuable? Within the service system, disability and disability labels are valuable to people who are labeled, and their family members, because a label is a passport to services.

Is the concept of disability useful and valuable within society? Yes and no. It's useful when it focuses public attention on needed societal changes advanced through the Disability Rights Movement. It's not useful and valuable (it's actually harmful) when it stigmatizes, marginalizes, and devalues a significant portion of our nation's population.

However, the concept may become more useful and valuable if we move it from administrative and legal usage to a universally-accepted idea that simply represents natural differences in the human body.

In essence, having a disability simply means a person has a body part that works differently from "the norm," which in no way diminishes the humanity, the wholeness, or the importance of the person. And because all of our bodies work somewhat differently, we could say we each have a disability. Think about it. A disability simply means a body part works differently.

Changing perceptions about disability and people with disabilities has been, and continues to be, a long and slow process. Even though I personally reject the idea of "normal" as applied to human beings, it's still an accepted concept across our society and within our government. Programs and services are based on the notion that because people with disabilities are different from the norm, they need services, entitlements, and other benefits.

We live in a world of "norms." At one time in our country, being Euro-American was considered the norm. Since normal is always the default position, anyone who wasn't Euro-American was considered different or deviant from the norm. At another time, being male was the norm in employment. A worker who was a woman was different or deviant from the norm. But norms can and do change, don't they?

Ethnicity, religion, age, gender, and other characteristics are no longer seen as deviance from the so-called norm. In these instances, we've either expanded the parameters of norms or we've discarded them. Our job is to help society expand or discard norms about bodies, minds, and abilities so that our children and others are no longer placed outside the boundaries of those norms. First we must see for ourselves, and then we must show others, that the way body parts (including the mind) operate is just one of an infinite number of natural human characteristics.

We can accept the traditional views of disability and continue on the rocky road we've traveled since the beginning of time. Or we can adopt new attitudes about disability that will translate into actions and behaviors, which will blaze new trails to inclusion for people with disabilities today and forevermore.

My hope is that one day, recognizing and accepting differences in each others' bodies will be common practice. Measuring and comparing abilities will no longer be seen as important. At some point in the future, disability will no longer be a relevant or useful concept within society.

OUT WITH THE OLD; IN WITH THE NEW

When we think about traditional beliefs—disability is the problem, people with disabilities need specialized help, the system can meet our needs, and others—it's significant that most of us have simply accepted these as facts. Moreover, we've accepted them without one shred of proof that they're accurate or truthful.

We've accepted them because embracing the *beliefs of the majority* is easier and safer than questioning them. In addition, we were never given alternatives to the conventional views because there weren't any, but now there are.

Even when conventional beliefs begin to tear at our souls and the fabric of our families, and even when we question and fight them, most of us don't reject them as outright falsehoods. We continue to hold on to them as acceptable foundations which simply need to "improve," as evidenced by our efforts to "change the system."

Seldom do the strongest disability advocates—leaders we follow into combat with policy makers, skirmishes over funding, and protracted sieges against educators—publicly and loudly reject the conventional wisdom. Instead, they seek modifications, alterations, and additions to today's current practices and systems. And most of us follow in lock step, believing if we fight long enough and hard enough, our side will eventually prevail.

Changing the system is a good and worthy goal. Systemically, we *do* need advocates and agitators who can battle the bureaucracy and shake up the status quo. But personally, we cannot ask our children to wait even one more day on the systems that were created to help them, but which have failed them, miserably, time and time again. We cannot allow our children to be dehumanized by the beliefs (and our actions) that they must be worked on, fixed, made more "normal," or that they achieve some artificial level of readiness in order to be fully human.

The system, no matter how much it changes, cannot bestow dignity, freedom, and opportunity on our children. Instead, it takes away the inherent hallmarks of what it means to be human. And the system cannot give our children what they really need. As is true for all children, the success of children with disabilities rests in the hearts and hands of their families and their communities.

So let's get rid of the old paradigms and replace them with new ones. Disability is natural. The "problem" of disability originates in societal attitudes. There is nothing "wrong" with a person who has a disability. The "cause" of disability is in the environment, not the human body. The system cannot meet the needs of children with disabilities.

Adopting these new ways of thinking, and others that are presented in the following chapters, will lead us to new ways of seeing our children, new ways of behaving, and new ways of doing things.

INTERNALIZING A NEW BELIEF

Each of us must move toward a new belief system in our own way and own time. Some will do it quickly—by the end of this chapter—for others, it will take longer. That's okay. We're all different, and we're learning that it's okay to be different, right? As you're learning new beliefs, you can practice some mental exercises.

Rejecting Normalcy

Is there a universal definition of what it means to be normal? No. In fact, people are considered normal by default. If a person does not have a characteristic that society, doctors, educators, or any other group considers abnormal, he's considered normal. Thus, the definition of normal is infinitely changeable. Normal can become abnormal or abnormal can become normal. Sometimes the process is cyclical: normal becomes abnormal becomes normal and so on. Major shifts in perceptions of normal/abnormal can result in social change, technological advances, or a variety of other developments.

For example, at one time, it was normal for parents to whip and beat their children for disobedience. Today, we call this child abuse and see it as an abnormal practice. Having a mouth full of decayed teeth was normal before the advent of modern dentistry; today it's abnormal. Slavery was once normal; today it's not.

Long ago, people in "proper" society protected themselves from the sun to preserve their pale skin tones. Rough, suntanned skin was the mark of laborers and those of low-birth; lily white skin was a sign of high society and good breeding. Over time though, skin bronzed by the sun announced one's membership in the jet-set strata of society. Even if a person couldn't really claim membership in the ranks of the rich and famous, you could look like you "belonged" by sporting a tan. When my sister and I were teenagers, we spent long hours lying in the sun—burning our skin—in order to look cool. But this trend has reversed itself again. Hats, long sleeved-shirts, and sunscreen are now used to protect our skin from cancer causing ultra-violet rays.

Think about other situations when normal changes position with abnormal, or better yet, when a belief or principle goes full circle: abnormal, normal, abnormal, and so on.

When the normal/abnormal concept is applied to people, it's almost always directed toward individuals or groups who are already marginalized. In fact, we could ask: are people marginalized because they're considered abnormal or are people considered abnormal because they're marginalized? Maybe both.

But let's exercise our minds by applying the concept to people or groups who are usually exempt from judgments about normalcy. And remember, there is no accurate definition of normal; the status is achieved by default: if a person or group does not have a perceived abnormality or difference "from the norm," then normalcy is assumed. Ready to exercise? Here we go!

- Mrs. Smith, the school principal, is very abnormal.

  Translation: the other members of the IEP team are difficult and hard to get along with. This is the norm at Mrs. Smith's school. By virtue of Mrs. Smith being a kind and helpful educator, she's different from the norm—she's abnormal.

- There are several abnormal senators in Congress.

  Translation: the majority of senators routinely miss one or more votes. But five senators (out of one hundred) have never missed casting a single vote. They are, therefore, different from the norm—they are abnormal.

- Mr. Carter is a very abnormal teacher.

  Translation: the majority of teachers at the high school teach the same way. They stand in front of the class and lecture. Mr. Carter's classes, however, take place in the parking lot, on the football field, and in other locations around the school. Mr. Carter roams among his students with enthusiasm and encouragement, as he helps them learn experientially. His difference from the norm makes him abnormal.

- Bureaucrats are an abnormal group of people.

  Translation: most Americans dislike the red tape and inefficiency of government agencies, and try to stay as far away from the system as possible. Thus, anyone who would choose to become part of the bureaucratic mess must be abnormal.

If the first three situations were real, the individuals who were different from the norm would certainly stand out. But most of us wouldn't use the term abnormal to describe them. In fact, the descriptors we use would reflect our positions and our viewpoints.

Parents would call Mrs. Smith an "extraordinary" principal, but her staff might call her a "pushover." Constituents and the media might call the five senators "dedicated public servants," but other senators might describe them as "do-gooders." Students may see Mr. Carter as "the best teacher in school who makes learning fun!" Other teachers may see him as "a weirdo who has no respect for traditional methods of teaching."

In the example of the bureaucrats, it is—once again—our *positions* that dictate our perspectives. People who feel the system helps them may see bureaucrats as "saviors." Those who are frustrated with the red tape of the system might see bureaucrats as a "bunch of do-nothing pencil pushers." Bureaucrats may see themselves as public servants who are "trying to make things better." What's important to realize is that all these perspectives are right!

Being considered abnormal isn't necessarily a negative. Whether we see something as normal, abnormal, or something in between depends on our position, as demonstrated in the previous examples.

When it comes to people with disabilities, however, abnormal is always perceived as a negative. This opens the door to seeing people with disabilities as deviant, not worthy, and worse. It also leads to efforts to make people with disabilities normal. Let's reject these descriptors when thinking or talking about people with disabilities.

We must also reject the concept of normal when it comes to how or when children with disabilities do things, what are families are like, and more. For example, parents and professionals often talk about making sure a child learns to do things the normal or "right" way. How ever a child does something is the right and normal way for him. We may think our families are abnormal, or we don't "feel" like a normal family because of all the baggage that goes with a child's participation in the service system, or for some other reasons.

From now on, let go of the concept of normal. In fact, remove the word normal from your vocabulary! There is no such thing as a normal human being, a normal family, a normal body, a normal mind, or anything else!

Chew on all this for awhile. Converse with yourself in your head. Discuss the concept of normal/abnormal with your husband or wife, children, neighbors, and others. When we question traditional ways of thinking, new ways of thinking can emerge.

Rethinking Disability and Differences

Another important mental exercise is to question what defines a disability or a difference. By now you know disability is officially defined by laws or by the agencies who provide services. But let's look at disability and differences through a wider lens.

My husband and I both wear glasses. If we weren't able to purchase thin line lenses, we would both be wearing "Coke-bottles" (super thick lenses, for those readers who are too young to remember this derogatory term). Because of the strength of my husband's lens prescription, I could say my husband is "almost blind," based on one or more of the definitions of being "legally blind."

It's possible my husband could go from *not* having a disability to having one if/when his visual acuity changes ("worsens"). But this is all dependent on the service system. He might qualify as having a disability under one federal or state program, but not necessarily others. In this hypothetical situation, my husband might choose not to invoke his disability status. In that case, he doesn't have a disability after all!

Think about a person who has multiple sclerosis, diabetes, or arthritis. These conditions and others may not be considered disabilities, in and of themselves. They may "become" disabilities within the contexts of (1) how they impact the person's life and/or (2) if the person chooses to say the condition is a disability. In the first context, a person could conceivably move in and out of having a disability, depending on how the condition affects his ability to do things, work, and so forth.

In the second context, let's consider two individuals (Mary and Elizabeth) who both have the same type and intensity of arthritis. Mary feels her condition is a disability (and can prove it, if need be) and she wants the services she is entitled to, as well as the legal protections afforded her by law. She sees her condition as problematic and seeks remedies. Elizabeth, on the other hand, doesn't feel her condition is a disability. She does not want entitlements, preferring to continue using the natural supports of friends, family, and co-workers. Elizabeth sees her condition as a natural part of life.

How many other situations or conditions can you think of in which a disability label is contingent on a person's individual beliefs about his condition, the manner in which the condition affects the individual, the way the person with the condition is treated by others, or any other variable? Think about these questions as they apply to your own child and his environments at home, in school, in the community, and other places.

Let's go back to Mary and Elizabeth again. Imagine they're both fifty years old and they're each employed by different stockbrokers in high-pressure offices. Mary's arthritic condition impacts her on the job because of the office environment. On the days when her arthritis flares up, she's unable to move as fast or work as hard, and her boss won't accept anything less than 100 percent. In order to keep her job and receive job accommodations she's entitled to under the ADA, Mary must choose to invoke her disability status.

Elizabeth's arthritis is the same as Mary's, and so is the workload. But Elizabeth has explained the situation to her boss, who understands and accepts her condition as a natural occurrence. On the days when her arthritis flares up, the office staff pitches in to modify the work load and give Elizabeth whatever assistance she needs. She has no need of entitlements and services, and she doesn't need protection against job discrimination, so she doesn't need to call her condition a disability.

Mary and Elizabeth have the same condition, and one has a disability, but one doesn't. What makes the difference? Environment and perception.

Now, think about your own child as I describe my son's situation. Because Benjamin doesn't receive any services (by our choice), we don't need to invoke his disability status, and I can, therefore, say he doesn't have a disability (even though he has the medical condition of cerebral palsy). If he should go back into the service system or if he ever needs the protection of disability laws, we could "activate" his disability status.

Here's another example. A child with autism may communicate just fine with her family at home, by using some speech coupled with hand movements and specific behaviors. In this environment, we could say she does not have a disability—she faces no barriers in communicating effectively. But when she goes to school, an environment in which teachers have not learned her communication patterns, she faces many barriers, she's perceived to need special help, and therefore, has a disability.

This may make sense to many readers, but some may be thinking, "Yes, these ideas are great for Kathie's kid or kids that have [whatever], but they won't work for my child. My Ian has a G-tube, he's non-verbal, and functions at the level of a three-month-old. In any environment, Ian has severe disabilities."

No, he doesn't. He has disabilities within the construct of the service system and the medical model, but that doesn't mean he's abnormal, nor does he have severe disabilities in every environment unless that's what we choose to believe and/or if we don't provide him with the tools, modifications, and accommodations he needs.

Let's look at the various descriptions of Ian. He's fed through a G-tube. We can see that as a significant deviance from the norm and be sad, mad, or frustrated about it, or we can yell, "Hallelujah!" and be thrilled we have a way of giving Ian vital nourishment. If we see this as a problem, other people will, too. And consider this: being fed through a tube is "normal" for Ian. If this perspective is held by Ian's parents, and if they share this perspective with others (at school, for instance), people will view Ian differently. Ian is fed through a tube; that's the way it is; that's what's normal for him; it's not a big deal.

His mom says Ian is non-verbal. Being non-verbal isn't the same as being unable to communicate. Ian probably communicates all the time, through sounds, eye movements, or body language. If other people don't understand Ian's communication, their lack of understanding causes a disability, not Ian's inability to speak. But when Ian is around people who understand his communication, we could say he doesn't have a disability.

Ian is said to "function at the level of a three-month-old." Gag. This type of description is so inaccurate and so demeaning. Ian, an eight-year-old, has eight years of life experience! How could anyone think of him as a three-month-old? He may not walk, talk, feed himself, or go to the bathroom by himself, but that doesn't mean he's like a three-month-old! Unfortunately, if people treat him as an infant, he may act like an infant. But no one, and I mean no one—not even his parents—can accurately peg Ian's intellectual abilities since no one has found an effective way of discovering what Ian knows. Unfortunately, professionals have measured Ian using a developmental scale and made an outrageous pronouncement that his parents believe.

While Ian may do things differently than other children, and he may not be able to do some things at all, his disability status is dependent on his environment. If Ian is provided with tools and accommodations, if his environment is modified, if he's treated like an eight-year-old, and his differences are seen as natural, Ian may not be seen as having "severe" disabilities; he may not be seen as "functioning like a three-month-old."

 Disability is not a fixed or permanent position. It's a variable status that's dependent on (1) the environment of the person with a given condition, (2) how that person views himself and/or how others view him, and (3) an individual's need or desire for assistance from the service system, entitlements, legal protections, or health care services which can only be accessed with a disability label.

Theoretically, disability is anything we say it is. Concretely—as a sociopolitical passport to services—disability is whatever policies and laws say it is. Further, the conditions we label as disabilities have been occurring since the beginning of time and many, if not most, will continue indefinitely (and new ones will be added), so disability is natural.

Can there be any doubt in your mind that the disability label attached to your child—regardless of its medical name or its "severity"—is a natural condition? Your child may have Down syndrome, autism, cerebral palsy, Williams syndrome, spina bifida, or any other congenital or acquired condition. But whether he or she has a disability is contingent on a set of variable circumstances.

HOW DO WE CHANGE OUR HEADS, HEARTS, AND LIVES?

How do we put this knowledge to use within our own families? What needs to happen in our heads, hearts, and lives? Because we're all unique individuals, we must each change in our own way, but I'll share some suggestions for you to consider.

No More Comparisons

One of the ways we can change is to stop comparing our children with disabilities to other children. It's detrimental to our children and our families, and it stands in the way of believing our children can be successful.

Making comparisons is another behavior we've been programmed to do. Specialists measure our children against developmental scales, comparing them to the mythical "average" child—to see how "far behind" they are—as a way of deciding which services they need. We continue the practice by comparing our children to other kids we know at school or in our neighborhoods, as well as to their brothers and sisters. Resolve not to do this anymore. Nothing good comes from this practice.

Comparing children with disabilities to their brothers and sisters is extremely harmful. These comparisons can cause great stress, and for many parents, it leads to great sadness. (This is especially true when the child with the disability has younger brothers or sisters who "pass him up" in physical or mental abilities.) Worse than the parents' sadness, however, is the pain it inflicts on the child with the disability. His parents' attitudes will cause him to believe he can never achieve as much as his brothers or sisters. Simultaneously, these comparisons create an atmosphere where brothers and sisters feel sorry for the sibling with a disability, they behave in patronizing ways, and/or they resent the child because of the extra attention he gets because of the disability.

Many of us are very good at recognizing our children who don't have disabilities as unique individuals—each is one-of-a-kind. Samantha is the only one in the family with red hair. Brett stands out as an artist; no one knows where that inborn ability came from. Julia is shy and a late-bloomer. Damon is a natural athlete. But we're often unable to see the unique characteristics that make a child with a disability one-of-a-kind. Most of the characteristics ascribed to him are disability-related, which means they're usually negative characteristics.

Think about this: except for height and weight scales when they're tiny babies, children without disabilities are seldom, if ever, systemically and routinely measured, judged, or compared to other children. If they were, we would be outraged! "Well, Mrs. Jones, little Tommy is not drawing as well as other children his age." "Mr. Smith, we're sorry to tell you that Jenna is not as good a ballet dancer as other girls her age." In reply to such ridiculous observations about our children, we might want to tell the speaker to "stuff it." Hopefully, we might actually say something like, "Well, Tommy's not real interested in art and drawing, so we're not too concerned about this," and "We're very pleased with Jenna's efforts at ballet. She may not be 'as good' as the other girls, but she's not taking this class to win any contests, she's there because she enjoys it." Shouldn't we respond similarly when professionals critique the progress of children with disabilities as compared to others?

Comparing our children with disabilities to other children, measuring their lack of progress or accomplishment, and seeing them as being different or abnormal because of a disability label prevents us from seeing and valuing their many wonderful characteristics. We—like professionals in the system—often let the perceived deficits overshadow positive characteristics.

Begin now to change these types of behaviors. Instead of comparing your child to any other child, compare him only to himself. What's she doing now that she wasn't doing six months, six weeks, or six days ago? This is what we usually do with children who don't have disabilities. We recognize individual differences, we don't constantly compare them to others; we compare them to themselves. My daughter loves to weave. I don't look around for other fifteen-year-old girls who weave to judge Emily's abilities. In this instance, I don't even compare what she's doing now with what she was doing six weeks ago. It's not important how she's doing it. What's important is that she enjoys doing it, that she's found something she likes, and so forth.

Take a few moments and think about what positive characteristics make your child unique. What are her gifts and talents? Is she curious, caring, funny, happy, kind, or what? What does she do better than anyone in your family? (Benjamin has the best memory or anyone in our family!) Is she the most patient, the most generous, or what? What does she want to be or do? Become a movie star, learn to ride a bike, go to the prom, or what? Your child's collection of positive attributes are far more imporant than the collection of "deficits" identified by professionals.

See the Ordinary

Don't view everything about your child through the disability lens. Many parents describe their children with disabilities by providing a laundry list of "what's wrong" with them. The list often includes characteristics or behaviors that are absolutely typical, but when viewed through the disability lens they're seen as aberrant, abnormal, and so on.

For example, most of us are familiar with the characteristics of the "terrible twos." But children, whether they have disabilities or not, don't necessarily go through this stage of development from the date of their second birthday through their third. And all children exhibit various characteristics of emerging independence during their early years. But over and over again, I've heard parents describe their young children with disabilities as having "inappropriate" or "manipulative" behavior during the toddler years. These negative characteristics are attributed to their disabilities instead of to the natural and positive struggle for independence.

Similar situations occur in the lives of school-aged children. Children at various stages are curious about body parts, sex, and other subjects many adults consider taboo. This is an absolutely ordinary part of growing up. But when children with disabilities, especially those with cognitive or behavioral labels, express interest in these subjects, parents (who have been influenced by the system) often see these typical behaviors as deviant or inappropriate and this deviancy is attributed to the disability. We must celebrate the ordinary, typical milestones, at whatever age they occur, and see them for what they really are.

I was delighted when Benjamin went through the "terrible two" stage. He was barely talking and he was unable to physically demonstrate his independence by doing the opposite of everything he was supposed to, but he learned to say NO! on a regular basis. However, the therapists and early intervention folks were most unhappy about this behavior. They didn't approve when Benjamin resisted them and yelled NO! as often and as loudly as possible. We cannot let the attitudes of others take away the pride and joy we have for our children and their achievements.

It wasn't until he was nine and confident in his power chair that he physically demonstrated his independence by "running away" from me in the mall and almost getting lost. (This is a behavior common to many two-year-olds.) Some might have viewed this as inappropriate for a nine-year-old. But I was ecstatic! Ditto when he acted like other boys his age by experimenting with "talking dirty" about body parts, checking out his own body parts, and engaging in other ordinary, growing-boy behaviors.

Don't see your child's actions or behaviors as abnormal or aberrant just because he does them on a schedule that's different from the norm! Celebrate every new thing he does, just as you celebrate what your other children accomplish. In addition, don't assume (or let others assume) everything your child does is a result of the disability. This is especially important if your child has behavior needs. Recognize that many behaviors might be typical for the age, part of your child's innate personality (irrespective of the disability), or something else. Remember: see the ordinary and celebrate it!

Unconditional Belief

The beginning of successful lives for children is our unconditional belief in them and their potential for success. For many parents, this belief is often conditional, based on conventional wisdom and the system. For example, a parent may think a child can only be successful if or when he learns to walk, talk, take care of himself, or whatever. Or we may think success will only come when or if we find the appropriate treatment for her condition (medication, surgery, cure, or whatever).

When we believe our children's success is dependent on external remedies, we're delivering our children's lives and their futures into the hands of a society that will continue to marginalize them because of their perceived imperfections and deficits. In addition, we're preparing for failure. For the "if" or the "when" may never happen.

If we're heavily invested in therapies, interventions, and the expertise of professionals, we're hoping and waiting for experts to help our children reach their "maximum potential." Belief in a child may be contingent on whether this potential is ever reached. But we must be very careful. When experts talk about maximum potential, they're usually talking about a child achieving normalcy or near-normalcy. To achieve this, they focus on changing or fixing the child.

This gives our children a profound sense of loss and unworthiness. Put yourself in your child's place. Hear the powerful message she must hear: you're not OK the way you are. And all the love and affection we shower on them cannot erase their feelings of inadequacy and unworthiness, and, worst of all, of being unlovable just the way they are. The only way off this one-way street of spiritual impoverishment is to believe that disability is natural.

What does it mean to unconditionally believe in your child and his future? It means that right now, regardless of your child's label or the severity of his disability, you believe he will be successful and will live the life of his dreams. It means you don't wait for something to happen or change before you believe he can be successful.

Many of us have a generalized attitude that, "I'll believe it when I see it." But when it comes to our children, we must adopt the attitude, "I'll see it when I believe it." Unconditional belief is another way of saying we have faith in our children, just as we have faith there's a God, faith the sun will rise tomorrow morning, or faith in anything else we can't see or know for sure. We *believe* there's a God; we *believe* the sun will come up again tomorrow. These are unconditional beliefs. There are many things we can't see or know with absolute certainty, but still we believe. We must take the same attitude about our children's success. Unconditional belief in your child's success will cause you to behave differently toward your child. You will begin to see new possibilities, which will result in your doing things to help ensure his success.

We do this in other areas in our life all the time, without knowing it. For example, if you believe you and your family will never take a dream vacation to Hawaii, it will never happen. But if you get the idea in your head, "We're going on that trip one of these days, one way or another!" you will automatically begin doing things to ensure this belief becomes a reality. You begin to "see" your family on the sunny beaches of Hawaii and this vision drives your actions: you find ways to put a little money away here and there and you investigate budget travel accommodations. You start figuring out *how* to make it happen.

The same thing will occur when you say, "My child is going to be successful, one way or another!" *See* your child as successful—at home, in school, in the community—right now and as an adult. But remember not to gauge success by the acquisition of functional skills (the way professionals do). The successes of children who don't have disabilities aren't thought of this way, so let's not do that to kids with disabilities. For example, we don't look at a typical ten-year-old and say, "Heather is successful because she can walk." Instead, we believe Heather is successful as a ten-year-old because she has friends, gets along well with others, is active in Girl Scouts, and by other ordinary achievements. We believe Heather will be successful as an adult because she has dreams of going to college, she wants to be a teacher or a ballet dancer when she grows up, and she talks about getting married and having children one day. Heather's parents "see" her as a successful adult because they've helped her dream. They "see" the success first, and then they believe it.

So begin to see your child as successful. Think about what the characteristics of success are for typical children who are your child's age. Now think about your child being successfull in similar ways. A two-year-old is successful if he's learning independence. A five-year-old is successful if she's becoming more helpful around the house and learning responsibility. A ten-year-old is successful if he's enjoying himself on the soccer team or has friends over on the weekend. A teenager is successful if she's thinking about what to do when she finishes high school. These are just examples, of course, and narrow ones at that. There are many ways typical children see themselves as successful, and many ways their parents see success, and the two ways may be very different!

Create some pictures in your head of what success would look like for your child. Think big and, at the same time, think ordinary. What are the typical things other children and young adults do that makes us see them as successful? Things such as helping around the house, being involved in community activities, learning how to use a computer, and other ordinary activities. What are the typical *characteristics* of successful children and young adults? Kindness, good manners, struggling for independence, dreaming about the future, and more.

Don't worry right now if you don't know *how* the success will be achieved. Just begin to *see* your child as successful. The vision must come before anything else. Then, between your own common sense and the suggestions in several of the following chapters, you'll figure out *how* to make it happen.

Share Your Beliefs

Your mind and your heart will be changed when you believe that disability is natural, when you stop comparing your child to others, when you celebrate the ordinary, when you believe in your child and his success, and when you take any other steps to see your child as a precious one-of-a-kind kid. Good things will happen to your child and your family when you share your beliefs with others.

Put your new beliefs to work by talking about them to your husband or wife, your family (including the child with the disability), friends, professionals, and anyone else who touches your family's life. Verbalizing your beliefs puts them into the consciousness of others. New ways of thinking results in new ways of behaving.

Call a family meeting (including the child with the disability) and talk about old and new attitudes. Discuss how new beliefs will be incorporated into your home environment. Ask how each family member can think differently. Talk about how you can support one another as you make the transition to new beliefs. Create a simple plan of action to put your beliefs to work: how will your family talk the talk and walk the walk? Help all members of your family "own" their new beliefs by encouraging them to contribute to the family plan.

Share your beliefs with your child's doctors, therapists, teachers, friends. As much as possible, let your child communicate the new principles to the people who influence his life. In a positive, proactive way, outline new parameters based on these beliefs, such as: "So in the future, we want to compare Robert's progress to what he did in the past, instead of comparing him to developmental charts or to other children."

Be prepared for resistance. This is new stuff to most people (heresy to some) and they may initially reject your beliefs as being unrealistic, pie-in-the-sky, denial, or any number of other characteristics. That's okay; this will pass. Your patience, persistence, and firmness will pay off. Everyone is capable of change; we all move at different speeds. Even when others don't agree with you, model the beliefs and the language you want them to adopt. Don't force it down their throats or it will just come right back out. Give them the opportunity to change. Most will accept.

WILL NEW ATTITUDES MAKE A DIFFERENCE?

When we accept disability as natural, we think differently and we behave differently. As parents, we begin to treat our children differently. We don't see them as a collection of body parts that need improvement; we see them, sometimes for the first time, as whole beings. This causes us to rethink what's really important.

Do we need to talk about our children's disabilities all the time or do we need to be talking about our children as unique individuals?

Are our children's labels the most important thing other people need to know about our children or should we be sharing our children's personalities, gifts, and talents with others?

Do our children need to spend hours being worked on by therapists or do they need to be experiencing typical childhoods?

Should the lives of our families be driven by our child's disability or by the wants and needs of the family as a whole?

How will believing your child's disability is natural affect your own family?

THE LARGEST MINORITY GROUP

People with disabilities constitute the largest minority group in the United States— an estimated 54 million Americans. It's a group that includes people of both genders, of all ages, and from all ethnic, socioeconomic, and religious groups. And it's the only minority group that anyone can join at any time.

The incidence of disability is on the rise. As Americans live longer lives, many of us will acquire disabilities through the aging process or through illness. Every year, thousands of Americans acquire disabilities when they're injured in accidents. Every day, babies are born with congenital disabilities. The disability community is truly inclusive and non-discriminatory: anyone can belong. In fact, an individual can join in the split second of an accident. Most American families will be touched by disability at one time or another. Can there be any doubt that disability is natural?

One of the ways we can promote this belief is through language. That's where we'll go next.

People First Language
New Ways of Thinking and Talking

> THE DIFFERENCE BETWEEN THE RIGHT WORD
> AND THE ALMOST RIGHT WORD
> IS THE DIFFERENCE BETWEEN LIGHTNING
> AND THE LIGHTNING BUG.
> *Mark Twain*

Our perceptions and attitudes live in our heads.
What's in our heads comes out of our mouths.
What comes out of our mouths reflects what we believe.
What we believe drives our behavior.
Our behavior affects our children.

The way we've thought about and talked about our children in the past—using their labels more than we use their names, spewing a laundry list of perceived deficiencies, and portraying them as needy and unable—may have gotten them a ton of services (or maybe not), but it has done little to ensure their success.

If we want our children to be successful, we must think and talk and behave in ways that reflect dreams of success. Using People First Language and focusing on the person first can move us in the right direction.

The way we think and talk about our children reflects our attitudes about our children. Many of us have doubted our children's potential for success. We've been caught in a cesspool of negativity that swirls around us. The way we (and others) think and talk about our children drives our behavior. Until our children are adults and/or on their own, *our* actions dictate our children's success or failure. Our thoughts, the way we talk, the way we act, and our children's lives are all connected. What we believe about our children will most likely come true. Believe in failure, get failure. Believe in success, get success.

WHAT IS PEOPLE FIRST LANGUAGE (PFL)?

In its most basic form, People First Language puts the person before the disability. In addition, PFL uses words to describe what a person "has," not what a person "is." But it's much, much more. Using People First Language means ridding our vocabulary of words that have become meaningless, words that presume or denote inferiority, words whose original meanings have become corrupted, and words that create invisible barriers.

Some parents and people with disabilities dispute the importance of using People First Language, saying it's just political correctness (PC), and is therefore worthless. Don't believe this. People First Language is about dignity and respect. It has more in common with the Golden Rule than with political correctness; it's about treating others the way you want to be treated.

Many people take politically correct language to extremes, but some PC terminology is valuable and appropriate when it helps promote equality and fairness. People and groups who have been disenfranchised *should* be able to right the wrongs that were perpetuated through language. At the same time, some use pseudo-PC terms to mock People First Language. Referring to someone who is short as "vertically challenged," someone who can't follow a map as "directionally challenged," and other humorless descriptions marginalize honest efforts to promote dignity and respect through language.

THE POWER OF LANGUAGE

Words matter; they can build up or break down. Words can create powerful, but invisible barriers that separate people with disabilities from the mainstream of society. *Attitudinal barriers are the single greatest issue facing people with disabilities today.* If society had different attitudes about people with disabilities, we wouldn't be in the mess we're in today!

Let's take a look at some words that are frequently used to describe people with disabilities, and their definitions from the 1995 Webster's New American Dictionary.

Handicap, as a noun, is defined as "[{from the} obsolete English handicap, a game in which forfeits were held in a cap, from hand in cap] (1) a contest in which an artificial advantage is given or disadvantage imposed on a contestant to equalize chances of winning; (2) a disadvantage that makes achievement difficult." As a verb, handicap, handicapped, and handicapping means "(1) to give a handicap to; (2) to put at a disadvantage." As an adjective, handicapped means "having a physical or mental disability that limits activity."

Thus, a person who is perceived to be at a disadvantage is "handicapped." We know, however, that the disability doesn't cause a person to be at a disadvantage. The disadvantage is caused by societal and environmental barriers!

An unpublished legendary origin of the word refers to a centuries old practice in Europe of people with disabilities having to beg on the street with "cap in hand" to catch the donations thrown their way. When translated into English, the word order was changed and the phrase became "handicap." This origin, however, has not been documented.

Webster's defines the verb "disable" to mean "(1) to disqualify legally; (2) to make unable to perform by or as if by illness, injury, or malfunction." "Disabled," as an adjective, means "incapacitated by illness, injury, or wounds; also, physically or mentally impaired."

The verb "impair" is defined as "to diminish in quantity, value, excellence, or strength: damage, lessen." "Impaired" as an adjective, means "being in a less than perfect or whole condition; esp: handicapped or functionally defective—often used in combination [hearing=impaired]." The noun "defect" is defined as, "blemish, fault, imperfection;" the adjective "defective" means "faulty, deficient."

This grammar exercise could be continued indefinitely in a review of terminology used to describe people with disabilities. Many of today's descriptors have evolved. Language is not static; word meanings and usages evolve over time. For centuries, "defect" was used as a descriptor of things, such as a defect or blemish in a bolt of cloth, a machine part, and the like. But today it's also used to describe disabilities as in "birth defect." How can we talk about a newborn baby and imply that she is blemished, faulty, imperfect, or deficient?

A variety of disability-related words are commonly used in derogatory, negative, or insulting ways. People in the news media, policy makers, and others use metaphorical phrases, such as:

- He turned a blind eye. (chose not to understand)
- Oh, that's lame! (stupid)
- He's a lame duck president. (ineffective, powerless)
- A disabled vehicle is blocking traffic. (broken down, doesn't work)
- Management is handicapped by the strike. (has problems, is unsuccessful)
- They turned a deaf ear. (chose to ignore)
- Don't be a retard! (don't act stupid)

I'm sure you can think of many more disparaging phrases that are used every day. People who use such phrases aren't demonstrating overt prejudice toward people with disabilities. They may not even connect the word they're using with disability. (My daughter came home from school one day and began telling me how "lame" something was. When I asked her what the word meant, she replied, "I don't know—stupid, I guess. All the kids say it.") But these words could not have evolved into insults unless they were perceived as negative terms to begin with. Prejudice and discrimination are hidden within the words, but they're there, nonetheless.

Disability-related words have gained common usage because they paint a vivid picture, they get the point across quickly, and they're easy to use. They're powerful and explicit descriptors! What is the absolute worst insult one child can hurl at another on the playground? "You're a retard!"

The relationship between attitudes and language is circular: our attitudes are reflected in the language we use; the language we use influences attitudes. My friend, Chuck, who happens to use a wheelchair, makes the point very succinctly: "What you call me is how you see me!"

THE BASICS OF PEOPLE FIRST LANGUAGE

Put the person first. We're all people, first. We're all individuals.

Don't use any form of "handicapped," as in, "the handicapped," "he's handicapped," "handicapping condition," etc. Remove this ugly word from your vocabulary. It's an old, antiquated term that's got to go!

Don't use "disabled." The original usage of this word has been corrupted. At one time, it may have been appropriate for people with disabilities to describe themselves as "disabled." Specifically, many adults who acquired disabilities have said, "I'm disabled now," because this is what a doctor or bureaucrat told them. In addition, some of us have substituted "disabled" for "handicapped," since the H-word was seen as stereotypical and prejudicial. But during the last ten or fifteen years, the word "disabled" has been used more and more to identify things that are broken or don't work.

During rush hour traffic reporters say, "We have a disabled vehicle in the right lane." Years ago, we heard, "There's a stalled car." But today, "disabled" is the adjective of choice to describe a broken down car.

Flight attendants routinely announce, "It is against federal law to tamper with, disable, or destroy the smoke detector in the lavatory." In this context, "disable" means to make the smoke detector inoperable. And in computer vernacular, "disable" is frequently used as a command to make something inoperable.

People with disabilities aren't broken down, like "disabled vehicles." They're not inoperable, like "disabled controls" in a computer. Because *society* uses "disabled" to describe things that are broken or don't work, do we dare use the word to describe people with disabilities? No, no, no!

We'll discard "handicapped" and "disabled" altogether. Instead, we will use disability, as in "people with disabilities" or "I have a disability." A disability simply means a body part works differently.

Don't use euphemisms such as "physically (or mentally) challenged." What does this mean, anyway? That a disability is something to be overcome? That a disability challenges a person, like one sword fighter challenging another to a duel? Is a person in a fight with the disability? Using this term puts the "problem" of disability squarely in the lap of the person with the disability, when we know the problems are within society. We might go so far as to say society is "challenged" by people with disabilities!

"Challenged" is a descriptor that's easily denigrated when people corrupt it into so-called humor. As I mentioned earlier, people joke that someone who's shorter than average is "vertically challenged." A person who gets lost easily is said to be "directionally challenged." These descriptions are always accompanied by laughter. And, intentional or not, they ridicule People First Language and our attempts to inject dignity and respect into language about people with disabilities.

I've asked many adults with developmental disabilities about the use of the word "challenged" and none like the term or think it's appropriate. *They never refer to themselves that way.* Remember, your child will grow up to be an adult with a developmental disability. Let's learn from those who have real-life experience living with a life-long disability.

The descriptors adults with disabilities use on themselves varies. Older Americans who have acquired disabilities often call themselves "handicapped" since that's the word they grew up with. Younger adults with acquired disabilities often call themselves "disabled." But the vast majority of adults who were *born with developmental disabilities* are vehement supporters of People First Language.

Unlike adults who have acquired disabilities, most adults who were born with disabilities have experienced exclusion, prejudice, discrimination, and isolation—to one degree or another—all their lives. They're more aware of the importance and power of language than people with acquired disabilities. People who didn't have disabilities as children had typical opportunities to define themselves. When they acquired a disability as an adult, their lives were impacted by the disability, but many have been able to hang onto the positive image or success they enjoyed prior to the disability. The same is not true for adults who were born with disabilities. Because their labels defined them as children, they've had to fight against labels and negative attitudes all their lives, making them more sensitive to and aware of the power of language.

As you may recall from the history chapter, adults with developmental disabilities introduced People First Language when they demanded to be known as people, not their labels. Our children will grow up to be adults with developmental disabilities. Let's be respectful of the wisdom of today's adults with developmental disabilities. They've been where we, as parents, can never go; they've been where our children are now.

People First Language always refers to what a person *has,* not what a person *is.* For example, say "My child has autism," instead of "My child is autistic." *A person is not his disability.* Disability is simply one of many human characteristics. If you describe your child by what he "is," you're telling your child and the world that's what you think he is! How do you want others to see your child? More importantly, how do you want your child to see himself?

When we use People First Language, we use words not as definers of human beings, but as descriptions of characteristics. Put another way, we'll use descriptors in the same way other people use them. For example, a person who has cancer doesn't say, "I'm cancerous." He says, "I have cancer." A mother doesn't say, "My daughter is freckled." She says, "My daughter has freckles." Let's learn from this. Instead of saying, "My daughter is disabled [or handicapped or retarded or whatever]," say, "My daughter has a disability."

Certainly, there are exceptions to this. Some people say, "I'm a diabetic," while others say, "I have diabetes." While I can't provide a definitive reason for this, I believe it must be because diabetes (and many other conditions) have never carried the pervasive stigma of developmental disability labels.

During some of my workshops, I'm occasionally questioned by someone who takes things to extremes, by asking "But what about someone saying 'I'm a doctor' or 'I'm a brunette'—aren't they using labels to say what they 'are' not what they 'have'? Are you saying the way they talk is wrong?" Of course not. The difference lies in societal attitudes. In general, doctors, carpenters, computer programmers, and most other employment labels do not carry negative connotations. And there are multitudes of other things we routinely say about ourselves or others that do not carry negative stereotypes. We just need to use our common sense about this or we could argue ourselves into oblivion!

Our goal—and my personal hope—is that soon we won't even need People First Language. As more and more people with disabilities are included in schools, jobs, and communities, they'll become known simply by their names. Labels will be irrelevant in society. (Unfortunately, we'll still need them in the service system.) But we're not there yet; change takes time. In the meantime, PFL provides a vehicle to rid our language and our attitudes of the demeaning, stereotypical views about individuals who happen to have disabilities. Following are details and suggestions about specific disability labels.

Congenital Disability

"Birth defect." Ugh. "Brain damaged." Double ugh. What do we do when we bring a new toaster home from the store, plug it in, and it doesn't work? We march right back to the store, take our toaster to the customer service counter and say, "This toaster is defective. I want another one."

What does defective mean? That something doesn't work or is flawed. And we don't *want* a thing if it's defective or damaged. Do we feel that way about babies who are born with "birth defects" or with "brain damage"? Should we send them back for new ones? I don't think so. Instead of using the stigma-laden "birth defect," say congenital disability.

Why is "damaged" so frequently used when talking about the brain, but not all body parts? If you break your arm, do you tell the doctor you have a "damaged arm"? No. You would probably say, "I injured [or hurt or broke] my arm." Instead of "brain damaged," let's say brain injury.

Cognitive Disability

Many adults with the label of "mental retardation" (MR) are ready to toss this label in the trash heap and I heartily agree. The MR label has become an all-encompassing term that means everything, and so really means nothing. Professionals typically use IQ scores as the criteria for assigning this label. But we know IQ tests are misused and don't accurately indicate a person's abilities. Even if professionals want to use this criteria, we don't have to agree with or accept the MR label. The descriptor that reflects dignity and respect is cognitive disability. This simply means a person's brain works differently; a person learns differently.

"Retarded" is a word whose time has come and gone. Dictionaries define "retard" as "to slow" or "to hold back," and many folks think the word is acceptable. "Hey, retarded just means he's slower," a parent might say. But when we say someone is "slower," we're back to the model of measuring a person's deficiencies against the "norm." When we say someone is "slower," what are we really saying? Slower than who? Under what circumstances? In what environment? In the long run, how important is speed? Remember the tortoise and the hare? Slow and steady won the race! Let's not use "retarded" or "mental retardation" about people with disabilities anymore. Excise that term from your brain right now. Cognitive disability is more dignified and more accurate, as in "people with cognitive disabilities" or "My child has a cognitive disability."

Autism

Let's not use "autistic" anymore. Say, "My daughter has autism," not "My daughter is autistic." Say "My son has PDD," not "My son is PDD." Our children are children, first. When a parent says, "My daughter is autistic" what visual image do we have? A child who flaps her arms all the time, perseverates, self-stims, doesn't make eye contact, and on and on. A child with autism may demonstrate some of these characteristics some of the time, but is this all there is to her? No. She loves music, hates asparagus, is a great artist, and more. She has a name. That's who she is.

Have we ever stopped to think that many of the characteristics attributed to children with autism spectrum conditions are also characteristics of people who *don't* have disabilities? I know several people who perseverate on a regular basis. Don't you know people who don't make eye contact? And who doesn't self-stim? Smokers (me), nail biters (my husband), hair-twirlers (my daughter), beard-rubbers (my brother), nose-pickers (my son—well, no comment) and . . . the list could go on and on. Perhaps most of us have a degree of autism. So let's put these things in their proper perspective. Besides, aren't you ready for people to stop saying, "Oh, your kid is just like Dustin Hoffman in *Rainman*."?

Down Syndrome

Please say, "My daughter has Down syndrome," instead of "My daughter is Downs," or "My daughter is retarded." Your daughter is Mary or Susie or Jessica. She has big brown eyes, beautiful hair, loves Barbie, and happens to have Down syndrome.

Physical Disabilities, Wheelchairs, and More

My son has cerebral palsy (CP). I know others who have sons and daughters with spina bifida (SB), muscular dystrophy (MD), and other conditions. Children with physical disabilities are not "lame" or "crippled" (no more Tiny Tims), physically challenged, paralyzed, or anything else.

They are not "wheelchair bound" nor are they "confined" to a wheelchair. I don't recall ever binding my son to his chair, nor confining him to it. I have confined him to his room, but never his wheelchair. My son's wheelchair is not confining. On the contrary, it gives my son freedom and independence. People with physical disabilities *use* wheelchairs, so let's say, "My son uses a wheelchair." And with all the high-technology today, the most accurate descriptor is that my son uses a mobility chair. He doesn't passively sit in a chair that has wheels. He moves. All the time. Whenever he wants. To go wherever he wants. To go in circles as fast as he can in the driveway.

Some children have acquired physical disabilities through injuries sustained in accidents: a spinal cord injury (SCI) or a traumatic brain injury (TBI). These children are not "quads" (paralysis of all four limbs) nor are they "paras" (paralysis of the legs). They're children who *have* quadriplegia or paraplegia. They are also not "brain damaged" or "brain injured." They have a brain injury.

Disorders and Disabilities

This section includes learning disabilities (LD), attention deficit disorder (ADD), attention deficit with hyperactivity disorder (ADHD), sensory integration disorder (SI), emotional disorder (ED), oppositional-defiant disorder (ODD), and any other "D."

"My kid is LD," is a description used by many parents. No, no, no. Your child *has* a learning disability. If we say, "Lauren is learning disabled" does that mean she can't learn anything? No. Does it mean her learning is disabled? No. It simply means Lauren learns differently. Perhaps her learning disability only affects her in reading, but not in math or art or the computer. So, when it's absolutely necessary to talk about her disability, we might want to say, "Lauren has a learning disability in reading." It makes absolutely no sense to give Lauren a generic LD label when that label is so ambiguous. On its own, it means too many negative things to too many people. Most importantly, though, what does it mean to Lauren and the way she feels about herself?

Ditto the above about kids who have ADD, ADHD, SI, ODD, ED, or anything similar. We need to make sure we say, "My child *has* [whatever]." not "My child *is* [whatever]."

I've heard many parents say, "My son, Tommy, is hyperactive." What's the image there? A kid who runs around like the proverbial chicken with its head cut off? Why do we want to portray our children in a negative way? Besides, aren't we all hyperactive sometimes? If I'm running late for an appointment, hyperactivity is good. It helps me get out the front door on time. And there are many times my husband exhibits signs of ADD, like when he swears I didn't tell him something when I know I did! Instead of saying what your child "is," say, "My son, Tommy, *has* hyperactivity."

I'm going to digress for a moment and urge you to be vigilant if your child has been assigned one of these labels or any other condition in which the diagnostic methods are iffy. Take some time and really think about what behaviors your child exhibited that led a professional to assign one of these particular labels to your son or daughter. Many labels represent "catch-all" generic diagnoses that really don't tell us much about the condition or the child who's been given the label. What often happens is that doctors or educators observe certain characteristics or behaviors (or are told about them) and then make these traits fit into some category.

I've met many parents with children who have been given one or more of these labels. Many have told me stories about how "severe" their children's disabilities are. Because I'm very curious (okay, nosy!), I often asked questions about their children's lives. The answers parents give are often surprising, even to themselves. Some begin to question and even doubt the diagnoses applied to their children. Following is a composite of various conversations on the subject:

> Mom: Oh, yes, my son has ADD [or LD, ADHD, SI, ODD, etc.]. It's so bad he's having trouble staying in the classroom. He can't pay attention, then he gets into trouble, and now the school thinks he's also got behavior problems. Anyway, they're having to pull him out more and more and he hates going to the special ed room.
>
> KS: How would you say the ADD affects your son?
>
> Mom: Oh, it affects everything. He just can't seem to stay focused on anything.
>
> KS: Have you seen him at home or other places besides school where he *does* stay focused on something?
>
> Mom: No, not really.
>
> KS: What are his favorite things to do?
>
> Mom: Oh, he loves computer games [You could substitute any other activity.]
>
> KS: Does he stay focused on his computer games when he plays them?
>
> Mom: Oh, definitely! He'll play this one game for hours and hours.
>
> KS: Then he doesn't have ADD all the time, does he?
>
> Mom: No, I guess not. I never thought about it like that.
>
> KS: Then would you say he shows signs of ADD mostly at school?
>
> Mom: Yes, come to think of it, I think that's right.

KS: Perhaps the school should use what your son loves to do and does well—like computers —to help him be more successful.

Mom: Yes! If he could use the computer to do his work at school, I'll bet he could really stay focused. I think he must get bored when he's having to listen to the teacher lecture. Then he gets in trouble. Hmmm—why didn't I think of that?

KS: Probably because you've been brainwashed and you lost your common sense. But now you're getting it back.

Education will be covered in Chapter 17. But I share this story now to illustrate that many children essentially "acquire" disabilities such as LD, ADD, ADHD, SI, ODD, ED, and others when their learning styles or personalities don't mesh with the public school system; when there are unresolved conflicts between their personalities and the structure of the classroom; and/or when their needs are not being met. In essence, these are often "school induced" disabilities! This is another example that demonstrates the cause of disability as being in the environment, not in the person.

Interestingly, many children—especially boys—are not identified as having these conditions until they reach the upper grades of elementary school or the middle school/junior high level. Early elementary education (kindergarten through third grade) often includes hands-on activities, group activities, talking, sharing, movement, and fun projects. This is a good match for a child who is very active. In many schools, however, the classroom environment changes in the fourth or fifth grade: children are then supposed to learn by sitting still and listening instead of actively doing. And this practice usually continues through middle and high school.

Kids who don't learn well this way may do poorly in school; they may become very bored. Their boredom leads to frustration and that often leads to what educators call disruptive behavior. *Voila!* We've now *created* kids with disabilities (LD, ADD, ADHD, etc.). Instead of looking at the school environment, society (educators and physicians and even parents, sometimes) look at the child. When children don't "fit" into the structure of a classroom, we say it's the child's fault and we try to modify the child instead of modifying the environment. This is very dangerous. Efforts to modify the child are usually unsuccessful (as well as disrespectful). When the child rebels against this invasion of his mind and spirit, and when he chafes at the insults to his dignity, he may acquire a behavior label.

A young mother told me her two-year-old daughter had been labeled with Oppositional Defiant Disorder (ODD). I was shocked. Most parents would agree that *all* two-year-olds have oppositional-defiant characteristics. That's the nature of being two. This mother seemed to be relieved—almost glad—that her daughter had this label. Was it because the mother could now attribute her daughter's behavior to some medical reason? What message was being sent to this little girl? Are we giving her license to always be "difficult" because that's what her label says about her? Will she, indeed, live down to the expectations of her label? What kind of doctor would give a two-year-old such a label?

Short Stature

Snow White and the Seven Dwarfs might be a catchy movie title, but we don't want to use the terms "dwarf" or "midget" anymore. People whose bodies are shaped differently prefer the term short stature. So for a child with the medical condition of "dwarfism," let's say, "She is of short stature."

Other Conditions and "Afflictions"

If I haven't provided examples of how to describe your child's condition using People First Language, just remember to say what your child *has,* not what he *is:* "My child has [a developmental disability or the name of the specific condition]." Instead of saying, "My child is medically fragile," say, "My child has significant medical needs."

"Suffering," "afflicted with," and similar terms have got to go! Instead of using these negative terms, just say, "has." So instead of, "My daughter suffers from [whatever]." say, "My daughter has [whatever]."

"Special Needs"

Don't all children have special needs? Have you ever considered that your child's so-called special needs are normal and ordinary needs for her? When we say we have a "special needs child," we might as well be using a megaphone to shout, "She different, doesn't belong, can't cut it in ordinary situations or with typical kids. She's special!" At one time, special was a nice word, a good word. But in today's usage in disability circles, it only serves to separate and segregate (special education, Special Olympics, and others). It's also one of the best sympathy-invoking terms to use. Saying "I have a special needs child," automatically triggers pity and paternalism in the listener.

"Special" covers such a huge landscape, it's really an irrelevant term in describing needs. If my friend, Charmaine, and I both say we have children with special needs, are we saying our kids have the same needs? This can't be true since our children have needs that are unique to each of them. In the minds of many, "special needs" is just another way of saying "handicapped." Let's bury both of these terms.

There is no replacement term for "special needs." Just don't use it anymore, period. As you'll see later, we're going to change the way we talk about needs altogether.

Exceptions to the Rule

Some people with sensory disabilities don't like People First Language for themselves. They've told me, "I'm deaf," or "I'm blind." But there are others with visual or auditory disabilities who support People First Language and say, "I have a hearing impairment," or "I have a visual disability." Many of us have heard the terms "the deaf community" and "the blind community," (meaning groups of people who share these similarities, not geographical communities).

Not everyone who has deafness or blindness claims membership in these intangible communities. But many who do have chosen not to affiliate themselves with the overall disability community. Specifically, many deaf people (as they like to be called) propose that being deaf is not a disability; it simply represents a different culture—the Deaf culture—which has its own language (Sign).

I want others to respect our family's wishes in how Benjamin is described, so I must be respectful of the wishes of others. In this regard, I usually make a point of asking persons who have sensory disabilities how they describe themselves instead of assuming my descriptors are appropriate.

Level of Disability

Let's eliminate "mild, moderate, severe, and profound" descriptors. They're really meaningless. One person's "moderate" is another person's "severe." Sometimes parents use descriptors as "badges of honor." "Oh, your son just has mild [condition]? Well, my son is severe!" Gag!

In some instances, these descriptors may get us more services, but they also increase the stigma and prejudice directed toward our children. As I've mentioned previously, a classroom teacher may welcome a child with the label of "mild mental retardation," but may reject a child with the label of "severe mental retardation" even though she's never met either child!

Instead of trying to use a one-word descriptor, simply describe your child's specific needs; not as "special needs," but as needs that are usual and normal for him. Speaking this way provides more accurate details, and is more dignified and respectful. I'll share some examples on how to do this toward the end of the chapter.

Typical Children

If you want your child with a disability to be included in a regular ed classroom, please don't say, "I want my daughter to be with normal kids." If you do, what are you saying about your child? That she's abnormal? Let's use the terms typical kids (because no one ever says its opposite: atypical) or simply, children without disabilities. When talking about typical children, stay away from the terms "healthy" or "regular." This implies that children with disabilities are "unhealthy" or "irregular." Our children are normal, healthy, and regular. They just happen to have disabilities.

Special Ed Language is Not So Special

When we talk about school issues, many of us say something like, "Oh, yes, we have three children and one of them is in special ed." Do we ever say, "We have three children. Two are in regular ed and one is in special ed."? No, we usually don't. Our focus tends to be on the negative, the special, or the different. In the future, don't make this distinction, period.

In both of those statements, the words we use—"in special ed"—reinforces the idea that special education equals segregation. While it's true that many children *are* physically segregated from their typical peers in resource and special ed rooms, special education is not supposed to be a place. Let's begin speaking *the way we want things to be*, the way things should be, by saying "My child *receives* special education services."

Accessible Parking, Restrooms, Etc.

All across the country, blue and white signs emblazoned with the universal access symbol of a wheelchair user can be found in parking lots, on ramps, in restrooms, and other places. Unfortunately, many of the signs also include the words "Handicapped Parking," or

"Handicapped Restroom" or "Handicapped Ramp." This has always puzzled me. Does this mean the parking lot or the restroom or the ramp has a disability?

This type of signage is a perfect example of how the term "handicapped" has been misused as a generic term for all people with disabilities. For example, does a person who only has a hearing impairment (1) need to park in a "handicapped" space or (2) qualify for a placard or license plate entitling him to park there? The answer to both questions is no.

The purpose of close-in parking, wider stalls, ramps, and other accommodations is to provide access to persons with physical disabilities. Individuals who use mobility devices, and those who have difficulty walking due to a physical condition, heart or lung limitations, or other physical needs are afforded greater access and independence when these accommodations are provided. So the appropriate terminology is "accessible parking," "accessible restrooms," "access ramps," and so forth. Starting now, replace the saying, "handicapped parking" with "accessible parking."

The word "handicapped" is used to cover all manner of accommodations. But there are many distinct differences. Braille symbols added to signs or menus, elevators and traffic crossing lights that emit audible signals, and similar accommodations provide access and independence to persons with visual disabilities. Telephones and alarm clocks with flashing lights and other modifications are helpful to people with hearing impairments.

When making reservations for a family vacation, I tell the reservation clerk we need a wheelchair accessible room. "A what?" he asks. "A wheelchair accessible room," I politely repeat in my best teaching voice. "Do you mean a handicapped room?" he asks, hopefully. "Yes," I reply with a sigh, recognizing we're speaking two different languages.

The motel does have a wheelchair accessible room. Yippee! But, oh-no, it only has one double bed. I digress for a moment to wonder how the hotel/motel industry has come to the conclusion that a person who uses a wheelchair always (a) travels alone or (b) always wants to sleep in the same bed as her traveling companion or (c) would never travel with more than one person. Obviously, my family does not end up in the wheelchair accessible room since the four of us are unable to sleep in one double bed.

Usually, the effort to reserve a wheelchair accessible room is an exercise in futility. Ending up in a standard room with two double beds, we rearrange the furniture. Even then, it's not uncommon to see one of the bedspreads mysteriously sliding off the bed. Oops! A corner of it is caught in Benj's wheels. I always remind Benj it's the housekeeper's job to change the bed, not his!

Now back to the issue of the generic usage of "handicapped" again. Why does a hotel presume a wheelchair accessible room is a "handicapped" room? Is the room appropriate for someone with a hearing or visual impairment? In addition to the room having a wider doorway, roll-in shower, grab bars, turn-around space in the bathroom, and other modifications (in our dreams), does the room also have a vibrating or light-emitting alarm clock, a TDD, and a captioned TV for people with hearing impairments? Does it also have Braille signage on the television guide, the room service menu, and similar modifications for people with visual impairments? I don't think so.

Again, "handicapped" is such an all-encompassing term no one is sure what it really means. We need to educate the staffs at hotels, motels, and other businesses about accessibility and accurate terminology.

It's hard to eradicate the H-word from society's vocabulary when millions of Americans are face-to-face with the word every time they search for a parking space and when businesses proudly proclaim they have "handicapped" rooms, provide assistance to "handicapped" customers, and so on.

To remedy this situation, we need to write to sign manufacturers and educate them. Stores don't create their own parking signs, they buy them from sign companies. We can begin by searching in our telephone books and public libraries to identify sign manufacturers in our areas. A nice letter to the owner of the company about the importance of eliminating the word "handicapped," along with the suggestion to simply use the universal wheelchair symbol with either no words or the words "accessible parking," is the right step in eliminating this derogatory label. (And we don't need "Disabled" parking on the signs, either.)

In many cases, we need to learn what words are used in state and local laws. The word "handicapped" is no longer used in federal regulations, but it's still common at the state and local levels. It's possible that signs with the word "handicapped" are purchased to meet a city or state regulation. Let's educate state and local policy makers and bury this word once and for all.

There's one more way to get rid of the H-word on parking signs. Put on a jumpsuit or some other outfit that makes you look like a construction worker. When it's dark, and there are few cars in the parking lot of your local shopping area, remove H-word or the D-word with the swipe of a paintbrush! Act like you're supposed to be there—you've been hired by store management to work on the signs, right?

THE PROBLEM WITH "PROBLEM"

Throughout this book, I've repeatedly stated that having a disability is not the "problem;" that the real problems are attitudinal and environmental barriers. In general, however, society continues to believe the myth that the "problem" of disability lies within the person who has the disability. In all fairness to society, people with disabilities and family members (that means us) must bear some of the responsibility for perpetuating this myth. Our language tells the tale.

The one word we seem to use most often when talking about our children with disabilities is "problem." "He has a problem using his right hand." "She has lots of behavior problems." "He has problems with reading." Problems, problems, problems. We don't realize what outcomes are generated when we speak this way.

We try to help our children by getting as many services and supports as possible. And it seems the only way to get all these benefits is to describe all our children's "problems." Just as disability organizations portray people with disabilities as unfortunate or pitiful in order to get donations, parents paint vivid and detailed pictures of all their children's "problems" in order to get services. The language we use has two extremely negative side effects.

"Problems" Activate Exclusion

We set our children up for exclusion when we detail all of their "problems." In an IEP meeting, for example, a mom provides the IEP team with her child's laundry list of "problems" in her attempt to get the appropriate services and supports. In response, the special ed teacher informs the mom that all these services are available only in the resource room. Bye-bye, inclusion.

Conversely, a parent may be making great strides in her efforts to have her child included in a regular ed classroom. But when the classroom teacher hears about all of the child's "problems," she's overwhelmed by the enormous task and declines to have the child in her classroom. She says she can't handle all the child's "problems." So long, inclusion.

When we want our children to participate in typical community activities—whether it's day care, preschool, park and rec activities, or anything else—we tell everyone about all of our children's "problems" so our kids will receive the right supports, adaptations, and so forth. But what we're really doing is setting the stage to be told, "Oh, we don't take children like that," or "I think there's a special program for kids like yours."

Talking About "Problems" Wounds Our Children

Talking about our children's "problems," sends very clear—but unintended—messages to our children about what we think of them. It was years before I realized what I was doing to my son by the way I talked about him. (I'll tell you that story in a moment.) Do you realize how often we talk about our children—in front of them—as if they were not there? We also talk about them in ways we would never talk about our other children.

As soon as our children our diagnosed, we begin talking about their body parts and their "problems," because this is how professionals talk. When our children are tiny babies, before they learn to understand language, talking about them in front of them might be okay. But we forget that they grow and begin to understand what we're saying. Many of us think if our children don't speak, they don't understand. But they do. Our children, regardless of their disabilities, hear us or interpret our behaviors, even though they may not respond or react to what we're saying or doing at the time.

In our children's presence, we talk about them and their "problems" to other family members, doctors, therapists, educators, and many other people. Most of us would never do this to our other children. If we did, hopefully they would say, "Hey, don't talk about me like I'm not here!" Unfortunately, children with disabilities don't often speak up about this because they've grown up with this awful practice and they think it must be okay.

Please take a few moments to think about what you say about your child and her so-called problems in front of her and to her, directly. Now here's my story.

When Benjamin was about eighteen months old, he began walking in a pediatric orthopedic walker. For the next two or three years, while in the grocery store or at the mall, we were stared at by the majority of people we encountered. While hardly any adults spoke directly to us (they just stared), many young children came right up to me and said, "What's wrong with him?" The first few times this happened, I responded, "There's nothing wrong with him. He has a disability [or cerebral palsy]." But I soon realized this was a meaningless response to children. They didn't understand what I meant, so they often gave me a confused look and followed up with, "Well, why does he have that [the walker]?"

I realized I needed to come up with a "stock" answer. You know what I mean. When we're asked questions, we often can't think of the right thing to say at the time. I spent a fair amount of time thinking about what would make sense to young children, and came up with a couple of variations along the same theme. For the next year or two, when children asked me about Benjamin, I said, "He has a problem walking and the walker helps him," or "His legs don't work as good as yours and the walker helps him." Yep, these answers made sense to other kiddos, because they nodded in understanding. (As soon as he could, Benjamin took the responsibility of answering for himself, but when he was very young, it was hard for him to stop for a conversation while trying to maintain his balance and posture in the walker.)

I can't remember what caused this next event; perhaps it was a conversation with an adult with a disability or perhaps something in my subconscious floated into my active mind. At any rate, when Benjamin was about four, I finally heard myself. I heard—really heard—what Benjamin had been hearing me say (and what he said about himself, thanks to my teaching). When I spoke these words, "He has a problem . . ." and "His legs don't work as good as yours . . ." what was Benjamin hearing? What did these words mean to him? Could he, as a young child, separate his legs from who he is as a person? He was hearing—over and over and over again—that *he* was the "problem," that *he* was not "as good" as others.

I was horrified and guilt-ridden. How could I have been so stupid, so thoughtless, so uncaring, and so unaware? I had learned from adults with disabilities about the long-lasting pain and devastation parents unknowingly inflict upon their children by their language and behavior. But I had forgotten what they taught me. Or maybe I didn't think what I was doing was the same thing they were talking about. But what had I done to Benjamin's mind and his soul? What had I done to his image of himself, his self-confidence, and his belief of who I thought he was? Children see themselves through our eyes.

Guilty, ashamed, and disgusted with myself, I decided it was time for some serious thinking about my language and my behavior. When I thought about parents I knew from therapy and parent support groups, I sadly realized my behavior was common. We all spent most of our time talking about our children's "problems" in front of our children, as if they were invisible. Did I do this to my daughter? No. Did I hear or see parents talking about their other children this way? No. What, I wondered, are we doing to our children with disabilities? I consciously decided to never again talk about Benjamin using words that told him he's not good enough, that he's not OK, or that he is a "problem."

Trying to figure out how to do things better, I fished out a ton of material I had received during my Partners training and from other conferences and workshops. I came across bits and pieces of information about disability that included words about limited function, malfunction of body parts, and differences in body function.

At that time, I didn't know about the words in the DD Act that clearly describe "disability as a natural part of the human experience." But I *did* know about my son and his body. I knew other children with disabilities. And I had met adults with disabilities and learned from them. When I thought about my son and the others with disabilities I didn't think of them as being "unable" or having limited function or malfunctioning body parts. Instead, I thought of them as doing things differently or of having body parts that operated differently than the average person. Similar descriptions were in some of the reading material I was searching through. Having a body part that works differently; that's what a disability really was.

I realized it wasn't a perfect definition, since anyone could split hairs with me by saying, "What about someone who doesn't *have* any legs? How can you say a disability means a body part works differently if there *are* no body parts?" Well, so be it. I'd worry about hair-splitting later. I forged ahead with my new way of thinking.

My new answer to children who asked about Benjamin and his walker was this: "His legs work differently than yours and his walker helps him walk." Bingo! This made sense to me, it made sense to Benjamin, and it made sense to children who asked the questions.

More importantly, the words were respectful toward my son and put things in proper perspective. His legs didn't need to be "as good" as someone else's. Who was I to insult him and hurt him by telling others—in front of him—that his legs weren't as good as theirs? He didn't have "problems" with his legs; they simply moved differently than other children's. To Benjamin, his legs were perfectly normal; it was the way he was born; they're the only legs he's ever known! When I stopped using the word "problem" when talking about Benjamin, I also stopped sending the message that he was the "problem."

My next step was to call a family meeting and discuss this with four-year-old Benjamin, six-year-old Emily, and my husband. I apologized to Benjamin for saying things the wrong way. I told him we were all learning together and we would say things differently from now on.

Not only did I need to change the way I responded to other children's questions about Benjamin, but I needed to stop talking about him in front of him, as if he wasn't there. I notified the professionals of what I was doing and why. At therapy, in the doctor's office, or at school, I made sure that in Benjamin's presence, conversations about him included him.

This was a transition I had to work hard on. Talking about Benj in front of him had, unfortunately, become a habit. But it was an even harder transition for some of the professionals. When, in Benjamin's presence, the therapist, doctor, or educator forgot to include Benjamin in conversation, or began talking about him like he wasn't there, I politely interrupted with, "Well, let's ask Benjamin about that," or I addressed Benjamin directly, "Benjamin, what do you think about . . ." When the discussion moved in a direction that Benjamin could not or should not participate in, I told the professional we would talk about that later, on the phone out of Benjamin's earshot. (Regarding telephone conversations, it's just as important that our children don't hear our phone conversations about them. They only hear one side of the conversation, which can be worse than hearing the whole thing.)

This opened up a whole new world for me, for Benjamin, and for every one who was involved in his life. People began seeing him as a person; not a set of problems. And it made me realize this was Benjamin's life and he should be included and actively involved in all the issues affecting his life. Certainly, this didn't mean that as a four-year-old, he was competent to make all the decisions in his life. But I realized how parents and professionals take over a child's life from the very beginning.

Do we need to wonder why many young adults with disabilities have difficulty making their own decisions and thinking for themselves? It's because their parents—us—and the professionals who surround them do all the thinking and decision-making for them! This must stop!

Our Children See Themselves Through Our Eyes

Talking about our children's "problems" and everything they can't do is devastating to their souls and, ultimately, to their opportunities for success. All children, including our children with disabilities, see themselves through our eyes. Most of us are familiar with the philosophy that children live up—or down—to our expectations. If our words and actions tell our children we believe they're wonderful, capable, talented, kind, generous, loving, and lovable, that's how they'll see themselves. Sure, they don't always behave the way we want them to, but that's the nature of children (and adults, for that matter). But the beliefs we communicate to them lay a strong foundation on which they can grow.

If our words and actions send the message that we think our children are incapable or not good enough, that's how they'll see themselves. Our parental influence is the strongest influence in their lives. How do we want our children to see themselves?

As they grow, our sons and daughters will also be influenced by people in other environments (school, community activities, etc.). Sometimes these outside influences are negative, but if we've given our children a good foundation, they can successfully weather emotional storms.

Most of us understand the importance of our influence on our sons and daughters who don't have disabilities. But when it comes to our children with disabilities, we're caught between a rock and hard spot, and our children pay the price. In our efforts to help our children, we focus on their perceived deficits and try to help them via interventions, therapy, and other services. We see our actions as helpful, loving, and beneficial. But our children see them differently.

If children see themselves through our eyes, how do our children with disabilities see themselves, based on our words and actions? When we talk about their "problems" and what they can't do, they see themselves as "problems." When we (along with therapists and educators) focus on what they can't do and try with all our might to get them to do what they can't do, they see themselves as not good enough and not-OK. They see themselves as disappointments because they cannot live up to our expectations. Let's look at some examples.

Judy wants little Zach to learn to walk, so she takes him to therapy and play groups day in and day out, makes him do exercises at home, and instructs the teachers and therapists at school to make sure he gets therapy there. It's hard on Zach, but he tries his best because he wants to please his mommy. Sometimes he cries and doesn't want to go to therapy. Sometimes it hurts physically and sometimes it hurts emotionally. He tries to tell his mommy this, but he doesn't have all the right words. His mommy keeps making him go. She's says she knows it's hard, but it's important that he learn to walk. Zach wants his mommy to love him and he knows therapy and his learning to walk are really important to her. He doesn't want to disappoint her any more than he already has. He'll keep trying.

Zach might not ever be able to walk independently; perhaps he'll be able to walk in a walker, but not very fast and not for very far. He wonders if this be good enough for his mom. If not, when will he be good enough? How long will it take? What will it take to make himself OK in his mom's eyes? Can she ever love me just the way I am, Zach wonders.

We do things to children with disabilities we would never do to other children.

Let's look at Judy and her family in a different scenario. Judy wants Marissa (who doesn't have a disability) to learn ballet. She enrolls her daughter in a class that meets once a week. Marissa likes it at first; she's never done anything like this before and all her friends are doing it. But after a month or so, Marissa begins to complain that ballet is hard and she doesn't want to go. Judy tells her to keep at it; she'll get better. Marissa hangs in there awhile longer, but it's just not going to work. She cries and begs her mom not to make her go. Judy really wanted Marissa to do well in ballet; it was a dream she always had for her, ever since Marissa was a baby. But she realizes how unhappy Marissa is and she knows Marissa stayed with it as long as she did just to please her.

Judy finally lets go of what she wants for Marissa and lets Marissa drop out of ballet. Marissa, believing she's a disappointment to her mother, cries and apologizes for not being any good at ballet. Biting back her own tears, Judy hugs her precious daughter and tells Marissa it's not important; she loves her just the way she is. Marissa, unlike Zach, no longer needs to wonder if she's good enough.

All children want to please their parents. They want and need our approval and our unconditional love. Sometimes they behave in ways that makes us feel they don't give a darn about us, but that's just on the outside. Inside, children never lose the need for parental love and approval, even when they're adults.

When children who don't have disabilities experience failure or disappointment, and when they're sad because they feel they've let us down, most have a supply of self-confidence to shore them up. We've given them the original seed that grows self-confidence and we've watered and nurtured it. As our children grow, they nurture it themselves as they experience success and as they rebound from failures and disappointments. Their self-confidence grows.

But this is not always true for children with disabilities. Many don't have a deep sense of self-confidence or self-esteem. What self-confidence they do have may come and go. When they feel they've pleased us by learning to talk, walk, behave, or by achieving improvement, their self-confidence grows. But when, as so often happens, they try over and over again to do something we want them to do and they're unable to do it, they feel they've disappointed us, they're not good enough, and their self-confidence and self-esteem evaporates. Then the roller coaster starts all over again. They master a skill or improve on one. Mom's happy, a child thinks, I must be OK, now. But no, I guess I'm still not good enough because now I have to do [something else].

Children without disabilities acquire self-confidence when they're successful at running, throwing a ball, playing, talking, interacting with other children, and doing other typical childhood activities. But children with disabilities who cannot experience these or similar activities are often unable to acquire a well of self-confidence to draw from. We must step in and create environments and experiences that will enable our children to believe in themselves and enjoy success. I'll show you ways to make this happen in later chapters. But the first step in this process, getting back to where we began, is using language that promotes our children's sense of self-worth.

Is It a Problem or a Need?

We're still not through with the word "problem." We're so accustomed to thinking a certain way we say the word without thinking. So let's think about what it is we're really trying to say.

I wear glasses. I don't say, "I have a problem seeing," or "I have a problem with my eyes." I say, "I need [or wear] glasses."

About my son, I *could* say "Benjamin has problems eating, walking, writing, reading, going to the bathroom, and. . ." (shall I go on?). But I don't say those things. If I don't use the word "problem" about myself, why would I use it about my son?

Instead of describing my son's "problems," I describe what Benjamin needs or uses. He *needs* adapted utensils for eating, he *uses* a wheelchair for independent mobility, he *uses* a computer for writing, he sometimes *needs* larger print in books, he *needs* assistance in the bathroom, and so on.

Get it? When we talk about our children's "problems," we're really talking about their needs! Whatever we normally describe as "problems," we need to describe as needs. And we must be specific. When we talk about so-called problems, we tend to make them global even when they're not. For example, a parent might say, "My daughter has problems paying attention." But I doubt this is true all the time, in every setting. She may pay lots of attention when watching a video, playing with a friend, or during dinner. Maybe the only time she doesn't pay attention well is when she's bored in school! (Pretty typical behavior for all of us!)

Sometimes we don't use the word "problem," but we describe what our children cannot do. Instead of doing this, describe what your child *can* do and what he needs to do it successfully. In a moment, I'll show you how we can redefine our children and how to rephrase problems into needs.

You and I don't usually spend a lot of time talking about everything that's "wrong" with us—telling everyone about our "problems" or listing what we don't do well. I don't introduce myself to you and say, "Hi, I'm Kathie. I have a problem seeing. I smoke too much. My thighs are flabby. I don't eat enough green leafy vegetables. I can't always balance my check book correctly. There's soap scum in my shower and a ring in my toilet bowl."

But we do this to children with disabilities all the time! We describe and define them in terms of their disabilities and what they can't do. Seldom do we spend much time—if any—talking about who our children really are.

To tell you about myself, I might say, "I'm Kathie. I love to read. *Law and Order, NYPD Blue,* and reruns of *Murder, She Wrote* are my favorite television shows. I love wearing sweatshirts and jeans. And I love to travel—I'd like to visit every continent." I could go on, telling you about other things I love, how I like to sew and paint when I make the time; I could tell you all about my family and our pets and places we've been and things we've done. I would describe myself in positive ways.

If you asked, "Tell me something that's wrong with you, tell me something you're not good at, something you have a problem with," I would most definitely be offended. What bad manners you'd be exhibiting! But this is what we do to children and adults with disabilities. We spend more time thinking and talking about what they can't do, what they do poorly, and what their "problems" are, than describing what they like, what they want to do, what they're good at, and all the things that make each of them perfectly human and wonderfully unique.

What we think comes out of our mouths. Our thoughts are intangible, invisible, and are ours, alone. But when our thoughts are turned into spoken words, they become concrete statements and beliefs that are picked up by anyone who hears them. Our children accept our words as truth, our beliefs as reality. What beliefs do we want our children to have about themselves? That they have lots of "problems," they're not good enough the way they are, and they're more incapable than capable?

Parents often ask for my opinion or advice at workshops, and they begin by spewing out their children's labels and problems, followed by questions about their children's education or treatments. My first response is always a question: "What's your child's name?" Many gulp, embarrassed they haven't even bothered to identify the child by his name. Others rush on, quickly giving me the name and then pressing for answers. We behave this way because this is what we've learned; the disability and all its "problems" become more important than the child or any of his other characteristics.

Spend some time thinking about how you've thought about and talked about your child. Have you spent more time talking about your child's problems than who he is as a person? Has he heard himself described in mostly negative ways? How does your child see himself, based on how you've talked? Think about all this for the next five minutes.

Okay, you've spent enough time thinking about what you've done. There's no more time for guilt. Resolve to do things differently and don't waste another moment on self-recrimination; we have too many other things to do!

STOP APOLOGIZING! NO MORE WHINING!

Another way we promote negative images of our children is by apologizing and whining. We do it all the time and we don't even know it. Sometimes, we really do say "I'm sorry." At other times we use different words and phrases that are apologetic or whiney.

Parents of children with autism, PDD, or other disabilities in which behavior is an issue might be familiar with the following example. You're in the grocery store and your child with a disability goes ballistic. Everyone around you freezes, their attention focused on your child. You quickly try to remedy the situation as you take little Johnny by the hand and begin to lead him away. With an apologetic look on your face, you glance at the strangers around you and in a voice that's slightly above a whisper, you say, "He has autism . . ." and you walk away as quickly as you can.

Are you thinking, "So what? What else am I supposed to do? People need to understand why my child acts the way he does." No, they don't. Consider this: what does a mom do when a child *without* a disability goes ballistic in in the grocery store? Does she meet the eyes of all the onlookers and say, "He takes after his father!" Or does she say, "Oh, I'm such a bad parent!" Of course she doesn't! She usually doesn't say anything. It's nobody's business! She doesn't need to apologize or explain for her child, and parents of kids with disabilities don't either.

Parents "apologize" in a variety of other ways, as in this example. Your daughter, Marisol, has been invited to Leah's ninth birthday party. You're so excited for Marisol! In your heart, you wish you could just drop her off at the party, like other parents do. But you feel you can't; no one knows how to help Marisol like you do. You assume Leah's mom knows Marisol has a disability since the two girls are in the same third grade inclusive class at school. Still, you're worried about how this will all work out. You call Leah's mom and begin your liturgy of apologies and regrets.

"I'm so glad Marisol has been invited to Leah's party. Are you sure it's okay if she comes? I mean, I'll come with her cause she can't go to the bathroom by herself and she really can't talk very well." Without giving Leah's mom a chance to reply, you breathlessly forge ahead before you lose your nerve. "I'll try to stay in the background and not mess up Leah's party. I know I'll probably be the only other mother there, but Marisol's so excited about going I don't want her to miss the party. You know this is the first birthday party she's ever been invited to and I want to make sure everything goes okay. And I don't want all this to mess up the party, but I want you to know what to expect, you know. Marisol's a pretty messy eater and sometimes it grosses people out, but I'll help her when it's time for the cake and ice cream and—well, uh, do you want to ask me any questions before the party?"

In the best case scenario, Leah's mother will know all about Marisol since Leah gives her daily reports about her friends at school; your apologies and explanations weren't necessary. In the worst case scenario, you've scared the pants off Leah's mother. Worse, you've set Marisol up for Leah's mom and others to feel sorry for her, be afraid of her, or see her as a problem.

All of this is unnecessary. You certainly need to educate Leah's mom about how Marisol does things and what help she may need, but the *way* you do it is critical. If you're upbeat and enthusiastic, showing your excitement about the party, while providing Leah's mom with details in the most positive way possible, you're sending the message that Marisol is just fine and that Marisol, Leah, and Leah's mom are competent to handle this. Wouldn't the following conversation be more effective and more respectful?

"Marisol is so excited about Leah's birthday party! She can't wait to go shopping for Leah's present. Barbie doll stuff, right?" you ask, and continue the chit-chat about girls and Barbies and birthday parties. "I'm so glad our girls are friends. Marisol would love Leah to come over and spend the night sometime soon. By the way, if Marisol needs to use the restroom during the party, she'll need some help. If it's okay with you, I'll bring Marisol to the party a little early to show you how to help her."

In this conversation, you've painted a picture that illustrates how Marisol is just like other girls her age: she loves birthdays, buying presents, and Barbies. Then you casually mentioned that Marisol might need help in the bathroom, sending the message that this is perfectly natural, and you let Leah's mom know that she can handle it. You don't need to tell Leah's mom anything else about Marisol's speech or her ability to eat. Those issues can be covered—in the most positive and natural way possible—when you take Marisol to the party early. No doubt Leah, being Marisol's friend, will reassure you and her mother that everything will be fine!

Bob, a dear friend who happens to use a power wheelchair, says, "I'm sorry," more than any person I know. If we're leaving a restaurant and I hold the door open for him, he says, "I'm sorry." If he drops something, I pick it up for him without waiting for him to ask, and I hear, "I'm sorry," again. During a long visit with Bob, I was sick of hearing this and asked him to stop apologizing. I asked him why he did it—why he didn't just say, "Thanks," instead. I told him that when someone holds the door for me when my arms are full, I don't apologize, I just say, "Thank you."

After a few minutes of thoughtful silence, he said, "Kathie, I've always needed so much help from my parents and other people that I've always felt like a burden. No one ever told me I was, I just felt like it. Since people had to help me so much, I never wanted to ask for more help. It's like—that would just be too much. I guess I apologize all the time because I feel like I'm causing trouble for others—that they have to take time away from their own lives to do stuff for me." I was stunned. I learned so much from his words.

We must make sure our children don't grow up feeling they're burdens, causing trouble for everyone around them. If, like Bob, our children already feel they're burdens because they need lots of help, we must make every effort to erase this attitude from their minds.

When we apologize on their behalf or when we make excuses for them, we make them feel even worse about themselves. We're also teaching others to see them in a negative light.

After Bob shared his feelings with me, I assured him I didn't see him as a burden, and I didn't help him because he was a "needy" person with a disability. I told him I help because he's my friend. His disability is irrelevant.

Bob's words also taught me that we have to help our children learn to ask for help. Because Bob didn't want to ask for help, he really never learned *how* to ask for help. He would often go *without* help because he didn't want to "burden" anyone. On the few occasions when he did ask, he was apologetic and whiney about it.

Many of our children don't often need to ask *us* for help since we know everything they need (or think we do, anyway). We routinely step in and help without a lot of conversation. But we're not going to be around forever (a fact many of us have difficulty facing), so our children need to (1) learn how to ask for help in ways that are not apologetic and whiney and (2) be able to describe exactly what kind of help they need and how it can be provided.

We struggle with this in our own home. Being a stay-at-home mom, I'm with my kids more than my husband is, so I'm more familiar with what Benjamin needs and how to best provide assistance. For years, we dressed Benjamin as he lay on the bed. Over time, as he's been able to help more, I realized we shouldn't treat him like a baby, and our routine evolved. Benjamin took a more active role in dressing himself, sitting on the side of the bed or in his chair. Because I helped him five mornings out of seven, he and I had the routine down pat.

After a change in the routine, I briefly explained it to my husband, Mark. On the next Saturday morning, Mark was helping Benj dress when I heard screaming from the bedroom. I ran to see what the ruckus was. Benj was mad that his dad wasn't doing it the right way—the way Benj and I had been doing it. When I asked Benjamin why he didn't just *tell* his dad the right way to do it he replied, "Because I don't know how!" He meant he didn't know the right words and the right sequence of steps to properly explain it to Mark.

I should have been more thorough in explaining it to my husband. But more importantly, I should have helped Benj learn how to explain what needed to be done. Right then and there we all three reviewed the dressing process: saying what needs to be done and who does what, and physically demonstrating the different steps.

One of these days—sooner than we think—Benj will need to count on others for help. Unless I invent a dressing machine, he'll probably always need help getting dressed. If Benjamin doesn't have the power and the ability to ask for the help he needs, and to describe exactly how the help should be provided, he'll either be without any help or he'll be at the mercy of people who will help their way, not his. Our children must be in control of their own lives. In Benjamin's case, being in control doesn't mean he must be able to dress himself. It means he must have the power and the ability to ask for and receive the help he needs.

REDEFINING OUR CHILDREN

Who are our children? How do we want them to feel about themselves? How do we want others to see them? How do we want them to be treated? What matters most about our children?

Our children, like everyone else, should be known by their names and their positive characteristics. When describing our children to others, we should first focus on what's important about them—what they love, what they're interested in, what they dream of doing, and more. And when we need to talk about how their disabilities affect them, we need to speak of needs, not problems. Whatever you've previously described as a weakness or a problem, rephrase it and describe it as a need, or simply relate the way your child does things, as shown in the following examples.

From:	To:
Christina has problems writing.	Christina writes with jumbo crayons. [or] Christina writes on the computer.
Carlos can't talk.	Carlos communicates with his eyes. [or] Carlos uses a communication device.
Jolene can't feed herself.	Jolene needs help when she eats. [or] Jolene eats finger foods.
Chris has problems with solid food.	Chris eats [or drinks] liquids. [or] Chris is on a liquid diet. (Don't say "special" diet. It's not special to Chris; it's his normal diet!)
Jaynie has problems with math.	Jaynie needs math manipulatives instead of workbooks.[or] Jaynie does math on her calculator.
Rob has behavior problems.	Rob needs support during the Scout meetings. (Remember not to speak in global terms. Rob may not need support all the time. Be specific and describe when or under what circumstances he needs behavior support.)
Wendall can't copy from the blackboard.	Wendall needs to sit in the front row. [or] Wendall copies best from teacher notes.
Keesha has problems paying attention.	Keesha needs a buddy during sports.[or] Keesha listens best when you're close to her. (Again, be specific about when and where.)
Kevin has reading problems.	Kevin uses large print books.
Faith can't read.	Faith uses audiotaped materials. [or] Faith learns best by listening.
Jamal can't use his left hand. [or] Jamal's left hand doesn't work.	Jamal does most things with his right hand.

It's all about perspective: is the glass half full or half empty? When we use different words, we paint a different picture, and this makes all the difference in the world in how our children see themselves, how we see them, and how other people see them. How our children see themselves directly impacts their success. How we and others see our children directly impacts how we treat them and what we expect from them.

Most of the usual ways we describe our children are negative because they're referenced against the norm. In the examples I provided, we're moving away from comparing our children to the so-called norm and stating what's normal or right or authentic for them.

Who Are Our Children?

In its simplest form, redefining our children is an attitudinal adjustment. Let's use "Is the glass half empty or half full?" again. When we see the glass half full, we can confidently present a more accurate, favorable, and dignified image of our children. Let's quit defining our sons and daughters by their so-called deficits and describe them by their assets.

Parents of children without disabilities describe their children by their assets all the time. "Oh, let me tell you about my son, Sam!" a mom or dad says. "He loves baseball, he collects all kinds of sports cards, and when he grows up, he wants to be a veterinarian. He's so good with animals, you know." We didn't hear about Sam's faceful of pimples, his quick temper and forgetfulness, or any other unflattering characteristic.

Let's compare the traditional way many parents and professionals often describe children with disabilities using the deficit model, with a new way—the asset model. We'll use my son as an example. After you've finished reading this, write your own comparison chart.

Who is Benjamin Snow?

Deficit Model Thinking in Jargon	Asset Model Thinking in Plain English
• Male, age 13	• Benjamin, age 13
• Spastic diplegia cerebral palsy	• Excited he's finally a teenager
• Level of physical function: eight months (can't walk, crawl)	• Loves to write plays; family performs
• Level of mental function: varies	• Good manners; helpful
• Poor fine motor skills, can't write	• Fantastic imagination
• Non-ambulatory; wheelchair bound	• Very independent in his power chair
• No independent toileting skills	• Curious mind; asks lots of questions
•Poor visual tracking skills	• Works part-time at Dad's office
• Below grade level in several subjects	• Outstanding memory
• Performs few independent daily living skills	• Loves to play MadLibs
	• Interested in math; enjoys using calculator
	• Loves James Bond, Zorro and Superman
	• Great mimic: does movie dialogue/voices
	• Proud owner of a parakeet and many fish
	• Uses computer for games, learning, writing
	• Adores Stephen Hawking as a role model
	• Likes to make up his own spelling lists
	• Writing his life story; wants it published
	• Has Christmas lights in his room
	• Made a short video for parents of kids with disabilities
	• Goes in circles in his chair to get dizzy
	• Wants to be a newspaper reporter when he grows up

Do you see two different children in these comparisons? The first list is how most professionals would see Benjamin. The second list is who he really his; it represents how he sees himself and how others see him, because that's the way we've helped him define himself. We don't pretend he doesn't have cerebral palsy and needs lots of assistance, but we don't let his disability define him or limit his dreams or potential. We don't think about his disability a whole lot. We don't let the disability mask the real Benjamin.

Pretend these lists actually represent two different children. If you showed these lists to children, which Benjamin would be seen as the more desirable playmate? What if you showed them to a classroom teacher? Which Benjamin would she want to include in her classroom?

Most importantly, if I showed the two lists to Benjamin, which one would he say is accurate? If he believed he was the child described in the deficit list wouldn't his spirit be crushed?

If your real child is hidden behind a disability, scrape off the veneer of labels, imperfections, and deficits, so his true self can be revealed. When you do, the world will change before your eyes.

In a moment, make your own lists. Put the Deficit Model on one page and the Asset Model on the other. Take your time and do a thorough job. You can probably zip through the Deficit Model quickly. You know the jargon; you know how your child has been described and defined up to this point.

You may have a harder time with the Asset Model. Some parents have never viewed their children this way. Understand that professionals may view assets differently than what I'm recommending. For instance, their list of assets would most likely include functional skills: walking, talking, eating, etc. Those are fine assets. However, we don't describe people without disabilities that way, so why should we do it to people with disabilities? Our children's assets can be their likes and interests, things they enjoy doing, things they do well, things they want to do, or anything else.

Most children with disabilities are considered "behind" in one or more areas. Don't let this get in the way of identifying all the wonderful characteristics of your child. Don't judge your child's assets in comparison to what she "should" be doing. Your son or daughter is one-of-a-kind: there's not another person in the whole wide world like your child! What is it that makes your child unique? What's important to your child? Music? Movies? Painting? Dancing? Action figures? Barbies? Back Street Boys? Football? Ice cream? Burger King? Look at the common and the uncommon. What are your child's dreams? What does he want to learn how to do? Where does he want to go on vacation? All these are assets.

When I present this exercise in workshops, some parents are stumped. They say things like, "My child doesn't talk or walk; they say he's 'severely retarded.' I can't think of anything to list." Here, here! Get creative and think with your heart. Does your child smile when you hug him? "Likes to hug" or "Is affectionate" are assets. What's his favorite television show? Toy? Food? What excites him? Pleases him? Don't wrack your brain trying to find assets professionals would view as "valuable." Just get started, put *something* down, and the rest will begin to flow. (And everything you list *is* a valuable asset!) If it's hard thinking of the big picture, start small. Think of earlier today. What did your child do or say that was wonderful, funny, or exciting?

As you're listing your child's assets, use plain English, not professional jargon. Some of us (me, at one time) can sound more like professionals than professionals. Eeek! Using People First Language and redefining our children means erasing professional jargon from our vocabularies. If we're ready to stop viewing our children through the lens of the medical model, we must not use medical model language. For example, you may want to list some functional abilities if they're really important to who your child is. If so, list your child's desire and attempts to talk, for example, as an asset by writing, "trying hard to talk." Don't write, "attempting to acquire verbal skills" or "attempts to vocalize."

Never, ever use the words "function" or "functioning" when talking about your child. This is professional jargon that relegates our children to machine-like automatons. Our children don't function, they *live*. Would therapists or doctors or educators ever describe themselves that way?

Take some time now and make your two lists. When you've finished, carefully review them. Then take the Deficit Model list, fold it in half, stand over a garbage can, and rip it to shreds. Then shed some tears, jump for joy, or do both at the same time. You have just ended the practice of describing your child by his perceived deficits. Next, take the Asset Model and show it to your child. Ask her what else needs to be added to the list. Then tape it to the door of your child's bedroom, on the mirror in the bathroom, or on the refrigerator. Add to it regularly. Keep it handy, for we'll come back to it later.

While you're at it, create lists of assets for your other kids, too. Do one for yourself, your spouse or significant other, and anyone else who's meaningful in your life. Wallpaper your house with them. They're more precious than gold.

Are you beginning to see a different child already? Once you've redefined your child in your head, in your heart, and on paper, it's easy to help others know your child based on her assets instead of perceived deficits.

PROTECT YOUR CHILD'S PRIVACY

Changing how we describe our children is only part of the equation. Being careful about when and to whom we talk about our children is also critically important.

To ensure your child will be treated with dignity and respect, and to keep the focus on him and not his disability, don't talk about your child's condition, his needs, or anything else pertaining to the disability *unless it's absolutely necessary*. We're so accustomed to spilling our guts about our children to professionals, we do the same with many others we come in contact with. But your child's condition is nobody's business! You child's life should not be an open book.

Yes, with professionals or educators, and in certain other circumstances, we need to discuss specifics, but we should only give the information that's required. If, for example, you want to enroll your child in a park and rec activity, don't ask if they take kids with disabilities. Simply ask your questions about the activity and sign your child up, without saying anything about his disability. Then prior to the first day of the activity, talk with the person who will be leading the activity and describe what your child needs to be successful (accommodations, supports, and so forth). Make sure to speak in ways that promote your child's humanity instead of verbally dissecting his body or mind.

When talking to neighbors, acquaintances, or others, there's no need to divulge personal information. We don't do it to ourselves, so we shouldn't do it to our children. Would you, for example, tell someone you just met or someone you know very casually, that it's hard for you to sit down right then because you have a big, fat boil on your butt? (Please don't say yes.) It's nobody's business! And if you choose to sit with one cheek off the chair and one cheek on, let 'em wonder why. If they're rude enough to ask why you're sitting in such a strange position, you can (a) give them a graphically detailed explanation and offer to give them a close-up look at the left cheek or (b) tell them you're practicing a new yoga position.

Even with those we're close to—relatives and friends—we need to be careful. Would you tell your mother the personal or intimate details about your spouse's inverted nipple or the way he/she likes to take a twenty-minute air bath in the privacy of the bedroom on Saturday mornings? How would your spouse feel about this betrayal of privacy?

Would you tell relatives or friends that your burly sixteen-year-old son who is a linebacker on the football team still sleeps with a night light on in his room? You and your immediate family know this and it's not a big deal. But how will your son feel when he learns you blabbed about his private needs?

We do things to children with disabilities we would never do to others. Protect your child's privacy and humanity. *Our children have never given us their permission to lay open their lives for public consumption.* We must not betray their trust. We must not talk about them in ways that reduce them to malfunctioning body parts. We have no right.

We do things to our families others would never do. Protect your family's privacy and dignity. As clients of the system, we're often compelled to share a great deal of confidential information about our finances, family history, and other personal issues. Too many people know too much about our private lives as it is. Don't subject your family to any more prying eyes and ears than is absolutely necessary. Your child and your family are not public property.

For some odd reason, people often see a woman's pregnant belly as public property: "Oh, you're carrying it low. It must be a boy!" Whether they're strangers or distant relatives, some folks have no qualms about staring at it, asking about it, or wanting to touch it. To keep unwanted people from invading their personal space, many pregnant women must extend an arm to keep an interloper away.

We must do the same. We must defend the personal space and protect the spiritual space of our children and families by not making our lives open books. You do not owe anyone an explanation about your child's disability or his needs. It's nobody's business!

EDUCATE, GRIN, GIGGLE

Most of us have endured unpleasant and awkward experiences related to our children and their disabilities. Eyes stare, fingers point, and voices whisper as we pass by. We're asked odd questions, given free advice, and offered unusual tokens. There's no sense being upset by the curiosity or ignorance that people may exhibit when they see us. Take it in stride and turn unpleasant moments into teaching opportunities.

In the grocery store once, a lady approached my kids and me, looked closely at three-year-old Benjamin, who was sitting in the shopping basket. Staring hard at his leg braces, she said, "Poor dear. When was the accident?" "What?" I asked. "The accident," she repeated. "Didn't he break both legs in a car accident?"

I was in a good mood that day, the kids were calm, and she had a nice face. I took the time to explain what cerebral palsy was and why Benjamin wore leg braces. When I finished, the lady had a sad face (as if she was sympathetic for our "plight"). But I steered her away from that place by focusing on factual information about CP and orthotics, purposely keeping Benjamin out of the conversation. She listened intently and when I was through, she patted Benjamin on one knee and asked, "But will he be all right?" "Sure," I happily answered, "he's fine just the way he is. He's a typical three-year-old boy who happens to have cerebral palsy." "Oh," she brightened, "I guess you're right. Well, thanks for explaining all that to me. Your kids sure are cute. Have a good day!"

She learned something that day. So did I. Curiosity, I discovered, sometimes wears the mask of rudeness. It's how we see it that makes the difference.

When we take an uncomfortable situation and turn it into a learning experience, we can be proud that our children are instruments of change. Whenever possible, we should make the effort to educate others, by taking the time to explain about a child's disability in an upbeat, positive fashion. Provide facts and information about the condition, and stay away from specifics that will evoke pity toward your child.

But we may not always have the time, energy, or inclination to do mini-lessons on disability. And that's okay, too. Humor can turn an awkward situation into a pleasant and funny interchange.

Debbie was in the produce department of her neighborhood grocery store, and two-year-old Danielle was in the shopping cart. Mom and daughter both have dark brown hair and brown eyes. Danielle has Down syndrome and her eyes have a very pronounced slant. This, coupled with her skin, hair, and eye color, gave her a very exotic Asian appearance. As Debbie bagged apples and oranges, Danielle babbled away just like other two-year-olds. Very happy with the sound of her own voice, Danielle was delivering a variety of sounds at a rapid fire pace. A middle-aged lady pushed her basket closer to Danielle and exclaimed, "What a pretty baby!" Debbie thanked her and gave her a big smile while Danielle maintained her fever-pitch delivery of consonants and vowels.

"Never in my life," the lady continued, "have I heard a baby speak Chinese!" (She was seriously impressed.) Without missing a beat, Debbie chimed in, "Oh, that's nothing! Next week, she's going to begin French lessons." "My, my," clucked the lady, shaking her head in amazement as she moved toward the tomatoes, "that's just wonderful!"

"If somebody gives you lemons, make lemonade," is a most appropriate philosophy when we're faced with goofy situations. Whenever possible, seize the opportunity to teach others. But if you're not up to it at the moment (you're tired, the kids are cranky, you're in a hurry, or whatever), then use humor.

Speak gibberish that sounds like a foreign language, as if you don't understand or speak English, and wave your hands around a lot. Practice this at home, it's fun. For inspiration, watch reruns of *I Love Lucy*.

Question the questioner in a serious, respectful manner, which will usually bring the interchange to a screeching halt. "Was he born like that?" a stranger asks, pointing to your child. "Who?" you ask. "Him," the stranger replies, pointing again. "Ohhhh, you mean *him*," you say, followed by, "I'm sorry, what was the question again?" At this point, the questioner will probably give up—embarrassed—and tell you never mind as she turns away. If she's persistent, however, the conversation could continue as she repeats her question, "I asked if he was born that way." "What way?" you ask, keeping a straight face. "You know, like *that*." she says. "I'm so sorry," you reply in a very friendly manner, "I'm not sure what you mean." That will most likely end it.

Be outrageously silly. "What's wrong with her?" someone asks. You reply, "You know, I haven't the faintest idea. A small asteroid fell in our neighborhood a couple of weeks ago and every kid in the neighborhood got the same thing. Do you know what it could be?" Who knows, this could get you on the cover of a national tabloid—talk about getting disability issues into the media! Or answer this way, "Oh, she has the Albert Einstein [or Babe Ruth, Tarzan, Marilyn Monroe, etc.] syndrome." Most people will just nod their heads in agreement and say, "Ohhhh, I see."

A really curious person might continue with, "What's that?" Then you ask, "You've never heard of that? Gosh, I thought everyone knew what it was! I can't believe you've never heard of it. Well, I don't have a lot of time right now, but if you'll give me your phone number I'll be happy to call and explain it to you in great detail." Begin digging in your purse and say, "Let me just find a pencil and some paper—" By now, the questioner will be backpedaling as fast as possible.

If you and your spouse are together when someone asks what's "wrong" with your child, make your response a family affair. Simultaneously point at each other and reply, "He/she did it" and giggle hilariously.

When you're asked questions about your child, make it a teaching opportunity if you feel up to it. As soon as your child is able, let him do the educating. These teaching opportunities provide great benefits to the questioner. If a teaching moment isn't appropriate or do-able, use humor. This will protect your spirit by preventing feelings of hurt, embarrassment, or anger.

Never, never, never take other people's ignorance personally. Most don't know any better. Don't respond with anger or sarcasm. Those negative feelings will eat you up. If you can teach them, do so. If you can't, let humor or silliness raise you above ignorance. You're not only protecting your own spirit, you're also protecting your child and your family. And by your actions, you're modeling positive, effective methods to deal with awkward situations.

One more word of caution: please do not hand out business cards that describe your child's condition. Parents of children with autism have shown me cards they carry in their wallets that came from a national autism organization. They're supposed to be used when a child goes ballistic in public or in other situations when parents feel the need to explain their child's behavior. On one side of the card is a description of autism; the other side lists a toll-free number to call for more information.

Let's think about this for a moment. I'm in the grocery store and my child with autism loses control. I mumble my apologies to the onlookers and hand each person the autism card. Do we really think people are going to go home and call the 800 number to learn more about autism? From observing my child's behavior in the store, they probably think they know more about autism than they want to know!

I previously described the reasons we don't need to apologize for our kids. Parents of children without disabilities don't do this. Yes, if a child—with or without a disability—knocks over a shelf or pulls all the magazines out of the rack, we should apologize or help them learn to apologize. But we shouldn't apologize for who our children are!

SOLUTIONS TO STARES

Remember Ed Roberts, father of the Independent Living Movement, who was described in the history chapter? Let's follow his lead: when he was being stared at, he chose to believe people stared because he was a "star."

When our family is out and about, we get a lot of stares, like the time a lady stood transfixed by the appearance of four-year-old Benjamin in his walker. She clucked her tongue and shook her head in sadness as he walked by her. Then she looked up at me with those still-sad eyes, patted me on the arm, and said, "But he's so cute . . ." In her mind, I suppose, the "tragedy" that had befallen Benjamin was made even greater because he was cute, while if he was ugly it wouldn't have been so bad!

Then there are the stares that say to me, "What an angel you must be to take care of him." You know the look: a small smile accompanied with eyes that don't smile, but that are turned down in sympathy, the head cocked to one side. And, of course, there are all kinds of looks and stares in between. You've probably experienced your fair share of stares.

When you're with your child and you get a pitiful smile or an extra long stare from a stranger, smile back—a big, friendly smile, the kind that shows your teeth and crinkles your eyes in friendship—then wave, wink, or call out, "Hi, how are ya?" or "Don't we know each other from somewhere?" Instead of ignoring stares, acknowledge them! This technique is very effective when you and the starer are moving, as you pass each other in the mall or in the supermarket, for example.

But if you're both stopped, as when you're in parallel check out lines that are slow as molasses, a different approach might work better. After you smile your biggest smile at the starer, break eye contact for a moment. Then look back at her and smile again. She'll break eye contact this time, but you keep looking at her. She'll look back one more time and when she does, pretend you're not sure she's really staring at you. Turn your head and look behind you as if you're looking for the person she's really staring at, or continue looking at her in a friendly, questioning way and point your finger at your own chest as if to say, "Are you looking at me? Me?"

Initially, you mind find it hard to believe you could use any of these methods to successfully deal with uncomfortable situations. But consider the alternatives. If we feel sad, angry, or frustrated to begin with, we merge those feelings with the hurt and anger brought on by stares and stupid questions. Then we either let these volcanic emotions erupt in anger directed to others or we hold them inside our hearts where they simmer and bubble and hurt us even more. But when you've redefined your child in your own head, it's easy to be friendly and helpful to strangers (the teaching mode) or funny and light-hearted (the humor mode).

As soon as your child is able, let him handle the stares. If another child (or an adult) stares, teach your child to smile, say "Hi!", or even say something like, "Are you wondering about my [whatever]?" Help your child learn self-advocacy as early as possible. He'll need to speak for himself all his life; the sooner he learns how to do it, the better.

PRACTICE MAKES PERFECT

If People First Language and the suggestions in this chapter are new to you, understand that change may not come overnight. The way we speak and the words we use are habits. For some of us, replacing an old habit with a new one is easy; for others, it's harder and takes longer. Reread this chapter on a regular basis until these methods feel natural.

When I present this material in person at workshops, many parents embrace the ideas right away, but their words don't automatically change. They often have to catch themselves when old words or professional jargon slip out. That's okay. Keep practicing. Many times we have to stop and think about which new words to use or how to respond in ways that use People First Language. The new words may not come naturally at first. Practice makes perfect. Be patient and kind with yourself. It's just like starting and maintaining a new diet or an exercise program. Keep at it. Don't give up. It will come.

WHAT ABOUT OTHER PEOPLE'S LANGUAGE?

We're changing our own language, but what about the way other people talk? We start in our own homes, first. Sit down with your family (including all your children), your friends, and other people who are close to your family, and share this information with them.

Some in your inner circle will be very receptive to new ways of thinking and talking. Others might be resistant to change. That's okay. Don't fight over this. Model the appropriate language and most people will eventually begin to use words that are more respectful.

Do whatever works. Make lists of the words and phrases that apply to you and your family and post them around the house. Give copies to your friends and family. Make it fun. Invite everyone over for a potluck dinner and give a mini-presentation. It's much easier to tell a lot of people at once than to tell every person individually. Write a family letter and send it to those who live far away. Be excited about this new way of promoting your child's dignity and share the excitement. And let your child do as much of the teaching as possible!

The next group to influence is the army of professionals who impact your child and your family. Many professionals use a basic component of People First Language, by saying "children with disabilities." But few are aware of, or understand the importance of, moving from the Deficit Model to the Asset Model. Give a mini-presentation to professionals, in a group or one-on-one, about new ways of thinking and talking. In addition, model the language you want others to use; they'll learn by osmosis. When you first became involved with professionals, none of them ever told you, "Talk this way. Use these words." We learn to use professional jargon because we hear it so often. The same can be true in reverse.

If educators, therapists, and others repeatedly hear you using People First Language—words and descriptions that focus on your child's assets—they'll begin to think and talk differently. It might not happen overnight, so be patient. Don't beat people over the head with it. Don't get mad and don't take it personally when people use inappropriate language. They haven't had a chance to learn it yet. And remember, some professionals might be "slow learners." Model the language you want, gently correct people, and give people a chance. Here are some examples of modeling and reinforcing appropriate language:

Professional: Well, the program for the mentally retarded is at Wilson Elementary.
Mom: So Wilson provides services for children with cognitive disabilities . . .

Neighbor: You know, my sister has a Down's kid like yours.
Mom: Oh, really? So you must know a lot about children with Down syndrome. (As the conversation continues, Mom keeps repeating the appropriate phrase.)

Schoolmate: What's wrong with your brother?

Girl: What do you mean?

Schoolmate: Well, you know, is he retarded or something?

Girl: Oh, no. Brandon has autism. It means his brain works differently. That's just the way he was born. He's like you and me; he just does some things differently. You know "retarded" isn't really a very nice word.

In later chapters, I'll share the details on how to influence people's perceptions in specific instances (IEP meetings, day care settings, etc.). In certain situations, using Deficit Model language might be a prerequisite to getting services: children must be labeled a certain way and exhibit specific "deficits" before they're entitled to services. This will also be covered in more detail later.

OUR CHILDREN ARE TEACHERS

The following two stories represent the power and influence our children can exert over their own surroundings. We have an obligation to help our children learn to speak for themselves as early as possible.

"I'm Not Handicapped"

It's allowance day, time for a trip to the five and dime store in our small town. Six-year-old Benjamin, in his walker, is ready to pay for his toy at the register. In a highly coordinated effort, I put my hand on his right side to help him maintain his posture, he lets go of the walker with his right hand, I quickly put his money in his hand, he proudly thrusts it at the clerk. He grabs hold of the walker again, I get his change for him, take the small sack from the clerk, and we mosey out the front door. Our van is parked by the door in the accessible parking spot. I pick Benjamin up and put him in the front passenger seat. As I snap the seat belt in place, a man comes up behind me and taps me on the shoulder.

"Excuse me," he says, "I see your son is handicapped." I turn around and start to respond, but before I can, Benjamin's arm snakes toward me and gently shoves me out of the way. Face-to-face with the stranger, Benjamin begins, "Sir, sir—I am not handicapped." With his pointer finger wagging for emphasis, his small but determined voice continues, "My name is Benjamin. I have a disability, but I'm not handicapped. Handicapped is an ugly word and we don't use it in our family."

The man smiles an embarrassed smile, gulps, and stammers, "Oh, uh, yes, uh, you have a disability—that's what I meant. Sorry. Well, anyway, I wanted to tell you about a camp for handi—uh, kids with, uh—"

"A camp for kids with disabilities?" I finish for him.

"Yes," he sighs in relief. "Anyway, I didn't know if you knew about it, but I thought maybe your son would enjoy it."

"Yes, we've heard of it, thanks," I reply. "Benjamin already participates in the regular activities of our park and rec. We think it's pretty important he participate in regular activities, not special ones. He likes to be with his friends."

"Oh, yeah, sure," he says. "That makes sense. Well, nice talking to you. Bye, Benjamin."

"Bye," Benj says, "Have a nice day."

My son helped this stranger learn a new attitude, and he did it in a way that was far more powerful than anything I could have done.

"Handicapped is an Ugly Word."

Benjamin's second grade teacher, Mrs. M, really listened to her students. When a problem arose, any student could call for a class meeting to immediately discuss the situation. On a regular basis, children called meetings when teasing was going on, when children weren't sharing, and for a variety of other issues. Several pieces of Benjamin's adaptive equipment were in the room—a floor chair, a stander, and other things. One day, as several children gathered in the corner for an activity on the floor, a classmate of Benjamin's loudly called out, "I'm going to sit in the handicapped chair."

Across the room, Benjamin heard this and, in an even louder voice, called out, "Mrs. M! Mrs. M! It's time for a class meeting. Clayton just said 'handicapped'!" Mrs. M called the students together and Benjamin reminded his classmates—especially Clayton—that "handicapped is an ugly word." A lively discussion ensued, which ended with Clayton apologizing and saying he just forgot.

Benjamin regularly helped his friends learn better language, so he was accustomed to doing this. He was patient with them; he knew not everyone learns at the same speed or in the same way.

On the following page is a reference chart of examples of People First Language. Use it as a guide, inserting the appropriate words or phrases which will describe your child with dignity and respect.

Using People First Language and redefining our children are the first steps on the road to ensuring successful lives for our children in the real world. We've begun transforming ourselves and the fun is just beginning; it continues in the next chapter!

EXAMPLES OF PEOPLE FIRST LANGUAGE

Say:	Instead of:
children with disabilities people with disabilities	the disabled, the handicapped
he has a disability	he's disabled; he's handicapped
she has a cognitive disability	my daughter is retarded
people with cognitive disabilities	the (mentally) retarded
my son has autism	my son is autistic
she has Down syndrome	she's Down's; she's mongoloid
he has a learning disability	he's learning disabled; he's LD
I have paraplegia	I'm a paraplegic
my son has a physical disability	my son is disabled
she is of short stature	she's a dwarf
she has an emotional disability	she's emotionally disturbed
he uses a wheelchair (or mobility chair)	he's confined to a wheelchair he's wheelchair bound
typical children kids without disabilities	normal kids or healthy kids
he receives special ed services	he's in special ed
he needs behavior supports	he has behavior problems
congenital disability	birth defect; brain damaged
accessible parking accessible bathroom	handicapped parking handicapped bathroom
she needs . . . she uses . . .	she has a problem with . . . she can't . . .

Transformation
Association, Cooperation, Negotiation

EVERYONE THINKS OF CHANGING THE WORLD,
BUT NO ONE THINKS OF CHANGING HIMSELF.

Leo Tolstoy

Evolution. Growth. Conversion. Metamorphosis. The slowly creeping caterpillar becomes a hard-shelled cocoon and is then miraculously transformed into the magnificent butterfly. Like the butterfly, we need to transform ourselves to ensure our children's success in the real world.

Using People First Language and redefining our children are significant transformations. These efforts will help our children shed the cocoon of disability labels, allowing them to spread their wings and soar. But we, too, need to emerge from our own cocoons. The roles we've assumed in our efforts to advocate for our children have entrapped us as surely as our children's labels entrapped them. Redefining and transforming ourselves will allow us to soar, too.

Most of us want things to change. Specifically, we want improvements in the service system, the educational system, and any other systems that impact the lives of our children and families. Parents and other advocates have been very successful in changing laws, policies, and funding. But these changes don't always equate to changes that affect our children. Because the system doesn't run on its own. The system cannot exist without people (professionals and bureaucrats) to run it.

It's not always the system that needs changing; in many cases, it's the *people who run the system* who need to change. For example, as I described in Chapter 8, even though early intervention provisions mandate services in natural environments, many EI professionals have yet to make this change a reality. Unless people change along with systems, no improvements occur. But we can't change people. People must change themselves. This chapter is devoted to ways we can change ourselves, change our relationships with professionals who run the system, and promote an atmosphere in which professionals can change themselves.

Few would argue that relationships between parents and professionals need to improve. But some might wonder why parents should be the ones to change. Shouldn't professionals change? Yes, we all need to change. All parents and all professionals can do better. But parents will almost always be the ones to *initiate* change because we're the ones who *want* change! For us, the need for change is very personal, and there's a great deal at stake: our children's lives.

When we change ourselves, we can change the outcomes of our relationships with professionals. Transformation will come when we cultivate and maintain positive associations with others, practice cooperation, and use negotiation strategies.

THE GOAL OF RELATIONSHIPS: HELPING OUR CHILDREN

In our dealings with educators and other professionals, our ultimate goal is to help our children. We all start from this point, but far too many of us quickly shift our focus. When our focus changes, our methods and behavior change, as well.

During team meetings and in conversations with professionals, we sometimes feel we're being ignored; other times we feel we're being attacked. We frequently feel hurt, frustrated, angry, or betrayed. It's not uncommon for us to take things personally, and we want to strike back. Far too often, proving our point at any cost, getting even, proving someone else wrong, or achieving another personal (emotional) victory, becomes our primary goal. We may not even be aware when the shift in our goal takes place. Even if we are, we may not be able to admit it to ourselves.

On the other hand, some of us announce (or think): "They're not going to get away with this!" While trying to help our children—by working with professionals—we add in our own personal goal of revenge, retribution, or domination. We escalate our efforts and use strategies that may give us a sense of power—for the short term—which may or may not lead to success in getting what we need for our children. When this happens, our common sense has been replaced by our emotions.

Make this a cardinal rule: when you deal with professionals on behalf of your child, leave your emotions out of it. It's hard, but not impossible, to do. When our emotions—our egos—take over, we're unable to stay focused on the ultimate objective of helping our children.

When we react or respond to negative or hurtful comments made during meetings or during one-on-one conversations with professionals, we get off track. We begin arguing *their issues* instead of promoting ours. Once off-track, it's very hard to get back on. Avoid this dilemma. When you feel insulted, hurt, resentful, angry, or anything else, *let it go.* Let it roll off your back and stay focused on what's important—your child.

STAYING OUT OF THE MUCK

When Andrew was in kindergarten in an inclusive elementary school, his teacher—Mrs. T—wasn't making the appropriate modifications, even though his mom, Carolyn, had been working very closely with her. Rather than calling repeated IEP meetings, Carolyn met with Mrs. T informally on a regular basis to try to resolve the issues. This worked for awhile, but some other problems were festering, so Carolyn asked for a meeting with Mrs.

T and the principal. Again, Carolyn chose not to call a formal IEP meeting. (When possible, we should try to solve issues in the most informal ways possible.) The meeting was scheduled during class time, so a substitute teacher was called in to take Mrs. T's place in the morning kindergarten class.

Carolyn began the meeting by thanking the principal and Mrs. T for their time. She detailed her concerns in a calm manner, providing details of what had and hadn't been done. She even gave Mrs. T the benefit of the doubt, by saying things such as, "Perhaps you didn't understand the importance of [blah, blah, blah]" and "Maybe I wasn't clear on how to do [such-and-such]." Carolyn referred to her notes as necessary, to make sure she covered everything important. When she finished, the principal looked at Mrs. T for her response.

Bear in mind that at the IEP meeting at the beginning of the school year, Mrs. T seemed enthusiastic about Andrew being in her classroom. In fact, she had a nephew with the same disability as Andrew's. When the year started, Carolyn truly believed Andrew was in very good hands.

Like many kindergartners, Andy was nervous about going to school and leaving mom every day. Carolyn planned to be an active volunteer in the classroom, but decided not to volunteer until after the winter break. She felt Andy would cling to her and not bond with the teacher if she volunteered from the beginning. In hindsight, she realized that by not volunteering, she missed opportunities to observe in the classroom and see how Andy and Mrs. T were faring.

Now, back to the meeting with the principal. During this meeting, which was taking place in January, Mrs. T responded to Carolyn's concerns. First, she defended herself by talking about how much of her time Andy took and how she had twenty other students in the class. The principal reminded Mrs. T that she also had more support than any other teacher in the school: a teacher's aide who was there most of the time, as well as a speech therapist and a special ed teacher who were in and out of her class every morning.

Undeterred, Mrs. T continued, revealing the following sentiments: (1) Andy didn't belong in her class; (2) he shouldn't even be in the school; and (3) he should be sent to some other school. Mrs. T also announced that Carolyn needed to "come to terms" with Andy's disability and recognize that he wasn't ever going to be a "Rhodes scholar." The longer she talked, the more emotional she became. Mrs. T capped her sermon by saying, "This isn't about Andy at all. This is about you trying to tell me how to teach and trying to run my class. Your son's condition has obviously made you dysfunctional. In fact, your whole family is screwed up!"

When Mrs. T first started her monologue, she was calm. Midway through her lecture, she became very tense. But by the time she finished, she was angry, in tears, and out of control. Carolyn wasn't. She was cool as a cucumber—on the outside. "Mrs. T, " Carolyn replied, "you're entitled to your personal opinion of me and my family, and I'm entitled to my opinion of you. But that's not what we're here to discuss. We're here to talk about my son's education. Now, I know you're a good kindergarten teacher. His public education starts with you, in kindergarten, and I know this can be a great year for him and for you. It's 11:30 and the bell is about to ring, so I've got to pick him up and take him home. I know you and I will be able to work together, so we'll just both have to try a little harder. We can work this out. Thanks so much for your time. I'll see you tomorrow!"

Carolyn left the principal's office, picked up Andrew, took him home, got him a bite of lunch, and put him in front of the television. Then she went out to the garage to sob and scream at the walls.

As badly as Carolyn wanted to yell and scream at Mrs. T during the meeting, she restrained herself. She knew if she ranted and raved, she'd be no better than Mrs. T. But the most important thing Carolyn knew was that she needed to keep the discussion focused on Andrew's education. How could she ever solve the problems of Mrs. T not doing what her son needed if she and Mrs. T both behaved like two alley cats? If their relationship degenerated into mutual disgust, there was no hope. Let Mrs. T be rude, ugly, and hateful; Carolyn would have no part of it.

She briefly considered taking Andrew out of Mrs. T's class and putting him in the other morning kindergarten class, but that would have been unfair to Andrew. He had lots of new friends and he was finally feeling good about going to kindergarten every morning. To move him to another class would have been harmful and disruptive. And what would she tell Andrew, that his teacher didn't like him? That would be a terrible thing to do.

When her tears finally stopped, she began to replay the whole episode in her mind. Carolyn wondered why the principal hadn't intervened when Mrs. T began attacking her and making it personal. He let her rant and rave and say all those cruel things. At first Carolyn was confused about this because the principal was a man of integrity; a wonderful leader, and a believer in inclusion. He had always been kind and helpful to Andrew and Carolyn. Then she realized that his lack of intervention was intentional.

By letting Mrs. T get everything out of her system, the principal allowed her true feelings to surface. It dawned on Carolyn that once she and the principal were aware of what was really going on inside Mrs. T, they could both figure out better ways of dealing with her. The principal *let* Mrs. T "shoot herself in the foot."

Later that day, the principal telephoned. "I just wanted to let you know how impressed I was with your professionalism in the meeting today, Carolyn." he said. "I know it must have been hard for you to listen to some of that, but I really admire how you stuck to the issues, even when Mrs. T got way off the mark. I think the three of us should continue to work on these issues together. I'll be visiting her room on a regular basis. I think between my visits and your volunteering, we'll be able to resolve these problems."

The rest of the year wasn't perfect, but things did improve. Carolyn and Mrs. T were able to work together with some degree of harmony. In fact, Mrs. T was very pleasant to Carolyn for the rest of the year. Carolyn never knew if this was because the principal had a little talk with Mrs. T or because Mrs. T's conscience finally kicked in. Carolyn never reminded Mrs. T of that awful meeting. By letting it go, she allowed Mrs. T to "save face." Carolyn could have made a lot of trouble for Mrs. T if she wanted to. But she didn't, and Mrs. T was probably eternally grateful.

By her actions and her attitude, Carolyn carved a powerful, positive reputation for herself. She was known as a mom who remained calm in the face of turbulence, who didn't let emotions (hers or other's) steer her off course. Carolyn had a strong ally in the principal, and in succeeding years, she developed great relationships with her son's teachers. As a result, the rest of Andrew's elementary school years were wonderful.

FIGHTING FOR RIGHTS VS. DOING WHAT'S RIGHT

Many of us spend a great deal of time advocating on behalf of our children. And the driving force behind much of our advocacy is fighting for our children's rights. In the process, many of us make enemies. Parents across the country have told me stories about their relationships with professionals. I've heard tales of parents who spend the majority of IEP meetings trading insults with one or more educators; who hate the men and women on their child's team; who never get to the really important issues about their child's education because they react emotionally to negative comments; and who won't go to an IEP meeting without an attorney. Parents have told me of disagreements with day care centers, neighborhood preschools, community programs, and other entities.

Some of us are very good at advocating for our children's rights: we know the laws, we know the procedures to follow, and we call on other advocates for assistance. But frequently, something's been lost in the process of advocating for rights. We've forgotten about *doing what's right*. We've ignored the human component and forgotten our manners. In demanding that educators and others follow laws and procedures, we've discounted the importance of relationships. From afar, it seems relationships and the human component have nothing to do with laws and rights. But up close, whether we want to admit it or not, we know they do. It takes *people* to implement policies and procedures and laws.

In our determination to ensure our children's success, we've sought rights and justice. And this is an important and noble action. But the assurance of rights doesn't guarantee our children's success. The right to a free and appropriate public education, for example, may be achieved, but that right doesn't necessarily mean a child will be treated with love and care by his teachers, or that he will enjoy social equality in a public school setting. These are not possible unless parents have positive relationships with educators. While working to ensure a child's rights are upheld, we permit—and sometimes even accelerate— the deterioration of our relationships with people who touch our children's lives.

Furthermore, when we fight with people, we're reacting with our hearts instead of our heads. And when our emotions drive our behavior, we've lost control, and then we lose sight of our goals. It might be *our feelings* that get hurt, but it's our children's lives that are really harmed. They pay the price for our misbehavior.

To ensure our children's success, we're obligated to do more than fight for their rights; we're obligated to *do what's right*. And suggestions in this chapter will demonstrate many ways to accomplish this.

PLAYING THE GAME

In the traditional ways of disability advocacy, we are, in a sense, playing a game. Parents are on one side; professionals are on the other. Like other games, this game has rules and each side plans a winning strategy. Parents play the game quite well. We keep our eyes on the prize (laws, rights, entitlements, etc.) and we develop our strategies (advocacy). But even though we're good at the game, we seldom "win." The other side not only has more players, but also more power. We become bruised and battered, but we're also determined, so we continue to play.

Unfortunately, the games we play aren't really about the best interests of our children. Egos, power, laws, internal politics, revenge, the status quo, and just about everything but the kitchen sink get in the way of the real issues. And in this game of "us vs. them," no matter who wins, our children ultimately lose. Enough is enough. The time has come to end competition and begin cooperation.

It bears repeating: for our children's sake, we are obligated to do more than fight for rights; we're obligated to do what's right.

When I present this information at workshops, some parents recognize the danger and futility of this unending competition. Others, however, find it difficult to let go of their anger or forgive professionals. They're stuck in the role of victim and they're determined to receive justice. Many parents resort to legal action and sue their school districts.

My recommendation is this: if you decide to sue your school district, go for it, as long as you're willing to move to another city or another district. If you lose the lawsuit, you'll be branded forever as a troublemaker and it will be difficult, if not impossible, to ever work cooperatively with the school. If you win, school personnel will be forced to follow the orders of the court—as long as someone watches over their shoulders—but trust and cooperation will be forever gone. In either case, your reputation will both precede and follow you in future dealings with educators and other professionals. But winning or losing and the status of your reputation are less important than this: why, oh why, would you want to send your children to a school where educators hate your guts? Can we afford to take the risk that negative attitudes toward us might impact our children?

We do things to children with disabilities we would never even consider doing to our other children. Would you ever, under any circumstances, send your children who don't have disabilities to a place—day in and day out—where the people who are entrusted to take care of your child are your enemies? Would you drop your daughter off for a ballet lesson if you and the ballet teacher disagreed on just about everything? Would you send your son to a martial arts class if you didn't trust the instructor? Would you allow your child to be with any adult who you're angry with most of the time?

Most of us wouldn't allow our children to go near adults we didn't like and trust. In the example of the ballet teacher, for example, you would look for another ballet school. If there wasn't one, you would probably encourage your daughter to take gymnastics, tap, or some other form of dance. Alternatively, you might decide to repair the relationship with the ballet teacher. Ultimately, you would take whatever steps were necessary to ensure your child's safety and success. And I seriously doubt any of us would allow a child to continue taking ballet lessons while we're filing a complaint against, or suing, the ballet school!

While we can choose which community activities would be best for our children, we're usually not allowed to choose which schools our children attend. So when we can't change the *place,* we must attempt to change our relationships with the people at those places.

Parents who believe lawsuits or other legal proceedings are effective methods of change may strongly disagree with my position. I understand their feelings. At one time—although I've never personally sued anyone on my son's behalf—I believed invoking our due process rights was a good and proper action to take. But I've seen too many parents who—even when they win—feel they've lost. The emotional and financial drain, the alienation they experience, and the constant monitoring they feel compelled to do, takes a heavy toll.

If parents win a due process lawsuit, the hearing officer's decision can force a school to follow the law, but seldom will the ruling change people's hearts. For long-term change to occur, we have to help people change their basic attitudes—their feelings about children with disabilities and parents. Consider, for a moment, if you or your employer were sued and then forced to follow the directives of the court. How would you feel about the people who sued you? Would you be interested in working collaboratively with them in the future? Or would you deal with them only when it was mandated, and with the greatest reluctance and barely disguised anger?

When professionals are not doing what we know they should—like following the law or anything else—we can choose to *not* respond or react with words or actions that make the situation worse. We can get out of the game-playing mode. We can rise above the muck. And we can be more professional, more polite, more reasonable, more positive, and more persuasive than educators and others who influence our children's lives. Most importantly, we can provide leadership. The time for change is now.

RELATIONSHIPS RULE THE WORLD

We all have voluntary and involuntary relationships. My relationships with my husband, my best friend, the grocery store clerk, and many others are voluntary—I have *chosen* to form a connection with them. I can have voluntary relationships with professionals, if—and it's a big if—I'm free to choose which teacher, therapist, doctor, or other professional will work with my son, and if I'm free to terminate those relationships when I choose.

Usually, however, we're not able to choose all the different professionals who will have influence over our children's lives. We're forced to work with certain people, whether we like them or not, whether we choose them or not. And it works both ways: many professionals are forced to work with us whether they like us or not.

Traditionally, the position of professionals is paternalistic: they have the authority and the power; they dole out what we need. They play the role of "givers." This puts us in the position of "receivers." Needless to say, this is an unequal relationship. There's nothing inherently wrong with unequal relationships. They're fine as long as both parties are satisfied. Some relationships are almost always unequal, to one degree or another: parent and child, employer and employee, and so forth.

Parents who are content in unequal relationships with professionals may be getting everything they want and need for their child, or they may be glad to let someone else assume responsibility. But when we're unhappy in an unequal relationship, we take on a new role. We throw off the cloak of "receiver" and step into the body armor of advocate.

Advocates or Parents?

Let's digress for just a moment and think about that word. In Webster's New American Dictionary, 1995, advocate—as a noun—is defined as "one who pleads another's cause; one who argues or pleads for a cause or proposal." As a verb, it's "to plead in favor of." Plead means "to appeal earnestly" or "to argue for or against something." Further, appeal is defined as "to plead for help, corroboration, or decision" or "to arouse a sympathetic response."

Do our actions—in the name of advocacy—fit these definitions? I know many of us do a lot of arguing with professionals and that doesn't usually get us anywhere. I don't think we want to "arouse a sympathetic response." I don't want sympathy, I want equality, nor do I want to "plead" for anything. Maybe we "appeal earnestly" sometimes.

It's good to call ourselves advocates in terms of working to change the big picture about people with disabilities. But I'm not sure we always want to use the word "advocate" when dealing with professionals who work with our children. For one thing, it often sets off alarms in the minds of educators and others. Ask an educator or a service provider what an advocate is and you may get a slew of answers that wouldn't mesh with the dictionary definition, nor would they be complimentary to parents.

However, the bigger issue is this: parents of children *without* disabilities deal with educators, medical professionals, park and rec coaches, ballet teachers, day care providers, and others, all the time. But these parents don't call themselves advocates. They call themselves parents. They simply do what parents do: take good care of their children. Isn't that what we're trying to do on behalf of our children?

One of the interesting things about using the word advocate when we're in team meetings (IEP, IFSP, etc.) is that we may use the word *only when we anticipate problems*. When things are going well, we don't need to advocate. But when a contentious meeting is coming up, not only do we arm ourselves in advocacy, but we often bring a couple of extra advocates with us (other parents, experts, lawyers, etc.). We might as well fire off a couple of warning shots while we're at it. We're sending the message: get ready for a fight, the advocates are coming. Let the battle begin.

Most parents don't want to fight with educators and other professionals. We're simply trying to do our best on behalf of our children. We would prefer to have mutually beneficial partnerships with professionals that include respect, equality, and reciprocity. But when disagreements cannot be resolved, when personality conflicts fan the flames, and when effective communication ceases, relationships disintegrate.

The roles we play—advocate, parent, and others—exert a powerful influence on our relationships. And the roles we play are ever changing. Like beauty, roles are in the eyes of the beholder. We see a person in a certain way and our behavior is based on our perception (not the reality) of that person's role. Professionals do the same thing. Our perceptions of one another—whether they're accurate or not—set up invisible barriers. But we don't need X-ray vision to see beyond these barriers. We just need to fine tune our thinking.

A psychologist once told me, "When you're in a relationship with another person, it's like you're slow dancing together. If one dancer changes dance steps, the other dancer has to change, too." If we change our dance steps, our dancing partners (professionals) will change theirs, too. Let's dance a new dance. Let's make things better. Starting now.

THE ROLES WE WEAR

For several years, my fifteen-year-old daughter Emily has worn the same Halloween costume. She becomes Gumby, of Gumby and Pokey. The costume covers her from head to toe, which is important in the Colorado mountains at 8,600 feet elevation. October 31st is usually cold and windy, and a few snowflakes often find their way into the candy bags of trick-or-treaters. To make it a little easier for kids to get as many goodies as possible in the shortest amount of time, the two small shopping centers in our town transform themselves into a "neighborhood." Kids from all over town dart in and out of the grocery store, dime store, laundromat, health food shop, and other businesses to get their treats as they dodge the wind and the cold.

The mask of Emily's Gumby costume is like having a paper bag over her head. It's big (and green, of course), covers her entire head, front and back, and the stiff, foam-backed material rests on her shoulders. When the costume and the mask are on, Emily is not Emily anymore. She's Gumby!

As she makes her way through the throngs of pirates, fairies, monsters, and other characters, little kids run to her, yelling, "There's Gumby! There's Gumby!" They stare up at her Gumby face, wave at her, squeeze her hand, and hug her around the knees. She waves in return, squeezes hands back, and gives pats on the back. Parents, with babes in arms, approach Gumby to give the littlest trick-or-treaters a closer look. "Eeeeahhhyowwww," they wail, not liking Gumby one bit. Tender-hearted Emily jerks the mask off to show the babies they don't need to be afraid. With a couple of gulps of air, eyes darting between Emily's face and the Gumby mask, the babies' fear turns to relief. When she slides the mask back on, she's assumed the role of Gumby again.

While it's my sweet daughter that's behind the mask, children and adults aren't responding to Emily. They're responding to the role she's playing—Gumby.

When we put on Halloween costumes and masks, we assume new roles. In our relationships with educators and other professionals, we assume new roles. Others react to the roles we wear; our behavior is dictated by the roles we choose. We can change our roles. We can take off our masks and work with one another as human beings.

Let Go of the Role

Whatever roles you've been playing, it's time to let them go. Take off the mask of Wanda the Whiner, Cathy the Cryer, Terry the Terrible, Dan the Man, Laura the Legal-Beagle, Ross the Boss, Betty the Beggar, Norman the Nag, Patty the Professional, Deanna the Demanding, Steve the Strong, or Annie the Advocate. Be yourself. Be your kid's mom or dad. Redefine yourself.

Some of us use our roles as weapons. As in a truce after a battle, we may not want to lay down our weapons unless the other side lays theirs down first. But we must take the first step. Others will follow our lead. It will happen.

When we change our roles by taking off our masks, we help others take their own masks off. All of us assume many different roles throughout the day, taking them on and off depending on what we're doing and who we're with. At home with my kids, wearing sweats and yesterday's mascara, I'm Mom. On the airplane, with my two appropriately sized carry-on bags, I'm a Business Traveler.

The role-changing process is not static; it's not fixed. It's flexible, responsive, and ever-changing. Role changes can equalize relationships, ensure reciprocity, and open the door to friendship and success. They allow us to develop long-term, sustainable, positive, and co-operative associations with professionals and others, now and in the future.

The Roles of Others

You can't force other people to change their roles, but—in your head—you can change the *perceptions* you currently hold. Many of us know professionals by their job titles, but we've also ascribed other, less formal roles to them as well. Mr. B carries the title of special ed director, but you also know him as the jerk. Mrs. V wears the mask of the principal, but you've assigned the role of witch to her.

Let go of these roles in your head. If I could jump in your brain right now and pull them all out, I would. But you can do it on your own. It's important. We don't want our children to be defined by their perceived deficits, so we can't define others by theirs.

Our imaginary Mr. B isn't just the special ed director *or* the jerk. He's also a loving and beloved husband, a good father of twin sons and a daughter, a reader of mysteries, a dad who can put the bow in his daughter's hair the right way, a fan of professional football, a thoughtful son who helps takes care of his aging mother, and more. Our Mrs. V is a widow, the mother of two college kids, a lover of history, and a great cook who specializes in Northern Italian cuisine. She plays tennis, has two dogs, is lonely, likes old movies, and goes to church on Sunday mornings and Wednesday evenings.

Professionals are people, too. They're not one-dimensional characters. They're not their roles, just as Emily is not Gumby, just as our children are not their disability labels. You might think of yourself as the Mother-From-Hell but that's not who you really are. That's simply the role you wear in certain circumstances; it's the role you assume. You're not a one-dimensional character either. You're you! You have many wonderful virtues that can ensure positive relationships with professionals. When we redefine ourselves *and* the professionals we work with, we create "new and improved" associations that can guarantee our children's success.

It's always best if we can start off on the right track. But what about the current relationships you're in—the ones that are causing the most problems? They have to be repaired. You can do it. If, however, you choose not to repair them, expect more contentious meetings and unpleasant interactions. Expect continued exclusion, segregation, and lack of services and supports for your child. Not quite sure if you're ready to do this? Give it a try. What have you got to lose? Already made up your mind you want things to improve? Then let's go for it!

Many of the suggestions that follow focus on our relationships with educators. But the techniques can be used with any professional.

REPAIRING RELATIONSHIPS

The first step in repairing relationships is letting go of the past. This may be hard—very, very hard. Many of us have endured years of frustration, stress, and anger after being treated unfairly or with disrespect. But holding on to these wrongs is poisonous: it contaminates our spirits, corrupts our basic goodness, and pollutes our hopes and dreams. Use whatever method works for you to let go of the past: forget; forgive and forget; shake it off like a bad dream; release it like it's a balloon floating up, up, and away; wad it all up and throw it in the trash; burn it like a log in the fireplace; or do any other exercise that will help you let go and move on.

The next step is believing you will be successful. Without sounding overly simplistic, accept this as fact: failure is not an option. Do not say you'll "try" to succeed. This leaves the door open for failure, so you can say, "Well, I tried." If you can't convince yourself at this very moment that you'll succeed, then pretend to believe it for now. The small successes you'll enjoy on your way to the big success will provide the proof you need to believe.

Communicating your intentions is the next step in the process. Let professionals and others know you're ready for a positive change. This takes a lot of courage. But you can do it. If making positive overtures to people you don't like causes you to grit your teeth in disgust—or worse—focus on why you're doing this: for your child. Most us us are willing to walk over hot coals for our children. If we'll do that, then certainly we can do whatever it takes to have positive interactions with those who influence our children's lives. Isn't your child's success worth whatever bruises your ego might take?

There are any number of ways to do this. You can pick up the phone and call people. You can wait until they call you. You can approach them the next time you see them. But I suggest you make an effort to see them in person, as soon as you feel comfortable—and the sooner the better—to let them know of your intentions. What should you say? Whatever feels right. Here's an example:

> Hello, Mr. Harris, this is Kate Webster. I know we've had some difficult times in the past, but I'd like to put all that behind us and work at having a better relationship. I hope we can get to know each other a little better. I know that both of us want what's best for my daughter and I'm sure that together, we can make good things happen!

If you're gagging on these words, take a deep breathe and keep a picture of your child's success in your head. If you have the courage to argue with people, you also have the courage to be polite.

If you can really let go of the past and if you can open your heart (remember, this is all for your child), add in an apology. Your apology is not for anything you've done, but for the poor relationship. To the example above, you could add, "I'm really sorry we've had a hard time getting along."

If you can open your heart as wide as possible, do apologize if you've done wrong: "At the last IEP meeting, I was really rude and I'm sorry. I want to have a great relationship with you. We're both working for the benefit of my daughter!" Other examples of making amends include saying such things as:

- We've had a troubled relationship. I'd like us to start over.

- I've let my emotions get the better of me and I'm going to do what it takes to keep our relationship positive.

- I haven't done all I can do to ensure a successful relationship with you. That's going to change. I look forward to cooperation and friendship in the future.

Say whatever you feel is appropriate to open the door to a new relationship. Be creative. Be as sincere as possible. Even if you don't *feel* like saying the words, say them anyway—fake it, if you must. Authentic sincerity will come soon enough. The reactions and responses to your overtures will both surprise and please you. Many parents have told me that simply *stating their intentions* to have a positive relationship has brought immediate improvements.

STEPS TO SUCCESS

Now, let's look at other steps we can take to ensure positive relationships. Use these in new and existing associations. I'll start with the simplest steps and work up to those that are more complex.

Use First Names

A totally different atmosphere surrounds you when you're on a first name basis with professionals. During your next visit with the doctor, specialist, educator, or other professional, make the change.

For example, if the doctor greets you with, "Hello, Mrs. Smith, how can I help you today?", smile a big smile and say, "I'm so glad you're our doctor. Please call me Sarah and I'll call you Ted." (Notice you're not asking; you're stating.) There's a slight chance he'll respond in the negative. If he does, laugh it off, and follow up with, "Okay, then how about Dr. Ted?" If that doesn't work, repeat the procedure at a later time or look for another doctor! In any case, on your way out the door, say, "Thanks, Ted!" and give him a big silly smile and a wink. Throw in a hug for good measure.

If he already calls you by your first name, try this after he greets you: "I'm so glad you call me Sarah instead of Mrs. Smith! I'd like to call you Ted." If your child's therapist calls you Mrs. Smith, but you call her Cindy, change it. "Cindy, we're so close, please call me Sarah."

Do the same thing during professional telephone calls. When you call the principal or the special ed teacher or someone else, use the example above. Keep it simple, keep it light, keep a smile on your face and in your voice. *It's much harder to be angry with someone when you use first names!* Using first names in one-on-one situations helps equalize relationships. It adds a touch of intimacy and friendship.

It's even more important to use first names in team meetings. Begin now to get on a first-name basis with every person who is involved in your child's team meetings. During telephone calls, in one-on-one meetings, when you see a teacher at school, or in any other situation, take the opportunity and make it happen. Using first names lays a good foundation for successful team meetings.

Share Something Personal

The relationships we have with educators, physicians, therapists, and others start off as professional relationships, but our connection to them is very personal: our precious children. Our children unite us with others whether we like it or not, so let's develop personal connections with those who touch our children's lives. Let them know who you really are.

Whether you're creating new associations or repairing old relationships, give the gift of familiarity. Make small talk about where you're originally from, your hobbies, your favorite TV show, the books you love to read, how many brothers and sisters you have—anything that makes you a real person, that tells someone you're more than a "special ed parent" or "tough advocate."

Learn Something Personal

When you're making small talk about yourself, use the give-and-take of conversation to find out something personal about the professional you're dealing with. If you say, "I watched the most interesting 'whodunit,' last night. I love mysteries! Did you see it?", you might learn you share a love of mysteries, or you may discover the person doesn't *ever* watch television. On the other hand, you may learn she didn't see the mystery show because she was watching ballet on PBS. In any case, you'll learn something you didn't know before.

With all the little "somethings" you learn, you'll better understand the person and discover new ways to connect with her. If necessary, jot these down as soon as you're able and start keeping dossiers on the folks you deal with. Pretty soon, you'll know a great deal about them. On a foundation of familiarity, we can build positive, personal relationships.

In my own district, during a meeting with the special ed director in his office, I noticed some photographs hanging on his wall. There he was, all decked out in a helmet and a flashy outfit standing next to a motorcycle. Never in a million years would I have guessed this serious professional sitting across the table from me in his three-piece suit was a motorcycle racer! I took the time to ask Sam about it and learned he raced motorcycles on weekends. I was fascinated; it seemed so out of character. I *had* to find out more: how long had he been doing it, how did he get started, did it worry his wife, and so forth. Sam really enjoyed talking about his lifelong hobby. In the process, he revealed a side of himself that was very different than his professional persona.

During our conversation, Sam described being in a very serious accident several years before. While he was recovering from his injuries—being immobile for a time, receiving therapy, and needing lots of help—he said he "learned a little bit about about what it was like to have a disability." This revealed still another side of himself. I began to see who really lived in the body of the person I knew as the special ed director. During that one conversation, I learned more about him than most of his colleagues (and other parents) knew.

From that point on, I asked him about his cycle and his weekend races when we saw one another. For example, when I attended IEP meetings with other parents, I made a point of asking Sam about his latest escapade. It changed the tone of the meeting, relaxing tensions and creating an atmosphere of friendship. It also demonstrated to others that Sam and I had a personal, as well as professional, relationship. Even if he and I disagreed about something during the meeting, the motorcycle stories kept us connected.

Redefine Yourself

Professionals often see parents as "problems." Why? Because the majority of the time, the only time they see us is when we have problems. In the eyes of many, we're one-dimensional characters—The Special Ed Parents—because *that's the way we've presented ourselves*. Sharing something personal about ourselves is one way to redefine ourselves, but there are many others.

At school, shed your special ed parent persona in favor of another. Become the mom or dad who: brings freshly-baked (or store bought!) cookies to the staff meeting every Tuesday morning; volunteers at school during the day or performs volunteer work for the school at home in the evenings; helps out with athletics; serves on the school improvement team or other school committee at the building or district level; or becomes the PTA president. Create one or more roles for yourself that are *not* related to special education.

Every school needs many parent volunteers. After-school activities can't be done without help from volunteers. Extracurricular activities such as sports teams, drill teams, and others all depend on volunteers. Find something that's interesting that fits in with your schedule and get busy. It's not absolutely necessary that you volunteer for an activity in which your child participates. You might want to choose something your child *would like to do;* volunteering ahead of time will give you good insight into what accommodations your child might need when he does participate. The connections you make while volunteering can lead to inclusion, friendships, and more. Recognize that every person you come in contact with through your volunteer efforts is a potential ally.

Volunteer to do presentations at the school's "career day." If such an event isn't on the agenda, offer to coordinate one. Many schools regularly invite adults to share their professional or personal expertise with students. Even if a school doesn't officially sponsor such programs, many individual teachers seek out adults for this purpose. Don't look to participate only in your child's class. Offer to do this in any class. Most employers willingly give employees time off to participate in such activities; it's good public relations.

Contribute to the overall well-being of your child's school; demonstrate your value to the school and you'll be repaid in kind. Imagine walking into an IEP meeting as the PTA president, the booster club volunteer, the cookie lady, the science club advisor, or some other persona, instead of the role you've been playing: the special ed, troublemaking, angry parent. It's very, very difficult for an educator to tell you "no" at or before an IEP meeting when you've been making valuable contributions to the school or the district. Your efforts will be repaid a thousandfold in goodwill directed to you.

You may be thinking this isn't "right," that schools should follow the law and do what they're supposed to do whether parents contribute to the school or not. And you're probably correct. But the simple reality is one you already know: you can catch more flies with honey than vinegar. I'm much more giving, kind, and considerate to people who are nice to me than to those who are rude or uncaring. I'm much more willing to go out of my way to help people who have shown an interest in me or were kind and helpful. Educators and professionals are no different.

There are a zillion other ways to redefine yourself. Every school district has many, many committees that parents serve on. Most of these committees are also composed of teachers, administrators, and other educational staffers. Not only do you become known as a member of such-and-such committee, you also get to know educators and other parents who can become your allies. If you're in tight with administrators and school board members, consider the possibilities.

Call the school and the district offices to learn more about committees and volunteer opportunities. "Ha! They hate me," you may be saying to yourself, "They'll *never* give me this information." If your current reputation with the school is that bad, have a friend get the information for you. After you've improved relationships, this will all change.

When you're redefining yourself through new activities, don't make the mistake of interjecting your special ed connection in the early stages of your new relationships. You don't want to be known as "Susan, the Special Ed Mom Who's Now Also the Volleyball Volunteer." Be Susan, first, and then Susan, the Volleyball Volunteer. Wait until you know people better before talking about your child's disability or special ed experiences. Identify and develop commonalities before introducing differences. Of course, you might already be known to others as "Joshua's mom." That's fine. Use that as an opportunity to present positive images of Joshua and your family.

Become More Visible

Even if you can't volunteer, you can redefine yourself in other ways. If your child currently rides the bus, and if you're able to take your child to and from school, do it. When you drop your child off or pick him up, run into the building once a week, once a day, or whenever you can, and greet teachers, the school secretaries, the principal, the custodian, and any one else you come across. Be seen in school as often as possible. Introduce yourself. Chit-chat whenever you can. You never know how these connections can be used in the future. Start looking at regular ed teachers not as strangers, but as your child's future teachers, next year or the year after that.

While running in and out of a school building is quite easy in the elementary grades, it can be a little harder when your child is in middle or high school. Many kids don't want their friends to even know they *have* parents, much less see them in school. No matter; it's still possible. Be creative and think of "excuses" to go in to school. In fact, you could let your kid out at the curb, go park your car, and pretend you don't even know each other. That will make your kid happy and you'll accomplish your goal of making connections with folks in school.

Nurture New Connections

As you're redefining yourself through volunteer and other activities, you'll be meeting new people. Cultivate these new connections. Nurture them. Take the time to get to know folks. When you leave a meeting, walk to the parking lot with a new friend and chat by the car for a minute before leaving. Better yet, join your new friend(s) for a cup of coffee on the way home. You never, ever know what will develop. These new friends can connect you to others. Your circle of friends, allies, and supporters will grow exponentially.

Never underestimate the help these new folks can provide, nor the amount of help you may provide to others. And never prejudge the influence others can have over your child's education. One of the best connections I made when my son was in elementary school was with Sheila, the school custodian. When I was in and out of the building, I made a point of speaking to everyone I saw, including Sheila. Every Christmas, I gave presents to all my children's teachers, as well as the librarian, the cafeteria ladies, the school secretaries, and Sheila. Sometimes my presents were baked goods; other times they were small trinkets or something the kids and I made to show our appreciation.

One day, we decided Benjamin needed a desk easel/book stand to hold papers and books in the right place. I showed the principal and the teachers pictures of easels in speciality catalogs. Needless to say, they were expensive. When we began discussing all the red tape we needed to go through to purchase one, we brainstormed other ideas. *Voila!* We talked to Sheila and she enthusiastically agreed to figure out if she could make one. Not only did she make a wonderful easel for Benjamin, she made two more at the same time for other students. I was thrilled at how quickly she got it made, the district was happy at the minimal expense for the raw materials, and Sheila was proud of her contribution. Sheila became quite an expert on the equipment needs of kids with disabilities in the school. Her help was always beneficial.

Go Beyond Schools

Schools are not the only places we can redefine ourselves. In some cases, *creating* an identity is as important as redefining ourselves. Just as we can become more involved in our children's schools, we can insert ourselves into community activities as a way of helping our children. Help out with park and rec activities. Sit on community committees and boards. Volunteer at any of the many, many community organizations and activities in your area.

Widen your horizons beyond disability issues. Your efforts will pay big dividends. It's much easier to have your child included in park and rec activities if you're a park and rec volunteer or a committee member.

Your role in the community can cross over and have a powerful effect on your relationship with educators. Imagine walking into an IEP meeting not only as Terry's mom, but also a park and rec board member. You're not one-dimensional, only caring about special ed issues; you're a park and rec expert. You'll be perceived as a leader who shapes the community. And you never know how the connections you make in these activities will help in the long run.

Redefine Others

Remember the suggestion to learn something personal about the people in your child's life? Take what you learn and build on it to redefine the professionals you deal with. Who are the people you least enjoy dealing with? Start with them first!

Sometimes we don't want to let go of negative perceptions and feelings about people we have difficulty getting along with. Because of their actions, some folks genuinely deserve our contempt or anger. Others may not be as bad as we make them out to be, but they make good targets for our frustration and fears. Regardless, our children will benefit when we have better relationships with professionals. If we continue to view influential people as our enemies, we won't be very successful in our efforts on behalf of our children. Redefining others can help change this.

When you discover something interesting about evil Mr. So-and-So, or an intriguing tidbit about obnoxious Mrs. What's-Her-Name, you'll start seeing them in a different light. Maybe one is a scout leader or a park and rec coach. Maybe one painted the pictures hanging in the office. If you discover you have something in common with them, or when you learn something positive, you might actually see them as (gulp) friends. Yes, friends. If not friends, then at least associates who you can work with comfortably.

What do you know about the people who attend your child's IEP meeting or the ones who act as the gatekeepers to community activities? Put on your detective hat and start sleuthing.

The first place to learn more about a person is from the person, directly. You can start by learning something personal, as previously described. Take it a step further and find out as much as you can in casual conversation. Obviously, you don't start interrogating a person about her personal life. When you make time for chit-chat, simply interject something about yourself and follow it with a related question for the other person.

Here are some examples on ways to use casual conversations to learn more. While these conversations might look stilted on paper, in real life the wording would be more natural.

Principal: Hello, Mrs. Smith, how are you?

Parent: Oh, fine—just a little tired this morning. By the way, please call me Sandy. Anyway, Jim, I was up late last night baking cookies for church— yummy chocolate chip. That's our favorite. What's yours?

Principal: Hmm, I guess chocolate chip is my favorite, too.

Parent: Great! I'll bring you some this afternoon when I pick Kevin up. I have some extras. I needed to bake five dozen for the church bazaar this weekend. You're welcome to come! By the way, do you and your family go to church?

Parent to teacher: Kendra's great-grandmother from West Virginia is sending her a new doll and she can't wait to bring it for show-and-tell.

Teacher: Oh, you have family in West Virginia?

Parent: Yes, that's where my family is originally from, but we have family in California and Minnesota, too. What about you? Where are you from?

Parent to educator: Wow! Did you see the Cowboys beat the Raiders on Sunday? That was some game. Do you follow pro football?

Educator: Well, some. I really like college ball better. I went to Ohio State.

Parent: Oh, did you grow up in Ohio?

Educator: Yes and no. When I was young we lived in Illinois, but we moved to Ohio when I was twelve.

In real life, the dialogue in all of these scenarios could continue far beyond what I've put on paper. Think of casual conversations as lubricants. Just as oil lubricates your car engine to keep it running smoothly, casual conversations are the lubricants of relationships. How often do most of us typically engage in small talk with folks at IEP meetings and in other potentially tense situations? How would our IEP meetings, and our relationships with educators and others, be different if we shared in friendly conversations based on commonalities?

In addition to learning about individuals by direct conversations, we can also talk to people who know them. Ask a teacher where the principal attended college. Ask the principal where the teacher is from. Ask other parents about educators and professionals they're familiar with.

Learning more about individual people won't automatically change your relationship with them, but it *will* open the door to change. Amazing things can happen when we learn about the "real" people who live inside their professional roles. We all have so many wonderful attributes. I know you can find something in common with most of the people you deal with, even those you like the least.

After I learned the wife of an educator was a potter, I was interested and impressed with her vocation. I shared my feelings that I love to look at handmade pottery and would like to collect it. The educator then began to let me know about pottery shows and when his wife's work would be exhibited and sold. Little bits of familiarity like this make us more than professionals and parents; they make us friendly acquaintances and, in many cases, friends.

When you've learned more and more about the people you interact with—whether it's trivial tidbits or life histories—you're able to redefine them in your mind. Even before you've taken active steps to change the relationship, you can start to change things in your head. If you learn the special ed director loves Mexican food, imagine him dipping his tostada chips in salsa. Begin to replace the negative images you have with pictures in your head of folks being real people—real people who are more like you than they are different.

Gather information during formal and informal interactions and use it to build bridges. Next time you see the principal, whether you pass him in the hallway at school or when you're facing him at an IEP meeting, ask him if he's been to any new restaurants, if he's seen the latest movie, or some other casual, but relevant, question. This is how friendly relationships grow and develop. Why shouldn't the people who influence our children's lives be our friends and allies? We can help make it happen.

Improving our relationships is one step in our transformation. The next one is using cooperation.

COOPERATION

When we wear the role of advocate, we're often unwilling to work cooperatively. We feel we must be firm and rigid in our positions to avoid being pushed around by the powers-that-be. Some of us want what we want and we're not willing to give an inch. We may work cooperatively up to a point. But when we've had enough of half-truths and broken promises, we give up on the give-and-take of cooperation.

It *is* hard to cooperate with people we perceive as our enemies. But once we begin to redefine ourselves and others (turning professionals and adversaries into friends and allies), cooperation becomes easier and our efforts will greatly benefit our children. Cooperating doesn't mean giving up or giving in. It simply means we work *with* others to achieve success for our children.

Winners and Losers?

When we're attempting to work with others on behalf of our children, we often believe the only outcome can be win or lose. When this attitude drives our behavior, we set ourselves up for failure, even when we win. For when one side "wins," the other side "loses." If we're on the "losing" side, we feel angry and don't want to cooperate. Some of us are not only angry, but we think about revenge. If we feel we've won, we gleefully leave a team meeting, often gloating about our success and the failure of the other parties. Sometimes we even rub the loser's nose in it. It's no wonder so many relationships fail. But when we work cooperatively, it's a win/win situation, and everyone feels successful.

Consensus-Building

Taking cooperation a step further, we can work with others and make decisions based on consensus. In consensus-building, we don't focus on getting what we "want;" we focus on what we can "live with."

Several years ago, our district's special education advisory committee (SEAC) decided to draft a mission statement on inclusive education. Our goal was to create a statement that the school board would approve and include in its annual report. While the statement wouldn't have the power of a directive from the school board, mandating that every school in the district practice inclusion, it would be a starting point—a philosophy that could point educators in the right direction. The SEAC was composed of a few parents of children with disabilities (including myself), several special educators, an occasional regular educator, and the special ed director.

As with IEP/IFSP teams, our group was not always of one mind. It seemed everyone had his or her own agenda to follow. We knew we would probably never be able to arrive at a statement that everyone agreed with 100 percent, so we decided to use the consensus method: we would write a statement that we could all "live with."

After discussing the ideas we wanted in the mission statement, and then deciding how to state these ideas, each person would say, "I can live with that," or "I can't live with that." We purposely avoided extreme positions such as "I love [or hate] it." or "That's wrong [or right]." Had our goal been to write something that each of us found perfect, we would still be meeting! Many revisions were made during the six months it took to wordsmith the mission statement until it was something everyone could live with.

By using the consensus method in IEP/IFSP meetings or in discussions about community participation for your child, you recognize that total agreement is impossible, but that compromise and cooperation by everyone will ensure success. Many parents have learned that even the *offer* of compromise and cooperation can change the dynamics of their relationships. It demonstrates flexibility, empathy, and leadership. How would a meeting be different if we stated, "Well, I never considered that before. Let's talk about it," instead of saying, "Absolutely not!"?

Cooperative Behavior

Cooperation requires us to be respectful of others, listen well, keep the lines of communication open, and be problem-solvers.

Show respect for others

Do this even if you don't feel you're getting respect. Remember the axiom about the slow dancers: if you change your dance steps, your dancing partner must change his. Don't dance their dance of disrespect; get others to dance your dance of respect. Keep showing respect to others *out of respect for yourself.* Maintaining your dignity and your composure enables you to keep a tight hold on your own self-respect.

Respecting others means we don't trade insults with them, we don't interrupt them, and we have good manners, even when—especially when—they don't exhibit those behaviors! Remember what your parents taught you when you were young and you'll be fine: "Treat others the way you want to be treated," and "Don't sink to their level!" Too often, we simply forget our manners—we become highly uncivilized, in fact—when we're hurt, scared, or angry.

Listen Well

We often hear what we want to hear, not what's really being said. If we've had bad experiences with Mr. So-in-So in the past, we assume everything he'll say in the future is negative or against us. We might also read more into what he's saying than what he really means, based on our own emotional state or previous experiences. We embellish his words with our own ideas and opinions. Sometimes we don't hear what someone really says because our brains are not focused on the person speaking: we're too busy thinking about what we're going to say next.

When I was a television producer years ago, the hostess of our interview show was a very poor interviewer because she didn't listen well. To remedy this situation, we jointly prepared a list of questions for her to use during an interview show. But even this didn't always help. Instead of listening to the guest's answers, she was thinking about her next question, how she looked, where the camera was, or who knows what. So when she asked questions during the interview, she would inadvertently ask something the guest had already answered. For example:

> TV Interviewer: Mrs. Adams, how did you get involved in writing children's books?
>
> Mrs. Adams: Well, I loved making up stories for my three children when they were young—I have two boys and a girl—and my husband encouraged me to write them down for others to enjoy.
>
> TV Interviewer: Oh, and how many children do you have?
>
> Mrs. Adams: Uh, uh, three—two boys and a girl.

We often see similar situations on national news magazine programs. (We're not the only ones who don't listen well. Million-dollar television hosts do it, too!) Most interview guests have such good manners they don't embarrass the interviewer by saying, "You must not have been listening. I already answered that question!"

We need to hone our listening skills to ensure we really hear what's being said. Sometimes we feel *our* words are more important than the words of others, so we don't even give them the courtesy of listening. How, then, can we know how important their words are? Assuming others' words aren't as valuable as our own is a subtle form of prejudice.

Listening well means asking for clarification when we don't understand. If there's any confusion or doubt about the words someone said or the meaning intended, ask for clarification. Say, "Let me make sure I understand . . ." or "So you're saying that . . ." followed by your interpretation of what was said. Continue this procedure until you're absolutely certain you heard and understand what the person really said and meant.

Keep the Lines of Communication Open

Keep talking. When frustration mounts, tension escalates, or tempers flare, don't launch verbal assaults. They'll either inflame the situation or shut communication down entirely. Don't get up and storm out of a meeting. Don't give ultimatums or use threats. Every problem is solvable if we keep talking.

In an IEP meeting, for example, it's much better to keep going and try to complete the IEP than end the meeting in anger and reconvene again later. It's perfectly all right to say, "How about a five minute break?" or "Can we all do deep breathing exercises for two minutes?" Wouldn't that bring a laugh and relieve the tension? Or, "Let's all stand up and stretch." Better yet, call out, "Time for a group hug!" then jump up and hug several people at a time.

A moment of silence with heads bowed can have a calming effect. In one-on-one situations, we can use similar techniques. Saying, "Let me take a deep breath and think a moment before we continue," can be a big help when things are tense. We don't always need to have immediate responses; we can take the time to think.

All of these techniques send the powerful message that you're a leader who is committed to keeping the lines of communication open. You're demonstrating maturity, respect, and a determination to succeed.

Be a Problem Solver

We often know what we want for our children, but we don't know how to make it happen. Other times, we identify needs for our children but educators or other professionals don't have the solutions. Since you're the true expert on your child, you have a greater ability to provide creative solutions to your child's needs than any professional.

When it comes to inclusion—whether in a classroom or in a community activity—don't expect professionals to always know how to make it happen. Many have no experience. Special educators may have lots of experience with kids with disabilities, but if they've always taught in a resource room they may not have good solutions for including a child with a disability in a general ed classroom.

In these situations, it would be ideal if a professional would say, "Gee, I don't know how to do this. Can you help me with some ideas?" You could then share your wisdom, or the two of you could brainstorm together. Unfortunately, the majority of professionals seldom give such a response. A few brave souls might feel comfortable admitting they don't know something, but most are simply unwilling to do so. As a result, professionals will come up with some solution—in many cases one that's a variation of something that's been done before, something they're comfortable with—that may be very inappropriate or unacceptable for your child. This begins a verbal interchange that can lead to serious problems: you state a need, the professional describes the solution, you reject the solution, and the professional feels hurt, insulted, angry, or embarrassed. To "save face," especially in the middle of an IEP meeting, the professional may refute your rejection and forcefully push his solution. A stand-off begins and things start to fall apart.

When you identify your child's needs, always be ready with possible solutions. The way you present your solutions is critically important, however. When we take our cars to the quick-lube for an oil change, we have a need and the mechanic has the solution. But most of us wouldn't dream of standing over the mechanic's shoulder and telling him how to do his job. This is how we often appear to professionals. If we attempt to "tell" professionals how to do things, many feel threatened. Others think we're implying they're incompetent. In either case, this provokes anger and defensive behavior on their part. The solution is to *suggest* solutions in a respectful manner. Let's look at three different hypothetical situations during an IEP meeting:

Scenario #1: Estella says she'd like 15-year-old Maria to be included in the sophomore biology class. Educators on the IEP team say this isn't possible: the placement is not appropriate since Maria can't read the materials. Estella argues that, under the law, accommodations should be made, but the educators stand firm. It's highly possible educators don't have any ideas on how Maria could be included in the class. It's never been done before; they just can't picture how she could be successful. Therefore, the answer is no. (In this example, Estella is presenting a "need" or a "problem to be solved," but doesn't offer any solution or method to address the issue.)

Scenario #2: Estella states that Maria can be successfully included in biology if the textbook and other lessons are modified to her reading level. (This is good: Estella isn't just telling the IEP team members she wants Maria included and then leaving the rest up to the them. She's telling the team *under what circumstances* Maria can be successful in biology. However, the educators don't think they have the time, manpower, or expertise to make the modifications.)

Instead of telling the truth, however, they say Maria can't be included because of her disability or her lack of readiness. Estella can stand on principle and demand that the school provide the modification she recommended, but she'll be arguing a moot point if she's outvoted by the majority of the IEP team.

Scenario #3: Estella states that Maria can be successfully included in biology if the textbook and other lessons are modified to Maria's reading level. Estella has anticipated the negative response of the team members. Before anyone has time to refute this suggestion, Estella provides the solution and explains how the modifications can be made:

> "I just found out that the 'State Services for the Blind and Learning Disabled' has modified textbooks. They work with public schools and I'm pretty sure Maria qualifies for these services. Why don't we look into this?" or

> "A friend of Maria's brother is a biology student at the junior college. He'll be happy to work with the biology teacher to modify the lessons for Maria. That would work, wouldn't it?" or

> "Maria has two friends who will be in that class. They've both said they could work as a team with Maria during class and in study hall every day. What if we talk to the biology teacher about this?"

Under any of these circumstances, how can the school refuse to *consider* Estella's request? Her approach will—at the least—keep the dialogue going, which will improve her chances of success.

There are many, many creative ways to meet our children's needs. You may not think of yourself as having expertise in education, curriculum modifications, or accommodations across a variety of settings, but neither did Estella. She was simply being resourceful, she used her common sense, and she remained determined to find the solution that was right for Maria. Parents have a distinct advantage over educators in this area: each of us only has one student to think about—ours! And we care so deeply for our children that we'll take the time and make the effort to find the right solutions. Regardless of laws, it is unrealistic to believe educators could or would spend time and make the effort to find the best solutions for all the different students they work with. Similarly, we can't expect T-ball coaches, for example, to know what accommodations a child with a disability needs to be successful if he's had no experience in this area.

Who better to come up with great solutions than us? Shall we stand on principle and demand our children's rights; demand that schools take all the responsibility for our children's success? Or shall we focus on finding the solutions—since we know best—and help professionals and our children at the same time?

NEGOTIATION

When we're in adversarial positions with professionals and others, we often don't consider negotiation as a valuable tool. We don't need to beg, cry, cajole, or threaten people anymore. We need to negotiate. We need to *see ourselves as negotiators*. And there are two key components to using negotiation in team meetings and in other situations when we're working on behalf of our children: negotiating the details through compromise and negotiating around the word "no."

Negotiating Through Compromise

We often hear stories on the news about a union whose members are on strike against management. A negotiator is called in to help both parties arrive at a mutually-agreeable settlement. Before the two sides begin negotiations, they both "posture" for the news media—touting their demands and making their positions clear. But this posturing doesn't reflect the true positions of either side, and both sides know it. In reality, management and the union are both willing to settle for less than they officially demand. They exaggerate in the public forum intentionally. Then, once they arrive at an agreement, after "giving up" some of their demands, they appear "reasonable." Public relations plays a huge role in these situations.

Behind the scenes, the negotiations include thoughtful deliberations, give-and-take, and each side accepting what they can live with. Once a settlement has been reached, the negotiator and the two sides detail the compromise through the news media. Seldom, if ever, do we hear that one side won and the other lost. This, too, is a public relations maneuver. If the union announced that it won, management would look bad, the company's stock price would fall, and any number of negative outcomes would result. If management announced that the company won, union members would garner support from other unions, dissension would begin to grow and another strike would be in the works. Through compromise, both sides have won: it's a win/win scenario.

We can use some of these strategies in our dealings with educators and in other situations in our communities. However, we don't want to strut around "posturing." Unlike unions and management, we don't have a public spokesperson to do the talking for us and handle public relations. We must deal with our adversaries face-to-face. When we publicly announce our demands—by bragging to other parents, threatening educators, and so forth— we inflame an already tense situation and we must bear full responsibility for the outcome. Furthermore, we've shown our hands and can then be outmaneuvered at an IEP meeting.

But we can and should use the give-and-take components of compromise and negotiation. We should always go into an IEP meeting (or any other type of discussion related to our children) knowing which small things we're willing to give up in order to get what's most important to us. We can bargain with others: "Okay, we're willing to drop the request for this, so long as this happens . . ." Successful negotiation requires flexibility. We may not get everything we want, in the way we want it, when we want it. But if educators, professionals, and gatekeepers are able to meet us part way, we need to accept what's offered in good faith. And the same is true in reverse.

How we perceive such a negotiation, however, is very, very important. If we feel angry about only getting part of what we asked for, our emotions will drive our behavior, and we'll alienate the very people who are potential allies.

Our anger will make them sorry they did the good thing they did. It's not unlike the situation in which a mom works as hard as she can to get something her child wants and then the child complains it's still not enough. Mom feels angry because her efforts aren't appreciated.

Getting part of what we want puts us that much closer to getting the whole. Too often, we work from the "all or nothing" perspective. If we don't get everything we're asking for, our egos or our anger prevents us from accepting a "partial victory." If you're generous with appreciation and thanks for a partial victory, it's that much easier to go back in a month or so to discuss the items you didn't get the first time. But if you were angry and threatening after the partial victory, your second attempts will most likely be unsuccessful. By appreciating others' efforts and nurturing relationships with them, we're improving our ability to help our children get what they need. Remember: is the glass half-empty or half-full?

Negotiating Around "No!"

When I've presented these ideas about transformation to parents in workshops, many are excited about trying new methods of influence. Invariably, however, several come up to me absolutely thrilled about this next tip. They say, "That's the best piece of advice I've ever heard!" So here it is: from now on, never ask a question that can be answered "yes" or "no." Instead, ask questions that begin with, "What would it take?"

Here's the way this method works. First, when you ask, "What would it take?" the person you're talking to can't answer "yes" or "no," because either reply is grammatically incorrect! But that's not *why* this strategy works. It's a successful method because *any* reply will provide information you didn't know before—information you can use to learn even more. Let's compare the way we often ask for things at an IEP meeting, for example, with this new way of asking.

Typical method:

> Parent: Eric needs a computer next year.
>
> Educator: I don't know if that's such a good idea. I mean, Eric can't really use a computer, so—
>
> Parent: Yes, he can use the computer. He's been working on our computer at home all summer and—
>
> Educator: That's nice, but we don't think he's ready to do any school work on the computer. He still needs to learn the basics.
>
> Parent: But he needs a computer to do all that. And under the law, you're required to provide the assistive technology he needs.
>
> Educator: We know what the law says. But the team agrees that Eric wouldn't benefit from a computer at this time. Maybe next year.
>
> Parent: But—
>
> Educator: Now, let's get back on track. Where were we?

And so it goes.

"What would it take?" negotiating method:

> Parent: Eric has been doing great on the computer over the summer, especially with math and language skills. I know he could benefit from having a computer in school this year. What would it take to get him one?

Educator: Uh, uh—[He's taken by surprise; he's never been asked a question like this.] Well, uh, we just don't have that kind of money.

Parent: I understand completely. Computers can be expensive. I believe the school has lots of computers, though, in different classrooms and in the library-media center. What would it take to move one of those into Eric's classroom and designate it for his use?

Educator: Well, I don't know if we could do that. All those computers are already being used by other students and teachers.

Parent: Yes, I see what you mean. Well then, how about if we talked to the library/media director to see if he could free up one of the computers for part of the day?

Educator: Well, I guess Eric's teacher could talk to John about this.

Parent: Great! I know you'll all be very pleased when you see the great work Eric's capable of.

Here's a different variation, picking up after the educator tells Eric's mom all the computers are already being used by other students and teachers:

Parent: Yes, I understand. Learning how to use computers is an important skill for all the students.

Educator: It certainly is! It wouldn't be fair to take a computer used by many children and give it to just one student.

Parent: Oh, I agree. And since the school doesn't have money to buy a new computer, I wonder about looking for a used computer that Eric could use in his classroom.

Educator: Well, I don't think we have the money for a used computer either.

Parent: I see. Well, what would it take to see about a company donating one of their old computers—I hear lots of companies do this. Do any of you know anything about this kind of stuff?

Educator #2: Actually, I think my husband's company donates their old computers. I'll talk to him about it tonight.

Parent: That would be wonderful! In the meantime, could we all put our thinking caps and see how we could make this happen? I'll check with the Rotary Club and some other community groups to see if they could help.

Educator: Actually, I probably could check with the district to see if we have any funds available for this type of thing. I think we could work something out. I'll make some phone calls today and get back to you.

There are other avenues Eric's mom could take. She could ask what it would take for the school to rent a computer for $40 or $50 dollars per month. This might be very acceptable to the school. They might be able to "find" that amount of money. She could ask about the possibility of the principal checking to see if an extra computer could be found somewhere in the district. She could ask what it would take to find out just how much money the school *could* allocate. Once she got a firm commitment, she could discuss ways to supplement those funds with money from other sources—businesses, volunteer organizations, or other groups in the community—in order to buy Eric a computer for school use. (In Chapter 17, I'll show you how many of these issues can be resolved before the IEP meeting.) In the examples presented above, the issue of the computer is not yet a done deal. Still, Eric's mom has helped the team move in the right direction.

When we use this negotiating method, there are several key points to remember:

Acknowledge what the person said by saying, "Yes, I see" or something similar and then follow up with another "what would it take" question. To avoid sounding like a parrot, use phrases like "what would happen if we," "I wonder about " or similar phrases, taking care not to use questions that can be answered yes or no.

Don't argue about the responses you're given. Use them as springboards for your next question. Arguing gets you off track and it's hard to get back on.

Keep a positive "can-do" attitude. Your enthusiasm and determination are contagious. Others sense you're trying hard to find a workable solution and they soon join you instead of fighting you. If you get stuck, turn to others for help. Ask something like, "Does anyone else have an idea on what it would take to make this happen?"

Be creative and plan ahead. Have some firm solutions before you engage in conversation and be flexible enough to think of others as the conversation goes on. It's okay to take time to think about this during the conversation. We don't always have to have snap answers. It's okay to say, "Well, let's think about this for a minute. How would this work?"

Parents who have tried this method of negotiation have experienced success beyond their wildest dreams. Try it! You'll like it!

In fact, you can use this method with anyone. Instead of yelling at your kids, ask "What would it take for you to clean your room today?" Or use it with your husband, as in, "Honey, what would it take for you to clean out the gutters this weekend?" How can anyone tell you "no," give you "back talk," or argue when you've asked a question that gives the other person a feeling of power and control?

IT TAKES TWO TO TANGO

The success of our children rests in our capable hands. But none of us can do it alone. We're all interdependent on one another. Positive relationships with educators, professionals, and others will result in success for our children. It takes two to tango. Negative relationships produce negative effects. Shall we continue to dance the dance of anger and frustration, or shall we assume leadership positions and move beyond pettiness and personality problems? We can no longer let ourselves be provoked into behaving in ways that are detrimental to our children. Nor can we let our emotions drive our actions. Our children's lives are at stake.

The ways we think, act, and relate to others don't just happen. They're choices we make. We can all make better choices. And every choice you make is based on your attitude. Attitude is everything.

It's said that behind every successful man is a good woman. Perhaps behind every successful child with a disability is a parent who has good relationships. Self-determination is another step on the ladder to success, and that's next.

Self-Determination: The Foundation of Success

THEY ARE ABLE BECAUSE
THEY THINK THEY ARE ABLE.
Vergil

ACT AS THOUGH IT WERE IMPOSSIBLE TO FAIL.
Dorthea Brande

Making decisions about their lives is a routine practice for most adults. It's a skill we learned growing up. Our parents let us assume more and more responsibility for directing our own lives as we grew. Making our own choices and taking responsibility for our actions lays the foundation for living a successful life of one's own choosing.

For many adults with developmental disabilities, however, the practice isn't routine, and it's been given a name: self-determination. In workshops and through one-on-one interactions, many adults with developmental disabilities are being taught self-determination skills. This is a good. They *should* make their own choices and take responsibility for themselves.

Why, though, do they need this training? Because since childhood, their lives have been controlled by others: parents, service providers, special ed teachers, voc-rehab counselors, service coordinators, institution and group home staff members, and a variety of others.

In small towns and big cities, good work is being done to provide adults with disabilities with the lessons, opportunities, and supports they need to control their lives and their destinies. In the best cases, training is highly individualized; everyone has different experiences, so one size doesn't fit all. Some folks need help learning how to make decisions about what type of job they want or where they want to live. For others, however, the training is even more basic: how to make decisions about things most of us consider mundane activities of daily life. What time should I go to bed? When should I eat? What should I eat? What time should I get up?

It's not that adults with developmental disabilities are inherently incapable of running their own lives; it's that many have never been given the opportunity to do so. From the time they were young children, they were viewed as incapable of making decisions because of their disabilities, so parents and/or professionals made decisions for them. Many of today's adults with developmental disabilities grew up with exclusion and isolation. They weren't allowed to participate in or benefit from typical activities, environments, or experiences.

Throughout their lives, many learned helplessness. They also learned not to trust their own minds and hearts. Instead of gradually taking more and more control over their lives as they grew up, they were kept in a perpetual state of infancy and dependency.

Within the last thirty years, all of this began to change. The Independent Living Movement was a rebellion against the prevailing wisdom that saw people with physical disabilities as "patients" and "helpless cripples" who were incapable of taking control of their lives. The Self-Advocacy Movement was a rejection of the philosophy that adults with cognitive disabilities are unable to think or speak for themselves. The ongoing efforts of both of these movements continue to provide the foundation for the paradigm shift about adults with developmental disabilities: they do not need others to direct their lives or determine their futures; they are capable of doing it themselves.

In many ways, the world of our children is different than the one today's adults with developmental disabilities grew up in. Our children have many more opportunities for inclusion and participation in schools and communities. Assistive technology increases our children's independence. And we're recognizing that children with disabilities are more like other children than they are different. So it's surprising that even in a vastly different landscape, many of our children are still being denied the opportunities to develop self-determination.

While much is being done to increase the capacity for self-determination of adults with developmental disabilities, what about the self-determination of children with disabilities? What are we doing to ensure our children won't need training in self-determination when *they're* adults?

Many parents and professionals still do not look at children with disabilities and presume competence. We still don't expect them to be responsible. It's almost as if we think it's all right to keep children dependent, for parents and other adults to control their lives; we'll wait until they're adults to worry about their capacity for self-determination. But we can't wait! And we must not make our children wait!

It's difficult for children to achieve self-determination, however, unless they come from families who are self-determined. In the past, families who were were controlled by the system produced children who were helpless and dependent. If we don't want this practice to continue, we must understand the critical need for families to be in control of their own destinies.

Self-determination for adults with developmental disabilities has been a hot issue for the past quarter century. It's time to put self-determination for families and children on the front burner of disability issues. We'll look at both.

FAMILIES AND SELF-DETERMINATION

Families have typically not experienced the forced helplessness and isolation that many adults have endured in sheltered workshops, institutions, day activity centers, group homes, and other segregated environments. Families do, however, experience loss of control, autonomy, and choice when they're in a system that is unresponsive to, and incapable of, meeting their needs.

In the system, members of a family are not stripped of making decisions about when to eat or what time to go to bed, but they *are* often stripped of the opportunity to make choices, for there are few or no choices to make. They're often stripped of dignity and autonomy by a system that fosters dependency on professional expertise and bureaucratic programs. Families are often unable to achieve or maintain self-determination because the system has already determined the what, how, and who of services and assistance.

A powerful sensation flowing in and out of many families is loss of control—lack of self-determination. This sensation manifests itself in feelings of anger, frustration, sadness, guilt, incompetence, and more. However, all these emotions may be replaced (temporarily, at least) with joy and happiness when the system works and we get what we need for our children. What we fail to recognize, however, is that whether we're satisfied or angry with the service system, our sense of well-being is still dependent on the system. When things are going along fine, we (and our families) are at peace; when things are not going well, we're in crisis. Our lives ebb and flow not by our own actions, but by the whims of the system.

We don't seem to mind dependency as long as things are going our way. But dependency on the system, even when things are going well is harmful: we're unable to attribute our success and our sense of well-being to our own abilities. Instead, we often owe our success and well-being to professionals, services, programs, and bureaucracies. Belief in our capacity to control our own lives is eroded. A family's autonomy and privacy slowly evaporate. Our lives are no longer our own; they belong to the system and professionals who prescribe solutions to the "problems" of our children's disabilities. When families choose self-determination, they assume responsibility for their lives.

There is no official definition of self-determination for families. Each family is unique, so what it looks like may be different from one family to another. But in general, self-determination simply means that we—not professionals, agencies, or organizations—are in control of our lives. We make the decisions that affect our family members. Further, we decide what's important, what's right, and what's normal for our families.

When we're self-determined, we don't automatically accept the conventional wisdom about our children, nor do we make decisions based solely on the expertise of others. Instead, we make thoughtful decisions based on our own intimate and expert knowledge of our children and families, taking into account the wants, needs, and opinions of the child with the disability and other family members.

When we choose self-determination, we accept and utilize the expertise of professionals only if we decide such expertise is appropriate for our family. We use the services of professionals and the system only if the services are better than the natural supports and generic services available in our communities.

To help our children achieve self-determination, we must model the behavior we want them to acquire. When we trust ourselves to know what's best for our families, our children learn self-confidence. When we reject the control of others in favor of personal choice, our children learn self-respect. When we reap the benefits of our communities, and sow seeds of inclusion and reciprocity, our children learn citizenship. When we reject dependency on the system and choose interdependency in the community, our children learn self-determination.

What's your family's level of self-determination today? Are you and your family dependent on the system, interdependent in your community, or somewhere in between?

- Do you feel the system has too much control or influence over you and your family?

- Do you often feel victimized by professionals and/or the system?

- Do you usually take the advice of professionals even though you may not agree with them?

- Do you accept services from the system even if you're not sure they're right for your child or family?

- Do you spend a great deal of time arguing with professionals or bureaucrats about services and programs for your child?

- When your child or your family needs assistance, do you go to the system first (before investigating what's available from family, friends, neighbors, and natural sources in your community)?

- Do you believe the system (doctors, therapists, professionals, bureaucracies, etc.) is the only place you can go for help?

- Do you feel you must be careful about how you interact with people in the system to avoid jeopardizing your position?

- Are you often upset, sad, or angry because you can't get what your child or your family needs from the system?

- Does the stress of working with the system infect your family? Does your stress rub off on your spouse and children?

- Is your entire family affected by the services provided to the child who has a disability? For example, is the family's schedule impacted by the schedule of services, therapies, and interventions prescribed for your child?

- Are you unable to be the parent and/or the spouse you want to be because most of your energy or time is spent advocating for services or taking your child to services?

If you answered "yes" to one or more of these questions, you need to increase your family's self-determination. If we don't devote energy to this issue today, we shouldn't be surprised when our children, upon reaching adulthood, need training in self-determination. Our children learn from us—from what we do, not just what we say. They model their behavior on ours. If our children have grown up in families that are dependent on the system, they'll learn that, as adults, *they* should depend on the system.

Self-determination isn't rocket science. The first step is to see your family as a normal, average, typical, run-of-the-mill family. Don't let your child's disability and/or your relationships with professionals and the service system define your entire family. This change in perception will get you moving in the right direction. Next, look around at families you know who are not dependent on a human services system. They have self-determination without really trying. They're simply living their lives and making their own decisions. When they need help, they go to their extended family, friends, neighbors, and to the natural supports in their communities because there is no system for them to become dependent on! (In Chapter 15, you'll learn how to use the natural supports and generic services in your community.)

To be self-determined, families need to regain control and autonomy, and they need to protect their family privacy. To a great degree, a family's self-determination is contingent on the child's. How parents perceive their children and their children's needs, as well as how parents decide to meet those needs, will shape the self-determination of the child and the family. The two are intertwined.

"Sibshops"/Sibling Associations

When parents see their child with a disability—and the family as a whole—as aberrant, abnormal, or unusual, they're frequently concerned about the effect of the child's disability on their other children. As a result, some enroll their children without disabilities in a "sibshop" or a group composed of children whose siblings have disabilities. These organizations may include regular meetings with trainers, social activities, and other get-togethers. The rationale behind these group meetings is that the siblings of children with disabilities may have "a lot to deal with," and being able to talk with other kids who are "in the same boat" may be helpful.

Like many other things we do, this effort is done with the best of intentions, but a beneficial outcome is not always guaranteed. Like other components of today's conventional wisdom, the premise of sibshops is based on disability being a "problem." The message to brothers and sisters is, "Your sibling is so different, and your family's life is so adversely impacted by your sibling and the disability, that your life is being negatively affected and you need help to deal with all this."

I'm sure some children may benefit from friendships with other children in these circumstances. However, the message of sibshops is so detrimental that I'm not sure the benefits outweigh the negative outcome. How does the message affect how a brother or sister feels about the sibling with a disability? Sibshops don't usually promote the notion that disability is natural or that a brother or sister with disability is more like other children than different; instead, they do just the opposite. If we want unity and self-determination within our families, we don't want our typical children to receive negative messages about their brothers or sisters. I've met several families whose typical children have been told they have psychological problems because of their siblings' disabilities!

Let's carefully consider what message we want our typical children to have about their brothers or sisters with disabilities. If one or more of your other children has been involved in a sibshop or something similar, it's never too late to make a change, especially if you're beginning to implement some of the changes I've suggested in previous chapters.

CHILDREN AND SELF-DETERMINATION

Children who don't have developmental disabilities learn self-determination unconsciously, through the typical experiences of home, school, friendships, activities, and the like. As they grow and develop in these various environments, they gain more and more power and control over their own lives; they begin to make their own decisions; and they assume responsibility for the directions their lives will take.

But from the time they're very small, many children with developmental disabilities are prevented (purposely or unintentionally) from experiencing typical activities. As a result, they don't have the same opportunities for learning self-determination. Social and environmental barriers stand in their way. For example, a young child's universe is greatly expanded when she learns to walk and explore—learning every step of the way. In the case of a very young child with physical disabilities, the lack of mobility interferes with the child's ability to learn and explore.

Today's conventional wisdom rarely addresses this crucial issue. Interventions, therapies, and even much of special education focus on "deficits" or body parts in isolation, ignoring the whole child. While parents and professionals are busy trying to fix or improve those body parts, minimize the effects of the disability, maximize the child's potential, and get the child "ready," life and learning experiences are whizzing by. Children are prevented from participating in typical childhood activities because they're considered not ready, delayed, unable, incompetent, and on and on. Far too many professionals and parents overestimate the value of a child mastering "normal" functional abilities and underestimate the value of a child mastering his environment *in any way he can*. When children are unable to have power over their environments and when they're prevented from making choices, they cannot achieve self-determination.

WHERE DO "DELAYS" ORIGINATE

Children with developmental disabilities are often labeled as being "delayed" in functional abilities, such as walking, talking, feeding, and so on, as measured by developmental scales. We typically believe these so-called delays are caused by the child's disability. In some cases, a child's condition *does* cause specific developmental delays. For example, having cerebral palsy is the cause of my son not being able to walk.

But we should question whether all delays are caused by the child's disability. So-called delays in social, cognitive, and emotional development are often attributed to the child's disability. Have we ever considered that delayed development may not be caused by a disability, but by the lack of opportunities to learn, which is, in turn, a result of social or environmental barriers?

We also don't consider that deviations from the "norm" may simply be unique personal characteristics that have no connection to the child's disability. We like to wrap up every difference in one package and say they're all caused by the child's disability. By focusing on the disability instead of the child, we overlook the child as a whole being.

There is a devastating consequence to this paradigm. When one body part finally reaches a particular developmental milestone, we attach a functional or developmental age—based on developmental scales—not just to that body part but to the whole child!

Routinely, professionals assign a developmental age to a child, based on an isolated body part or specific characteristic, even though the child may be far above this age physically, emotionally, socially, or cognitively. When we accept this nonsense as truth, we set the stage for our children to acquire global delays, as I'll describe in a moment. When this happens, children have little or no chance of developing the deep roots necessary for the natural, evolutionary growth of self-determination. Following are scenarios you may be familiar with.

Communication is More Than Talking

When children without disabilities begin talking, they achieve great power. Saying "NO!" and asserting their independence are the forerunners of self-determination. Similarly, when a child says "I want a cookie, please," and her father gives her one, she's learning that she and her words are valued, and that her words can make things happen. This, too, is a critical component in a child's ability to develop self-determination. Children learn they can exert control over their own lives through their words. Communication connects children to their world and the people in it. Throughout all of our lives, communication is the key to relationships, and relationships are the essence of life.

What happens when a young child with a disability fails to develop understandable speech? Typically, we enroll him in speech therapy. We focus on verbal speech without realizing that the *real need is communication.* Emotional, social, and cognitive growth can be delayed if a child cannot exert control over his environment through communication. When a child has no effective means of communicating, he's at the mercy of those around him; he learns he has no power. Some children become docile and helpless. Others try to exert control through physical actions, which often results in professionals giving the child a "difficult behavior" label.

We shouldn't be surprised at this turn of events. What would *you* do if someone took away your voice this instant? Most of us would become frustrated and angry when we could no longer say what we want or didn't want. Yet too many of us haven't made the connection between lack of communication and "problem behavior."

If a child is able to make sounds, we seize on the notion that (1) he will learn to talk and/or (2) if he doesn't do it on his own, we can make him talk. We may send a child to speech therapy for years waiting for those sounds to become understandable words. In the meantime, the child is missing crucially important opportunities to direct his life and impact his environment through communication. By focusing on speech, we overlook the many other methods of communication—from the simplicity of picture cards to the high technology of augmentative communication devices.

In our society, we mistakenly use oral communication as a barometer of a person's overall competence. This is so ingrained in our society that we consider people with the largest vocabularies as the smartest and most competent and, therefore, the most valuable. People with smaller vocabularies are considered less smart and less competent and, therefore, less valuable.

People with no speech or with incomprehensible speech have been perceived as having incompetent minds. They're unable to demonstrate competence through the medium that's most valuable in our society: speech. Thus, children who don't develop speech at the expected time are often presumed to be incompetent in other areas of development. As a result, we prevent them from having opportunities to develop and grow. We have failed to recognize that the real issue is communication, not speech.

What's Really Delaying Kyle?

Imagine six-year-old Kyle. After four or five years of speech therapy, he's still unable to communicate effectively with people outside his immediate family. His parents, therapists, and other professionals have focused exclusively on oral communication. Other children his age have had years of experience exerting control and acquiring self-determination through communication.

Kyle's inability to communicate effectively has resulted in a variety of negative outcomes. With his parents, he can communicate simple needs through behavior. When he wants a glass of milk, he takes his mother's hand and leads her to the refrigerator. But often, his parents must spend a lot of time guessing what Kyle wants or needs. This results in a great deal of miscommunication, which then leads to frustration and stress for Kyle and his parents.

When Kyle is unable to have his needs met, he cries, screams, and behaves in ways that are unacceptable to his parents and others. This has led his parents and professionals to see Kyle as having "behavior problems." In addition, his family often treats him like a baby. After all, when babies need attention, they get it by crying, right?

Because he has no means of effective communication, Kyle hasn't learned how to play with other children or interact with adults, so his social development is affected. Because he doesn't speak, Kyle is presumed to not understand or be interested in written words, so he's missing out on many learning opportunities. Professionals and his parents have assumed he's not very smart. They're beginning to wonder if Kyle also has a cognitive disability.

Within the realms of professionalism and developmental scales, six-year-old Kyle is considered to be greatly delayed in his cognitive, social, and emotional growth. The original disability was his inability to speak. But now, he's given more labels. His parents and the professionals in his life say Kyle is delayed cognitively; he doesn't know what other six-year-olds know. He's delayed socially; he doesn't behave the way other six-year-olds do. He's delayed emotionally; he doesn't have the maturity of other six-year-olds.

How could Kyle's speech disability cause all these other disabilities? It didn't. What created the other delays was Kyle's inability to communicate, not his inability to speak. Because Kyle's parents and therapists focused on speech, they did not help him find an alternative method of communication. Thus, Kyle was unable to participate in and learn from ordinary, but crucial, childhood experiences. The cognitive, social, and emotional delays Kyle is now labeled with were *environmentally induced*.

If Kyle's parents had asked, "Kyle, do you want to talk or do you want to communicate?" how do you think he would have answered? If *you* lost the ability to speak today, what would you want? Would it be acceptable to spend years not being able to make your wants and needs known to others? Would you want to spend years in therapy, hoping one day your speech would be understandable to others? Or would you want some other means of effective communication *right now?*

Using alternative methods of communication doesn't mean we ignore or give up on a child's potential for verbal speech. We can give him tools to communicate and still continue our efforts to help him talk.

When Kyle was two, he needed to be able to tell his parents "No!" without having to scream and cry to get his message across. When he was three, he needed to be able to tell his dad his wanted a cookie. Today, Kyle needs the ability to communicate effectively with his parents and family members, with children in the neighborhood and at school, and with other people in his life.

He needs to experience control over his life—the control that emerges as children use communication to make things happen. With effective communication, Kyle can demonstrate his cognitive, social, and emotional development. Perhaps most importantly, would "I love you, Mommy," expressed through sign language, picture cards, or a communication device be any less precious than the spoken words?

Our Focus is Misdirected

Why do we still see children who have no means of effective communication? Oh, let us count the ways! Because we focus on speech to the exclusion of other forms of communication. Because we underestimate a child's potential to communicate in alternative ways, especially if the child has a real or suspected cognitive disability. Because we allow ourselves to be limited by the solutions offered by the system, including special education services. Because we don't explore or create a variety of methods that will give a child the power of communication. And finally, because we don't recognize the importance of communication (in whatever form) as one of the cornerstones in the development of self-determination.

Great harm comes to adults and children with disabilities who have no method of communicating effectively. Other people make decisions for them—from the simplest decision about when and what to eat to life-altering decisions about education and employment—so they have no power over their own lives. They're labeled "retards" because they're unable to demonstrate their cognitive abilities. They're ignored because people think they have nothing to say. They're abused because they're unable to say "no" to protect themselves and because they can't tell anyone what's happening to them. All of this constitutes a cruelty we can no longer tolerate.

When we don't give children the ability to communicate, we must bear some of the responsibility for their delays in development. Our children must be able to communicate. We must help them achieve self-determination through communication.

MOBILITY IS MORE THAN WALKING

Children without disabilities are typically upright and on the move by the time they're twelve to eighteen months of age. They're everywhere. Moving their bodies through space, having the ability to move away from Mom and then return just as quickly, and making decisions about where to go in the house or the yard are just some of the hallmarks of toddlers. Everything they do is important to them; everything they do is helping them learn and grow. Like communication, movement helps children exert control and power over their own lives, which helps them achieve self-determination.

But what happens to children with physical disabilities who are unable to move around on their own? Most of us do not give them the tools (mobility), nor we do alter the environment (our homes and other places), which would allow them to explore and learn and move in the ways that are best for them. Instead, professionals and parents focus on getting the child to crawl and walk—to move according to the accepted norm. We inadvertently delay their overall development. In essence, we're telling them, "We will not let you experience being an eighteen-month-old until you can move the way other eighteen-month-olds move."

Let's assume Jocey doesn't learn to walk until she's four. It's time to celebrate! Now she can explore to her heart's desire! But guess what? That's not what a four-year-old does. It's what an eighteen-month-old baby does. Four-year-olds are on to bigger and better things. They've been exploring for years and they've learned a great deal during that time.

While Jocey's parents and caring professionals focused on particular body parts and functional skills, Jocey's overall development has been put on hold. Like Kyle, Jocey will probably be saddled with some other labels that reflect her delayed development.

How do we expect four-year-old Jocey to act like a four-year-old when we haven't given her the opportunities to develop into a four-year old? Think of all the things two and three and four-year-olds do through movement. They go to mommy for a hug or run away when they're mad. They feel powerful and strong because they're more like grown-ups than babies (they move around on their own; they're not being carried or pushed in a stroller like a baby). They have power over their environments and their lives. Every minute of the day, they make scores of choices about where to go or what to do in the house or the yard or at day care.

But Jocey hasn't experienced most of the same things other kids her age experience. She's been carried by her parents, pushed in a stroller or wheelchair, left in the same spot when she wanted to be somewhere else, and she's had little or no control over where her body is. Because she's had no means of effective mobility, she's been prevented from experiencing typical childhood activities that promote learning, social development, and the capacity for self-determination. Professionals may soon label her as having cognitive, social, or emotional delays.

Children who are unable to move themselves need independent mobility at the chronologically appropriate age in order to grow and develop. I wanted Benjamin to have a walker when he was eighteen months of age, but the physical therapist said no, since his body wasn't "ready" (he hadn't mastered all the pre-walking skills). But when I asked the orthopedic doctor about it, he said we *should* get Benj the walker, that eighteen-month-olds were upright and moving around, that Benjamin's *body* might not be ready to do this, but his *mind* was. The doctor's wisdom showed me that one specific delay shouldn't be allowed to cause other delays, and we shouldn't presume a child has delays in other areas.

If we don't want a physical delay to cause other delays, we must give children independent mobility so they can learn, experience typical activities, be self-determined, have power over their lives, and interact with others in a variety of environments.

How do we give Jocey independent mobility? First, her parents must give her the appropriate tool(s): a wheelchair (manual or power), a power scooter, a walker, or whatever will get her upright and able to move *when and where she wants on her own*. Second, her parents must alter the environment so Jocey can move around freely. Her parents may need to rearrange furniture, widen doorways, or make other alterations so Jocey has the freedom and the power to master her home environment the way other children do.

When Jocey has independent mobility, she'll have the opportunity to develop self-determination. She'll be in control of her body, she can play with other children and develop social skills. She can learn and do and become more independent, just like other children.

Giving Jocey a mobility device doesn't mean we give up on her learning to walk. But if Jocey's parents asked her what she wanted: "Jocey, the goal is to get from Point A to Point B. After two or three more years of therapy, you might be able to get there by walking. Or, you can use this power wheelchair starting right now to go the distance. Which do you prefer?" What do you think Jocey's answer would be?

If you lost the ability to walk today, what would you want? Would you choose to go to therapy for years in the hope you would regain the ability to walk? And while you were in therapy all those years, would it be all right that you had no control over where your body was? Would it be acceptable that you could not move from the living room to the kitchen unless someone was there to move you? Or would you choose to use a mobility device that would restore your freedom and dignity?

Our Focus is Misdirected (again)

Why don't we see more young children with physical disabilities in mobility devices? Because we believe that walking is crucial to a child's success. Because we believe if we do enough therapy, he'll walk one day. Because we believe that very young children cannot operate wheelchairs and/or are unsafe in them. Because we limit ourselves to the solutions offered by the system, professionals, and/or our insurance coverage. Because we believe that providing a child with a mobility device means he'll "never learn to walk." And finally, because we don't recognize the importance of independent mobility as a cornerstone in the development of self-determination.

QUESTIONING PROFESSIONAL WISDOM

These illustrations represent only two scenarios out of many, but we can apply the concepts to virtually any disability condition. Over and over again, parents have told me their children don't have communication or mobility equipment because professionals have told them not to give these devices to their children. In some cases, parents have made the decision, on their own, not to give their children tools for success. We must question the rationale behind these decisions.

I've already described my family's experience: Benjamin's therapists told me not to get him a walker, a scooter, or a power wheelchair. No one, except Mark and me, could see Benjamin as a whole child who needed these devices to grow and develop.

Many parents whose children have physical disabilities have had experiences similar to mine. Some parents even said their gut instincts told them to go against the therapists' advice, but they didn't have the courage to buck the experts.

Other parents have shared their stories about communication devices. Several parents who have children with autism described an intensive intervention prescribed for their children. Their stories were similar: five or six adults came to the home five days a week, eight hours a day, for hands-on therapeutic intervention for the child with autism. According to the parents, the greatest need their children had was communication. When I asked,

"Why don't you just get your child a communication device?" their answers were always the same. "Well, we thought about it," they replied, "but the professionals said it was the worst thing we could do. They said if we did that, Joe would never learn to talk."

When we accept this type of thinking, we've lost our common sense. Why in the world would we deny our children the opportunity to communicate effectively, have independent mobility, or experience other critically important components of life? How can we, in good conscience, prevent our children from experiencing power and control over their lives and force them to remain dependent? We expend far too much effort on helping our children acquire one or two skills while ignoring the development of the whole child.

The next time a professional says you should not provide your child with the tools for self-determination, why not ask him what he would want if he needed those tools? Or perhaps you could just ask if it would be acceptable to take away his car, his computer, his telephone, or any other tools he uses to make his life better.

SELF-DETERMINATION IS A MOST VALUABLE ASSET

Self-determination is not about functional abilities. It's about being in control of your life. It's an asset most people zealously guard. On a regular basis, many Americans balk at government interference in their lives. We see parents who don't want schools teaching children moral values; parents feel this is their responsibility, not the school's. Teenagers and young people struggle mightily to exert control over their lives. Self-determination is a cornerstone of life in a free society.

Being self-determined is more important than any functional ability. Within our midst are adults with disabilities who cannot walk, talk, feed themselves, or go to the bathroom independently, yet they are self-determined and in control of their lives. To succeed, they depend on tools (wheelchairs, communication devices, and such) as well as help from family, friends, and, in some cases, paid attendants. Is their situation any different from people without disabilities who depend on tools (computers, cars, and the like), as well as help from their friends and family?

WHAT WE OWE CHILDREN

Parents are responsible for setting their children on the path to self-determination. Providing our children with tools and accommodations ensures a physical environment that's conducive to self-determination. But we must also provide an emotional environment that allows children to grow into responsible adults. Most of us routinely do this for our children who don't have disabilities. We must do the same for children with disabilities.

Equal Treatment

After yelling at eleven-year-old Emily to clean up her room for the umpteenth time in a week, nine-year-old Benjamin approached me and said, "Mom, do you want me to go clean up my room?" Actually, Benjamin's room seldom got messy, because he couldn't stuff clothes under his bed, pile junk in the closet, or hide things instead of putting them away. But that was irrelevant. Benjamin wanted to be treated in the same way Emily was. He wanted to be held accountable, too. After recovering my composure, I yelled at him the same way I did Emily, "Yes, Benjamin, get in there right now! Don't come out until your room is picked up the way it's supposed to be!"

With a huge grin on his face, he skedaddled as fast as he could and attempted to rearrange things. In a few minutes, he called me to his room and said he didn't know where some of his stuff should go. With a stern look on my face, I showed him what needed to be done (which was very little) and told him to call me when he was ready for my "inspection." He was thrilled!

Children with disabilities don't want to be treated as though they're "special." They don't want to be coddled and they don't want to be able to "get away with things" because they have disabilities. We often treat children with disabilities differently because we feel sorry for them or we think they're incapable. When we treat them the way we treat our other children, they learn they're as valuable as their brothers and sisters.

Treating them equally doesn't mean we expect them to do everything their brothers and sisters do. It *does* mean we demonstrate, through our actions, the belief that children with disabilities are competent and responsible. Our children see themselves through our eyes. If we don't give them equal treatment, they perceive themselves as unequal.

Choice and Trust

On a sidewalk in front of one of the great museums in our national's capitol, we gawked at the magnificent buildings along the Washington Mall. Four of us were doing a little sightseeing after a full day at a disability training conference. Three moms of kids with disabilities and thirty-something Sharon—a funny and exuberant lady who happened to have cerebral palsy—were trying to cram in as many sights as possible into an hour. After half an hour, we slowed our pace a little. Sharon, who walks "funny" (her description), was tiring. When the sidewalk narrowed, we could no longer walk four abreast. Sharon and I fell back and took up positions behind our friends. I noticed Sharon's feet: with each step, her feet rolled inward toward her arch. It looked painful. The sides of her shoes were scuffed where they continually scraped the concrete.

At the time, Benjamin was three. I was still in my Therapy Mom role, Benjamin was still wearing his knee-high ankle-foot-orthoses (AFOs). I had worked closely with the therapist and the orthotist over the years, and had suggested an unusual design for Benjamin's AFOs. They then used my suggestion when making ankle braces for other children. I saw myself as an "expert" on the feet of people with cerebral palsy.

I really liked Sharon and was impressed with her life. She had earned two college degrees, was working in a great job, and had a boyfriend. She had it all together. But I couldn't figure out why she wasn't wearing AFOs or some type of braces to help her walk better. I thought I could help. "Sharon, you know my son has cerebral palsy, too. The braces he wears really help his legs and feet. Have you ever thought of getting some? I think they could really help you."

She stopped in her tracks, looked me straight in the eye and asked, "No kidding?" "No, I'm not kidding," I said, eager to share my knowledge. "This guy called an orthotist makes casts of your feet and—"

"Hey," she interrupted, "that's not the kind of 'kidding' I meant. I thought you were trying to be funny telling me I needed braces. I know all about braces, Kathie. My mom made me wear them for years. I hated them! When I was ten, I took them off for the last time. I told my mom I wasn't wearing them ever again and I threw them in the trash!" She gave me a little chuckle and a big grin, then patted me on the back to let me know there were no hard feelings.

Wow! So much for my expertise, right? Embarrassed and ashamed, I apologized for my stupidity. I then peppered her with questions, knowing she could teach me a great deal. "But, Sharon, what about your feet? Does it hurt to walk the way you do? Are you worried about contractures? Benjamin's therapists are always telling me if he doesn't wear braces and do all this other stuff, he'll get contractures and deformities. What did your mother say when you threw the braces away? If you wore braces today, would it help you walk better?"

With a big sigh and a great deal of patience, she answered my questions, "No, it doesn't hurt to walk this way. This is just the way I walk. I don't worry about contractures. I'm thirty-four and I haven't gotten them yet. If I get them, I get them. I'll figure out what do if and when that time comes. It's not a big deal. Professionals make a big deal of it, but I don't worry about it. Braces might help me walk 'better,' but I think I walk fine. If it doesn't bother me, why should it bother anyone else?

"About my mom—at first she was really mad at me. She wanted me to wear my braces because everyone told her I needed them. We talked about it a lot when I was a kid and she finally realized it was my body and that I knew best. At the time, I thought, 'Wow, my mom's really cool for letting me be in charge!' But later, it meant more than that.

"In public school I was with a lot of other kids with orthopedic disabilities. I was the only one who had the support of my parents about braces and therapy and stuff. My mom supporting that one decision was just the beginning of a new relationship between us. She really began to trust me to know what was best for my body. She let me make the choices. Listen to your son, Kathie. He knows his body better than all the doctors and therapists in the world."

We have a responsibility to care for our children. We also have a responsibility to give them choices and to trust in the choices they make. There's a fine line between caring for our children and running their lives. Letting our children make decisions about therapies, braces, equipment, and other services and interventions sets them on the path of self-determination. (By the way, when Benj resigned from therapy, he threw his braces away, too, and hasn't worn a pair since.)

High Expectations

Sherri and I were discussing some strategies to use at her son's IEP meeting. The school was planning on placing seven-year-old Christopher in a segregated class because he has Down syndrome. Sherri wanted him included in a regular class; she wanted Chris to have the same wonderful opportunities as his two older brothers. I suggested she address the IEP team this way: "We want Chris to have the same experiences as his brothers; we want him to learn and have friends, to go to college, get married, have a good job—"

"No, Kathie, no," she interrupted. "I can't tell them that. How can Chris go to college? He has Down syndrome!"

We talked. Sherri admitted she regularly spoke to her nine and eleven-year-old sons about their future, saying such things as, "When you're grown up and go off to college . . ." and similar statements. I asked if she included Chris in these statements, if she talked about dreams to him, as well. "No," she replied, as tears welled up in her eyes. "Kathie, I really don't think he could ever go to college. Wouldn't it be unfair to talk to him about that when it will never happen?"

I explained the greater unfairness was not letting Chris know they had high expectations for him. Chris was receiving the message—loudly and clearly—that his parents didn't expect him to be as successful as his brothers. In Chris's mind, this probably meant his parents didn't love him and value him as much as they loved and valued his brothers. Children can't dream for themselves until we dream for them, first.

It's not possible for Sherri to know with certainty that her other two sons will attend college, get married, or do anything else. By the same token, she doesn't know what's possible for Chris. But high expectations set a course for our children. Without dreams and expectations for success—without high hopes—our children experience hopelessness.

A key component of self-determination is being able to believe in yourself because others believe in you. Can Chris believe in himself if his parents don't believe in him, and if he thinks he's less than his brothers?

Our children see themselves through our eyes. Even if, right now, you're unable to see how your child will go to college, have a great job, get married, have children, or achieve anything else, pretend! Have high hopes! We do this for our other children. We don't know what's really ahead for them. Still, we believe in their potential. Believe in the potential of your child with a disability. Have the same great expectations for him as you do for your other children.

Opportunities and Experiences

Nine-year-old Tyresha had orthopedic surgery and was in a lower body cast for six weeks, making her completely immobile. She was usually pushed around in a manual wheelchair and had never been free to explore her home the way her three-year-old brother did. While the cast was on, Tyresha couldn't sit in her chair; she could only lie on the sofa, floor, or bed. When she needed to be moved, her dad picked her up and carried her.

One night as Tyresha's dad was carrying her to bed, he detoured to the refrigerator for a drink of water. He shut the refrigerator door and began to walk away. "Stop, Daddy, go back!" Tyresha yelled. "I want to open the refrigerator." Dad pivoted and took the two steps back to the refrigerator. "Hold me tight, Daddy," Tyresha said, as she leaned closer to the door, grabbed the handle, and pulled it open. Then she immediately shut it. Dad turned and began the trek to Tyresha's bedroom.

He didn't get very far. Tyresha had reached over his shoulder and grabbed the handle again. "Wait, Daddy," she yelled again. Dad stopped and turned back toward the refrigerator. Tyresha adjusted her grip and opened the refrigerator door again, then began closing the door very slowly. As she did, she leaned forward, trying to get her face as close as possible to the one inch opening. Her dad was beginning to have trouble holding her in this precarious position. The casts were heavy and Tyresha's leaning was putting Dad off balance. Still, he maintained his hold.

Tyresha closed the door all the way, opened it a tiny bit, and stuck her nose into the opening. Again, she closed it very slowly. "What are you doing, Tyresha?" asked Dad, with a grunt and a groan. "The light, Daddy, the light!" Tyresha shrieked. "Yeah," Dad replied, "what about it?" "It goes on and off when you open and close the door!" Tyresha exclaimed.

This was a bigger discovery than Columbus discovering the New World. At age nine, Tyresha had just discovered the mystery of the light in the refrigerator.

Tyresha's dad was both ecstatic and miserable. He was thrilled with his daughter's discovery and her excitement. He was miserable at the realization that he and his wife hadn't done all they could to reduce the barriers that limited Tyresha's exploration. Tyresha's three-year-old brother had discovered the mysterious refrigerator light when he was about eighteen months of age.

Immediately, they began to remedy their oversights. They spent a great deal of time looking at their home the way it must look to Tyresha. They looked at what she could see and do and get to. It wasn't much. Even in their own home, their daughter's exploration was limited. They got her a power wheelchair and made changes to their home. Soon, Tyresha knew her home as well as her little brother.

Children with disabilities need to savor ordinary life. Opportunities and experiences—not functional abilities—are the stuff of life. Children need to master their environments and own a variety of experiences before they can achieve self-determination.

Responsibility

Dinner time at Maggie's was always stressful, even though her children pitched in and helped before and after the meal. Eleven-year-old Ryan, who has autism, seemed unable to sit through the meal, participate in suppertime conversations, and have good manners like his brother and sister. Tantrums, food all over the place, constant interruptions, and other behaviors disrupted the peace.

Sara and Robert each had responsibilities before supper—setting the table, pouring the milk, and the like—and after supper they helped clear the table and load the dishwasher. But Ryan had no responsibilities. Before supper, Ryan was either off by himself doing his thing or disturbing those who were bustling around in the kitchen.

When everything was on the table, Ryan was called to supper. Conversations that had started in the kitchen moved to the table. But these were conversations Ryan was not really a part of, and he usually interrupted them to get attention. In his own home, Ryan was an "outsider" during the evening meal. Things changed when Maggie realized the family had unintentionally excluded Ryan.

Maggie, Sara, and Robert helped Ryan experiment with the different tasks that needed to be done before, during, and after dinner. Of all the jobs, Ryan liked setting the table best. He set it more perfectly, more precisely, in fact, than Sara had ever done. It took Ryan longer to do it than others, but that wasn't important. Ryan, like his sister and brother, now had an important responsibility and was able to contribute to the welfare of his family.

As more time passed, Ryan's family began to expect more from him. He began to participate in the conversations taking place in the kitchen and at the dinner table. Ryan learned it was everyone's responsibility to ensure dinner was a pleasant experience. And very soon, it was.

Giving our children the gift of responsibility lets them know we value them. More importantly, they learn they are capable. Children and adults with disabilities have been told over and over again that they're incapable. But they *are* capable and we need to create opportunities and situations where they can demonstrate their capabilities to themselves, as well as to others. To achieve self-determination, they must believe they're capable of assuming responsibility.

Unconditional Love

Of course we love our children. But they need to *know* we love them. We need to tell them, over and over again, "I love you!" We need to show them with hugs and kisses, doing fun things with them, laughing and reading, and doing all the other things that say, "I love you." But there's more to unconditional love. I'm no philosopher, nor am I a poet who can wax eloquently on how to love. But the personal stories of adults with disabilities teach us what it feels like when a child doesn't feel *unconditionally* loved.

Lena, a 30-year-old woman, reflected on her childhood. She was born with a right arm that ended at the elbow. There was no right hand, but three fingers protruded from the end of her arm. Doctors assured her parents that when Lena turned six, they would see if she was a candidate for a prosthetic lower arm and hand. If so, they would amputate the three fingers and part of the lower arm before fitting the prosthesis.

The years went by and when Lena turned six, the doctors confirmed that a prosthetic arm could be made for Lena. They would not perform the surgery, however, unless Lena agreed to it. Her cooperation was absolutely necessary, for after the prosthesis was fitted, Lena would have to undergo months of therapy to learn to isolate and use the muscles that would operate the lower arm and fingers. In addition, she would need larger (and more sophisticated) prostheses throughout her childhood to accommodate her growth. Lena and her family could expect at least fifteen years of intense medical intervention.

At age six, Lena told her parents she didn't want the surgery or the artificial arm and hand. She understood that if she had the surgery, the three fingers that had served her well for the past six years would be cut off. If, after getting the prosthesis, she decided she didn't want to wear it sometimes, her right arm would be useless to her. Lena's arm might be short, but with the three fingers on it, she did just fine. Her parents accepted her decision.

When she turned seven, however, her parents asked her again. And again, she said no. This continued every year on her birthday. After ten years, on the day she turned sweet sixteen, she didn't just say no. She asked her parents, "Why do you keep asking me if I want an artificial arm? Why aren't I good enough just the way I am?"

Lena expressed deep sadness, tinged with anger, about these events. She knew, of course, that her parents were operating from the position of, "We just want what's best for you." That didn't change the message Lena received that she "wasn't good enough" just the way she was. She knew her parents loved her, but she always felt they would have loved her more if she had agreed to the prosthetic arm. She spent many, many years being torn apart by her desire to please her parents and her need to be accepted as she was.

What about Lena's parents? Were they doing what was best for Lena? It's difficult to question what's in someone else's heart. It's painful, for when we try to look into another's heart, we must also look in our own.

Lena's parents thought they were doing what was best for her. But if they plumbed the depths of their reasoning and emotions, perhaps they would have discovered they were "doing their best" for Lena based on the medical model and the notion that Lena was "abnormal." With deep understanding and not a trace of bitterness, Lena reported that her parents didn't really know what it was like to have a short arm with three stubby fingers. All they knew was that Lena had difficulty with some things, she was teased, she was stared at, and the "problem" of her right arm would never go away unless they intervened with the prosthesis.

Lena often wondered if her parents wanted her to have the prosthesis because it would be best for *them*. Perhaps *they* would feel better if Lena looked more normal. Their lives would be more peaceful if they didn't have to deal with a variety of situations relating to Lena's disability. Perhaps they would have been prouder of their parenting if they could make Lena normal.

Because Lena was born this way, this was the only way she knew how to be. She was all right with who she was. She could handle the teasing; other kids got teased for other reasons. She figured out how to do things with her short arm and stubby fingers. Any feelings of being not-OK were caused by her parents' desire for her to have a "real arm." This hurt her deeply. To Lena, her right arm *was* a real arm. Her disability caused more problems for her mom and dad than it did for her.

It may seem harsh to question the actions of Lena's parents. But doing so will help us learn. It's not enough to have good intentions. We all know the road to hell is paved with them. Lena's story reinforces the maxim that perception is greater than reality. The reality was that Lena's parents loved her deeply and thought she was a wonderful person. Lena's perception, however (based on her parents actions, not just their words), was that she was not-OK and she was not loved unconditionally.

Unconditional love gives our children the strong foundation of knowing they're loved just the way they are. When we love a child unconditionally, we respect her individuality, her innate wisdom about herself, and her determination to be in charge of her life.

WE MUST DREAM

Every precious human life in this universe is dependent on hopes and dreams. The hope of a good day is what gets us out of bed in the morning. Dreaming of an exotic vacation makes difficult days easier. Hoping the school doesn't call again today is a worthy dream. Ditto hoping the baby takes a longer nap than yesterday. Hopes and dreams come in all shapes and sizes. They're vital to our emotional well-being. They're also a critical part of self-determination.

Dreams about our children give us hope for the future. We dream that our children will have better lives than our own. Some feel this isn't realistic for a child with a disability. But it is. Once we internalize the belief that disability is natural, we can once again dream big dreams for our children with disabilities. Let's look at the differences between dreams for kids with and without disabilities.

When Jennifer (who doesn't have a disability) is born, her parents dream she'll one day become a doctor, a lawyer, or an astronaut. Her parents don't really know if she has the abilities to attain one of these lofty dreams, but they know before any great thing can happen, a vision must be created.

As Jennifer grows up, she dreams of becoming an artist, not a doctor, lawyer, or astronaut. Are her parents heartbroken over this turn of events? Will they give up on her because the dreams they once had are gone? Probably not. They'll change their dreams to mesh with hers.

Soon, however, Jennifer's parents begin to feel she doesn't have any natural talent for art. Jennifer thinks she's a great artist, but her parents aren't so sure. Will they tell her, "Sorry, honey, but you'll never be an artist. You're just not good enough. We really don't know what you'll be good at, but we're sure art is not in your future." Of course they wouldn't tell her that! If they love her and believe in her, they'll continue to support her dream, knowing that one of two things will probably happen. Either Jennifer will blossom into a successful artist through hard work and determination, or one day she'll decide art is not for her and she'll find something else to dream about.

When the dreams we have for our typical children don't come true, most of us don't fall apart, nor do we give up on our children. But many of us have discarded our dreams for children with disabilities.

If Jennifer had been born with a disability, would this scenario have played out the same way? For most parents, no. As soon as the disability diagnosis was made, the big dreams would have died. Depending on Jennifer's disability, her parents may never dream for her again. Or they might dream itty bitty dreams: that one day Jennifer may become "independent enough" to live in a group home. They may also secretly hope that Jennifer will die before they do because they don't know what will happen to her if they die first.

We absolutely must dream big dreams. If we don't dream for our children, how can they dream for themselves? We must trust in our children with disabilities, just as we trust in our children who don't have disabilities. If we believe in our children, they can dream big dreams. As they grow, they (like their brothers and sisters) will change their dreams many times. And when the time is right, they'll decide which dream to follow.

In my younger days, I dreamed of being a teacher, nurse, mother, fashion model, police officer, and many other occupations. As an adult, though, I became acquainted with a variety of opportunities that I was unaware of as a child. Sometimes our dreams lead us to opportunities, but just as often, opportunities find us. I have been a secretary, bank teller, switchboard operator, casualty insurance specialist, camera operator, television producer and director, writer, disability advocate, public speaker, and wife and mother.

Think about your own childhood. How many different dreams did you dream? Did your parents dream for you? Did they dream big dreams? If they didn't, you know how much harder it was to dream for yourself. If they did dream big for you, you know what it felt like to believe anything was possible.

Detail Your Dreams

Grab a pad of paper and write down the dreams you had for your child before you found out he had a disability. Write down every memory you have about those dreams. Next, write down the dreams you currently have for your child with a disability.

If your current dreams are the same as your original dreams, good for you! Keep dreaming those big dreams. To your list, add the dreams your child has for herself, regardless of how realistic or unrealistic they seem. Post the list of dreams on the refrigerator so you can see them every day. Add to the list when you or your child think of another dream. While you're at it, create similar lists for all your children. Take down some of the other stuff cluttering your refrigerator, buy some new magnets, and make a fresh palette of dreams where everyone can see it!

If your current dreams are not the same as your original dreams or if you have no dreams at all, that's okay for now. If this makes you sad and you need to cry right now, that's okay, too. This will pass. By the time you finish this book, you'll have new dreams. Then you can make your list and post it on the fridge. (If you need to cry, put this book down, cry for two minutes—and that's all—blow your nose, and then start reading where you left off.)

Grieving, feeling sad about your child's disability and what he cannot do, or fearing the future is a waste of your valuable time and it saps your energy. Self-pity is destructive. Once we've fallen to the bottom of that dark tunnel, we have to somehow find a way to climb out of it. And while we're feeling sorry for ourselves, we're encouraging others to feel sorry for us. Snap out of it! A day from now, a week from now, or a month from now, you'll see things very differently.

We Need Others to Dream With Us

If we've felt sorry for ourselves—sad, mad, or ashamed—because we have a child with a disability, we've probably shared these feelings with our parents, brothers, sisters, and friends. They've probably decided the source of our emotional pain is our child, because that's what they've learned from us. They don't understand that the "problem" is not the child's disability, but attitudinal and environmental barriers. Unintentionally, we've taught others that dreaming big dreams is an exercise in futility.

Our parents want to protect us from being hurt. If our parents feel the child is the source of emotional pain, how might they feel about the child? Many parents tell stories of grandparents who coddle and cuddle all the grandchildren except the one with a disability. Are these grandparents inherently prejudicial and unkind? Probably not. They might simply be reacting to the hurt they think the child with a disability is inflicting upon their own son or daughter. They may be physically uncomfortable around the child, not understanding that he's more like their other grandchildren than different. Or they may be afraid to hold, touch, or play with the child since they don't know "what to do."

Grandparents may be at the opposite extreme: they coddle grandchildren with disabilities too much. Their actions may be driven by pity or worry. If they feel the grandchild with a disability has a "terrible" life, they might overcompensate and give too much: too much time, too many hugs, or too many presents. This can cause the other grandchildren to resent the child with a disability.

We can help our family members and friends learn new attitudes. Teach them what you're learning; spend time wondering and pondering with them. Give them the freedom to change at a pace that's comfortable for them. We can't dictate the speed with which others learn new ways of thinking. Once we change, we'll want those closest to us to change right away. But it doesn't always happen the way we hope. Be patient and give others time. It will happen. As you model a new way of thinking about your own child, other people will learn from you.

After you've helped others learn new perspectives, share your dreams with them. Ask what they dream for your child. Tell them they don't have to be realistic!

Publicizing our dreams helps make them become real. When we share our dreams with others, we've carved a little niche in their minds and hearts. They are then in a position to help. Who knows what opportunities may come into your family's life simply because you've shared your dreams with others?

We need our friends and family to dream big dreams for our child. None of us can get through life's ups and downs alone.

Help Your Child Dream

Our children learn to dream big dreams for themselves by seeing us dream for them. So it's important that parents and children share their hopes and dreams with one another. But for our children to believe they can dream, they must feel good about themselves; they must feel worthy and valuable and important. Our attitudes about disability, in general, and our children, specifically, must promote these ideals. No child can dream if he sees himself through the lens of incompetence, inability, or other negative perceptions about people with disabilities. Our children see themselves through our eyes. Make sure your child sees himself for the wonderful, successful, lovable child he is.

WHAT WILL IT TAKE?

When you think about what it will take to help your child achieve self-determination, think about how other children learn to be in charge of their own lives. Don't make this hard, it's not. Whatever your child's age, look at what's typical for the age and give your child opportunities for the same or similar experiences.

The first thought that jumps into the minds of many parents is: "But my kid can't [walk, talk, or whatever], he can't do what other kids his age do." You're probably right, up to a point. Your child may not be able to do everything *in the same way* that other children his age do, but he certainly can have the same or similar *experiences!*

When Benjamin was very young, at the age when all children are either carried or pushed in a stroller, I learned something very valuable about him. We were running really late for an appointment and I ran from the car to the building's front door, holding him tightly in my arms and hoping I didn't trip and fall. All of a sudden I heard Benjamin laughing and screaming with glee. He loved running!

From that time on, we ran with Benjamin a lot. I did it for fun (at home or in the yard) not just when I was running late for an appointment! But this activity became more important as Benjamin grew and we realized he might not be able to run on his own. He needed to experience wind blowing through his hair, his body moving quickly through space, and his eyes seeing unfocused shapes whizzing by. When he got his first manual wheelchair at age four, we pushed him at a run. Since he's had his power chair, he often drives as fast he can. And he also goes in circles as fast as he can to get dizzy, not unlike what other kids do when they turn around and around until they fall down in joyous dizziness.

Benjamin has never been able to run—the way other children do—but he's had many *experiences* of moving fast, getting dizzy, and being in control of where his body is.

This is one tiny example. Every day, there are zillions of situations—both ordinary and extraordinary—that our children are prevented from experiencing. Pretend, for a moment, that your child doesn't have a disability. What would he be doing? Whatever it is, that's what he needs to be doing, in whatever way he can.

Does your child know about the light in the refrigerator? Has he ever felt the bark on a tree? Has he jumped up and down in a mud puddle and gotten all dirty?

Can he express "NO!" in whatever way is best for him? Can he communicate his wants and needs? Can he express his feelings?

Is she learning to wear make-up and pantyhose? Is her hairstyle one she has chosen? Does she pick out what she's going to wear every day?

Do you expect your child to be responsible? Does he help around the house?

Does your child participate in his own IEP meetings? Do you allow him to make decisions about the services he needs?

Is he allowed to make choices, even if they're wrong? Is your son or daughter expected to succeed and fail, just like everyone else?

Start by examining your own thoughts. Examine your own home. Examine your child's life. What needs to happen that will change the trajectory of your child's life from helplessness and dependency to self-determination? Will a power wheelchair or a communication device make the difference? What about giving your child more responsibilities and more choices about his life? Should you have higher expectations for her? Can you look beyond the disability and see what your child really needs? Talk to your child; it's his life.

Our children must be allowed to make their own decisions, speak up for themselves, and say no to protect themselves. And they won't be able to do these things in the real world until they can do them successfully in their own homes.

When your child is grown, will he thank you for protecting him from life? For focusing on one need to the exclusion of others? For not expecting him to do much or be much since he has a disability? Or will he look back and be grateful for your belief in him? For allowing him to experience all he can, including success and failure? For trusting him to be in control of his life?

We know what to do about our children's disabilities. We learn the lingo and the laws, and try to put them to good use. We advocate for more services and more supports. We take our children to therapies. In general, we do everything possible for the good of our children. But few, if any, interventions, therapies, or professionals address the most fundamental need of our children: self-determination.

We know professionals are not the true experts on our children. And we—the parents—are not the most qualified experts either, although we're close. The most competent experts are our own children, as well as adults who have grown up with disabilities. Learning from our own children and from adults with developmental disabilities can endow us with wisdom that far exceeds theories, authoritative research, and principles of conventional wisdom.

If we listen carefully, we can hear our children telling us their hearts and souls need more of our attention than their bodies and brains. They're telling us they want to be in control of their lives. What will it take for us to finally hear them and heed their wisdom?

As we listen carefully to our children, we can also hear them telling us what they really need to be successful. That's next.

Tools for Success:
Meeting Needs and More

TREAT PEOPLE AS IF THEY WERE
WHAT THEY OUGHT TO BE AND
YOU HELP THEM TO BECOME WHAT
THEY ARE CAPABLE OF BEING.
Johann von Goethe

Conner needs to walk. Samantha needs to talk. Ethan needs to behave. Olivia needs to feed herself. Austin needs to read.

Traditionally, when we talk about the needs of children with disabilities, we describe what a child can't do and/or what he needs to be able to do so he'll be more "normal." But if we reject the concept of normal, we must rethink our concept of needs. Let's not see "meeting needs" as a way of achieving normalcy. Instead, let's look at meeting a child's needs as a way of ensuring his success.

In this context, we can take the examples above and say: Conner needs independent mobility; Samantha needs a way to communicate; Ethan needs support (or Ethan needs ways to calm himself); Olivia needs assistance with eating. Austin needs adapted learning materials. (This way of describing needs was described in Chapter 11.)

I've said it before, but it's worth repeating: our children's needs are not special. They are perfectly normal, routine, and common for our children! When we say our children have special needs, we're implying that our children's needs are uncommon, unique, or different, as compared to the norm. This is another way language separates children with disabilities from the mainstream of society. Let's stop thinking and saying our children's needs are "special."

TOOLS FOR SUCCESS

The needs of children with disabilities have been called special or extraordinary because they're different from the ordinary or common needs that typical children have. But the concept of what's ordinary, common, or routine is ever changing.

At one time, having a computer in one's home was considered uncommon and extraordinary. It was, in fact, a luxury for only a few. Today, home computers are common, and many of us seem them as *necessities.* We can say the same thing about electric lights, microwave ovens, air conditioners, cars, calculators, telephones, and every other tool that has improved our lives. Most us us would strongly agree we need all of these tools. Thinking about your child, aren't his needs—whether they're assistive technology devices, environmental modifications, or behavior supports—things that improve his life in one way or another, just as telephones, computers, and other devices have improved your life?

Parents and professionals may not see how the needs of a child with a disability are comparable to the common needs shared by typical adults. Many of us continue to see the things needed by children with disabilities as expensive luxuries which will be provided only if they fit into someone's budget. Other times, we see them as something to be provided only as a last resort. So, let's compare some needs and the tools used to meet those needs. In the pairs below, the first description is of an adult without a disability and the second is of a child with a disability.

- To write his book, an author needs a computer.
- To write his spelling list, a student needs a computer.

- To be understood clearly, a public speaker needs a microphone.
- To be understood clearly, a child needs a communication device.

- To learn from written materials, a reader needs books written in the language he understands.
- To learn from written materials, a child needs books written in Braille.

- To learn from management books, a busy executive needs books on tape.
- To learn from books at school, a child needs books on tape.

- To balance the company's accounts, a bookkeeper needs a calculator.
- To add, subtract, multiply, and divide, a child needs a calculator.

- To get to work, the store, and other places he needs to go, a man needs personal transportation: his own car.
- To get around the house, the school, and other places he needs to go, a child needs mobility: a wheelchair he can use independently.

Most of us never question the importance and usefulness of tools used by typical adults and children, whether they're common or uncommon. Businesses need telephones; dentists need drills; gardeners need hoes and rakes; children need toys. And we usually don't let the *cost* of tools determine whether we get them or not. *We find a way to get what we need.*

Unfortunately, however, we don't routinely do the same for children with disabilities. In schools, educators frequently deny tools of assistive technology because (1) they say they don't have the money, (2) they think the tool isn't necessary, and/or (3) they think the child won't benefit from having the tool. Parents and professionals often see equipment (tools such as wheelchairs or communication devices) as symbols of a child's failure (to walk or speak) that should be used only as a last resort. In other situations, parents, educators, and professionals are unable to visualize how tools (adaptations, modifications, or individualized supports) can promote a child's success. The conventional wisdom of the medical and readiness models plays a crucial role in this dilemma, as does our unwillingness to recognize what our children really need.

I've told you the story about Benjamin walking out to recess in his walker every day when he was in the primary grades. Everyone (including me, at first) thought this was a great idea. It was "informal" therapy. Except by the time Benjamin got to the playground, recess was over! Not only that, by the time he walked back to the classroom, he had missed academics, and he was exhausted. We were focused on what we thought he needed (to learn to walk). But what he really needed was effective mobility so he could play during recess, get to and from class on time, and be as independent as possible.

At the time, however, we didn't see a power wheelchair as a tool. We saw it as a failure of Benjamin's legs to walk. We also saw it as a sign that *we* had somehow failed. And we saw it as an admission that (sniff) Benjamin would never be "normal." If I knew then what I know now, Benjamin would have been using a power wheelchair when he was two.

At age nine, he finally had independent mobility, the independence he should have had at age two! About six months after he started using the power chair, he chose not use his walker anymore. As the true expert on himself, he realized that walking in the walker was not an efficient form of mobility. Yes, he could get from point A to point B in his walker, but it took him a long time and it was very tiring. He learned that in the power chair, he was master of his own fate: he could go when he wanted, as fast or as slow as he wanted, he wasn't tired when he got to where he was going, and he could do it by himself.

Using the power chair was more than a replacement for walking, however. It became a magical tool that changed Benjamin's life in many ways. It opened the door to more friendships: Benjamin could chase kids on the playground and they chased him. It facilitated Benjamin's emotional growth: he didn't see himself as dependent, needing to be pushed in a manual chair or assisted in the walker. Benjamin's learning was enhanced: he could do things he had never done before. And the power chair enabled Benjamin to assert himself as his own person: he could choose where to go, when to go, and what to do—he had power! Overnight, shyness and uncertainty were replaced by strength and determination.

But none of the professionals in our lives saw a power wheelchair as a tool for friendships, emotional growth, learning, or self-determination. They only saw it as a poor substitute for walking independently. When Benjamin was younger, we saw it the same way. But after learning from adults with disabilities and recognizing what was really important (independent mobility), we finally saw the power chair as a tool that could give Benjamin independence and freedom.

Under the medical model, we were supposed to fix Benjamin by making him walk. That functional skill was to be achieved, no matter the cost to Benjamin (acquiring more delays, social isolation, dependence, and more). In the medical model, the need was walking, not independent mobility.

The readiness model, including the rigid adherence to sequential skills development, also presents barriers to providing children with the tools they need for success. We often insist that children learn things in the prescribed manner. We don't let them learn in ways that are best for them, and we prevent them from using alternative methods of doing things.

Math has always been hard for Benjamin. In his early school years, most of his classmates progressed through addition and subtraction. But Benjamin had difficulty with the basics. It was hard for him to use math manipulatives and he couldn't write equations, since he didn't use a pencil. Because he was unable to demonstrate his understanding of math in the traditional ways (counting objects, writing equations by carrying and borrowing numbers, and so forth), it was assumed he wasn't learning math. As a result, he was instructed in the basics, over, and over, and over again. He began to hate math.

But one creative teacher changed all that when she suggested giving Benj the power to do math by using a calculator instead of trying to force him to learn math using traditional methods. In second grade, a calculator gave Benj the ability to "compute." He didn't need to write numbers and didn't need to know about carrying and borrowing. Not only could Benj do math with the calculator, but he enjoyed math for the first time. The calculator and fun math programs on the computer enabled Benj to learn math, his way.

We're often shortsighted. We look at what our children can't do—based on the norm, the traditional, the expected—and attempt to help them do those things. Many of our children, however, may never be able to do things the way other people do. (And that's okay!) Our repeated efforts to force our kids to do things the "right" way bear no fruit. Worse, our actions and attitudes are demeaning and hurtful to our children.

We need to consider what's most important. We need to be farsighted and look at the long term goal. Which is more important? Walking or the ability to move about independently in the most efficient manner possible? Is talking more important than being able to communicate? Is reading at grade level more important than learning the subject in the manner that works best for the student?

Let's look at one more example. Daniel is said to have "sensory integration deficits." He's unable to effectively "process" written language. Educators and his parents believe Daniel will be unable to learn in a regular classroom because first grade curriculum focuses on learning to read, and Daniel isn't demonstrating the appropriate prereading skills. The IEP team places Daniel in a special ed room so he can get the special help he needs. Sounds good in theory. Daniel's parents believe after he learns to read in the special ed room during first grade, he'll go on to a regular second grade class.

What's wrong with this picture? The focus is on getting Daniel to read, not on learning in general. As a result, his placement in a special ed room will result in diminished opportunities for learning; this will have a negative effect on his overall development. He won't be exposed to typical first grade curriculum, since the special program has its own curriculum for children with SI "problems." Thus, he won't be "ready" for second grade, whether he learns to read or not.

In addition, Daniel is facing many negative experiences in this environment. He's not exposed to typical school experiences of other children his age. A special ed room, especially one that includes children of varying ages, is very, very different than a regular ed first grade classroom. Since he's only with other children who have "problems," he'll learn lots from them, like inappropriate behaviors. Before long, *he* may acquire a "behavior" label.

Daniel is also learning he's very different from his brothers and sisters and other kids in the neighborhood. His school day is very different from theirs. Friendships don't develop and birthday party invitations don't come his way. The kids in the special ed rooms are kept apart from others and Daniel quickly learns he and his classmates are different and don't belong. The result is a sad, angry, and frustrated child. That "behavior" label is now more of a certainty than ever.

In essence, Daniel has been given a one-way ticket to segregated special education classes for the rest of his years in public school. After one or two or three years in the special program, he won't be "ready" for inclusion in a regular classroom; he'll be so much further behind globally that educators will insist on keeping him in special (segregated) settings. With the best of intentions, his parents agreed to the initial segregated placement since it focused on helping Daniel's needs with reading. But this placement can not enhance Daniel's opportunities for success, it can only diminish them.

Let's look at the real issue. What's most important is for Daniel to have the opportunity to learn what other first-graders are learning, to experience being a first-grader, and to be included with his peers. That's what his parents really wanted. But they were brainwashed into believing that before Daniel can learn—before he can benefit from the traditional first grade curriculum—he must be able to read like other children.

Have we ever considered the extraordinary amount of learning that occurs from birth until a child is five or six? It's all achieved without reading!

Schools are very traditional and, in many respects, way behind the times. Learning in public education is based on reading, but in the real world, people learn lots of different ways. Employees in a bank learn about new procedures from an in-service workshop where the presenter talks and uses graphic overheads to illustrate important points. Factory workers learn a new technique by watching a video and by hands-on experience. A busy executive learns new management techniques by listening to a book on tape in his car. All of these people are learning, but they're using methods other than reading.

Daniel can be successful in an inclusive, regular education classroom if he's provided the tools that enable him to learn in the way he learns best. Perhaps he needs large print books. Maybe his books need to be recorded on audiotape so he can listen and follow along in the book. All the while, educators still help him with reading skills. And because he's in a regular classroom, he'll be learning what other first graders are learning; his overall academic achievement won't be delayed just because he can't read the way other children do.

Let's assume Daniel is included in a first grade classroom led by a supportive, creative teacher. Daniel might be the only child with a disability label in the class, but he's not the only student that finds reading difficult. To help all her students become confident readers and feel good about reading, the teacher regularly divides the class into mixed ability reading groups. In this way, emerging readers receive naturally-occurring assistance from more experienced readers.

In addition, the classroom teacher and the special ed teacher work together to create learning opportunities that don't require reading. This benefits Daniel as well as other students who are not visual learners. Some students learn best through hands-on activities; others learn best by listening.

THE VICIOUS CYCLE

We must be aware of the vicious cycle we put our children through. Under the current system of the medical model, professionals and parents often play a role when a child's development is delayed.

When a child has a "delay" or "deficit" in a particular area, we focus on the so-called deficit to the exclusion of the child's overall development and then use the "deficit" or "delay" as the basis for saying a child is "not ready." In either case, we prevent the child from benefiting from typical childhood activities, experiences, and education. This results in the child acquiring additional delays. The cycle continues: when these additional delays are identified, we focus on them and continue (and even expand) the child's exclusion from typical and natural childhood experiences. The more a child is excluded, the more delays he will acquire. The more delays he acquires, the more excluded he'll be.

It doesn't have to be this way. We can stop the cycle by recognizing that (1) all children are different and (2) a delay in one area doesn't mean a child is delayed in all areas. The cycle will also be stopped when we give our children whatever tools they need—from assistive technology to behavior supports to environmental modifications—to ensure they have opportunities to live typical childhoods.

The ideas that follow represent only a miniscule number of the many ways we can help our children. We'll look first at assistive technology devices, and then go on to a variety of every day tools, accommodations, and modifications.

ASSISTIVE TECHNOLOGY

What is assistive technology (AT)? Anything that enables a person with a disability to be more independent or any device to make life easier or better.

High-tech assistive technology, such as power wheelchairs, communication devices, and other items are important tools for our children. But low-tech devices can also contribute to a child's success. Homemade communication cards, talking calculators, toys operated by switches, and much, much more can significantly enhance a child's independence, learning, opportunities for growth, and self-determination. Our family couldn't live without the low-tech assistance of hook and loop fasteners and non-slip fabrics!

When considering a need that can be met through a low *or* high-tech device, investigate the low-tech device first. Low-tech devices are less expensive and often more effective. Professionals may recommend high-tech, well-known devices because that's what they're familiar with. But there are as many solutions as there are people who need them.

We live with our children every day; professionals don't. When looking into AT devices, don't take their words as the gospel truth. We know our children best. Take the time to investigate, experiment, and think out of the box. Then do whatever it takes, using proactive and creative strategies, to get what your child needs.

AT Centers

Assistive technology centers, funded by federal and state grants, can be good sources of information and help. Some AT centers are very, very good: they have loaner equipment, they may help with locating sources of funding, and they may provide assessments. But others aren't so good. If the AT center in your area or state is not helpful, find other sources of help. Some disability-related organizations (Easter Seals, United Cerebral Palsy, and others) offer AT assistance.

AT Assessments

Your child may receive an AT assessment through an AT center, some other organization, or through the school system. Some schools use their own personnel to perform the assessments; others contract this service to a state AT office or another agency. In any case, recognize that no AT professional is familiar with every device and every possible solution. Some are experienced with only certain devices, and that's what they'll recommend, even if the device is not the best choice for your child.

There are a variety of barriers within the professional AT arena that may prevent children getting the devices they need. An expert may declare your child isn't able to use or operate a device and wouldn't benefit from it, *even though your child has never had the opportunity to try it!* Some experts may make AT recommendations on the basis of the disability label instead of your child's unique situation. Also, professionals may have reviewed erroneous material in your child's file. In some cases, a school may pressure an AT expert to *not* recommend a device because the school says it doesn't have funding to pay for it. Don't let any of these dilemmas stand in the way of getting what your child needs.

Some "assessments" may be nothing more than a collection of opinions. In a truly accurate AT assessment, a child would need to actually use a piece of equipment for a day, a week, a month, or however long it took to determine if the device is appropriate.

For example, it's not uncommon for professionals and parents to decide a child wouldn't benefit from a communication device or a computer because the child can't use a keyboard. But how can anyone know whether a child can use a keyboard unless he's provided with the appropriate modifications and then given lots of opportunities to try? Also, professionals have been known to say a child with a cognitive disability could not benefit from a device because of the child's "low IQ." They're making inaccurate assumptions based on a test score, without ever giving the child an opportunity to become familiar with a device.

In these instances, people have lost their common sense. These actions are analogous to a parent telling a child, "I'm not going to buy you a bicycle until you know how to ride one." A parent purchases a child's first bicycle *knowing* the child doesn't yet know how to ride. First-timers buy computers before they know how to use them. What if you went to buy a computer and the salesperson sized you up and said, "I'm sorry, but I won't sell this to you because you don't look like you're competent to use it." You'd go ballistic and you'd have every right to do so. Yet this sort of thing happens to children with disabilities all the time! In the real world, we all buy things we don't know how to use. We buy them in the belief we'll learn how to use them. We presume competence!

If someone says your child can't benefit from an assistive technology device, don't waste your time arguing with them. There are many ways you can do your own assessment.

Do-It-Yourself Assessments

If you know what type of device you're interested in, call the manufacturer or distributor and ask to borrow a demo. The company may work with you directly, or they may agree to loan you a demo only if a professional (therapist, teacher, physician) is involved. If this is the case, do not ask for help from the professionals who have already told you no. Instead, get help from someone who's your ally. Call your family doctor, for example. He may not know anything about the device you're interested in, but he's got the professional credentials you need.

If you can't get a demo or a loaner, try to find out (from the manufacturer or distributor) about other families who live close to you who have purchased the same or similar piece of equipment. Then visit those families so your child can experiment with the device. Sales people will probably not give you a list of customers in your area since it's a privacy issue, but they may be willing to ask customers for permission to give their names and phone numbers to you.

Funding for Assistive Technology Devices

Finding the right piece of assistive technology is one thing; funding expensive items is another. Many of us depend on the system to provide funding for AT devices. But this isn't always the best way.

For example, under special education law, the school system may be legally responsible for funding AT equipment which a child needs for school. Some schools are easy to work with and parents have no trouble getting what their children need. But for most parents, counting on the school system to provide AT equipment is fraught with potential difficulties. The school may simply say your child can't benefit from the equipment and refuse to buy it. You may have to jump through hoops to get approval to purchase the equipment. The school may buy a product for your child, but not the exact one you know is best, or your child might have to wait months before he finally gets what he needs.

Some parents, influenced by the entitlement mentality, dig their heels in for a long battle with schools over funding AT devices. But while they're battling, their children are going without. None of us could go one day without the tools we need: telephones, computers, electricity, and so forth. Why are we willing to let our children go months or years without the tools they need? Winning battles with schools should not be more important than our children's ultimate success! Use special ed services for AT devices only as a last resort. There are better ways to get our children what they need.

If you have private insurance, approach them first about funding the device or equipment your child needs. If your insurance will pay for the device, it will belong to your child, now and forever. If the school pays for the equipment, it belongs to the school. Educators may sign it out to your child for use at school and home, but it still belongs to the school. At some schools, educators may agree to fund an AT device, but when it arrives, your child is only able to use it during the school day (not at home). An even worse situation exists when educators decide the device must be shared with other children.

The parents of eight-year-old Angelique were finally successful in getting the school to purchase a communication device. But their victory was short-lived. After the device was delivered, the special educators in Angelique's segregated classroom decided the device should be shared equally among the five or six other children in the class who had not yet acquired speech. This was equivalent to telling typical children: you may each talk two times each day for twenty minutes each time.

The efforts of Angelique's parents didn't produce the intended outcome. However, if Sonja and Jose had gone to their private insurance for the communication device, it would have belonged to Angelique, at home and at school, no ifs, ands, or buts.

If your insurance will pay for the device, make sure the school knows it belongs to your child and not the school. Understand, too, that some educators are quite stinky when the device doesn't belong to the school. Parents have reported that when their children arrive at school with a communication device, educators have said, "If it breaks or it doesn't work right, we're not responsible." Yuck! Even under these conditions, it's still best if any AT device belongs to your child and not the school.

In some areas across the country, private insurance carriers and Medicaid programs are in cahoots with school systems when it comes to therapies, assistive technology, and other services. Some schools are successfully billing a family's insurance for therapy provided at school. This is a controversial and dangerous practice. It's possible school administrators might agree to "fund" an AT device, but they're really going to bill your insurance for it. The possibility then exists that educators presume the device belongs to the school and not your child. If this insurance/school partnership exists in your district, don't even get the school involved. Work with your insurance directly; keep the school out of it.

Get the right prescription from the right person. If insurance will pay for the AT device, you'll need to submit a prescription from a doctor. Make sure your plans don't fall apart at this point in the process.

Some physicians depend on a recommendation from therapists or other professionals before they write a prescription. If this is how your child's doctor operates, be careful. If the therapist has said your child can't use the device, but you know better and you're going to get it anyway, don't go to your child's doctor for the prescription. Before he writes it, he'll call the therapist for her recommendation. She won't give it to him and you may not get the prescription. Or, he may overrule her and give you the prescription after all, but then you've created a sticky situation between the doctor and the therapist, and you're in the middle of it. Or, the doctor may write the prescription for a communication device, for example, but not the one you want, since he (or the therapist) "knows" about another one he thinks would be more appropriate.

Many parents (including myself) have found it easier and more beneficial to work with a family doctor or a "general" pediatrician who is not a specialist. In the best case scenario, the physician knows he's not an expert on your child's disability; he recognizes your expertise and he trusts you. When you ask for a prescription, he'll say, "Okay, tell me what to write." He won't argue with you or try to talk you into something else!

If your insurance or Medicaid won't pay for an AT device, buy it yourself. If you don't have the cash, charge it on your credit card and pay it out. So what if you don't have money for extras during the next several months? In the big scheme of things, it's a small sacrifice to make. If a typical child needs glasses or orthodontic braces, we usually find a way to pay for those things, with or without insurance or public funding. Do the same thing for your child with a disability.

If the item is too expensive for your household budget or a credit card, borrow the money from the bank. Many banks offer low-interest, long-term loans for equipment for people with disabilities. That's the only way we could afford a wheelchair accessible van. The longer term of the loan put our monthly payments within reach.

Talk to friends and family about pitching in to help financially. You may be able to pay them back, you may not. If you can't pay them back financially, pay them back with your time or some other way. Work something out; make it happen.

Ask service clubs in your community to help: Kiwanis, Lions, Rotary, and so forth. Each service club could donate funds for the cause or members could use their connections to help find a solution. You can "repay" them by giving disability presentations or by having your child attend their meetings to demonstrate the new equipment. Invite the media to cover the "story;" your benefactors will love the great publicity.

Go to the PTA, Scouts, a youth group, your church, a school booster club, or a student group for help. Our PTA regularly gave scholarships for a variety of needs: paying expenses for parents or teachers to attend workshops, paying for students' summer learning programs, and more. Parent-teacher organizations routinely work for the benefit of students. Shouldn't students with disabilities be the beneficiaries of these good works?

Don't feel like this is charity (it isn't) and don't feel like a beggar (you're not). Your child is a citizen of your community. Anything that helps your child helps your community. Let others have a stake in your child's success. People love doing good works. How many boxes of cookies have you bought from Girl Scouts? How many tins of popcorn from Boy Scouts? How many other ways have you supported children in your community? Turnabout is fair play.

Investigate how disability organizations or other community groups could help. Many disability groups have storehouses of donated equipment: wheelchairs, standing frames, and more. A community organization may provide cash donations to help families purchase equipment.

In addition, you may find help with the design and/or construction of a device at engineering, electrical, and other classes in highs schools, colleges, and on military bases. Many classes routinely do volunteer projects for people in their communities.

Think outside the box. Remember the goal: to help your child be more independent and achieve success. If you'll lay down your life for your child, surely you're willing to do whatever it takes to get him the tools he needs!

Shop Smart

Research AT devices by requesting product information from manufacturers. Search catalogs and the Internet. Be determined and don't give up. Try to ensure your child has as much as experience with a product or device before you buy it, especially if it's expensive. You must take the ultimate responsibility for knowing if something is right for your child.

Let's say an AT professional recommends a certain device for your child and you go along with the decision. Your insurance or some other funding program agrees to pay for the device. Two months after you get it, you discover it's not right for your child. You're probably stuck with it for at least a couple of years. An insurance company, for example, may only pay for a new wheelchair every two to five years.

If you had paid for the device yourself, you most likely could return it within a reasonable length of time, no questions asked. But when someone else pays for it, things are different. It's almost as if there's an unwritten "no returns" policy.

Check all this out before you buy. Ask what happens if, once your child has used the device for thirty days, you decide it's not the right piece of equipment. Can you return it? Ask the manufacturer, the distributor, and, especially, ask the insurance company or whoever is paying for it. Be an active participant in this process. Don't let an insurance company, a therapist, or the school handle all the details. You need to know everything!

Low-Tech and Do-It-Yourself AT Devices

Expensive, high-tech devices are critically important tools in the lives of many of our children. But low-tech devices and things we can make for our children can have as big an impact as sophisticated razzle-dazzle items.

You might not think of yourself as an AT expert, but you really are. You may not have the training of a professional, but you know your child best. You know what your home life is like, and you know what's important to your child and your family. Most importantly, of all the people in your child's life, you're the one with the greatest motivation to find what's best for your child! Your common sense and the ideas here will enable you to identify, find, or create the things that will make an incredible difference in your child's life.

Shop generic stores, first. We may need to go to medical supply companies for some things, but our first places to shop should be stores in our neighborhoods. At specialty stores, our choices are limited and the prices are higher; that's the way all niche markets are. At mass market outlets, we can often find greater selection at lower prices. The same or similar item from a medical supply house will cost more and take longer to get than the same item from a regular store. Use specialized outlets as a last resort.

Benjamin's talking clock and talking calculator came from Radio Shack. Hook and loop fasteners for his clothes, non-slip fabric, and his large display digital watch are from Wal-Mart. His clock radio—with extra big knobs—is a Nickelodeon product from the toy store. Since we consigned his custom-made orthotics to the back of his closet, I've found a variety of "off-the-shelf" orthotic inserts in footwear catalogs.

Raised toilet seats can be purchased from durable medical equipment (DME) companies, but they may also be found at local drug and discount stores. Grab bars can be ordered from specialty catalogs, but hardware and home stores have them, too. The list goes on.

In addition to buying things off the shelf, we can make devices that are helpful to our children. I've made Benj a bath chair out of PVC pipe, a door closer out of string and screws, and I've learned how to do many repairs on his manual wheelchair and his super high-tech power chair. If I didn't know how to make these repairs, Benj would probably be without his chair for several weeks of the year.

Become an avid collector of all types of catalogs (a list is included in the appendix). You'll find low-tech (and low cost) solutions to meet your child's needs in many general and specialty (non-medical) catalogs. You'll also get ideas about things to make and ways to make them. We're all more talented and creative than we know. Let's put those characteristics to work for our children. They're counting on us.

In the following sections, I'll focus on specific areas of need. Later, I'll describe a variety of ideas, modifications, and accommodations that may be helpful to children with disabilities and families, regardless of the type of disability.

COMMUNICATION

If your child needs help in the area of speech, widen your focus to effective communication, not just talking. You've heard me preach about this throughout the book. Being able to speak is good, but being able to communicate is more valuable. We can help our children communicate with a variety of low and high-tech devices, which I'll describe. But first, let's review some issues about communication.

As I've described in previous chapters, some parents and professionals are adamantly opposed to exploring alternative methods of communication. Their rationale is that if a child uses a communication device, picture cards, or some other form of communicating, the child will "never" learn to talk. There is no way to substantiate such a claim and I don't know how we've come to believe such hogwash. Don't ever believe professionals who say your child will "never" do something. How do they know? Do they have a crystal ball? Do they know what's in your child's heart and mind? How dare they insult our children by using the word "never." Don't all of us continue learning all our lives? Are *you* not doing things today you never thought you could do? We give such little credit to the human spirit.

If a child is going to talk, he'll talk when the time is right and in his own way, and communication aids will not get in the way of his desire and ability. Giving a child tools will enhance—not detract from—his ultimate method of communication, whether that's speech, signing, or using a device of some kind. When we deny communication to children, we're robbing them of opportunities for learning, social interactions, freedom, independence, and self-determination.

A child is often described as non-verbal even though he talks. For example, if he makes sounds that are unintelligible to us, regardless of his age or disability, we say, "Oh, he's just babbling. It doesn't mean anything." Wrong! He's talking and *he* knows what he's saying. We don't understand his words because we haven't figured out his speech patterns. The problem is ours, not his. What sounds like gibberish to us means something to *him*.

We also make the outrageously unfair assumption that if a child doesn't speak he doesn't understand. Imagine you're a child who is talking the best way you can. What would you feel if you heard your parents say, "She's just babbling. She can't talk yet." Would you be hurt? Would you be angry? Would you feel valuable and loved? Our children understand far more than we think they do.

Benjamin didn't talk until he was almost three. When he was four, he asked me about a trip we took when he was an eighteen-month-old: "Mom, remember when we went to the beach and we rented that white Ford Taurus station wagon?" I was stunned. At the time of the trip he was "non-verbal," but he remembered words and things that happened. He continued to surprise us by talking about other things that happened and things people said during his "non-verbal" years. Presume your child understands. Presume competence.

If children do not vocalize at all, or if we don't understand their speech patterns, they communicate in other ways. We may have figured out what a look, a touch, or some other action means. Other times, we guess, trying to figure out what a child is trying to tell us. Hopefully, we're successful most of the time, but sometimes we're not. For example, Jamie's parents assume they know what she wants. They act on their assumptions, but Jamie goes ballistic. What happened? Jamie's parents assumed wrong and Jamie is upset. Without effective communication, her outburst is the only way to express her frustration.

Children who have no speech—or speech that's not intelligible to others—may end up with behavior labels. A child experiences extreme frustration when no one understands him. But many "inappropriate behaviors" diminish when a child can communicate effectively. This doesn't mean Jamie must be made to talk; it means we must help her find a way to communicate so others know what she wants and needs. The Jamies of this world must have ways to effectively interact with others so they can form relationships and acquire social skills.

Specialists in behavior whom I respect (Joe Schiappacasse; Herb Lovett, who has passed on; and others) have spent years teaching that—for all of us—behavior is a form of communication. Behavior and communication are intertwined; it's hard to separate one from another. Many communication specialists estimate 90 percent of all communication is non-verbal! Body language, facial expression, tone of voice, and silence all send clear messages.

For example, when making up with my husband after an argument, if I say, "I'm sorry, too" with sarcasm, gritted teeth, and angry eyes, my behavior says far more than my verbal communication. My facial expression and tone of voice are more truthful than my words: I'm telegraphing that I'm still angry and I'm not really making up. The same would be true if I answered his apology with silence.

All of us communicate through behavior, to one degree or another. Children with disabilities may communicate through their behavior more than others. But many people don't see the behavior as communication. Instead, they see "inappropriate behavior" or "behavior problems." A little later, behavior supports will be examined in greater detail.

Expressive and Receptive Language

Professional assessments used to measure a child's expressive language (what he can communicate to others) and his receptive language (what he can understand) may lead us to incorrect beliefs about children.

Obviously, a child who has no intelligible speech will do poorly on an expressive language test. But if he also does poorly on a receptive language test, professionals may assume he could not benefit from any communication devices or tools. The logic is that if a child cannot understand language, he's inherently incapable of communicating to others. But tests can be wrong!

For example, during the receptive language test, four-year-old Mario was asked to do certain tasks—pick up the red ball, point to the telephone, and so forth—to demonstrate his understanding of other people's language. But on this particular day, Mario didn't feel like doing everything the tester asked him to do and he didn't understand some of the requests. He was frightened and nervous. Since he doesn't have speech, he couldn't tell the tester he didn't understand.

Mario's receptive language abilities may be just fine. But he wasn't able to demonstrate his abilities through the methods used by the tester. To get the recommendation for a communication device, it may be left to Mario's parents to "prove" he can understand language by describing how Mario comprehends language at home. When his mother asks him to put his toys away he does. When his dad asks if he wants to watch a video, Mario grabs his favorite tape and puts it in the VCR.

Presume competence. Regardless of what your child is or is not doing right now, and regardless of professional expertise, presume your child does understand oral communication and that this ability will grow and deepen. Don't let negative opinions (your own or others') of your child's capacity for expressive or receptive language stand in the way of your child acquiring tools for communication.

There are many, many ways to help children with communication. The ideas presented here have been used successfully by many families. Customize these and/or use more than one method to give your child the right tools to communicate.

The World's Best Speech Therapists

Every parent is a born speech therapist. Think about it. Speech is a very complex activity, and most children (including children with disabilities) learn to talk without ever being formally taught! They learn by hearing other people talk, by imitation, and by experimentation. The best (and easiest) way to help your child acquire speech is to talk to him, all the time. Even if he is unable to talk back to you, talk to him as if he could.

Think about what we do with newborn babies: infants can't talk, but we talk to them all the time! They don't understand the words we're saying, but they're soaking up our words, tone of voice, facial expressions, and more.

In addition to talking to your child as much as possible, have fun with sounds. Be silly. Sit facing your child and make funny faces and funny sounds that he can try to imitate. Play cars, play baby, play school or any other game of imagination. Encourage family members to help. A brother or sister a year or two older can also be the best speech therapist in the world. Children are tireless, exuberant, and excited about everything, and it all rubs off.

Play music. Some children learn to sing before they learn to speak. Try the audiotaped reading programs that help children practice phonics. Experiment with computer games that talk. Buy books on tape and let him listen. Experiment to see if radio talk shows or television might help. When Benjamin was very young, he sat transfixed in front of the evening news, but ignored *Sesame Street.* I think he liked watching the news anchors and hearing them talk. Expose your child to as much language as possible.

Presume competence. Before Benjamin could say words we understood, I did dumb things because I didn't know any better. At the dinner table, he would grunt and point to something on the table. Trying to figure out exactly what he wanted, I pointed to a variety of things, saying "This?" for every item until Benjamin nodded his head or grunted.

After describing this scenario to the speech therapist, she asked, "Why did you call everything 'this'?" The question caught me by surprise; I had never thought about it. After a moment of reflection, I answered, "I guess because I didn't think he knew the names of all the stuff on the table." "Well, he might not right now," the therapist replied, "but he never will if you keep calling everything 'this'!" From then on, I never called anything "this;" I called everything by the right name.

Assume your child is learning from your words. For many years, while driving Benjamin to therapy several days a week, I talked constantly, hoping he'd learn to talk. I spent lots of time as a tour guide in the car: "Look, there's the church." A block away: "That's the way to grandmother's house." Three blocks away: "There's a grocery store," and so on.

Imagine my shock one day when, in the midst of babbling sounds, Benjamin blurted out, "There's the church!" He pointed to it as we drove by and then went back to the babbling sounds. Staring at him wide-eyed and slack-jawed, I almost wrecked the car!

When your child begins talking, she'll pronounce many words incorrectly. Don't correct her pronunciation by saying, "No, you say it [however]." Instead, model the correct pronunciation by repeating the word back to her, "Yes, I like the [whatever], too." When we correct children's speech, we embarrass them. To avoid being embarrassed, they'll give up.

Communication Cards

Using communication cards is a simple, but highly effective method of expression for many children with disabilities, and they're appropriate for children of all ages.

A wide variety of picture-symbol cards (they may be called by various names) are available from specialty catalogs, but you can also make your own. Don't confuse communication cards with flash cards. Communication cards convey messages, while flash cards essentially teach word recognition and spelling.

Communication cards feature a drawing, symbol, or picture of an action, a feeling, or a thought. The words to describe the picture are written across the top or the bottom of each card. For example, a card might show a glass of milk with the words, "I want milk, please." The written words help a child associate sounds to letters.

If your child has been exposed to written language, the words may be important and relevant to her. If she isn't familiar with written words, don't worry about that right now and don't try to force your child to be interested in them. That will come later. Initially, the focus is on giving your child the power of communication. Use your own intuition and take your cues from your child. If she's interested in the words, point to them as she uses the cards. If not, wait awhile.

However, you *do* want your child to know the sounds that go with each card, so every time he uses a card, say the phrase that's printed on it and encourage your child to repeat it to you. Don't worry if he doesn't make the sound just right. If he even attempts the sound, he's succeeded. We climb the mountain one small step at a time!

Homemade cards may be best. While a wide variety of manufactured cards are on the market, many parents have found their children do best with homemade cards. If you make your child's cards, you can personalize them to your child, his needs, and his environment. You can make them simple or sophisticated, depending on your child's needs:

- Hand draw symbols and pictures on note cards. Use a thick black marker on white; or outline the drawing in black and fill in with bright colors.

- Make cards on the computer, drawing pictures or symbols freehand or by using clip art.

- Cut out pictures from catalogs and magazines to use on the cards.

- Take photographs of your child doing the action. For example, take a photo of your child drinking milk, making sure to frame him in the viewfinder so there's room to write words across the bottom or the top. Then put a piece of tape or a sticky label on the photo card with the words, "I want milk, please."

Photo communication cards may give children a greater sense of power as they learn to communicate: they feel a sense of ownership and they're more interested in the process of communication. Also, seeing themselves in the picture cards makes it more fun!

Laminate communication cards so they'll be sturdier and easier to keep clean. Do-it-yourself laminating sheets can be purchased at office supply stores or you can pay to have it done at a copy store.

Organize the cards in a way that makes sense to your child. You can sort them by category (activities, food, feelings, etc.) or by frequency of use (most frequently used, least frequently used). Many parents punch one hole in a corner of the cards and use a round snap ring to keep them together. Alternatively, you can put the cards in a small format photo album. The cards should be organized in a way that's best for your child.

Your child's stash of cards will change as he does. With new experiences and abilities, your child will need new cards. By the same token, you'll need to remove cards that are no longer necessary. For example, once your child can get his own milk he'll no longer need that card.

Make as many cards as your child needs to communicate effectively. Start with the basics: an image of a plate of food with "I'm hungry" written on it; an image of the television set with "Watch TV," and so on. Make "emotion" cards, too. Many children have great difficulties communicating their feelings or states of being. Make cards that represent feelings of being sad, happy, angry, scared, tired, in pain, etc. Wouldn't it be great if your child thrust an "I'm angry" card at you instead of throwing a tantrum? Don't forget to make "conversation" cards: "thank you," "I'm ready to go," and, of course, the most important card, "I love you."

Make this a family affair. If someone in your family is a great photographer, let him take pictures. If your teenager likes working on the computer, she can help. If you don't have anyone at home to assist in this activity, ask for help from extended family and friends.

Sit down with your whole family (including the child who will use the cards) and explain the benefits of the cards. Be enthusiastic and excited. Don't make this a serious lesson about what the child must do from now on; he might decide to resist! Talk to him about how grown up he is or use whatever words will be encouraging to him. Don't focus on how the cards will help his "problem;" let him know the cards are to help you and others.

Reassure him that you'll help him learn to use the cards. Give him a chance to become familiar with all the cards; let him play with them; review what each card means. Practice using them: "Let's pretend you want to go outside, Jonathan. You'll show me this card." And, "Jonathan, when you're mad from now on, you don't need to bite yourself or throw something—just bring me this card." Helping your child communicate is an exciting opportunity. Bring enthusiasm, joy, and fun to this important endeavor.

Start slowly. Like the rest of us, children with disabilities don't always welcome change. If they're comfortable with their way of communicating, they may balk if they feel pressure to change. If this is the case, start slowly with only one or two cards.

Success will come easier if you start with something that's important to your child. If he has a favorite book he likes you to read to him, make a card for that book. Make one for juice or milk, cookies or pizza, swinging in the backyard, going to a fast food place, or getting a hug. As your child becomes accustomed to the cards and enjoys using them, make more. The way you introduce your child to the cards is critical. Let's look at an example in which you're the mother of Elias.

Three-year-old Elias loves apple juice. Several times a day, he leads you to the refrigerator, opens it, and points to the bottle of juice. So, the first card you'll make is a picture of a cup of apple juice (or a photograph of him drinking juice) with the words "Apple juice, please" or "I want apple juice, please," printed in big block letters.

When you're ready to introduce the card to Elias, be excited: "Look Elias, this is a picture of your cup of apple juice! When you want juice from now on, you don't have to take me to the refrigerator. All you have to do is show me this card! Now, where should we keep this card? Should we put it on the refrigerator with a magnet? Or would you like to wear it around your neck? See, I have this rainbow cord we could put in on and you could wear it. What do you think?" (If you think this last idea will fly, get one of those lanyard neck straps with a hook on the end. You can punch a hole in the card and hook it to the lanyard.)

Hopefully, Elias won't balk at learning to use the card. But it must stay within easy reach, or he'll forget to use it since it's not a habit yet. If he's agreeable, but he forgets to use the card the next time he wants juice, be positive and say, "Oops, where's your card?"

If he balks at using the card, stay calm and don't show any disappointment. Put the card away and try again in a week or so, or continue in a very low-key fashion: stick the juice card on the refrigerator with a magnet. The next time Elias leads you to the refrigerator, pull the card off the refrigerator before you get the juice, and say, "Oh, look! This is what we're doing, isn't it? I'm getting you apple juice and here's a picture of it!" You may need to repeat this several times before Elias decides to bring you the card. That's okay. Be consistent and stay hopeful. We learn by repetition, so give Elias lots of opportunities!

Some children adapt to change easier than others, so be patient. They might not see the benefit of using the cards, they might not understand how the cards work, or maybe they're just not interested in them. A big "Ah-Ha" moment may be the key to helping them embrace something new. If so, create such a moment by making a card for something important to your child: a toy he wants, a place he wants to go, or something else very wonderful. There are at least two different ways to make this "Ah-Ha" moment happen.

Let's say Elias has been wanting a new Mickey Mouse doll. In private, make a Mickey Mouse card by drawing it or cutting out an ad. While Elias is asleep, put the card on the refrigerator or wherever he'll see it throughout the day. Don't say a word about it. The next day—probably within minutes of seeing it—he'll lead you to the card, take the card to you, or somehow direct your attention to it. When he does, say, "Yes, that's a picture of Mickey Mouse. You've been wanting one haven't you? Shall we go buy it today? I'm so glad you showed me the card to tell me that!"

This will help Elias understand the value of the cards. Assuming this method works, the next day reintroduce the juice card again, "Remember how I knew what you wanted when you showed me the Mickey Mouse card? If you show me the juice card, I'll always know when you want juice."

Another way to produce an "Ah-Ha" moment is to make the Mickey Mouse card, show it to Elias, and say, "I know you've been wanting a Mickey Mouse doll. I'm going to put this card on the refrigerator. When you're ready to go to the store to buy Mickey Mouse, give me this card, okay?" If he tries to take the card out of your hand, gently resist, and quickly post the card on the refrigerator. Then begin washing the dishes or busying yourself somehow. Most likely, he'll immediately grab the card and give it to you, letting you know he wants to go right now! Follow the recommendations above, saying something like, "Oh, I'm so glad you let me know you wanted to go today. Okay, we'll go right after I finish washing these dishes. I'm so glad you gave me the card to tell me what you wanted!" Later, reintroduce the juice card.

Adjust these scenarios for the age and interests of your child. Experiment, be patient, and know that you'll find a method that works. If/when your child forgets or chooses not to use the cards, casually say, "Can you give me the card?" or "Did you lose your cards?" or "Here, let's get your cards and then you show me, okay?"

It's important to give your child opportunities to use the cards with everyone he comes in contact with and in all settings. If he likes to go to McDonald's, make a card that says, "A cheeseburger meal and a root beer." Then take him to McDonald's, give him a couple of bucks, and let him go up to the counter and order his own meal. How exciting!

Make cards that are specific to other members of the family. A card for Dad might need to say, "Swing me" or "Let's go fishing." If your child is attending public school, you'll need to work closely with your child's teachers so the success your child enjoys at home will transfer to school. Involve your child in the process of making the cards to the greatest extent possible. If he's involved, he'll be more invested in using them.

If your child has an orthopedic disability, you'll need to create cards that are user-friendly. For example, a child who cannot walk to you and hand you the card will need his cards organized so they're always with him. A child who has difficulty holding things in his hands may need cards put in a large photo album. By putting stiff tabs on the edges of each album page, a child could use the back of his hand to flip the pages to find the right card. Some children may need a mouth or head stick to accomplish this. Put your thinking cap on and try different methods until you find the one that's best.

Signing

Using sign language may supplement oral communication or it may become a child's primary form of communication. Many people assume signing is only for people with hearing impairments. But children with Down syndrome, speech delays, autism, and a variety of other conditions use sign language, too.

To supplement oral communication, some children and families make up their own signs and teach them to grandparents, day care workers, and others in the child's life. Others take a course in American Sign Language (ASL) to learn the real thing. Regardless of the type of signing, it must be a family affair. If the child can only communicate with mom, he'll continue to be frustrated by the lack of communication with others. Children who use ASL can be included in regular education classes and in typical community activities, either by the addition of an interpreter or when other people around the child learn Sign.

Some children use sign (formal or informal) along with other methods of communication early on. For example, a child might use some sign, some picture cards, and some speech. As the child grows, one form of communication often becomes more dominant.

Facilitated Communication

Many children are successfully expressing themselves through facilitated communication (FC). In a nutshell, FC is a process in which a child uses a typewriter or computer to communicate. A facilitator provides sensory support, by lightly placing her hand on the child's hand. As the child becomes more proficient, the facilitator may gradually move the support from the back of the child's hand to the wrist, then to the elbow, then the shoulder, and then support may be removed entirely. This physical support has enabled many individuals to successfully communicate for the first time in their lives!

In some quarters, there's a great deal of controversy about FC. Some people say the facilitator, not the person with the disability, is really doing the typing. But I have never met anyone who's actually tried it and believed this. On the contrary, I've known several children who are successfully using facilitated communication. After a six-year-old girl with autism began using FC, her parents and teachers discovered she could read, write, and do math, even though no one had formally taught her these things. She had often spent long hours looking at books and everyone assumed she was just looking at the pictures. They were all ecstatic about her many capabilities.

Some children with disabilities may be able to speak, but they're unable to express personal feelings or needs. As a result, they may exhibit "problem behaviors" out of frustration, anger, sadness, or fear. But with FC, they're able to express their deepest feelings. Parents have said FC enabled them really know their children for the first time.

Learn more about FC from the variety of books and papers written about it. Search the Internet, and talk to parents, educators, and therapists who have experience with FC.

Communication Devices

Augmentative communication (AugCom) devices—also known as speaking devices, communicators, or talkers—come in all shapes and sizes. Basically, they're machines that use computer-generated or synthesized speech to talk for the user.

Those made for younger children feature symbols and large buttons that are easy to push. At the other end are sophisticated keyboards that can be programmed to deliver speeches! Many can be hooked up to computers so children can do their school work with them. Some have tinny robot-sounding voices; others have more natural sounding voices. Look for a communication system that can be customized to your child's needs, is easy to use, and easy for your child to transport. If the thing weighs twenty pounds, your thirty pound child won't be able to tote it around!

Learn about communication devices by talking with other parents, speech therapists, and AT specialists, and from information in catalogs and on the Internet. Try to find children in your community who are using them so you and your child can see them up close.

Insurance or other programs will often pay for communication devices, but with restrictions. For example, they may only pay for one every five years or one per lifetime! Learn all these details before making a selection. Anticipate your child's growth and development. Buy one he will grow into, rather than one he will quickly outgrow.

Laptop computers can also be used as communication devices. A variety of computer programs have speech output. This requires the user to type in the words. But even if a child can't write or spell yet, there are word prediction programs that "learn" how the user communicates and suggests a variety of words to choose from. In addition, children can begin by spelling words the best way they can (invented spelling).

Alternatively, a parent could help the child program sentences or questions that would enable the child to initiate conversations, as well as phrases, words, or sentences that would be used frequently. By the time this book is in print, there may well be software that uses symbols instead of words for use by people who don't know letters or words yet.

A laptop computer may provide advantages over a traditional communication device. It will probably weigh less and cost less. It could serve multiple purposes: communication; learning, via software for history, math, and so forth; writing, in lieu of a pencil and paper; Internet access; and games. With the addition of operating programs, peripherals, or upgrades, a laptop could be appropriate for many years to come.

Devices That Don't Communicate

Some children are provided with switch-activated or other simple devices for communication. But we need to be wary of so-called communication devices that don't really allow communication.

Ten-year-old Natalie, for example, had two five-inch discs mounted on her wheelchair tray. Her mom could ask, "Do you want an ice cream bar or a brownie? Touch the yellow button for ice cream or the red one for a brownie." Natalie could indicate her preference by a swipe of her hand on the appropriate disc, which made a beeping sound when touched.

But the limitations of this system are obvious. What if Natalie didn't want either of the goodies offered? The device was totally useless for situations involving more than two choices. In addition, Natalie could not *initiate* communication; she could only respond and she could not express her feelings.

When Natalie was very young, she communicated with her family by facial expressions: a smile, a frown, or an eye gaze. Her parents didn't see any need to find a more effective way since *they* knew what their daughter needed most of the time. But when Natalie started school at age five, her parents bought the beeping discs on the recommendation of therapists. Because Natalie didn't have a lot of control over her arms and hands, and because everyone believed she had significant cognitive disabilities, no one thought Natalie could use a more sophisticated device. Of course, no one ever gave her the opportunity to try other devices, so there's no way to know what her capabilities were. And because Natalie had no means of effective communication, no one ever knew what her cognitive abilities were.

Natalie used a manual wheelchair she could not push herself, and no one thought she was capable of using a power chair. As a result of not having effective communication and independent mobility, Natalie was often treated like a baby. She was included in her classroom at school and other children cared about her, but it was impossible for her to initiate conversations and difficult for her to play with other children. In addition, no one seemed to be able to find meaningful ways for Natalie to participate in the classroom. She was a passive observer of life. But the sparkle in her eyes sent the clear message that she wanted to belong. Sadly, no one saw Natalie and presumed competence.

With the right assistive technology to meet her needs, Natalie's life could be very different. She could be independently mobile in a power wheelchair, operating it through a knee switch (or a switch activated by any other body part). A communication device modified for Natalie's abilities could enable her to giggle with girlfriends, participate in class discussions, and tell her mother what she wants for breakfast, lunch, dinner, and dessert!

Remember the Goal

Whether your child needs communication aids to supplement his emerging oral speech or as his primary form of communication, remember the ultimate goal: to enable your child to have an effective and appropriate method of communication that will enable him to experience typical, age-appropriate activities.

A two-year-old needs to be able to say "no," as well as "please" and "thank you." A three-year-old needs to tell you about her nightmare. A four-year-old wants to have a birthday party with all his friends and family present. What's typical for other ages? Thirteen-year-old boys needs to be able to talk sports or computers. Fifteen-year-old girls need to be able to talk music and make-up. What can you do to make sure your child has the tools for self-expression and communication that will enable her enjoy typical, age-appropriate experiences—experiences that are the keys to her social, emotional, and cognitive development?

Never underestimate the importance of communication. The right to free speech should not be denied our children simply because we haven't taken the time or made the effort to help them acquire the tools of communication. Whether our children communicate orally, with cards, communication devices, through signing, or by any other means, communication is the basis of all relationships. The ability to communicate is probably more important than walking, seeing, hearing, or any other "functional" ability. Communication enables us to express our needs and wants, to tell others who we are and what we think, to share our lives with others, to say "no" to protect ourselves, and to say "I love you."

BEHAVIOR

Many children are labeled with disabilities that have a "behavioral component," such as autism, pervasive developmental disorder (PDD), hyperactivity, attention deficit disorder with or without hyperactivity (ADD, ADHD), oppositional defiant disorder (ODD), cognitive disabilities, and others, including specific emotional disabilities. Children who carry these labels are all unique individuals. But the behavioral component shared by many of these disabilities is the one characteristic that's perceived as the most problematic. I'll use the terms "behavioral disability," "behavior issues," or "behavioral component" in this section as catch-all descriptors to avoid renaming a variety of different disabilities.

Children *without* disabilities exhibit a variety of behaviors, many of which could be considered aberrant, difficult, or challenging. We don't get too concerned about these, however; we chalk them up to age, personality, circumstances, and so on. Some children are shy and don't talk much (that was me, believe it or not); some are loners at very early ages (this was my daughter); and others are boisterous, loud, and in constant motion (I've known my share). We acknowledge that even within the same family, two children can be as different as night and day in their personalities and behaviors.

But when children with behavioral disabilities exhibit unusual or unacceptable behaviors, we often see the behaviors as part of the disability. Seldom do we consider that the behavior might be circumstantial, a typical stage of growth, or part of the child's innate personality. All behaviors are attributed to the disability.

Many people believe that for every "inappropriate" behavior, there must be a treatment, intervention, pill, or some type of remedy or response. For example, a child with autism may be a quiet loner because that's part of his personality. But no one sees it that way. We see it as a characteristic of the disability and work furiously on behavior "management" techniques to force the child to become more socially active.

A child with ADHD may be a super active kid who talks non-stop because that's part of his personality. But, again, we don't see it that way. Professionals and parents see the behaviors as characteristics of the disability, so drugs, interventions, and "behavior modification" plans are prescribed to remedy the behavior "problems."

Attributing all personal or behavioral characteristics to the disability is very unfair to our children. When we do this, we don't allow them to be who they really are. When we focus on remedying the perceived deficits, we overlook the child as a whole. And just like kids with other disabilities, children with behavioral disabilities are often not allowed to experience the fullness of childhood because of the way we treat them.

If your child has a disability that has a behavior component, reexamine how you see your child. Take a closer look. Pretend you don't know much about your child's disability.

Or go further and pretend your child has never been given a label. Now, step back and do a lot of wondering: wonder if a particular behavior is truly a manifestation of the disability or if it's simply part of your child's personality, a stage he's going through, or something else. You may begin seeing your child through different eyes.

Many typical children display unusual behaviors. David, a four-year-old without a disability label, absolutely hates going to the big discount store. Every time Laurie walks into the store with David, he screams, cries, and tries to run away. But he loves going to the mall, restaurants, and dozens of other places, including other discount and grocery stores.

Who knows why this happens? Laurie has tried to remember if something once occurred to make David frightened of the store. She can't recall anything and even though David talks very well, he's unable to tell her why he's so uneasy. Whatever the reason, Laurie knows something makes David very anxious in that store. His tantrums communicate his extreme discomfort.

Rather than make a big deal out of it, Laurie simply doesn't take David to that store anymore. She doesn't spend a lot of time trying to discover the reason for David's discomfort; nor does she try to devise a plan to modify his behavior. Instead of seeing his tantrums as "aberrant" behavior, she respects David's feelings and his individual personality traits. She'll wait a few weeks and try again.

Of course, Laurie *could* take David to a specialist who would probably diagnose some disability or another, followed by a behavior modification plan. Millions of people could be labeled with behavior disabilities if we shared every unusual behavior with experts!

When a child has an orthopedic or other disability that's visible, it's often easier to distinguish whether a characteristic or behavior stems from the disability or the personality. But for parents of kids with invisible disabilities, the task is not so easy. Making these distinctions may be difficult, but it's critically important to make the effort.

Do all behaviors we find unusual or unacceptable need to be treated? No, sometimes we just need to learn to live with them or make accommodation. Who among us has reached a level of maturity and self-control that ensures perfect behavior?

Some children with behavioral disabilities are perceived to have so many imperfections they're seen as unlovable. Parents and professionals struggle to find the smallest shred of goodness. Many mothers have cried as they described all of their children's "behavior problems" to me. But what do our feelings do to our children? How do we expect them to cope with our disappointment in them? Even if we've done our best to hide our feelings, our children know—they know!

We must take the time and make the effort to let our children's true personalities emerge from the shadow of the disability label. Choosing to see every behavior as disability-related and in need of some form of treatment is an inhumane way to treat children.

Behavior as Communication

The first and most important thing we can do is see behavior as communication. Whatever our children do and however they behave, they're communicating with us. What we often see as "problem behavior" may simply be a child's form of expressing frustration, anger, pain, boredom, or loneliness, as well as excitement, joy, anticipation, and everything in between. The "problem" in "problem behavior" is really our problem: we find the behavior inappropriate or unacceptable; it causes us discomfort, shame, or pain.

Trusted experts have taught me that behavior is learned. As newborns, we come into the world "knowing" little. Our first behavior is crying. It's a behavior that's not learned; it's instinctive. Crying is also our first form of communication. Crying is both behavior and communication: it's behavior that communicates! Babies cry to have their needs met. Think about this: all children first communicate in what we consider a "negative" fashion (crying) before expressing joy and happiness through smiles and laughter. We recall a baby's crying as routine. But baby's first smile is remembered as extraordinary, a long-awaited gift.

At birth, we're all wired with the ability to express frustration, anger, pain, boredom, or loneliness *as a way of ensuring our own survival.* A baby cries when he's hungry: his tummy is empty and it hurts. He's angry, too, when he hurts and no one comes to help. Parents respond to the baby's anger and pain with a breast or a bottle. If the parents didn't respond, the baby would die. If a baby's needs are never met, he'll spend a great deal of time crying. At some point, he may stop crying because he's given up; he's lost all hope. Only when a child's needs are met—when he feels secure and safe, with a full tummy and loving arms around him—does he achieve the ability to smile and communicate contentment.

Think about these foundations of behavior and communication as they apply to children with behavioral issues. Regardless of the child's disability—whether it's autism, ADHD, cognitive disabilities, or anything else—a child who behaves or communicates in ways we consider unacceptable *is attempting to have his needs met.*

Too often, no one listens to the behavior or understands it, so the child's needs go unmet. In the process, children become frustrated that they're not listened to or understood. The frustration turns to anger and emotional pain, and "unacceptable behaviors" escalate, often to the point that the child is punished, restrained, or both.

Some parents recognize their children's behavior may always be considered unusual and they're okay with that. They focus on understanding their children and helping them learn to get along in the world. Other parents, however, are striving to make their children behave according to some norm. *Our job is not to make our children's behavior acceptable to other people or to make them behave like other children.* It's good if our children's behavior is not offensive to other people, but our primary obligation is to help our children find ways to have their needs met. Once children are successful in having their needs met, "inappropriate behaviors" often miraculously subside or disappear altogether.

At all times, we must look for the *purpose* in a child's behavior. And we don't have to be specialists to do this. We can all become armchair "behaviorists" by carefully observing our own behavior, the actions and behaviors of others, and the environment.

While writing this book, I reached the half-century mark. I think of myself as a mature adult woman. But when my needs aren't met, I occasionally "misbehave." When I'm stressed out, tired, or overwhelmed, I need my family to nurture me, take care of me, and "baby" me for a little while. In the best case scenario, I'm able to communicate these needs.

But when my frustration is at its highest point, I don't always have what it takes to calmly state my needs. Instead, I rant and rave at my husband and two teenagers about how messy they've let the house get, or I angrily demand to know why they expect me to do all the work! In other words, I lose it, I go ballistic. As soon as my outburst is over—after the volcano has exploded—I'm calm and I'm also horribly embarrassed and remorseful. Then I cry and apologize. I hug my family and they hug me back.

What happened here? I ultimately got what I needed—some loving attention—but I certainly could have communicated my needs differently. If I had held it all together, I could have asked for what I needed, and received it without hurting my family and being rude. As a mature adult (most of the time), I can examine my behavior, learn from it, and hopefully not repeat my mistakes.

My "inappropriate behavior" is similar to the actions of some children with disabilities. Perhaps the only differences are that they behave this way more often, they may not be able to calm down after the eruption, they may not feel remorseful, and they may not be able to examine their behavior and learn from it. When we look at the *purpose* of a child's behavior or actions, we can learn a great deal.

I've never had any long-term concerns about Benj's behavior, although he's had his share of "temper tantrums" (wonder where he learned that—couldn't have been from me, could it?). But he does do something that many people may consider aberrant.

Benjamin talked "late," but once he started talking, he spoke in long sentences and paragraphs, not in single words and short phrases. It was almost like he had stored all his thoughts from the time he was born and when he was finally able to speak, the thoughts came pouring out. He's always had a great auditory memory, so when he hears something that interests him, he memorizes it verbatim.

When he was about three, he would begin telling me a long story about something that happened, a book or video, or something else. But three-fourths of the way through his monologue, something would distract him and he would stop talking for a moment. Then he would start again, but he wouldn't pick up where he left off; he would start at the beginning! At first, I tried to tell him he'd already told me the first part and he just needed to tell me the end of the story. But he couldn't do it, so I listened as he retold it from the beginning again. Sometimes, he would get distracted two or three times, so he'd go back to the beginning each time. And, amazingly, each version was exactly the same. I don't think I could ever repeat the same story two times in precisely the same way, but he could.

It took me awhile to figure out what was going on. I believe his brain is wired in such a way that a group of thoughts was a whole and always had to be. He wasn't always able to separate a story into individual pieces that could be put together like a puzzle. I think this particular characteristic reflects the combination of the way he processes information and his extraordinary auditory memory.

At age thirteen, it's still important for him to complete an entire thought or story. If he's interrupted or distracted, he still needs to start over from the beginning. Additionally, he often tells the same story or thought again and again, not always at the same time, but a few days, a week or two, or a month later. The more I've learned about Benjamin, I've realized this is how he learns things. It's as if he needs to *hear* his thoughts or stories out loud as a way of internalizing, understanding, and owning them. And he needs to hear them repeatedly. Many times, after he's told me the same story numerous times, he asks me questions about the events or people he's described. He wants to learn more or understand something more fully. After I give him the answers, he often changes the story for the next time, incorporating this new information.

Some people may loosely call this perseveration, even though it's different than repeating the same word or phrase over and over in one sitting. Some would see this as attention-getting behavior or as a way Benjamin monopolizes conversations. And other people would just see it as "crazy." But I know this is Benjamin's way of learning, of making sense of things, and of organizing things in his head. By repeating the story out loud, he learns it better, it sparks other questions, and he processes the information better than if he just thought about it. This behavior meets a need for Benjamin.

In your own child's situation, think about the purpose of his behavior. What is he trying to communicate? What does he need? What does he want? What need is the behavior fulfilling?

Behavior issues can be very complex, but we shouldn't let them overwhelm us into believing that nothing can be done. Behavior needs are frightening to parents, educators, and other adults because they don't know what to do.

It's not uncommon for some people to believe a child is simply *choosing* to be out of control, or that the child is inherently bad or evil. Because we can't "see" behavior disabilities, the way we can see a wheelchair as an indication of an orthopedic disability, it's often difficult to get our arms around behavior as a disability. It's frustrating for parents to know that a wheelchair can change the life of a child with a physical disability, but there's no magic bullet or remedy that can change the life of a child with behavior disabilities (although effective communication may often be that magic bullet).

Some children's brains are wired differently (aren't all of our brains wired differently, though?) and it's our responsibility to seek understanding. Some children need their environments to be a particular way, others need help in learning how to handle frustrations and anger, and some may need medicines for chemical imbalances.

When we're looking at ways to help our children, let's start our search with the simplest methods that are doable in the most natural ways, before moving on to more complex, sophisticated methods.

Communication, First

The way to help varies from child to child and sometimes from moment to moment. But the experiences of parents all across the country indicate that many "inappropriate behaviors" disappear when a child is provided with effective communication, whether in the form of cards, communication devices, or other methods. So focus on communication first, using your own ideas or some of the suggestions presented earlier.

Change the Environment

Another important step is to carefully analyze, and change when necessary, a child's environment. For example, our house (Benjamin's primary environment) must be free of physical barriers that prevent him from going where he wants to in the house. As I already mentioned, we remodeled parts of the house to eliminate barriers. But every member of our family must take responsibility to ensure our home *remains* barrier-free. Our furniture needs to be arranged against the walls to give Benj free and clear pathways. We don't leave things in the middle of the floor that would block his movement. We didn't create an environment that works for the three of us who walk, and expect Benj to fit into that world. We changed the environment to ensure Benjamin's success and independence.

We could view this from a selfish or self-righteous perspective: "We're not going to change our lives around just for Benjamin." An observer might look at our family's situation and think, "Can you believe that? They let that kid run the family's life." Or, "Oh that poor family, they sure have to do a lot for that kid."

If a family feels it's at the mercy of, or is somehow victimized by, a child's disability, members of the family can easily slide into selfish and self-righteous behavior. We must recognize that every member of a family needs support, every member is responsible to everyone else, and compromise and cooperation are the keys to successful families. Each family of a child with a disability must be secure in the beliefs that (1) their actions can have a profoundly positive or negative influence on the child and (2) only they can define what's right and normal for them. We need to let go of any stereotypical views of what our families "should" look like.

As I mentioned before, parents may find it hard to see behavior disabilities in the same way we view physical disabilities. For example, if they consider making accommodations and modifications in the child's environment (the child's home life), they may feel they're "giving in" to "bad" behavior. They may think they should not let the child's behavior control the rest of the family, or that members of the family shouldn't have to change—the child needs to change. But consider this. The environment of a child with a physical disability is crucial to his success. The environment is no less crucial for a child who needs behavior supports. That child's need for support and accommodation are no different than Benjamin's need for a clear path and wider doorways.

How can we change and/or manage the environment of our homes to ensure the success of a child who needs behavior supports? Many children with autism and other disabilities may have heightened sensitivities to sounds, sights, smells, touch, and so forth, which may cause them great discomfort and even pain. If a child's brain is wired a certain way, there's not much we can do about that and we should make accommodations. At the same time, we can help the child learn strategies for coping with this world that's full of sounds, sights, smells, and so forth. This difficult situation is exacerbated if a child is unable to tell his family about these invasions to his peace; he communicates his discomfort through behavior that's seen as aberrant or inappropriate.

For example, if the sound of the vacuum cleaner makes a child go ballistic, then we shouldn't run it while the child is at home. We cannot say, "He must learn to tolerate the sound of the vacuum cleaner." This would be equivalent to me saying, "Benjamin must learn that we're going to put the furniture the way we like it. If he can't get around in certain rooms, that's just too bad!"

It's all about compromise and cooperation. We can vacuum the house when the child is at school. If visitors are coming right away, we can provide an accommodation by changing the child's environment: while Mom vacuums, Dad takes his son for a drive around the block. If that doesn't work, to heck with vacuuming for the time being!

Even as we make accommodations, however, we can try to lessen the negative effect the vacuum cleaner has on the child by giving him power over the situation. Efforts to help the child cope with the vacuum cleaner are not just about the vacuum cleaner, though. This may be the start of a child learning to better cope with other irritants and intrusions.

Here's a possible scenario. Tony's parents place the vacuum cleaner in the living room, unplugged. At first, Tony may be scared and tense in anticipation of the vacuum cleaner being turned on. Just the sight of it may trigger an outburst. If so, the vacuum can be moved to a more out of the way place, but not put totally out of sight. During the next few days, the vacuum is moved a couple of feet a day until it's back in the living room. By this time, hopefully, Tony is accustomed to seeing it and knows that it doesn't always make the noise he fears.

Without ever speaking about the vacuum cleaner, Mom can begin to work on it one day: opening the cover and changing the bag, wiping the dust off the insides, turning it upside down to clean the gunk off the roller, and so on. Mom could even ask Tony to take the full bag to the garbage, or find some other way for him to become more familiar with the vacuum monster. She might ask Tony to help her remove the threads that are wrapped around the carpet roller.

If he balks at any time, Mom stops and lets Tony go on his way. She leaves the vacuum cleaner where it is and goes back to it in a day or so. The next time she begins to work on the vacuum cleaner, she pushes it over the carpet (still unplugged) as if it's not working right and she's trying to figure out why. "Tony," she asks, "will you push it for a minute and let me get down on the floor to see what it's doing?" If he can grab hold of the handle, even for a moment, he's winning the war against the vacuum monster. He might even decide he likes pushing it around the house (turned off, of course); this gives him a sense of control over the monster.

At this point, Mom begins to talk with Tony about the noise: "This vacuum cleaner is really loud when we turn it on, isn't it? Sometimes it bothers me, too. You know, I think the next time I turn it on, I'm going to wear a pair of ear plugs. Maybe then the noise won't hurt my ears. And if that doesn't work, I think I'll wear your sister's headphones and listen to some soft music on the radio while I vacuum. Would you like to try these things, too?"

This, perhaps, could be the beginning of Tony achieving mastery over this particular part of his environment. If he's been unable to say exactly why the vacuum cleaner scares him so, we can only imagine. The sound, of course, is irritating to most of us. But to him, the sound may cause physical pain, or it may sound like a train about to run over him. He may also be afraid the vacuum cleaner will attack him or suck him up. Who knows?

All of us are afraid of things and we try to avoid them as much as possible. At the same time, we know there are some things we can't avoid, so we try to manage our fear. Children with autism or behavior disabilities are no different. We may not be able to take all of our children's fears away, but we can help them manage some fears by demystifying them or giving the child some control over them.

Behavior Management: Cruel and Unusual Punishment

Many professionals recommend "treatments" that force a child to confront his fears. Others use aversive methods as a way of controlling a child's behavior. Some so-called treatments include inflicting physical pain as a form of desensitization. If some of these same "treatments" were performed on typical adults, the perpetrators could probably be arrested for assault and battery. How can we let our children be hurt in the name of treatment? We must not allow their bodies, spirits, and hearts to be scarred and ruined by people who profess to know "what's best."

While writing this chapter, I received a call from a father who wanted some advice and information about how to handle the difficulties his son was facing at school. Eight-year-old Sean was labeled as having a sensory integration disorder. In a nutshell, the school was not making the accommodations and modifications Sean needed to be successful in the classroom; his needs were not being met and he became frustrated and angry. Educators listed Sean's behavior for his dad: talking back, ignoring the teacher's requests, refusing to "cooperate." Sean's dad felt (and I concurred) that these behaviors were Sean's way of communicating that his needs weren't being met; no one at school was hearing his cries for help. Sean felt powerless and overwhelmed, and he was trying to hold on to the only power he had left: the power to resist.

The principal and teachers at the school saw Sean's behavior as manipulative, inappropriate, and obsessive. They unofficially gave him an obsessive/compulsive label. Their "treatment" for Sean was isolation in a six foot square room (a closet), with a teacher's aide standing by as his guard. He was incarcerated in this fashion for several days in a row, during which time he was expected to "think about" his misdeeds. In addition, he was told to write letters of apology to teachers and classmates he had "offended." This "treatment" was directed by the school principal who had been a special ed teacher!

Sean's father and I agreed the isolation and demeaning treatment would only aggravate Sean's frustrations. But the learned professionals at school insisted their method was valid and beneficial: "Sean would learn that bad behavior would result in loss of privileges." Their form of treatment wasn't treatment at all; it was abusive punishment.

In their well-meaning efforts to help their children, some parents bounce their children from one treatment to the next, looking for a "cure" or some method that will put an end to unacceptable behaviors. Many methods use harsh, coercive treatments that are downright brutal and threatening, while others systematically peel away a child's sense of dignity and humanity. Parents must proceed with great caution. We must be very careful about methods that may do more harm than good.

Our sons and daughters aren't robots that need to be controlled. They are children who need to learn how to get along in the world. They need the ability to communicate in ways that will enable them to have their needs met. And we need to listen to what they tell us. Their behavior doesn't need to be perfect. It doesn't even need to "look" like other children's behavior. Children with physical disabilities move differently than other children and that's just fine. It's also fine if children with behavioral disabilities behave differently than other children.

The web site of the Autism Network International (an organization run by adults with autism) reflects the belief that supports should be aimed at helping people with autism compensate, navigate, and function in the world, and should not focus on changing them into "non-autistic" people or isolating them from the world. We'll become wiser if we learn from adults with disabilities.

A disability is simply one characteristic of a human being. But many parents of children with behavioral disabilities bemoan that their lives are impacted more negatively by their children's disabilities than are families whose children have orthopedic or cognitive disabilities. Parents who feel this way continue to see the problem of disability within the child instead of in the environment.

Supportive Environments

My friend and behavior specialist, Joe Schiappacasse, praises the use of videotape in trying to help us discover more about our children's behavior. He recommends videotaping over several hours or days and then watching the video over and over and over again. Of course, you don't follow your child around all day with a camera. You set up the camera and leave it for several days so the child becomes accustomed to it. When it's become just another piece of the furniture, you start recording without notifying everyone. Joe has described how he's viewed the same video tape again and again, and every time he watches it he learns more. The first time you see the obvious. The second time, you see things you didn't see the first time, and so on. This technique can be used at home or school. When we observe the total environment, not just isolated behavior incidents, we can learn what provokes a particular behavior, how the setting or its dynamics affect the child, and much, much more.

In our neighborhood inclusive elementary school, children with behavior disabilities were successfully included because the school focused on providing supports, as well as creating environments that *prevented* inappropriate behaviors from occurring. For example, in one classroom, Taylor, his mom, the teacher, and all his classmates discussed what Taylor needed to be successful. They also talked about things that might upset Taylor which could lead to outbursts of anger and frustration. Everyone in the classroom assumed responsibility for supporting Taylor and ensuring the environment was conducive to Taylor's success.

One day, as one of the fifth-graders walked to the pencil sharpener, he nonchalantly rapped his pencil on every desk he passed by. Most of the kids ignored it, but it really upset Taylor. A class meeting was held immediately and the Pencil Boy and everyone else agreed to (1) not rap the desks with pencils and (2) be more aware of other things that could surprise, distract, or upset Taylor.

No one considered this special treatment. It was simply an act of courtesy and support in a classroom where everyone was valued and everyone cared enough about each other to create an environment that worked for them all.

Children who bite themselves, bang their heads, or do other things to hurt themselves are communicating anger, frustration, boredom, loneliness, or something else. If we study the environment, we can often figure out what's causing the child's feelings. When negative influences are replaced with positive ones, and when the child's needs are met, self-injurious behaviors usually stop.

While we're trying to discover what's happening in a child's environment, we don't have to sit back and watch him hurt himself. But trying to restrain a child usually only makes matters worse; it's a temporary solution to a long-term issue. The ways a child behaves may have become a habit, just as smoking, finger-tapping, and other behaviors are habits. Trying to stop a habit simply doesn't work; one habit must be substituted for another. In the case of children who hurt themselves, we can suggest new habits.

If a child bites herself, she could be given something to bite on so she won't bite her arm: a folded washcloth or other safe object. If a child pinches himself, his parents can suggest other things to do with his hands. When he's upset, he can clap his hands, make a fist and pound the table, or hit a punching bag. Substituting one behavior for another is most effective if we ask the child what suggestions he has. He needs to "own" the solution.

It's important to realize that not all behaviors are fixed and permanent; a particular act may be transitional. However, if we focus all our attention on stopping a particular behavior, we probably guarantee it will become fixed and permanent. In an attempt to maintain some control over his life, a child may hold on to a behavior even tighter as a way of preserving power and autonomy.

Who Doesn't Self-Stim?

Self-stimulation is a great concern to many parents and professionals. We view rocking, arm waving, wrist shaking, perseveration, and other actions as disturbing and aberrant. But these behaviors must be serving a need or the child wouldn't do them. We need to respect a child's humanity as we try to discover ways to help him cope. And consider this: a child's behavior that stresses *us* may actually be calming to him!

People without disabilities self-stim all the time. Smoking, fingernail biting, hair twirling, beard stroking, nose picking, finger tapping, leg shaking, crotch rubbing, doodling, rocking in a rocking chair, and a variety of other actions are all common behaviors. All meet some need or we wouldn't do them! We see the behaviors of children with disabilities as aberrant only because they're not common and/or socially acceptable. If smokers gave up their habit and replaced it with arm flapping, society might very well begin to see arm flapping as socially acceptable behavior!

Few of us would let someone try to take away our self-stimming behaviors. We would angrily resist their efforts, and more importantly, we'd hold onto the behavior more tightly than ever and it would become even more important to us. Our kids are no different.

Like other behaviors, self-stimulation may fulfill a sense of power and control. And we all need to feel we have power over our lives, our bodies, and our environments. People without disabilities find various ways of coping throughout the day. When we're bored, stressed out, angry, lonely, scared, or anything else, we use coping mechanisms. And we each know how these behaviors help us, but other people may interpret our behaviors differently.

For example, in a company business meeting, the vice-president doodles as the president speaks. From our perspective, the vice-president must be bored. But worse, his doodling and lack of attention are perceived as disrespectful and rude. In reality, however, the vice-president is listening to every word. He doodles because it helps him concentrate on what the president is saying!

Pick your battles. If a self-stimming behavior isn't hurting anyone, learn to ignore it and let it go.

However, if you feel your child doesn't really want to continue the behavior but he's unable to stop on his own, then figure out positive, supportive ways of redirecting his actions, or help him find a substitute behavior. Some children feel locked into a behavior and they may want and need help to change it. We can show them alternatives and support their efforts to choose how and when to change.

Maybe we should provide a child who rocks with his own rocking chair. When a child is flapping his arms, maybe we should turn on some music so he can move to the beat of a song. These actions will let a child know we accept his behaviors and we're supportive of his need to do these things. When he knows his behaviors are okay, he doesn't have to hold on to them so tightly; he can change them, replace them, or stop doing them.

The child who stares off into space for hours ("zones out") may be organizing his thoughts about what happened yesterday or what's going to happen in an hour. Or maybe he's daydreaming, taking himself to some far off place that's peaceful and fulfilling. Maybe we should sit quietly next to him and stare off into space ourselves, letting our minds wander and our bodies be still.

Perhaps it's time to see our children as teachers. We can best help them by learning from them. Instead of making them try to walk in our shoes (by making them behave "normally") we should walk in theirs some of the time.

I'll never forget the day I walked in Benj's shoes and had my eyes opened. He was four and going to therapy all the time. The PT was trying to get him to maintain erect posture while seated on a bench. She wanted his torso, neck, and head aligned straight as his feet were flat on the floor and his palms rested on the bench next to his thighs.

His feet were where they should be, but the therapist couldn't get his palms to stay flat and his torso upright at the same time. Kneeling behind him, she would press his palms flat against the bench, but then his shoulders, neck, and head would droop forward. When she pulled his head, neck, and shoulders up straight, his palms would come up off the bench. It was like he was a puppet and she couldn't pull the right strings to get his body to do what she wanted it to do.

This went on for several more minutes: palms flat, good; uh-oh, shoulders, head and neck are drooping; pull them all up straight, but then the palms come up. Benjamin was getting tired and frustrated and so was she. I suggested she do something else.

Then I sat on the bench, trying to figure out what had been happening. I pretended to be Benjamin, with my feet flat on the floor, my palms flat on the bench and my torso, head, and neck maintaining upright posture in the "proper alignment." Guess what? I couldn't do it either! My feet were flat on the floor, but to get my palms flat on the bench, I had to drop my shoulders forward. I did it again and again, trying to hold my torso, shoulders, and head up straight while keeping my palms flat on the bench.

I was puzzled. What was going on here? Then it all became clear. My arms simply weren't long enough to keep my hands flat on the bench and sit upright! I showed the therapist and she was amazed. She had never considered that a child's arms might not be long enough to hold that posture.

At home that evening, I asked my husband and daughter to sit in a chair and assume this position. They could both do it. In fact, they could even flex their wrists so that part of their lower arms were touching the seat. I showed them what happened when I tried to do it and they were also amazed. "Gosh," my husband said, "I never knew you had such short arms!" Perhaps my arms *are* out of proportion to my tall body, but it's not something you'd notice if you saw me walking down the street. But I guess I am different from what we call the norm. Or could it be my husband and daughter are the ones who are different?

After that incident, I wondered how many other times people (including myself) tried to make Benjamin do things that his body simply wouldn't be able to do. From then on, I always tried to step into Benjamin's shoes in an attempt to learn how things were from his perspective. I've learned a lot, an awful lot. Step into your child's shoes; see things from his point of view.

Become a Good Detective

Many children with behavior needs are often unable to tell us what they need. In these circumstances, we need to become really good detectives.

Tyler, a fifth-grader with autism, was included in a general education classroom. An aide had been assigned to him, per his mother's request. From the perspective of his parents and teachers, things seemed to be going well for Tyler. What this really meant was that

Tyler wasn't "causing any problems" in the class. The aide, who was glued to Tyler, made sure he didn't disrupt the class.

Maggie, the parent of a child with a disability who also attended the inclusive school, was a sharp cookie who had the respect of the principal. She had provided teachers lots of good ideas on how to help her daughter. The principal asked Maggie to observe some of the classes where students with disabilities were included. He wanted her opinion about how well the school was supporting these students.

When Maggie observed Tyler's class, she saw things differently than Tyler's parents and teachers. The aide sat next to Tyler for most of the day. When he fidgeted or talked too loud, the aide whispered to him or put her hand on his arm. Tyler's body was a mass of movement: knees bobbing up and down, feet tapping, fingernails being chewed. Tyler spent most of his time looking around the classroom instead of paying attention or doing the work that was in front of him.

Every few minutes, Tyler attempted to get up, but the aide gently and firmly placed a hand on his shoulder to keep him seated. Watching all this, Maggie felt Tyler wanted to be anywhere than where he was. The aide was a very nice lady, but it really bothered Maggie that not enough was being done in the way of curriculum modifications and adaptations. Maggie thought if Tyler was engaged in meaningful and interesting activities he wouldn't want to get up every few minutes.

When it was time for a spelling test, the teacher called out a list of words. Because Tyler's handwriting was illegible, the aide wrote for him. Tyler liked spelling and was good at it, so he quickly rattled off the correct spelling of the words on the test.

A little later in the morning, the teacher (Mrs. Holmes) announced it was time to watch a filmstrip. Maggie was glad the teacher had picked up on Tyler's interest in mechanical things: Mrs. Holmes took Tyler with her to the library to get the AV cart. When they returned, Tyler pulled the screen down, loaded the filmstrip, turned off the overhead lights, and started the silent film. As Mrs. Holmes talked to the class about the scenes on the screen, Tyler quietly roamed the room.

She allowed Tyler to move around the darkened room while filmstrips were being shown; he never showed any interest in them and this was a good time to let Tyler expend some of his pent-up energy. Several times he walked between the projector and the screen. Once he stopped, curiously studying his shadow as it obscured the images on the screen. "Tyler, you need to move out of the way. We can't see," Mrs. Holmes instructed.

A minute or two later, Tyler moved toward the screen again, this time walking right up to it and pointing to a car in the city scene that was on the screen. "Hey! I've seen a car like that!" he reported with great pride and excitement. Maggie was thrilled to see Tyler showing interest in the filmstrip. But her joy was short-lived. "Tyler," Mrs. Holmes said firmly, "we're not talking about cars right now. Please move out of the way." Maggie couldn't believe it! Tyler was showing interest—he was trying to participate in his own way—and the teacher blew him off. Maggie's heart sank.

During lunch, Maggie walked the perimeter of the playground thinking. On her way back to Tyler's class after lunch, she detoured to another classroom, spoke with a student who has a disability, and left the class carrying the student's laptop computer. Arriving in Tyler's classroom, she asked Mrs. Holmes, "Would it be all right if Tyler and I sat at the table in the back? I want to show him something." Mrs. Holmes agreed. Tyler knew Maggie, so he was glad to sit with her and get away from the aide for awhile.

Opening the laptop, Maggie told Tyler about the different activities he could do on the computer. She showed him how to open the various programs and then she sat back and let Tyler explore the math, geography, and other fun activities.

For the next three hours, Tyler never tried to get up, never bit his fingernails, never shook his legs, and never took his eyes off the computer screen. He even skipped recess to continue exploring the computer. No one had ever seen Tyler be still for this long.

Near the end of the school day, Tyler discovered the computer's word processing program. Hesitating slightly, he found the five letters he was searching for and proudly typed his name. Maggie showed him how to increase the font size to make his name bigger on the screen. Tyler grinned, the biggest grin Maggie had ever seen. His blue eyes shining, he looked at Maggie and said, "Miss Maggie, if I had one of these, I could do my own spelling words, couldn't I?" Maggie's eyes misted ever so slightly.

Tyler, like all children, was successful when he was interested in what he was doing. His teachers and his parents saw Tyler's behavior—the constant motion and the apparent disinterest in his surroundings—as symptoms of his disability. Tyler was unable to verbally tell anyone, "I'm bored! This stuff doesn't interest me!" But his actions were screaming these exact feelings. No one but Maggie saw that. Why? Why didn't his parents or his teachers see it? Perhaps because they viewed Tyler through the lens of his disability label. Maggie saw him as a ten-year-old boy.

Discovering that a computer could fulfill many of Tyler's needs was good detective work on Maggie's part. But it was also Maggie's common sense and positive attitude. She viewed the environment through Tyler's eyes and she viewed Tyler with no prejudices or preconceptions.

Redirecting Exuberant Behavior

Some children are labeled "destructive." Their parents install gates all over the house or even lock their children in their rooms to keep them from tearing up the house. It's highly possible that children who turn over furniture, pull things off tables, or do other things that create chaos are trying to communicate frustration or boredom, or they may be trying to prove (to themselves or others) they have power over something. Children with behavior disabilities are just like other children in that the more parents make something a big "no-no," the more the child wants to do it.

Sherry described how her eight-year-old son regularly turned every chair in the house upside down. Why, she constantly wondered, did Josiah do this? I had no answer when she described the situation to me, so we batted around a few ideas.

Several days a week, Sherry's home was filled with a variety of professionals (behavior modification experts, therapists, and others) who provided "interventions" for Josiah. Between his hours at school and the hours of home therapy, Josiah had little free time. Perhaps he flipped the chairs over because he was sick and tired of being manhandled all the time; or because it was the only thing he felt he had control over. Maybe he did it because that's what he felt people were doing to him—therapists and professionals manhandled him all day, so he'd do the same to the chairs. Or maybe he flipped chairs because it was the only fun he had all day.

What if Sherry didn't make such a big deal out of Josiah turning the chairs over? What if she let Josiah know he could do it as long as he turned them back up the right way when Sherry asked him to? What if they made a game of it? Sherry and Josiah (or everyone in the family) could have a contest to see who could turn the most chairs over and then upright again in the shortest amount of time? What if, when Josiah turned the chairs over, everyone in the family tried to sit in them that way? When they fell out or hurt their behinds, they could all laugh and be silly. Sherry decided to try these ideas. In addition, she was going to consider letting go of some of the professional home therapies, and she also planned ways to give Josiah more control and power over his environment.

Just as children who use mobility devices may need the house arranged a particular way to ensure their freedom of movement, children with behavior disabilities may need their homes arranged in particular ways, as well. When typical children are small, parents don't usually leave breakables and other untouchables on the coffee table. We don't expect young children to have the self-control to stay away from things that are so very appealing. We need to use these same techniques if older children haven't yet acquired self-control.

Chemical imbalances may contribute to certain behaviors, so medication may be helpful. But children who are on medication—and their parents—are often on the roller coaster ride of their lives. A medication may initially work, then it doesn't, so another med is added, the behavior changes again, and so on and so on and so on. We must proceed with caution. We must also heed the little voices inside us that tell us what feels right and what feels wrong. Our gut instincts are usually right.

Let's frame behavior in a different way, as I described in the section on People First Language. Don't talk about your child's "behavior problems" or use other descriptions that are demeaning and degrading. Instead, describe your child as needing communication support or behavior support or something similar. Put the focus on what your child needs, not on what "problems" he has.

More Ideas for Behavior Supports

Following are ideas that have worked for parents whose children need behavior supports:

- If your child runs away from you while going to the car, in the mall, etc., have him march in step with you like soldiers do. Make it fun. Be silly. Swing your arms, let your child say "hut-hut." March side-by-side or have your child walk directly in front or in back of you.

- If your child runs away while he's in the yard (assuming you don't live on a busy street), enlist the help of all your neighbors. If you don't know all your neighbors, there's never a better time than now for your family to meet them. Let them all know wonderful things about your child, as well as the fact that he tends to bolt. Work out a plan with them: if they see your child in their yards or in the street, they can (1) call you immediately, (2) walk him back to your home, or (3) invite him in for a cookie while they call you to pick him up. And why not try running with your child one day? See the neighborhood from his perspective. Try to figure out what he's getting from the activity.

- Another option if your child runs out the front door or leaves the yard without your permission is to put a marker in the yard next door or two doors down. Ask the owner of the house if you can stick a pink flamingo (or something to get your child's attention) in the yard. Let your child know you understand his need to fly like the wind, but when he sees the pink flamingo, he needs to fly back home.

- For children who need to burn off energy or run around unfettered, set up a "running course" in your yard (or in the house, if possible). Use orange plastic cones (find them where bikes are sold) to define the course and let your child help set it up. When he needs to run, he can run through the course to his heart's content.

- If he likes to run in the grocery store, give him the responsibility of pushing the basket so he has something important to do. If he's not a good "driver," shop early in the day or during other times when the store isn't too crowded. Buy him his own small basket and tote it to the store with you.

- Try "reverse psychology." If your child likes to run out the front door, give him a reason to do it. Ask him to run and get the mail or the newspaper and run back as fast as he can. Or have him run to the neighbor's house to borrow something. In the grocery store, have him walk as fast as he can to the produce section to pick up three apples. In school have your child's teacher assign him jobs that require him to move around during the school day: taking the attendance slips to the office, taking books back to the library, etc.

- Some children might benefit from having a punching bag on which they release their energy or frustrations. In toy departments, you can also find a weighted, blow-up "dummy" which stands on the floor, that can be pummeled on a regular basis.

- Some children need to be calmed through "vestibular" (whole body) movement, like swinging. Hang a hammock sit swing in your child's room or the den. Encourage him to use it when he feels stress building. Also, rocking horses are good for some children.

- If your child needs his own quiet space when he's upset, raise his bed up on blocks, hang a dust ruffle or length of fabric from the bottom of the bed to the floor, and create a dark, cozy space for him to retreat to. Let him take a flashlight, pillow, or any other goodies he needs.

- Instead of making a child wear a harness to keep him close to you, utilize the wireless electronic devices that you both wear. When the child gets too far away from you, it beeps to let you know. Find them at electronic stores or through catalogs.

Many parents of children with behavior disabilities are learning to see beyond the disability label and understand that many aspects of their children's behavior are quite typical. Children *without* disabilities regularly push the limits, and they're looking to their parents for boundaries. They're simply being kids, doing what kids do. Children with behavior disabilities are no different. Parents and professionals often believe every naughty behavior is disability-related, when it could simply be typical age-appropriate behavior or unique personality characteristics. We must presume competence in, and have high expectations for, children with behavior issues, just as we do for other children.

MOBILITY AND POSITIONING

Crawling, creeping, rolling over, sitting up, pulling up to stand, walking, running, jumping, falling down, getting up and starting over again. Typical children do all these things and they're learning with every move they make. They're learning about their bodies, about moving through space, about their own power. They're learning what's dangerous and what's not. They're learning to pull the dog's tail, get their own juice, ring the front doorbell and giggle as they run away. They're learning they don't have to come every time their mothers call: they can hide in their rooms and yell "Boo!" when their moms come looking for them. They're learning about freedom.

Crawlers, walkers, crutches, and wheelchairs are all great tools that help many kids with disabilities move through space. Children need these tools at the proper time in their lives. Think independent mobility; think age-appropriate. A three or four-year-old shouldn't have to be pushed by her parents in an orthopedic stroller or a manual wheelchair. If she can't wheel a manual chair herself, she needs a power chair. A child who can walk in a walker, but is unable to have fun on the playground or in his own backyard while using it, needs the independent mobility of a manual chair (if he can push himself) or a power chair. Ditto a child in a walker who can't transfer into or out of his walker.

Providing your child with independent mobility doesn't mean you're giving up on your child walking, transferring, or anything else. You can still find many opportunities to help your child exercise and do other activities to help with leg strengthening, balance, and so forth. Put yourself in your child's shoes and consider what's really important. Would your daughter rather move slowly and with great caution through the hallways at school in her walker, or would she rather zoom past all the other kids on the way to recess? Would your son rather be stuck in one part of the house until someone takes the time to move him? Or would he like to wheel into the kitchen on his own to visit with you while you prepare dinner? We often focus on what *we* want without considering the child's viewpoint.

Think Freedom

When we think about independent mobility for our children, keeping the big picture in mind is critical. Parents often take the the narrow view that's shoved down their throats by the gatekeepers (physicians, professionals, and insurance companies) about "medical necessity." If we had the cash to buy our children what they need, we wouldn't even consider medical necessity as a criteria. But we're forced to follow the rules of the insurance companies which require the obligatory "letter of medical necessity" from the prescribing physician. So, let's play the game and follow the rules while thinking big at the same time.

If we limit our thinking to the medical necessity concept as the basis for selecting which mobility device our children need, we're essentially looking at getting the "minimum." To keep their costs down, insurance companies would prefer to pay the least amount of money on a claim.

An insurance company (and perhaps even doctors, therapists, or parents) often use the child's disability and prognosis as the determining factor in which type of mobility device is appropriate. But your child's current or future dreams are also critically important, as is your family's lifestyle. A mobility device that meets the child's minimum needs may not meet the child's overall needs for independence, freedom, and self-determination.

For example, if your child wants to play sports, take dance classes (yes, there are dancers who use wheelchairs), go bowling, or participate in similar activities—now or in the future—which mobility device is more appropriate: a walker, a manual wheelchair, or a power wheelchair? Ditto if your family enjoys outdoor activities: going for walks, cookouts and picnics, camping and so forth. What good is a mobility device if it doesn't allow your child to live a full life with the family?

Think long and hard, and consider what kind of life your child wants to lead when considering mobility. When it's time to deal with the insurance company about "medical necessity," do whatever you must do or have the physician write whatever he must write on the prescription pad to give your child more than the minimum. Give him freedom and independent mobility across all areas of his life.

Crutches and Walkers

Today's crutches have come a long way from the bulky wooden crutches of yesterday. They're lightweight, come in a variety of colors, and look cool! Some children may do well on crutches, but feel unsteady when leaning on the crutch tips. A variety of catalogs feature replacement tips that are larger, as well as other accessories to make crutches more comfortable and safer.

Pediatric posture control (reverse) walkers and traditional push walkers are helpful for many children. Pediatric reverse walkers are different than push walkers. They go around the back of the child and the child pulls it instead of pushing it. The design enables a child to stand up straighter as he walks. They can be outfitted with a variety of accessories, including forearm and torso supports.

The two-wheeled reverse walker has wheels in front and flat tips in back. Benjamin always used a four-wheeled model (the rear wheels are ratcheted so the walker won't roll backwards) because it rolled more smoothly and was easier to use.

It would seem the longer a child uses a walker, the better chance he'll have of walking independently one day. However, this isn't always the case. The long-term effectiveness of orthopedic walkers is a mixed bag.

A child's ability to walk with a walker is not always an indicator the child will one day walk unaided. Every child is different. Children who need walkers mainly for balance may be able to walk independently one day. Other children need walkers for balance and strength: their legs aren't strong enough to hold them up, but the strength in their arms—as they hold onto the walker—enables them to stay upright. As children grow and gain weight, their arm and leg strength may not increase enough to compensate for their heavier bodies. These children may or may not be able to one day chunk the walker and walk unassisted.

For many children, the limitations of a walker become obvious. For example, a child who always needs to hold on to the walker with both hands cannot open or close a door, pause for a snack or a drink, scratch his nose, or do anything else with his hands. A child may be unable to get in or out of the walker without assistance, so he always needs someone close by to help. Other children tire quickly or get cramps, and they may move so slowly they're unable to get where they want, when they want. In these instances, they have limited mobility, not independent mobility. For all these reasons and more, many older children choose to exchange their walkers for wheelchairs so they'll have independent mobility and freedom.

For some children, however, walkers are a very efficient form of independent mobility. They're able to run, play soccer, and engage in other physical activities. For them, walkers may provide independent mobility throughout their lifetimes.

It's important to look at the long term impact of our decisions. I'm glad Benjamin had the experience of walking in his walker when he was younger. At the same time, I wish we knew then what we know now. If we did, he would have enjoyed independence in a power chair at age two instead of having to wait until he was nine. His early years would have been much different had we done that.

Orthopedic Strollers

When Benj was about two, we bought (with help from insurance) a razzle-dazzle, expensive orthopedic stroller. It was easy to use, great for Benj's body, and it came with a lap tray and other helpful accessories. It didn't have that "institutional" look and I was often stopped in the mall by parents of typical children who said, "Oh, I love that stroller! Where did you get it?" Their jaws always dropped when I told them how much it cost.

However, we soon realized it wasn't so great after all. When other children saw Benjamin in the stroller (including kids who were younger than Benj), many approached us and said to their mothers, "Look at the baby, Mommy." At the time, I tried to believe Benjamin didn't hear or understand what they were saying, but in my heart I was afraid he did. We didn't want him to think he was a baby, but that's what he looked like in a stroller. We realized we should have bitten the bullet and purchased a wheelchair instead of the stroller, but we were stuck with it for awhile: insurance wouldn't pay for anything else for at least a year or so.

More importantly, however, in hindsight I realize how we limited Benjamin's opportunity for learning and discovery. He was positioned wonderfully in the stroller, but he had no way of moving on his own!

Knowing what I know today, I wouldn't recommend an orthopedic stroller to anyone. Children with disabilities under the age of two usually do fine in a regular stroller. There are so many on the market today, one is bound to be almost perfect. If necessary, we can use little pillows and rolled up blankets to help our children maintain their posture in regular strollers. But by the time a child is two, we need to be looking at equipment that will give a child independent mobility.

Manual Wheelchairs

There are incredible wheelchairs available today! Getting the right one requires research on your part. Don't count on the experts to know what's best for your child. The salesman who recommended the first manual wheelchair we purchased assured us Benj would be able to wheel himself "once he got the hang of it." But Benj never could move himself more than a few feet in that chair. Since it was our first experience, we didn't know what to look for, so it seemed natural to trust the salesman's wisdom. What we learned from watching Benj was that he couldn't get his arms back far enough to grab the wheels and give them a good stroke. When we bought his second manual chair, we found one with adjustable wheels that could be moved forward.

But even with the second manual chair, we were still not pleased. Around the house and at school, Benj could get around by himself pretty well, although he could never get from place to place as fast as wanted. This new chair was state-of-the-art and lightweight, but pushing was hard work for Benj. He tired easily and then needed a push. We were happy to help, but he didn't like it. I'm sure he felt trapped between a rock and a hard place. With no more energy, he would ask us to push him, but then he wasn't in control.

It wasn't until my good friend Tom chastised me for my shortsightedness that we decided to get Benj a power chair. (Benj did have a power scooter in the meantime. These devices are described next.) Tom also has cerebral palsy and his life experiences gave me more wisdom than I ever received from professionals.

Tom didn't have independent mobility until he got his first power chair at age twelve. He described how it changed his life and how, for the first time, he felt in control of his life. Ed Roberts, who you met in the history chapter, always told a similar story. On a network television interview, Ed related how when he was being pushed, people always talked to the "pusher," ignoring Ed as if he wasn't even there. When Ed got his power chair, people had to talk directly to him. For the first time in his life, he felt powerful.

Tom helped me see into the future. "If Benjamin can't push himself well in a manual chair, Kathie, how do you think he's going to feel when he's in middle school?" Tom asked. "How's he gonna get a girlfriend? Think he wants to meet some girl and say, 'You don't mind pushing me, right?' If Benj has a power chair, he can say, 'Come sit on my lap and we'll ride off into the sunset!' Which will Benjamin want, Kathie?"

Duh! It didn't take me long to figure out how right Tom was. And Ed's tales of independence and power came to the forefront of my thinking. Their real-life experiences helped me understand what was really important in Benjamin's life.

A manual wheelchair is the right choice if—and it's a big if—the child can push herself successfully for more than a short distance and over a variety of terrains. But even if a child can push herself well, can she do other things she wants to do? Can she play at recess, chasing other children or letting them chase her? Can he shoot baskets or move quickly across the soccer or softball fields? As a teenaged babysitter, can she carry a baby on her lap and wheel herself? *Independent mobility is more than efficient movement; it's being able to live the life you want!*

Ron's mother described how his manual chair was perfect until he met new friends when he entered high school. This group of boys hung out in their yards, sitting around talking, tossing a football, and so forth. But Ron was unable to get through the grass on his own. He wanted to be part of the group, but he didn't want to be seen as powerless and dependent, always having to ask a friend to push him across the lawn. Ron knew his friends didn't mind pushing him, but that wasn't the point. He needed to feel competent and powerful, and he didn't in the manual chair. His mom got busy and got him a power chair so he could be "one of the guys."

A manual chair is right for your child only if she can truly be independent in it. If she is unable to push herself over a variety of terrains, for longer distances, and in a variety of circumstances, forget the manual chair and get her a power chair instead.

Unfortunately, parents often don't know if a manual chair is right until they've already bought it! To avoid this dilemma, get a demo or loaner chair from a dealer and try it before you buy. If you do get a manual chair paid for by insurance, then find it's not right for your child and want to get a power chair, your insurance may still pay for it. The physician would need to write a letter of medical necessity saying why the child needs a power chair. In other words, the physician would need to describe how "unable" your child is in the manual chair to "prove" a power chair is needed. If that's what it takes to get it, go for it!

If a manual chair is right for your child, do your homework. There are many, made by a variety of manufacturers. There's lots to research: frame types, seating systems, arm rests, foot rests, seat belts, brake types, and more. Don't leave anything to chance.

If your child currently uses a manual chair but she has difficulty pushing herself, there are several products on the market that turn a manual chair into a power chair with the installation of a small motor and steering device that attach to the chair. I've not personally known anyone who has used these products, but they might be worth a closer look.

I recently came across an ad for a manual wheelchair that, instead of pushing it with your arms, you pedal it with your feet! It really looked interesting. The advertisement showed an adult using the chair, so I don't know if a pediatric version is available. The ad stated only a slight push of the feet was needed to propel the chair.

Scooters

A three-wheeled power scooter is a great option for many children. If you're not familiar with these, they're similar to the adult scooters provided for shoppers at Wal-Mart and other stores. Against the therapist's advice, we got one for Benjamin when he was in the first grade. It was a life-changing experience for him and us. For the first time in his life, at age six, he went outdoors all by himself. Previously, someone always had to be close by. If he was in his walker, I needed to be near in case he got stuck or his knees buckled. In his manual chair, I needed to be there to push when he tired.

The day we brought the scooter home, Benj went out the front door by himself. Watching from the window, I saw him drive to the end of the driveway and back again. Then he did it again, and again, and again. The glow on his face was as bright as the sun and I couldn't take my eyes off this exciting sight. At one point, my eyes teared up as I saw Benj mosey to the edge of the driveway, where he bent over and pulled a handful of wildflowers up. He drove to the porch, clutching them tightly. When I opened the front door, he thrust the tiny blooms at me and proudly announced, "Here, Mom. I picked you some flowers." At age six, Benj finally had the ability to do things his sister and other children did when they were two. As I've said before, we inadvertently delay our children's development when we don't provide them with the tools they need, at the appropriate time! I've done it plenty of times, but I'm finally wising up.

In the scooter, there were other things Benj could do for the first time in his life. In the grocery store, for example, he and his sister roamed the aisles without me. Soon, Benj would find me, racing up to my basket at warp speed. In the little basket attached to the front of his scooter would be something Benj wanted me to buy him. "Please, Mommy, please can I have this?" he would ask. He wasn't walking, but he was doing what he wanted to do, going where he wanted to go, on his own! Again, this was an activity done by typical three or four-year-olds. Benj didn't have the ability to do it until he was six.

At school, he could finally race out to the playground and actually play, instead of sitting, hoping someone would hang out by him. He chased his friends and they chased him. He was, in fact, the envy of the playground crowd. Other kids routinely begged, "Benj, can I have a ride on your scooter?" Why, I berated myself, didn't we get him a power scooter when he was younger? You know why: because we had listened to professionals who focused on walking instead of mobility.

The only downside of the scooter was that Benj couldn't use it to sit at his desk or the dinner table. The seats on most scooters rotate 90 degrees, enabling the user to get on and off easier. We tried having Benj park his scooter parallel to his desk, with the seat rotated so he was facing the desk the right way, but it didn't work well. His feet weren't supported, he had to park exactly right every time, and kids had to position their desks away from Benj's. As a result, he always had to transfer into a regular chair or his manual chair in the classroom and at home. This was fine with me and the folks at school, but it wasn't fine for Benj. When he wanted to move, he wanted to move, and he didn't want to have to wait for someone to transfer him. Still, the scooter brought Benj his first taste of real freedom.

Scooters are probably best for children who can (1) transfer themselves, (2) bear weight, and (3) walk with crutches, a walker, or independently for short distances. The scooter can then be used for longer distances, for having fun on the playground, and so forth. Most scooters don't provide the level of posture support that wheelchairs can, so that's something to take into consideration.

Many scooters can be easily disassembled and transported in the back of a van (or a car with a large trunk). I could pop the seat off Benjamin's, remove the batteries (always get two), and easily pick up the frame and place it in the back of a mini-van. In a van with a ramp or a lift, the scooter could be transported without disassembly.

Power Wheelchairs

Many power wheelchairs are marvels of technology. Benjamin's Permobil is. He can push one button and the chair will stand him up, with his knees supported by a knee pad. A chest bar, to keep the torso upright, can be attached. Standing is good for weight bearing and it enables him to reach things or rise to be face-to-face with someone else. The push of another button will raise the entire seat up, which also enables him to get up higher to see or reach.

For younger children, Permobil makes a similar power chair that—with a push of a button—will lower the seated child to the floor. It's so cool! The seat moves forward and then down. This feature was designed with young children in mind: they play on the floor and sit on the floor in circle time at school. Today's power chairs feature a variety of accessories that give children the ability to participate in typical activities and be more in control of their lives. A power chair that will go *up and down stairs* is being developed. Fitted with multiple wheels, gyroscopes to keep it level, and all sorts of other wizardry, it's expected to be on the market soon. Benj is getting one of those!

Investigate power chairs carefully and try to get a loaner or a demo for your child to try. When we looked into the Permobil, the distributor had a demo chair Benj tried out at home for a week or so.

Parents and professionals often believe some children with disabilities won't ever be able to use a power wheelchair. But I can't think of *any* physical condition that should prevent a child from achieving independent mobility in a power chair. Nothing is impossible! The joystick that controls the chair can be modified in numerous ways. It can be mounted anywhere on the chair, so that a slight push of a finger, hand, chin, head, wrist, elbow, knee, foot, or any other part of the body can get the user on his way. A puff and sip breathing tube will also work.

Many parents believe a child with a cognitive disability doesn't have the "intelligence" to operate a power chair. But walking is actually a much harder skill than using a wheelchair! Let's think about a child (Laura) who has only a cognitive disability. None of us would say, "Laura is unable to walk because she has a cognitive disability." This would be a ludicrous statement. Once Laura has learned to walk, she's able to go forward, sideways, and backward. She knows to watch out for other people; she doesn't routinely walk into walls; she knows to go around, slow down, or stop when something or someone is in her path. All of these are actually quite difficult skills, which require the integration of mental and physical abilities.

Using a power wheelchair is a less difficult skill than walking. There aren't as many body parts involved and coordination and balance aren't as important. If a child with a cognitive disability can learn to walk, how can we say a child with both cognitive and physical disabilities is unable to use a power wheelchair?

The same issues are involved when a child has a visual disability. I don't know anyone who would say, "Kenneth can't walk because he's blind." Of course he'll learn to walk! He learns to move around his house initially by touch, and over time, he navigates without touch, assuming no one has moved the furniture. In other places, he may use a cane or a guide dog, or he may hold the arm of a companion. But his visual disability doesn't prevent him from walking. Why would it prevent him from using a power wheelchair?

A child with a visual disability who is unable to walk can operate a power chair while holding one arm out to feel, just as he would if he was walking. Small, flexible tubes or springs may be affixed to the sides of the chair so he can feel or hear when he gets close to something, like the devices on cars or trucks. Sonar-like devices that emit an audible beep to alert him to obstacles could be used. He could hold a cane out in front of him or use a guide dog, just as he'd do if he walked.

When presented with the independence afforded by a power chair, children become highly motivated and can show us just how capable they really are. For children with mobility impairments, there is no greater power, no greater magic, no greater freedom than what a power chair can provide. If you want to see a miracle, put your kid in a power chair and observe the shining eyes and the euphoric smile as he savors the sweet joy and awesome power of independence.

Wheelchair Accessible Vans

If your child gets a power wheelchair, an accessible van is a must. Even with a manual chair, an accessible van is helpful.

We've had two accessible vans. The first was a factory-modified mini-van and the second is a full-sized Ford van we had modified. In the mini-van, the middle bench seat was removed to make room for Benj's chair. There were two bucket seats up front and the bench seat in the back. But when we wanted to go on trips or haul a bunch of kids somewhere, the mini-van was just too small. In addition, when the four of us were together, someone always had to sit in the way back and conversation was almost impossible.

We sold the mini-van and bought a used full-sized Ford van. It was a "custom" van, so it already had a raised roof. A company that specializes in accessible vans lowered the floor and installed a telescoping ramp. Many full-sized vans have a wheelchair lift, but the ramp worked best for us to ensure family togetherness.

If a wheelchair lift had been installed, both middle seats would have been removed to accommodate the lift. We wanted to keep the seat behind the driver in place so the four of us could all be closer together for conversation. The telescoping ramp (which we open and close manually) didn't take up as much room as the lift, allowing us to keep the seats the way we wanted. The seat closest to the side doors was removed and this is where Benjamin sits in his power chair when we travel.

After we bought our second van, I learned that used wheelchair accessible vans are often available at very reasonable prices from state agencies that serve people who use wheelchairs. If you're in the market for one, check with your state voc-rehab office, organizations that serve people with mobility impairments, the para-transit system, and other state or private agencies.

Is Your Home Wheelchair Accessible?

Not only do we need accessible vehicles, we also need accessible homes. Unfortunately, some families are able to transport a child's chair, but the chair stays in the car or the garage because the home isn't accessible. Children must have independence and freedom in their own homes!

Consider the situation of many older people who are forced into nursing homes when they can "no longer care for themselves." The reality is that many people *could* continue living in their own homes, with little or no outside help, if their homes were accessible.

When we don't create barrier-free environments, we limit our children's independence. It's our responsibility to do whatever it takes to ensure our children's success in our homes. A variety of modifications can make our homes accessible.

Wider doorways are essential. If you own your own home, replace narrow doors and door frames with thirty-six inch wide doors and frames. If you, your spouse, or other members of your family are the least bit handy, you can do this. Call on your neighbors or other members of you community for help if you can't do it yourself. Perhaps some local handymen, a high school shop class, or a Scout troop could help if you provide the materials.

Alternatively, you can widen doorways by two inches simply by replacing the hinges. Several mail order catalogs (I've never seen them in hardware stores) sell an offset hinge that allows a door to be opened two inches wider than the standard hinge allows.

Floor coverings may make the difference between an accessible home and an inaccessible one. In a power chair, a child can easily roll over any surface. But in a manual chair, a child may be unable to wheel across carpet. The weight of the chair and the child causes the chair to sink into the carpet, making movement difficulty. It's equivalent to always having to push uphill. The easiest surfaces to roll across are wood floors, vinyl, ceramic tile, or flat, tightly woven carpet with no pad underneath.

We replaced our worn out shag with a commercial grade flat berber in our living room and den (with no pad). Doing it yourself is not hard. When no pad is used, the carpet is simply glued down. (Just get a good pair of knee pads.) Ditto other floor coverings. I installed ceramic floor tiles in the hallway and kitchen. Home stores have all kinds of products to enable you to do a "professional" job.

A larger bathroom, with enough space to turn a chair around, is important. In our house, the kids' long and narrow bathroom was inaccessible. Beyond the vanity area, the toilet and tub were enclosed in a tiny space with a twenty-eight inch door. We knocked out that wall completely to open up the room. Then we knocked down the wall between the bathroom and the den, took three feet from the den, and built a new wall. This gave Benj the room to turn around. If you can make your bathroom larger, do it. If not, figure out ways to modify it so your child can get in and out of the bathroom while using a mobility device.

Steps and high thresholds may be barriers to children getting in or out of their homes or moving between different rooms. There's not much to do about a flight of stairs (until the stair climbing wheelchair comes out), but we can eliminate smaller barriers.

In our home, there was a four inch drop from the kitchen door into the garage. With a big bucket of ready-mix concrete, a trowel, and a couple hours of my time, we soon had a ramp so Benj could come into the house from the garage. A similar condition existed from the sliding glass door onto the deck. I was prepared to build a simple wooden ramp, when—lo and behold—my brother presented me with one. He had bought a house from an older couple and they had a small ramp from their back door to the garage. Since my brother didn't need it, he bequeathed it to us and it fit perfectly.

A variety of portable aluminum ramps are available through catalogs. If you have a split-level home, you may be able to make it wheelchair accessible with a ready-made ramp or you could build a wooden ramp. Use your good judgment. If the ramp is too steep, not only will your child not be able to negotiate it, but it'll be dangerous for everyone.

If you're not able to make your home barrier-free, and you want your child to be independent, you might have to bite the bullet and move into a different home. Before we bought our current home, I told the realtor: don't show us any homes with steps or sloped yards. In the mountains of Colorado, where the majority of homes are split level or two story, this was a tall order. The first five houses she showed had two or three steps up to the front door, steps between rooms, or a yard that was part of a mountain. The last house—the one we bought—only had the two minor barriers I described above. We moved into this house from a full two-story, totally inaccessible home in Texas.

Parents have told me they "know" they should get an accessible home, but they "don't want to give up the family room in the basement" or they "can't afford to move, and besides, they don't mind helping their child move around the house." There are times when we need to make sacrifices for our children and this is definitely one of them. We can't expect our children to become independent adults if they don't learn how to be independent as children. There's no magic switch to flip when they turn twenty-one. It's far better for us to make sacrifices now, than to ask our sons and daughters to sacrifice a lifetime of freedom and self-determination.

Imagine you needed to use a chair after car accident or stroke. Would independence in your own home be important? Would you want to be dependent on others simply because you couldn't get around in your own home or yard?

Seating and Positioning Devices and Other Ideas

Seating and positioning devices help children sit up and be properly supported. But being upright isn't just about helping our children's bodies, it's also about helping their minds. When in an upright sitting position, children can experience typical activities, which helps them grow and develop.

Babies without disabilities are usually sitting up unassisted between five to eight months of age. A baby's view of the world is very different when he's sitting up than when he's lying down. He can see and touch things in different ways, and he learns from these new experiences. Think about the opportunities babies without disabilities have and try to replicate those opportunities in your baby's life.

When children are small, they'll fit in regular baby carriers, strollers, baby walkers, and other devices. We can stuff little pillows or rolled up blankets around them for posture support. As our children get bigger and grow out of these typical products, we need to look into corner chairs, positioning seats, and other equipment. These can enable children who can't sit independently to see the world from a different perspective, interact with others, and learn from their environments. Many kind and loving parents inadvertently delay their children's development when they don't find ways to help their children sit up and participate in the world around them.

Lorraine thought she was doing the best for Sasha, her four-year-old daughter. Sasha had a feeding tube and other medical needs, and the doctors warned Lorraine that Sasha could easily get infections that would land her in the hospital again.

Lorraine's house was a busy one; Sasha was the youngest of five children. To protect Sasha from germs, Lorraine kept her daughter in the "safest" room in the house—the master bedroom. And because Sasha "couldn't do anything" (sit up, talk walk, etc.), she stayed in her crib all day. The room was bright, and the crib was filled with mobiles and toys for Sasha to look at when she wasn't asleep. Lorraine and other family members regularly visited the room to read to Sasha, play with her, hug her, and such. But except for visits to the doctor's office, Sasha never left the room!

By the time she was four, doctors threw in a "severely mentally retarded" label. This beautiful four-year-old child didn't know there was a world outside her parent's bedroom. How could she *not* have cognitive delays under these circumstances?

Lorraine got connected with parents who supported her efforts to protect her daughter, while simultaneously allowing Sasha to be a four-year-old. Little by little, Sasha's world changed. For example, after her mother got her a floor chair, Sasha began watching videos and children's TV shows with her six-year-old sister in the family room. When Dad played in the yard with the other children, he took Sasha out, too, to let her feel the grass between her toes and the sunshine on her face—for the first time in her life.

Sasha began sleeping in a regular bed with her sister, she joined her family at the table for meals, and took her place as a valued family member. The metamorphosis is on-going. Friends who haven't seen Sasha in awhile can't believe she's the same little girl they knew in the crib. Neither can her mother: Lorraine watched her daughter go from a somber, quiet "baby" to a laughing, engaged four-year-old.

When a baby or child is sitting up, people treat her differently. It's difficult for interactions to take place when a child is always lying down. When she's sitting up, she can see the world around her, learn new things, play with toys, and interact with mom, dad, brother, and sister in ways that are impossible when she's lying down.

As children with physical disabilities grow and change, the devices they use must change. A two-year-old, for instance, even if she's small for her age, shouldn't be using baby equipment. People (including her parents) will see her as a baby and treat her as one. If she's not able to walk, she needs independent mobility in a wheelchair. The positioning chair she used as a one-year-old might still fit her and provide good support, but she'll still look like a one-year-old in it. Instead of putting her in this "baby chair" when she's not in her wheelchair, buy a child's rocking chair and pad it as necessary. Or use a bean bag chair or some other type of seating that's appropriate for a two-year-old. With a bean bag chair, someone needs to be close by if the child cannot move herself. She could be in danger of suffocating if she somehow turned her mouth and nose into the vinyl and couldn't move.

Another option is to use the big back rests with arms, the ones people use to sit up comfortably in bed. To help Benj sit up on the floor, we placed one of these against the base of the sofa. It prevented him from tipping backwards and sideways.

When Benj and Emily were young, a child-size table and chairs were perfect. They played, had snacks, and looked at books together. The therapist made a heavy cardboard insert that supported Benj in the right places.

Do whatever it takes to enable your baby or young child to participate in life from an upright position. Search catalogs and roam stores for chairs, the backrest bed pillows, and other seating and positioning devices. While many products have been specially designed for children with disabilities, products found in regular stores may work just as well. They cost less, we can take them back if they don't work out, and they enable a child to benefit from a more natural environment.

If your eight to twenty-four-month-old baby can't move around on the floor by crawling or rolling, give him the opportunity to explore his surroundings the way other babies explore. Instead of leaving him in a play pen, the crib, or in one spot on the floor, move him to different places throughout the day. Put him under the kitchen table, up close to the sofa, in the corner by the bookshelves, or any other safe place a crawler would go. Put him on a blanket and drag him around the house. Go fast, go slow; make it fun!

Mimic what he'd be doing if he could move on his own. Where do crawlers love to go? Everywhere they're not supposed to! But, oh how they learn when they're there. Drag the blanket into the bathroom so he can see what's behind the toilet. While you're cooking supper, let him play in the lowest cabinets, pulling everything out. And don't forget to do the same thing in the yard, at the park, and other places outdoors.

At the typical age when children learn to stand, help your baby stand any way he can. Look into buying a standing frame. If you don't have the money and if insurance won't pay, make one out of PVC pipe, lawn chair webbing, and a big piece of plywood. Look at pictures of standing frames in speciality catalogs as a model. When kids are at the age they typically learn to stand, their minds need their bodies to be upright, one way or another.

What can they do in a standing frame? Watch TV, have a snack or play with toys on the table you pull up in front of her, play at the sink in the bathroom or the kitchen and splash water everywhere (as you grin behind her back and tell her to not make a mess). We had two standing frames for Benjamin: a free-standing one that could be placed anywhere and one that leaned against the kitchen or bathroom counters where he played with water and cups and stuff, and got water, water, everywhere.

It's important for children to stand and bear weight so their bones will grow and become strong. Even if they're never able to walk, they still need strong bones. Weight bearing also helps their bones grow in length. Many children who never bear weight on their legs don't grow in height the way they typically would.

Children who push themselves in manual wheelchairs often find their feet sliding forward off the footrest. When this happens, the child's entire posture may be affected, and she may not be able to use her arms and shoulders or hold her head up. To remedy this, get a two or three inch wide piece of webbing and attach a plastic buckle set to it (webbing and buckles are available at fabric stores). This "leg belt" will be used to keep the child's feet from slipping off the footrest. Decide the best placement for the belt: at the ankles or the knees (for Benj, we put this belt up by his knees). As your child is seated in the chair, run the belt behind the upright tubes of the frame, then bring it around to the front and buckle, pulling it tight. Make sure the belt is in front of your child's legs, not behind. Wrap some tape or a small bungee cord around the tubes, just below the placement of the belt to keep the belt from sliding down the frame.

Cover the seat cushion in your child's wheelchair (or other seating surface) with slinky fabric. This will make it easier for you to position him and easier for him to move his bottom around in the seat. The slinky fabric reduces the friction, enabling his bottom to slide more easily.

If your child has difficulty moving around in bed, buy or make sheets that are slinky (high quality cotton or polyester). Make sure to use fabric that breathes so your child won't perspire all night. You may also want to buy or make slinky pajamas. Benj sleeps in long underwear that's "silk-like." Slinky-to-slinky fabrics enable a child to roll over and move around easier.

When children wear plastic orthotics, their feet often perspire a great deal, which can lead to athlete's foot and other conditions. Sprinkle foot powder inside the sock so it doesn't go everywhere. Antiperspirant doesn't just work on underarms; it works great on feet, too!

If your child has trouble holding her head up, let her wear a soft cervical collar (the kind people wear after getting whiplash in a car accident). Some children will tolerate wearing these, some won't. The therapist may or may not like it, but if your child likes it and if it helps her keep her head upright, go for it. You can find these in drug stores and catalogs, available without a prescription.

A transfer board can save your back and your child's bottom when moving your child from the bed to a wheelchair. A variety of devices are available from catalogs and medical equipment outlets. The simplest ones are smooth wood, about a foot wide and two or three feet long. One end is placed under the child's bottom on the bed and the other end is placed in the wheelchair seat (while the chair is parked next to the bed). Instead of picking your child up to transfer him into the chair, you simply help him slide from the bed to the chair, then remove the board. A fancier model is plastic and has a round disk fitted into a channel that runs down the center of the board. The user sits on the disk, and the disk slides down the channel.

Transfer belts may also be helpful. These can be purchased or you can make one with sturdy fabric or wide webbing. In its simplest form, the belt is buckled around the waist of your child. Attached grips on each side allow you to hold onto the belt (instead of your child's body or clothes) when helping him transfer. Alternatively, you could take a long canvas belt (like a martial arts belt), wrap it around your child's waist a couple of times, tie it in front or back, and grab one of the layers to move your child.

SUCCESS BEGINS AT HOME: HELPERS FOR ALL KIDS

Your home is your family's castle. Make sure it's an accessible, user-friendly castle, regardless of your child's age or disability label. Your child will learn more in his own home environment than in any other. If he can't be successful at home, we cannot expect him to be successful in other settings. Professionals often try to make our children fit into a particular environment, instead of changing the environment to fit the child. Let's not do that to children in their own homes!

From the kitchen to the bathroom, there are many ways we can help meet our children's needs and ensure their independence, self-determination, and success. First, I'll review some basic guidelines for all around the house, then we'll look at different rooms in the house.

Electrical Things On and Off

Reaching the switches on table lamps and then turning the little knobs can be almost impossible some children. We purchased "touch discs" at Wal-Mart for about $8.00 each. The device consists of a gold-colored disc about two inches in diameter which is connected to a small transformer box via a thin electrical cord. The disc can be placed on a table top. The lamp is plugged into the transformer box, which is plugged into the wall. A slight touch on the disc will turn the lamp on and off.

You can also buy do-it-yourself thumb switches at your local hardware department to replace traditional on/off switches on lamps, radios, and other electrical gizmos. Benjamin's lava lamp, for example, didn't have an on/off switch. It was on when plugged in; off when unplugged. He couldn't reach down to plug it in every night, so a thumb switch, placed about six inches away from the base of the lamp enables him to turn it on and off by himself.

If the light switches on the wall are too high, lower them by installing a new switch plate several inches lower than the existing plate and connect the wires behind the wall. Then cover the old switch plate with a flat cover. This is not hard to do; get a do-it-yourself book or ask a handy friend to help. An alternative is to purchase plastic rods that attach to the existing switch plate. They hang down low enough for a child or someone using a wheelchair to operate.

Environmental control units (ECUs) can be programmed to turn a variety of electrical devices and appliances on and off with the touch of a button or a remote control. Find them at Radio Shack, home stores, and through catalogs.

Going In and Out

Lever door handles are easier to use for those who have difficulty grasping and turning round door knobs. They're also better for everyone in the family! When my arms are full, I can push the lever handle with my elbow to open the front door.

A keyless front door lock can be a great solution for many children who have difficulty holding small objects or for those with visual disabilities. These locks use a touch pad instead of a key. Punching in the right code unlocks the door.

In the Kitchen

Children with disabilities will one day be on their own—yes, they really will. There's no time like the present to help them learn how to cook and clean and do all the rest of the stuff we do in our kitchens every day. For many of us, the kitchen is the heart of the home. It should be a heart that embraces our children with disabilities.

Family dining is important. In a family's life, eating doesn't just fill a biological need, it also fills a social need. When we're together at mealtimes, we fill our bellies with food and our souls with companionship. Babies and young children should be provided with seating or positioning aids that enable them to sit at the table with everyone else. If a typical high chair doesn't provide the right support, use cushions or other supports around your child. Also, some orthopedic positioning inserts can be used in regular dining chairs.

As children grow, they may not fit into a high chair any longer, but a regular dining room chair is too big. A bar stool with arms can provide a secure feeling. Cushions or foam can be inserted to help keep the child balanced. Some bar stools have height-adjustable legs, or you can cut the legs down to size to fit your table.

Consider making a seat insert that can be strapped into an adult-sized chair. First, take measurements. With your child seated and his hips and knees each at a ninety degree angle, measure the width of his shoulders and bottom, the seat depth (from the tailbone to the back of the knees), and the leg length from the soles of feet to the back of the knee (for a leg support/footrest). Using these measurements, make a custom-fitted insert out of plywood. Make the back support as high as your child needs; it could surround his shoulders if necessary. Paint it or stain it, and add cushions and a seat belt to hold your child in place. Next, place the seat insert in the adult-sized chair, and construct a seat platform and a back support that will hold the seat insert in the right place for your child. Add straps to keep the seat insert firmly attached to the chair.

Some children need support for many parts of their bodies. A footrest gives a child a sense of stability; it's something to keep him steady, something to push on. Armrests can also be extremely important for many children. Soft but sturdy supports at the rib cage, around the waist, and at the hips and thighs can also make the difference between a child sitting up straight and secure or leaning precariously. Wedges to separate the hips and knees, or soft bands to keep them together may also be important.

Eating Aids

High-tech feeding machines can help children eat with little or no assistance. Found primarily in catalogs, these machines have a mechanical arm to scoop the food and bring it to the mouth.

Children may need spoons, knives, and forks with built-up, non-slip handles. Some can be bent or angled to help a child guide the food to his mouth. You can use the utensils you already have and make your own built-up handles by using soft foam insulation tubing from the hardware store. Alternatively, visit a craft store and buy the clay you can bake in your home oven. Form the clay around the handle of a typical spoon or fork, then let your child grip it tightly while it's soft. After the impression of his hand is made in the clay, bake the whole thing in the oven. After it hardens, it will be a perfect match for your child's hand.

Even with adapted utensils, many children may still be unable to feed themselves. If that's the case, serve as much finger food as possible, and make frequent exceptions to what's appropriate to eat with fingers and what's not. Green beans are hard for Benjamin to pick up with a fork or a spoon, so they're finger foods for him at home. When we go out to eat, he usually orders chicken strips and fries, so his table manners (eating with fingers) are just fine. Children need to be able to feed themselves in whatever way they can.

Plates with built-up sides allow a child to scoop food onto a fork or spoon without pushing it off the plate and onto the table. These are available from specialty catalogs. For less money, however, you can find comparable items in regular stores: children's plates and bowls with one side higher than the other, and divided plates with high sides (made for the microwave). You can use your own plates, and purchase a metal or plastic edge that clamps onto the plate. These are found in specialty catalogs.

Plates and bowls with non-slip bottoms are available from specialty catalogs, or you can make your own. Cut non-slip fabric to fit the bottom of a dish and glue it on.

To keep everything in place at the dinner table, cut a length of non-slip fabric for a placemat (find it at Wal-Mart or other general merchandise store, in the housewares department). In our family, it's always been important that Benjamin doesn't feel he's the only one who needs extra help. So I bought a large roll of non-slip fabric and snipped off four pieces to make place mats for all of us. This miraculous stuff comes in various colors and it's inexpensive. We couldn't live without it. It keeps just about anything from sliding: dishes, books, toys, and more. Benjamin's classrooms were never without a supply of it. It kept him from sliding off the bench in music class, so it holds bottoms securely in place, too.

Cups with weighted bottoms reduce the chance of spills, as do drinking glasses with lids. If your child uses a straw but constantly bites on it, purchase rigid plastic straws (called "soup straws") from a medical supply store. They come in two foot lengths and can be cut to the desired length with a hacksaw. I use one in my big sports bottle, and Benj can gnaw on his all he wants and it doesn't get ruined. If a rigid straw isn't suitable, buy a length of flexible vinyl tubing (from the plumbing department in home stores).

Make sure a complete set of whatever your child needs for eating (utensils, plate, non-slip placement, straw, etc.) is always with your child for use at school, in restaurants, or other eating places. At school, your child's pals can get these things out of his backpack and put them back to be taken home. If the cafeteria ladies are really nice, they might be willing to keep these items in the school kitchen so you don't have to send them every day.

If your child takes her lunch to school, pack food she can eat with little or no help, and wrap it so she can open it herself. Plastic containers with lids, bags that zip, and even plastic wrap can be difficult for some children to open. Use zip bags, but don't zip them closed, or wrap sandwiches in wax paper. If she wants a hard-sided lunch box, but can't open the latch, replace it with hook and loop fasteners. Experiment at home to see what works best.

The Dining Table

A child's wheelchair and the dining table sometimes don't match up very well, but there are solutions. Most dining tables have a piece of wood—called the apron—that runs right under the table top. This slat may only be three or four inches high, but that's sometimes just enough to prevent a wheelchair from fitting in close. The armrests on the chair or the child's knees may hit the apron. Because this slat is a structural piece of the table, you can't permanently remove it. But you can take it off, cut out a notch where you child's chair needs to go and put it back on. Alternatively, you could replace the slat with a narrower one.

When Benj got his power chair, he sat up much higher than in his manual chair. As a result, he was too far away (heighth-wise) from the dining table. I found a cardboard box that was about five inches high, eighteen inches wide, and twelve inches deep. I taped the box closed, covered it in contact paper, taped a piece of non-slip fabric to the bottom, and it became a small table on top of the dining table. This brought Benj's plate closer to him, making it easier for him to feed himself.

Bibs

No one wants to see a ten-year-old wearing a bib, but we also don't want him wearing his spaghetti for the rest of the day. Let's allow our children to maintain their dignity by not putting bibs on them unless they're babies. There are other alternatives.

In our house, my husband always wears an apron during mealtimes. Don't ask me why, he just does. I don't. Perhaps that's why his clothes stay cleaner than mine! (On occasion, I've had to remind him to take it off before he leaves the house.) At any rate, Benjamin will not tolerate a napkin tucked into his neckline. But since he wants to be like his dad, he'll wear an apron when he eats. I've made him aprons in the past, fun ones using Power Rangers and other children's prints, but any type of apron will work. We shorten the neck strap so the apron covers him from neckline to knees. If everyone in your family—or maybe just Dad or Mom—wears an apron, your child will agree to it more easily than if he's the only one. Make it fun! Buy or make aprons for everyone in the family, personalize them with fabric paint, and wear them when cleaning, painting, or whatever.

If the apron idea won't fly, try this: take a shirt your child likes, and cut it all the way up the back. Finish the raw edges, sew some hook and loop fasteners at the opening and *Voila!* Your child has a bib that doesn't look like a bib. If food goes everywhere, make it a long sleeved bib. You might consider using a shirt that's a size or two larger than your child's regular tops. If you need to protect just the torso area, make it look like a vest. Cut the arms off the shirt and finish the edges, or use a real vest and cut it up the back.

A User-Friendly Kitchen

Rearrange the contents of drawers and cabinets to make it easier for children to be more self-sufficient in the kitchen. Most people put their silverware in the top drawer. This is what we always did until we realized Benj could see and reach utensils better if they were in the second drawer. If your plates and bowls are in the upper cabinets, move them to the lower cabinets so your children can get them on their own. Move the pots and pans to the upper cabinet. Won't these changes make it easier for all your children to set the table and put away the clean dishes?

When you can, do a little remodeling and either replace your cabinets with drawers or insert drawers into the cabinets. We converted a crowded combination kitchen/breakfast room into a roomy kitchen with no breakfast room, which gave us space for a wall of three columns of floor to ceiling storage. (My husband and I did all the work; you can, too.) From about chest high to the ceiling we built shelves, while below are large drawers. This solution was good for all of us.

With regular kitchen cabinets, stuff gets pushed to the back and disappears into a black hole. But with large drawers, nothing gets lost. In our home, plates are in one drawer, drinking glasses in another, bowls in yet another. In the next column of drawers are snacks, canned goods, boxed foods, and other stuff Benj can get to. Anything he needs access to goes in the drawers. Everything else goes in the upper shelves.

Replace your double-handle faucet with a single lever faucet; it's much easier for everyone to use. When we remodeled, we added a second sink and counter top that were at a height appropriate for Benj in his chair. He needs to learn to wash dishes, right? There's no cabinet under the second sink so he can get his chair under the sink and counter.

If cabinet doors under the sink prevent your child from wheeling up close to the sink, remove the cabinet doors (along with all the cleaning supplies) to create knee space and provide better access. If you don't want this big space to be visible all the time, leave the doors on, carefully cut off the center vertical bar and attach it to the edge of one of the doors. When you close the doors it will look the same as it did before. You'll still need to clear out all the cleaning supplies to make room for your child's knees. Don't forget to wrap the hot water pipe to so your child's legs won't get burned.

You may be thinking, "Even if I did redo my kitchen, my kid still couldn't do anything for himself." When we remodeled our kitchen, it was several months before Benjamin began to do more for himself. We remodeled based on our belief Benjamin *would* become more self-sufficient if we gave him opportunities to do so. Remodeling gave him this opportunity. It's been about five years since we finished the year-long project and Benjamin continues to learn to do new things for himself.

After Santa brought a new microwave for the family one Christmas, we were delighted at how fast it cooked our favorite popcorn. And I was thrilled when I heard Benjamin rummaging around in the kitchen a few days later. "How many minutes do I cook this stuff?" he yelled. The new microwave was easier to use and the popcorn was in a drawer he could reach. He had never tried this before. It made my heart happy. Make yours happy by doing whatever it takes to help your child be more in control of his world.

If I didn't know any better, I would think microwave ovens were invented for people with disabilities! Professionals tell many young adults with disabilities they must stay in a group home until they learn how to cook. Hey! Sticking a TV dinner (or breakfast or lunch) in the microwave *is* cooking! Help your child learn to use kitchen appliances; start with the microwave since it's easiest.

Ask all your children which night they'll prepare dinner each week. Let them decide what to prepare and who will do what. Make sure your child with a disability has some responsibilities. Whether they prepare TV dinners, warmed up leftovers, or a gourmet meal of boxed mac and cheese, wouldn't this be a treat?

Rearrange the inside of your refrigerator so everyone can have access to the most frequently used items. Make it easy for your child to get what she needs by putting favorite items on shelves in the door. If possible, reverse which side the door opens if that makes it easier for a child to get stuff out of the fridge.

Transfer food into containers that are easier and safer to use. Benjamin loves pretzels, but has difficulty getting the large zippered bag open. So we pour the pretzels into a large, clear plastic jar that has a wide-mouth flip lid. These jars are great for cereal, peanuts, and many other foods. If a plastic gallon jug of milk is too heavy or unwieldy, pour some of it into a smaller pitcher or bottle your child can handle. Or, use a large plastic jug with a push button dispenser on the bottom that can stay on the shelf in the fridge.

The safest stove for families with young children is the type with the controls at the back. But this same stove may be inaccessible and dangerous for children who use chairs or those of short stature. They may not be able to reach the controls at all. If they can, they must reach across hot and steaming pots or pans. When our old stove bit the dust, we replaced it with a model with the controls in front which everyone in our family can reach.

If a child is not tall enough to see the contents of a pan on top of the stove, he can stand on a large, sturdy step stool. To ensure a child who uses a wheelchair can see what's happening on top of the stove, affix an unbreakable mirror to the wall behind the stove top, at an angle, like the ones in the produce department at grocery stores.

Kitchens can be dangerous places and children must learn how to be safe in the kitchen. We don't want our children to hurt themselves, but we've all been burned or cut while working in the kitchen. Teach your children safety, but also teach them where the bandages are. We can't protect our children from all harm, and we don't want to protect them into the arms of helplessness and dependency.

See your kitchen through your child's eyes. What needs to be changed and what tools need to be added so your child can get a snack on his own, help cook and clean up afterwards, and learn how to be master of his world?

In the Bedroom

Of all the places in your home, your child's bedroom needs to be a model of accessibility, whether she has a room alone or shares one with a brother or sister. What can't your child do for herself in her own room? Talk with her, experiment, and come up with solutions so she can be successful and independent in her room. It may end up looking very different from typical bedrooms, but so be it. Let go of preconceived notions about how things "should" be.

Rearrange the closet so she can get to her stuff. If necessary, replace the clothes rod with built-in shelves or plastic cubes and fold your child's clothes. Remove the closet door if that helps. Use large plastic bins for toys, books, or anything else if dresser drawers or shelves are hard to manage.

Children who use wheelchairs need things at just the right height since it's difficult to reach items that are too low or too high. We got rid of the desk, dresser, and bookshelf in Benj's room and replaced them with kitchen counter tops along two walls, placed at the right height for Benj. Counter tops are made to be supported by cabinets, but this wouldn't work because Benj couldn't get up close and he wouldn't have any knee space. So we built a wooden frame attached to the wall to support the counters. Containers of books and toys, his CD player, and gobs of other things line the counter tops, and Benj can reach them all.

How and where our children sleep may be critical factors that affect the whole family. Find solutions that work, whether or not these methods are typical for other families.

Many babies and children with disabilities often have nervous systems that are hypersensitive and/or less developed, which results in them being fretful and anxious. In addition, many children with orthopedic disabilities are very aware of their inability to get out of bed by themselves. Thus, a child may be afraid of sleeping by himself because he knows he can't get out of bed in the middle of the night and run to his parents' bed when he's afraid.

There's nothing wrong with a baby or young child sleeping with family members. Benjamin slept with my husband and I until he was four! He had his own bedtime (which was much earlier than ours), but he needed the security of sleeping in our bed. Many people disapprove if this practice, but it worked for us. (In many societies around the world, it's common for babies and young children to sleep with their parents. Children need our comfort and love. Only in "modern" nations do we force little ones to be alone at night!)

Benjamin was ready to sleep in a bed by himself when he was four. But he still wasn't ready to be alone in his room. The solution was to outfit each of our children's rooms with trundle beds. One night, both kids slept in Benjamin's room with Benj sleeping in his bed and Emily sleeping on the trundle bed on the floor. The next night, it was reversed: they both slept in six-year-old Emily's room, with Emily sleeping in her bed, and Benj sleeping on the trundle on the floor. When Benj was six, he was finally able to sleep in his own room, alone. Because he needs help getting out of bed, we purchased an inexpensive inter-com system. He can beep us or call us when he needs help during the night.

Lynn's Bedtime Story

When I first met Lynn, she asked, "What do you know about group homes?" I gave her my opinion (not a good one) and assumed she must have a young adult child with a disability. "Could you tell me why you're considering a group home?" I asked.

With a shaky voice and tears brimming from her eyes, Lynn described difficulties at home: she and her husband had not had a full night's sleep since their daughter, Melanie, was born with cerebral palsy. She went on to say that members of their extended family were urging her to place Melanie in a group home for the sake of Lynn and her immediate family. Lynn said she didn't really want to do it, but she didn't know what else to do. She and her husband both worked full-time, they were exhausted and stressed out trying to take care of Melanie and her older sister, Janelle. I still assumed Melanie was a young adult, but something told me I was wrong.

"How old is Melanie?" I finally asked. When Lynn replied, "Four" I was shocked. "Why are you thinking about a group home for a four-year-old?" I asked. She began repeating her story until I asked her to give me specifics, not generalities.

In a nutshell, this was the situation: Melanie and five-year-old Janelle each slept in their own rooms. Melanie still slept in a crib; her mom and dad thought this was safer than a regular bed because Melanie had difficulty with balance. During the night, Melanie often got turned the wrong way. One of her legs would get caught under the other leg, or some-thing else would wake her up. Because she was unable to reposition herself, she cried out for help in pain and frustration. This had happened every single night, sometimes more than once a night, for four years straight. I certainly understood why Lynn and Bob were exhausted and stressed out.

After many more questions by me and many more answers from Lynn, I proposed a solution which she eagerly agreed to try. A week or so after our initial meeting, Lynn reported the solution worked. She and her husband were sleeping through the night for the first time since Melanie was born. The solution wasn't rocket science. It was just common sense; common sense that Lynn had lost during the four years she had been involved in a system that portrayed her daughter as a helpless, pitiful creature who would never grow up to be anything. Have you guessed the solution?

Lynn put a twin mattress on the floor in Janelle's room for Melanie to sleep on. If Melanie rolled off the bed, she wouldn't hurt herself since the floor was just four inches down. When she got turned the wrong way and cried out, her sister woke up, took two steps to Melanie's mattress, and straightened her sister out. Then the sisters went back to sleep.

The solution was great for everyone. Lynn and Bob were getting the rest they needed. Melanie felt like a big girl since she was out of the crib and sharing a room with her big sister. Janelle thought she was an even bigger girl since she was given the important responsibility of helping her little sister. Even better, Janelle began seeing her sister through different eyes. She didn't see Melanie as a baby anymore, since she didn't sleep in a crib. And they had fun at bedtime! After Lynn and Bob turned out the lights, Janelle pulled out Barbies and other toys and she and Melanie played in the dark before they dozed off. They became closer than they had ever been.

This incident was a significant turning point in Lynn's family. Up until this time, Lynn had pretty much accepted the professionals' view of the situation: Melanie would never walk, talk, or do much of anything, and when caring for her became too difficult, her family would need to place her in a group home. But once Lynn and Bob were not so stressed out, and as they watched the changes in their two daughters, they saw things differently. They realized that with accommodations, Melanie could be just as successful as her sister. With assistive technology, Melanie could have independent mobility and communication.

But perhaps the biggest change was Lynn's attitude about herself. She admitted she had gone back to work after Melanie's birth and diagnosis because she didn't feel competent to meet Melanie's needs. In her first four years of life, Melanie was shuttled back and forth to therapies, early intervention and early childhood programs, and day care. Lynn felt professionals were better suited to help Melanie than she was. But when she saw that a simple change in Melanie's life—changing where and how she slept—could produce such wonderful ripples of change in their lives, she realized she *did* have the capacity to meet Melanie's needs.

During this metamorphosis, she tearfully but joyously said, "I've decided to quit my job and be a stay-at-home mom. I think it's time I get to know my daughter." I got goose bumps then and I've got them now retelling this story. The loss of Lynn's salary was hard in many ways, but they learned to make do. Lynn gave up a professional position and good money, but regained control over her family's life and her children's destinies.

If your child—regardless of age or disability—has difficulty getting to sleep or is unable to sleep alone, explore solutions to ensure everyone gets the rest they need. Sleeping with you, on a mattress on the floor in your room, or sharing a bed or a room with a brother or sister are options to explore. If the first idea you try doesn't work, keep trying!

At the other end of the spectrum are children who sleep by themselves but who wake up in the middle of the night. A child may be lonely or afraid, or he might be ready to get up and he wants everybody else up, too! Again, look for creative solutions. Change the environment. Set some ground rules that work for everyone.

If your child wakes up and just needs companionship, let him crawl into bed with you or another member of the family. If he's wide awake and not prepared to go back to sleep, tell him you need to continue sleeping, but he can look at a book with a flashlight while lying in bed with you or on a pallet of blankets on the floor in your room. If he makes too much noise, leave him in your room and go crawl in his bed to sleep!

One mother told me her daughter regularly woke up about four in the morning wanting microwave popcorn. The solution: teach the hungry girl how to use the microwave so she could make her own early morning snack without waking everyone else up.

Many children sleep better when there's "white noise" in the room. A small fan will do the trick, as will high-tech sound machines that feature a variety of sounds (rainfall, ocean waves, etc.). Soft music, a night light, a lava lamp, or other environmental accommodations may help some children sleep more soundly.

If your child has difficulty getting in and out of bed, consider buying an adjustable bed, the type with a control that will raise the head and foot of the bed, as well as the entire mattress. A trapeze bar may also be helpful. We didn't like the institutional look of Benj's adjustable bed, so we covered the headboard and footboard with white contact paper to match the white counter tops in his room.

In the Bathroom

If your child can sit up in the tub, but his bottom slides, line the bottom of the tub with a piece of non-slip fabric. For children who are unable to sit up in the tub, a bath chair that rests on the floor of the tub may be helpful. If you can't afford one and insurance won't pay, make your own with PVC pipe. Look at pictures of these chairs in catalogs, then design your own. Visit your local home store for the PVC pipe, connectors, pipe cutter, and glue. Because PVC is relatively inexpensive, if you mess up and have to start over, you'll still have spent far less than the cost of a ready-made bath chair.

For suction cups to hold the chair securely to the floor of the tub, visit an auto parts store and look for suction cups made for car top carriers. Drill holes in the PVC pipe to attach the suction cups and use rustproof stainless steel screws.

Buy lawn chair fabric (the plastic/nylon mesh stuff) in your child's favorite color and hand sew it onto the frame of the bath chair. In the spring and summer, this prepackaged material is available at stores that sell lawn furniture. Year-round, it can be found at many fabric stores. Buy webbing and plastic buckles at the fabric store for a seat belt. For about $50.00 for all the materials, your child will have a custom made bath chair.

Power bath chairs will lower a child into the tub and then raise him up again. There are even bath tubs that have a door in the side for easier access. Insurance may pay for these expensive items.

When children get bigger, as Benjamin is now, lifting them in and out of the tub can be difficult and dangerous. Shower/bath chairs may provide a safe alternative, although your child must take a shower instead of a bath since the chair sits high in the tub. These come in all shapes and sizes, and are available from catalogs, medical supply houses, and some drug and discount stores.

One of these days, we'll probably rip out the tub in the kids' bath and replace it with a roll-in shower. If you've never seen a roll-in shower, imagine removing the tub, tiling the area where the tub was, and building up a small ridge on the floor where the long edge of the tub rested. The ridge keeps the water from spilling out onto the main part of the floor. A child can sit in a regular shower chair or can roll in using a wheelchair made for the purpose (a rustproof chair with quick-drying upholstery).

Tooth decay is a concern for many children with disabilities. If your child has trouble holding a regular toothbrush, build up the handle using the suggestions described for spoons and forks. (Built-up handles on combs, hair brushes, pencils, and anything your child needs a good grip on can make a huge difference.)

An electric toothbrush can be a big help, whether your child brushes his own teeth or if you help. We found one (made by Oralgiene) that has bristles in a cup-like shape to clean all sides of a tooth at once. Electric flossers, plaque-removing mouthwash, a fluoride rinse, and other goodies can be wise investments. Because of the difficulties getting Benj's teeth really clean, the dentist coats all his molars with sealant.

Children who use wheelchairs are often unable to use the bathroom sink if a cabinet underneath blocks their access. If necessary, remove the cabinet doors or modify them using the techniques described in the kitchen section.

Install an easy to use single lever faucet in the bathroom sink. Better yet, install a kitchen faucet with a high spout and a built-in sprayer. It's high enough so a child can wash her hair in the sink. And a child in a chair (who is lower than a child who stands) won't bang her head on the faucet when she leans in to rinse her mouth (I speak from my son's experience!).

Replace the bathroom sink, too. A shallow sink that's rectangular, longer from the front edge to the rear, is better than traditional sinks. This puts the plumbing pipes as far back as possible to provide more knee space.

Diapers and the Toilet

Many children with disabilities, especially those with physical disabilities, may have difficulty with toileting skills. In some cases, children may be delayed in this area simply because they haven't had opportunities to explore the bathroom the way other children do. Typical two-year-olds become very familiar with the bathroom. They follow their parents in, watch older brothers and sisters go, and try to flush things down the toilet! We need to give young children with disabilities the same familiarity.

Summer time is always the best time to teach potty skills since a child doesn't need to wear as many clothes. Putting a child on the pot once every hour or so will give them a feel—so to speak—of what this is all about. And, of course, being patient and understanding is important. Additionally, we may need to use the toilet seat inserts that make the toilet seat opening smaller to fit a little one's bottom. Or the small portable potty that sits on the floor may be appropriate. Some children may need toilet rails to hold onto and a footrest or foot stool for balance.

If a child with a disability isn't able to use the toilet around the same age other children learn, we must ensure he isn't made to feel bad about himself. Also, we shouldn't advertise the fact that a child is still in diapers to everyone we know. The only people who need to know are folks who help a child with bathroom needs.

When Benjamin started kindergarten in an inclusive classroom, he was still in diapers. But I didn't want all the kids in his class to know this. To help preserve Benjamin's dignity and to ensure his privacy, I didn't want the teacher's aide (TA) to change his diaper in the back of the classroom, or even in the boys' bathroom down the hall. The nurse's office would have provided privacy, but he would have missed a lot of class time and his classmates would wonder where he and the TA went every day.

The solution was to let Benj wear a pull-up diaper and insert a diaper doubler in the crotch. Diaper doublers are like a sanitary pad, but they're made for babies, not ladies! Because Benj didn't usually have a bowel movement (BM) until he was home after lunch, all the TA had to worry about was him peeing. The diaper doubler absorbed the urine, so the pull-up diaper stayed relatively dry. A couple of times during the morning kindergarten class, the TA accompanied Benj to the small bathroom in the classroom. She put Benj on the pot to see if he could go. If he had already peed in the diaper, the TA simply pulled the diaper doubler out while Benj was sitting on the pot, and replaced it with a dry one, leaving the pull up diaper on. Benj could wear the same pull-up until he came home from school at noon. It worked great!

Over the next summer, between kindergarten and first grade, Benj learned to pee in the toilet. He couldn't get to the bathroom and sit on the toilet by himself, so every hour or so I put him on the pot. After a few weeks, he began telling me when he needed to go. I let him know he needed to give me plenty of time since it took a moment or two to wheel him into the bathroom, get him out of his chair, and pull his pants down. We had plenty of accidents: sometimes he wasn't fast enough in telling me and sometimes I wasn't fast enough doing my part. But he was out of diapers!

We've tried a variety of other methods of helping Benj go to the bathroom and I want to share them with you in the hope they might be helpful to your child or other children you know. Condoms, yes, condoms may be the answer for some boys. Have you ever thought about how male astronauts pee in space? Or how long haul truckers drive for hundreds of miles without stopping to go to the bathroom? They wear condoms that have a small opening at the end which is attached to a long, narrow tube, which runs to a collection bag worn around the ankle under long pants! This device is also used by many men who have spinal cord injuries.

I found all those goodies in a medical supply catalog. There are many mail order companies that specialize in "incontinence" products. The condoms come in a variety of sizes, since one made for a grown man wouldn't fit a small boy! I had a funny telephone conversation with one of the sales reps during my first call about these products. He asked me what size Benjamin would wear. I wondered if he wanted me to go measure Benjamin's penis! I asked him what sizes were available. He replied, "Pediatric; adult small, medium, large, and extra large; and geriatric." He then went on to give me the dimensions of those sizes in millimeters or centimeters or something. I was writing all this down and stopped dead in my tracks when I realized the pediatric size had the same dimensions at the geriatric size. I thought I must have written it down wrong, so I asked him about this, trying not to giggle too much. "Are you telling me pediatric and geriatric are the same sizes?" I asked. He was a good sport and said, "You got it! Tell your husband what he has to look forward to when he's an old man!"

So, we tried the condoms (also called external catheters), experimenting with a variety of types and brands. Just like other condoms, they're rolled on and off, and most have adhesive to hold them in place. Benj could wear the same one all day, unless it accidentally came off. A couple of times a day, he drained the leg bag into the toilet.

However, Benj didn't like the condoms. He didn't like going through the routine we needed to do every morning: putting the condom on, attaching the tubing, strapping on the leg bag, and so forth. But this system might work for your son or other boys you know. Insurance usually pays for these items. Before buying a month's supply, ask the medical supply company for free samples of different types.

A similar alternative for males consists of a pair of cotton underwear with a plastic ring in the front. The fabric within the cotton ring is cut out. A soft plastic sheath (one-size-fits-all) is attached to the ring, and then to a drainage tube and leg bag. Benjamin liked this system better, since it was faster. However, it didn't work because the sheath was too big and his penis didn't stay in place, so he sometimes peed on himself. I'm saving it all in the event he wants to try it again when he's "bigger."

Collection bags may be an alternative to diapers for very young boys or girls. You might have seen these at doctor's offices or hospitals where they're used to collect urine specimens. It consists of a small plastic bag attached to a cardboard frame that adheres to the skin. After the child pees, the bag is removed and replaced with a fresh one.

For older girls, there aren't as many options. Women who are incontinent because of spinal cord injuries often use internal catheters: a slender tube is inserted through the urethra into the bladder. The other end is connected to a leg bag. This may be an option, but be aware that inserting the catheter is not a pleasant feeling and infections are possible since a "foreign object" is put into the body.

An alternative to traditional child or adult diapers that may be appropriate for girls are incontinent pads. Some attach to the crotch of panties with adhesive. Others are worn with an elastic belt that has hook and loop fasteners. What's nice about this method is that a girl who wears these instead of diapers will feel great about being able to wear cute panties, just like other girls. In addition, the pad can be changed in a more dignified manner than a diaper; the girl wouldn't need to lay down and be changed like an infant. The pad could be pulled out and changed while she sits on the toilet.

The pee method currently working for Benjamin is extremely low-tech and low cost. He pees in a sports bottle! Benj wears extra large sweat pants with an elastic waist. In his power chair, he stands himself up, uses one hand to pull the pants away from his body, sticks the pee cup around his penis, pees, and then empties the cup. No more getting him in and out of his chair, and he can do it by himself. Like lots of movie stars (so we've heard), Benjamin chooses not to wear underwear. They get in the way with this method! He started out using a portable urinal. But we switched to a sports bottle for a couple of reasons. The urinal was too big for Benj's hands and it couldn't be cleverly disguised. Benj keeps the sports bottle in a cup holder attached to his chair, and no one but us knows it's a pee cup.

This system might work for a girl who used a chair if her clothes were modified. If her slacks had a flap in the crotch area that could be opened, she might be able to get a female urinal in place. She would probably need to go without underwear, too.

Before deciding on the pee cup method, we experimented with funnels and tubing at the toilet. I attached a long piece of clear plastic tubing to a regular kitchen funnel. Benj could wheel up to the edge of the toilet, put the funnel up to his crotch to pee, and the urine would flow down the tubing, the end of which was in the toilet bowl. The basic premise worked, but it was hard for Benj to get the funnel on and off wall hook it hung on. If you try something like this, make sure the funnel and the tubing are large enough. We started out with a small funnel and tubing, but it didn't drain quickly enough and the urine backed up onto Benj. Look for flexible plastic tubing and funnels at hardware and home stores, and make sure they fit together snugly.

We also tried using a length of stiff piece of plastic plumbing pipe, about eighteen inches long with a two inch diameter. Benj would wheel up to the toilet, open the fly on his pants, position the tube so one end was around his penis and the other end rested on the lip of the toilet. When he peed, the urine ran down the tube into the toilet! But this didn't work for us (at the time) because Benj had difficulty getting the tube out of and back into the waste basket I used as a holder. We might try this again in the future when I figure out a better way to store the tube. You could experiment with different lengths and diameters of pipes. If standard plumbing tubes aren't the right size, check out clear plastic flexible tubing, as previously described.

Now let's move on to the other part of bathroom activities: the BM, or Big Job, as we call it in our house. (This was a term my husband's mother used when he was a boy!) Benj is able to tell us when he needs to make a Big Job, so we simply put him on the pot, wipe his bottom when he's done, and get him back in his chair. He'll probably always need help getting on and off the pot; that's life. (By the way, don't stop using pre-moistened baby wipes when your child stops using diapers. They're better than toilet paper for everyone.)

Most children want to get out of diapers and most can. For some children—and I think Benj was one of them—it simply takes longer to develop a sensitivity of what an impending BM feels like. It might be helpful to describe those feelings (a sense of fullness, gas moving around in our tummies, pressure) so a child has a point of reference.

Some children seem to be perpetually constipated. With spastic cerebral palsy, for example, we tend to think of children having tight muscles in their legs, arms, and hands. But they may have tight muscles everywhere in their bodies, including the muscles in their intestines. When Benj was younger, bowel movements were difficult and painful, and he was often constipated. One solution was to give him lots of yogurt and prunes. As he grew, he balked at eating prunes, but when offered a choice of prunes or a suppository, he always chose the prunes!

Another way to help children who are constipated is to change their positions throughout the day. Sitting in a wheelchair all day, for example, can contribute to constipation. Using a standing frame for part of the day, sitting on the sofa instead of the wheelchair, and assuming other positions can help.

Some children with Down syndrome or other conditions involving low muscle tone often have very loose bowel movements that seem to come out of their own volition. Cutting back on apple juice and fiber-filled foods may help. Experiment with your child's diet to see what makes a difference.

There are no products like condoms for Big Jobs. But if we're creative, we can still find alternatives to diapers. Boys or girls could wear regular underwear, with incontinence pads. The pad could be positioned so it's toward the back. Or the child could wear two pads: one positioned in the regular place for pee and one toward the back for poop. Unless a child had diarrhea or very loose stools, the pad would probably "catch" the poop. When he pooped, someone could simply remove the pad, flush the poop, discard the pad, wipe the bottom, and put on a new pad. When he peed, the wet pad could be discarded and a new one put in, and all this could be done while he's sitting on the toilet.

Another alternative is to use the disposable bed or chair pads that are made to protect sheets and upholstery from urine. One side is a soft absorbent paper, the other side is soft plastic. They're usually about eighteen inches by two or three feet and you can find them at drug or discount stores. You could cut these to fit inside a child's panties to catch poop, pinning it or somehow attaching it to the underwear so it wouldn't move around and get all bunched up in the crotch area. As in the previous example, a child could be changed while sitting on the toilet: someone could take off the old pad, dump the poop, wipe his bottom, and put a new pad on. It's worth a try—anything's worth a try—to help our children preserve their dignity and get out of diapers.

When diapers are the only option, we must make sure children are not treated like babies. It might be easier on the caregiver to have a child lie down, spread his legs, expose his privates, and be cleaned up, but it's embarrassing and undignified for the child. We need to find other ways of changing children's diapers. For instance, a child who can walk should be taken to the bathroom and changed while he's sitting on the pot or standing up. It can be done—I've done it with some of my friends' children. The child should be encouraged to help as much as possible, by helping to pull down his pants, ripping the tape off the diaper, and so forth.

If child uses a wheelchair, her diaper can be changed while she sits in her chair. The helper can lift the child into a standing position (keeping the child's feet positioned on the footrest) and pull her pants down around the knees. (This would be easiest if the child wore elastic waist pants that aren't too tight.) Then she sits the child back down in the chair and pulls apart the adhesive strips on the diaper. Next, she raises the child back into a standing position—the diaper remaining on the seat—and wipes the bottom. While holding the child in the standing position, she removes the dirty diaper and places a clean one on the seat, then sits the child on it, and attaches the adhesive tapes. Finally, she lifts the child once more to pull up her pants and it's done. I know this sounds like a lot of lifting and many steps, but once it's done a few times, the process will become streamlined. This would be relatively simple if the child can hold on to the caregiver's neck while standing, and if she can bear some weight.

If the child is unable to do either of these things, ways could still be found for this or a similar method to work. For example, if the child's pants were modified to open down both side seams (closed with hook and loop fasteners or zippers), the child wouldn't need to stand for his pants to be pulled down. The caregiver could open the sides of the pants and pull the front part down to get to the diaper. With the child still seated, the diaper adhesives could be undone. Then, the caregiver could lift the child just enough to clean the bottom, pull the dirty diaper out and slide a new one in. She sits the child back down on the diaper, attaches the adhesives, pulls the front of the pants back up, and it's done.

Regardless of who changes your child's diaper—you, another family member, someone at school or day care—your child's dignity and personal privacy are critically important. We often don't consider our children's feelings when we decide how to do things. We focus on efficiency and speed. But this is one activity in which a child's feelings should be paramount. All children go through periods when they don't want anyone to see their bodies. But children who need help with toileting and dressing don't often get to say, "Don't look at me! Don't come in my room when I'm dressing."

Our children aren't inanimate objects or pieces of meat that have no feelings about this. They may not be able to express their feelings, but assume they're there, nonetheless. Protect your child's privacy. Experiment to find the most dignified way to help your child with toileting issues. If a teacher's aide or other helper balks at new methods, patiently, firmly, and persistently explain the importance of dignified assistance and respect for your child's privacy.

Because children who use wheelchairs aren't able to exercise the way other people do, they often run a great risk of becoming overweight. I never would have thought this when Benjamin was younger, with his scrawny little arms and legs, but at thirteen he's growing a paunch like his dad's. It's important to watch our children's diet as they get bigger, for if they become overweight they're at risk for a variety of dilemmas as adults.

I have several adult friends who use wheelchairs and who are extremely overweight. When they were younger and at an average weight, one person could help them transfer to the toilet and they were able to help some, too, by bearing some weight, holding on, and so forth. But as they grew heavier, one helper couldn't do the transfer alone. As a result, they had to start wearing adult diapers.

To change the diaper in this situation, the helper must use a mechanical lift to transfer the person from his chair to a bed, where he lies down to have his diaper changed. He knows when he needs to poop, but there's no way one helper could get him out of his chair and onto a toilet in time. He's stuck wearing adult diapers. It's embarrassing and potentially dangerous. A woman in this situation may get frequent urinary tract infections because she sits in the poop and the germs get into her urethra. One of my male friends was on an airplane trip and had diarrhea. He had to sit in it for several hours, which greatly irritated his skin, and the odor filled his part of the plane. He was horribly embarrassed.

There are many ways to help our children with peeing and pooping that are dignified and sanitary. Let's take the time to find the ways that work best.

CLOTHING

Rearranging our children's rooms and closets gives them more opportunities to pick out their own clothes. But even if your child can't physically grab the pants and shirt he's going to wear, he should still be the one to make the decision about *what* to wear.

Regardless of your child's disability, encourage him to pick out his clothes at the same age he'd be doing this if he didn't have a disability. If your child is above the age of three or four and he's not choosing what to wear every day, change that!

Long past the time I should have been doing it, I continued to select Benj's clothes for him. He couldn't get them off the hangers, and it was faster and easier for me to make the choices. Something clicked when he was about six and I realized how dependent I was making him.

The first time I asked Benjamin what he wanted to wear, he just looked at me. I pointed to his closet and said, "Tell me which shirt and pants you want to wear." He still just looked at me. It dawned on me that he didn't know about the routine decisions most of us make every day, because I had never given him the opportunity to pick out his clothes!

When I got more specific with him, it started making sense. "Do you want to wear black pants or these blue ones?" I asked. "The blue ones," he answered. "Okay, let's see which shirt would go with those. Do you like this striped one or this sweatshirt?" I asked.

"The sweatshirt," he replied. After a few weeks, he became adept at choosing his clothes and didn't want me to offer choices. Success!

Encourage your child to select her own outfits. It will give her a wonderful feeling of power and it's good practice in decision-making. And when shopping for clothes, let your child make choices. For years, I bought Benjamin's clothes for him, since I was the one who dressed him and I knew what worked. How thoughtless and disrespectful I was!

Getting Dressed

Many children have difficulty dressing themselves; some may never be able to dress without some help. Regardless, they should be encouraged to help as much as they can. For years we dressed Benj while he was lying on the bed—just like we dress tiny babies. It was wrong, wrong, wrong. But not only was it wrong, it prevented Benj from helping. There wasn't much he could do while flat on his back. Now we help him get dressed while he's in his chair, and he can help some by pulling the sweatshirt over his head, getting his arms inside the armholes, and so forth. Even if it's faster and easier for you, don't let your child be as still as a mannequin while you dress him. Encourage him to do as much as he can.

Children may learn to dress themselves easier in front of a full length mirror. Many people can dress themselves without thinking, but for children with disabilities, the steps involved may be mind-boggling. Start out with one piece of clothing and help your child master that one piece before going on to others. And start with the piece that's easiest for your child.

A child may learn a new task better if it's broken down into a series of small steps. This technique may be extremely important in a child learning to dress himself, as well as for other tasks that require sequential steps. We may need to talk through the different steps if it's hard for a child to get the sequence down. (In therapeutic vernacular, this is called motor planning: getting the mind to know which parts of the body do what and when.) For example, "Okay, Stephen, see this tag in the neck of the sweatshirt? This tag is always in the back of a shirt. That means this is the back of the sweatshirt and this other side is the front. You always want to put the back of the sweatshirt on your back and the front on your front. So put the sweatshirt on the bed like it's going to lie down on its tummy. Now, pick it up by the bottom here with both hands, lift it up high, and pull it over your head . . ." and so on. Giving a child these verbal cues helps him learn the different steps of the routine.

As Stephen becomes more proficient at dressing himself, his mother streamlines the verbal cues: "Sweatshirt down on its tummy, grab the bottom. Lift it high and then pull it down . . ." This is great progress. However, in looking at this situation broadly and over the long term, it's important to wean the child from dependence on verbal cues. If he needs the consistency and repetition of the verbal cues given the same way each time, he will always need his mom to help.

The next step is to replace the verbal cues with sensory cues. Later, the sensory cues can be faded back until they're no longer needed. For example, once Stephen has learned to put on his sweatshirt with the help of verbal cues, his parents let him know he doesn't need to be told each step anymore, that a touch or a signal will do the trick.

Stephen's mom starts out giving each verbal cue and a corresponding sensory cue simultaneously. While she's doing this, she encourages Stephen to mimic the sensory cues. To replace the verbal cue of laying the sweatshirt face down ("Lay the shirt on its tummy."), mom touches her tummy. Next, she could make her hands into fists ("Grab the sweatshirt here."), lift her hands above her head ("Lift the shirt up high."), and lower her hands down to her shoulders ("Pull it down.").

For awhile, Stephen's mom gives him both sets of cues each time he gets dressed. Then, depending on Stephen's self-confidence and comfort level, she begins dropping one or more of the verbal cues and uses only the sensory cues. She might have Stephen practice the sensory cues, in the correct sequence, several times a day when he's not getting dressed. The goal is for Stephen to give himself the sensory cues so he can dress without his mom's assistance.

It's vital that Stephen participates in the development of sensory cues. It may make more sense to Stephen, for example, to touch the bed instead his tummy as a way of knowing how the sweatshirt should be placed so he has the front and the back the right way. It's also important that other family members learn and take part in the process so Stephen is not dependent on only one person.

The sensory cues, given in the same order every time, help Stephen learn or memorize the routine. Whether we realize it or not, routines fill our days. At some point in the past, I had to think about my shower routine: do I wash my hair or body first; at what point do I shave my legs; when do I put baby oil on my face to take off yesterday's mascara? After figuring out which routine is best, I do it the same way each time and no longer have to think about it. This is essentially what we're doing when we help a child learn how to do something by breaking it down into small steps.

Be aware that the way we dress ourselves (or do anything else) might not be the best way for a child to do it. For example, you might put on a sweatshirt by pulling it down over your head first. But your child might find it's easier or makes more sense to put his arms in the sleeves first, and then pull it over his head. Let your child guide you. He knows best. If he isn't able to verbally tell you what's best, listen to his body language and his behavior.

A variety of dressing aids can be found in catalogs. Sock pullers allow a child to put a sock over a form and pull it on with the two long strings that are attached. Short poles with hooks may help a child get the shoulder of a shirt or coat pulled around to the front.

Don't worry about whether your child will ever be able to dress herself completely. Help her do the best she can do. Benjamin will probably always need assistance dressing. So be it. When he's a young adult, we'll look for a friend to help. When he's married, his wife will be there for him. It'll all work out.

Clothing Adaptations

Buttons, zippers, snaps and other doodads are often barriers to our children being able to dress themselves. Get rid of whatever might be standing in your child's way!

Hook and loop fasteners can replace just about any type of closure method. For shirts that button up, use small circles or squares of hook and loop fasteners. Tack the buttonholes closed, snip off the buttons, and sew them on top of the buttonholes, giving the appearance of the shirt being buttoned up. Sew one piece of hook and loop fasteners where each button was, then sew the other piece under the buttonhole. No one will know the buttons are non-functional. Do the same thing for buttons or snaps on the waistbands of jeans or slacks.

Rip out zippers in pants and replace with hook and loop fasteners. Some children may not be able to pull the opening apart if the fasteners run the length of the fly opening. In this case, use several small squares instead of a long piece. Don't use the *sticky back* hook and loop fasteners; they'll come off in the washer or dryer. Use the sew-in type, stitching it in by hand or with a machine.

If your child approves, buy elastic waist pants since they're easiest to get on and off. Styles of today's clothing are so varied that elastic waist pants aren't always "uncool." Kids today wear plaid, flannel "lounging" pants to school because they're cool. Sweats and wind pants have elastic waists and are favorites of many kids. Sweatshirts, t-shirts, polo shirts and other tops that pull over the head are easier to put on than button up shirts. Also, clothes that are a size or two larger are easier to put on. This works out great, style-wise, since loose is "in."

Children who use wheelchairs need pants that are longer since pant legs ride up when they sit. (Benjamin hates it when his socks are visible. "Pull my pants down, my socks are showing!" he'll yell.) In addition, they need pants that have a longer seam in the seat since they're seated most of the time. If you sew, you can make clothing that works for your child.

Sew fabric loops inside the waistband of pants at each side so children who have difficulty grasping can hook their thumbs or fingers into the loops to pull up their pants. Sew brightly colored pieces of fabric or small buttons inside the back neckline of tops and the back waistband of bottoms to help children better distinguish the front from the back.

For children with visual disabilities or children who have a hard time knowing which tops go with which bottoms, code the clothing by sewing in buttons or color coded tags. Or organize the closet or dresser so he knows which clothes go together. Be creative!

Help your child dress for success. Our kids need to take pride in their looks the way other children do.

ACADEMIC LEARNING BEGINS AT HOME

Learning begins at home. You might not think of yourself as a teacher, but you are. Your child learns more from you—from just being around you—than from any formal teaching.

Schools cannot do everything. We should not expect them to, but more importantly, we should not want them to. I want my children's lives to reflect *our family's* interests, values, and goals, not the school's.

You can ensure your child gets the most out of public education if you lay the groundwork for academic learning at home. You know how your child learns best. If you don't, start getting a handle on this by reading books about different ways of learning, watch your child, and talk to her about this. You know things about your child a teacher may never know. In a public school setting, it often takes a teacher months to get to know your child well enough to know how to help her. But you know and you can teach others.

If we take the time to discover our children's learning styles and needs at home, we can send our children to school with the tools they need to succeed. If, for example, you're able to educate a teacher about the unique characteristics about your child, months of trial and error in the classroom could be exchanged for months of real learning. In the best case scenario, we wouldn't spend hours in IEP meetings haggling over "how" to do things. If we leave it up to the school to figure out how to help our children learn, we're asking for trouble. In too many cases educators don't try to figure out how to help your child learn best; they try to make your child fit into the teaching styles or classroom structures that are already established.

There are many ways to help our children learn at home. In parts of this section, there is overlap between home and school, because learning occurs in many places.

Reading and Writing at Home

Read to your child as much as you can, regardless of her age or disability. Read to her about subjects she's interested in, not just what you think she ought to be learning. Benjamin has always been more interested in stories and books about real or fictionalized people. He disliked the "cute" books that were used in the primary grades. Thomas the Tank Engine was the exception! Like anyone else, Benj had no use for subjects he wasn't interested in. But he loved books about real or fictional people (Benjamin Franklin, Zorro, Paul Bunyan, and others).

Buy your child as many books as you can afford. It's money well spent. When he has his own library at home, *he'll see himself as a reader,* whether or not he reads at "grade level." And that's a big step in the right direction. Many public libraries have annual book sales where customers can buy used library books cheap, cheap, cheap. Also, shop at used bookstores. If you can't buy books, check out books from the library on a regular basis.

Regardless of your child's age or disability, help her select books that are readable. Emerging readers typically need large print books; most "easy reader" books feature large print, while traditional children's books, such as Little Golden Books, may not. Watch out for books that have type printed over pictures in the book; these can be hard to read.

Older children who need large print may not be interested in traditional children's books that feature large print; the subject matter isn't interesting to them. If so, look for large print adult books in libraries and book stores. *Reader's Digest* has a large print edition.

If they're appropriate for your child, use books that come with an audiotape of the story. Many adult-level books can be purchased on audiotape, including popular fiction and non-fiction books that middle or high school students may enjoy.

Don't be concerned if your fifth or eighth or tenth grader is reading books that are below grade level. Be proud that he's reading, period. Children don't have to be ace readers to be successful. There are many different ways to learn.

Some children with disabilities may have difficulty reading black letters on white paper. The contrast is too great or the white paper is too bright. To some children, the black/white combination causes the black letters to look jagged, while to others the black letters seem to move or jump on the page, making reading difficult, if not impossible. Changing the white background to another color is often helpful. Experiment with copying books onto pastel colored paper, or use colored transparency sheets over the white book pages to lessen or change the contrast. Some children may benefit from wearing prescription or non-prescription glasses with colored lens to change the contrast. Optometrists who offer vision therapy often have experience in this area.

If large print books still don't have print that's big enough, you can enlarge books on a copy machine. You could also retype the text on your computer in a large font and make a brand new book by pasting your new pages over the original pages, leaving any illustrations uncovered. Alternatively, a new book could be constructed by cutting out illustrations and pasting them on your large print pages.

Magnifiers may help. Inexpensive ones can be found in many stores and specialty catalogs. Whether your child does or does not need prescription glasses, think about buying your child a pair of non-prescription reading glasses. Take your child to the drugstore, along with her favorite book. Let her try on the different strengths to see if this helps.

Experiment with a magnifier that's worn around the head. Attached to the headband is a flip-down magnifier for both eyes. This is what jewelers and others use for close work. They're available at many hobby shops and fabric stores.

There are high-tech devices that enlarge print onto a video screen. The user places the book under a magnifier and the image is transmitted onto the attached video screen. The print can be made huge! These devices were invented for adults with visual disabilities and they may be most helpful to people who already know how to read. When Benj tried one in first grade, it wasn't too helpful. He could pick out individual words, but he couldn't read for content since very few words were on the screen at one time. If you think this device might help your child, request a demo. Look for it in specialty catalogs.

Tricks of the (Reading) Trade

One of Benjamin's primary grade teachers, Mrs. M, was also a reading specialist and she helped me understand a great deal about reading. Many children with and without disabilities (especially boys) aren't wired for reading until they're eight or nine, but we put great pressure on them to read in first grade. Unfortunately, this pressure causes children to resist reading, especially if they feel they're not very good at it. They learn to hate reading and this feeling may last a lifetime. Mrs. M recommends lowering the pressure.

Mrs. M used a combination of phonics and whole language techniques, depending on what worked best for each child in her class. She taught me to help Benjamin read for content, instead of just sounding out words. Prior to her help, I did what most parents do: when Benjamin got stuck on a word we'd go through the "sounding out" game. Sound by sound, syllable by syllable, I would urge him to figure out what the word was. But Mrs. M pointed out that interrupting the flow of the story causes children to lose interest in the whole, as they focus on one specific word. Many children find this process so stressful they give up right then and there.

The alternative Mrs. M suggested was to go ahead and tell Benjamin what the word was and allow him to continue reading. Individual words and sounds will come. We need to let our children learn to love reading for content. When I put myself in Benj's place, Mrs. M's suggestion made sense. As adult readers, we often come across words we're unfamiliar with. But if we're reading a good book, and we stop every few minutes to look up a word in the dictionary, we'd probably lose interest in the story. The same is true for children when the flow of the story is constantly interrupted.

As a child, Mrs. M had been called a slow reader. She painfully remembered what it felt like to be labeled. Her childhood experiences gave her deep insight and understanding, and helped her develop creative methods to help children become successful readers. I'm sure when she was little, her parents and teachers never thought she would grow up to be an excellent teacher with an extraordinary ability to help children learn.

Mrs. M taught me that in the minds of some children, other people's written words (in books) don't mean anything until *their own words* mean something. When Benjamin was struggling to learn to read, she encouraged him to write stories on the computer at school as well as at home. How, you may be wondering, could this possibly work? Traditionally, we believe children must be able to read (and spell) before they can write. If a child can't read, if he doesn't know what words are and how to spell them, how can he possibly write? Surprisingly easy.

During writing time at school, Mrs. M helped everyone in the inclusive first grade classroom learn to write. The purpose of the activity wasn't spelling, handwriting, or grammar. The purpose was to gain a sense of power over words and learn how to put ideas together.

Many children already knew how to read and spell, others didn't (including Benjamin). Regardless, all the children were able to write stories using "invented spelling:" spelling words however they thought the words were spelled. They started out writing a word or phrase, then progressed to putting their versions of sentences together. Because they were given the freedom to write in whatever ways worked for them, they were bold and creative. At school and home, Benj was encouraged to write stories about things he cared about. He loved Thomas the Tank Engine books and videos, so he often wrote his own versions of Thomas stories.

As Benjamin became confident in his writing abilities, Mrs. M and I helped him with spelling. Like his classmates, Benj knew his spelling was often inaccurate. When children have confidence in their ability to write, however, they want to make their stories "better," so they're eager to learn the correct spelling.

After Benjamin wrote a story, he read it to me. This was an important step. Had he simply given the story to me to read, I may not have been able to accurately decipher what he wrote. But *he* knew what he wrote. When he read it to me, I was able to see how he spelled certain words and understand which group of words made up a sentence, since there was little or no punctuation at first. Once he read the story to me, I could then read it back to him. He loved it! These were his words, his story, and his ideas.

Mrs. M was absolutely right. Once Benjamin's own words meant something to him, the words of other writers—in books—meant something to him and reading became easier.

Another way to help a child with reading, writing, and spelling is to have him write lists: grocery lists, Christmas lists, lists of errands to run, or anything else. A child can do this by hand or on the computer. I routinely ask Benj to write my lists and I call out things as I'm running around the house. Sitting at the computer, Benjamin often asks, "How do you spell that?" My first response is usually, "How do you think?" He spells it the best he can and we correct it later. If has no idea how to spell the word, I tell him. We started doing this when he was six and age thirteen, this continues to be mutually beneficial: Benjamin learns and makes an important contribution to the family, and I get the lists I need.

Creativity is the key to helping children learn to read. But first, recognize a couple of things. If a professional has said your child is not reading, but your daughter can recognize the McDonald's sign or a stop sign, the professional is wrong! Your daughter *is* reading! This is prereading, for in its simplest form, reading is the recognition of symbols (letters) that we interpret as ideas (words).

The second thing to remember is this: being a good speller is not a sign of high intelligence and being a poor speller is not a sign of low intelligence. Educators have taught me that spelling is a visual memory skill. Some of us have above average visual memory skills; others don't (but they have skills in other areas). I have friends who are excellent teachers, great hairstylists, and enterprising business people who, in their own words, "can't spell worth a darn." Nevertheless, they're all successful.

Help your child learn by filling your house with words. Take note cards and, in block letters, print the names of things in your home, one thing per card: television, sofa, bed, counter, table, chairs, etc. Then tape each card to the appropriate object. As your child (all your children, actually) moves around the house, he'll learn how to spell things without formal lessons.

Take another set of note cards and print a variety of words, one per card, that your child can use to make sentences. Start with words that are meaningful and relevant to your child; words that are in his favorite book or video. Or write the names of everyone in your family, along with words that describe what happens in your family's life (Mom, Dad, Bobby, work, soccer, hamburger, eat, ice cream, and so forth). Write nouns, verbs, and more.

Start by sitting down with your child (or have an older brother or sister do this) and put the cards together to make a short sentence: "Bobby loves ice cream." Read it to your child and encourage him to say the words with you in order. Have him "read" the sentence to you. Make this fun and let your child take the lead. Don't force anything. He may want to focus on one or two words, or he may want to focus on the whole thought. Be silly and rearrange the words so they don't make sense, read it out loud, then put them back in order.

Encourage your child to put different cards together to make his own sentences. Make more cards as needed. Ask your child what words he wants on the cards. Even if your child isn't writing by hand or on a computer, this activity will help him compose, by putting words together to create a sentence. In toy stores and in catalogs, you can buy sets of magnetic words that stick on the refrigerator. These might be all you need. However, by making your own, you'll have more cards, and they'll be meaningful and individualized to your child's life.

Letting your child dictate to you (or other family member) can assist your child with reading. Have him tell you a story or dictate a letter to grandma. In large block print or on the computer, write it just the way he says it. Afterwards, help him read it back to you. He'll remember the gist of what he dictated. Don't worry if he doesn't do it perfectly. After he's "read" it out loud, you do the same, pointing to the words as you go.

Pointing at words while reading is okay. Using a ruler to keep the eyes focused on a certain line of type is okay, too, as is any other technique that helps your child. Don't listen to experts who insist that there's a "right" way to do things. What's "right" is whatever works for your child. If your son still points when he reads when he's twenty, so what? By the time he's forty and needing bifocals, pointing to the words might serve him well!

Make reading a family affair. Pick a regular time every day and have the whole family sit down and read a book together. Let everyone take turns. If it's a book with characters speaking dialogue, let family members assume a role and each can read his or her part. Don't forget the narrator's part!

Take one of your child's favorite books, read it out loud and record it on an audiotape. Then have your child listen to the story as he looks at the book. Or let your child tell you a story and record his voice on audiotape. Transcribe his words to written form to make a "book." Let your child listen to the audiotape he made as he looks at the book he wrote! How exciting! Take the book and the cassette with you in the car when you're running errands to give your child more opportunities to read.

384   Disability is Natural

Have your child record his favorite book on audiotape. Children love to hear their own voices. So that the tape matches the text in the book follow this procedure: with the tape recorder off, read the first sentence of the book to your child, quickly turn the tape recorder on and have him repeat it back to you. Continue this process to the end of the book. If he has a great memory, he might be able to recite the story without much help.

In many states, children with disabilities are eligible to receive modified reading materials (large print books and/or audiotapes) from the state office "for the blind." Look in your telephone book under state offices and find out which agency handles this in your state. You might want to get materials for use at home, at school, or both.

Ways to help your child with reading and learning are limited only by your imagination. Listen to your child, ask him how best to help. Our children know more than we think they do!

Writing

For children who can't write with a pencil or for those who have great difficulty writing, learning to use a keyboard is a must. Many parents want their children to be able to write on a keyboard, but they say their children don't have the physical or mental ability to do so. But they can if we're creative!

First, a few words about keyboards in general. If you don't have a home computer, just about any type of keyboard will do for a start (typewriter or word processor). Investigate what's available (new or used) at computer or office equipment stores.

If you don't have the moola to buy anything like this, spread the word about what you need. Someone you may not even know could be an angel in disguise. Businesses get rid of their old computers. Service clubs (Kiwanis, Lions, and others) raise money or provide things for people in their communities. There are all kinds of ways to get what our children need. Be brave; go out and ask for help! Neighbors, friends, and people in our communities can help us more quickly and more effectively than any system can.

Some children have difficulty seeing the individual keys or finding the right keys. Modifying the keyboard can help.

When Benjamin first started using the computer, he just couldn't find the right keys and he would get so frustrated he'd want to give up. I used colored dots (available at office supply stores) to customize our keyboard. On yellow dots, I wrote the individual letters of Benjamin's name as large as possible with a black marker. Then I stuck those letters to the B, E, N, J, A, M, I, and N keys on the computer. The circles were a little large, so I trimmed them to fit. Next, I used red dots on the top row of keys. Green dots went on the next row, blue dots on the row after that, and orange on the bottom row. On each dot, I wrote the letter or number to correspond with the key. The yellow dots with the letters of Benjamin's name were interspersed throughout the rainbow of colors.

I sat with Benjamin and helped him learn to type his name first. "Just find the yellow dots," I said. He was now able to focus on something—the yellow dots—instead being overwhelmed by keys that all looked the same. Very quickly, he learned to peck out his name with his pointer finger. As he began writing other words, I helped him find each letter of the word by saying, "Look on the red row. Good, now look on the blue row," and so on. After a few weeks, he didn't need the dots any more.

At computer outlets or in catalogs you can find similar ready-made keyboard stickers. The letters of each key are in larger print to make them easier to see. But these are more expensive than the ones you can make yourself and they don't come in bright colors.

If your child has difficulty using a keyboard because her hands stay fisted or she can't separate her fingers, try this trick. Take a pair of thin gloves and cut off the pointer finger part. Then sew the tip of the thumb and the tips of the middle, ring, and little fingers to the palm of the glove, as if the hand was making a fist with all except the pointer finger. When your child puts the glove on, the point finger will be isolated and she can type, point, finger paint, or whatever!

Alternatively, take a mitten, cut a small hole for the pointer finger and sew the tips of the thumb and the finger part to the palm. If, after sewing these down, the glove or mitten is too hard to get on your child's hands, take out the stitches and use hook and loop fasteners or snaps to hold the two parts together. If this doesn't work, use gauze, a support bandage, or other soft material to wrap her fingers and thumb out of the way to isolate the pointer finger.

Needless to say, don't force any of these measures on your child. If she balks, try different approaches gradually. You could start by holding your child's hand in yours, with her hand in a fist, except for the pointer finger. Move her finger over the keyboard, typing out her name or play a computer game. If she's not interested, type your child's name on the computer while she's sitting with you and make a big deal out of what fun it is, saying the letters out loud. Print it up and read it to her with great enthusiasm.

If your child can't use her pointer finger, put your thinking cap on. Maybe another finger will work better. If she keeps her hand in a fist, she could hold a pencil (or some other type of pointer or stick) in her fist and use the object to strike the keys. Some children do well with a head stick: a pointer is attached to a band around the head and the child pushes the keys with a movement of the head.

There are many accessories to make computers easy to use. With touch screens, children simply touch the screen instead of the keyboard. If your low-tech modifications of the standard keyboard don't work, a variety of modified keyboards are available; keyboards that are colored or have larger keys. And many types of modified "mice" are available, as well.

At the very high-tech end are computers that use a child's eye gaze. Another computer program puts a variety of words on the screen. When the user sees the word he wants, he taps a switch to select the word. (This is what British scientist Stephen Hawking uses.)

Recognize how important computers are today: in schools, in jobs, and at home. The sooner children learn to use them, the better. If your child is not interested in writing on a computer, try games. Exciting graphics, sounds, and action may intrigue your child.

Borrow software from friends or from the public library to try out. Check out educational software catalogs that offer a thirty-day money back guarantee. Regardless of what your child's interests are, you'll be able to find a computer program that he'll find enjoyable: art, music, cars, Barbie, movies and television, phonics, reading, math history, and just about anything else you can imagine.

Don't give up if your child isn't interested in the computer right at this moment. Our children are always growing and changing. Every couple of weeks or so, give your child the opportunity to try it again. And don't get discouraged if your child doesn't do a computer program exactly the way it's supposed to be done.

When Benjamin was younger, I would sit down with him at the computer to instruct him in how to use a new program. He hated that! He would yell and scream and then not want to do it at all. I learned that computer programs are just like new toys: children may need to do things "their way" first. After Benj was through checking it out on his own, he would ask me to show him what to do.

Handwriting

Many children need assistance holding a pencil. For some kids, simply adding pencil grips is enough. Mail order catalogs feature many devices to enable a writer to get a good grip. Giving children extra fat pens, pencils, paintbrushes, and other writing instruments may be all that's needed. And don't listen to experts who say your child must hold a pencil the "right" way. How ever your child holds the pencil is the right way!

A variety of paper and paper aids are also available. Paper with two different colors of lines helps children "stay in the lines" when they're learning to print. On other types of paper, the lines are raised with ink so a child can feel where the line is with her pencil.

"Masks" are helpful, too. These are heavy plastic or cardboard sheets with rectangular holes that correspond to a line in a notebook, for instance. Place the mask over the paper and the child writes within the small rectangular area. Make your own with card stock.

In an earlier chapter, I described buying Benjamin a name stamp in first grade. This was a much more efficient way of getting his name on his papers. You might also consider buying a set of alphabet stamps. Children can learn to spell their names and other words with these handy devices.

If handwriting is a laborious, time-consuming task, or if your child's handwriting is illegible, move on to a computer as soon as possible. Few of us hand write anything anymore. If your child cannot write fast enough to take notes or complete a test, he needs a computer at school.

Try out handwriting tools at home, then share your wisdom with educators. Without your guidance, teachers may spend too much time on handwriting at the expense of academics and other important areas of development. The most handwriting you and I do is writing checks and signing our names. If your child can sign his name as well as a doctor signs a prescription pad, that's perfect!

Use an Easel for Reading and Writing

Just as some children need to be positioned properly, they also need the things they use in the right positions. It was always hard for Benjamin to maintain his posture and balance when he tried to finger paint or hold a book. A desk easel was the answer. It brought the paper or book close to him, and it was adjustable so we could position things just right. When he was in elementary school, the custodian made one for him. If you or someone you know is handy, you can easily make one. Find a picture of one in a catalog for a model.

When Benjamin was drawing or finger painting, we found it helpful to tape his paper to the easel to keep it in place. Even if your child doesn't use an easel, it might be helpful to tape the paper down. It's hard for some kiddos to hold the paper with one hand and paint or write with the other at the same time.

With the easel, Benjamin could position a book close to his eyes and at just the right angle. In addition to bigger easels that are good for several purposes, you can find small easels just for books. Some have a spring-like device that holds the pages flat so the child doesn't have to worry about holding the book wide open as he reads. Check out office supply stores, book stores, and general merchandise stores for these items.

Math Tools

Most adults use calculators, so why shouldn't our children learn to use them as early as possible, especially kids who have difficulty with math to begin with? Educators often argue that children need to know the basics of rote addition, subtraction, multiplication, and division. Yes, it would be nice if all children could learn these, but some may not. Just because a child can't do math the traditional way doesn't mean he should be denied a tool to help him do math his own way!

There are a zillion ways to learn math at home. Setting the table: how many people are there and how many forks do you need? When the pizza is delivered, how many pieces are there altogether and how many can each person have? Take your child to the grocery store and have him add up your purchases on the calculator or teach him how to round the numbers to the closest dollar to arrive at an approximate total. Cook together; measure and count as you follow a recipe. Think about the math you use during the day and teach your child those basic skills. Board games, card games, dice, and dominoes are great math tools.

Buy fun math books or borrow them from the library. There are many great books to give you ideas about helping your child learn math in fun and relevant ways. Check out computer games, electronic handheld math games, counting sticks, and other devices.

History, Social Studies, Geography, and Other Academics

Computer games, board games, interesting books, videos, and television shows can all be used to help your child learn at home. If it works at home, send it to school; teach the teacher what works best.

Use natural methods to help your child learn. Don't call it "geography;" just talk about what you see when you're driving to the store or going on vacation. Read newspapers and current events magazines together and teach your child history, social studies, government, and more. Make up family games: let your child be the President of the United States and make decisions that are supported or vetoed by the Congress (the rest of the family).

The Home-School Connection

We can help our children be more successful in school by supplementing what they're learning at school with learning opportunities at home. If something works at home, send it to school. For example, if a sixth grade class is studying American history, a child who reads at a lower grade level could study an easy-reader book at home about George Washington or the American Revolution.

Videotapes can be used in lieu of textbooks. There are many great educational videos on the market. You probably won't be able to find a video that exactly matches a school textbook, but if your child is learning the basic information of the subject, it shouldn't matter what source he uses. Many good educational programs are on cable television stations (*Discovery Channel, The Learning Channel-TLC, History Channel,* and others). Record shows on your video recorder at home and develop a library of videotapes that can be used by all your children. Offer to send the videotapes to school for the whole class to view. If you make the offer in the right way, your child's teacher will love you.

Find out what videos are available from the school library and your public library. Search the Internet for video companies and request a catalog. Work with the librarian or the teacher about finding funds to buy videos every child in the school could learn from.

Computer programs are an ideal way for students to learn when reading text books is difficult. Using the American history example again, your child could probably learn more (and in a more interesting way) from a computer program or video than from a textbook that's boring or hard to understand.

Think Out of the Box!

Think back to your own years in school. What would have made learning more fun and enjoyable? Talk to your child and get her expert advice on how best she could learn. If we do our parental homework, our children will be the beneficiaries.

Do all you can to help your child (all your children, for that matter) learn at home. We should not expect public education (regular or special) to provide our children with the best education possible. Schools are overcrowded, teachers are overworked, the curriculum isn't always exactly what you want your child to learn, and much of the subject matter isn't interesting or meaningful to your child.

Learning should be a fun and exciting lifelong journey of discovery, but for many children it's hard, meaningless, or boring. Keep the flame of discovery burning bright in your child's spirit. Counter the negatives of school with positive and exciting learning opportunities at home.

COMMON SENSE AND CREATIVITY

When we use our common sense to find the right solutions to meet our children's needs, we're giving them tools for success. The system cannot provide everything. The system can't be in our homes (surely we don't want them there, anyway) to help us figure out what works best for our children. We can—and we must—be the ones to do it. All of us can reclaim our common sense and come up with creative solutions that are good and right for our children and families.

Sometimes the best thing to do is to sit and think and ask yourself, "What if?" What if you did this or that or the other? If the first idea doesn't work, try something else. You'll learn so much by trying.

If no creative ideas are bouncing around in your brain or if you can't do everything yourself, that's okay. Describe the situation for friends and family members. Ask for help. Need to pour a ramp? Need assistance altering clothing? Need ideas on behavior supports or ways to help your child learn? Tell everyone you know what you need and be specific. You'll be surprised at all the help you'll receive from people in your community. In addition, the community is where you'll find natural lives and inclusion for your child and family, as I'll detail next.

Natural Lives
in the Community

Pretend there was no service system, no therapy, no special programs. What would you do? Would you let your child go without the help he needs? No, you'd find it—one way or another—in your own community.

Buckle your seat belt, sit back, relax, and enjoy the journey. We're heading off into the sunrise of a new day. Our destination? A Natural Life. On the way, we'll pick up some of the common sense we misplaced awhile back, we'll exchange some of our old ways of thinking for new, and we'll use the vocabulary of community—People First Language. Our journey begins at home, for the sanctity of our homes and the love in our families are the most crucial components in achieving natural lives for our children.

On the journey, our families will participate in common, every day experiences; we'll use natural supports and generic services when we need them; we'll make new friends along the way; and we'll detour through the maze of the system only as a last resort. Community is a place where children with disabilities and their families live natural lives. It's a place where our children are children, first; where the demons of segregation and exclusion have been exchanged for the spirits of participation and inclusion; and where the dark hopelessness of low expectations is replaced by bright and shiny opportunities for success.

"COMMUNITY-BASED" SERVICES VS.
NATURAL SUPPORTS IN THE COMMUNITY

The paradigm shift from life in an institution to life in the community has been going on for several decades. Deinstitutionalization mandates created what the service system called "community-based services." But we need to be careful.

Don't confuse using community-based services with inclusion in the community. They're not the same thing! Community-based services are still part of the system. They're simply services that are provided somewhere other than an institution. They often have little or nothing to do with *inclusion* in the community.

The majority of people with disabilities, now and in the past, live in communities, not institutions. And most use community-based services, but a majority are still not *included* in their communities. They're invisible, just as people in institutions are invisible. Why? Because community-based services are still specialized (segregated) services created specifically for people with disabilities. People who don't have disabilities don't use these services.

BEING IN THE COMMUNITY VS. BEING PART OF THE COMMUNITY

Children and adults with disabilities, and their families, are often *in* their communities, but they're not *part* of their communities. Special programs, private and agency therapies, group homes, voc-rehab assistance, and other services are community-based, but they seldom ensure inclusion in the community. Just the opposite is usually true. Physical, social, and psychological segregation are common when people use community-based services.

It's very difficult to assume the role of citizen and achieve inclusion in the community when one is still dependent on the service system. Just about the time you're feeling like a citizen, the system reels you back in to let you know you're still a client. Still, many of us continue to wear our client-roles because it feels safer. We're probably not getting everything we need, we might hate the system and all its rules and regulations, and we might be continually frustrated and angry. But at least we're familiar with it all. Community-based services are predictable. There aren't too many surprises. We feel safe, since we're tethered to service providers, therapists, or other professionals who are in charge of our lives.

Being included in one's community is sometimes unpredictable. You never know what might happen. No one is in charge but you and your family. When you go to the edge of the cliff to see the beautiful view, there's no professional to grab you and save you. But the people in your community will protect you; they won't let you fall. They're not paid to do this. They do it because they're your friends. They do it because, in community, people care about one another. In community, we replace the artificial services and supports of the system with the natural supports and the generic services that already surround us.

When we're ready to move from being clients in the system to taking our rightful places as citizens in our communities, we must do it in the manner that's best for us. For some, it will be as simple as saying "no" to the system and "yes" to community. Others will need a plan of action. Regardless of how you get to community, every member of your family will be successful if you're determined to live natural lives of freedom and dignity.

COMMUNITIES ARE RICH; THE SYSTEM IS POOR

As clients of the system, our children and families are expected to fit into the paltry assortment of existing services. As citizens in communities, we can find and/or design what we need from the rich array of services and supports that meet our unique needs. Most communities already have just about everything we need. But most of us haven't taken the time to discover what's available. If the exact things we need don't already exist, we can fine tune what's there to meet our needs.

Every time you, your child, or your family participates in your community, every time you help someone learn what supports your child and your family need, and every time you contribute to your community, in whatever way you can, you're increasing the capacity of your community—the capacity to support and meet the needs of others with disabilities. Capacity-building is a work in progress.

In the system, we're recipients of help. In community, we're both recipients and providers of friendship, assistance, volunteerism, and more. Community means reciprocity. We don't want charity, we want equality. We don't want to only receive; we also want to give. This is natural. In community, we focus on the inherent worth of all citizens, not on the perceived deficits of individuals with disabilities. In community, we live real lives.

INCLUSION AND THE SYSTEM

Inclusion, like love, is hard to find when we're looking for it in all the wrong places. The programs and services designed to help our children usually keep them excluded and segregated. Many of us keep banging our heads against the wall of the service system, demanding inclusion and insisting on change. We're sad, angry, frustrated, and tired. Day after day, our children are growing up in the very unnatural environments of the service system, surrounded by professionals who are paid to help them. And all the while, our precious sons and daughters are missing out on the joys of birthday parties, friends, sports, dating, a good education, and other ordinary activities that lay the foundation for success.

If we can't find inclusion within the service system, where can we find it? In our homes and communities.

WHAT IS A COMMUNITY?

A community is more than a geographical location. We're surrounded by numerous communities. Some are separate and distinct from one another; others overlap. They're like the stars in the night sky: they're always there, but we don't always see them.

Communities are places you and your family are currently involved in or places you want to be involved in: the church community, the job community, the neighborhood community, the school community, the sports community, and more, much more. Communities are never static; they're living, breathing entities that change and grow, along with the people in them.

Not only are children with disabilities often outsiders in their own communities, but their families are, too. Unfortunately, many parents who are connected to the service system have cut themselves off from their communities. All this can change. If you don't feel you're a part of any community, don't worry. It's never too late to become a member.

WHAT IS INCLUSION?

Being included is not a privilege to be earned, nor a right that is given to individuals. Inclusion is—first and foremost—a state of mind. Do you *feel* you belong: in your home, at work, in a classroom, at church, in the PTA, or at a T-ball game?

Do you do what it takes to be included? Do you participate, make others feel welcome, and share? Inclusion is always reciprocal. Everyone in an inclusive setting contributes for the good of the whole. If a member receives (or takes) but does not give, he is not included. He's a recipient of charity, a guest, or a thief.

Inclusion in the community looks different for everyone, because we're all individuals. But generally, it means people with disabilities are participating, valued members of their communities. They enjoy the pleasures, rights, and responsibilities of full citizenship; they are known by their names and their interests, not their disabilities; and they contribute to, and enjoy the benefits of, the naturally-occurring supports and services that exist in their communities.

Because there's not an exact definition of inclusion that's appropriate for everyone, it's probably easier to define exclusion than inclusion. To exclude means to prevent from participating, to leave out, or set apart.

In communities, inclusion is the default position: being included is the natural state of being. Individuals don't have to look a certain way or act a certain way to be included. Nor do they need to meet a particular standard. People are included and they belong simply because they're present. Whether inclusion *continues* is dependent on the actions of each individual: does the person contribute, participate, make others feel welcome, and so forth.

Communities—whether they're within neighborhoods, churches, recreational activities, places of employment, or anywhere else—are filled with individuals who are different from one another. But their shared participation in a given community connects them to one another. People with diverse characteristics (that's all of us) are included *because they expect to be included.* They expect they can join a church, participate in community activities, join the PTA, get a job, play in the softball league, or do whatever else they want to do.

So why are so many people with disabilities not included in their communities? Why are people with disabilities often invisible? Why are some excluded? Certainly, some are prevented from participating because of prejudice and discrimination. But this is the exception and not the rule. In general, children with disabilities (and their families) are not included because they *don't expect to be included!* Unfortunately, many parents expect their children will be *excluded,* and this attitude permeates their actions: the expectation becomes an unfortunate reality.

Let's look at the lives of parents whose children do not have disabilities. Many parents are included in a variety of communities because of their children's lives and activities. They're included in the communities of their children's schools as PTA members, volunteers, or because they meet other parents in the school parking lot mornings and afternoons. If their children play sports or participate in other activities, parents are included in those communities. They meet other parents at games, while volunteering or carpooling, and in many other ways.

It's easy to see how parents of children with disabilities may feel isolated and disconnected from their communities; easy to understand why they don't expect inclusion. If their children are segregated in the public school system, parents don't see themselves as part of the school community. And poor relationships with educators exacerbates this painful situation. When children are excluded and isolated at school, parents often feel isolated and excluded, too.

In the community-at-large, many children with disabilities don't participate in activities because their parents feel they're not "ready" or not capable. Parents may feel their children could not be properly supported or included in youth organizations or activities. Others don't have time for their children to participate since they're too busy taking their children to therapies. In some cases, children don't participate because their parents have been told "we don't take kids like yours." Regardless of why children don't participate, their parents feel excluded, isolated, and disconnected.

Most importantly, parents and their children with disabilities are not part of their natural communities because they're dependent on the service system. They don't go to their communities for help and support; they go to paid professionals in the system. The service system has taken the place of their natural communities.

Most parents of children with disabilities want to be part of their communities. They want to belong; they want to be included. They don't like feeling isolated, disconnected, angry, and lonely.

We can make it happen. When we say goodbye to the conventional wisdom of the service system and look to our communities for support, inclusion happens naturally. Inclusion doesn't require that we change our children. It does require a change in perception (seeing our children's gifts and talents as more important the the disability) and a change in attitude (believing our children can be successful in typical activities).

WHAT IS A NATURAL LIFE?

Most people who don't have disabilities live natural lives. Like inclusion, living a natural life is the default position for people without disabilities, so it's probably easier to define an unnatural life than to define a natural life. People who live unnatural lives are those who are dependent on the service system, having ceded control of their lives and destinies to others: professionals in medicine and education, bureaucrats in the service system, and other gatekeepers.

People living natural lives use the common and ordinary resources in their communities to achieve success and have their needs met. If they can't find what they need, they create it with the help of others.

People living unnatural lives depend on the limited resources of the system to achieve success and have their needs met. If they can't find what they need, they either agitate for change or give up.

THE COMMUNITY VS. THE SYSTEM

Living a natural life in the community means taking a different path than the one we've been on. When we use the system, we have to follow the rules of the system. We must take the single path (eligibility and red tape), approach the gatekeepers (service providers), and shout the correct passwords (disability labels) to enter the kingdom of services.

In community, there is not just one path to take, there are many. There are no rules, no passwords, no gatekeepers. In community, we get what we want and need using the same methods as others: using the existing resources in our cities and towns, depending on friends, networking, calling on old connections and making new ones, offering to give, being creative, thinking out of the box, and being both flexible and persistent.

We recognize that what we need is already there, we just haven't been seeing it. We've been looking at our communities through a knot hole in the fence of the service system. When we climb over the fence, go around it, or knock it down, we see the community as it really is.

Limited Menu or All-You-Can-Eat

Using the service system is like going to a fast food place. At McServices, there's a basic menu to pick from. The food is okay, but there's not much choice, and the menu seldom changes. Ho-hum.

Using the natural resources in our communities is like going to a full-service buffet. At the Community Cafeteria, there's a huge, tantalizing selection. With so much to choose from, there's something delicious for everyone. And you can get all you want. The menu's always changing, too. Yummy!

Which do you want? McServices or the Community Cafeteria?

Disability is Irrelevant in Community

When our children participate in typical, age-appropriate community activities, they're living natural lives and achieving success. Our children are seen as real people, not their labels. In community, disability is irrelevant.

When nine-year-old Jeremy takes his place on the softball field, he's known as the left outfielder, not the kid with a disability. His label is irrelevant. What's important about Jeremy is that he's a real team player, is always on time, likes to bat more than anything, and his mom always brings chocolate chip cookies for players on both teams.

In her Girl Scout troop, Megan is seen as leader. Her disability is insignificant. Megan's twelve-year-old friends admire all her badges. Several ask for advice on the latest project. Another wants to room with Megan at camp this year. What's important about Megan is that she's the first one to offer to help when one of her fellow Scouts needs assistance, she never gives up, and she always makes new girls feel welcome.

During Tom's part-time job at the neighborhood pack-and-ship store, he's known for his attention to detail and his skill in boxing and wrapping packages. His disability is inconsequential. At fifteen, he's the youngest employee and the one with the most energy. What's important about Tom is his willingness to pitch in and help others, his positive attitude, and his friendliness.

The four members of the Johnson family volunteer every other Saturday at the Care-and-Share food distribution center. When ten-year-old Kara puts the fresh vegetables in the customers' bags, her label is meaningless. She's part of the food crew and she handles the tomatoes and corn very carefully so she won't bruise them. The Johnson family is known by its contributions to the community, not by the disability label of one of its members.

How do you want your child to be identified? In the system, our children are known by their disabilities, labels, and perceived deficits. In our communities, they're known by their assets and contributions. When our children become involved in typical community activities, they assume new roles that open up new opportunities for success. Children with disabilities have earned the dubious privilege of carrying around years of medical and special ed baggage. File cabinets all over the country are overflowing with our children's diagnoses, prognoses, assessments, and histories. The current roles our children wear are based on these biased and unfair credentials. These are the same credentials that provide entrance to the service system, including special education. Our children's labels, perceived deficits, and identified needs are what's most important to the system, so that's how our children are known.

When our children participate in typical, age-appropriate community activities, they become known by their assets, strengths, and interests. What might happen if these impressive credentials permeated the attitudes of those in the special education system? What might happen if Jeremy's softball coach, Megan's troop leader, and Tom's boss participate in their IEP meetings? Consider the possibilities.

For parents, the inclusion of their children in the community brings powerful emotions. We can puff out our chests with pride over our children's accomplishments. Tears of joy can be shed when we see—sometimes for the first time—that others think our kids are really neat.

But what's it like for our children? How might these experiences feel to them? To feel like you're really somebody for the first time in your life? To be a part of something where people like you because you're you, where they're counting on you because you're needed and valued? What does it feel like to have real friends? To share a giggle or a raunchy joke with a best buddy?

How can we measure the value of these treasures—the precious gems of fellowship, contribution, and reciprocity? And can we afford to withhold these gifts from our children any longer? If our sons and daughters live natural, interdependent lives in community, they're on the path to successful lives as adults.

THEY ARE CHILDREN, FIRST

The conventional wisdom of the system—that professional intervention is necessary to meet the "special needs" of children with disabilities—has done a great disservice to parents and their children. In addition to undermining parents' confidence and usurping parental influence, the excessive focus on "special needs" often causes us to disregard our children's basic needs. As I've pointed out earlier, many interventions yank our children out of childhood and thrust them into clienthood. Our children are children, first. A child's greatest need is to be a child, not a defective thing to be repaired, not a body to be manipulated, not a client to be served.

Regardless of the labels assigned to them, our children are blossoming and developing right before our eyes. Each is unique, each deserves every opportunity and privilege we can provide, and each has distinctive needs. Differences aside, all children with disabilities have the same basic needs as other children: to be unconditionally loved, valued, and respected for who they are; to love, value, and respect themselves as they are; and to grow up knowing they can and should participate in, and contribute to, the world around them.

When my son was very young and I was still enamored with therapies and interventions, I justified my actions with this thought: when Benjamin was thirty years old, I wanted to be able to look back on his life and know I did everything I could for him. Translated, this meant I would spare no expense or effort to help him walk, talk, and all the rest. Today, I know what's really important is that when Benj is thirty, I can look back and know I did everything I could to give him the same things his sister—and all children—need: a sense of belonging, belief in himself, and the capacity for self-determination.

The system may entitle our children to certain rights, but their humanity bestows upon them the greatest right: the right to a full and natural childhood. Childhood is fleeting; once it's gone, it's gone forever. We must protect our children's childhoods.

Many of our children are hurt by the system. They're turned into clients; viewed as body parts in need of repair; made to feel unworthy; and their childhoods are lost in the maze of services and interventions.

The injuries to our children's spirits don't happen in one swift, bold move. It's not like the pain and injury of being cut once—deeply—with a sharp blade. It happens, slowly, over time, in ways that are almost imperceptible. It's like being nicked with a dull knife, over and over, for years. The milder, but constant pain becomes a normal part of life. And instead of one deep cut, we're left with many smaller wounds. Some may heal and others may fester, but eventually, they take their toll: our children's spirits are permanently scarred. We must protect our children—and our families—from the interference of interventions. They must be allowed to be children, first.

ON BECOMING ORDINARY

The lives of children with disabilities should look like the lives of children who don't have disabilities. Take some time and think about what your child would be doing if he didn't have a disability. Two-year-olds explore the house. Seven-year-old girls play with dolls. Thirteen-year-old boys are into music, sports, or computers.

Typical children spend lots of time doing things that meet their needs. A two-year-old *needs* to explore to learn about his world. A seven-year-old *needs* to play with dolls to learn about caring and love. A thirteen-year-old *needs* to learn more about himself through social interactions.

Children with disabilities have the same basic needs as all children. However, most of us don't focus on basic needs and allow our children to enjoy typical childhoods. We focus on the so-called special needs and our children live unnatural lives. Meeting these needs keeps the service system in business and keeps parents in a constant state of "busy-ness."

Beyond "Special Needs"

In the previous chapter, I recommended going from just "meeting needs" to providing our children with tools for success. Now let's go a step further.

There's more to having a wonderfully successful life than just having our needs met. It's time to go beyond meeting the needs related to a child's disability. When assessing your child's needs, has anyone ever said, "He needs to have fun!" or "He needs to experience a typical childhood."? It's time to address what our children and families really need: fun and excitement, rest and relaxation, and the simple pleasures of an ordinary family life.

I don't want my son and my family to be special. I'm tired of special. Special is not really so special, after all. I want ordinary, plain, regular, average, natural. I want my family to be woven into the fabric of our community, not held aloft as a shining example to be admired, nor pushed aside to the tattered edge because of differences.

Becoming ordinary and using more natural ways of helping our children provides many benefits. We reclaim our family's autonomy, unity, dignity, and privacy. We don't structure our lives around therapies and interventions. We begin living regular lives. Perhaps most importantly, helping our children in natural ways sends a clear message to our children: we value them just the way they are. This doesn't mean we don't help them with their unique needs. It means we use natural methods—not artificial ones—of helping our children, based on their strengths and interests.

EVERYONE IS "READY" IN COMMUNITY

Before we can help our children assume natural lives in the community, we must consciously decide they're ready for life just the way they are. We must presume competence.

We must discard the philosophies that have promoted exclusion. We must reject the deficit and medical models of disability, as well as the concepts of readiness and developmental age that were covered in previous chapters.

If we let these detrimental philosophies accompany our children into the community, we'll set them up for failure. The majority of people in our communities aren't familiar with these concepts and *that's the way it should stay*. We don't want a Scout leader to know, for example, that a nine-year-old boy has been judged "not ready" for troop membership because he "functions" at the level of a five-year-old.

The way we present our children determines how others view them. Many parents eagerly embrace using People First Language and they're excited about redefining their children by their gifts and talents. But parents may still hold on to some of the old ways of thinking. Specifically, many of us still accept the validity of the readiness and developmental age concepts. This subject has been discussed in previous chapters. However, it's important to examine it within the context of community, for your efforts to have your child included will be diminished if the readiness and developmental age philosophies follow him around. When we reject the developmental age concept, our children are able to assume new and different roles within their families, as well as in their communities and schools. Let's look at how children without disabilities are usually perceived.

If You're Six, You're Six

Children without disabilities are always thought of in terms of their chronological ages, even when they don't "act" their age and even if they can't or don't do what's considered "normal" for their age. Seldom do we cut typical children into pieces based on specific characteristics.

For example, most parents and professionals don't look at a typical six-year-old and say, "Physically, John is the size of a five-year-old, has the motor abilities of an eight-year-old, the speech of a nine-year-old, and the manners of a three-year-old."

We don't look at one characteristic and let that define John. When looking at his manners—his social development—we don't say, "Because John functions at the level of a three-year-old, we'll treat him like a three-year-old." Typical parents (who have no formal training in child development) know how wrong this would be. Using their common sense, they know if they treat John like he's three, he'll act like he's three instead of six. If they treat him like he's six—if they expect him to act like a six-year-old—John will become more like a six-year-old in his manners and social skills. He will, in essence, rise to their expectations.

Typically, his parents would look at John as a whole child and say, "He's six. That means he's going to first grade, we're taking the training wheels off his bike, he's going to join Cub Scouts, we'll sign him up for T-ball, and he's old enough to spend the night at friend's house." And when he doesn't always act like a six-year-old, his parents recognize this as a natural occurrence. He's not defined by his actions or behavior.

For example, when he goes to his friend's house for his first sleep over, his parents are understanding when he calls at midnight, in tears, and says he wants to come home to his own bed. Six months later, he still doesn't want to sleep over at his friend's house. Even under these circumstances, his parents still see him as a six-year-old, even though he's not doing what other sixes may be doing! But children with disabilities aren't always so lucky.

Many are routinely given two ages: their chronological age (actual age) and a developmental age (an age based on the child's abilities as compared to a scale of average development). Children with disabilities are frequently denied participation in typical, age-appropriate activities (at home, in school, and in the community) because they're not perceived to be at the appropriate developmental level. When this happens, our children are prevented from experiencing opportunities for success and for living natural lives. And parents may be part of the problem. When we buy into the developmental age model, we're asking for trouble.

The difference between a child's chronological age (CA) and his developmental age (DA) takes on progressively more importance as he grows. When children are very young, the differences aren't critically important. But once children reach school age, wide differences between a child's CA and his DA often lead to segregation and exclusion. For example, a twelve-year-old with a developmental disability is excluded from seventh grade because her developmental age is eight. A twenty-five-year-old is told he cannot leave the group home and live on his own because he "functions" like a fourteen-year-old.

Contrary to conventional wisdom, an individual's developmental age is *not* a reflection of the actual impact of the disability. Instead, it reflects the limited opportunities for growth and learning afforded that person. The individual was given a developmental age and was then treated as if he was really that age. As a result, he was denied opportunities to "be" his chronological age.

The developmental age often becomes more important than the disability label and it's often all-encompassing. Let's say a professional identifies thirteen-year-old Kara as having a developmental age of nine in the area of cognition. However, in physical abilities Kara's developmental age is the same as her chronological age, and in her social skills, her developmental age is two years above her chronological age. She's a very mature and responsible thirteen-year-old. However, these last two measurements are irrelevant to many professionals and maybe even her parents! All they see is the cognitive function is of a nine-year-old, so that's who they think Kara is.

Another scenario is also possible. Once Kara's DA was fixed at nine, her social skills and physical abilities may not even be tested. Some people may assume Kara is at the nine-year-old level in every area. It's possible her physical abilities and social skills are not perceived to be as important as cognition.

The intent of measuring children with disabilities on a developmental scale is to identify those areas of development in which a child needs help. But the measurements are constantly misused: children are categorized and defined by their developmental ages, which leads to exclusion and lost opportunities. The whole concept of developmental age should be scrapped. It's caused more problems than it's solved for children with developmental disabilities. It's a tool adults use to judge children.

Why aren't there developmental scales for adults? Do we stop developing once we hit a certain age? I hope not. But if someone ever came up with a developmental scale for adults, we wouldn't stand for it.

If there was such a thing, I would be very upset if *my* developmental age was *always* the same as my chronological age. At the age of fifty, I sometimes act silly like an exuberant six-year-old and sometimes I need to be babied like an infant. At other times, I strive to have the wisdom and insight of an eighty-year-old. If it's okay for adults to operate at many different levels, why isn't it okay for children with disabilities?

What would happen if we used developmental age as a criteria in business and government? Membership in the American Association of Retired Persons (AARP) is limited to people aged fifty and above. But what if they changed it to a *developmental age* of fifty or above? Perhaps some thirty-year-olds could join. And maybe some eighty-year-olds would never qualify because they still act forty-five!

What if states made laws requiring a developmental age of sixteen for all drivers? There might be some twenty-year-olds who wouldn't be able to get a license! And in which area should the developmental age of sixteen apply? Cognition? Visual-spatial? Social skills? Perhaps we would decide social skills are most important: if people behaved with more manners and respect toward other drivers, we could end road rage.

Developmental readiness creates a vicious circle. We don't let our children experience typical age-appropriate activities because they're not "ready," but they're never able to be "ready" because they don't experience typical age-appropriate activities. This detrimental process must end.

We don't inflict the developmental model on children *without* disabilities. Why do we allow it to harm children with disabilities? We do things to children with disabilities we would never do to children without disabilities. How can we expect our children to fully grow and develop when we put restraints on them?

Let's go back to the imaginary scenario with Kara. If, at age thirteen, we treat her like a nine-year-old, what do we expect from her? What will happen to her if we put her with nine-year-olds—even in an inclusive classroom—because that's the level of academic work she can do? How will she behave? How will she ever learn how to be a whole thirteen-year-old if we don't treat her like one? She cannot rise to our expectations, since our expectations are low. But she will probably live *down* to our expectations.

Worse, though, is the effect of this action on Kara. What does Kara think about herself? How can she believe in herself? How can she like herself under these conditions?

We need to change the way we treat our children. We need to give them experiences appropriate to their chronological ages. This doesn't mean we should expect a child to do all the things children his age do. It simply means we give him *opportunities* to be his age; we expose him to *experiences* of children his age; and we give him the *respect and dignity* his chronological age affords him.

In order to treat our children the ages they really are, many of us will need to change the way we do things. We'll need to meet our children's real needs and provide them with tools for success, as described in the previous chapter. We can't expect a nine-year-old to be like a nine-year-old if he has no form of effective communication. He needs to have his own "voice." Similarly, we can't expect a sixteen-year-old to be his actual age if someone has to push him around in his wheelchair like he's a baby. He needs independent mobility.

We need to change our children's environments, not our children. If they're given age-appropriate opportunities, our children will grow up just fine. A six-year-old should not still be in a special ed preschool. She needs to be in an inclusive first grade classroom. A three-year-old should not be in the church nursery on Sunday mornings just because she's still in diapers. She needs to be in the three-year-old Sunday school class.

The benefits of age-appropriate experiences extend far and wide. When children are successfully included within their own homes and their own communities—when they're living natural lives according to their chronological ages—they're far more likely to be successfully included in age-appropriate public school classrooms.

Our children can lead successful lives only if we let them. You and your child need to decide what's important for your child to learn and do based on his chronological age, not the developmental age assigned to him. This is critically important to your child's long-term success. Presume competence. Systems use developmental and readiness models to decide our children's fates. We must not.

NATURAL LIVES BEGIN AT HOME

Everything starts at home. Our homes must be inclusive environments. Children need to achieve success living natural lives in their own homes first. This will make the paths to natural lives in communities and schools much smoother.

What's your child's role at home? Is he the "baby" of the family, regardless of his age and birth order? Does he contribute to the overall of success of the family? Is he expected to help with chores? Does he have responsibilities? If the other kids in the family get an allowance, does he? Does he participate in family decisions? Is he consulted? Is his voice heard? Does he participate in family activities? Does he go on family vacations or does he stay home with a sitter or go to grandma's? Is he dependent only on Mom or Dad, or does everyone in the family pitch in to help everyone else? Are younger brothers and sisters made responsible for him? Or is he expected to help take care of his little brothers and sisters? Does anyone in the family seek him out for assistance? Does he have what he needs for typical age-appropriate experiences?

We can all do better to ensure our children with disabilities are participating, contributing, included members of our households. Sometimes it takes a little work to make it happen, but aren't they worth it? Their future is in our hands; they're counting on us.

Being Needed; Assuming Responsibility

One of the many blessings a family bestows on us is the very important feeling of being needed. All of us feel valued and loved when we're needed.

Children with disabilities need to be needed. Regardless of age or disability, your child needs to be a responsible member of the family, who—like everyone else in the family—contributes to the family's overall success. One of those responsibilities is helping around the house. Two-year-olds can help. Children who use chairs or have breathing tubes can help. Our children should not be made exempt from obligation and contribution because of their disabilities. They need to feel useful, not useless.

Call a family meeting and make a list of everything—and I mean everything—that needs to be done in your home on a daily, weekly, and/or monthly basis. Start with the jobs that must be done by an adult: earning money, paying bills, and so on. Children don't usually know how many things their parents are responsible for, either because they don't think of them as chores or because they don't see us do them. So list everything done by adults in your home.

If you start your meeting by listing the jobs already being done by you and your spouse, your children will see you're already overworked and you need their help: "Dad works all day to earn money and Mom works half the day. Dad gets the cars serviced. Mom pays the bills." Don't stop there, keep going. Your children will probably be amazed at everything you do.

Then begin talking about all the other chores that need to be done. In our home, one of the first questions we asked after the "parent-only jobs" was, "Who wants to clean the gutters?" That brought no response from the kids. "Okay," Dad says, "I'll do that. Let me read off some of the other chores and tell me when you hear one you'll take responsibility for." The children spoke up and stated their preferences. Now we were getting somewhere.

There are many things Benjamin is unable to do around the house. But guess what? We all have things we can't do. I can't go into the crawl space under the house. It hurts my back and gives me claustrophobia. So there's never any discussion about who should do that. My husband or my daughter volunteer since they know I can't.

If your children aren't accustomed to doing chores, they might balk. That's to be expected. When Benjamin sets the dinner table, he sometimes whines about it, but he loves that he's important and valued. If anyone tries to help him do it, look out! "It's my job!" he yells. "I'll do it!"

When you have family meetings and each member agrees on what he or she will do, everyone is making a commitment to other members of the family. If children resist doing the things they've agreed to do, simply remind them of their commitment. You might even say, "I know this is not your favorite job, but I really appreciate your willingness to do it. Our next family meeting is in two days. We can makes changes then, okay?"

Let everyone choose what to do for a specified length of time—a week, for example. If your child with a disability volunteers for something you don't think he can do, let him try, unless it's something dangerous. He might surprise you. Modify the task, if necessary. Let your children do things even if you could do them faster or better. I can set the table faster than Benj can, but the point isn't to get everything done fast. The point is to create an environment where everyone contributes and belongs.

Let go of the notion that things have to be done a certain way. If your daughter empties the dishwasher differently than you, that's okay. Don't criticize her efforts. If you've shown her how to do it and she chooses to do it a different way, accept her way as long as it gets done.

Have the next family meeting in a week and talk about how things went. Get comments and suggestions from everyone. Let each person pick again for the next week. And let each member of your family take turns *leading* the meetings. Leadership starts at home.

I recently spoke to a mom who was having trouble getting help from her twelve-year-old son who has autism. It was just the two of them after the death of her husband a couple of years before. She had already done a good job of making her son feel needed by letting him know he had to help more since his daddy was gone. She cooked dinner for the two of them every night when she got home from work, and her son was responsible for cleaning up the kitchen and taking out the trash.

One day, he angrily announced he was "sick and tired" of helping her. His attitude made her feel hurt and frustrated. I suggested she sit down with him and tell him she understood his feelings, because she also got tired of doing chores. Perhaps she could ask him, in a friendly and respectful manner, if he'd like to switch responsibilities: he could have dinner ready when she got home and she'd clean up the kitchen and take out the trash.

At this, she gave me a big grin and said she felt pretty sure he would decide his responsibilities weren't so bad after all.

As children grow and develop, or when circumstances change, we need to modify our expectations. Once Benjamin got his power chair, he had far greater abilities to help than he did in the manual chair. I had become accustomed to asking Emily or Mark for more help than Benjamin, simply because there were many things he couldn't do. But when he started using the power chair, I had to rethink things.

Instead of automatically asking my husband or my daughter for help, I'd give myself a minute to figure out if Benjamin could do it. As an example, everyone was expected to pitch in and help clear the table after dinner. But we never expected Benj to help with that, because he couldn't wheel himself in the manual chair and hold dishes at the same time. But in his power chair, he could hold a ketchup bottle in one hand or a couple of plates in his lap. Proudly, he began helping with this task, calling out, "Here you go, Mom!" as he rolled up to the sink. Being asked to help made him feel important, valued, and worthy.

A hint about chores: forcing the issue doesn't work. Children will just procrastinate and balk even more. Tell your children you *need* their help. Whenever it's called for, I throw my hands in the air and plaintively announce, "I can't do it all by myself! I need your help." And I really do. I don't like to beg for help. I also don't appreciate the help if I had to coerce someone to help me. When I tell my family I need their help, I get a much more positive response than when I try to force them.

We're All Responsible for One Another

If one parent provides most of the help for the child with a disability, that needs to change. Every member of a family should be helping every other member. In many families, this is a common practice, except when it comes to the child with the disability. For example, brothers and sisters without disabilities may help each other do many things, but they may provide little, if any, help to the child with the disability; that's left to mom. When I've asked parents why this happens, they mumble something to the effect of, "Well, it's not their responsibility. He's not their child."

If we accept this reason as valid, then the following statements are also valid. It's not your sixteen-year-old's responsibility to mow the yard. It's not his yard, it's yours. It's not your ten-year-old's responsibility to take out the garbage. It's not his garbage, it's yours. Do these statements make sense? Of course not.

Every member of a family should be responsible for and to every other member. Parents cannot do it all. Many mothers are exhausted, tense, and frustrated because they're trying to do it all. Just stop. Get help from your children, your spouse, and any other members of the household. Everyone needs to pitch in and help. Helping each other is a basic responsibility of being a member of a family, it's valuable experience, and it demonstrates love and caring. Isn't taking care of one another the essence of a family?

Emily has grown up helping Benjamin. When they were very young, they both spent a lot of time playing on the floor. If she wanted Benj to come in her room, she didn't come ask me to move him. She simply took his arms and dragged him down the hallway. If Benjamin didn't like this I would have stepped in. But he actually thought it was quite fun. They both giggled all the way down the hall.

Today, Emily knows how to help Benj get on and off the toilet if they're home alone, how to help him get dressed, and how to do other things Mark and I usually do. When it's time to go out, whoever is closest to Benj helps him put his coat on.

The best relationships are based on reciprocity. We need to be able to give and receive. When we only take in a relationship or when we only give, the relationship is uneven and it doesn't feel good. The helper feels resentful at always having to give and never receiving anything back. The recipient of help feels inadequate and may even feel resentful towards the helper. Thus, our children cannot only be recipients of help; they must be allowed the *privilege of giving.*

While Emily helps Benj on a regular basis, he also helps her. If she needs help with a computer game, Benjamin is there for her. When the phone rings, Benj is happy to answer it, even though most of the calls are babysitting jobs for Emily.

If your other children aren't helping your child with a disability, why not? Why shouldn't they be expected to do many of the same things you help your child with? Don't most parents hope that after they're gone, their children will stay connected, to love and help each other? Don't we need to make sure these deep relationships develop when our children are young? And because reciprocity is so important, what can your child with a disability do for his brother or sister? If something doesn't jump out at you this moment, think about it for awhile and be creative. There's nothing wrong with manipulating or modifying a situation so a child with a disability can help his brother or sister. It's vital our children learn about responsibility to others and reciprocity.

Don't Overdo It

When it comes to helping our children with disabilities let's not smother our children or create dependency. At some point, we had to let go of the bicycle seat when a child learned to ride without training wheels. We watched as she fell, we watched as she gained more control over the wobbly front wheel, and we watched, with a big lump in our throats, as she finally mastered the art of riding a bicycle. With children with disabilities, there are times when we shouldn't help, times when we need to pull back and let children struggle as they master something new.

To that end, we sometimes need to wait for our children to ask for help. Family members shouldn't automatically take over and do "for" all the time. When we let children try to do for themselves, even if they're unsuccessful in a task, we've given them a sense of trust that we believe in them. When they ask for our help, we can do "with" instead of "for." And when children learn to ask for help, they need to be able to tell a helper what type of help they need and how to provide it. As adults with disabilities, they'll be getting help from people other than family members. They need to learn these skills at home, starting with parents, brothers and sisters, friends, babysitters, and others who are close to the family.

A Child's Role in the Family

Is your child's role in the family appropriate for his or her age? In families where the child with the disability is the eldest or is in the middle, younger brothers and sisters sometimes "pass" the older child in certain abilities. Parents often make the mistake of putting a younger child "in charge" of the older child with the disability. Please don't do this. It sends very negative messages to all your children. It tells the younger child that she's more valuable and more competent than the child with the disability. It tells the child with the disability that he's more like a baby than a big brother. Explore ways the older child can be responsible for his little brother or sister: "Paul, I'm getting in the shower now. Will you please watch over little Susie for a few minutes?" Don't worry if Paul can't really take care of little Susie. Create the illusion and it can become a reality.

In our own family, thirteen-year-old Benjamin feels he's way too big for fifteen-year-old Emily to "take care of him" when I go out of town and they're home alone during the day until my husband comes home. Benj doesn't like Emily having more responsibilities just because she's older. He wants as much or more responsibility! So I say, "Benjamin, you do [such and such] and Emily, you do [this and that] while I'm gone. I'm counting on you two to take care of each other, and Dad too, until I get back."

Take whatever steps are necessary to ensure your child with a disability is a needed, responsible member of your family. Further, make sure your child has a variety of roles, just like everyone else in the family. Don't allow him to be only the special child, the baby, or the dependent one. Your child is more than that. In our family, Mark is the official garbage-taker-outer, the music buff, the cover-to-cover newspaper reader. Emily is a different kind of music buff, a busy baby-sitter, the dishwasher unloader. Benjamin is the computer-meister, the playwright, the dish-bringer. I'm the pet-feeder, the mystery buff, the seamstress.

You cannot make all this happen by yourself. Every member of your family is responsible for making sure inclusion is a reality in your family. And everything done to ensure your child's inclusion, participation, and contribution to your family's well-being will help ensure his success in the community and in school.

RETHINKING THERAPY

We take our children to therapy in the hope they'll acquire new skills and abilities (walking, talking, chewing, controlling their bodies, improving their behavior, and so forth). Our intentions are good. But the outcomes of therapy are often questionable. As detailed in Chapter 9, we have no guarantee therapy will work, it sends negative messages to our children, and it disrupts family life.

One misconception we have about therapy is that it's the only way our children will learn certain things. But that's another myth! Children can and do learn from a variety of experiences. The alternative to professional therapy is simply to help our children in the most natural ways possible. And the ways to accomplish this are infinite.

We can give our children the help they need. We don't need to know everything a therapist knows. Think about it. Their training covers a very wide spectrum. They're trained in treating all different types of conditions in children. You only need to know how to help one child: yours.

Is it better for your child to receive intensive physical therapy sessions twice a week or for you to integrate the assistance your child needs into her daily routine? Skill development, range of motion exercises, strength training, proper positioning, auditory training, behavior interventions, and other types of therapeutic activities can be done by parents, day care providers, grandmothers, and even brothers and sisters. These activities can be done at home, in front of the TV, at day care, preschool, in the backyard, or anywhere your child happens to be. I'll share examples of "non-professional" interventions later in the chapter.

There's no reason to believe your child will do something with or for a therapist she won't do at home with you and others who love her. There is no magic in a therapy session. The magic is in your child. Her body and mind will do what's right at the right time, with or without a therapist. Furthermore, she wants to be with *you*. She wants to please *you*. She wants *your* help and companionship more than a therapist's.

In addition, our children can get the help they need in the natural settings within our communities. Ballet, karate, park and rec sports, and other activities can provide them with the exercise they need for their bodies and minds.

If you're not ready to replace therapy with more natural activities, you can still effect positive change by shifting the role of the therapist from a direct service provider to a consultant. You can combine your intimate knowledge of your child with the professional expertise of therapists, to help your child in more natural ways.

A New Role for Therapists: Consultants

The first step is talking with the therapist: "Mary, we're making some changes in our family life. We want to be able to help Jessica throughout the day in more natural ways. We want everyone around her to know what to do. So instead of you providing hands-on therapy twice a week, I'd like you to become our consultant, to teach me, my family, and the other people in Jessica's life how to do things with her at home and in other settings."

Use this as an example. Certainly, these exact words won't fit your unique situation. The example is meant to emphasize the importance of *stating what you want*. You don't ask permission; you don't ask if it's okay. You simply state your position.

The therapist may be upset by your proposal. She doesn't want to lose your child as a client, she might feel you can't do as good a job as she can, and she may feel insulted you think you could replace her. She might even see this as "neglect" on your part. On the other hand, she may be excited about this new opportunity.

Let her know you value her expertise. Be enthusiastic about all the ways she can help you help your child. Be firm, be friendly, be positive, and then be firm some more.

When a therapist becomes a consultant, the service she provides will be very different—and the roles you each assume are vastly different—from the old way. Hands-on therapists do what they think is best for your child. Consultants provide you with the help you ask for. Here are some examples of what a consultant therapist might do:

- Teach you (and others) about natural activities to do at home, or wherever your child is, that are integrated into your child's natural environment(s).

- Share ideas about assistive technology; teach you how to modify things for your child.

- Survey your home and make recommendations about accessibility and/or other issues that promote independence.

- Give your child a "check-up" on a regular basis (monthly, every two months, etc.) to monitor progress or note additional needs.

- Visit your home and/or wherever you child is during the day to demonstrate the best ways to help your child do things (get out of bed, brush her teeth, use the toilet, feed herself, etc.).

- Give a mini-training to your whole family, the day care or preschool staff, friends and relatives, or others you choose, about the things you want them to learn about your child and her needs.

The possibilities are endless. Be creative and thoughtful about what you need from your consultant therapist.

Potential Barriers to the Role Shift

You might already have a therapist who provides consultation instead of therapy, or one who already visits your home. If not, be prepared for potential barriers to this strategy.

One barrier involves funding. Consultation is usually billed differently than hands-on therapy. Some funding agencies (Medicaid, private insurance, HMOs, and others) may require a doctor's prescription for consultation. Insurance may pay for many therapy sessions, but for only one or two consults. If this is the case, creative thinking by you and the therapist is in order. A new therapy plan could be written in such a way that what you need from the therapist still falls under the umbrella of therapy. I'm not suggesting we ask therapists to do anything unethical or illegal regarding the billing and funding processes. But we can usually find appropriate solutions if we work at it.

On the other hand, the funding source may be delighted to pay for one or two consult sessions per month instead of numerous therapy sessions. We're in uncharted territory here, so there's no way to map every possibility. You'll need to put on your detective hat and do some sleuthing to find out more.

Another potential barrier involves travel. If you currently take your child to a therapy center, the therapist may not be able to leave the premises to provide services. If appointments are scheduled every thirty minutes, there's no way she can drive to your home (or wherever), and get back in time for her next appointment. In addition, she might not receive mileage reimbursement for her travel, and the therapy clinic's insurance may not cover her when she's away from the building. If she can leave the building, schedule your consult sessions at the end of the day. When the session is over, she can mosey on home from your place.

If there's absolutely no way the therapist can leave the premises, you might have to find a new one who can travel. If you want to stay with the one you have, even if she can't come to you, alternatives could include you and your child seeing her once a month at the clinic for an hour. During this time, she wouldn't provide hands-on therapy. Instead, the two of you would discuss what's been happening and what you want to happen. You might bring things from home to show her, demonstrate how you're doing things for/with your child, and so forth. If you wanted her to train your child's day care or preschool teachers, they might be able to go to her office. Think it out. Solutions are there.

Using therapists as consultants can help us wean ourselves of our dependency on professional intervention. If you're ready to make the switch, you may decide you only need the therapist for a few more months. Perhaps you don't want regularly scheduled meetings or sessions; maybe you want her "on-demand." And still another option is to end your relationships with therapists all together. You may realize you already know what your child needs and you're willing to trust yourself, knowing you can use more natural methods.

Alternatives to Professional Therapy

If we put our thinking caps on, most of us can figure out how to help our children on our own, and with the natural supports and generic services in our communities. Zillions of ideas will come to you if you spend lots of time thinking, daydreaming, wondering, and asking others for ideas. Use every available means to arrive at good solutions: your intimate knowledge of your child, good old common sense, ideas from others (including your child), and information within this chapter and from Chapter 14. You'll be proud and amazed at your success, delighted at the changes in your family's life, and pleasantly surprised by your child's achievements. In this section are ideas that can be done by you or another caregiver in a natural setting. However, later in the chapter you'll find examples of how typical community activities (dance classes, martial arts schools, and so forth) can be used for exercise.

As you use natural methods to help your child, keep these three principles in mind: (1) do not try to replicate a therapy session in your home; (2) do not take on the role of therapist; and (3) let your child lead you.

If you replicate a therapy session in your home, you'll be sending your child the same message he received in therapy: "You're not OK the way you are, so let me fix you." Instead of an intensive hour of hands-on home therapy, incorporate a variety of activities throughout the day in your child's natural environments. By making these pleasant and enjoyable; your child will be getting "therapeutic assistance" without knowing it! Focus on doing things *with* your child instead of *to* your child. In addition, preserve the sanctity of your home. Do not set up a therapy room and do not acquire a stash of therapeutic equipment. Your child shouldn't feel he's "in therapy" in his own home.

Stay in your role of Mom; don't become your child's therapist. Your child needs you to be Mom, no one else. When your child was receiving therapy, he looked to you for relief when therapy was uncomfortable. If you become your child's therapist, who will your child turn to for comfort?

Listen to your child and follow his lead. Instead of trying to make your child do what you think is important, take what he's interested in, and what's relevant and valuable to him, and build on it. At the same time, expand his horizons by exposing him to many different experiences and opportunities.

Don't focus on your teaching, focus on his learning. Your child—like all children—was born to learn. He may need more repetition, more assistance, more time to learn, and adaptive devices, but he will learn. We all learn best by doing; focus on creating learning opportunities in which your child is an active participant instead of a passive recipient.

Recognize that just as your child learns through trial and error, you'll learn how to help through trial and error. Benjamin is thirteen, and we're still learning how to help him do and learn many things. Often, the method I think is going to work doesn't. So I ask Benjamin to show or tell me how I can best help him. We try different things and keep trying until we get it right, or until we realize it's not going to happen. Then we find alternatives.

Traditional therapy usually focuses on helping a child master a particular skill. In "natural therapy," you'll be doing much more. Not only will natural activities help improve your child's physical abilities, they'll also have a positive impact on his mind and spirit.

Following are some examples to inspire you and get your creative juices flowing as you consider natural ways to help your child grow and develop as a whole child. These examples reflect our children being in natural environments and receiving informal assistance.

Oral-Motor and Speech

Help your child learn to drink from a straw. If he chews up the ends of straws, buy the hard plastic straws (described in Chapter 14) available from medical supply stores. They're chew proof.

Buy bottles of bubbles. Blowing bubbles is fun for kids of all ages and it helps your child develop the muscles in his mouth and face. Buy sugarless chewing gum. Have a contest to see who can chew gum the longest. Make faces at each other. The sillier the better. Laugh a lot. Good for the mouth and for the spirit. Make animal sounds. Imitate the sounds of nature: the plip-plop of raindrops, the whoosh of wind, or the roar of thunder. Buy kids' music and sing or hum along.

Let your child lick the beaters of your mixer when you whip up brownies or anything else. Buy sugar-free suckers for your child to lick. Good for oral motor and fine motor.

Drop small bits of food (raisins, M & Ms, small bits of bread or whatever is best for your child) on a plate. Have your child stick her tongue out to pick up a piece of food. Then take a turn and do it yourself (or let another member of your family play this fun game). Be silly about it. In the first round, each player gets one piece. In the second round, each player gets two pieces, etc. Next, play the game using the lips instead of the tongue. Be creative! Make up your own fun games using mouth, teeth, lips, tongue!

Fine Motor Skills

Teach your child how to use the remote control, the buttons on the TV and VCR. If your child can't use the remote you have, buy a universal remote with large buttons. Kids are highly motivated to handle these goodies and it's great hand and finger exercise. Be "lazy" or "busy" and ask your child to switch the stations for you. Get the remote out of Dad's hands and into your kid's. I've always thought it strange that therapists continue to make kids stack blocks and plastic donuts to improve their fine motor skills. But at home, a child demonstrates great fine motor skills: isolating his pointer finger to pick his nose, using the remote control, digging coins out of the bottom of your purse, and more! Why don't we see these realistic activities on a therapy plan?

Keep art supplies out all the time. Coloring, drawing, and painting are great activities and an artist's inspiration can happen anytime. Paint one wall of your child's room white (or cover it with butcher paper) and let it be his personal canvas to write or draw on at will.

Don't try to force your child to hold the pencil or the hairbrush or the spoon the "right" way. Show him the conventional way, but if he can do it better a different way, let him. The "right" way is the way he can do it best.

Give him the sensation of writing by holding his hand as he holds a marker and write for him "hand-over-hand." Buy alphabet stencils or make your own for writing practice.

Finger paints are wonderful for learning about colors and textures and writing and drawing. Ditto shave cream. Squeeze out a glob and squish it, smear it, draw on it. Buy an Etch-a-Sketch or a Magna-Doodle.

Let your child help you make cookies. Stirring, pouring, and dropping the dough onto the cookie sheet are great exercises and it's much more fun than sorting beads. Let her eat the dough for chewing and swallowing activities.

When trying to help your child learn to feed herself—with fingers, utensils, or both— let her try to feed you, dad, brothers, and sisters. It's good practice and she can see what she's doing. And what fun you'll all have. The big people get to wear bibs while they're absorbing nutrients through the skin on their faces!

If your child can't cut with regular scissors (and *if* this is an important skill), check out all the different types of scissors at fabric stores and in catalogs. You'll find scissors that only require a squeeze (they release by themselves), rotary, battery-operated, and others.

Use Play-Doh, Silly Putty, and other stuff you can smooth, flatten, roll, and pull. Make homemade bread (buy the raw dough that's frozen) and let your child knead the dough.

Buy or make a dart board that uses hook and loop-covered balls instead of sharp darts. Everyone in the family can play. Throwing the ball is good arm and hand exercise, and it's great for hand-eye coordination.

Buy a Gertie ball, the kind you blow up with a straw. If you blow it up not quite all the way, the ball can be held and thrown easier. It's the kind of ball that's safe to toss in the house. Roll the ball while sitting on the floor. Toss the ball while sitting or standing.

If you have a cat or dog, help your child brush the pet or give the pet a massage. Help him learn how to keep his hands open, how to rub, isolate fingers, and more. Let your child give you a massage. Benj can't write with a pencil very well, but he gives great shoulder rubs, and they're good for both of us!

Give your child a massage. While he's watching his favorite TV show, or in bed before he goes to sleep, rub lotion into your hands and massage his arms, pulling down and stretching gently. Do the same thing with his hands and fingers. Make massages more fun by getting everyone in the family involved. Have everyone sit in a circle, front to back, and each person massages the shoulders or back or the person in front. Great family togetherness!

If your child needs range of motion exercises in his shoulders, make it fun. Tell him he's a helicopter. Sit behind him on the bed, couch, or floor. Put your left arm across his chest to keep him steady. Put your right hand under his right armpit and slowly and gently rub your hand toward his elbow and wrist, bringing his arm up and out. If you can, rotate his arm in a circle. When you're through with that arm, reverse and do the other. If it feels better, do this with lotion on your hands. If your child's shoulders pull up, sit behind her and gently push down on her shoulders, then give them a little shake. Do it to music (sing your own songs) or while watching TV.

Whatever skills your child needs to learn to do to himself, let him practice on you and other family members first. Let him brush your teeth, comb your hair, put your T-shirt on, and . . . keep thinking! It's often easier to do something to someone else than to yourself. (It was much easier for me to French braid my daughter's hair than my own.)

GROSS MOTOR SKILLS

Help your baby roll over by putting a toy just out of arm's reach and roll your child over to help him feel what it's like. If he likes rolling over, roll him over and over and over from one side of the room to another. Then roll him the other direction.

When your child is at the age when typical children are learning to pull up, arrange your furniture so he has more things to grab on to. If he can't do it himself, give him a hand. Whether he does it on his own or with your help, he needs the experience of moving from the floor up to the sofa or chair. Of course, once he's up, he'll want to go back down. That's what babies do. So help him slide back down to the floor. Do it over and over. It's possible his body will never be able to do this on his own. That's okay. His brain needs the experience.

Once your child is at the typical age for learning to stand, help him stand, even if he may never be able to do it by himself. He needs the sensation. When Benj was little, we stood him in a corner of the sofa. He loved being upright. Once he accidentally fell to the side, landing on the seat of the sofa and from there he rolled onto the floor. Pillows had been placed on the floor just in case this happened. When he landed on the pillows, he laughed and laughed. "Do more, do more," he squealed. We boosted him up onto the sofa, then helped him stand and he fell again—this time on purpose—and rolled off the sofa onto the pillows, delighted with every sensation. Guess what we did for the next hour? And the next day and the next and the next?

When Benj got too tall to stand on the sofa, we used a corner of a room and did the same thing. We'd stand him up and the corner walls would support him. He'd stand for four or five minutes, grinning and talking. Then his knees would buckle and I'd catch him or let him land on pillows on the floor. More squeals of delight. Buy or make a standing frame so your child can play at the sink, stand up to catch and throw a ball, and do other activities.

If your child can't stretch her own muscles through typical daily activities, you can do it for her and make it fun at the same time. If she's young, watch *Sesame Street* together and exercise her arms and legs in time to the music or mimic what the characters are doing on the show. Or play some fun music and move her arms and legs in a "dance." As your child grows, modify these activities so your child is doing movements similar to what other kids his age are doing. For older children, do it to music or while watching a favorite TV show.

Get the whole family involved and make it fun. Have your child lie on her back on the floor. One person holds your child's hands, another the feet. Now pick her up and swing her from side to side. Don't drop her when you all start giggling. Add some music for even more delight. What other ways can you help your child stretch? Ask her.

Massage your child's legs or feet. Use the ideas described in the "fine motor" section. Do this before your child goes to bed to help with relaxation or while you're all watching *Jeopardy!* Tickle him: on his feet, under his arms, or anywhere else that's comfortable. It gets the muscles moving.

To help your child develop leg strength, have him sit or lie down and let him push his feet against your hands, your back, or whatever part of the body works for you. Sit him on the sofa or a chair and put a ball in front of his feet. If he can't kick the ball on his own, move his leg for him.

Instead of taking your child to hippo therapy (horseback riding), just let him ride a horse! Make it a family affair at the local stables, or invite a friend to go along. If your child can't safely sit on the horse alone, ride with him. If he can sit, but he leans to one side or the other, let him. He's still getting the benefit of the horse's movements.

If your young child cannot yet walk, pick her up and run with her as fast as you can. Give her the sensation of movement—the wind rushing through her hair, the landscape disappearing behind her. Hold her up so she can stretch to feel the bark on the tree. Bend her over and let her pick some flowers for you. Other two-year-olds scale the kitchen counter to reach the great height where they discover the dust bunnies and other goodies on top of the refrigerator. Help yours find the dust bunnies by lifting her high enough to see what's on top of the refrigerator.

Play hide and seek and hide your little one in the corner of the closet or under the bed—places he might never be able to get to by himself. Help him stretch out under the bed or roll himself into a ball in the closet. Give your child the same experiences other children his age are enjoying while helping his body at the same time.

Instead of doing water therapy, just go swimming! Why shouldn't everyone in the family do fun things together? Use the arm floaties (or other devices) to help your child keep his head above water. Children with disabilities can do many things in water they can't do on land. Heated pools and warm soothing hot tubs will be fun for everyone. Join the YMCA or find a hotel or motel with a hot tub or heated pool and ask the manager if you can visit the pool frequently.

Do stretching and range-of-motion activities while you're helping dress your child. It's the most natural time and place to do it.

Dance with your child. If your child uses a wheelchair, let him "dance" with his arms and upper body. If he's little, pick him up and carry him around while you dance. We put on the Pointer Sisters and Benj boogies in his chair—great arm exercise.

If your child liked being on the big balls at therapy, buy a small one for home and let everyone in the family take turns sitting, rolling, and bouncing on it.

If your child needs to develop upper body strength, buy a portable pull up bar from a sporting goods store and wedge it in a doorway. Kids in chairs can do this, too: they can pull up from a sitting position or they can lie on the floor and pull up. Everyone in the family can get big biceps.

Other Therapies

If your child receives art, music, drama, gardening, or other types of professional therapy, do it yourself at home, naturally. If music calms your child or helps him focus or communicate, make music part of your daily routine. Have it playing most of the time. Buy your child his own portable cassette or CD player, with headphones, and let him wear them around the house.

Instead of making your child do "art therapy," have a family art activity, when everyone paints at the same time. If your child uses art to express himself, have other members of the family draw or paint to express themselves, too. Make it a shared experience. The next time anyone in your house is angry or upset, have the person draw what he's feeling instead of saying it. Then let him share the drawing with everyone.

Do your own vision therapy by shining a flashlight on the ceiling and walls of a darkened room, and have your child follow the light. Turn it off and let him tell you where to shine it next. Mimic what the vision therapists do, but make it fun and let your child have more control.

Find ways to make the components of other types of "hobby" therapies part of your home environment. Make them accessible to your child at all times. If your child doesn't respond to your presence during these activities, let someone else be the one to help: another adult family member, brother or sister, or friend.

If doing these activities at home doesn't work, enroll your child in an art class or music class, let him help the neighbor with her garden, or find some other way of enabling your child to benefit from these activities in fun and natural ways. Remember, there's no magic in therapy. The magic is in your child. She knows what's helpful to her. Trust her.

Potpourri

Wrestling and "fighting" are great ways to exercise children's bodies and minds. Most boys love to wrestle with their dads or other men and boys. Go for it! If your daughter is a "tomboy" (I was), help her do this rough-and-tumble stuff, as well! Getting physical is especially important for children with significant physical disabilities. Just because a child can't do something doesn't mean he doesn't want or need to do it. Children who are unable to move their bodies may need our help to experience typical activities. A child might look "frail" on the outside, but inside a tiger is trying to get out.

Benjamin's favorite thing to do with his dad is "fight on the bed." They both take their glasses off and go at it. My husband "pins" Benjamin and then lets Benjamin "throw" him off the bed. Then Mark puts Benjamin on top of him (Benjamin has "pinned" dad), and Mark has to try to throw Benjamin off. Great exercise, great fun, great time spent with dad. I love hearing the screams and laughter coming from the bedroom.

Let other children help you and your child. Brothers or sisters and kids from school or the neighborhood—especially those just a year or two older than the child with the disability—can be a big help. Use their valuable expertise!

Imagine and Make it Happen

The ways we can give our children the help they need are limited only by our imaginations. Have a family meeting and brainstorm creative and fun ways to help your child. Let everyone share ideas and encourage everyone take part in the fun and the exercise activities. If your family has been stressed out because of a hectic therapy schedule in the past, and if your other children have felt left out because of all the attention that's been paid to the child with a disability, working together and having fun will restore your family's peace and unity.

Right now, you may be thinking, "I don't have time to do all the things you've suggested!" And, right now, you may be right. But if you stop taking your child to therapies and interventions, your schedule will change immediately. You'll not only have time to help your child, you'll have more time for your other children, your spouse, and most importantly, yourself!

If you're a single mom with only the one child who has a disability, you're shaking your head, knowing this won't work for you. But it can. Call on friends, family members, and neighbors for help. If you don't feel comfortable doing this right now, you will by the end of this chapter.

The best assistance your child can receive is the informal help you can provide in your home and other natural environments. But there are many other ways to help our children by using natural supports and generic services in our communities.

DISCOVERING COMMUNITY

Where can your child be valued for who he is? In community. Where will he be known by his name and not by his disability label? In community. Where can your child be included, have friends, and be successful? In community.

Our communities are full of natural supports and generic services that can enable our children and our families to live successful, natural lives. We can move from dependency on the system to interdependency in the community. Remember that none of us is truly independent. We are all interdependent. Each of us needs help and support to survive and thrive.

The differences between the system and the community are mind-boggling:

In the system, we are clients.
In community, we are citizens.

In the system, we're recipients.
In community, we're participants.

In the system, professionals make decisions for us.
In community, we make decisions for ourselves.

In the system, we must follow their rules.
In community, we make our own rules.

In the system, we feel weak and vulnerable.
In community, we are strong and powerful.

In the system, we get what's offered.
In community, we get what we need.

What are Natural Supports?

Contrary to popular belief, natural supports are not cotton underwear! They are, in fact, the common, every day people and organizations in your community.

You may have an idea of what natural supports are from the vignettes on page 394. Natural supports differ from one community to another, from one family to another. But I'll share some examples to get you started thinking about what's in your community. In some cases, the organization is the natural support; in others, support comes from the individual people in the organization.

Friends • Neighbors • Church • Scouts • Youth Organizations • Preschools
Day Care Centers • Nursing Homes • Public Schools • Park and Rec Centers
Service Clubs (Kiwanis, Rotary, etc.) • Chamber of Commerce • Sports Groups
Colleges • Symphonies • Theater Companies • Musical Groups • Libraries
Computer Clubs • Businesses • Special Interest Groups and Organizations
(acting groups, environmental organizations, bridge clubs, and many others)

What are Generic Services?

Generic services are the ordinary businesses, associations, and groups that are used by citizens in your community. In every city and town, public and private services exist to serve a variety of needs. Following is a basic list of generic services that are found in many communities. There can often be overlap between natural supports and generic services. For example, the park and rec department might provide a variety of learning, social, and sports activities (generic service), but it's also a source of friendships and networking (natural support).

Park and Rec • Ballet Classes • Karate/Martial Arts Classes

Gymnastics Schools • Preschools • Day Care Centers

Museums • Music Classes • Employment Agencies

Community Colleges • Art Classes • Libraries

Adult Education Classes • Swimming Classes

Start Your Journey

Think of your journey to community as you would a vacation. Let's say you're on your way to Fun City. You've heard great things about it. There's so much to do there. But before you head out, you need to plan. For your journey to community, you need to decide what your child and your family want to do once you're there.

In Fun City, you'll need tickets for all the events and attractions. In community, your child's tickets will open the doors to inclusion. But unlike the tickets to Fun City attractions, tickets to inclusion don't cost anything; we have them already. Your child's tickets are his assets.

When you get to Fun City, with your tickets in hand, different people will show you around—experienced guides, natives of Fun City, folks familiar with the lay of the land. In community, folks who can provide your child and your family with natural supports and generic services will be your friendly tour guides to inclusion.

Later in this chapter, you'll practice drawing up your own plan. First, though, look over the following examples to learn how other families have successfully discovered the riches in their communities.

The process is simple. The first step is identifying your child's wants or needs. Right away, however, think out of the box. Identify real life needs—not just the needs identified by those in the service system. Put aside professional jargon and don't use the paradigms of conventional wisdom (deficit, developmental, readiness, sequential models).

The second step is to identify your child's "tickets." Everyone has tickets: they're the assets and characteristics that make us who we are. A child's tickets can be anything: what he likes, what he does well, what he wants to learn, hobbies, interests, and more. Back in Chapter 11, you wrote a list of your child's assets. You'll need that list for your plan of action.

The third step is to figure out how to use a child's tickets to open the door to natural supports or generic services that can meet her specific needs. Following are some general guidelines that may help you think differently:

- Instead of professional help, use the expertise of friends, neighbors, and community members.

- Instead of therapies, do fun things with your child at home, and use community activities to meet his needs.

- Instead of special ed preschools, use neighborhood preschools.

- Instead of respite, identify and use people in the community for child care—people who will care *for* your child because they care *about* your child.

- Instead of voc-rehab, help your child use networking and community connections to find her dream job.

As you read the following examples, you'll notice that some of the needs described may traditionally be the responsibility of the school system under special education law. But since we know schools aren't always successful at meeting our children's needs, there's no reason not to look elsewhere for help. Schools cannot be all things to all students. It's time we recognized that. Our goal is to meet our children's needs; quibbling over who will provide those needs is a waste of time and energy.

Kiley, age four, along with her parents and others who love her, have identified a variety of things she and her parents need. Kiley needs friends, her parents need a babysitter a couple of times a month, and Kiley needs to be able to communicate more clearly. Following are their ideas.

Need/Want	Ticket	Natural Support/ Generic Service
Friends	Loves Barbie dolls. Has kiddie pool. Friendly. Likes to dance.	Go to park-take Barbies. Preschool 2 x week. Park & Rec ballet.
Babysitter 2 x month.	Mom can barter. Mom can help at church.	Teen neighbor. Church "parents' night out" Parents of Kiley's new pals.
Clearer speech	Loves books. Loves to be read to. Wants to read.	Library story time. Buy/borrow "Phonics" game. Preschool 2 x week.

Kiley's tickets in the friendship column are characteristics that are probably typical of most young girls her age. They're not extraordinary skills or abilities, they're simply commonplace characteristics that will open the doors to friendships for Kiley. When Kiley and her mom, Lisa, visit the neighborhood playground, other young girls will be attracted to Kiley's Barbie dolls. That makes it easy for Lisa to meet the parents of these other girls. From there, it's natural to invite new playmates over for a dip in the backyard kiddie pool.

Enrolling Kiley in the park and rec ballet class also creates new friendship opportunities. If the other little ballerinas see some Barbie dolls poking out of Kiley's ballet bag, so much the better. Again, Lisa can get to know the other mothers through the ballet class. Perhaps little Samantha will go to Kiley's house after ballet one day for a dip in the pool. If Samantha's mom has a few hours to herself while her daughter is at Kiley's house, she'll probably return the favor and take Kiley home with her after class one day. Kiley's mom has now identified a potential babysitter for Kiley. In addition, these experiences (being with other children at the park, in her home, and at ballet) will help Kiley's speech.

If Kiley attends a typical preschool two mornings a week, she'll have opportunities for friendships. But money is tight so Kiley's parents will try other things first.

Lisa and Jim want to enjoy an evening out a couple of times a month. Respite care services are not available, but Kiley's parents know there's a thirteen-year-old girl in the neighborhood. Lisa and Jim have decided one of the outings each month will be low-cost, so they can afford to pay a babysitter. They'll simply go for a drive, to a fast food restaurant, or window-shopping at the mall. The other night out will include going to a movie or a restaurant, which won't leave any money for the sitter. On that night, they'll barter for babysitting services. Lisa will talk to the thirteen-year-old about babysitting in exchange for a variety of things the teenager might need. Lisa will offer to drive Kristin and her friends to the mall, tutor her in school work, or do something else that's valuable to the teen. Lisa can also offer to take care of Kiley's new friends when their parents need a babysitter; these moms and dads will reciprocate when Jim and Lisa need a babysitter.

Another option for child care is the nearby church that provides drop-in child care—Parents' Night Out—every Friday night. Since Lisa and Jim don't have the money to pay the babysitting fee, Lisa will offer to work at the Parents' Night Out on the two Friday nights she and Jim aren't going out, in exchange for the two nights they use the service. Hours are from 6:00 to 11:00 PM. If this works out, Lisa will take Kiley with her for part of the evening so her daughter can meet new friends and be around other kids who are talking. At 8:30, Jim will pick Kiley up and take her home.

Kiley loves books, loves being read to, and wants to read. These are tremendous assets. Lisa will begin taking Kiley to story time at the library every week. Listening to an adult read a book in an exciting fashion will keep Kiley's interest and help her learn appropriate speech patterns. Lisa knows she'll probably pick up some tips on being a better "storyteller," herself, by listening and learning from the readers at the library. Kiley and Lisa will make some new friends here, too.

Lisa is interested in the phonics programs that claim to help children read. Since the audiotapes feature voices repeatedly pronouncing letter sounds, they might help Kiley's speech. Lisa will see if the library has one. She's also going to ask around to see if anyone she knows has one she could borrow or buy used. Maybe some of Kiley's new friends would have fun listening and playing the phonics games with Kiley. Preschool is another option to help Kiley with her speech, but Lisa will try that only if the others don't work out.

Lisa and Jim are excited about the outcomes of using natural supports and generic services. Lisa can get lots of help for Kiley—and have fun doing it—and she and her family can retain their freedom, privacy, and family autonomy. And, of course, they'll all be making lots of new friends and acquaintances along the way.

Because Kiley and her family are doing typical things in the community without the stigma of special programs, it will be far easier for Kiley to be included in the neighborhood school when it's time for kindergarten. She won't be bringing any special ed baggage with her; she'll bring a history of inclusion along. In fact, Lisa isn't even going to go through the IEP process. She'll just register Kiley for kindergarten, like all other parents do. When and if Kiley's teacher decides Kiley needs some extra help, Lisa will suggest ways to provide natural help in the classroom. It's easier to stay out of special ed than get out.

Ryan, age eight, needs friends, wants to play softball, and needs a power wheelchair.

Need/Want	Ticket	Natural Support Generic Service
Friends	Computer at home. Outgoing, friendly.	School computer lab. PTA meetings. Park/rec computer class. Computer club.
Play softball	Great desire to play. Plays at home with big brother.	Park and rec team
Power wheelchair	Wants to be independent. Dad knows lots of people.	Service clubs: Kiwanis, etc. Community groups.

Like most children with disabilities in his district, Ryan doesn't attend his neighborhood school. He's bused to the elementary school that houses "special programs." He has no real friends at school and doesn't know any children in the neighborhood. Bobbie and Paul know their son's expertise on the computer, along with all the great software they have, would be appealing to other boys who like computers.

Bobbie decided to use the neighborhood elementary school (where she wants Ryan to attend) as a natural resource to identify potential friends for Ryan. She begins volunteering in the library/media center and becomes friends with the computer teacher. One of Bobbie's duties is to help students learn how to use the computers; she's met a variety of seven, eight, and nine-year-old boys that could become her son's new friends.

Another option she considered (but which she ended up not needing) was attending PTA meetings, in hopes of meeting other parents from the neighborhood school who might have young sons. If that didn't produce results, she planned to boldly ask the whole group if they knew of any elementary school boys who love computers, then she'd try to meet their families.

Bobbie was also going to investigate the computer classes offered through park and rec. Another idea was to find a computer club in her area that Ryan could join. But she didn't need these options. After volunteering in the computer lab twice a week for several weeks, Bobbie sought and received permission to bring Ryan with her. During a three-week period, she pulled Ryan out of his school for a couple of hours and brought him to the computer lab once each week on the days she volunteered. She introduced her son to the different classes. Right away, a couple of boys his age became acquainted with Ryan. Soon, they were coming over to play on the home computer. Before long, Ryan had more than computer buddies; he had real friends.

Ryan and his sixteen-year-old brother, Tim, often played softball in the backyard. Ryan couldn't throw the ball very well, but he loved to smack it with the bat, and he gave it his all as Tim pitched.

Before they decided to use natural supports, Bobbie and Paul hadn't ever considered enrolling Ryan in the park and rec softball team. They just didn't think the program would accept Ryan, even though they know discrimination based on disability is illegal under the ADA. Other children with disabilities had always been referred to the special softball league. That wasn't appealing to Paul, Bobbie, or Ryan.

Being a plumber, Paul knew lots of people around town. Several had children who participated in the park and rec softball games. Since the spring league was about to start, Ryan's family decided to attend the games as spectators. Several of Paul's customers were there; they greeted Paul and his family, meeting Ryan for the first time. Bobbie and Ryan were glad to see some of the boys from the computer lab in the league. It was like old home week. After attending several games, they were seen as "regulars."

Ryan's family always arrived at the games early, to ensure they got seats on the bottom row of the bleachers next to Ryan in his chair. As the players were warming up on the field, Ryan and Tim did a little practice of their own on the side of the field. Everyone could see that Ryan was able to hit the ball. Before long, some of the team members began greeting him, giving him a high five, and talking to him before and after the games. Coaches, too, began to get to know Ryan.

At the end of the last game of the spring session, the coaches were passing out registration forms for the summer session. When Tim pushed Ryan up to the group of boys, the coach gave Ryan a registration form—along with a wide smile. When the summer league started, Ryan was part of the team.

Bobbie made connections with other softball moms and they arranged visits to each other's homes. Several of the boys had heard about Ryan's computer games and couldn't wait for their turn to visit.

There was a potent and surprising benefit to Ryan's inclusion on the softball team: the parents of Ryan's new friends began a push for Ryan to be included in their neighborhood school when school began in the fall. Paul and Bobbie had a new group of influential allies.

Ryan doesn't qualify for Medicaid and the family's insurance will not purchase another wheelchair for Ryan for at least two more years. Ryan can push himself for short distances, but his parents know a power wheelchair would give Ryan the independence and freedom to be the active boy he wants to be. But where would they get the $10,000 to buy the chair Ryan needs? This is too much for Bobbie and Paul to handle by themselves.

They called on old friends and new (including some of the parents they met through the computer lab and the softball league). After a few brainstorming sessions, several plans emerged.

Throughout this process, Bobbie and Paul bared their souls, but asking for help from others wasn't as hard as they thought it would be. Their friends really did want to help; that's part of what being a friend is all about. The process wasn't about pity and charity; it was about the excitement of teamwork and contribution. It was also about everyone wanting Ryan to have the freedom and independence he needed.

By thinking outside of the box, the group discovered bold and creative solutions. Jim and Lisa could come up with $4,000 ($1,000 from savings and $3,000 borrowed from the bank). The durable medical equipment (DME) company offered to knock $500 off the price of the chair. Since the chair wouldn't be paid for by private insurance or a government program, the DME agency agreed to reduce the amount of the profit they normally made on the chair. Cash talks. Paul and Bobbie still needed $5,500. Their friends brainstormed and used their connections to network with others who might help.

Four different service clubs agreed to contribute a total of $3,000. A disability organization gave $500. Several local businesses were approached by Paul and Bobbie's network of allies. Another $1,700 was was raised. The final $300 was provided by the business that sponsored Ryan's softball team.

Giving back to the community that had given so much to them was important to Paul and Bobbie. Being the expert plumber that he was, Paul offered to give several presentations at the service club meetings. Everyone was pleased to be getting free advice from a plumber! He also offered to discount his services to the local businesses who had contributed. Bobbie volunteered to give presentations on disability issues to the service organizations. And Ryan would provide technical assistance to the local businesses on how to make their places more accessible to people with disabilities. It was a win-win situation.

Bobbie, Paul, and their network of friends were daring, determined, and resourceful. They asked and they received. And then they gave back.

Amber, age thirteen, also needs friends, she wants a job to earn her own money, and she dreams of being a model some day.

Need/Want	Ticket	Natural Support Generic Service
Friends	Wants to look and be like other girls.	Typical 13-year-olds at school.
Learn to model	Likes to dress up and "strut her stuff." Is bold and funny.	Modeling school.
Wants a job	Willing to work. Likes little kids.	Typical girls at school. Red Cross child care class.

Amber, who has a cognitive disability, has spent most of the last two years in the middle school resource room, but was allowed "visitation" in art, PE, and music. She didn't really have any girlfriends. While she was acquainted with classmates in the resource room, she had yet to spend the night at a friend's house, nor had anyone ever spent the night at her home. And never had she been invited to a friend's birthday party.

Several days a week, Amber arrived home overflowing with adoration for a few of the girls in the regular ed classes. Sometimes it almost broke her mother's heart. Anne had been told over and over again that Amber would "never be like other kids." When Anne began thinking about Amber from the assets perspective, she began to realize how similar Amber was to other girls her age.

Being in segregated classes for most of her school life, Amber hadn't had many opportunities be around typical peers in her age group. Still, she was chomping at the bit to be like other girls: to begin experimenting with make-up, to dress like some of the other girls, and more. And like most parents of young teenage girls, Anne was a little nervous about Amber's budding development. She recognized the importance of taking an active role in helping Amber become a real thirteen-year-old.

Anne didn't have the best relationship with the special ed teachers at Amber's school. Going to them for help in facilitating friendships for Amber simply wasn't an option. But she wanted to know more about the students Amber admired, to determine if they were girls she wanted in Amber's life. She wracked her brain trying to figure out a way to visit the art, music, and the gym classes. In middle school, volunteer parents are a rarity. She thought about finding an excuse to "drop in" on the classes, but that might arouse suspicion and it would also conflict with her job schedule.

Finally, she bit the bullet and called all three teachers (art, music, PE). She laid it out: she wanted to help Amber make friends with the some of the girls in these classes. She asked the three teachers about the girls Amber talked about. She also wanted their opinions on the relationship Amber had with the girls.

The gym teacher wasn't too helpful, but the art and music teachers both gave her good reports. There were three particular girls both teachers singled out as friendly and caring toward Amber. Even better, they weren't too "far out" for thirteen-year-olds. All good news, but now what? Middle school is tough; the cliques are often tightly formed. Anne decided a slow and steady approach was best.

First, she encouraged Amber to exchange phone numbers with the girls. What thirteen-year-old female doesn't like to talk on the phone for hours? That week and the next, Amber called all three girls after school. The calls were relatively short. This was a new experience for Amber; she was just learning the art of telephone conversation.

The third week, one of the girls called Amber. Anne and Amber were ecstatic. The fourth week, calls between Amber and two of the girls were reciprocal. Amber, with Anne's assistance, invited Marcie and Jessica to a "make-up party" and sleep over. Amber excitedly told her new friends she could now wear a little lipstick and mascara, and she wanted them to help her learn how to do it. Anne met the parents over the phone and they finalized the arrangements.

On the big night, Anne met the parents of the two girls face-to-face when they brought their daughters to Amber's "party." Things were really starting to happen! Amber was making new friends and Anne was meeting new people, as well.

After devouring pizza, the girls decided the make-up could wait. One had brought her CD player and some CDs. They retreated to Amber's room to listen to music, giggle, and talk. Behind the closed door, Anne heard the joyous sounds of friendship. The next morning, a beaming Amber emerged from her room with a new hairstyle and make-up—a little too much make-up, actually—followed by two new friends who were helping her achieve her dream of being a "regular" teenager!

Amber was anxious to have a job and earn her own money. Anne didn't need to look too far for help with this need. Babysitting is the obvious moneymaking opportunity for many teenage girls. Amber's new friends had babysitting careers. Anne and Amber talked to Marcie and Jessica about what it takes to be a babysitter. They had both taken the one-day Red Cross babysitting course offered by park and rec. Anne signed Amber up for the class, and Jessica attended with Amber. Jessica knew the instructor, and she was a great bridge between Amber and Mrs. McNeil. An unofficial "babysitters club" soon emerged for the trio of friends. Before long, Amber was going along on some of the babysitting jobs, earning half the money. Amber was being transformed and her mother's heart was bursting with pride.

Amber vowed to save her babysitting money to buy a CD player, but she couldn't resist spending some of it on make-up and hair stuff. As Anne watched the changes in Amber, she felt no hesitation signing Amber up for a modeling course offered in town. She didn't know if Amber would really grow up to be a model, but that didn't matter. What mattered was Amber knowing she had the opportunity to make her dreams come true.

The modeling school had never enrolled a student with a disability before, but the staff was charmed by Amber's friendliness and determination. The three-month course changed Amber's life. She developed poise, self-confidence, and pride in herself. She was also the envy of her friends. Her modeling school attendance became a "ticket" to more friendships: when some of the classmates in art and music heard about it, they began approaching Amber to talk about it.

As the school year ended, Anne had high hopes for the next fall. Amber would be moving to the high school with her new friends. The negative relationships Anne had with the middle school special ed teachers would be a thing of the past. With the help of their new family friends, Anne began planning strategies to ensure Amber would be included in regular classes with her friends.

Nineteen-year-old Joshua wants to assume his role as a young adult. He wants to live on his own, have a real job, and his own set of friends.

Need/Want	Ticket	Natural Support Generic Service
Own apartment	Determined to move out; doesn't want to depend on parents; wants to live alone.	Unsure at this time.
Job and job skills	Good with hands. Dependable. Likes cars, animals, gardening and yard work.	Auto repair places. Zoo, humane society, pet store.
Friends	Loyal and giving. Friendly. Loves music.	Places where others hang out, college? Volunteer work. Where else?

Joshua "graduated" from high school, with a "certificate of attendance"—standard issue for most students who receive special ed services. Joshua started out in life with a physical disability that caused him to have an awkward style of walking. Later, he was diagnosed as having significant learning disabilities, and still later, he was classified as having a behavior disorder.

His parents knew Joshua had difficulty learning in school, but they always felt the behavior label was ridiculous. Joshua never had significant "behavior problems" at home, only at school. Was it possible the so-called unacceptable behavior identified by educators was, in fact, caused by the school environment?

Under the law, Joshua could continue receiving special ed services until he turned twenty-two. But Joshua and his mom and dad—Peggy and Dean—agreed it was time for Joshua to get on with his life. The special ed teachers urged Joshua and his parents to stay connected with voc-rehab for help with job training and/or placement. But Peggy and Dean needed a break from the system. In addition, they hadn't heard too many voc-rehab success stories involving students with disabilities who Joshua had known in high school. In the two years the voc-rehab counselor and the special ed teacher had been working on Joshua's behalf, no opportunities for employment had emerged. Peg and Dean didn't want Joshua's special ed baggage to follow him into the real world. They decided to try the assets approach.

Joshua wanted his own place to live. His older brother and sister had moved off on their own after high school, and Joshua felt it was his turn. His sister had gone on to college full-time and moved into a dormitory; his brother had entered the military. Joshua wasn't interested in pursuing either of those options. He just wanted his own place to live, a real job, and real friends. Peggy and Dean knew there was no way Joshua could live on his own unless he had money to pay for an apartment, and they didn't have the extra money. Joshua was in the real world now. Getting a job had to be the first order of business.

Peg and Dean called friends and neighbors to a Dream Party at their home to brain-storm ideas. A little timidly at first, Joshua told everyone his desires: to live on his own, to have a job, and to have his own set of friends. Everyone at the party knew about Joshua's love of animals, the pride he felt in a job well done after doing the yard work, and his enjoyment in successfully changing the oil in his Dad's car. These were all valuable assets.

While Joshua could be very friendly at times, he really enjoyed spending time alone. Educators and professionals had seen this as a sign of a "troubled personality"—a defect. Peg and Dean knew it was a personal characteristic that had nothing to do with Joshua's disability labels.

At the end of the Dream Party, Joshua was excited about the opportunities that lay ahead. To help him decide what type of job he wanted, several non-paid internships would be arranged. Through existing personal connections, as well as new ones in the making, some of the Dream Team members contacted "quick-lube" oil changing shops, pet stores, the zoo, and the humane society about Joshua interning. Different individuals made the initial calls, then accompanied Joshua to the businesses for interviews.

Some businesses were more receptive than others. Liability was an issue: what if Joshua got hurt? He wasn't really an employee and so wasn't covered by Worker's Compensation. At the zoo, the problem was easily resolved: Joshua joined the corps of existing volunteers. Then he got permission to spend three days "visiting" the lube shop after a Dream Team member went up the company's corporate ladder. At the local pet store, the owner was helpful and agreed to let Joshua intern alongside the employees who worked with the puppies, kittens, birds, fish, and reptiles. What an exciting problem Joshua faced! He had to decide how to allocate his time.

Simultaneously, plans were created for Joshua to start his own lawn care business. He loved the idea of being his own boss. In his part of the country, homeowners needed lawn care about nine months out of the year. Peg helped Joshua prepare flyers advertising his lawn care service, and Joshua distributed them in a wide area around his neighborhood. He began getting a few calls.

The internships and volunteer work were successful. There were no immediate job openings, but the lube shop and pet store managers both encouraged Joshua to check back on a regular basis and apply for the next open position. Joshua kept his volunteer position at the zoo. He began meeting a variety of people of all ages who liked him, invited him out, and introduced him to other people. Joshua soon had the set of friends he had always wanted.

Soon, Joshua's lawn care service kept him as busy as he wanted to be and he was earning good money. He even bought new lawn mowing equipment with some of his profits. Not only did he continue changing the oil on his dad's car, he began learning how to maintain and repair the small motors in his mower and edger. He's becoming quite the expert in motors; these skills will help him land a new job if and when he chooses to leave his lawn care business.

Peg, Dean, Josh, and the Dream Party members came up with a great idea to fulfill Josh's dream of living on his own. Since he wasn't making enough money to pay a typical monthly apartment rental, they thought up a unique alternative: a garage apartment on the site of a large home where Josh could take care of the yard work and help with maintenance in exchange for paying a monthly rental. They haven't found just the right place and just the right homeowner yet, but they know they will. Josh's "investigators" are scouting locations on a regular basis. The community is a good place to be.

The steps for you to create a plan for your child will be detailed in a moment. First, review the following information about friendships. When presenting workshops on community, the majority of parents painfully reveal their children with disabilities don't have friends. Friendships are a natural by-product of community inclusion, but a little extra attention to friendship issues at this time may be helpful.

FRIENDSHIPS

Sadly, many children who are in segregated educational settings have no friends, and their parents see little potential for their children to make friends. In other cases, parents don't see how their children *could* have real friends because of the type or level of their children's disabilities: "My child can't walk, talk, or play. How could she have a friend?" All children can have friends and we can help.

There's a wonderful connection between friends and inclusion. Friends in the community can pave the way to inclusion in public schools. Simultaneously, getting our children out of segregated classes and into inclusive classrooms in public school will lead to friendships in the community. And there are many things we can do to facilitate friendships for our children.

- Beat the bushes in your neighborhood. Go for walks and look for children playing in their yards. When you're driving to and from the store, look for signs of children living nearby: bikes in the yard, a basketball hoop near the garage, and so forth. Be bold! Knock on those doors and introduce yourself as a friendly neighbor. Get to know children and families in your neighborhood. If you've already met other families but don't have positive relationships with them, start over! Invite another mom over for coffee, offer to pick up something for her when you're at the store. Once you're friends with her, your kids can more easily become friends. Be creative!

- Talk to the parents of your other children's friends. Invite those families over for a pizza night to meet the other children in the family.

- Volunteer in community activities for children and teens. Become familiar with opportunities in which your child could participate. Meet other children and their parents.

- Enroll your child in scouting, 4-H, sports, dance or martial arts classes, or other youth activities.

We like to think making friends occurs naturally. And parents may believe a child's disability is a barrier to friendships. But both of these assumptions are myths. Developing friendships *doesn't* come easily for many people, whether they have a disability or not. And people with disabilities can and do enjoy real friendships. Between friends, disability is irrelevant. Parents can and should take an active role to help their children with disabilities enjoy the richness of friendships.

When making friends doesn't come easily, parents can step in and manipulate or massage the circumstances to promote real friendships. Some parents feel awkward doing this or, worse, they feel it's wrong. They may believe if a friendship has to be "helped along," it's somehow not a true friendship. But this just isn't so.

When my daughter was in second grade, there were only seven girls in her class. In classes where there were ten or more girls, two or more groups usually evolved. But with only seven, there was, in effect, one group. Unfortunately, this group was heavily influenced by the unofficial leader of the group, a big, strong, powerful girl who physically and verbally intimidated the other six on the playground.

Emily often came home crying, saying, "No one will play with me." She was not athletic and she preferred the company of one friend instead of a group. The "leader" of the group regularly insisted they all play tether ball or do some other activity. Sitting on the playground and talking, or swinging side-by-side wasn't part of the "leader's" plan! Girls who weren't good tether ball players (like Emily) were regularly teased or left out.

Emily and I talked this over and decided there were probably other girls in the group who felt the way she did. I suggested she start taking some Barbie dolls to school to play with during recess. "Just sit by yourself and play with them," I advised, "and I'll bet some other girls will join you." And that's exactly what happened. Emily and some of the other girls learned they didn't need to be a part of the other group to belong, they formed their own group.

Friends open the door to social and emotional growth, they help smooth the rocky road of life, and they let us know we're valued. Because many children have been segregated in public schools, they haven't had opportunities to learn how to make friends. Many children, both with and without disabilities, need guidance and support in creating and maintaining friendships. It's a skill, just like any other, and there's nothing wrong with helping our children learn this skill.

If you think your child's significant disability is a barrier to friendship, fear not. Help other children learn about your child's abilities and disability in a positive way. Point out the similarities between your child and a new friend: things they both like to do, toys or other things they both like, and so forth. Then teach the new friend the best ways to play, communicate, and understand your child in a positive way, without pity or worry. Then let the magic of friendship take over.

Make your home a haven for your child and her friends. If it's Friday night, it's time for pizza, movies on the VCR, and a sleep over! Got a tent? Have a kids' camp out in the back yard. If you don't have a basketball hoop attached to your house, get one. It's a magnet. Patch that kiddie pool and fill it up. Even big kids like to cool off on a summer day. Help your child invite a friend over to play on the family's newest computer game.

Initially, it's often better for a child to have one friend over at a time. If two or more children are invited at the same time, especially if those two are already friends, the two may stick together and unintentionally exclude your child. When only one child is invited, the friendship can be cemented more easily. This is not a hard and fast rule, however. Experiment and see what works best for your child. Some children do fine in groups and everyone's included. Others do better with just one friend at a time.

If you have more than one child, it's sometimes better and easier if each of your children has a friend over at the same time (especially if your children are close in age). When our children were younger, we learned this through experience. If Emily had a friend over to spend the night and Benjamin didn't, he'd bug her and her friend, and Mark and I had to referee. The same happened if Benj had a friend over and Emily didn't. But when they each had a friend over to spend the night at the same time, these problems evaporated. Since the playing field was even, neither cared what the other was doing.

As your child develops friendships, respect her desires and recognize that children change. Benj went through a period where he wanted and needed lots of friends. Then he went through a couple of years of not wanting anyone to come over to spend the night, but he did like talking on the phone. He's now wanting to have friends over again. At one time, Emily did better with just one "best friend." Now she enjoys having two or three "best friends" who all get along well together.

Another factor to consider is the reciprocity of friendships. Many parents have said they invite children to their home, but their children don't get invited to friends' homes. They then feel the friendships aren't genuine. But this may not be an accurate assessment.

You may be the kind of parent who enjoys (or can happily tolerate) other children being in your home. For whatever reasons, however, not all parents are like this. Some parents just aren't very hospitable. They might be nice people, but they don't invite *anyone* over for a visit! Don't be oversensitive about this issue.

On the other hand, parents might be afraid to invite your child over; they may think they don't know how to "handle things." Conversely, maybe your child was invited to a friend's home but you didn't let him go because you didn't think the other parents could handle things!

The key to solving this dilemma is educating other parents and trusting them. In a casual and proactive way, simply let others know what help your child needs. On the first visit, teach the parents what they need to know. Trust that your child's friend can help, or that he can teach his parents how to help. While your child is visiting, be available by phone so the mom or dad can call with questions if they arise. You'll discover what a wonderful feeling it is to know your child can be safe in the hands of friends.

With few exceptions, Benjamin's friends always came to our house. He seldom visited theirs for two main reasons: (1) the homes of his friends weren't very accessible for his power chair and (2) Benj was most comfortable at home. *Where* Benjamin played with his friends had no bearing on the depth of his friendships.

Having friends doesn't only benefit our children. There are also benefits for us. When we become friends with the parents of our children's friends, our lives our enriched in many ways. In addition, these parents can become great allies. And one of the greatest benefits is you'll have potential babysitters! As you get to know the parents of your child's friends, offer to watch their children when they have errands to run or need a night off. Then, when you need a babysitter, they'll be available for you!

Do whatever it takes to help your child enjoy the precious gift of friendship. Be creative. Have fun. Act natural. Ask for help. Trust. Your child is counting on you.

TIME TO PLAN!

Are you ready to plan? Ready to dream? It's your turn, now. The following suggestions will guide you on the journey to community. There are three main steps to the process:

Step 1: List your child's dreams, wants, and needs
Step 2: Identify and list your child's "tickets" (assets, gifts, and talents)
Step 3: Identify natural supports and generic services in your community, and brainstorm which of these will meet your child's needs. You may or may not need a "ticket" for community supports.

You can map your child's journey to community on your own, or you can get help from others (and I hope you will). You can involve your immediate family, as well as friends, neighbors, and others who know your child well (Sunday school teacher, babysitter, and so forth). In addition, you can involve people *you* know, but who may not know your child, who could contribute their networking abilities or community connections to the process (your husband's boss, a friend who works at the bank, and so forth). Most of us will have greater success if we call on the help of others.

Spend some time thinking about your child's Dream Party, including who you want involved and how you want to proceed. You and your immediate family can do all three steps, or you can do step one together and have a larger group of allies help you tackle steps two and three. Mix and match the steps and the people how ever you like.

To maximize your efforts, involve people—formally or informally—who are well-connected in your community. Use their influence and networking abilities.

In addition, recognize the value of getting others involved in all three steps of the process. When thinking about step two (identifying your child's assets), each person who knows your child sees him a little differently than you do. When my husband and I were identifying Benjamin's assets, we came up with different lists! Every person in your child's life can identify unique characteristics, interests, gifts, and talents to provide a more complete picture of your child.

Do not invite professionals from the service system. They might be very nice people, but they'll usually look for solutions within the system and that's not what you're looking for. If, however, a professional is ready to embrace community solutions, and you have a very close relationship with the person, consider making an exception.

Your child, of course, needs to be at the center of the process, regardless of how you choose to proceed. If your child is age two or above, talk everything over with him or her. Use your wisdom and your common sense: you'll talk about the process with an eight-year-old differently than an eighteen-year-old. Your son or daughter needs to contribute to this process to the best of his or her ability. In fact, your child could run the meeting if she feels comfortable doing this. And remember, they sky's the limit! Don't pooh-pooh any of your child's ideas no matter how impossible they seem!

Do whatever it takes to achieve a comfort level prior to tackling these activities. Spend time thinking about who you want to be involved. Plan a positive, upbeat get-together. Spring for pizza or make it a pot-luck supper with everyone bringing something to share. Think enthusiastically; your enthusiasm will be contagious!

At the Dream Party, whether it's an intimate family meeting or a larger gathering, begin by sharing your overall goal: "We want Mary to be part of her community, just like her brothers and sisters," or "Our whole family needs to be involved more in our community," or whatever is appropriate.

It's highly possible this process will lead you to looking at what your entire family needs from the community. If so, there's nothing wrong with including your other children's needs in the process. However, in most cases, they probably will have not faced the barriers your child with a disability has faced. The beauty of this process is that it's yours to make it work in the ways that are best for your child and your family. Now, let's look at the steps.

List Your Child's Wants, Needs, and Dreams

Remember the dreams you once had for your child? In an earlier chapter, I asked you to list those dreams. Get that list and begin to add to it. If you didn't make a list at that time, make one now. Take some time to think about what's important to your child and your family today.

In addition to dreams, list everything your child wants and needs, as well as what you and your family want or need to support your child's dreams (assuming they're not in direct opposition to what your child wants), including those things you've been told are impossible! Be bold. Dream big. Make sure your child is involved in identifying her dreams, wants, and needs.

List things that are related to friendships, community activities, wanting to learn a new skill, and anything else you can think of. Don't forget to list child care as a need of the family, if that's appropriate. If your child is a teenager, talk to him about needs or wants regarding transportation, jobs, college, or moving away from home.

You may want to list some categories to get you started, such as: Friends, Community Activities, Assistive Technology, Employment, Transportation, Child Care, and so forth. Then list the dreams, wants, and needs within each category.

If you're ready to simplify your life by taking a break (temporary or permanent) from therapies, or if you're ready to move your child out of the traditional types of interventions into more natural ones, list the types of things your child customarily receives from the service system (assuming these are things he wants and needs). But put them in a different perspective. Instead of saying, "Needs speech therapy," say, "Needs to learn typical speech," and/or "Needs communication device." Instead of saying, "Needs physical therapy," say, "Needs to swim," or whatever type of exercise or activity that may be appropriate. Be specific and think out of that box! To keep those creative juices flowing, or if you're stuck, the following list of examples may help:

Friendships: playmate...one best friend...girlfriends...sports friends...boy pals...computer buddy...someone to share hobbies with...dance partner

Community Activities: T-ball...basketball...football...soccer...swimming lessons...ballet...martial arts...gymnastics...art classes...Scouts...hanging out at the teen center...church...archery...volunteer at library...babysitting classes...volunteer at zoo...Campfire group

Employment: part-time job after school...full-time job...babysitting jobs...lawn care jobs... housesitting...take care of pets...college...vocational school

Housing: live alone in an apartment...share a place with a friend or roommate...live in college dorm

Transportation: learn to drive...car pool to and from work...ride the bus to work...own car...a ride to and from school

Assistive Technology: communication device...laptop computer...power wheelchair...bathroom accessories...talking watch...calculator for grocery shopping...adapted silverware...environmental controls

Dreams: learn to model...drive a race a car...run a marathon...meet the TV weatherman...get married...go to college...climb a mountain...see the ocean...go trick-or-treating...sit on Santa's lap...go to Disney World...see a movie once a week...join a club...go to the prom

Physical Abilities: communicate effectively...use the toilet...write name with pencil...dress independently...eat with utensils

Child Care: babysitter every Friday night...dependable neighbor to watch kids during short errands...extra help at home on Saturday mornings

Identify Your Child's Tickets (Assets)

In an earlier chapter, you had the opportunity to redefine your child by his assets. Retrieve that list and add to it. For a refresher, or if you didn't make the list before, go back to Chapter 11. We'll call your child's assets his "tickets to community."

When you're making your list, and when you speak to others about making their lists of your child's assets, remember to think very broadly. Don't focus on functional skills (the way most professionals do). Describe your child in ways that are unrelated to the disability, such as:

- Things your child enjoys doing: playing with trucks, listening to music, being read to, playing on the computer, shooting baskets, playing with Barbies, going to the zoo, watching sports on TV, helping in the kitchen, and so on.

- Things your child is good at: has good manners, loves to laugh, great imagination, good with the dog, great listener, good with younger children, understands money, memorizes Bible verses, and so forth.

- Things your child wants to do: play the piano, become a babysitter, learn to sew, mow the yard, travel, learn to wrestle, become an actor, learn to put on make-up, play sports, volunteer at a hospital, and so on.

Any or all of the assets you identify can be used as tickets to community, whether they're commonalities your child shares with others, gifts your child can contribute to others, or desires that match up with things offered in your neighborhood or town.

Identify Natural Supports and Generic Services

List people, places, and organizations you're familiar with: the neighbor who gardens, your co-worker who is a Scout leader, the local swimming pool, park and recreation, and the nursing home nearby. But don't stop there. Take out the Yellow Pages, drive around town, and talk to other people to get a better feel for what's in your community. You'll probably be amazed at how rich your community is with wonderful people and places you never knew existed! On the other hand, you may be aware of many people and places close by, but you've never thought about them in terms of natural supports and generic services.

Putting the Puzzle Together

By now you should have three lists: (1) your child's needs, wants, and dreams; (2) your child's tickets (assets); and (3) the natural supports and generic services in your community. Next, it's time to figure out which tickets will open the doors to natural supports and generic services to meet your child needs.

Whether you have a Dream Party or use a more informal method of putting the puzzle pieces together, transfer each list to large flip chart paper or something similar so the lists are easy for all to see. Alternatively, you could type them on regular size paper and make copies for everyone. I've found it easiest to place the three lists in the following order, from left to right: needs/wants, tickets, natural supports and generic services.

Start by looking at the first need on the list and see if something listed in the natural supports/generic services list jumps out at you. This often happens. In these cases, you don't need to use a ticket. For example, if a need is to have more friends, enrolling him in a Scout troop is the answer. However, once he gets in the troop, you may want to use some of his tickets to demonstrate how similar he is to other Scout members, to showcase his gifts and talents, and so forth. In other instances, a ticket will be needed as the entree, as in the following example.

Lee is a fourteen-year-old with autism, with no brothers and sisters at home. His parents still need someone to be with Lee when they're out. They've used respite care in the past, but when Lee turned thirteen, he flatly refused to have a babysitter; he says he's too big for a babysitter. Suzanne and Hal want to respect their son's emerging manhood, but they're not comfortable leaving Lee home alone. They decided to look at alternatives to traditional babysitting. In this instance, Lee's parents chose not to have a Dream Party to identify community supports. They didn't want Lee to know they were looking for a new babysitter.

Suzanne and Hal brainstormed. They knew Lee did better with people who were older, instead of kids who were the same age. What if Lee had young adult male friends he could spend time with? They thought this might work, since Lee wouldn't perceive this to be a babysitting situation. But how could they find young men who fit the bill? The answer was to use one of Lee's tickets: his love of music and desire to play the guitar would mesh perfectly with young men who played in bands.

With help from a couple of friends, Hal discovered several nightspots in their community that featured live bands. Two of these locations weren't just bars, however, they were also restaurants. On Friday and Saturday nights, families frequented these two places until about 9:00 PM; after that, it became more like a typical bar environment. In addition, most of the bands who played were local; the majority of the young men lived in the community.

Lee and his parents began going to the restaurants on Friday nights. They didn't tell Lee they were looking to meet "new babysitters." They were just going to have fun and let Lee enjoy watching live bands perform. During these evenings, when the band took a break, Lee and Hal approached the band members and introduced themselves. Lee was quite shy, so Hal explained Lee's interest in music and his desire to learn to play a musical instrument. Casually, Hal asked the band members several questions: did any of them give lessons, did they live close by, and so forth. He left it at that the first time. During the next two or three outings, Lee and Hal greeted the band members and struck up conversations, talking about Lee's interest and possible lessons. They exchanged phone numbers.

Hal took the bold step of calling the friendliest two members of one particular band and made the official request for lessons. Both said they'd be happy to help Lee learn informally; but they didn't feel qualified to give "real" lessons and charge a fee. Hal set up a time for the two of them to come over. The rest, as they say, is history. After two or three visits, Lee and the two band members were friends. They learned about Lee and his disability, and they recognized Lee's desire to seen as a "cool guy." In friendship, they asked Lee's parents to drop Lee off at the restaurant where they played in the early evening on Friday nights and pick him up by 9:00 PM. In addition to gaining new friendships, Lee soon became their unofficial helper, and he was learning to play the guitar and drums. He was a happy camper.

Lee's parents were ecstatic. Both young men were polite, as well as being clean and sober. One was married with a small child. Because they were in their early twenties, they were more mature and became great friends and supporters of Lee. On Friday nights, and other times Lee was with his new friends, his parents were able to have some time alone.

In this example, Lee's parents used one of his tickets as an entree to the community. Sometimes a ticket is necessary, sometimes it isn't.

During this process, take the time to share new paradigms with your helpers. Teach them that disability is natural, that all people are ready, about People First Language, and so forth. Review how we want to present children with disabilities: as children who are more like other children than different, who have the same basic needs, wants, and dreams. You don't want people "begging" for help on behalf of your "pitiful" child!

Use members of the Dream Team to help you unearth all the different natural supports in your community. Networking is the key! Then use common sense and creativity to arrive at solutions. Try to come up with multiple natural supports and/or generic services for each need. If your first option doesn't work out, you'll have other possibilities to fall back on.

Let your thinking processes flow. If a child needs help with reading, for example, ask yourself how children become better readers. The answer: by being read to and by reading to others. Where could a child get this type of help in a loving supportive environment in the community? If grandparents aren't near, how about an older neighbor, or people who live in a nearby nursing home? Think about it. This is what community is all about: reciprocity. An older person is giving to your child by listening to him read and reading to him. Your child is giving the gift of companionship to the older person.

You may want to address every need on the list during your Dream Party, or you may want to focus only on the needs you think you need help with. Do whatever makes the most sense to you and your family. But always remember to call on others when and if you need help. We're all stronger and better, together!

If you get stuck, go back and reread the various examples in this chapter. Share them with those who are helping. Think big, bold, and creatively. Be determined to succeed. Some solutions will come quickly. Others may take more time and effort, but failure is not an option!

Writing the Master Plan

As you arrive at solutions, record what you're doing on large flip chart paper. Create a heading like the one below and record the appropriate information in each column:

DREAM/NEED/WANT   TICKET   NATURAL SUPPORT/GENERIC SERVICE

Be very specific in everything you include on the chart. If an action will be taken by someone on the Dream Team, write those details. For example: "Erica (the next door neighbor) will contact youth organizations within one week." This will become the master plan, the map, the action plan for your child. Make sure all your helpers know what responsibilities they have.

Thank everyone for their help and adjourn the meeting. Don't forget to write thank you notes to all who are helping.

Next, everyone goes to work, doing whatever was decided. Some goals will be accomplished more easily with others. And some activities may need follow-up with one or more of the Dream Team members. Take whatever steps are necessary to achieve the follow-up. You may want to bring everyone back together in a month, or simply visit with specific team members on the phone. Your child is on his way to a real life in the community!

SYSTEM TEAMS VS. COMMUNITY TEAMS

Parents of young children are familiar with the individualized family service plan (IFSP); parents of school-aged children are familiar with the individualized education program (IEP) and the individualized transition plan (ITP). You may not be aware that similar plans are written for adults with disabilities who are in the system: the individualized habilitation plan (IHP), the individualized work/rehabilitation plan (IWRP), the individual program plan (IPP), and others.

These plans or programs focus on the individual with the disability (and the family, in the IFSP), but often, the individual whose life is being planned is *not* an active participant in the process! Other people (professionals and parents) frequently decide what's important, what the person wants and needs, what the person's goals should be, and so forth. And in too many cases, the person doesn't get what he needs; he gets what the system offers.

Person-centered planning, personal futures planning, and other person-driven methods, including the strategies in this chapter, go far beyond the system's efforts. Methods which include the person with the disability, and which are based on his assets and desires, were developed to meet needs that were unmet by the system. Person-driven methods go beyond basic needs to big dreams; they utilize natural supports and ensure the person whose life is being planned *is an active participant in the process.*

These planning styles did not come from the system. They came from persons with disabilities and their supporters.

In a community team (Dream Party) planning session, the individual with the disability is not only the focus of the meeting, but the individual (and/or the family) is *in charge* of the meeting. People who attend the meeting do so because they care about the person; they're not professionals from the system who are paid to be there. Community members find creative ways to provide the supports that are needed; they don't say "We can't do that," or "We don't offer that," or "We don't have the money." If solutions in the community aren't readily available, imaginative and resourceful Dream Team members can create the solutions. This is impossible in the system.

Some of us may be wary of teams or committees because we've had negative experiences with them in the past. Parents have been ganged up on, out-voted, ignored, and worse. So it's important to recognize the differences between teams in the system and teams in the community.

In the system, professionals are there because they're paid to be there. Many times, they may not even know the person whose life they're planning. System teams may be unable or unwilling to look outside the system for solutions. They operate under directives of federal and/or state laws, policies, and procedures. There are many rules to follow. The process is professional, structured, and formal.

Team members in community planning sessions are there because they care about and know the person or the family. They're involved because it's something they want to do. They invest their time and energy on the basis of friendship and community, not because they're being paid. They don't have hidden agendas, nor do they bring turf wars to the table. They listen to the person's dreams, wants, and needs, and don't talk about whether these are realistic. Possibilities are explored and solutions found. If something doesn't work, they regroup and try again. They don't wait a year to see if their efforts are successful. Community teams operate under the directive of the individual with a disability (or the family). There are no rules. Teams may choose to make guidelines that can be changed at a moment's notice. The process is friendly, informal, and anything goes!

But a word of caution is in order. When something works, someone, somewhere will try to duplicate and mass market it. Unfortunately, some agencies and professionals in the system have seen the benefits of community planning processes and have decided if they work in the community, they'll work in the system. Of course, they can't. It's like trying to mix oil and water. Community teams are successful because they're flexible, unconstrained, voluntary, spontaneous, inspired, and dynamic. Teams from the system are structured, deliberate, and static.

Be on guard—be a skeptic—if professionals and agencies from the system begin promoting or operating community-oriented processes. Be especially wary if an agency or organization of any kind begins employing people with job titles such as: "Person-Centered Planning Facilitator," "Natural Supports Coordinator," and the like. When the informal processes of our natural communities are co-opted by a structured organization (even if it's a non-profit disability organization), the processes are no longer natural and they are no longer community-oriented. They become institutionalized, organized services where professionals are in charge and where rules must be followed. They become part of the system.

PASS THE TORCH

When your child and your family successfully achieve inclusion in the community and when your child's needs are being met by natural supports and generic services, other families will want what you have. They may ask you to "coordinate" or "facilitate" their personal efforts or those of the planning team. Please decline this offer to "manage" the process or the activities. Instead of doing the job *for* someone, show them *how* to do it. Support their efforts, offer ideas and suggestions, but stay in the background. Attend the Dream Team meeting only as an observer or a technical advisor. Allow others to experience what you've experienced: the joy of cooperation, the pride of achievement, and the exhilaration of successful leadership.

TRUST YOURSELF

You are the expert. Trust in your ability to know what's best for your child. And trust in your child to know what's best for him. If your self-confidence has been shaken by the system—if you don't trust yourself—fake it for now.

Put aside what you've been told about your child and her disability. Listen to your child. And listen to that inner voice inside your heart, that small voice that wants to be heard. Sometimes our inner voices can't be heard because the big voices in our heads talk louder and longer. Quiet the big voice for awhile so you can hear the small voice.

You know more than you think you know. From personal conversations with hundreds of parents, I know that some of what's in this chapter is stuff you already know—in your heart. It's been buried down deep, covered up by the heavy dogma of conventional wisdom. When I've presented this information in person, parents approach me with, "This is what we've always wanted to do, but we felt such pressure to do what the experts told us," or "Yes! I can do this! Why didn't I think of it before?" You, too, can rediscover your own common sense and wisdom, and combine them with new ideas to make your child's life the best it can be.

Regardless of your child's disability, you have the knowledge and the capability to raise your child to live a natural, successful life in the community. Never, never believe myths about your child—myths based on the disability—and never believe the lie that professionals know more than you about your child and her needs.

HAVE FAITH IN COMMUNITY AND THE FUTURE

In the world of the service system, goals are set and the measurement of progress of bodily functions is an absolute must. We've erroneously believed acquisition of these goals will somehow make our children successful. Goals in the system don't focus on the true indicators of success: being able to get along in the world, having friends, believing in oneself, being self-determined, and so forth.

In community, goals and measurements are unnecessary and unnatural. In community, we focus on what's really important and we don't need or want to measure what our children achieve. Instead, we celebrate and value milestones such as friendship, freedom, and self-determination. How could we (and why would we want to) measure the value of friendship, the quantity or quality of freedom, or the importance of a future that's based on citizenship and self-determination?

Regardless of the ages or disabilities of our children, we all share one common concern: we care deeply about our children's futures. What kind of lives will our children have as adults? Will they be able to take care of themselves? Will they have friends? Get married? Can they be successful in college? Will they find good jobs? Where will they live? Will they be safe? Will they be okay when we're gone?

We usually don't worry about what will happen to our typical children after we're gone. Correctly or incorrectly, we assume they'll have friends and their own families, that they'll have jobs, and that they'll be able to take care of themselves after we're dead and buried.

But many parents, especially parents whose children are now young adults, don't believe their children will be successful or safe in the community without the official protections provided by the service system. No human being—with a disability or without—can ever be assured of safety 100 percent of the time, but we're all safest when we're surrounded by people who know us and who care about us. In essence, we're all safer within caring communities than we are in the artificial environments managed by the system. No system can guarantee safety. Physical or emotional abuse in group homes and respite care is not unusual. Further, isolation and despair often accompany the "security" of day programs and sheltered work environments.

After we're gone, we have no way of ensuring the personnel and regulations in the system we've depended on won't change. Certainly there are staff people in group homes who care about the people they work with, but their paid assistance can never take the place of the caring and safety provided by friends and neighbors. It's never too early and it's never too late for us to make connections in the community—using natural supports and generic services—that will ensure our children are surrounded by friends and neighbors who care. They will keep our children safe.

Using natural supports and generic services can restore your family and your child to "normal" lives again. When you've lifted the burden of dealing with the system off your shoulders, you'll experience a feeling of freedom like never before. And your child will be on his way to living a natural and successful life in community.

As detailed earlier in this chapter, many parents have discovered that inclusion in the community provides a valuable stepping stone to inclusion within the public school system. And that's where we're going next. First, we'll look at alternatives to traditional programs for babies and young children, and then we'll go on to inclusive education.

The Early Years
Alternatives to Special Programs for Babies and Young Children

16

THE MOTHER'S HEART IS
THE CHILD'S SCHOOLROOM.
Henry Ward Beecher

What kind of lives do we want for babies and young children with disabilities? The most natural lives possible.

In general, the lives of young children with disabilities shouldn't look much different from the lives of young children who don't have disabilities. While children with disabilities may have very unique needs, including significant medical needs, our goal should be to ensure our children live natural lives, included in their homes and communities, from the earliest possible moment. Unfortunately, the special programs and services many parents have come to depend on force children to live unnatural lives, isolated and segregated from the mainstream of their communities.

In Chapter 14, you learned about a variety of ways to meet the needs of children with disabilities, and Chapter 15 detailed strategies for children and their families to live natural lives in the community with the help of generic services and natural supports. In this chapter, we'll look at alternatives to the special programs that are offered to children with disabilities from birth to age five.

The service system separates the early years of children into two distinct categories: birth to three and three to five. But these are distinctions based on how laws are written and the accompanying funding streams; they are not logical distinctions related to childhood development. Lest the title of this chapter misleads you, I won't be suggesting "programs" as alternatives to traditional services. Our children need to be children. They may need assistance, but they don't need programs.

To that end, this chapter focuses broadly, simply, and briefly on how parents can ensure their babies and young children live natural lives. Keep in mind that greater details (covering children of all ages) on how to use natural supports and generic services are in the previous chapter. The last part of this chapter includes details about how parents can impact the early childhood education system.

DON'T WORRY

If I could see you in person right now, I'd give you a big hug and tell you not to worry about your child. I know it probably sounds trite, but I really mean it. When my son was very young, I wish another parent of an older child had told me what I'm telling you. As it was, I surrounded myself with other parents of very young children with disabilities and professionals. The professionals were nice people, but in "doing their jobs," they repeatedly told me negative things about my son. When I was with other parents of kids with disabilities, we loved being together for mutual support, but we spent a whole lot of time being worried about our children.

As I mentioned in earlier chapters, I wasn't able to see things clearly until I met adults with disabilities during the leadership training course I took when Benjamin was three. I met all types of adults with disabilities: some were very successful, had good jobs, and so forth, while others weren't—not much different than general society, right?

Before I met those folks, it was hard for me to think about Benjamin's future. I couldn't get a clear picture in my head of what he would be like as an adult. I tried not to think of it most of the time. When I did think about it, I was like other parents: I pictured my son as an adult *who did not have a disability*. It was as if I believed all the therapies and interventions would, indeed, "cure" him of the disability. In addition, I didn't have any frame of reference to picture him with a disability as an adult. But my attitudes and beliefs changed after I met adults with disabilities. I realized I didn't need to be scared anymore. I was able to visualize Benjamin *as a successful adult who happened to have a disability*. I no longer worried about his future.

So I want you to trust me for now, when I tell you that you really don't have to worry about your child's future (unless you leave everything up to professionals!). Your precious son or daughter can be as successful as his brothers and sisters or other children who don't have disabilities. Pretty soon, you won't need to trust me, your trust in yourself and your child will be all you need to feel okay about things.

Disability is always hardest on parents of young children because everything is so unfamiliar and frightening. Much of what's in this book may also be confusing and scary. I've met many parents of young children during workshops and they're always shocked when I recommend not using EI and ECE services. Their worlds were originally turned upside down by their children's diagnoses, then EI and ECE gave them a lifeline to hold on to, and then I come along and make things topsy-turvy again. So I apologize if I've upset you. Sometimes it takes shocking revelations to enable us to see things clearly. I hope you agree by now that it's critical we move away from the deficit, readiness, and sequential models—promoted by EI and ECE—and see our children for the wonderful, unique, and precious children they really are.

Know that as time passes, things get easier. Time has a way of doing that. But you can speed this process up by following the suggestions throughout this book. You should know that since Benjamin stopped going to therapy—since he started living a natural life—his disability has become irrelevant. I just don't think about it anymore. You know a lot about

Benjamin by now: he uses a power wheelchair, writes on a computer, needs help going to the bathroom, getting dressed, and more. Still, no one in our family thinks of him as having a disability.

What causes parents so much pain is the constant reminders of disability: therapy, professionals measuring our children against developmental scales, special interventions, and more. When my son was still getting services and therapy, I had to repeat his life history (including my prenatal history) over and over and over again, to every new person we saw. I hated it! But once we got out of Disability World, I haven't had to tell that story once! And do you know what else I haven't done since my son quit therapy? Cried about him having a disability. I haven't shed one tear about my son or his disability in the last seven years. You, too, can achieve these milestones. I promise.

Remember not to compare your child to other children—daily, on his birthday, or at any other time. He is growing and developing as he should. With your help and belief in him, he will have the life of his dreams. So don't worry anymore and don't feel sad. Your child is precious. Celebrate his life and his accomplishments every day!

I know what you've been though; I know what you're going through. And I also know how things can be: wonderful! Picture your child as a successful school-aged child, as a successful young adult, as an employee and as a husband or wife. Dream again and don't worry anymore, please. Do this for yourself and your child.

FOCUS ON YOUR CHILD; NOT THE DISABILITY

The best thing you can do for your child is treat her as if she doesn't have a disability. That doesn't mean you ignore her disability or her needs; it means you give her opportunities to live a full and natural life, experiencing typical childhood activities. If you have older children who don't have disabilities, think about what their lives were like when they were the age of your child with a disability. If you don't have older children, look at typical children in the your child's age group.

Chapter 15 detailed how children with disabilities can lead natural lives, so I hope you already have some ideas about how to make some positive changes. But since Chapter 15 didn't focus specifically on a particular age group, following are some principles to keep in mind about babies and young children with disabilities.

Natural Environments

Your child needs to be in natural, not artificial, environments. He should be wherever he would be if he didn't have a disability: at home, a typical day care or preschool, family day care, at grandma's, and so forth. Artificial environments include: early intervention/ infant stimulation classes and programs; therapy settings; early childhood special education programs; and other places that are only for children with disabilities.

It's somewhat disturbing that we even need to talk about natural environments. Parents whose children don't have disabilities would probably wonder what in the world we're talking about! Their children are in natural environments, but they don't have to call them that! The service system and its professional interventions have corrupted our basic sense of parenting.

When the service system started providing services for very young children in the 1980s, services were provided in unnatural settings. Babies and young children with disabilities were segregated and isolated from the mainstream. In 1997, however, legislation mandated that services for young children be provided in their natural environments. This language was included in the law to specifically counteract the trend of making young children spend time in artificial environments.

Presume Competence

Regardless of what any professionals have told you about your child and her disability, presume she's smart, can learn, and will be successful. At the same time, respect her individuality. Don't try to make her look like other children her age and don't worry if she's not doing the same things, and in the same way, other children her age are doing. Don't compare her to other children her age and don't let other people do it either. Just give her lots of opportunities to live a typical and natural childhood, and she'll do fine.

Have High Expectations

Dream for your child and let him know you dream for him. Once your child acquires speech or some other form of communication, ask him what he wants to be when he grows up. If he uses a wheelchair and he tells you he wants to be a fireman, don't tell him he can't! Over the years, Benj has told me he wants to be a professional basketball player, a pediatric orthopedic surgeon, the host of *Jeopardy!*, and a variety of other things. I've always said, "Good for you!" or "That's great!" just like I did when my daughter said she wanted to be President of the United States. As your child grows, he'll figure out what he'll be able to do and what he won't. Don't squash his dreams; there will be enough people in the future who will try to do that. He needs you to believe in him so he can believe in himself.

Meet Your Child's Unique Needs

Whatever your child needs to be successful, provide it for her. If your baby is fretful and needs to be held most of the time, do it. If she needs to sleep with you, let her. If your toddler still needs to be rocked to sleep, that's okay. Many professionals have told parents that children with disabilities learn to be very manipulative. They warn against "giving in" or "indulging" a child who has a disability. This is cruel and it's also baloney. Children with disabilities are no different than children who don't have disabilities: they need what they need! They are not more or less manipulative than other children. All children are different and all have different needs. Listen to your child and listen to your heart.

When we spend lots of time with our children, cuddling them, playing with them, and responding to their tears and fears, they learn they can trust us—that we'll be there for them. This is the foundation of self-confidence and self-determination.

Provide Tools for Success

To ensure your child has a wonderful childhood, full of opportunities and experiences, provide her with whatever tools for success she needs: independent mobility, communication tools, adapted equipment, assistive technology devices, and anything else that will allow her to learn and grow from typical childhood experiences at the appropriate age. The earlier you get her these tools the better.

Contrary to today's conventional wisdom, it is not services and interventions that will minimize the effect of the disability or prepare your child for a real life. Your child is ready for a real life right now! Providing her with the tools she needs is what will minimize the effects of the disability. Tools level the playing field; they enable children with disabilities to get on with the business of living.

Help Your Child Naturally

If you haven't already, try to let go of professional hands-on therapies and other interventions. You have what it takes to help your child with walking, talking, behavior, feeding, toileting, and so forth (go back and review Chapter 14 if necessary). I'm not implying we forego true medical help. But we can let go of the intrusive treatments that rob our children of their childhoods and send the negative message that they're not-OK. While your child is spending hours in therapy, he's missing out on a natural childhood!

Experience the Dignity of Risk

If your child has significant medical needs (a tracheotomy, oxygen, feeding tube, etc.), don't let these prevent her from participating in typical age-appropriate activities. For example, if you want to enroll her in a neighborhood preschool or a gymnastics class, don't assume her medical needs will be a barrier to her participation. Trust that she can be successful, whether or not she does things the same as other children. Trust, also, that the adults in charge of these activities will welcome her and will learn how to handle her medical needs. I'm not suggesting we ever put our children in danger. But we need to find a balance. Many children who have significant medical needs are prevented from living natural lives because parents fear for their safety.

In addition, if your child has an interest in doing something, support her desire and be willing to take risks. For example, if a young girl who uses a walker or a wheelchair wants to take ballet, go for it! Don't assume it won't work. If she wants to do it and she knows her parents are behind her, it will work out one way or another. If a boy who's blind wants to learn to play sports or do other "rough and tumble" boy things, let him give it a try. We never know what's possible until we do it! Be willing to experience the dignity of risk.

Anticipate Criticism

Parents of young children who *don't* have disabilities are often at the mercy of grandparents, neighbors, and other well-meaning people who feel the need to tell parents everything they're doing wrong. Parents whose young children do have disabilities sometimes get a double dose of this. We share stories about our children's disabilities and their experiences in therapy or EI/ECE services with family members and friends. Too many people know too many things about our children and our families. As a result, others feel qualified to give us free advice about our children and our parenting skills.

If you've decided to make some changes (getting out of the service system, quitting therapy, enrolling your child in a neighborhood preschool, and so forth), and you share this information with people in your life, be prepared for criticism and concern. Family members, especially our parents, often haven't learned to see disability as a natural condition. They're grateful and excited that your child is entitled to so many services. They may not understand why you would make changes or let go of entitlements and services. Be prepared to help them understand what you're doing and why you're doing it. At the same time, reconsider how much of your family's life you want everyone to know. Our family members may have learned a lot in the past because we've ventilated about frustrations with the system. But many parents who get out of the system find their lives so much calmer they don't need to ventilate as much!

Protect Your Child's Privacy

Your child's life and his disability are not an open book. As I've mentioned in previous chapters, parents have sometimes gotten in the terrible habit of telling everyone they know everything about their children and their children's conditions. Friends, family members, and strangers in the grocery store all want to look at, touch, talk to, or get close to babies and young children. They're irresistible! As proud parents, we love talking about our children. The problem is we may talk too much and inadvertently set our children up for exclusion, pity, or some other negative reaction. In certain circumstances, we do need to share specific information with specific individuals. But in general, your child's condition and what he can and can't do are no one's business. Use your own best judgment about who you tell and what you tell, but you don't owe anyone any explanations.

Listen to Your Inner Voice

After your child was diagnosed, you were probably told about the services your child was entitled to, as well as how badly your child needed those services. Like most parents, you accepted this information as fact. Now, perhaps, you feel differently: you're not as happy with the services as you once were; the intrusion into your family's life is too stressful; or some other issues are creating doubts. At the same time, you may be hesitant to drop therapy, early intervention, or early childhood education services. You may be frightened or nervous about what will happen to your child without professional assistance. I understand. I was there once.

I was often uncomfortable with early intervention, but I stayed with it for two more years. I did turn down infant stim classes, and later, ECE services. It took a lot of courage to listen to my inner voice. I first began questioning therapy when Benj was three; but it took three more years before I paid attention to my son's tears and my own nagging doubts.

When my son was very young, the pressure to "do the right thing" for him—as defined by professionals in the service system—was enormous. It was difficult to go against conventional wisdom: to stand up to professionals, question their judgment, and reject all the "help" that was offered to my son and my family. But once I began trusting my instincts, it was easier to take the plunge and say no. And my self-confidence in knowing what was best for my son grew each time I said no. The world didn't end when I rejected special services. In fact, the world got much better!

Listen to your inner voice. Do what's right according to your own beliefs, not those of professionals, educators, or others. You might feel comfortable scaling back on professional help as a way of weaning yourself from it permanently. Or you may be ready to let go of it all right way. Follow your intincts; you know best.

NO SPECIAL PROGRAMS

Your child doesn't need special programs and interventions. Yes, he may need help learning to do new things, and he may need assistive technology, accommodations, modifications, and support. But you, your family and friends, and others in your community are fully capable of providing for his unique needs. How do you get to this point, if you're not already there? It's not as hard as you might think.

BEYOND EARLY INTERVENTION AND THERAPY

If you're ready to take the big plunge, simply tell the service coordinator you no longer want EI services. It's that easy. You'll probably need to have an IFSP meeting to officially take your child out of the program.

If you're not quite ready to totally let go of EI services, but you are ready for less intrusion, have an IFSP meeting and rewrite a plan you're more comfortable with.

If you're ready to stop taking your child to therapy (or having the therapist come to your home), just do it. If you need to wean yourself gradually, cut back on the number of therapy sessions for the next month; cut them back again for another month; and so on until you can stop altogether. Alternatively, change the role of the therapist to a consultant, as described in Chapter 15.

Of course, you'll need to steel yourself for criticism. Many parents have been given dire warnings when they don't heed professional wisdom. If a tongue-lashing from an expert makes you weak in the knees, practice how you'll handle the situation ahead of time, or have a friend along for moral support. Then smile and thank everyone for all their help, and get on with living a life free from intrusion!

What will "replace" therapy and EI services? In a formal sense, nothing. Informally, you'll be helping your child in a variety of more natural ways. If you're a stay-at-home mom, use your own common sense and the ideas in Chapters 13, 14, and 15 as your guide. Ditto if your child is in a day care setting: help caregivers learn how to assist your precious baby with "therapeutic-like" activities and so forth.

BEYOND EARLY CHILDHOOD SPECIAL ED PRESCHOOL

If you're ready to make some changes regarding special ed preschool services, a variety of options are possible.

From ECE to Home or Day Care

If you're a stay-at-home mom, you can—in all good conscience—pull your child out of the special ed preschool program (today!) and keep him home with you. You do not need to replace the ECE program with something else. Just utilize your own abilities, and the natural supports and generic services in your community to meet your child's needs. If you're a working mom and your child goes to an ECE program and day care, you can pull him out of ECE and he can spend the whole day in the day care setting.

Contact the school and call an IEP meeting to formally "dismiss" your child from special ed services. The experts will try to talk you out of it; they may try to make you feel guilty. Don't listen to any of this. Know that, when it's time, your child will have a better chance of being included in a regular education kindergarten class if he has not been in an ECE program!

From ECE to Neighborhood Preschool

Another option is to pull your child out of the ECE program and enroll him in a neighborhood preschool or mom's-day-out program, with you assuming the financial responsibility for the tuition. Your child will do just as well (if not better) in a natural environment than in the ECE program.

Some parents face no barriers enrolling their children with disabilities in typical neighborhood preschools. But other parents may have difficulties, especially if their preschoolers are still in diapers or if their children have visible or behavioral disabilities. Following are some helpful hints.

Do Your Homework

Before you choose a preschool, do your homework. Talk to friends and neighbors. If you know another mom who currently has a child in a preschool you're interested in, go with her when she picks up her child and check the place out. Additionally, make unannounced visits to every preschool in your area. Don't be put off by the exterior of the building. Warm and loving staff may be inside. If your child uses a mobility device, scope out the exterior with an eye toward accessibility. One neighborhood preschool Benjamin attended wasn't the most accessible, but because it was the best overall, we put up with the inconvenience of the two steps leading to the front door.

Don't even think of calling a preschool for information until you've made a personal, unannounced visit. By "dropping in" you'll get an accurate picture of what the preschool is really like. And *don't* take your child with you on these "surveillance" visits. Be warm and friendly, introduce yourself, and tell the preschool director you'd like information about the school: what ages are served, schedules, tuition, etc. She'll probably ask you about your child, but only give basic information such as your child's name and age. Do not mention your child's disability at this point. More on this in a moment.

Child Care Settings, Potty Training, and the ADA

This next part of your homework is extremely important if your three or four-year-old is still in diapers. Some child care and preschool centers will not accept *any* children, ages three and above, who are still in diapers. Many parents have shared stories about trying to enroll their preschoolers with disabilities in a child care facility, but they're refused enrollment because the child is still in diapers. When this happens, parents think the center is violating the Americans with Disabilities Act. However, we need to understand the law before we jump to conclusions.

Under the ADA, businesses are required to provide accommodations, but they're not required to provide *extra* services to people with disabilities. What does this mean for a child care facility (preschool or day care)? If a preschool for three and four-year-olds does *not* provide the service of changing diapers for any child at the facility, it is not required to provide the service for a child with a disability. If, however, a facility serves children aged two and younger, and provides the service of changing diapers for younger children, the facility cannot refuse an older child who wears diapers. Simplified, if a facility provides a service for one child, it cannot refuse to provide the same service to other children.

So, if your older child is still wearing diapers, you need to know if the facility has younger children there who are in diapers. If so, it will have a room or a place where the diaper changing is done, and the facility can help with your child's toileting needs.

But couldn't a preschool without diaper changing facilities simply agree to accept a child in diapers? Not necessarily. The facility would first have to create a diaper changing area, per state regulations regarding sanitary conditions in child care settings.

If we're not familiar with child care regulations, we might simply assume a preschool without diaper changing facilities could just change a child's diapers in a corner of the room or on the bathroom floor. So when a preschool director tells us the school doesn't accept children who aren't potty trained, we often assume the facility is discriminating against children with disabilities who are still in diapers. As you can see, though, it has more to do with state health regulations than discrimination. If this is a situation you might be facing, I urge you to find out more by calling the child care licensing department in your state (or research this on the Internet).

Church Preschools and the ADA

The Americans with Disabilities Act impacts child care facilities in another way. Because of the separation of church and state, churches are exempt from ADA regulations. However, the relationship between churches and child care facilities are important.

If a child care facility in or on church property is operated by the church, it's exempt from the ADA. But if it's run by another entity or organization, it is not exempt from the ADA. So if you're looking at a preschool or child care program in a church building, find out who runs the program: the church or someone else.

Site Visits

Back to your site visits, now. Before you go on any site visits, create a checklist of things to look for at each preschool you visit. While you're at each facility, don't rush. Tell the director you'd like to sit and observe the class your child would be in. Picture your child there. What do you see?

As soon as you're back in the car (before you forget it all), write down what you learned. What ages are served? Are there diaper changing facilities? Is the building accessible? Is the environment suitable for your child's particular needs? Is it calm and quiet, with a lot of order? That might be right for some children and wrong for others. Ditto if it's wild and chaotic.

What's your gut instinct about the staff? Are they patient, kind, and loving? Stern disciplinarians? Or somewhere in between? Look closely at the teachers in the class your child would be in. Do they seem accepting of all their students? Can you see yourself developing a positive, cooperative relationship with them?

Many parents make a point of interviewing the preschool director during a site visit. But you may run into a director who turns the tables and decides to interview you on the spot. Her routine practice may be to ask a new parent lots of questions about the child. At some point, she might even ask something like, "Does your child have any special needs we need to know about?" Honesty might be the best policy, but you also need to use your common sense. You can't tell an outright lie, because if you do and then decide to use this facility, you'll have started the relationship off badly.

If the director asks, "Does your child have special needs?" in a way that leads you to believe she *wouldn't* accept children with disabilities, you're probably better off scratching this place off your list. If, however, she seems kind and genuinely interested in meeting the needs of all her students, you can probably feel free to answer truthfully. But remember to frame your child's disability in a way that doesn't present your child in a negative light. Rather than saying the name of your child's disability, provide a positive description.

If a preschool director asked me, "Does your child have any special needs?" which description would be more likely to make the director feel at ease: (1) "Yes, he has cerebral palsy;" or (2) "Not really. He uses a wheelchair, but I think he can maneuver around the classroom just fine. He's very friendly and knows how to ask for help, so I think everything will be just fine." (Once Benj is enrolled, I can work closely with his teacher to help her learn more about him.)

The first hypothetical response ("He has cerebral palsy.") may cause the director's stomach to knot up, especially if she imagines "the worst." The second response would probably stimulate questions from her, such as: can he feed himself, can he talk, and so on. I would provide answers that are truthful, and that also portray Benjamin in a flattering light.

If you have a child with autism, for example, when asked if your child has any "special needs," say something like, "Not really. Matthew communicates with picture cards, but he'll bring them when he comes to school and I'll be happy to help everyone learn more about them." Or, "Melissa has lots of energy. She does best when she's kept busy."

In any event, unless you know with certainty the preschool welcomes children with disabilities, don't mention your child's disability until the enrollment process is completed.

After Johnny is enrolled and you've paid the first month's tuition, and before his first day, call the director and tell her you'd like to bring Johnny by for a visit, to familiarize him with the people and the place. Don't mention your child's disability at this point either (unless it's already been disclosed when the director interviewed you). When you and little Johnny walk through the door, you want his shining smile, beaming eyes, and precious personality to define who he is, instead of the disability label defining him.

At the meeting (or a later meeting with the teacher), review your child's strengths, gifts, and talents before describing his needs. Reassure the director (or teacher) of your willingness to work with the school to ensure everyone's success: you'll volunteer on a regular basis, you'll stay with your child for an hour or so during the first few days, you'll be available if they need to call you at home with questions during the time your child is in class, and so forth. They're sure to have many questions, so appreciate their willingness to learn; don't become offended and insulted and don't wear your heart on your sleeve.

A One-on-One Aide?

Many parents unwittingly sabotage their efforts when they insist that a neighborhood preschool provide a one-on-one aide for their child as an accommodation. Often, the process of enrolling their child is going smoothly, but things hit a big snag when this issue is brought up. Know that your child doesn't need a one-on-one aide. If you want him to be included, he's got to be part of the class. In Chapter 7, I reviewed how aides get in the way of a child's inclusion. Reread that if necessary. Whatever help your child needs can be provided by his teachers and his classmates. In addition, modifications and adaptations can make a difference in the amount of support your child needs. Presume competence. Presume your child will do well; presume peer support will be helpful; and presume the preschool staff is qualified to meet your child's needs.

Under the ADA, you could ask the preschool to provide an aide as an accommodation. However, a preschool could be justified in refusing to hire an additional staff person because it wouldn't be a "reasonable accommodation" under the law. In other words, the cost of hiring someone would make the accommodation "unreasonable."

Conversely, a preschool may agree to enroll a child with a disability on the condition the parents provide (and pay for) a one-on-one aide. But again, your child doesn't need an aide. If, however, this is an option you've considered (and you have the money), would you really want to send your child to a preschool where the staff wasn't comfortable with him unless a "body guard" was present?

In the two neighborhood preschools Benj attended when he was three and four, he was still in diapers and he needed a great deal of physical assistance. In both preschools, everyone did fine. No one felt the need to bring another warm adult body in to help. The teachers and the directors all pitched in when necessary. In the church preschool, when the teacher needed an extra hand she simply went out in the hallway and yelled. The director was there in a flash.

The most important barometer of a good preschool for your child is the staff. If they're open and honest, kind and caring, and if they really love all children, you can work with them to solve any problems that arise. If, however, they're hard to get along with, you'll need to make a judgment call on how much effort you're willing to expend. If fear is what's driving their discomfort, acknowledge their fears and give them all your support. If you get the feeling they think your child is simply "too much trouble," cut your losses and find another preschool. Your child is too important to become a pawn in a game.

Using ECE Related Services Only

Another option is to pull your child out of the special ed preschool, keep him at home with you or send him to a neighborhood preschool, while still using the related services offered through the ECE program. How this might work depends on what you want and how the school usually operates. Some parents have been more successful than others; there are many variables.

Don't try to get every related service the school typically provides. For instance, if the ECE program provides bus transportation from your home to the school, don't expect the school to provide transportation for your child if you enroll him in a neighborhood school.

There are other related services (specifically therapies) that he may be able to receive in settings other than the ECE classroom. However, in some districts, it's simply not feasible to provide related services to children who are not in the ECE classroom.

Legally, you could take this to the extreme and sue the district if they refused to provide what your child is entitled to under IDEA, but I hope you won't. You'll be setting yourself up for years of bad karma, especially if this is the district in which your child will be spending many years. Suing over the meager related services the school can provide is probably a waste of time and energy! So, let's assume you're not going to sue over related services, and look at the different issues to consider.

Are the therapists who work in the ECE classroom itinerant therapists (driving from school to school) or do they only work in that particular school building? Do you want to take your child to the ECE classroom when the therapist is there for your child to receive PT, OT, or speech therapy?

If you're enrolling your child in a neighborhood preschool or if you're keeping her at home, would you want the therapist to go where your child is to deliver services? Instead of direct hands-on therapy, would you like a therapist to teach you or others (neighborhood preschool staff) how to help your child in his natural environments? If so, which would work better: for the therapist to make home visits or for you to visit the ECE classroom to meet with the therapist?

There are so many variables, it's impossible to describe every possible scenario. So put your thinking cap on and figure out what you really want and need, and what's best for your child and your family. Consider all the issues. If you decide to keep your child at home, do you really want to make a trip to school once or twice a week, or do you want the therapist coming into your home? If your child is going to attend a neighborhood preschool, will a therapist visiting the neighborhood preschool interrupt your child's day? Will she have a good relationship with the preschool staff? Most importantly, would the therapy be beneficial and relevant to your child?

Once you've decided what's what, call an IEP meeting to discuss the issues. Before doing this, however, read the next chapter to learn more about effective IEP meetings.

Using a Neighborhood Preschool with School District Funds

In a very few communities, school districts provide special education preschool services to children with disabilities in their natural environments. If the child stays home with mom, special ed teachers, therapists, and other specialists deliver services in the child's home. If the parents want the child to attend preschool, he attends a neighborhood preschool and the school district pays the tuition. Again, ECE professionals deliver services to the child in that environment. But this is not the norm. However, more and more parents are trying to make it the norm. Some are successful; some aren't.

In school districts where educators are unwilling to provide special ed preschool services in a child's natural environment, some parents are suing their school districts over the issue. Some have won these lawsuits, but the price they pay may be extremely high: creating life-long enemies of people in their district. Personally, I wouldn't want to send either of my children to a place where people hate my guts.

At any rate, when schools provide services in natural environments, the school district still receives federal and state funding, but the funding is directed to paying for the tuition and the services the child receives in a typical preschool or other setting.

If you decide to go this route in a school district that doesn't routinely follow this practice, be prepared for resistance. An educator, for example, may be willing to consider your request, but school administration may not go along. School personnel may be afraid of "setting a precedent:" if they do it for you, they'll have to do it for every parent and they're not prepared for the onslaught. Be persistent and determined (use strategies presented in the next chapter), but know when to cut your losses. Weigh the effects of this fight against the long term relationships with the school district.

CHANGING EARLY CHILDHOOD PRESCHOOLS

A more effective way to ensure young children receive ECE services in natural environments is to change the overall system. Unfortunately, the process may take longer than you have. If your child is four, and you start advocating for systems change today, she'll probably be in second or third grade by the time the change takes place (if it does take place). Still, it's a worthy goal that could impact thousands of children in the years ahead.

The easiest and quickest way for this to happen would be for the district's school board to make it policy: all children who receive special ed preschool services will be served in their natural environments. On their own, most school boards probably won't do this. They may know little, if anything, about the district's ECE program and/or they may let the special ed department take full responsibility for ECE policies and procedures. So, it's up to parents to initiate change. There are many ways to influence; following are some suggestions that may be helpful to parents who are ready to take the tiger by the tail.

This is not a one person effort. Parents whose children are currently enrolled in the special ed preschool, parents of babies with disabilities who may one day use the services, directors and teachers from typical preschools, and community members would need to form a coalition. If staff members of the special ed preschool are willing to look at alternatives, it would be beneficial to have them involved as well.

The first step is to identify typical preschools/child care centers who would be willing to work with the school district. We wouldn't want just one neighborhood preschool to take all the responsibility, for if all young children with disabilities went there, it wouldn't look much different than the existing segregated program. The population of the preschools should reflect natural proportions; the number of children with disabilities in any given classroom should not exceed 10 percent of the total.

The coalition would need to identify a variety of methods of collaboration between the school system and the neighborhood preschools. These recommendations could then be taken to the school board. In some school districts, the principal or special ed director should be included in the process. The more supporters, the better.

In a hypothetical situation, the coalition could propose the following: the special ed preschool staff will provide technical assistance and on-site support to all the participating typical preschools. Itinerant therapists will provide direct services to children, or technical assistance to the preschool staffs. Parents can enroll their children in the participating preschool of their choice, or geographic boundaries can dictate which children go to which preschool. The district will pay the preschools directly for all the children's tuition. Children who stay home with mom, instead of attending a preschool, will also receive services per their IEPs, in the natural environment of their homes.

Another option would be for the school district to issue vouchers to parents whose children are enrolled in the ECE program. In this situation, parents could send their children to any preschool in the area and use the voucher to pay tuition. The district would provide itinerant services.

After the coalition has decided how the mission can be accomplished, the recommendations would be presented to the school board. The goal is to have the board make new policies and procedures regarding ECE services. When presenting the recommendations, the coalition must not only present the "pros," but also the "cons." In all likelihood, one or more board members will play devil's advocate. Most school boards do not make sweeping decisions lightly, so the coalition must make sure to cover all the bases!

There is one more method to consider. If the parents of all the children in ECE classrooms in the whole district banded together, it's possible change could occur almost overnight. All parents would need to collectively meet with the special ed director and/or the school board and announce:

- Starting next Monday, we will no longer bring our children to the ECE classrooms.

- We are prepared to enroll our children in neighborhood preschools and we want special ed preschool funding to follow our children to those community locations.

- Related services will also follow our children to their natural environments (home, day care, neighborhood preschools, etc.).

This method might work, but only if *every single parent in the district banded together*. If just some parents joined in the effort, it would most likely fail because of logistics and economics. For example, the school district probably doesn't have enough staff people to split them into various locations: half staying in the ECE classrooms and half going out into community settings.

But if *all* children are served in community settings, the staff wouldn't need to be in the school building(s). Therefore, they could roam around town to deliver services to children in neighborhood preschools.

When services are provided in natural environments, they won't look the same as an ECE classroom. Instead of ECE staffers staying in the ECE classroom all day, they'll be out and about, dividing their time among the different community settings. Special ed teachers won't be classroom teachers anymore, they'll be consultants to the staffs at community preschools and day care facilities, as well as to parents. Therapists may provide some hands-on therapy, but will provide more assistance as consultants.

For this method of systems change to work, parents would need to be of one mind when delivering the ultimatum to school authorities. In addition, they would need to do their homework and be prepared to follow through. They couldn't just rattle their sabers with empty threats.

Prior to meeting with the special ed director or the school board, they would need to really have their children enrolled in community child care facilities. They would also need to present a written description of how this new method would work. If this isn't provided, school administrators will simply throw their hands up in confusion, wondering how in the world they're supposed to accomplish the goal. And none of this can be done in anger. The manner and style—positive and helpful, yet firm—in which the leaders of the group present the resolution is critical.

One of the dilemmas facing parents who might want to try this approach is getting all the parents in the district together in the first place! Because of the confidentiality of special ed services, it's often difficult for parents to find one another. But this is not an insurmountable barrier. It's easier to get connected to parents of other children than you think: volunteer; hang out before or after class to meet other parents; follow the ECE school bus through the neighborhood and see where it stops; plan an informal, initial "support group" meeting at your house and send invitations—in sealed envelopes—to all the other parents (you or your child can distribute them to his classmates).

If ECE classrooms are located in different elementary schools in your district, you'll have a little more work to do. Get other parents to help and try these ideas: follow the ECE school buses in the afternoon and note the addresses where they stop; make invitations to parents for a "support group" meeting, take them to the other schools and ask the principal or the ECE teacher to give them to the students in the ECE classroom, or put the notice of the meeting around town, in school newsletters, local newspapers, via PTA meetings, etc.

Anticipate that the sealed envelopes may be opened by school personnel. Therefore, on the invitations to the meeting, make no mention of what the "support group" meeting is about. Just call it the "ECE Parents Group" or something.

Once you get all the parents together in a meeting, however, you're still not home free. *You* may be convinced all preschoolers with disabilities belong in natural environments in the community, instead of the artificial settings of ECE preschools, but how do you convince others? Some parents may be emotionally invested in ECE; others are on the fence. It's important to educate them about the benefits of inclusion in the community, the negative messages of ECE, and a variety of issues that are included in this book. Remember that some people take longer to warm up to new ideas than others. And remember that even within a group of parents, it's important to make allies. Some parents may feel alienated, scared, intimidated, or outnumbered by the supporters of your proposal. Be patient and kind as you help them understand new ways of looking at things.

If you're unable to get every single parent to buy into this effort, don't go forward. It has to be all or nothing. If you try to do this with some of the parents, the school will use the divide and conquer strategy. You and your supporters will be seen as the enemy. The other group of parents will be seen as angels. You'll make enemies with educators and parents. But if you think there's a chance this might work, go for it!

In addition to influencing how ECE programs are implemented, we can also influence how typical preschools in our communities operate, regarding the inclusion of children with disabilities. In Chapter 21, strategies on how to work proactively with day care centers and preschools are detailed.

INCLUSION BEGETS INCLUSION

Based on the real life experiences of children with disabilities and their families, children who have not attended special ed preschools have a better chance of being included in regular ed kindergarten classes in their neighborhood schools than those who have attended special ed preschools.

In the transition to public school, special ed preschool teachers may recommend placement in special ed during kindergarten. Additionally, regular ed kindergarten teachers may be hesitant to include a child with a disability who comes to the class with two or three years of special ed baggage. The perception is that this child is too needy, too difficult, or too different, and the kindergarten teacher doesn't feel she can handle the situation. On the other hand, a child who has attended a typical preschool, or who has stayed home with Mom and/or participated in typical community activities, may be welcomed into the inclusive classroom. The perception is that he's capable and competent since he's been successful in typical settings.

If your child has been enrolled in an ECE program for the last year, don't think he's doomed. Just pull him out now, keep him home with you or enroll him in a neighborhood preschool. When it's time for kindergarten, he'll have a history of success in the community instead of special ed baggage.

The special ed process is often difficult; many parents dread IEP meetings, they must fight to get what their children need, and they're frustrated, exhausted, and angry. But inclusive education can become a reality and we can have positive relationships with educators, as the next chapter demonstrates.

Inclusive Education: Blueprint for Success

EDUCATION IS TOO IMPORTANT TO BE
LEFT SOLELY TO THE EDUCATORS.

Francis Keppel

Under federal special education law—IDEA, the Individuals with Disabilities Education Act—students with disabilities have the right to a free, appropriate public education (FAPE) in the least restrictive environment (LRE). But it's time to go beyond legal rights. Inclusive education is simply the right thing to do. Exclusion and segregation are more than potential violations of special education law. They are violations of the moral code that all children deserve the best we can give them. Our society constantly struggles to do what's best for its children. It is immoral to do less for children who happen to have disabilities.

In an attempt to ensure their children's legal rights are fulfilled, parents of children with disabilities often beat educators over the head with the law. And yes, schools should follow the law. But our efforts must be based on more than the minimum: the services and entitlements guaranteed by legal rights. We must be driven by the belief that all children deserve the best. When we rise above manmade legalities and operate from the highest principles of ethics and morals, we will no longer engage in a tug-of-war with educators.

THE SPECIAL EDUCATION PROCESS

Although most parents whose children receive special ed services are familiar with the special education process, I'll provide a mini-review as a refresher. Throughout this chapter, we'll study the specifics of the law as they apply to inclusive education. However, this chapter does not include explanations of all components of IDEA, such as mediation, due process, and other issues. To learn more about the entire law, check with your state's parent training and information center, protection and advocacy organization, or disability-related agencies about free or low cost manuals on the law.

The Ideal

The special education process can be initiated by parents or educators when they suspect (or know) a child has (or is at risk of developing) a disability that may affect a child's educational experiences. The first step is the assessment process, in which a child is evaluated to determine if he qualifies for special education services. If the child qualifies, an individualized education program (IEP) is written for the child by a team which includes the child's parents; the child, when appropriate; educators; and others who can contribute knowledge about the child.

The IEP is written during an IEP meeting in which all team members are expected to participate. During the meeting, the team shares assessment data about the child, reviews the child's present level of educational performance, and writes goals and objectives to meet the child's individual needs. The team also decides what related services the child needs (therapies, assistive technology, transportation, and other services). The child's placement (regular classroom, resource room, and so forth) is based on the IEP.

The Reality

Congress enacted a good law, but how schools implement the law leaves much to be desired. Typically, the IEP process is not smooth. It is a rough road filled with potholes, detours, and road rage. Parents and educators often interpret the law differently, which leads to miscommunication, misunderstandings, frustration, and anger.

Parents are supposed to be equal members of the IEP team, but usually they're not. They are often given little or no information about assessments, test results, and other important information about their children. Educators often write goals and objectives without parental input. The decision on which related services to provide is often based on funding, staffing, or some other criteria, instead of on the child's needs. Placement decisions are frequently made by educators—again, without parental input—before the IEP has even been written. Further, many placement decisions are based on the child's disability label instead of the child's IEP.

During many IEP meetings, parents are not considered equal members of the team, their opinions are ignored, and their expertise is belittled. At some point, educators and parents may begin seeing each other as enemies, and the special education process becomes a battleground. We can change all this.

WHAT IS INCLUSION?

Inclusion has been defined in many ways by many different people. In general, however, parents and educators who have experience with inclusive practices agree on general parameters. Following is a definition of inclusion in public school settings that is widely-accepted, and it's the definition used in this chapter and throughout the book:

> Inclusion is children with disabilities being educated in the schools they
> would attend if they didn't have disabilities, in age-appropriate regular
> education classrooms, where services and supports are provided in those
> classrooms for both the students and their teachers, and where students
> with disabilities are fully participating members of their school communities
> in academic and extra-curricular activities.

Inclusion is not children with disabilities spending the majority of the school day in a special ed room, and being "included" in regular classes for art, PE, and music. This is visitation. Inclusion is not children with disabilities attending regular education classes, but being repeatedly pulled out for special services throughout the day. This is part-time mainstreaming. Inclusion is not children with disabilities being in regular classes, but sitting in the back of the room with full-time aides. This is physical integration. Inclusion is not typical children (peer role models) visiting children with disabilities in special ed classrooms. This is reverse mainstreaming. Perhaps my son's definition of inclusion is best. He said, "Inclusion is being a regular kid!"

DOES THE LAW MANDATE INCLUSION?

While you won't find the word "inclusion" in IDEA, the law is very prescriptive about placement. IDEA '97 states:

> Each public agency shall ensure
> (1) that to the maximum extent appropriate, children with disabilities,
> including children in public or private institutions or other care facilities,
> are educated with children who are nondisabled; and
> (2) that *special classes, separate schooling or other removal* of children with disabilities
> from the regular educational environment occurs only if the nature or severity of
> the disability is such that education in regular classes with the use of
> supplementary aids and services cannot be achieved satisfactorily. [Section 300.550,
> General LRE Requirements] (italics and underlining added)

> Each public agency shall ensure that the child's placement
> (1) is determined at least annually;
> (2) is based on the child's IEP; and
> (3) is as close as possible to the child's home;
> Unless the IEP of a child with a disability requires some other arrangement,
> the child is educated *in the school that he or she would attend if nondisabled;* in
> selecting the least restrictive environment, consideration is given to any harmful
> effect on the child or on the quality of services that he or she needs and a child is
> *not removed from education in age-appropriate regular classrooms solely because of needed
> modifications in the general curriculum.* [Section 300.522, Placements] (italics added)

> In providing or arranging for the provision of nonacademic and extracurricular
> services and activities, including meals, recess periods, and the services and
> activities set forth in Section 300.306, each public agency shall ensure that each
> child with a disability participates with nondisabled children in those services and
> activities to the maximum extent appropriate to the needs of that child. [Section
> 300.553, Nonacademic settings]

Look what the key phrases tell us: "educated in the school as close as possible to the child's home" and "educated in the school he or she would attend if nondisabled." That's the neighborhood school, and/or the school other children in the neighborhood attend. "Special classes, separate schooling or other removal" from regular ed and "is not removed" from "age-appropriate regular classrooms" indicate placement in regular ed classrooms.

Is there any doubt that the intent of the law is for children with disabilities to be educated in the same school as their brothers and sisters and neighbors, in regular ed classes? Other language in the law refers to teachers and students receiving the appropriate supports, and nothing in the law says anything about pulling children out of regular ed classes for these services. Furthermore, "removal" (used twice) indicates children with disabilities are supposed to *start out* in regular classes; they are not to start out in the most restrictive settings and then *earn* their way out. All of this is what we call inclusion.

Many educators do not interpret IDEA this way, which leads to contentious battles in IEP meetings. Parents want their children educated in regular classrooms, per the law, while many educators insist a resource room or special program—both are segregated—is the most appropriate placement. Parents often attempt to enlighten educators about the intentions of the law (as described in Chapter 7), but these efforts bear no fruit.

AN ISSUE OF THE HEART

Inclusion won't become a reality in many schools unless and until educators *feel* differently about it. If educators don't have the heart to do inclusion, they can (and do) interpret the law to justify their positions. When educators believe in inclusion—when their hearts are in the right place—the law frequently becomes irrelevant. Educators include, educate, and support students with disabilities because it's simply the right thing to do!

In an attempt to force educators to follow the law, some parents use their due process rights and sue their school districts. Some parents win and some parents lose. But even when they win, the outcome is often not what parents expect. Generally, the due process ruling applies only to the child whose rights were being violated, and seldom do educators permanently change their policies in ways that impact all students with disabilities in the district. They simply comply with the decision for the one child, and compliance is assured only through constant monitoring.

When parents file lawsuits—whether they win or not—the hearts of educators are usually hardened, not just toward the parents who sue, but toward other parents whose children receive special ed services (guilt by association). The repercussions may be felt far and wide, and be long-lasting.

The strategies in this chapter are not about enforcement of the law. The methods I'm suggesting combine common sense, an understanding of the law, and parental leadership. When we change the way we do things, we'll achieve different results.

A TRAILBLAZING APPROACH

New and improved! Strategies for success! A new approach for the new millennium! Try it, you'll like it!

The trailblazing methods in this chapter will enable you to: identify which age-appropriate regular education classes your child should be in for the coming year; assist in the design and execution of non-standard assessments; write an IEP Blueprint for your child's placement in a regular ed class; share this report with members of the IEP team during pre-IEP meetings to hammer out details; host a dynamic and productive IEP meeting; and monitor your child's education and maintain effective relationships via monthly informal team meetings.

The first step in initiating this new approach is being careful with the words we use. In planning for your child's education, don't talk to educators about inclusion unless your child is already attending a truly inclusive school! Don't even say the word "inclusion." It's a flash point that provokes negative attitudes in the minds of many educators. Reactions may include: "it's too expensive," "it's not done at this school," "our staff is not ready," "your child is not ready," and on and on. Instead of *talking* about inclusion and hoping educators will come around to our point of view, we will *act*, using creative methods to ensure our children are educated and supported in regular ed classes.

It Works

I've shared many of these strategies with parents at education workshops. Many were open-minded and ready for a change. Others were doubtful the methods would work for them: "Yes, these ideas might work for some kids, but—"

After taking a great leap of faith and trying this new approach, even the "Yes, but—" parents have achieved success. Through letters and personal conversations, moms and dads have gleefully and enthusiastically shared their accomplishments. They have repaired bad relationships with educators; their children are included and supported in regular classrooms; and the IEP process is no longer a battleground, but a journey of discovery, cooperation, and true partnerships. Your investment in this new process will yield great rewards: your child's success.

While IEP is an acronym for Individualized Education Program, we could also use the letters to represent Innovative and Effective Partnerships. Your relationship with educators is critical in ensuring your child receives a good education. And the most important part of your role is your attitude. In fact, your child's education will be more profoundly influenced by your attitude (and the actions that follow) than anything else!

Never, never, never underestimate your power to influence the IEP process. But know that true, long-lasting power doesn't come from "winning." It comes from creating win-win situations in which you generously and wisely help others feel successful.

The recommendations in this chapter are based on the presumption you have good relationships with educators or that you're working to improve them. I'm assuming that, if educators have typically seen you in a negative light, you're taking steps to redefine yourself as a great volunteer, PTA president, delicious cookie-baker, school supporter, active committee member, or any other role that demonstrates one or more of your positive, personal attributes (as described in Chapter 12).

Before detailing innovative approaches to achieve inclusive education, I want to address two particular areas: therapy in school and the role of paraprofessionals. Both of these were addressed in previous chapters, but I include them here again, briefly, as they relate to children being included in regular ed classrooms.

THERAPY IN SCHOOL

The value of pull-out physical, occupational, speech-language, and other therapies during the school day is questionable (see Chapters 7 and 9). A more important consideration, however, is that children are far more likely to be placed in regular ed classrooms if they do *not* receive direct therapeutic services in school.

In some schools, a request for therapy automatically triggers placement in the special ed resource room because "that's where the services are." In situations where a regular ed placement is a possibility, regular ed teachers and/or therapists may not see how therapies or other related services can be provided in a classroom setting. When this happens, the child may be placed in a regular ed classroom, but is routinely pulled out of class and sent to the resource room for therapy. There are alternatives to these dilemmas.

Therapists as Consulltants

The first alternative is to use school therapists as consultants. Instead of providing direct, hands-on therapy, the therapist can meet with you, your child, and your child's teachers on a regular basis (monthly, for example) to provide guidance on methods to assist your child in the classroom, using more natural methods that are meaningful and relevant to your child and his education.

When therapists are consultants in regular ed settings, they—along with educators—can see the child as a student and as a whole child instead of a collection of body parts. If they've only been providing hands-on services in isolated settings, therapists may not be aware of what real assistance a child needs to be successful in school. By spending time in regular ed classrooms, therapists become more creative as they devise natural and informal methods of helping children be more independent, achieve new skills, and so forth. This experience makes them better therapists!

There are many ways to use the expertise of therapists as consultants. An OT can observe your child during handwriting time, in the computer lab, at lunch, or in any other setting where he's using his hands, arms, mouth, or whichever body part needs attention. A PT could observe a child as he moves around the school, transfers in and out of a mobility device, during PE class, and in other settings. A speech therapist can observe the child in the regular ed classroom, during reading group or other participatory activities. Then the therapist meets with you, your child, and your child's teachers to report her findings and everyone works together to devise natural strategies for assistance.

When therapists and educators collaborate, the needs of students with disabilities can be met in regular ed settings, in ways that are relevant and meaningful to the students. In addition, students can receive natural support from their friends and classmates. During reading, for example, a classmate can help a child learn to pronounce words. At lunch, another student can help a child with a disability learn to open his milk and use utensils. There's no end to peer support. And these natural supports spawn real friendships!

In second grade PE class, two of Benjamin's classmates who happened to be girls took it upon themselves to help him transfer from his wheelchair to his walker and back. If the teacher's aide or the PE teacher tried to step in and help, the girls would shoo them away. It was fascinating to watch the interchange. When an adult helped Benj transfer, he was often a big lump; he didn't help much and the adult had to do most of the work. But when Carrie and Jessica stepped in, Benj came alive. He liked their help more than an adult's. They were like little drill sergeants and didn't take any bunk from Benj. They regularly exhorted, "Come on, Benj! Hold on right here. Tight! Don't let go. Now let's turn you around! Come on, you can do it!" This type of help from classmates was far more valuable than hands-on therapy in a pull-out setting.

Therapy, But No Pull-Out

If you feel your child must have direct, hands-on therapy, at least make sure he is not pulled out. You can help a therapist design therapeutic assistance that is meaningful to your child and provided in settings that are relevant to the therapy.

For example, a PT shouldn't try to stretch your child's hamstrings during math class! Instead, her time could be spent working with your child during recess or PE. Even then, however, she shouldn't pull your child aside and stretch his hamstrings while the other kids are doing something else. The therapist, you, your child, and the PE teacher can figure out ways of meeting your child's needs while he's participating in regular activities.

In the third grade gym class, the PE teacher and the PT worked together to modify activities so Benjamin could participate and exercise. A favorite activity of the class was swinging from a long rope attached to the ceiling of the gym. One at a time, each child stood on a platform, grabbed the rope, and leaped off the platform to swing in big arcs. At a cue from the PE teacher, the child would let go of the rope and land safely on the mats covering the gym floor.

Benj did not have the physical ability to do this the way the other kids did. So the PT brought a mountain climbing harness for Benj to use. She strapped him in and hooked the harness up to ropes rigged to the ceiling. Then she or the PE teacher hoisted Benj up in the air until he could grab the swing rope. Once he had a good grip, they tugged on the harness rope to get him swinging and he flew through the air like the other Peter Pans. When it was time, he let go of the rope and the teacher rapidly lowered him to the mat to simulate the drop other kids experienced. Like his classmates, Benj was expected to learn how to land safely on the mats.

Some parents may be happily shocked that a therapist and a teacher would go this far to enable a child to experience the same activities as other children. But their actions simply reflected the beliefs inherent in inclusive schools: students with disabilities are expected to participate in typical activities and be successful.

As an itinerant therapist, the PT traveled to many different schools in our area which did not practice inclusion. We asked her to do things very differently—and more creatively—than what she routinely did at other schools (pull-out therapy). At first, this caused a great deal of tension. But as she became more accustomed to inclusive practices, and as we encouraged her to be creative, she got into the swing of things (no pun intended). I think she probably had more fun at Benj's school than she did at others.

PTs can work with students in PE class, during sports activities, or at recess. OTs can spend time in the classroom during handwriting time, in computer lab, or in other activities and settings relative to a child's needs. Speech and language therapists can be in the classroom during reading or at other times when language is the focus of the classroom. And in all cases, the therapist's efforts must promote participation in the general curriculum.

When therapists provide direct services in inclusive classroom settings, they not only help the child with the disability, they're also helping regular ed teachers and other students learn how to assist children with disabilities. In addition, if therapists are open to learning from others, classroom teachers and students can help therapists understand what's really important in any given classroom setting.

No Therapy, Period

Another alternative is to forego help from therapists in school completely. You know what works best for your child and you know what he needs. When you have effective partnerships with your child's educators, you can work with them to provide naturally occurring assistance.

For example, you can show teachers how to help your child with "OT skills," such as learning how to write with a pencil, using the keyboard, and so forth. (Don't think this is "asking too much" of educators. They routinely do these things for students in their classes who don't have disabilities!) If your child has an orthopedic disability, you can work with the PE teacher on ways to modify gym and other activities to suit your child. Remember, you're the expert.

At this moment, you may not feel any of these alternatives are appropriate. But by the end of this chapter, you may feel differently.

INSTRUCTIONAL ASSISTANTS AND INCLUSIVE PRACTICES

In Chapter 7, I detailed a variety of problems that arise when aides are assigned to children, and when the roles of teacher's aides or paraprofessionals don't support inclusion. Further, I described how students do not need aides, but teachers and classrooms may.

These dilemmas can be resolved with another paradigm shift: instead of seeing a support person as an aide, we need to see her as an instructional assistant (IA). But the paradigm shift will not occur by simply using a new name. It will happen only when the person's role changes from supporting one child to supporting an inclusive environment.

The concept of providing an aide to a student with a disability is grounded in at least two presumptions. First, that the student is so incompetent or needy that he must have an adult close by the majority of the time. The second presumption is that as long as another person takes charge of him, a child with a disability will not disturb or inconvenience the classroom (or the teacher). In other words, nothing in the classroom needs to change, and the classroom teacher will not need to take time away from "her students" since the student with a disability has his own "teacher." This is not inclusion!

For a classroom to become inclusive, a variety of changes must take place to ensure a child is really part of the class, and to ensure the child *and* the teacher receive the appropriate supports. Simply plopping a child with a disability into a classroom, with or without an additional adult, does not make an inclusive classroom!

To create an inclusive classroom, parents and educators must consider a wide variety of issues, including: physical characteristics of the classroom, teaching and learning styles, learning activities, leadership of the teacher and classroom dynamics, curriculum modifications, and more. In any particular classroom we can boil all this down to one question using my son's description of inclusion: *what will it take to ensure this child is a "regular kid"?*

Regular kids don't have aides, they get the help they need from their teachers, peers, and other adults in the room. Regular kids are expected to succeed and they're seen as competent learners. Regular kids are not exempt from participating and contributing. And regular kids are simultaneously individual students and part of the whole classroom.

Many components must come together to ensure children with disabilities are regular kids, and an instructional assistant may make the difference between the illusion and the reality of inclusion. This doesn't mean we lay the responsibility for inclusion in the lap of

IAs. It does mean educators and parents must work together to discover how an IA—under the direction of the classroom teacher—can support teachers, students, and inclusive practices in the classroom.

Excise from your brain any thoughts that your child must have an aide in a regular ed classroom. But what, you may be wondering, about a child who need intensive or personal help, such as assistance in the bathroom, with eating, or with behavior issues? Doesn't this child need an aide? No, he doesn't. Whatever assistance he needs can be provided by a variety of people in a variety of ways.

In many schools, a support person/aide has been seen as the only person who should be responsible for helping a child with a disability, whether that help was academic or personal (bathroom needs, eating, and others). Educators and parents have often been reluctant to ask anyone other than an aide to help. But this reflects an old—and narrow—way of thinking. It indicates a belief that the school, as a whole, isn't responsible for students with disabilities, the way it is for the rest of the student body. It also represents a belief that providing accommodation for students with disabilities is somehow beyond the responsibility of all personnel in a school building: it's to be done only by designated individuals.

If we widen our thinking, however, we'll realize that schools make accommodations for typical students and teachers all the time. It's just that no one sees these accommodations as unusual or extraordinary. For example, schools provide restrooms and cafeterias for students. In many schools, restrooms for children in primary grades feature toilets and sinks that are lower to the ground. Why? To accommodate the needs of smaller children.

In most schools, the faculty has its own set of restrooms, separate from the student restrooms. This is an accommodation for staff, as is the teachers' lounge. Why do faculty members have their own restrooms and dining area; why can't they just eat with the students and use the same restrooms as students? Because it doesn't meet their needs!

Now let's look at how adults—educators, staff members and volunteers—take responsibility for typical students whether the responsibility has been specifically assigned to them or not. A custodian repairing a swing warns two boys about fighting; a volunteer in the library shelving books helps a child who is upset; the school secretary quiets a group of noisy students as she passes them in the hallway.

Recognizing that accommodations made for students and teachers are ordinary responses to meet people's needs, it's time to view accommodations for students with disabilities in the same light. Meeting their needs should not be considered burdensome or extraordinary. Accommodations for students with disabilities might be new and different, but so—at one time—were indoor toilets in schools!

Realizing that all adults in a school can and do take responsibility for typical students, it's time to realize they can and should take responsibility for students with disabilities. To that end, the needs of students with disabilities in the regular ed environment can and should be met by a variety of people: classroom teachers, instructional assistants, special ed teachers, volunteers, other school personnel, and classmates.

A variety of people assisted Benjamin in elementary school. Several—not just one—instructional assistants helped him go to the bathroom, as did the principal, and a couple of teachers who were not his own! Classmates helped him in class, at recess, and during lunch; the librarian helped him in the library; and so forth. All of this occurred because, under the principal's leadership, children with disabilities were seen as members of the student body, not as "special ed students."

As I'll describe later in this chapter, it's up to parents to become familiar with the school environment so they can determine what it will take for their children to be supported and included. We must reject the automatic assumption that placing a child with an aide in a regular classroom guarantees inclusion. Instead, we need to look at how an instructional assistant, the classroom teacher, and others can collaborate to ensure inclusion.

The practice of *routinely* assigning a support person to a child or a teacher is slowly changing. Instead of starting from the presumption that the student or teacher will be unsuccessful without the intervention of an adult helper, many parents and educators presume competence and success. The school year begins with no support person, and the dynamics of the classroom are given time to gel. If, after a couple of weeks or a month, the teacher, the child, the parents, and/or others on the IEP team decide extra help and support are necessary, they don't automatically install a full-time IA. Instead, they add support components a little at time until the right amounts and combinations are in place.

Think of it as creating a new recipe: you add a little of this and a little of that, take a taste and see if it's what you want. You keep adding a little more of this and that until you get it just the way you want. It's much better to start with less and add more, than to start out with the most and try to take some back.

Parents must be ever vigilant that issues surrounding accommodations and supports don't become barriers to their children's inclusion. With curriculum modifications; assistive technology; help from peers; assistance from the classroom teacher, special educator, and/or instructional assistant; and other supports, children with disabilities can be educated in regular ed classrooms without being constantly shadowed or attached at the hip to an adult.

RELATIONSHIPS AND ALLIES

Many of the problems parents experience during the IEP process are rooted in their relationships with educators and in the dynamics of the IEP team. In Chapter 7, I detailed issues that muddy the waters and prevent members of the IEP team from working cooperatively and successfully. What drives many IEP meetings is not the education of the child, but the politics that envelop the team.

IDEA is a good law, but it is implemented by educators who are, first and foremost, human beings with human frailties, feelings, and egos. We often focus all our efforts on the law and school policies, while ignoring the human component in the IEP process. To many educators, the law is an inanimate object; a collection of words that are either misunderstood or irrelevant to them, personally and professionally. But we and our children are real. When educators think of the IEP process, they don't think of the inanimate object—the law—they think of us. What do educators see? Allies or adversaries? What kind of relationships do we want with educators who wield great influence over our children?

We have the responsibility to do whatever it takes to ensure our children have the best education possible. Doing whatever it takes does not mean filing lawsuits, issuing threats, or enlisting an army of advocates to help us fight our battles. When we send our children off to school every day, strict adherence to the law cannot ensure our children's success. The only thing that can is the kind attention of educators who care about our kids. To that end, educators must also care about us and we must care about them.

When we enlarge our frame of reference from legalities to relationships, the world will change before our eyes. But long before the IEP meeting takes place, we must cut a new path; blazing a new trail takes time and effort.

People or Problems?

Separate the people involved in the IEP process from the problems. Make a promise to yourself to deal proactively with *problems* instead of attacking *people*. Don't shoot the messenger when you don't like the message. Keep your focus on developing and maintaining good relationships. Simultaneously, never, never, never complain about a problem unless you have a solution. Anticipate problems and create an inventory of possible solutions.

Be a Leader

Lead by example, by demonstrating patience, good manners, and respect. Remember what your mama taught you about not sinking to other people's level. Do good, even if others don't. Never seek revenge or retribution. *Be the type of person you want others to be.* Your child learns by watching your actions; what kind of adult do you want him to become?

Seek to Understand

Learn as much as you can about people who may be involved in your child's education—from the actual IEP team members to others who might impact the special ed process. What are their experiences with children and adults with disabilities in general? What is the school's history in special education? What are the barriers to inclusion? How do regular educators feel about children with disabilities in their classrooms? How do special educators feel about supporting students and teachers in regular ed classrooms?

How is the school district set up? Are special ed teachers under the building principal or under the district's special ed department? Are they a part of the school community, or are they off in their own part of the building? Are special educators "included" in their own school? If not, students receiving special ed services won't be either.

What's the overall atmosphere at the school? Is parent involvement in the school welcome? Is there active collaboration between educators and parents? What's the school culture and environment really like?

Don't guess about all this! Don't assume you *know* because of something you heard. Don't buy in to any prevailing negative attitudes or gossip from other parents of kids with disabilities. Find out for yourself and learn the truth! Being active in your child's school will enable you to gain a meaningful understanding of the people you're dealing with.

Recognize Fears

Fear of failure and fear of the unknown prevent many educators from embracing regular ed placements for kids with disabilities. There are as many different fears as there are educators in your child's school. A classroom teacher may be fearful of stepping on the toes of the special education department. A special ed teacher may fear the loss of her life's work if she no longer has "her room" filled with "her kids." A principal may be afraid to include your child if he believes it will lead to a flood of other parents wanting the same for their children: one is okay, but more than that might overwhelm the school's resources. Don't take these fears as personal rejections or insults, and don't let them interfere with your goal.

Recognize and understand people's fears. They're not uncommon. What did *you* know or feel about children and adults with disabilities before your child was diagnosed? Don't ignore people's fears; acknowledge them. Let people know you understand. Tell them you didn't have a Ph.D. in disability before your child was born; you've learned by doing.

Become an Insider

The IEP process in most schools often relegates parents to the sidelines. Educators on the IEP team are colleagues and co-workers on the inside. Parents—who are supposed to be equal members of the team—are the outsiders. See yourself as an insider—as a colleague—by getting to know and working closely with the members of the IEP team and others in the school.

Move beyond professional, formal relationships where everyone holds tight to their roles and positions. Move to personal, positive relationships that are flexible, equitable, reciprocal, supportive, and forgiving.

Develop Allies

Surround yourself with people who support you, your child, and inclusion. The very best allies in your quest for inclusion are educators. Just one classroom teacher, one principal, or one special educator can make all the difference in the world.

The next best allies are other parents who are respected and valued by the school. Seek out and develop relationships with parents who have positive influence within the school system. If you can't be the PTA president or a valuable committee member yourself, align yourself with parent leaders who are well-connected with educators.

Identify children who might be your child's classmates in a regular education classroom and cultivate their parents as friends and allies. Teach these new friends about yourself, your family, your child, and the desire for your child to be educated and supported in a regular ed class. Parents of typical children often don't have a clue about the exclusion and isolation of children with disabilities in public schools. Nor are they always aware of the benefits of inclusion. They will rally to support you when they learn about the unfairness of segregated special education.

At Benjamin's inclusive elementary school, parents I knew casually were often curious about my out-of-town travels. When I explained I did workshops on inclusive education, they didn't understand at first. They thought *all* schools were inclusive like ours, and they were shocked and dismayed when I described how children with disabilities were isolated and segregated in special ed classrooms at many schools across the country.

Share your dreams of inclusion with family members, friends, and others. But don't bad mouth educators or tell tales. In the short run, it might make you feel better to share all the pain or difficulties you've had in the past. In the long run, however, the sympathy of your supporters may do more harm than good: you don't want allies to become accomplices in ganging up on educators. This will only inflame the situation. You want allies to provide moral support and common sense, not ammunition for more fighting.

PREPARE FOR SUCCESS

While IDEA is a great law, the process of planning and writing an IEP hasn't always worked the way it should. The process is based on the notion that a group of good people can come together and—within the hour or two that's allocated for the IEP meeting—take a huge amount of information about a student, digest it, make wise decisions, agree or compromise on most issues, and write appropriate goals and objectives. Furthermore, the process is based on the assumption that decisions will be made *during* the meeting, by the IEP team *as a group,* after discussion of all relevant information. Parents are often shocked and angry when they discover many decisions, including placement, have been made *before* the meeting without their input.

From the perspective of educators, it's logical to come to an IEP meeting with some issues already decided or at least considered. Pretend you're the principal. Would you walk into an IEP meeting with a completely open mind? Would you be willing to "upset the applecart" of how things are done at your school simply to accommodate one student or one set of parents? Would you have your school checkbook out, ready to purchase whatever a parent requested? Or would you come to the meeting with some firm ideas in your head?

Educators know, as do many parents, that it's virtually impossible to get everything done in the time allotted for most IEP meetings. When educators make decisions prior to the IEP meeting, they do so to save time, protect the status quo, avoid surprises, and for a variety of other reasons. We can impact this practice.

According to IDEA, placement is supposed to be based on the child's IEP; thus, placement could not be decided *until* the IEP is written at the IEP meeting. But educators frequently decide placement before the IEP meeting, based solely (or primarily) on the child's disability label, not the child's needs. Typically, a child is placed into an existing "program" the school has already set up for children with the same or similar disabilities. Both of these actions are absolutely contrary to the law. Instead of hoping for—or trying to force—placement in a regular ed classroom, parents need to take a page from the law and *presume* their child will be educated in an age-appropriate regular education classroom in the school the child would attend if she didn't have a disability. You'll learn how to turn this presumption into a reality in this chapter. Do not, however, shout your intention from the rooftop at this particular time. Keep it to yourself until you've finished this chapter! And if you've been brainwashed into believing your child cannot do well in a regular classroom, keep reading. I think you'll change your mind.

Reconnaissance

Most of us go into an IEP meeting with some degree of preparation, but the meeting still doesn't go the way we hoped. What we don't realize is that, no matter how well-prepared we are, educators are always more prepared for one simple reason: they're familiar with what happens in regular ed classrooms and we're not!

When preparing for IEP meetings, we visualize what we want our children's education to look like. But the image doesn't always become a reality, because it was created using incomplete or inaccurate information about classroom environments.

Educators are the resident experts, we are the visitors; they live and breathe at the school, we exist on the periphery. Many of us don't know what a typical classroom day looks like, don't know about the resources of the school, and don't understand the culture or dynamics of the school and its staff. But educators do. When we become more familiar with classroom environments, we can write effective IEPs that reflect placement in regular educational settings.

Suzanne wants her daughter, Chelsea, in a regular sixth grade class, but educators on the IEP team reply this is not an appropriate placement because Chelsea is not ready: she can't do sixth grade work and so forth. Suzanne may argue her case on principles of the law, but the IEP team argues based on their knowledge of what the sixth grade is really like.

When we propose a regular ed placement during an IEP meeting, educators shake their heads in disbelief wondering how in the world we came up with such a preposterous idea. They know what the classrooms look like and we don't. They cannot visualize a child with a disability fitting in a regular ed class or see how she could learn and be successful, because they know what the teacher is like, they're familiar with the curriculum, and more. Because we don't know these things, how—from an educator's perspective—could we possibly propose a regular ed placement? We can change this problematic situation, and the first step is understanding what the law says about IEPs. According to IDEA,

> The term "individualized education program" or "IEP" means a written statement for each child with a disability that is developed, reviewed, and revised in accordance with this section and that includes—
> (i) a statement of the child's present levels of educational performance, including
> —(I) how the child's disability affects the *child's involvement and progress in the general curriculum;* or
> —(II) for preschool children, as appropriate, how the disability affects the child's participation in appropriate activities;
> (ii) a statement of measurable annual goals, including benchmarks or short-term objectives related to --
> —(I) meeting the child's needs that result from the child's disability to *enable the child to be involved in and progress in the general curriculum;* and
> —(II) meeting each of the child's other educational needs that result from the child's disability;
> (iii) a statement of the special education and related services and supplementary aids and services to be provided to the child, or on behalf of the child, and a statement of the program modifications or supports for school personnel that will be provided for the child --
> —(I) to advance appropriately toward attaining the annual goals;
> —(II) *to be involved and progress in the general curriculum* in accordance with clause (i) and to participate in extra-curricular and other nonacademic activities;
> —(III) to be educated and participate with other children with disabilities and nondisabled children in the activities described in this paragraph;
> (iv) an explanation of the extent, if any, to which the child will *not* participate with nondisabled children in the regular class and in the activities described in clause (iii). . . (Section 300.347 Content of IEP) (italics added)

How can *we* know how the child's disability "affects the child's involvement and progress in the general curriculum," and how can *we* effectively participate in writing goals that "enable the child to be involved in and progress in the general curriculum," if *we* don't have personal knowledge of a regular ed class and its curriculum?

It's time to become a great detective. Several weeks before your child's IEP meeting, visit the regular ed classes you want him in during the next school year. Your visits should be to the grade level that's age-appropriate for your child, *regardless of her current grade.* Six-year-olds are in first grade; eight-year-olds are in third grade; ten-year-olds are in fifth grade; twelve-year-olds are in seventh grade; fourteen-year-olds are in ninth grade; six-teen-year-olds are in eleventh grade, and so on. Certainly, take into account when your child's birthday falls when figuring out which grade your child should be in.

Do not choose a grade level based on a subjective and arbitrary measurement of your child's "functional level." And if your child has been held back, he should be bumped up to his age-appropriate grade level. This means he might actually skip a grade (or two). That's okay. Don't worry if he's not "performing at grade level." Curriculum modifications and adaptations—as mandated in IDEA—will take care of this issue.

Does this sound unrealistic to you? Then remember that your child will live up or down to your expectations, as well as the expectations of her teachers. If a nine-year-old is in second grade, she will be treated like a seven-year-old. How can we expect her to "be" a nine-year old? More importantly, how will she feel about herself if her parents believe she belongs in a second grade class? Remember the dangers of thinking about our children in terms of developmental age instead of chronological age.

Not only do you need to be familiar with the classroom environment, you also need to have some firm ideas about which teacher(s) will be best for your child. If, for example, you want your child in a third grade class, you need to spend time in each third grade class, observing the overall atmosphere in the room and the relationship between the teacher and the students. In secondary grades, however, you may not have a choice of teachers: there may be only one eighth grade math teacher, for example. If so, a personal visit is still neces-sary for you to learn about the curriculum and the atmosphere of the class. Visit all the environments in which your child may participate as a "regular" student: art, PE, and music classrooms; computer center; library; cafeteria; playground; gym; and any other places your child, as a member of a regular class, might be.

Spend as much time as you can in these classes. Bring a video camera and record what you see (ask for permission first). Take good notes, writing everything in a way that will make sense to you later. If you don't, the different classes and teachers may all run together in your memory and your visits will be for naught.

During your visits, please don't think, "Oh, my Johnny could *never* make it in this class." Instead, figure out *how* Johnny could succeed. When the class is doing science, for instance, how could Johnny be participating and learning in ways that are appropriate for him? Look at the books and materials used by the class. Do they need to be modified and if so, in what way? How might the environment be modified or what accommodations could be made to the class to ensure Johnny's participation? If Johnny uses a wheelchair, would he need a certain type of desk to accommodate his chair? If Susie has ADD, would a seat in the front of the room help her stay focused on the teacher? Visualize how your child's needs could be met in ways that promote his participation, belonging, and dignity.

How does the teacher teach? Does she lecture most of the time? Does she use an overhead projector and the blackboard? Is it a static environment where students are ex-pected to sit still and listen most of the time, or are they actively learning through hands-on activities? Do all students work alone or are they part of small group activities? If small groups are used, are students grouped by ability level (not good) or are they mixed-ability groups (good)?

What about the curriculum in the classroom? Do the students use standard textbooks and worksheets? Has the teacher created an activity-based curriculum? Are all students working from the same material or is there a selection to choose from?

What are the dynamics of the classroom? Is it friendly and warm or cool and indifferent? Is the teacher exciting, calm, patient, caring, harsh, strict, or easy-going? Is she able to help students learn or is most of her time spent maintaining order? Are the students bored, excited, glum, or happy? Do you see conflict or cooperation?

Note the overall atmosphere, both the positives and the negatives. There are no perfect classrooms. Don't judge classrooms in comparison to your own experiences in public school, whether those experiences were good or bad.

In my children's elementary school, some classrooms appeared wild at first glance. But the longer I was there, I realized what *looked like* chaos was actually organized, hands-on, exciting learning activities. Other classes, in comparison, seemed dull and boring. But they, too, were actually the sites of quiet creativity. And, often, these two extremes were seen within the same classroom. Spend as much time as possible in each class so you can observe all the variables.

Strategies to Initiate Reconnaissance

There are a variety of ways to initiate these visits. The best method depends on your individual situation and your relationship with school personnel. You may need to plan your reconnaissance a month or two before the IEP meeting.

If you're already volunteering in school, if you have a great relationship with one or more folks at the school, if inclusion is almost a sure thing, and/or if parents are always welcome in classrooms, simply ask the appropriate person—principal, teachers, office staff—for permission to observe. (School secretaries are more powerful than you know. Cultivate positive relationships with them and your efforts will pay off.)

Use your connections with teachers you already know. If, for example, you have a good relationship with one of your other children's current or former teachers, ask for their help in connecting you to the teachers whose classrooms you need to observe.

Try to volunteer in the classrooms you're investigating. Offer to give awareness presentations (Chapter 20) as a way to meet various teachers. Help with a party or special project. Volunteer in the school office or in some other position that allows you to visit many classrooms. Your volunteer efforts may provide enough time to observe, or you may need to set up a particular time to sit in the back of the room and be a fly on the wall. As you get to know faculty members, it will be easy to casually ask about observing classes.

If the school discourages parent involvement, your task will be more difficult. It's hard to believe that, in this day and age when schools need all the public support they can garner, some schools are not parent-friendly. Often, the principal doesn't want "outsiders" in the school building. In some schools, several teachers may encourage parental involvement, while others do not. However, if you have a good relationship with the principal or the teachers of your other children, you may not be considered an "outsider."

If you can't get permission to visit the classrooms for the express purpose of observing, find some other way to get in by giving whatever explanation will do the trick. Once you're in, find a way to spend as much time there as possible. The year I wrote the PTO newsletter, I went from class to class delivering the newsletters each month. It would have been easy to ask a teacher if I could stay a few minutes to watch what the kids were doing because, "It looks so interesting!" If you're on shaky ground with people in the school, and if they want to know why you want to observe, give whatever reason will get you in the door without arousing too much suspicion.

Be creative and determined! One way or another, find a way to personally observe potential classrooms. This is the foundation of your efforts to achieve a regular ed placement for your child. If you go into an IEP meeting without personal knowledge of the classroom settings, educators can easily refute your claims that your child can succeed in a regular ed class.

If a personal visit is absolutely impossible, you need to at least learn about the curriculum. Find parents whose children are in the grade level you're researching and ask to look at the child's books and materials. Talk to the parent about her child's experiences.

Analysis

After you've done your reconnaissance of potential classrooms, it's time to analyze your data. If you have a choice of teachers, compare them. Which one taught in a style that your child would be most comfortable with? Who was friendliest to you? Which one had the closest relationship with the students? Which classroom offered the best opportunity for your child to succeed? Consider other issues that are relevant to your child.

For all the classes you visited, think about how your child could participate and progress in the regular curriculum. What adaptations, modifications, and supports might be necessary in the different settings (academic classrooms, art, music, the library, and others). Later in this chapter, we'll go over related services, which will help you figure this out.

Selecting/Confirming the Teacher

In inclusive schools, educators and parents usually match up students with disabilities with the most appropriate regular ed teachers. But if a regular ed placement is not a sure thing, you'll need to consider a variety of different approaches.

If you know the teacher (she taught one of your other children, you've volunteered in her classroom, met her through PTA, and so forth) and think she might be open-minded about your child being in her classroom, stop by her room at the end of a school day or some other appropriate time, and tell her you think she would be a great teacher for your child next year. If she's nervous or hesitant, ask, "How could I help you feel more comfortable with this?" Think about this ahead of time so you can immediately provide suggestions about how she and your child can be successful.

If she's agreeable, your next step depends on the climate at the school. You may need to ask her to keep this quiet until you've talked to the IEP team. On the other hand, it might be better for *her* to tell the principal she wants your child in her class; this might make it a done deal! If, however, she's flustered and doesn't know how to respond to your request (because she's scared, doesn't want to overstep her bounds, and so forth) reassure her that you'll be working with the principal and others to make this new endeavor a success for her.

In some situations, it may be prudent to *not* approach the teacher directly. If *any* of the fourth grade classrooms would be appropriate or, conversely, if you don't believe *any* teacher is initially willing to include your child, it might be better to use a different approach. Use positive methods during pre-IEP meetings to influence the principal or special educator regarding a regular ed placement, while simultaneously seeking their opinions about the most appropriate classroom.

In upper grades, where you may not have a choice of teachers, approaching educators may still be a valuable action. But depending on the circumstances, you may not want to tip your hand ahead of time.

Again, there are many variables to consider. Use all your resources to figure out the best way to go: your own knowledge, the experiences other parents have had with particular educators and the school overall, and your gut instincts and common sense.

ASSESSMENTS

The next step is assessments. But in this new way of doing things, assessments and evaluations will be done very differently. Instead of your child being assessed globally, he'll be assessed relative to his needs in the regular educational environment, as the law intends. Special education law (IDEA, Section 300.532 Evaluation Procedures) states:

> A variety of assessment tools and strategies are used to gather relevant functional and developmental information about the child, including information provided by the parent, and information related to *enabling the child to be involved in and progress in the general curriculum* . . .

Parents are first introduced to assessments and evaluations during the eligibility process. By law, students must be assessed (1) prior to initially receiving special education services, (2) before any change of placement, and (3) every three years. The three-year assessments may be waived if the IEP team agrees they're not necessary. However, if the parents request new assessments, the school must provide them. While parents may be familiar with assessments and evaluations, they often don't understand the critical role assessments play in a child's IEP. This is a grave error on our part.

The Problems with Traditional Assessments

Professionals often claim expert knowledge about our children based on assessment and evaluation data. Some educators may use this data to justify or deny services, accommodations, placement, and more. But what if these assessments are wrong? Disagreements between parents and educators are often rooted in inaccurate or incomplete evaluation or assessment data. Consider the following:

- The purpose of assessments is "to gather relevant functional and developmental information about the child." The purpose is not to identify "deficiencies," as a way to justify a restrictive placement.

- IDEA does not prescribe which tests educators should use. There are hundreds of standardized tests, and most parents have little, if any, knowledge about which tests will be used on their children. Was the test given to your child appropriate when considering his disability? Most testers will not deviate from the test rules because any change "invalidates" the results. What happens when a child who has difficulty using a pencil is given a test that involves drawing or writing? What happens when a child who doesn't have typical speech is given a test that's heavy on language skills? Before the assessment, does the tester search for the right test or does he simply grab the most commonly used test from his current inventory?

- We don't know the qualifications of the tester. We don't know what the assessment is intended to measure and what it cannot measure. We don't know if the test results are accurate measurements, or if different results would be obtained if the child was tested in another location, at another time, by another person.

- Diagnosticians, psychologists, and educators often assume there are hidden disabilities in addition to the "primary" disability and they test for these. On the surface, it seems parents should be appreciative of the efforts to identify all of a child's needs. More labels might mean more services. But typically, more services means placement in more restrictive settings.

Assessments are often misused. Educators don't always use them to learn about the child; they use them to prove *what they already believe to be true!* Educators may gloss over or minimize positive assessment results because they believe they already "know" about the child, based on preconceived ideas about the disability or characteristics of the child.

When we allow our children to be formally tested, we're opening the door to an unknown world—a world where our children's humanity is often battered and bruised. Traditional assessments usually produce bad news, not good. "Deficiencies" are identified, qualified, and quantified. Once the test results are analyzed and interpreted, educators believe they "know" what to do with or for a child. But the data often has little or no relevance to the real child and his environment.

For example, a multi-disciplinary team of experts finds that nine-year-old Robby has an IQ of 75, the social skills of a five-year-old, low muscle tone in his upper extremities, visual-perceptual difficulties, and delayed speech. Wow! Robby is eligible for all types of special education services. But these "deficiencies" have just earned Robby a first class one-way ticket to the special ed room.

If Robby's parents want him included in a fourth grade classroom, the assessments "prove" this is not an appropriate placement for Robby. Even though several professionals have evaluated Robby, no one has seen him as a whole child—a nine-year-old boy who is a potential member of the fourth grade class. They have tested him against abstract norms, in isolation from his natural environment, and he has "failed." But what if he was evaluated as a whole child, and more specifically, what if he was assessed relative to his needs *in a fourth grade class?* We'll find out a little later.

Think about this: if children *without* disabilities were subjected to a regimen of special ed assessments and evaluations, my guess would be that between 50 and 75 percent would end up being labeled with "deficits" or disability labels.

Inappropriate Tests; Inappropriate Testers

When Benjamin was younger (and before I knew any better), he was given a battery of tests. These experiences demonstrate the inherent flaws of using standardized tests for children with disabilities, as well as the incompetence of many professional testers.

At two, Benjamin was given a standard "intelligence" test. The tester asked me to wait outside the cubicle, but I politely declined. She said I could stay only if I was silent and didn't interfere. During one part of the test, she gave Benjamin two blocks and asked him to stack one on top of the other. He did. She added two more and he stacked four. She added two more and asked him to stack all six. He gingerly got the sixth and last block on top of the wobbly stack, but as he was letting go of it, the whole stack fell.

She asked him to do it again, and he did, but the same thing happened. I knew Benjamin did not have the dexterity to gently release the top block without making them all fall. When the stack fell over the second time, the tester sighed and shook her head in disapproval as she marked his score.

I "interfered" by asking, "Are you testing his ability to understand your verbal instructions [intelligence and/or receptive language] or are you testing his fine motor skills? He's proven he understands because he's trying to do what you asked. The fact that he doesn't have the fine motor skills to get the last one to stay up there isn't a reflection of his understanding!" She tersely said, "We need to continue with the test."

In another part of the test, she asked Benjamin to draw a straight line and a circle. At home, because he had difficulty getting a good grip on a crayon and holding the paper in place, we always gave him extra large crayons, taped the paper to an easel, and provided some physical support to his arm or shoulder when he wanted to draw. When these accommodations were made, he could draw a straight line and the beginnings of a circle. In the test environment, however, these accommodations were not provided, and Benjamin was doomed to "fail" this part of the test.

The tester placed a few crayons and a piece of paper on the table. She asked Benj to draw a straight line. The tester's crayons were the skinny kind, well-used and worn down to nubs no longer than two inches. They were useless to Benj! He tried and tried, but he couldn't get a good grip on the crayon. The tester pushed another one toward him and he tried again, but to no avail. With a big sigh, the tester marked on her score sheet.

I began to protest again but she waved me off, reminding me not to interfere. I held my tongue for the moment. After two or three more questions, the test was over. As we were leaving, I informed the tester I would write a letter to add my comments to the official test results, stating they were inaccurate since the appropriate accommodations weren't made. She replied she did everything right according to the instructions that came with the test.

At age three, when Benj was exiting the early intervention program, the EI case manager came to our home for the last time to assess him. She sat across from Benj at a table and said she'd call me if she needed me. In other words, shoo! I told her I'd be staying. Like the other tester, she said I could stay if I didn't interfere (in my own home, no less!). She took the test materials out of her briefcase and began. Things were going fine; she asked Benj questions, showed him pictures, asked him to do things, and so forth.

I sat back, observing in silence, until she asked, "Benjamin, is your mommy a boy or a girl?" Benj stared at her and said nothing. She repeated her question a second and a third time, and Benj said nothing. She was preparing to give him a zero on that question.

Knowing Benjamin was a very literal child, I whispered, "Ask him if I'm a man or a woman." She whispered back, "I can't. I have to follow the test exactly." "He knows what I am—a woman, not a girl!" I hissed. Reluctantly, she rephrased the question as I suggested and Benjamin said, "She's a woman." (I was afraid he would say, "She's a woman, stupid!")

Shortly after this episode and following the recommendations of school authorities (I still hadn't learned to say no), I took three-year-old Benjamin to be tested at the early childhood education (ECE) program. Their offices were in an old school that had become an administration building. In what had once been a classroom, assessments for intelligence, PT, OT, and speech were given.

During the intelligence evaluation, the tester showed Benjamin a variety of picture cards and asked him to identify them. Several of the cards showed cartoon characters and Benjamin was stumped. I didn't let my children watch cartoons when they were little, so he had no idea what he was looking at. Big zeros for that part of the test. Later, the tester showed him pictures of household items. When shown a picture of an iron and ironing board, Benj was stumped. He had never seen me iron; he had no idea what the funny looking contraption was! Another zero.

At one point, the tester showed him a picture and he answered "garbage truck." This was an incorrect answer and the tester had no idea why Benjamin gave that reply, but I did. Benjamin has an incredible auditory memory. Remembering words, accents, songs, and other sounds is one of his many strengths. At the moment the tester asked Benj to identify the picture, he heard a garbage truck go by (the windows were covered). When he said "garbage truck" he wasn't answering the question, he was telling us about the garbage truck.

I proudly pointed out Benjamin's skill in identifying sounds even when he could not see what was making the sound, but the tester was not impressed. She only knew he gave the wrong answer. His strength was irrelevant. Nothing in the assessment tested auditory skills, so there was no way this strength could be evaluated!

The PT assessment was next and it was satisfactory. Next came the OT assessment. As the OT took the place of the PT, Benj was lying on a mat on the floor. The OT asked me to sit him up so he could manipulate blocks and other tools of her test. I asked her where she wanted him to sit. "Just sit him up on the mat," she answered. "Well, he won't do very well like that," I responded. "He'll lose his balance when he tries to use his hands and he'll tip over. He needs to be supported properly in a little chair with a table in front of him." She looked around, perplexed, and said, "We don't have anything like that here." How did she think she could accurately assess Benjamin when he wasn't positioned properly?

I put Benj in his orthopedic stroller and attached the tray, giving him the support he needed. "Wow!" the OT exclaimed, "I'm glad you had that!" I wondered what happened to other children who were not positioned properly. How accurate were their assessments?

After these experiences, I said no to standardized assessments. But when Benj was in the upper grades at his inclusive elementary school, I allowed him to be tested one more time. Karen, the special ed teacher, and I were friends. She asked if she could try out a new assessment on Benj, to see if she liked it. Because she worked closely with Benj in school, she knew what his abilities were. The test results wouldn't go in Benjamin's file.

Overall, Benj did well on the test, but Karen was puzzled about several questions he did not do well on. He could not identify some of the picture cards. When she showed me the cards, it was easy for me to explain why. They were small, detailed line drawings. Benjamin simply couldn't make out what the pictures were. He uses large print books and he's always had difficulty with "abstract images." If the cards had been photographs of real things instead of line drawings, he probably could have identified the images. If a typical professional had given Benj the test, his "intelligence" would have been discounted, based on his inability to identify certain visual images.

We assume test results tell us a great deal about a child. Presumptions, conclusions, and decisions are made based on the outcomes of assessments. Judgments are made by professionals who may have only met the child once (during the assessment), and by other experts who interpret the data, who may have never even *seen* the child! Test results cannot tell us everything we need to know about a child. Nor can they accurately measure a child's abilities or predict a child's potential. Test results only tell us one thing: how well or how poorly a child did on a particular test, given by a particular person at a particular time and place. That's all! Would different results have been obtained if a different test was given, by a different person, at a different time, in a different environment?

Experts often try to construct a composite picture of the whole child by giving a battery of tests covering a variety of areas. But the way to really learn about a child is to (1) be with him, talk to him, listen to him, watch him, see him in his environments, and do things with him, and (2) learn from the "experts:" parents, brothers and sisters, and others who know the child well.

When Congressional leaders framed special ed law in 1975, their purpose in mandating assessments was to ensure that children's unique needs—not their disability labels—were the driving force behind services and placement. But most schools simply do not follow the spirit or the intent of the law. Instead, assessments are used to label, categorize, and determine placement. Overall, standardized tests for children with disabilities probably do more harm than good. But there is an alternative.

Non-Standard Assessments

Instead of subjecting our children to the tyranny of standardized tests, we can use non-standard or informal assessments (the two terms can be used interchangeably). What is a non-standard or informal assessment? It's any method used to learn about a child other than standardized tests, and it's perfectly legal.

IDEA (Section 300.532, Evaluation Procedures) states:

> If an assessment is not conducted under standard conditions, a description of the extent to which it varied from standard conditions (e.g., the qualifications of the person administering the test, or the method of test administration) must be included in the evaluation report.

The first step in making informal evaluations a reality is for you to think like a tester. IDEA requires that five areas be considered when planning special education services: physical abilities, communication abilities, thinking (cognitive) abilities, social and emotional behavior, and developmental or educational growth. In addition, the law says to consider other areas specific to the child.

If the school has been testing your child in several of the five areas, has this been appropriate? Maybe your child only needs testing in one or two areas, not three or four. On the flip side, if the school has been testing your child in only one or two areas, perhaps he should be tested in three or four.

Do not leave it up to educators or others to decide in which areas your child needs to be assessed. Educators have traditionally assumed this role and forged ahead with testing. The next thing parents know, educators are detailing the results of the assessments at the IEP meeting and parents are in shock as they hear the dire results. We can and should change this!

Assessments should focus on your child's needs *relative to his participation in an age-appropriate, regular ed classroom.* After you've learned more about regular ed classes through your visits and observations, you'll know in which areas your child needs to be assessed and how to design the assessments.

Informal assessments can be performed by professional testers, parents, teachers, and other people who know the child. Ask the principal to help with assessments. Many principals who are former teachers would welcome the opportunity to be involved. And a child can even assess himself!

Non-standard assessments can provide a more complete picture of the child, for they can be designed to demonstrate a child's strengths and needs. While the results of many standardized tests *may* show strengths, educators often ignore these and focus on "deficits" and differences. Informal assessments are *not* used to pinpoint what's "wrong" with a child. They can identify what a child needs to be involved in regular ed classes, while enabling the child to maintain his dignity and humanity.

Another advantage of informal assessments over standardized tests is the natural environment in which the assessments are done. When standardized tests are given by unfamiliar people in unfamiliar environments, children may be nervous and uncomfortable, which leads to inaccurate evaluation data.

Non-standard evaluations can take many forms. You, your child, and others who know your child well are the best judges of what and how to assess. In all cases, make sure the assessments take place in natural settings that are (1) familiar to and comfortable for the child and (2) relevant to the subject area being tested.

Informal assessments can be done at home; on the playground; in the lunch room, library, gym, music room, classroom; or any other place that will provide the most accurate results. Schedule the evaluation at a time that is right for your child. For example, if he is at his best after lunch, that's the time to do assessments.

Use your own judgment about what and how to tell your child about this new evaluation process. In the best case scenarios, your child will be participating in the planning and execution of the assessments, so he'll know all about them. Even very young children can and should participate. You might tell your five-year-old, "There's a nice lady named Mrs. Harvey at your sister's school. Sometimes she helps kids learn how to talk, just like Sissy's teacher is helping Sissy learn about numbers. Mrs. Harvey wants to talk to you and me about how we talk! We get to have a meeting with her! Should Mrs. Harvey come to our house for the meeting or should we meet her at Sissy's school? How should we do this?"

Tell your child as much as you think he'll understand, in words that make sense to him. Don't trick your child into participating in an assessment and don't lie. Give him opportunities to make decisions about the process. If he's had bad experiences in the past, explain that these are different types of assessments. Be upbeat and positive.

Most children hate to perform, especially if they're asked to do something they don't think they do well. Plan assessment activities that allow professionals to observe or interact with your child without focusing on the perceived deficits. If children feel inadequate or frustrated, they won't do as well and the results will not accurately portray your child's strengths or needs.

In thinking about the five areas listed in IDEA, how should you decide in which areas your child should be assessed? Let's assume Michelle has only a cognitive disability and her parents have no other concerns about her physical or communication abilities or social and emotional behavior. If Michelle has no needs in these other areas, why bother with those assessments? Michelle's parents may want her assessed only in the areas of cognitive abilities and/or educational growth. Assessments should be designed to discover Michelle's strengths, as well as the specific areas she needs help with (reading, math, or other subjects) *in a regular ed setting.*

Base your decision on what you know is best. In the example above, Michelle may not be at "age-level" socially, but this doesn't necessarily mean she should be assessed or graded in the area of social development. With typical children, there are often significant differences between a child's cognitive and social abilities. For example, ten-year-old Chad, who does not have a disability, has the academic skills of a ten-year-old and the social skills of an eight-year-old. But no one is concerned; everyone presumes competence and knows Chad will "catch up." Think about your child this way. Presume competence and only assess specific areas of need.

At the same time, however, consider assessing areas to specifically demonstrate strengths and abilities. Let's assume, for example, you and educators disagree on your child's intellectual abilities. Standardized tests have demonstrated "deficits" that have landed your child in a resource room. But you know your child is far more capable than educators believe. In this circumstance, it's critical to design an informal assessment that will show your child's abilities in contrast to the negative results of traditional tests.

Take the time and make the effort to ensure your child is assessed in the areas that are relevant to his participation in a regular ed setting, in ways that will demonstrate an accurate portrayal of his abilities and needs. This is critically important. The outcomes of assessments will have a direct bearing on the IEP.

Charlotte and the IQ Test

Educators were insistent about giving an IQ test to Charlotte's daughter—Meredith, a six-year-old who has Down syndrome—prior to Meredith's entrance in a regular ed first grade classroom. Charlotte didn't want Meredith tested this way; she didn't believe it was necessary, and she didn't want Meredith known by her IQ score. When Charlotte asked why this test was important, the special ed teacher responded, "IQ tests are standard for all students with Down syndrome."

Charlotte successfully dealt with the situation by declining the IQ test and recommending the first grade teacher do an informal assessment. By simply sitting down and talking with Meredith, the classroom teacher could identify Meredith's "current level of functioning" and could determine what types of extra help Meredith might need in the first grade class. (This is not rocket science!) This was all educators needed to know in order to write an effective IEP. They did not need the results of a global intelligence test which would have given them an IQ score and little else.

Informal Assessments in the Five Areas

Following are examples to help you think about how to create effective informal assessments for your child. You'll be delighted at both the simplicity and the effectiveness of informal assessments.

In most cases, you need to be present for the evaluation and participate in it to the extent that makes sense. You can provide information to the tester that may not be observable, and you may be able to elicit more or better responses from your child than a tester. If your child is older, get her perspective on whether your presence is needed or not. She might want you nearby, but not in the same room.

Physical Abilities: Instead of having therapists do hands-on formal assessments, let them assess your child through observation. If a therapist is looking at gross motor abilities (legs, balance, etc.), have her visit the school during your child's recess or PE class, or invite her to your home. A therapist can learn a lot by watching.

If she feels compelled to "test" specific skills, help her learn how to do it informally. Instead of singling your son out in PE class to see if he can "throw a ball overhand eight out of ten times with 75 percent accuracy," (gag) the therapist can join in the fun and play a game of catch with your son and some of his friends.

Have we ever considered that most children and adults without disabilities could not meet the standards set by professionals when they use silly methods of measuring an ability? In fact, would the therapist like her abilities measured in the same way she measures others? What if *she* were judged by, "Perform a PT assessment with 75 percent accuracy, eight out of ten times."?

A therapist who is assessing fine motor abilities (hands, arms, upper body), can observe your child eating, coloring, working on the computer, or doing any other activity that's relative to a child's needs in a regular ed environment. Encourage the OT to make it fun and natural. For example, instead of the OT telling your child to color and then sitting back to "professionally observe," the OT can color, too, while watching unobtrusively.

Identify and plan assessment activities that demonstrate your child's strengths. Let him "show off" the things he does well. In the real world—now and when he is an adult—his abilities are more important than his inabilities.

When your child's physical abilities are being assessed, focus on what's really important. Let's assume your child's fine motor skills are being evaluated and the therapist is observing how he writes with a pencil or marker. The therapist may decide your child has "deficiencies" because he doesn't hold the pencil the "right way" or because he's not forming letters the "correct way." Please reject this nonsense! How *ever* he holds the pencil is the "right way" for him; it's irrelevant if he doesn't hold it the way other children do. Similarly, if your child forms letters in ways that don't follow the prescribed method of handwriting, that's fine, too. (How many adults follow the handwriting rules taught in schools?)

Again, focus on what's really important. Is it important that your child do things according to an artificial standard or is it more important that he be allowed to do things in ways that are right for him, that allow him to feel competent and successful, and that allow him to progress in his own way?

When my daughter was young, I tried to teach her to tie her shoes the "right" way, but she couldn't do it. Then a preschool teacher taught Emily how to tie shoelaces in "bunny ears." It wasn't how I was taught to tie a bow, but that didn't matter. It worked best for Emily, and today as a teenager, she still ties her shoes that way. What difference does it make *how* she does it, as long as it works for her?

Communication Abilities: What better way to assess communication than to simply engage in conversation with a child? Have your child sing a song, recite rhymes, or read a book to you and the speech therapist. Let him talk to a speech therapist about his favorite subject. Have him describe his pet, your vacation, or his favorite things about school. Play the TV interviewer game. Pretend your child is a famous person who's being interviewed on television. You or the therapist can be the "interviewer."

For a child who doesn't communicate orally, you—as the expert on your child—need to design an assessment, or help a professional design an assessment, using your child's form of communication. Does he communicate by formal or informal sign language? Through eye gaze, facial expressions, or behavior? With communication cards, an augmentative communication device, or a computer with speech software? All children communicate *in one form or another*. You and those who love your child can teach others about your child's communication methods. Don't forget to create opportunities for your child to demonstrate his strengths.

Communication assessments usually involve receptive (what the child understands) and expressive (what the child can tell others) communication. Erroneous assumptions are made when standardized tests are given to children who use non-verbal forms of communication. Professionals and parents often assume if a child cannot speak, he doesn't understand and, therefore, has a cognitive disability. We should, instead, presume competence.

Thinking (Cognitive) Abilities: Because this is such a broad category, it's critically important to identify *which* cognitive abilities need assessing: reading comprehension, writing abilities, or math concepts? Understanding instructions? Following directions? There are many things to consider.

Instead of an "official" tester (special ed teacher, psychologist, diagnostician, or someone else), a classroom teacher can do the assessment, as in the example about Meredith and the first grade teacher. Whoever does the evaluation can learn a great deal by observing, engaging in casual conversations, role-playing, and asking questions in a natural and informal manner. Remember to create opportunities for your child to demonstrate his strengths.

Many sophisticated diagnostic tools focus on learning and reading difficulties. Typically, the results of these tests often lead to prescriptions for therapies and interventions to "correct the problem." However, we must look at the bigger picture. Do we need to focus on correcting the problem or on providing accommodation in a regular ed classroom? Trying to fix the problem may not be successful, it may take time away from a child's overall educational opportunities, and it may send negative messages. Instead of trying to change the child, we should accommodate his differences and enable him to be successful via curriculum modifications, alternative methods of reading/learning, and other methods.

Any cognitive assessment must accommodate the child's disability. When you consider how these modifications should be made, think about how he demonstrates competence at home. Use these same methods in creating a non-standard assessment. Does he exhibit knowledge via a computer? Through play activities? Personal interactions? Reading? Writing? By imitating others?

There are often great discrepancies between what educators *believe* about a child and what the parents know to be true. Standardized tests often show a child as "deficient" in cognitive abilities, yet at home, he exhibits competence all the time. Make the effort to create informal assessments that demonstrate your child's true competence. Stay away from global "intelligence" tests; focus on specific areas.

Social and Emotional Behavior: Educators seem to be more fearful of disabilities that have a behavioral component than any others. But many children who are labeled as having social and emotional "problems" only have them at school! In other settings, their behaviors are not seen as problematic. A child may come from a family where everyone, if tested, would be viewed as "hyperactive." In reality, they're just a fast-moving family. In a school setting, where children are expected to sit still and be quiet, the natural behavior of the child is seen as unnatural. Educators often see non-conforming behaviors as conditions which should be "remedied" or "controlled."

When there are concerns about behavior, you and your child have an incredible opportunity to demonstrate your child's strengths and abilities. Invite the tester to your home to observe your child engaging in an activity he enjoys, and which demonstrates his calmness, patience, perseverance, or other strength. Professionals need to see a side of your child they may not know exists. If educators are concerned about a child's inability to stay focused, they need to see that when he does something he's interested in, he *does* focus!

Help professionals understand your child's behavior. They can learn a great deal from you and through conversations with your child. Often, for example, no one has ever asked a child who is in constant motion, "Why does it feel good to move around the classroom most of the day?" Keep in mind that a professional might ask, "Why aren't you able to sit still when Mrs. Andrews is teaching?" Asking the question in that manner is sure to make the child feel inadequate. The first example is a more positive way to find the answer. If you don't think the professional can ask questions in a positive manner, you do the "interviewing" as the professional observes.

Developmental or Educational Growth: This category means different things to different people. It can refer to a child being "behind" in certain areas; it may also refer to the overall progress the child is making. Much of what this category covers, in a general sense, could also be covered more specifically in other categories. If you're unsure what this category means in your district, ignore it and assess your child in the other relevant categories.

Focus on What's Really Important

We've been brainwashed into some strange ways of thinking. A parent recently asked me if I thought she should let a school OT continue spending time teaching her child to tie his shoes. Lots of time was spent during the school day on this activity. In the meantime, of course, the child was missing out on academic learning and social opportunities. I advised the mom to tell the OT to let it go, and recommended she buy her son shoes with hook and loop fasteners! Tying shoes, putting on coats, and similar activities are things we should be helping our children learn at home. Their time in school should be spent on academics, social interactions, and other typical activities, not on mundane tasks that are relatively unimportant in the big scheme of things.

Supplement Your Child's Assessments

Informal assessments are not complete without information from parents. Home movies, or videos you've recorded just for the evaluation, are perfect supplements. Maintain a list of books your child has read and make copies of work he does at home. Write up details of things he's said or one, and ask others (Sunday school teacher, babysitter, neighbor, etc.) to do the same. You're a gold mine of information; document it to make it official!

Creating an Informal Assessment

You may feel comfortable coming up with evaluation strategies all by yourself or you may want the ideas of others who know and respect your child (former teachers, neighbors, friends, etc.). Suggestions from a therapist, educator, or other professional you feel close to and respect may be helpful.

An extraordinary benefit of you designing—and participating in—the assessment(s) is the opportunity to demonstrate modifications and accommodations that are beneficial to your child. Schools often deny regular ed placements if they believe the child is not at grade level, and they don't know how (or don't want to take the time) to modify the curriculum. Informal assessments can change this.

Remember Robby from earlier in this section? I asked, "What if he was evaluated as a whole child, and more specifically, if he was assessed as a potential member of the fourth grade class?" Let's look at an example of an informal assessment which evaluates Robby's abilities *and* demonstrates curriculum modifications at the same time.

In the primary grades, the IEP team had always denied a regular ed placement for Robby because of his "subnormal" reading level. Linda's goal is for nine-year-old Robby to be included in the fourth grade classroom in the neighborhood school. Robby is reading on about a first-grade level. Linda knows Robby will "fail" a fourth-grade level reading test. But she's prepared to help him succeed, as in the following two scenarios.

In the first way, Linda will get a fourth grade textbook prior to the assessment. She'll take several paragraphs from one of the chapters and modify the text to suit Robby's reading level. (Don't worry, this is not rocket science, and Linda doesn't have to be an English major to do this well.) She'll take the information from the textbook and rewrite it in words Robby can read for himself. Linda will type the modified text on her computer, using large print. (If she didn't have access to a computer, she could hand print the text in large block letters on notebook paper.)

Prior to the test, Linda will discuss the plan with Robby and practice the assessment exercises. When it's time for the real thing with the official tester, Linda will ask Robby to read the designated paragraphs from the fourth grade textbook. Robby will struggle with most of the words, but might get a few of the easier ones. Without expecting him to finish the paragraphs, Linda will stop Robby after a minute or two. Then she'll ask him to read the modified text, which he'll be able to do just fine. Next, Linda will ask Robby to tell her, in his own words, what the text means, or she'll ask him a couple of specific questions about what he's just read. Linda and Robby have just demonstrated that although Robby is unable to read at a fourth-grade level, he can successfully learn in a fourth grade environment with a modified curriculum.

In the second plan, Linda could use a different accommodation. Instead of modifying the text into written form, she could record the information onto an audio cassette. She could read the designated text verbatim, or she could read it in words suitable to Robby's auditory comprehension. The assessment would continue as described above, with the audio cassette substituting for the written text.

After you've visited potential classrooms for your child, and using the examples in this section as models, think about activities that can be used to assess your child relative to his placement in an age-appropriate regular education classroom in the neighborhood school. If you don't feel comfortable designing informal assessments—with or without help from others—you can still help your child avoid being tyrannized by standardized tests. Tell the various assessment personnel to evaluate your child without using standardized tests. The tester can decide how to do this or you can provide ideas. A tester could observe a child in the classroom to evaluate cognitive abilities or she might give your child oral or written tests based on classroom curriculum. There are many creative ways to determine a child's abilities and needs.

Educating Educators About Non-Standard Assessments

Let's assume you have identified the age-appropriate regular education classes in the neighborhood school that you want your child to attend. After visiting the classroom, you've determined what it will take for your child to be involved in and progress in the curriculum (accommodations and modifications). And, you've thought about and/or designed informal or non-standard assessments relative to your child's placement in those classes. The next step is educating educators about your plans. Every situation is different, so use your great common sense and intuition on exactly how to proceed. But I'll share some general ideas you can use as a starting point.

Many educators may be shocked when you propose non-standard evaluations. To prevent an outright rejection of your ideas, don't spring this on professionals. Talk about this informally, long before the time for assessments and/or the IEP meeting.

Typically, the person responsible for scheduling assessments and planning the IEP meeting is a special ed teacher or coordinator. For purposes of this discussion, we'll call this person the "meeting planner." A month or two before the assessments and/or the IEP meeting are usually scheduled, call the meeting planner and casually tell her how well your child is doing in such-and-such area. If you've redefined yourself and/or become more active in your child's school, this call won't seem unusual—you'll be in contact with this person on a regular basis.

Use this as an example: "Hi, Marge. This is Johnny Smith's mom, Chrissy. Just wanted to touch base with you and let you know how much I appreciate all your help. Also, I wanted to tell you great Johnny is doing in [whatever]. We've really noticed an improvement just by [watching him, talking to him, or whatever]. And [his teacher and the neighbor, etc.] have been telling me all the good things they've seen Johnny do. We're so excited about his progress." That's your first conversation.

Two or three weeks later, be more direct: "Marge, I'd like to try something a little different before the next IEP meeting. Instead of using standardized tests, I'd like Johnny to be assessed informally. I really think we'll get a better picture of his abilities and needs that way." Then share your ideas about informal assessments.

Professional reaction may range from mild concern to extreme indignation at the notion that anything less than standardized test is appropriate. Furthermore, if—for the purposes of demonstrating your child's capability to be in a regular classroom—you propose an informal evaluation done by the classroom teacher, the special ed teacher may be aghast that you're presuming your child will be in regular ed classes. Under no circumstances should you respond with anger or aggressiveness. There are a variety of ways to handle this situation.

You can simply repeat your request, adding, "I'd like to try it this time and see what happens. I'd really like to see how much more Johnny can show us if he's assessed informally. I know we would get a more complete picture." No one can argue with a goal that will benefit everyone: getting a clearer perspective on Johnny. Persevere and be positive.

You can negotiate using the "what would it take" method. Ask, "What would it take for us to use informal assessments?" The tester won't just say, "No" since that's grammatically incorrect. Instead, she'll give you a reason, such as, "We feel standardized tests are best." You reply, "Yes, I understand standardized tests are traditional, but what would it take to use informal assessments at this time?" This will initiate a dialogue to help you learn enough to move beyond the arguments.

Testers, especially those in charge of IQ or psychological tests, might argue that standardized tests must be used because the law requires accurate classification of students for funding purposes. They may say informal assessments won't provide the number of "standard deviations" off the norm. (Gag!) But remember, IDEA does not specify what types of assessments are to be used. The state education agency or a school district may have guidelines about testing, but nothing in the federal law mandates the use of standardized tests. Furthermore, a state cannot make laws that infringe on federal laws. If you're given this argument, ask why, who says, how did that come to be? You'll be given enough information to dismantle their arguments.

With traditional assessments, not only are parents often unaware of how their children are being assessed, they also aren't always informed about the results of the tests until the IEP meeting. This can be changed using non-standard assessments. After the informal evaluations are done, immediately review the results with the educator(s) involved. You want to make sure you and the tester both come away with similar information, and you don't want to be surprised if the tester presents results at the IEP meeting that are different from the results you saw.

The tester—alone or in collaboration with you—should prepare a written report, which will be reviewed at the IEP meeting and placed in your child's file. If you have provided supplementary evaluation data, include this, too. After the assessments are completed, it's time to write the IEP Blueprint (described shortly).

Independent Evaluations

Some parents may have their children tested by experts outside the school system: private physicians, therapists, and so forth. Parents are often driven to do this when the school's assessments are inaccurate or incomplete. And the law says we can do this. However, the law also doesn't take into account the human component in the IEP process.

Parents may call in an outside expert when they feel the school doesn't respect the information they present about their children's needs. We may think, "Well, the school won't listen to me, but they will listen to Dr. So-in-So!" But the opposite is often true. If the school has dismissed your ideas, there's no way most educators will accept your expert's opinions as valid. To do so would be the equivalent of you rubbing their noses in their mistake in not listening to you in the first place.

Many teachers and administrators resent "outsiders" telling them what they're doing wrong, how to do something right, or anything else. We shouldn't be surprised by this. It wouldn't be any different than if I looked over the shoulder of the mechanic changing my oil and I tried to tell him what to do! The resentment felt by educators results in rejection of the "outsider's" expertise and his test results.

In addition to providing independent evaluations, private physicians are also used by parents to officially identify and certify one or more particular "defects" or diagnoses, such as a visual-cerebral defect, auditory processing defect, and so forth. Then parents say, "See, my child has this condition, so you must address the needs related to this condition." The problem here is that the diagnosis is probably meaningless to educators. They don't know what it really means, they don't know how to address it, and so forth.

In some cases, professionals outside the school system can cause more harm than good. For example, a psychiatrist in private practice was working with Fran and her son, Will, regarding Will's behavior. The doctor created a form which listed numerous types of behavior, actions, responses, and so forth. The teachers were instructed to fill this out every day, and to add any other comments about Will's behavior. The doctor would then use the information as a basis for regulating Will's medication and coming up with behavior management strategies. The intent might have been good, but the results were disastrous.

Educators already saw Will as a "behavior problem" and they were pushing Fran to put him in a special school. Giving Will's teachers the power to monitor and record Will's behavior reinforced their belief that he didn't belong in a regular classroom. Instead of seeing much of Will's behavior as typical for a six-year-old, they saw *everything* he did as disruptive and abberant. If the teachers had monitored *every* child in Will's classroom the same way, they probably all would look like "behavior problems"!

Use private physicians as necessary, but keep them in the background. If, for example, your child has a "visual cerebral defect" (like Benjamin does), that results in her having difficulty reading, understanding worksheets in school, and so forth, don't have the physician attend the IEP meeting, and don't even give educators some big long technical report from the doctor. Instead, learn about the condition from the doctor, put it in plain English, and help educators understand what it means from your parental perspective.

For example, you and your child can meet with the classroom teacher to talk about the situation. Have your child look at books, worksheets, and other materials used in the classroom during the meeting. Ask your child what she sees, what she doesn't see, and what would make it better. Take a worksheet that has multiple activities on it and mask off all but one. Does this make it better? What if the problems on the worksheet were enlarged? Maybe your child needs a worksheet prepared differently, so that instead of having multiple problems on a page, there's only one per page. Maybe using a different colored paper would help. Perhaps a clip-on lamp with an incandescent bulb would be better than the fluorescent light in the classroom.

In Benjamin's classes, we tried many things to help him see better, using a lot of trial and error. He had a clip-on lamp at his desk, his materials were in large print, and we put colored tissue paper over the florescent fixtures above Benj's desk. (This worked great! All the kids wanted paper above their heads, too, so the entire ceiling was a rainbow of colors!)

In the vast majority of cases, we can help educators figure out what our children need using low-key, proactive strategies instead of calling in outside experts as our "hired guns."

WRITING THE IEP BLUEPRINT

After you've visited potential classrooms, you're ready to write a blueprint for success—an IEP unlike any that's ever been written for your child! The purpose of writing an IEP Blueprint is to create a document which will become the foundation of the official IEP. The suggestions that follow will help you practice the steps for writing the Blueprint. But you don't have to do this alone, and I hope you won't. At the end of this section you'll find ideas for getting input and support from others. After you've become familiar with the process, you'll feel competent to teach it to others and get their assistance.

The IEP Blueprint will focus on the main components of your child's education, but it will not be a replica of the school's official IEP forms. To fully prepare yourself for the IEP meeting, become very familiar with the school forms. Get a set of blank IEP forms from the school and study them while writing your Blueprint. IDEA says the IEP must include, "an explanation of the extent, if any, to which the child will not participate with nondisabled children in the regular class." Is there a place on the school IEP forms that covers this issue? This is a critical piece: it requires the school to *explain why* a child would not be educated in regular classes. Study the school IEP forms until you know them like the back of your hand!

Your IEP Blueprint will contain three main documents; one each for Present Level of Educational Performance, Goals and Objectives, and Related Services. Allow plenty of time to write the Blueprint. Think of the documents like you would a grocery list. Post them on your refrigerator door and add things as you think of them. Take a week, a month, or more. This isn't something to be done in one sitting. Take the time to carefully consider what's really important for your child to be successful in regular classrooms.

Your child needs to write his own IEP Blueprint to the best of his abilities. Talk to him about what the regular educational environment will look like, about his abilities, goals, and related services. Be specific to help your child understand what all this is about: "How could you best learn history next year?" or "Let's think about how you could do math—with a calculator or on the computer, or do you want to try with pencil and paper?" If your child is unable to write, let him dictate his ideas and you write them down.

It might be a good idea for your child to write two reports: one done with your help (or on his own) and one done with the help of someone else who knows him well. Others often have wider or different perspectives than we (mothers) have. Because our children want to please us, we may inadvertently influence them to want what we want instead of what's really in their hearts.

Regardless of the type or severity of your child's disability, and regardless of his age, he needs to be a part of this process. It's his life and his education, not yours! You and others who know your child well can figure out the best way for your child to write, or contribute to, his Blueprint. Don't worry if you don't know everything you need to know right now.

Get through this chapter, visit classrooms, look at curriculum, talk with your child, and brainstorm with others. You'll figure it out.

It's critically important that your child take ownership of his education and the IEP process. You'll see an amazing difference when he is invested in the process. In addition, you'll see an incredible difference in educators when they see how competent your child is as he participates in his educational plan. Even if he only contributes a little bit the first time, it will be more than he has done in the past. The more he contributes, the more he's taking charge of his own life, becoming self-determined and self-confident.

What the IEP Considers

Per IDEA, the following five areas are considered in the IEP process: physical abilities, communication abilities, thinking (cognitive) abilities, social and emotional behavior, and developmental or educational growth. In addition, the law states any other areas specific to the child can be considered.

While writing your IEP Blueprint, consider all these areas. At the same time, however, don't feel you *must* identify needs or goals in each area. If there are no concerns about your child's physical abilities, for example, move on to the next area.

Present Level of Educational Performance

At many IEP meetings, this is one of the first things on the agenda. In educators' jargon, this may be called Present Level of Functioning, Current Level of Achievement, or something similar. IDEA says the IEP must include (1) "a statement of the child's present levels of educational performance," which includes (2) "how the child's disability affects the child's involvement and progress in the general curriculum."

"Present levels of educational performance" should obviously include a review of a child's educational strengths and needs. (Use the word "needs" instead of saying "weaknesses" like many educators do.) However, many IEP teams don't even come close to following the law in this area. Some spend little or no time discussing a child's "educational performance." Instead, they focus on the child's disability, and present assessment results, outcomes of the previous IEP, and other information that details the child's perceived deficits and functional limitations. Think back to your child's last IEP meeting. Did the team actually review your child's educational performance, or was most of the discussion centered around the disability?

When a discussion of the child's "present level" is done accurately, the IEP team can easily discern what the child needs in order to participate and progress in the regular educational environment. But too often, educators don't go there! They only see that—because of the child's disability—a resource room or special program is the appropriate placement.

In addition, IEP teams seldom specifically address the second component: "how the child's disability affects the child's involvement and progress in the general curriculum." The two distinct components of this part of the law, as quoted above, are often merged into one. During the discussion of the child's "present level," it's assumed the child's "deficits" automatically prevent him from participating and progressing in regular classes. Your IEP Blueprint will address these issues separately.

Educational Abilities: During the discussion of a child's "present level," an educator might report, "Mary functions at the level of a four-year-old." If Mary's actual educational performance *is* discussed, an educator might say, "Mary has not acquired the concept of number conservation." In your IEP Blueprint, details of your child's "present level" will not be written in professional jargon, nor will they be limited only to the abilities focused on by many educators. You'll go beyond what educators usually do and, in the process, enlighten the IEP team about who your child really is.

Create a document with the heading: "Educational Abilities." This will be part of the "Present Level of Educational Performance" document. List your child's academic/educational abilities, keeping in mind the five areas IDEA says should be considered: physical abilities, communication abilities, cognitive abilities, social and emotional behavior, and developmental or educational growth. List any new information you learned during your child's informal assessments. In addition, list strengths and personal traits, interests, skills, hobbies, and more. And don't forget to include specific items as they relate to your child's participation in an age-appropriate regular ed classroom.

Following are examples to get you started. In parentheses, I've described what each example represents.

- Susie can add and subtract columns of two digit numbers. (cognitive ability; educational growth)
- Kenneth gets along well with others. (social and emotional behavior)
- Marta likes to color maps. (cognitive ability; personal interest/hobby)
- Jeff likes to read biographies. (educational growth/cognitive ability; hobby)
- Latoya wants to learn about chemistry. (cognitive ability; interest)
- Juan speaks for himself with communication cards. (communication and cognitive abilities; social growth)
- Stephanie learns best by imitation. (developmental growth; personal strength)
- Mark is a good speller. (cognitive ability; educational growth)
- Amber has a coin collection. (cognitive ability; hobby)

Do you see the wide variety of strengths that can be included in the listing of your child's "Educational Abilities"? It's important for you to open your mind very wide to see all of your child's gifts and talents. Some of us have been so brainwashed that we can't see the forest for the trees. We've been taught to see our children from the deficit model—the way professionals and educators see them. But this is just not right! You, the expert on your child, can paint an accurate picture with a long list of your child's many capabilities.

If your initial list is very short, don't despair. Put it on the refrigerator and add to it as more things come to mind. And ask others—who may see your child very differently than you do—for help. More about that a little later.

Strengths: Many of the strengths and abilities on your list can positively impact your child's education in a regular ed classroom. Look at the following examples to see how a strength can be used.

Matt is great at basketball. Basketball could be used as a vehicle to: facilitate friendships which could lead to peer helpers in academic settings, help Matt acquire improved interpersonal relationship skills via team sports, help him with math (score keeping, as well as geometry and shapes via the ways players position themselves on the court), and more.

Dylan is trying really hard to talk. This strength demonstrates Dylan's interest in words—which can lead to his interest in reading—and in communicating with others, which shows his desire to socialize. He can learn and be successful in a regular ed classroom with a communication device or cards, as well as with books on tape and other modifications. At the same time, Dylan's speech will improve from being around typical children, practicing phonics during reading, singing in music class, and participating in typical school activities. He'll be surrounded by great speech therapists: other children who speak!

Benjamin knows how to use the computer. Even though he can't write with a pencil, Benjamin can write, do math, and successfully participate in other subjects in the general curriculum by using a computer. In addition, the computer is a powerful magnet that will draw other children to Benjamin for natural support and friendship.

Emily likes to play board games with other girls. This strength demonstrates Emily's capacity for socialization, her understanding of sequence, respect for rules (all games have rules!), counting abilities, and more. In the third grade classroom, this strength can be easily tapped into: the teacher routinely uses learning games in small group activities to help all the students learn math, geography, and other subjects. Emily's love of games will provide a gateway for learning, friendships, and more.

Tony can calm himself by running. Tony's running has traditionally been seen as "inappropriate" behavior by educators and other professionals. Tony's parents, however, don't see it this way; they know it's one of Tony's strengths. Running helps Tony calm himself and get back on track when something upsets him. At home, he's learned to get on the treadmill and run, instead of bolting out the front door. By putting a treadmill in the second grade classroom—accommodating Tony's need—he can participate in the regular educational environment. And, Tony will be in charge of "managing" his own behavior.

Nicole has a great auditory memory. Her parents have recognized that Nicole learns best by listening. This is a great strength going into sixth grade because the classroom teachers use interactive class discussions in all subjects. In language arts, social studies, and history, students routinely take turns reading out loud from textbooks and the class engages in lively dialogue about the subject matter. This is a perfect fit for Nicole's way of learning. In addition, her classmates will record chapters of books on audio tape, and the teachers will modify other materials to Nicole's reading level.

Mario loves football. When he was eight, Mario discovered football. He and his dad are avid armchair quarterbacks. Because Mario uses a wheelchair, he has never been able to play on a team, but this hasn't prevented him from being a great passer and receiver. He and his dad routinely practice throwing "the bomb" in the back yard. For years, Mario and his dad have attended the high school football games and become friendly with the coach. Through this relationship, Mario and his dad can secure the opportunity for the ninth-grader to put his skills to good use and, for the first time ever, participate in extracurricular activities. He can be the equipment manager for the team, helping the team during practice and providing an extra set of hands when the quarterbacks and receivers are practicing throwing and catching. And on Friday nights, he can be on the sidelines instead of in the stands. The friendships Mario forms can lead to peer support in regular ed classrooms.

Isabella loves to watch television. Isabella doesn't have much patience for typical class-room lectures; she's easily distracted by other noises and movement in the room and can't stay focused on the teacher. But she's mesmerized by anything on a television screen. Focusing on the sound and pictures is her most effective way of learning. If educators use this strength creatively, Isabella can participate and progress in the regular educational environment. Her teachers can provide the tenth-grader with a variety of videos and movie-like computer programs that correspond to the curriculum. Then she'll be able to participate in class discussions on the subject. Isabella's parents, in a bold streak of genius, have come up with another idea. The teacher could wear a microphone and a video camera set up in the back of the room could be focused on her. The video image could be transmitted to a television monitor on Isabella's desk and the audio would be sent to headphones Isabella wears. By concentrating on the sound and picture, Isabella could learn from the teacher's lectures the way her peers do.

Create a document entitled "Strengths," and from your list of "Educational Abilities" document, select characteristics which can support or enhance (1) a regular ed classroom placement and/or (2) the goals to meet your child's needs. Then write descriptions on how these strengths can be used, as in the examples above.

The "Strengths" form is primarily for you to use in thinking about goals, accommodations, related services, and so forth. But it can also be a tool to educate educators. Use your own judgment about how and when to share it with people on the IEP team. Supportive educators may find the information extremely beneficial, and they'll appreciate your resourcefulness. On the other hand, if educators are not open-minded about a regular ed placement, sharing the contents of the "Strengths" document may be very important in proving your case and bringing them around to a new way of thinking.

Affect of the Disability: Remember that, per IDEA, the "Present Level of Educational Performance" should include a statement on "how the disability affects the child's involvement and progress in the general curriculum." Educators may use the "affect of the disability" to exclude a child from a regular education classroom. We, however, will do what the law says: identify how the disability affects the child. In the process, we'll discover what a child needs in order to be involved in and progress in the general curriculum, as shown in the examples that follow. Later, this information can be used in writing goals and identifying related services.

Alyssa's orthopedic disability results in her inability to write legibly. In order for her to be involved in and progress in the general curriculum, she may need any or all of the following: a computer to do her class work on; assistance in learning the computer; worksheets and tests scanned into the computer; a calculator for math; assistance to improve her hand-writing skills; oversized pencils, paint brushes, and markers; and shorter tests and/or an extended time frame for taking tests.

Because of his disability (autism), Robert cannot always maintain "appropriate" class-room behavior. He's unable to stay focused on the teacher during lectures, he cannot stay seated for long periods of time, and he frequently becomes upset and wants to run away. So he can be involved in and progress in the general curriculum, Robert may need the following: a rope swing in the classroom or in the adjacent hallway that he can use whenever he begins to feel agitated; the freedom to be able to move around the classroom instead of staying seated at all times; hands-on manipulatives and interactive activities to supplement the standard curriculum; and small group instruction and extra help during math and science.

MacKenzie has extremely low vision and will be unable to read the written materials used in the general curriculum. In order to be involved in and progress in the regular educational environment, she may need: books and other reading materials translated into Braille or recorded on audio tape; Brailled tests and worksheets and a stylus; Brailled copies of the teacher's overhead transparencies; orientation assistance to learn where things are in the classroom and the locations of other places in the school (art room, music class, library, cafeteria, etc.); and modified curriculum and materials in art class.

Writing a description of how your child's disability affects his involvement and progress in the general curriculum is a very important step. Many parents have been accused of being "in denial" or having "unrealistic" expectations for their children. This is your opportunity for "full disclosure" (we can be realistic!) of how your child's disability affects him in educational settings, while—at the same time—identifying strategies and supports that will enable him to be successful in the regular educational environment. Write your statement in plain English, not therapeutic or professional jargon.

Once again, your familiarity with the regular ed classroom is vitally important. Your visits to potential classrooms will provide you with the information you need to write an accurate description.

Did you notice that, in the examples above, nowhere was there a mention of a student having an aide? When writing this description about your child, do not get into specifics about who will do what or exactly how something will be done. All this will fall under related services. Don't let these issues bog down the process.

Create a document with the heading, "How the Disability Affects [Mary's] Involvement and Progress in the General Curriculum," and write your description.

At this point, the first stage of your IEP Blueprint is complete. You've created three separate reports: "Educational Abilities," "Strengths," and "Affect of the Disability." Together, they constitute the "Present Level of Educational Performance" document.

The "Educational Abilities" report will be shared with every member of the team during your pre-IEP meetings and at the official IEP meeting. It needs to go into your child's permanent file. The "Strengths" document could be for your use only, or you may want to make it a supplement to the "Educational Abilities" document. The "Affect of the Disability" document will also be shared with members of the IEP team.

From Needs to Goals and Objectives

In many traditional IEP meetings, the next piece of business is a discussion of the child's "weaknesses" or needs. When IEP teams operate from the medical model perspective, they identify a child's "problems" and try to provide the "cure" through goals. Unfortunately, many teams focus on "remedying deficits" while ignoring children's true educational needs.

IDEA does not require the IEP team to list needs; it *does* require the IEP team to write goals and objectives to meet a child's needs. Remember that IDEA says goals should be written related to "meeting the child's needs that result from the child's disability to enable the child to be involved in and progress in the general curriculum; and meeting each of the child's other educational needs that result from the child's disability." Translated, goals need to be written based on what a child needs to participate and progress in the regular ed classroom. This is in sharp contrast to the goals written by many IEP teams. We'll get to writing goals in a moment, but first we need to examine how things have traditionally been done, so we don't keep making the same mistakes.

Parents initially learn about the IEP process from educators, so we often let the disability label drive the needs (medical model paradigm). It's critical to understand that *needs are the foundation of goals.* If a disability label or a child's "deficits" drives the needs, it also drives the entire IEP, including placement. Furthermore, we often confuse needs with related services (especially therapy) and/or accommodations. Negative consequences result from these erroneous ways of thinking, as demonstrated in the first scenario below. In the second scenario, however, a very different outcome is achieved.

Scenario #1: Because Sara has a physical disability, the IEP team agrees she needs physical therapy twice a week. There's no discussion about why Sara needs PT or what the PT is supposed to accomplish. It's assumed children with physical disabilities need PT.

Sara may be automatically placed in a segregated setting because PT is only provided in the resource room at Sara's school. Alternatively, she may be allowed to participate in a regular classroom, but will be pulled out for PT and will then miss academics.

Because no specifics are attached to the need for therapy, it will be left up to the therapist, with or without input from Sara and her mom, to write therapy goals. There's a good possibility these goals will be meaningless and irrelevant—and even demeaning—to Sara since they focus on her body parts. The goals will probably be unrelated to Sara's overall school experience, and they may segregate her from participation in mainstream school settings or experiences.

Because the IEP team, including Sara and her mom, followed the traditional way of doing things, Sara's disability drove her needs, and the so-called need for PT cost Sara an inclusive full-time placement in a regular ed classroom. It also resulted in a need being turned into a therapeutic goal.

Scenario #2: Sara and her parents have thought very carefully about what she really needs. She doesn't need or want hands-on therapy, and she and her folks have shared this with the IEP team. However, she does still need the services of a physical therapist.

One of Sara's goals is: "Sara will play basketball, softball, and other sports in ninth grade PE class." Instead of providing hands-on therapy, the therapist can collaborate with the PE teacher on accommodations and modifications. In addition, the therapist can assist Sara when she requests help during class. In this scenario, physical therapy is not a need, nor a goal, but a related service. Sara's needs, related to her participation and progress in the regular ed environment, not the disability itself, drove the goal and the related services.

We must be careful how we state needs and goals. Saying a child needs an aide or a behavior plan, for example, promotes negative images and can provoke educators into making emotionally-charged assumptions about a child that may pave the way for a segregated placement. Always think about goals in relation to your child's participation in regular ed!

Therapies, supports, and interventions should not be written as needs or goals. They are, instead, related services which *support* the goals and objectives and enable the student to benefit from special education. In the example of a child needing a behavior plan, assistance or support for the child would be a related service the school provides to the child, not a need or a goal.

As previously mentioned, IEP teams often identify a long list of a child's "weaknesses" or needs based on the disability. Then goals are written to meet the child's needs in an attempt to fix the child's "problems" and/or get the child "ready" for placement in a regular classroom at some future date. This approach does not follow the law because the goals do not reflect how a child will participate or progress in the curriculum in the general educational environment.

A child's academic needs are far more important than needs related to functional abilities. I always told therapists and educators who tried to focus on Benjamin's functional skills, "It will be very nice if my son walks one day, but walking won't get him a job! He can have a great life even if he uses a wheelchair, but he won't have a great life if he's not educated!" If we expect our children to go to college or trade school or get good jobs, their academic needs must be our primary concern.

In our new way of doing things, we'll follow the spirit and intent of the law. We don't need to make a long list of "weaknesses" or needs related to a child's "problems." We simply need to write goals related to "meeting the child's needs that result from the child's disability to enable the child to be involved in and progress in the general curriculum; and meeting each of the child's other educational needs that result from the child's disability."

To accomplish this, parents, as well as other members of the IEP team, must be familiar with "the general curriculum." Educators—some more than others—already are. But parents typically are not, and that's why visiting potential classrooms and learning about curriculum and activities are critically important. When we write goals, our focus will not be on the child's disability, but on what the child needs to participate and progress in the regular educational environment. If, for whatever reason, you or someone on the IEP team feels compelled to have a list of needs, take the goals and wherever you see the word "will," substitute the words "needs to." Presto! You have a list of needs.

Writing Goals

Writing relevant and appropriate goals is critical: they're the foundation of your child's daily educational experiences. Goals need to be written in plain English. When they're written in professional jargon, they're nonsensical and meaningless to everyone except the person who wrote them. How can a regular ed teacher make sense of, "Jay will [do whatever] four out of five times with 80 percent accuracy, 75 percent of the time."?

At the other end of the spectrum are goals that are senseless because they're so broad. While helping parents with their teenaged son's IEP, I learned educators had written only one goal: "James will improve his behavior." What does this mean? Improve his behavior in what way? To whose standards? In which class? How?

Your child's IEP should be *a living document,* not a sheaf of senseless gibberish that is filed away as soon as the IEP meeting is over. Write goals for your child in language that is easily understandable to anyone who reads them. Effective goals describe real-life activities which your child can master, not isolated behaviors or skills. If your next door neighbor—

or someone else who knows nothing about special education—can read and understand the goals and objectives written for your child, they've been written well. And goals and objectives written in plain English are far more likely to be implemented than goals written in professional lingo.

Think of an IEP as a set of instructions for a substitute teacher. If, for example, the classroom teacher is absent one day and she hasn't had the opportunity to review your child's situation with the substitute, could the sub pick up your child's IEP off the teacher's desk first thing in the morning, read it quickly, and know what to do? If so, it's a useful and meaningful living document. And one way to ensure this is by writing activity-based goals.

The following recommendations from The Schools Project of the Specialized Training Program at the University of Oregon, detail valuable ideas for writing effective goals:

> The purpose of writing an IEP goal is to describe a complete picture of competence by identifying the activity-based outcome that you intend the student to achieve by the end of the school year. First, an effective IEP goal describes something a student will do as an outcome of instruction (i.e. by the end of the school year) that is typical of others the student's age. Second, it describes the parameters under which the student will do the activity (i.e. where, when, how often, or with whom?). Goals describe answers to the following three questions:
>
> 1. How will the student's competence change as a result of instruction?
> 2. When, where, or with whom will the student do the activity?
> 3. What kind of help or support will the student need?
>
> The goal is "good" if it includes the following critical features:
> *   The goal is an activity.
> *   The goal says what the student will do.
> *   The goal describes the natural conditions under which the student will do the activity.
>
> A goal is not an activity if it designates performance of isolated skills or behaviors, such as "Sue will read at a 3.5 grade level," or "Bill will learn the value of coins."
>
> A goal does not describe a student's competence if it describes staff behavior rather than student behavior, such as: "Monica will maintain adequate dental hygiene," or "Dianne will have more opportunities to be integrated."

Following are several goals I prepared using the guidelines above:

*   Benjamin will move around his homeroom, go to and from art, music, PE, lunch, and recess in his wheelchair, daily, without assistance from an adult.

*   Dylan will make choices about his lunch selection, his free-choice activities in class, and what games to play at recess using communication cards.

*   Emily will read easy-reader books of her choice and will retell the story to her teacher and/or her classmates to demonstrate her comprehension.

*   Matt will communicate with his classmates and teachers using words instead of gestures when he's angry, upset, or needs help.

What goals will enable your child to participate and progress in the regular ed classroom? Think about goals related to academics, physical, social, behavioral, and other needs.

A word of caution is in order. Just because a child is placed in a regular ed environment, we can't assume he'll be expected to participate and progress in the general curriculum. For example, Kim was ecstatic when the IEP team agreed to place her son, James, in a regular ed fifth grade classroom. During the first month of school, everything seemed to be going great. In the second month of school, a few glitches arose and Kim decided to visit the classroom to see what was what.

She learned James was pulled out of class several times a day for special help with certain subjects. When he *was* in the fifth grade room, an aide sat next to him and helped him do work that was unrelated to what the rest of the class was doing. Kim realized that— even though James was in the fifth grade class—he never participated in the general curriculum and he didn't really belong. This could have been the result of poorly written goals; or, if the goals *were* written well, a result of educators not following the IEP; or both.

While a regular ed placement may not automatically ensure a child will be involved in the general curriculum, we don't want to write broad goals that reflect only subject matter, such as "James will learn fifth grade social studies." Goals should be specific and activity-based, detailing *how* James will learn fifth grade social studies.

Think carefully about your child's goals and focus on what's most important and doable. If we write multitudes of goals, many may never be met simply because there's not enough time in the day! Furthermore, goals are often written that—in the big scheme of things—are not appropriate or important to a child's participation in the regular ed environment.

I've seen goals about children learning to tie their shoes, wash their hair, become more organized, and other unusual activities. We cannot expect schools to do everything. But more importantly, do we *want* schools to have power over things that are *our* responsibilities? We can and should take responsibility for being our children's first and best teachers. More importantly, what opportunities for long-term academic success do children lose when educators spend time on insignificant and irrelevant activities?

Goals that focus on isolated functional skill development, such as "Juan will increase his gait speed," should never be written. "Therapeutic goals" usually focus on isolated skills that are not relevant to a child's educational day. The therapist's role should be supplementary, not primary: she's there to provide assistance to a child (or his teachers) within the context of goals related to a child's participation and progress in the regular educational environment.

Let's assume, however, that Juan's parents and educators on the IEP team feel it *is* important for Juan to increase his walking speed so he can get to his classes on time. Before the IEP team writes a goal about this, Juan should be consulted. Is this important to Juan? In addition, the IEP team should decide whether a *goal* is necessary and appropriate, or if Juan's need could be met through related services and/or accommodations.

If Juan moves slowly because of an awkward gait, would "increasing gait speed" be a practical, doable goal? If the PT worked with Juan in PE class (the natural setting for PT assistance), would this really enable Juan to walk faster?

Instead of trying to get Juan to walk faster, would it make more sense to provide accommodations? Maybe a friend could carry Juan's books for him, enabling him to walk a little faster between classes. Perhaps Juan and a friend could leave each class one minute early. Or Juan might decide a mobility device would be a useful accommodation to use for changing classes. There are many issues to carefully consider.

If, after all your pre-IEP meetings (discussed in the next section), you're still negotiating a regular ed placement, write goals in such a way that the only place the goals can be met is in an age-appropriate regular ed classroom. For example, "Johnny will learn how to read," is written so generically (and it's not an activity-based goal) that the IEP team could say, "The special ed teacher can teach Johnny reading in the resource room." But the goal, "Johnny will read easy-reader books to his same-age peers in small reading groups in third grade," can only be implemented in a regular ed classroom.

This one goal, however, isn't enough to ensure a regular ed placement. If this was the only goal written this way, educators could still place Johnny in a resource room, but let him "visit" a regular classroom for reading. Therefore, *all* of Johnny's goals need to be written to reflect a regular ed placement. If you've visited the classrooms you want your child in, you'll know how to write goals that will reflect his participation in those classes.

Short Term Objectives

IDEA says the IEP must include "a statement of measurable annual goals, including benchmarks or short-term objectives" These are the "steps" a child takes to reach a goal. Goals usually have more than one short term objective, and the objectives build on one another. Once a child has mastered the first objective, he moves on to the next, and so on, until the goal has been achieved.

A variety of traditional methods, such as formal assessments, academic tests, and therapeutic evaluations are often used to measure a child's progress. But the best way, especially with activity-based goals, is the simplest: observation by the classroom teacher and by the student. Is the student doing it or not?

The measurement of objectives can be made more effective if we write them in plain English and put dates on them, as in the following example:

> **Annual Goal:** Benjamin will move around his homeroom, go to and from art, music, PE, lunch, and recess in his wheelchair, daily, without assistance from an adult.
>
> **Short Term Objectives**
> 1. Benjamin will turn in his assignments by taking them from his desk to his teacher's desk, using his wheelchair, measured by teacher and student observation; by October 1st.
> 2. Benjamin will go with his classmates, from his homeroom to the art room and back, using his wheelchair; measured by teacher and student observation; by November 1st.

These objectives would continue in increments until the goal is met.

Following are specific recommendations for writing effective short term objectives form The Schools Project:

> The purpose of writing instructional objectives is to define what the student will learn in order to support the achievement of a particular IEP goal. Remember that an IEP goal describes what the student will do at the end of instruction, while IEP

objectives define all the skills which will support the accomplishment of that goal. IEP objectives are derived from the goals, and need to be much more specific than the outcomes sketched by the goals. Instructional objectives need to answer the following three questions:

1. What are the specific conditions under which the student will perform the skill? In other words, how will the student know to perform the skill? When or what will prompt the student in naturally-occurring situations to perform the skill?
2. What are the specific behaviors the student will perform?
3. How will the student's performance by measured in order to know that she has learned the skill?

Short term objectives should satisfy these critical features:
• The objectives are driven by the IEP goal.
• The objectives are observable and measurable and easily understood by everyone.
• The objectives result in ordinary and individually meaningful outcomes.

Double check objectives by asking:
1. Is the objective related to the IEP goal?
2. Is the objective clear, concise, easily understood, and written in everyday language?
3. Do the objectives represent a broad range of skills that can be taught within the context of the activity, rather than simply being a task analysis of the activity goal?
4. Do all of the objectives say clearly what the student, not the teacher, will do?
5. Do the objectives support the student's positive image and involvement with peers who do not have disabilities?

Create a document with the heading "Goals and Short Term Objectives" and make a list of annual goals for your child, along with appropriate objectives. Begin each goal with your child's name. Make sure the goals are doable, meaningful to your child, and relevant to your child's involvement and progress in the regular education environment. Don't forget to check them against the recommendations from The Schools Project.

While you're thinking about goals, review your "Strengths" document and connect the dots between your child's characteristics with goals in the regular educational environment. If you need to, go back and reread the examples in that section.

Related Services

Related services are what the school will do to ensure the child benefits from special education. These can include therapy, (physical, occupational, vision, hearing, speech and language, etc.), transportation, counseling services, assistive technology, interpreters, modifications, accommodations, and more.

IDEA (Section 300.347) says a student's IEP must include:

A statement of the special education and related services and supplementary aids and services to be provided to the child, or on behalf of the child, and a statement of the program modifications or supports for school personnel that will be provided for the child—

(i) to advance appropriately toward attaining the annual goals;

(ii) to be involved and progress in the general curriculum . . . and to participate in extracurricular and other nonacademic activities; and

(iii) to be educated and participate with other children with disabilities and nondisabled children.

There is no set formula for the delivery of related services; they are to be individualized to the child's needs and goals, so don't be limited by what the school typically does or does not provide. In addition, don't let your child's disability label dictate related services. Here are some examples of related services:

- A child who struggles with math (or who can't write with a pencil) may need a calculator. This could be considered an accommodation as well as a curriculum modification.

- A child who needs help with reading may need large print books, a reading buddy, and books on tape, or books and other reading material could be modified to his reading level.

- A student may need longer time for taking tests, shorter tests, or oral tests (instead of written).

- Students who use mobility devices may need the classroom rearranged to allow easy access.

- Children with behavior needs may need support from the classroom teacher, assistants, and classmates, as well as environmental accommodations, as described below:

  The classroom teacher can allow Billy to move around the room even though the other students are required to sit. Billy might not look like he's paying attention to the teacher, but he really is. In fact, if Billy was made to sit still, he would not be able to pay attention.

  In Janie's classroom, the regular ed teacher has a plan in place to support Janie when she gets frustrated and upset: without asking the teacher's permission and at any point in the day, Janie can take a book and curl up in the bean bag chair under the windows. If she wishes, she can carry the bean bag chair and her book to the library where it is quieter. Janie can return to her desk and rejoin the class whenever she's ready.

- Brailled materials may be needed by a student who is blind or has low vision; a sign language interpreter may be needed by a child who is deaf.

- Students may need assistance going to the bathroom, eating lunch, with medical care, or other personal needs.

- Children who are hard of hearing or easily distracted, as well as children with low vision may need to have their desks positioned close to the teacher.

- A student who cannot write, or one whose writing is illegible or time-consuming may need a computer or word processor.

- Augmentative communication devices or other types of communication aids may be needed by children who do not use oral communication.

Remember that, per IDEA, related services also include "program modifications or supports for school personnel that will be provided for the child." For example, assistance to the classroom teacher so she can make curriculum modifications is a related service.

Educators and parents often have great difficulty with the concept of curriculum modifications. Many educators believe if a child cannot do grade-level academics, he cannot be a regular classroom. Many parents are afraid to put their children in regular ed classrooms because they feel they can't handle the curriculum. But that's why we have curriculum modifications! Their purpose is to allow students with disabilities to be involved in and progress in the general curriculum. Before continuing with related services, in general, let's look specifically at curriculum modifications.

Because classroom teachers don't know our children, they need our help in figuring out what curriculum modifications are appropriate. But parents don't always know everything they need to know about the curriculum. The solution is for the parent, the teacher, the instructional assistant, and the special ed teacher (along with the student, when appropriate) to work together and *review the teacher's lesson plans.* This discussion could take place during informal monthly meetings of the team. When the lesson plans are reviewed in advance, educators have time to make the modifications.

Some teachers make the mistake of trying to modify curriculum on the spot, which doesn't work. One of Benjamin's teachers, for example, thought she could review each day's lesson plan before school every morning to figure out what Benjamin needed that day. But there just wasn't time to do this before class began.

When children aren't doing "grade level" work, parents and educators are often at a loss about curriculum modifications. For example, fourteen-year-old Jack, an entering freshman, performs math at a "second-grade level." How could he possibly do ninth-grade math? Is it possible to modify the curriculum to meet Jack's needs?

Let's assume Jack is enrolled in a "general math" class in ninth grade. Even though Jack's abilities at computation are considered to be at a second-grade level, he has a much greater familiarity with numbers and math concepts than typical second-graders! He's had seven more years of living experience: with spending money, helping his dad with home repairs (measuring), and so forth. Some of the math lessons would definitely be relevant to Jack and wouldn't need any modifying; other parts would. When the class is studying a math unit that Jack has little or no experience with, he and his teacher can decide whether to modify the lessons or have Jack do a different math activity that is relevant. Modifying curriculum isn't brain surgery. We just need to be creative and use common sense.

How parents handle the issue of curriculum modifications is important. I urge you to offer help to educators any way you can, including sending things from home, assisting with the modifications, and more. At the same time, be careful how you provide the help. If you suggest curriculum modifications that don't make sense to the teacher and/or if the teacher feels you're trying to "tell her how to teach," your efforts will backfire. The classroom teacher is the expert on curriculum; you're the expert on your child. Merge your expertise for an effective partnership.

Characteristics of Service

Describing the what, who, when, and where of related services is called characteristics of service. *What* are the related services? Therapy? Consultation? Curriculum modifications? Physical adaptations to a classroom? A modified desk? Adaptive PE? Assistive technology devices?

Who will provide services, instruction, modifications, adaptations? The classroom or special ed teacher, instructional assistant, therapist? *Where* will the delivery of services or modifications take place? In the regular classroom, in music, art, or PE? In the library/computer lab, at recess, or during lunch? *When* will they be delivered? *How often and for how long?* Think about what related services will (1) allow your child to be involved in and progress in the general curriculum and (2) help him reach his goals.

Related services can make the difference between a child's success and failure. During all the years Benj was included in regular ed classrooms in elementary school, he had only five or six goals each year. But the many related services he received proved to be the critical factor in his participation and progress in the curriculum.

Before writing your "Related Services" document, prepare a worksheet. Create three columns. In the left hand column, list your child's daily school schedule (travel to school, arrives at school, math, language, recess, and so forth). In the center column, list the related services he will need in that setting, and in the right column, describe the characteristics of service. After you have all the details in place, you can use that format or transfer the information to another page and write it in sentence or paragraph form, as in the following examples. Notice that all the sentences begin with what the school will do.

- The school will provide cooperative learning groups in the fourth grade classroom to enable Matt to learn teamwork and model appropriate behavior.
- The school will provide a physical therapist two times each week in Benjamin's regular ed PE class, to assist the PE teacher in modifying activities and to provide direct physical assistance to Benjamin when necessary.
- The school will ensure that Nicole's science lessons are modified for her reading level.
- The school will provide communication cards for Dylan to use in all areas of his school day (academics, lunch, recess, PE, music, art).
- The school will provide a computer and software, dedicated for Stephen's daily use in the classroom, for writing, math, and social studies.
- The school will provide a support person to assist Sasha when she needs to use the restroom.

MAKE THE BLUEPRINT A GROUP EFFORT

Many heads are better than one! You already know your child needs to write his own Blueprint or contribute to the one you are composing. But don't stop there. Letting others contribute to your child's IEP Blueprint will result in a better, more accurate report. Ask your friends, relatives, neighbors, and other adults who know your child to share their ideas. In addition, ask your other children, your children's friends, and students who have recently been in the grade level you looking into, for help. Children often have more insight into what's really important than adults!

Invite everyone to your home for a Blueprint Party. Review the information about the classrooms you want your child to attend and share some information about related services. Then ask everyone to share their opinions about your child's strengths, possible goals and objectives, and related services, and record them on flip chart paper. Don't worry that your helpers are not experts in special education. You want their expert opinions about your child, not special ed! If a Blueprint Party isn't your cup of tea, make blank forms of the documents you're writing and ask folks to write their own versions.

You'll be pleased by the insight, common sense, and creativity of others. After you've gathered their information, combine it all into one report. Eliminate any duplications or suggestions that aren't appropriate. Review it with your child and keep the ideas that are most important and most relevant to your child.

THE FINISHED BLUEPRINT

Hooray! You've done it! Give yourself a pat on the back and take a breather! You now have a completed IEP Blueprint which consists of three principal documents: (1) Present Level of Educational Performance (includes Educational Abilities, Strengths, Affect of the Disability papers), (2) Goals and Objectives, and (3) Related Services. You can put it aside for awhile, but keep it handy in case you want to add things before the IEP meeting.

Before your pre-IEP meetings (described shortly), make a cover sheet with your child's name, your name, and the date. Then make a copy of the report for each member of the IEP team. If you're so inclined, copy it onto light blue paper (it *is* a blueprint!), put it in a folder, put your child's photo on the cover sheet, or do anything else that will turn your IEP Blueprint into a professional, polished format. And be very proud of your efforts!

COMPOSING THE IEP TEAM

In most schools, parents have little or no influence regarding which educators will be on the IEP team. Typically, a special ed teacher, coordinator, or case manager (the meeting planner) takes care of this as she plans the IEP meeting. Some school districts have a set formula of who is on the team: parents; special ed teacher; principal; therapists; special ed coordinator, supervisor, or director; school social worker or psychologist; and so forth. Many parents have reported they didn't know half the people at the meeting and didn't know why they were there! In our new way of doing things, you'll assume an active role in composing the IEP team. IDEA says the IEP team is composed of:

The parents, guardians, or surrogate parents of the child;

At least one regular education teacher of such child (if the child is, or may be, participating in the regular education environment);

At least one special education teacher;

A representative of the school or district who
—is qualified to provide, or supervise the provision of, specially designed instruction to meet the unique needs of children with disabilities;
—is knowledgeable about the general curriculum; and
—is knowledgeable about the availability of resources of the school or district;

An individual who can interpret the instructional implications of evaluations results, who may be a member of the team as described above;

At the discretion of the parent or the school or district, other individuals who have knowledge or special expertise regarding the child, including related services personnel as appropriate; and

Whenever appropriate, the child with a disability.

Experience tells us the best, most productive IEP meetings include the fewest number of people. This is a new concept for some parents. In many cases, every professional who has even the remotest connection to the student attends the IEP meeting. Parents often bring advocates with them. Before long, the meeting is moved to a larger room to accommodate the crowd. Some parents boast about the large number of educators in attendance, as if this indicates their power or importance. But very little in the way of writing an effective IEP will be accomplished. Instead, muscles will be flexed and egos will vie for power. Even when parents are on good terms with educators, the IEP team can be large and ineffective if it includes every person who has done an assessment or has something to contribute (therapists, diagnostician, social workers, and others).

The number of people at the meeting directly correlates to how much is accomplished. This is a case where less is more!

Educators on the IEP team should be those who are—or will be—intimately involved in your child's education and/or those who have valuable knowledge about your child, relevant to his participation in the general educational environment. In many cases, these will be one and the same. Hopefully, people who already know your child, or those who will be closely involved in his school day, will be the people you'll use in informal assessments (special ed teacher, regular ed teacher, and so forth). In this case, they will be valued members of the IEP team because they represent two different roles: as testers of your child's abilities and as educators who will work with your child on a daily basis. Their dual role will cut down on the number of professionals on the IEP team, since they will take the place of people who only do assessments.

Professionals who will not be directly involved in your child's education do not need to be on the IEP team. If, for example, you decide against hands-on physical therapy for your child, there's no reason for a PT assessment and, therefore, no reason for the therapist to be on the IEP team. However, if you want consult services from the PT, you may want her at the IEP meeting to coordinate her role with other school personnel. On the other hand, instead of her attending the IEP meeting, you, the PT, and your child's teacher could meet informally at a later date.

In some schools, the district psychologist or social worker may routinely be involved in every IEP in the district. The presence of these professionals (and the assessments they may perform) can often create dilemmas that weren't there before. In several districts I'm very familiar with, the district psychologist injects psycho-babble into the IEP process that often leaves parents, and some educators, reeling. Out of nowhere comes concerns about the child's (or the parents'!) mental health and more. Similarly, social workers frequently bring up issues that weren't previously mentioned, and which border on "socio-babble." Just be aware of this and act accordingly: if you don't need these folks there, don't have them!

Once you have a firm idea of who you want on the team, talk with the meeting planner to discuss the issue. How you handle this depends on your relationship with her. If things are going well, tell her you simply want to keep the team small to ensure the best outcomes:

more will get done, a better IEP will be written, and so forth. On the other hand, if your relationship is still a difficult one, you'll need to use a great deal of finesse and diplomacy.

Under any circumstance, politely reject efforts to make the IEP meeting into a world summit. If a variety of people (school psychologist, social worker, special ed director, district administrators, etc.) routinely attend every IEP meeting in the school district, kindly tell the meeting planner, "I know Dr. Curtis and Mrs. Tanner usually attend all IEP meetings, but they really don't need to attend my daughter's next meeting. I appreciate their interest, but these folks are so busy. Can you let them know they don't need to be there?"

If this doesn't work, call each person yourself and say, "I really appreciate your interest in my child's education and I know how valuable your time is. Instead of taking time out of your busy schedule for the meeting, I thought you and I could just chat on the phone about any concerns you have or contributions you want to make." Most busy people will thank you giving them "permission" to attend one less IEP meeting. They don't like them anymore than parents do! If, however, any of these folks are your supporters or allies, you *do* want them at the meeting.

Many IEP teams routinely include the educators prescribed in IDEA, with the exception of the regular ed teacher. Even when a child is in a resource room for most of the day, with visitation to regular ed art, PE, or music, those teachers are not usually invited to the IEP meeting, even though the law is clear that a regular ed teacher should be on the team if a child will be in regular ed classes! It seems educators choose to ignore this requirement because they don't expect regular ed teachers to take responsibility for students with disabilities; these students are thought to "belong" to the special ed department. Unless a child is already attending an inclusive school or—in a non-inclusive school—unless parents have been successful in influencing educators to try an inclusive placement, a regular education teacher is usually not present at IEP meetings. This will change.

During your visits to classrooms, you will have identified which teachers you want for your child. During pre-IEP meetings with members of the team (described next), you'll attempt to cement placement before the IEP meeting so you'll know which regular ed teacher(s) should be on the team and at the meeting.

Visualize an IEP meeting that includes you, your child (more about this in a moment), a very few family members or friends who can significantly contribute (a brother or sister, people who know your child well, and/or influential parents who bring common sense to the proceedings), the regular ed teacher, the instructional assistant (if one has been identified), the special ed teacher, the principal, and, if absolutely necessary, a very small number of professionals. If your child has a friend who will be in the regular ed class you want, make sure this child is at the meeting. He can provide invaluable wisdom!

If you're on good terms with the school and placement in a regular education classroom has already been decided, you probably won't need any allies at the meeting; the team could be composed of you, your child, his teachers, and the principal. An intimate, caring group of people can move mountains.

PRE-IEP MEETINGS

Two or more weeks before the official IEP meeting, it's time for individual pre-IEP meetings with everyone on the IEP team. The purpose of these meetings is to do the majority of the work that's usually done at the IEP meeting. Your mission is to achieve consensus with individual team members ahead of time so that, at the official meeting, everyone simply signs off on what's already been decided. Use your own good judgment on whether to convey this purpose to the individual team members. Some educators will be thrilled that you're thinking ahead and taking care of so many details. Others may want to hang on to the old ways of doing things. Again, use your best judgment!

When you're ready, pick up the phone and call, for example, the special ed teacher: "Hi, Sally, this is Joan Myers, Leah's mom. I'm so excited about the IEP meeting that's coming up next month. My family and I, including Leah, have done some work to prepare and I'd like to review it with you and get your opinions. Can you and I get together the day after tomorrow to talk?" If your child wants to attend these individual meetings and/or if your child's presence will positively impact the outcome of the meetings, have her attend and let her contribute as much as possible. There's no better way to demonstrate her competency!

At or just before these meetings, give a copy of your IEP Blueprint to each person, then review it together during the meeting. If a personal meeting is not possible, mail or hand deliver a copy of the Blueprint to the person and have a telephone meeting.

These pre-IEP meetings are critically important to creating an atmosphere of trust and teamwork at the actual IEP meeting. Team members spend more time in conflict over issues than cooperatively writing an effective IEP. Your individual meetings can eliminate this. The goals of these pre-IEP meetings include educating team members, learning from them, moving beyond personal differences, negotiating and compromising, and finding common ground.

As you share your child's IEP Blueprint, you'll be making the case for your child's regular ed placement, while removing the barriers you previously faced. In essence, you'll be "proving" how your child can be successful in a regular classroom. Unlike a typical IEP meeting where one parent unsuccessfully argues with a multitude of professionals, these pre-IEP meetings will enable you to meet one-on-one with folks to calmly and positively discuss the issues.

You want to describe what your child's placement will look like: "In the fourth grade classroom—" or "In the tenth grade math class—". Then you want to get feedback from the team member. Solicit her ideas, talk some more, and negotiate until an agreement is reached.

After you've met with all the different team members individually, revise your IEP Blueprint to reflect the changes that have been negotiated and agreed upon. Later, you'll make copies of the revised Blueprint and distribute to team members during the official IEP meeting. In the best case scenario, your IEP Blueprint will be the foundation of the official IEP.

WHEN TO MENTION THE LAW

Hopefully, you'll never need to mention the law during the IEP process. But there may be times when you need to educate educators about specifics in the law. Depending on your individual circumstances, you may need to bring up the law during informal assessments, in your pre-IEP meetings, or at the official IEP meeting. Vow to invoke the words in the law only as a last resort!

The *way* you present the information will make the difference in whether educators listen to you or tune you out. Never do we want to beat people over the heads with "what the law says." If your approach is heavy-handed, educators will not be awed into submission by your incredible knowledge or your subtle intimidation! Instead, they'll probably feel threatened and then angry, and will dig their heels in to maintain the status quo.

Bring up the law in a manner which appeals to an educator's highest moral sense. Your demeanor will reflect surprise—not anger—that the educator wasn't aware of the spirit and intent of the law, and you'll demonstrate a genuine interest in "doing the right thing." Here's a scenario to illustrate one way to handle a sticky situation.

Educator: I noticed these goals you wrote talk about Jon being in regular classes.

Parent: Yes, that's right. [That's all you say for now, and do it with a smile; don't do any explaining at this point. Wait to see what he says next.]

Educator: Well, I just don't know about this. Jon is in the MR program is at Kimball Elementary, so these goals aren't appropriate for him. He's not at a fourth grade level.

Parent [with a pleasant smile and an excited tone of voice]: Oh, you're absolutely right! These goals are not appropriate for a student in a resource room. I was simply trying to do the right thing according to the law. Let's see—[begin digging through your purse], I think I have it right here—[pull out a wadded up piece of paper that has the regulations about placement and goals] Yes, here it is. Sorry it's all wrinkled; I've been carrying it around and studying it every chance I get. Let me smooth it out. Okay, right here it says . . . [read the appropriate part(s)]

So, that's what I did. I wrote goals for Jon about how he could be involved in and progress in the general educational environment! I'm sure glad I learned about this! It's really important to do things right. You know, I wouldn't want us all to get in trouble by not doing what's in the law.

Modify this response to fit your circumstances. For example, if you need to bring up the law when discussing informal assessments, mention how IDEA states assessments should gather "information related to enabling the child to be involved in and progress in the general curriculum."

Your response needs to reflect excitement about what's in the law. The friendly tone of your voice projects your desire to have a benevolent conspiracy with educators to do the right thing. Invoke the words of the law to bind people together for a common cause, instead of using them as a battering ram.

Appeal to people's sense of right and wrong as human beings, instead of trying to argue bureaucratic policy. Remember, this is all about your child and doing whatever it takes to help him succeed. Instead of ranting and raving, use finesse and diplomacy—and yes, a little "acting"—to bring out the best in others.

CHANGE THE MEETING; CHANGE THE OUTCOME

Your IEP Blueprint will have a significant impact on the IEP meeting, but you can also impact the outcome by changing the dynamics of the meeting.

This is another area for which you'll need to talk with the meeting planner before the meeting has been set. Your approach should be friendly and non-threatening. Say something like, "I've been thinking about ways to make the IEP meeting more [enjoyable, productive, etc.]. I'd like to share my ideas with you." Then describe your plans regarding the time and location of the meeting using the following ideas as a foundation. Don't share all the details of your new way of doing things. Share only those items the meeting planner usually takes responsibility for. See yourself as the "unofficial" meeting planner or even the "party planner," because that's basically what you're planning: a party!

Location

IEP meetings are typically held in a conference room, the principal's office, or in some other "official" room. This often puts parents at a disadvantage since they're "visitors" to the educators' turf. Suggest a more neutral and informal setting: the cafeteria, the gym, the teachers' lounge, or the library. In nice weather, have the meeting on a grassy spot on the playground or the athletic field. If it's already been decided your child will be in a regular classroom, have the meeting in that classroom. It brings everyone closer to the reality of the next school year, making it easier to discuss accommodations, adaptations, and more.

In the best case scenario, have the meeting in your home. Yes, in your home, with all your family present, where educators can get to know your child and your family! My best friend, Charmaine, had several of her son's IEP meetings in her home. The IEP team loved it, and it gave Charmaine a good reason to thoroughly clean her house once a year—and I helped! And people on the team saw a totally different side of her son when he was on his home turf. If you don't have the meeting in your home, invite your child's teacher(s) for a visit to your home before the school year starts. It's important for the teacher to see your child in his natural environment.

When is the meeting?

If the school routinely schedules IEP meetings at the end of the school year, request a meeting at an "off-time." Instead of May, try late April. You may want to shift your child's meeting to August, a week or two before school starts. I always had Benjamin's meetings right before school started in September instead of in May. Kids change over the summer; I wanted Benj's IEP to reflect his current abilities and needs.

Regarding the time of the meeting, request the first time slot of the day or the first one after lunch. This way, you won't be caught in a schedule that runs later and later as the day wears on. If your pre-IEP meetings have gone well, a one hour meeting will allow plenty of time to write the official IEP based on your IEP Blueprint.

If you're having the meeting in your home, schedule it in the late afternoon, if possible, and serve a snack supper. Folks can end their work day on a positive note and head home after the meeting.

Who will be there?

In a previous section, I reviewed who needs to be on the IEP team. A few days prior to the IEP meeting, talk with the official meeting planner to double check who's been invited to attend. If you discover someone has been added without your knowledge, get busy finding out the who and the why, and do whatever it takes to ensure only those individuals who can truly contribute are at the meeting. If necessary, make those phone calls giving people "permission" to skip the meeting!

The most important person at the IEP meeting is your child. When your child is at her IEP meeting, the entire atmosphere is different. No one can talk about her; everyone must talk to her and include her in the discussion. When our children aren't present, they're abstract entities who are viewed in terms of their disabilities, assessment results, or perceived deficits. When your child is sitting among educators, her humanity takes precedence over her disability.

Only you and your child can decide the extent of her contribution and participation, but always strive for the most, not the least. Students—especially those in the upper elementary, middle school, or high school grades—can and should run the meeting to the best of their abilities. They're big enough to speak for themselves and provide leadership in ways that are right for them.

A young child may get ants in her pants and be unable to stay focused during the entire meeting. In this case, have her participate in whatever part of the meeting you and your child believe is best. It might be better for her to participate at the beginning of the meeting so she can describe her strengths. Or her participation might be more important when the goals are being finalized. After all, they're her goals, right? If your child *can* attend the entire meeting, so much the better. Take some books or toys to keep her busy during the "boring" parts. Include her as much as possible, by asking her questions, getting her opinions, and so forth.

Imagine how very different an IEP meeting would look with your child present. Some parents are horrified at the thought, believing their children would be traumatized by the words and behaviors of educators. But parents who have included their children in IEP meetings tell a different story. They were amazed by the change in educators! And by supporting your child to lead and/or take part in her own meeting, you're sending a very clear and powerful message that you respect her and others should respect her, too.

I've explained why the IEP team needs to be small in order to be successful. However, there's a partial exception to this rule. Benj's first grade year was going to be very different than kindergarten. During half-day kindergarten, he and his class went to the library once a week for a very brief time and the teacher stayed with them the whole time. They went to gym once a week for thirty minutes of pure fun. But in first grade, the classroom teacher escorted her students to the library, gym, art class, and music room, where she turned them over to other educators. The students needed to become accustomed to these different adults, and to the cafeteria ladies and other faculty members they saw throughout the day.

I was concerned that all these folks didn't know Benj and didn't know about his wheelchair and walker. It was important for them to learn about Benjamin so they could successfully take responsibility for him, just as they would his classmates. I didn't want the teacher's aide to have to follow Benj all over the school unless he really needed her.

To remedy this, I invited all of these people to join us for the first ten to fifteen minutes of the IEP meeting. (It was held the week before school started, so all staff members were in the building every day.) I introduced Benjamin and he demonstrated how his walker and wheelchair worked. I showed them how to help him transfer between the two, as well as how to help him transfer into a regular desk chair. They asked questions, which (with my help, sometimes) Benjamin answered. It was important for them to learn to deal directly with Benj. After their questions were answered, we thanked them for coming and they left.

I must digress and explain the full story. When I contacted the music teacher about coming to the IEP meeting, he said he was too busy and added, "I don't really need to know all this stuff because the teacher's aide will handle it all."

"Yes," I responded, "but I believe it's important for *you* to know all about Benjamin, too." He repeated that he was too busy. Persisting, I said, "If you can't make the IEP meeting, could Benj and I visit your classroom to go over everything sometime before the first day of school?" He declined, repeating he was too busy.

"I understand, Mr. L," I responded. "But it's very important that you and Benjamin know each other before he comes to music class so you both start off on the right foot. There are things you need to know about him and vice-versa. By not going over these things ahead of time, there may be misunderstandings or confusion. So here's what we'll do. Once school starts, I'll ask the classroom teacher to keep Benj with her during music. When you find time for a short meeting with Benj and me, let me know. After we've had the meeting, Benj can come to music with his classmates."

Hiding my frustration, I politely thanked him for his time and ended the call. I wasn't happy about the situation, but I was determined to help ensure a positive beginning for my son and the music teacher.

I knew things only a mother would know and Mr. L needed to know these things, too. For example, from my daughter's experience in Mr. L's class, I knew the children sat on little benches, not at desks. First graders could sit three to a bench. I knew Benj would want to sit on a bench instead of in his wheelchair. For this to happen, someone would need to transfer Benj; he would need to sit in the middle of a bench so kids on each side of him could provide some support (I knew he'd have a death-like grip on the legs of each of these kids); and he would need to sit on a piece of non-slip fabric since the benches were finished with glossy, slick paint.

Imagine my shock when the very next day, Mr. L called! He apologized for his abruptness during our previous conversation. He still couldn't attend the IEP meeting, but said he could meet with us for a few minutes in his classroom.

Two days later, Benj and I went to the music room, accompanied by his wheelchair, walker, and a piece of non-slip fabric. We spent a few moments exploring the room. Then Benj and I began talking to Mr. L about the benches, transferring, and so forth, and I presented him the non-slip fabric to keep in the music room.

To my dismay, Mr. L was too busy to give us his full attention! While Benj and I tried to tell him things, Mr. L dug through his desk, arranged papers, and grunted occasionally. When we finished going over everything, he thanked us and said everything would be fine since the teacher's aide would always be in class. Grrr! I was really irritated, but I maintained my composure, stayed polite, and thanked him for his time. I resolved to stay on top of things.

About three weeks into the school year, I was once again shocked and surprised by Mr. L's behavior. After picking the kids up from school one day, Benjamin began singing, "Deedle-deedle dumpling, my son, John, one shoe off and one shoe on . . ."

"Is that a new song you learned in music today?" I asked. He grunted in assent and continued singing. When he finished the song, he excitedly told me how everyone in class sang the song and marched around the room with one shoe off and one shoe on. I found it hard to believe he had done this. At the time, Benj was wearing toe separators, socks, leg braces, and high-top, lace-up athletic shoes. I frequently reminded the PE teacher and others to never take his shoes or braces off because they'd probably never get them back on the right way!

I was curious about what really happened. You know how after-school conversations usually go: mom asks questions, kid answers in monosyllables or grunts. Here's how this one went:

Me: So all the kids were marching around with one shoe off and one shoe on?

Benj: Yes!

Me: What were you doing?

Benj: Marching, marching!!!

Me: You were marching with one shoe off and one shoe on? [I'm assuming the teacher's aide pushed him in his chair.]

Benj: Yes! Marching! [He started singing the song again.]

Me: Did you have one shoe off and one shoe on?

Benj: Yes! Everyone did! [He's still singing and is very impatient with my interruptions.]

Me: Did Mrs. B [the teacher's aide] take your shoe and brace off one foot?

Benj: No! [Still singing.]

Me: I'm sorry, Benj. I just don't understand. Did Mrs. B take your shoe off and push you around in your chair? [I knew he couldn't walk in his walker with one foot bare.]

Benj: No, Mom! Mr. L did it!

Me: Mr. L? What did he do? [I'm trying not to sound shocked.]

Benj: [By now he's exasperated with me and my apparent stupidity. He begins explaining it to me.] Mr. L said we should all march around the room with one shoe on and one shoe off while we sang the song. So Mr. L took mine off and he helped me march in the line! See?

Me: [Withholding my extreme shock, surprise, and joy, I stayed calm.] Oh, I see. And did he put your toe separator, sock, brace, and shoe back on or did Mrs. B?

Benj: No, Mr. L did it. Mrs. B wasn't there.

Me: Wow! That's really cool. I'll bet it was fun, wasn't it? [I was thrilled, but wondered why the teacher's aide wasn't there.]

Benj: Yep. [He went back to singing.]

The next day, I couldn't resist stopping by Mr. L's class on my way to pick Benj up after school. Although I felt like doing it, I did not run up to him, hug and kiss him, and yell, "Thank you, thank you for including my child!" Instead, I stuck my head in the door and casually said, "Benj said he really had fun learning that new song and marching around the class yesterday." "Yeah," Mr. L replied, "we had a great time! I wanted Benj to do what the other kids were doing, so I held him under the arms and marched him around in the line. It worked out great!"

"I'm glad everything went well," I said. "Was Mrs. B out sick yesterday?" His answer did more than touch my heart; it demonstrated that every human has the capacity to change and go beyond their perceived limitations. "Oh, Mrs. B was at school, but she wasn't in class with us. About a week ago I told her I didn't need her anymore!" he proudly announced. "I told her she could take a long coffee break instead of coming to class with Benj. I know what do to—I can handle everything!" I couldn't resist the urge any longer; I gave him a big hug and thanked him for all his good work.

This was the man who was too busy to meet with us, then too busy to pay attention; the man who wanted Benj to be the TA's responsibility, not his. But he showed me how—when you least expect it—people can and do change. Educators who are afraid of our children, those who may be fearful or resentful of additional responsibilities, and those who appear to be callous and uncaring, can evolve right before our eyes. They do not change because of the law or because they're forced to by angry parents. Instead, their hearts are changed by by our children.

At one time, my best friend, Charmaine, and I believed what many parents and educators still believe: that inclusion isn't possible until educators have been trained or until they are "ready" for it. But experience has shown that educators are "ready" for inclusion just the way they are, just as children with disabilities are "ready" for inclusion just the way they are! Few of us ever know what we're ready for until we try something new!

Now, back to the subject of having extra folks at the IEP meeting. If your child will be moving from a segregated, resource room to a regular ed class, or if he'll be interacting with a whole new set of people who are unfamiliar with him (and vice-versa), invite these folks to join the IEP meeting for a few minutes at the beginning. Alternatively, you and your child could have a separate meeting with this group or have brief individual meetings, prior to school starting.

Think about everyone in the school who may interact with your child: cafeteria ladies, librarians, computer experts, custodians, secretaries, nurses, specialty teachers (art, music, PE, etc.), coaches, and many others. They can all contribute to your child's success. In our case, the custodian became an important ally. She made an easel for Benj, and educators frequently called on her to tighten the screws on Benj's wheelchair, and for other important duties. In hindsight, I should have invited her to the meeting as well.

There was an unexpected benefit to Benjamin meeting people ahead of time. When school started, his classmates were impressed that Benj already knew all these people. He looked really important!

Positions

How people are positioned—physically and psychologically—can make a big difference in the dynamics of the IEP meeting. Create an environment that promotes real teamwork, equality, and friendship.

Be the first one to arrive at the meeting. This puts you in the position to welcome all the other team members. Greet each person warmly, shake hands or give hugs, and thank each one for coming. Encourage your child, your spouse, or anyone else who came with you to do the same. Even if the meeting is on the school's turf, welcoming team members as they arrive positions you as the host.

Don't sit at a table. It's a physical and psychological barrier. Sit in a circle so no one is at the "head of the table." You and your supporters (spouse, friends, etc.) should not sit next to one another as a group. This promotes the "us vs. them" mentality. Mix everyone up. Before all the educators arrive, arrange the meeting space the way you want: move chairs into a circle, have your supporters "save" their seats so educators are on either side of them.

You and your child should sit next to the most influential educator. This person may or may not be the highest-ranked professional. If the special ed teacher wields more influence than the principal, have her sit next to you. You may not know who the power broker is right now, but you will after you've had all your pre-IEP meetings.

Name Tags

People attending the IEP meeting don't always know each other. Be prepared for this by bringing stick-on name tags and a marker. As folks arrive, make each person a name tag using first and last names—and no titles! In a friendly, personal, and helpful manner, peel off the backing and stick it on each person's shoulder yourself. While you're up close and personal, give a pat on the shoulder or a big hug. Better yet, have your child put each person's name tag on. The physical closeness adds a dimension of warmth and familiarity. If you're so inclined, make the name tags ahead of time and decorate them in bright colors and simple artwork; set the stage for fun.

Food and Fun!

There's nothing like sharing food to create an atmosphere of fellowship and fun. If the IEP meeting is scheduled in the morning, bring fruit, bagels, and/or pastries. A pizza delivered for a mid-day meeting will put everyone in a happy mood, and cheese and crackers will lift everyone's spirits in the afternoon. If your relationships with others on the IEP team are friendly, ask one or more of them to bring some goodies. Otherwise, spring for the munchies on your own. Coffee is usually available from the teachers' lounge at school, but you may want to bring soda pop, ice, and a few plastic cups, along with napkins and paper plates. Can you imagine the surprise and delight of educators when they walk into an IEP meeting and are greeted with tummy-pleasing snacks? They'll actually look forward to your child's IEP meetings! One mom recently shared the experience that as educators entered the meeting room and smelled her freshly-baked banana bread, the atmosphere of the meeting was totally different than any previous meetings. The educators were delighted to be there!

A Positive Beginning

Ultimately, your child is in charge of the meeting—it's his IEP, his education—and you are second in command. (Remember, though, to lead not by overt power, but by easy-going strength.) Because you and your child are the informal leaders of the meeting, not only can you begin the meeting, but you can start things off with optimism.

Once everyone is present and seated, let your child say some opening remarks. Even a "Thanks for coming!" accompanied by a big grin is a powerful message.

Then you can add something like, "I want to thank everyone for coming today. I know you're all very busy, so I appreciate the time and effort you're investing in Janie and her future. To make this meeting as beneficial as possible for Janie and everyone else present, I hope we can do things a little differently. Let's all speak plain English, instead of jargon so we can all understand better. Also, since this is Janie's meeting, we'll need to make sure she participates and contributes. She'll start the meeting by telling you her dreams and then I'll share our family dreams for Janie."

At this point, your child takes center stage to say what's most important to her. Obviously, the two of you will have talked about this ahead of time. She might describe what she wants to be when she grows up, how she wants to have friends, what she wants to learn, and/or anything else! This is her moment to shine.

When she's finished, present your long-term, big dreams. Too often, we focus on short term solutions which fragment the whole child into body parts, perceived deficits, and specific needs. Members of the IEP team need a clear view of the big picture.

One of my statements to team members was: "Our dreams for Benjamin are the same dreams we have for Emily. We want him to go on to college or other training to help him get the job he wants. We expect him to move away from home when he's a young man and live on his own with whatever natural supports he needs. We expect him to have friends, get married, have kids, be involved in his community, and take care of us when we're old!"

Contrast that big dream for Benjamin with this puny one (read with a whiney voice): "We hope Benjamin will walk within the next year, that he'll learn to go to the bathroom by himself, and that he'll be able to write his name with a pencil."

Think big, think long-term, and share your vision. People will see your child through different eyes once they have the big picture.

After you've finished describing your family dreams, continue with, "Before we get started with official business, would everyone take a turn and share something wonderful about Janie? We're always interested in hearing great things we might not be aware of. I'll start and we'll each take turns. If you can't think of something right off the bat, we'll come back to you."

Set the example by sharing something wonderful about your child. Don't limit yourself to describing a functional skill; think about a hobby your child is interested in, a dream she wants to pursue, something funny or exciting she did or said, or anything else to demonstrate your child's gifts or talents. Then go around the table and let others share their wonderful opinions about your child.

There are other ways to start the meeting on a positive note. Charmaine always took a gift box to her son's IEP meetings. She wrapped a shoe box and its lid, separately, with beautiful shiny paper and put a big bow on the lid. Inside the box she had placed note cards, and on each, she had written one positive characteristic or interesting fact about Dylan. During her welcome, Charmaine passed the box around and each team member took the lid off, removed a card, and read it to the whole group. People learned a great deal about Dylan this way.

Anything you do to lay a foundation for positive, personal interactions will pay big dividends. Use humor and a light touch to put people at ease. After your opening statements, pass out your IEP Blueprint and begin discussing your child's bright future!

The Progression of the Meeting

How the meeting actually progresses is dependent on many factors. If your pre-IEP meetings have been successful, you may be able to review the IEP Blueprint with the team, make any revisions, transfer it (or attach it) to the official IEP forms and you're done!

If your pre-IEP meetings haven't gone as well as you hoped, that's okay. During the meeting, regularly refer to your Blueprint during the different discussions (Present Level, Goals, Related Services, etc.). Lead the meeting yourself, if you feel comfortable doing so. Or co-lead it with the special ed or classroom teacher. You don't need to ask permission to do this; just gently take the reins: "Okay, let's get started. First is the . . ."

Negotiate, Compromise, and Focus

The goal of your pre-IEP meetings is to iron out all the wrinkles ahead of time and achieve consensus on your plans. The official IEP meeting is then a formality. However, you still need to be prepared for the unexpected. An issue that's already been resolved between you and one or more team members may unravel prior to or during the formal meeting.

Think of yourself as a trial lawyer. During a trial, lawyers never ask questions they don't already know the answers to. The IEP meeting should proceed the same way: you don't want any surprises! Try to anticipate any issues that may come up. Be prepared to negotiate. Ask many questions for clarification. Don't let your bridge-building fall apart over one issue. Compromise in the short-run to ensure long-term success.

If the IEP team doesn't initially agree on the regular ed placement you hoped for, don't give up and don't get mad. Utilize the "what would it take" approach. "If Gloria can't be in Mrs. Johnson's class all day, what would it take for her to be there for half the day?" Keep asking questions and offering alternatives. As difficult as it may be, don't lose your temper. Also, don't feel all your hard work has been wasted. It hasn't; some nuts are just harder to crack than others. Persevere.

Be ready to let go of one or more "wants." This makes you seem reasonable which, in turn, makes educators more willing to be reasonable. Go to the meeting knowing you'll be satisfied if the overall outcome is "what you can live with." This is the basis of consensus building: it's not that we all get everything we want, it's that we can "live with" the agreed-upon outcomes.

Remember, the IEP is not written in stone. If necessary, you can agree with something even if you're not 100 percent satisfied with it, knowing you can call another IEP meeting (or even make informal changes without an IEP meeting) in a month or two. Parents often go into the meeting as if they're negotiating some type of permanent solution, and they're determined to get everything perfect. In the end, however, they often make enemies and may lose more than they gain. Don't see the IEP as a permanent, inflexible document. Think of it as a work in progress that can be changed!

Be positive. Don't talk about the past and what the school has or hasn't done. What's done is done; let go of the past and stay focused on the future. If your opinions are ignored or dismissed, be a broken record and repeat yourself in a polite tone. Don't argue their points; that gets you off your points. Don't get suckered in to any argument, whether it's about you, your child, the school, or anything else. You're not there to argue; you're there to educate others and impact your child's future.

If you, or anyone else at the meeting loses control, take a five minute break, have everyone stand up and breathe deeply, or do anything else to halt the breakdown in communications. Then start again. Maintain your leadership by positive example.

If the IEP meeting doesn't go as well as you hoped, don't despair and don't make enemies. People can and do change. Resolve to do whatever it takes to successfully interact with educators who have "challenging behaviors."

Maintain your dignity and good manners in the face of disappointment. Share this disappointment if you wish ("I'm disappointed that—"), but don't let frustration degenerate into angry words you can't take back. If you didn't get the placement you hoped for, put things in their proper perspective: your child is not facing the guillotine, nor will he be permanently scarred by the situation; he's just not where you want him to be right now. Continue building relationships. You know more now than you did before the IEP meeting. Take what you've learned and keep going. As hard as things may seem, know your efforts are more valuable than precious gems. Your child's future is in your hands.

Schedule Monthly Meetings

At the end of the IEP meeting, when you're thanking everyone profusely for all their good works, suggest the following: "The best way we can ensure my child's success is to stay in touch. Why don't we schedule informal monthly meetings with [the classroom teacher, instructional assistant, and others who work with your child every day] to stay on top of things. We can set the times and dates before we leave today. How about the first Monday of each month, for no more than one hour after school. Would that work for everyone or is there a more convenient time?"

Try to get this out all in one breath. If you simply ask if people want to have monthly meetings, some might say no. Assume they'll want to, and give them the option of when, not if. Not all team members need to attend these monthly meetings; for instance, you probably don't need the principal there. Limit the attendance to a very small group of people who work with your child on a daily basis.

In our case, monthly meetings to stay on top of Benj's education included me, the classroom teacher, the instructional assistant, and the special ed teacher. Sometimes Benjamin was there, depending on what issues we were planning to discuss. Occasionally, the PT and/or the OT were there on a "consult" basis. We agreed on the one hour limit, and sometimes we were through in fifteen minutes. Other times, we had much to cover, so we talked fast, prioritized the issues, and kept the chit-chat to a minimum. Someone always brought snacks and we enjoyed friendly, productive meetings.

Mark your calendar with the dates of the informal, monthly meetings you've proposed. Stay in close contact with those who will be at these meetings and call them a few days ahead of time to make sure everyone remembers the date. Arrive early with goodies to munch on. Make these meetings fun. Ask everyone how things are going and work proactively to solve any issues. If everything's going well, share the food and chit-chat for a few moments, then everyone can leave the meeting early! If there are many issues to discuss at a particular meeting, prioritize them to ensure the most important ones are covered first. Keep the meeting going at a fast clip and don't let it run long.

If these monthly meetings become lengthy and contentious, you'll lose the support of the other team members. It's better to end each meeting on time and call an additional short meeting if necessary. The purpose of these meetings is not to rewrite the IEP each month, but to resolve small issues before they become big issues.

Staying in Touch

After the IEP meeting, write thank you notes to everyone who attended, taking care to be especially courteous to anyone you like the *least*. Keep the lines of communication open and continue to demonstrate leadership. Have your child write thank you notes also. Let him include a picture he drew or something equally wonderful, such as a photo of himself. Kill 'em with kindness!

While you're marking your calendar for the monthly meetings, mark some dates for sending notes to educators. Once a month, for no particular reason, send a note card with a warm message to your child's teacher, the principal, and others at school. Fertilize and water those blossoming partnerships!

There are other ways to stay in touch with your child's teachers. Some parents and teachers send a spiral notebook back and forth to school each day. Parents often like this, but this method is often difficult for teachers. We did this when Benj was in first grade. Sometimes the classroom teacher, the instructional assistant, and the special ed teacher all wrote something the same day. But the next day, there would be nothing. I didn't know whether they forgot to write or if they had nothing to report.

When I sat down with Benj's teacher one day, she apologized and said she sometimes just didn't have the time. From volunteering in her class, I knew she was truthful. She said when important things came up she always took the time to write, but if it was a routine day, the notebook slipped her mind. If you think the traveling notebook might be a good solution, don't expect your child's teacher to write a lengthy report every day. Instead, propose that she write only when she needs your help with problem-solving and when she wants to share something wonderful! I used the notebook to give teachers a heads-up on unusual situations. For example, if Benj didn't sleep well or if other things occurred that could impact his school day, I wrote those in the notebook.

And there are still other ways to stay in touch. If possible, take your child to and from school every day. When the afternoon bell rings, be waiting outside the classroom to greet your child. Benj's teachers and I resolved many issues in the space of five minutes at 3:45 PM. Volunteer in the classroom. Meet the teacher for lunch every week or two, or arrange for a fifteen minute phone call every Friday afternoon. Do whatever it takes to maintain a close personal relationship. Your child will be the winner!

IEP BLUEPRINT RECAP

1. Visit regular ed classrooms
2. Plan informal assessments
3. Write the IEP Blueprint
4. Identify the IEP team
5. Have pre-IEP meetings
6. Revise IEP Blueprint
7. Plan the IEP meeting
8. Host the IEP meeting
9. Stay in touch with educators
10. Enjoy your success!

CREATIVE SUPPORTS: ADDITIONS TO THE IEP PROCESS

In addition to the formal IEP process, we can use other methods to ensure our children are included and supported. But how these supports are identified and used is critically important.

Beyond the Circle of Friends

The Circle of Friends concept is a way of identifying classmates who can provide friendship and assistance to a child with a disability. However, many thoughtful people, including adults with disabilities, have questioned the value of this method.

Here's one example of how this concept is put into practice. A teacher in an inclusive classroom talks to the class about how the students can help a classmate with a disability. She asks for volunteers to form a circle of friends. The child with the disability may or may not be present for this discussion.

A paradox exists. The efforts to include a child with a disability actually result in his being singled out and set apart!

The "circle" approach typically focuses on the "special needs" of the child and how he's different. In some instances, the child unintentionally becomes the "poster child" of the classroom or even the entire school. The benevolent effort to help a child can actually be harmful: it stigmatizes the child as being different from, and more needy than, his peers.

All children in a classroom, whether they have disabilities or not, need support, help, and friendship. It's a disservice to the child with a disability to single him out. In addition, some of his classmates may feel resentful toward him: "Why is he getting all the attention? What about things I need help with?"

An alternative is to focus on the needs of all students in the class, by having a class meeting at the beginning of the year, and then as often as needed throughout the year. The teacher and one or more parent volunteers facilitate the meeting. Every child speaks up and describes what he needs: a pal to help with math, a buddy to play with at recess, two friends to sit with at lunch, or anything else. The needs are recorded on a flip chart.

If the teacher is aware of individual student needs that have not been mentioned, she brings them up in a very delicate and dignified way. She asks Leigh (a shy girl who has not spoken at all) if she would like a reading buddy. Then she asks Elijah (a boy with a disability) if he would like help from a classmate getting his jacket on and off every day. After all the individual needs of children have been identified, the teacher asks for volunteers to fill those needs and adds this information to the flip chart.

Next, the teacher or parent volunteer leads a discussion about needs that affect the whole class and other issues that need to be resolved. For example, the teacher might talk about the importance of everyone having having a playmate at recess so no one is left out. She can ask the class to brainstorm solutions.

When the needs of everyone in the class are discussed, the needs of a child with a disability are simply part of the mix. In addition, the stage is set for *all* students to give to one another and take responsibility for the success of the class as a whole. Friendships develop naturally from mutual support.

It's important that students with disabilities have the opportunity to *help* others, instead of only being recipients of help. If, during classroom meetings, a student with a disability doesn't offer to help, or is not asked to help by another student, the teacher or parent facilitator can make suggestions. Because of Benjamin's familiarity with computers at an early age, he often helped other children with computers in the classroom. Regardless of a child's disability, there's *something* he can offer to others. If this something isn't readily apparent, it's up to adults to figure out how a child with a disability can contribute to the well-being of his classmates.

Individualized Planning Session (IPS)

Another alternative to the "circle" approach is the IPS. Many parents choose to do an IPS prior to the IEP meeting and then incorporate the outcome into the IEP.

The IPS is similar to person-centered planning processes: the individual who is the focus of the meeting is in integral participant of the meeting. Questions are posed, answers are recorded, and a plan of action is agreed upon. A facilitator hosts the meeting and asks questions of the group. A recorder writes what occurs during the meeting. In my state, IPS facilitators are trained by the Colorado Department of Education (CDE). Any parent or teacher can request an IPS and CDE will provide a trained facilitator. The facilitator then selects a recorder. The IPS is a voluntary process, not governed by laws and official policies, but by people's good will.

An IPS meeting can be very valuable when children are moving into new situations. When Benjamin entered kindergarten, we had an IPS for him, and my friend, Charmaine, recently had an IPS for her son, Dylan, when he moved on to middle school.

The parents and the child decide who will be invited to the IPS. Only people who know the child and/or those who will be directly involved in the child's education are invited to participate. Others may be invited as *observers,* but they may not participate. The number of participants is equally divided between children and adults. If, for example, there will be six adults participating (two parents, classroom teacher, special ed teacher, next door neighbor, Sunday school teacher), there must be six children in attendance (child with the disability, brother, sister, and three friends). Observers might include the principal, counselor, special ed director, or other educators.

Prior to the IPS, the facilitator meets the child, the parents, and the child's classroom teacher(s). Together they decide what questions the facilitator should ask at the IPS meeting. In addition, they discuss what hopes they have for the outcome of the meeting.

At the meeting, the participants sit in a semi-circle and the facilitator and recorder stand at the front of the room with a flip chart and markers. Observers sit in the back of the room. I'll describe parts of Benjamin's IPS to give you a feel for what one is like.

The facilitator asked, "Who is Benjamin?" The recorder useds words, pictures, and symbols in brightly-colored markers to record all the responses on flip chart paper. She recorded Benjamin's vitals (five-year-old kindergartner in Mrs. White's class; uses a wheelchair and walker), and added the descriptions provided by the participants (adults and children): cute little brother, friend who likes Thomas the Tank Engine, happy child, son who is determined and loves to talk, friend who's good at the computer, and others. Benjamin, of course, contributed who he thought he was. Every description painted a positive image of Benjamin—a far cry from the mostly negative descriptions brought up at typical IEP meetings.

The facilitator then asked, "What are your dreams and hopes for Benjamin?" followed by "What are your nightmares and fears?" Later, steps were included in the action plan to make sure dreams came true and nightmares didn't. The children had no nightmares, but adult responses included fears that Benjamin would be left out or not have real friends. When the children heard these responses, they interrupted and yelled that would never happen! (What's interesting is that the nightmares for parents whose children don't have disabilities are often the same nightmares we have. They, too, worry about their children being left out, teased, and so forth. Often, our nightmares have nothing to do with a disability, even though we think they do.)

The next question was "What are Benjamin's gifts?" The children's answers and the replies from my husband, daughter and I were eye-opening for the other adult participants and the observers. They saw a side of Benj they didn't know existed, a side that was very different from the medical model perspective.

From this point on, the questions posed were those we had agreed on with the facilitator, and included things like:

- How does Benjamin learn best?
- What will Benj need help with in kindergarten?
- How can he best play with other kids at recess (in his wheelchair and walker)?
- How can he get books off the shelf in the library?

In an IPS, the sky's the limit when it comes to problem-solving ahead of time. Parents know what general issues their child might face; educators know the specific issues during the school day. Together, they can figure out what questions the facilitator should ask; then solutions are brainstormed. In Benjamin's meeting, the youthful and no-nonsense wisdom of his sister and his peers (children who had been in his class at the neighborhood preschool) led to solutions the adults couldn't have come up with in a million years!

Once all the questions were asked, answered, and recorded, the action plan was devised and agreed upon. The recorder listed what needed to be done, who would do what, and by what date the actions would be completed. Everyone left the meeting happy and excited at the prospect of success.

Benjamin's kindergarten IPS took about three hours and was held in the school cafeteria. How, you might be wondering, did we manage to keep six young children happy and occupied for three hours? By being flexible. Benjamin, as it turned out, was never bored. He was mesmerized by the process. He wanted to talk all the time! Occasionally, the facilitator had to gently tell him that she needed to let others talk, too. When the other children got antsy, they got down on the floor and played with some toys and books we brought, had snacks, and did whatever else they needed to do to stay happy. When it was time for the kids to answer another question, they were ready and willing to talk again.

As Benjamin's meeting demonstrated, an IPS with very young children can be quite successful. Benjamin's five-year-old peers demonstrated great wisdom and creative solutions. Imagine all the good that can come out of an IPS when children are older!

While the IPS focuses on the child with a disability, just as the Circle of Friends does, you can easily see the differences between the two, and understand why one is better than the other. The child's presence and participation, the focus on gifts and talents, the participants (only people who know Benj, not strangers in a new classroom), and other components of the IPS ensure the child is seen in a positive light and treated with dignity and respect.

BOLD ALTERNATIVES TO SPECIAL EDUCATION

Some parents are doing the "unthinkable." Instead of starting with the special ed process, they're starting with regular ed by simply enrolling their children with disabilities in the neighborhood school, in age-appropriate regular education classrooms. Then the parents, classroom teacher, and others observe the child to determine if special ed services are absolutely necessary. If so, the special ed process is initiated. Perhaps this is what Congress intended when it originally passed special ed law in 1975.

If a preschool aged child has no connection with the special ed department in the school district—in other words, if she has not entered the special ed world yet—her parents could simply sign her up for kindergarten. If the child is older and the family moves into a new school district, the parents could register the child for the age-appropriate class in the neighborhood school. (These approaches may not be feasible if the parents and student are already known by special educators and principals!)

If you're in one of these situations, use your own judgment about whether to take your child to registration. Do your homework about the school. If inclusion is already being practiced, you're home free. If not, you may not want to take your child to registration if his disability is easily observable. For instance, if a child who uses a wheelchair or has some other visible disability accompanies his mom to registration, the principal or some other educator might take one look and tell the mother she can't register the child since "he belongs in special ed and needs an IEP." If your child's disability is relatively invisible and you take him with you to registration, don't mention the disability at this time.

Once your child is enrolled and begins attending school, there are a variety of responses educators might have once a disability is observed or suspected. If your child's disability is visible, the principal might frantically call you the first day of school to say your child can't stay in the regular classroom, that he needs to "be in special ed." If this happens, calmly state that you'll come in *immediately* to talk with the principal, the teacher, and/or special educators. At the meeting, politely state that your child *does* belong in the class: he's the right age, he lives in the neighborhood, and so on. Request that he remain in the classroom and that appropriate personnel (classroom teacher or special ed teacher) observe him to assess what he needs *in the regular ed class*. Do everything you can to help educators learn how to provide the supports for your child without special ed services. If that's not possible, initiate the special ed process, and presume your child will stay in the regular ed classroom.

If you child's disability is not immediately apparent, it could be days or weeks before the teacher notices he's having difficulties in certain areas. When she does notice, however, she'll probably call in a special educator to observe. At that point, the special ed teacher would ask permission to test your child, activating the special ed process. If she assumes you don't know about the suspected disability, she may gently break the "news"!

You want to avoid this scenario since things could spiral out of your control very quickly. To prevent this from happening, you would need to stay in close contact with the teacher so she'll feel comfortable telling you about any "problems." You can then lead her in the right direction, by suggesting ways she can help your child. In the best case scenario, you and the teacher could work together to determine how to provide what your child needs without special education services. If, however, she insists on asking for help from special educators, you can intervene immediately to ensure your child remains in the regular classroom and receives the necessary supports.

Postponing or Declining Special Ed Services

If you're a risk taker, at your child's next IEP meeting tell the team you want to see how your child will do in a regular classroom without special ed services. Then after the first few weeks of school, your child can be observed in the classroom to determine his needs in that setting. In many ways, this makes more sense than trying to determine what a child's needs are before he's in the class!

You might also consider declining special ed services altogether. This can work if (1) you're willing to forego therapies and other related services, (2) the classroom teacher is supportive, and (3) you're willing and able to work collaboratively with the teacher to provide your child with curriculum modifications, identify natural supports in the classroom, and assist in whatever ways are necessary to ensure your child and the teacher are both successful. If, at any time, you decide your child needs the services mandated by special ed law, you can invoke the special ed process.

On behalf of our children, we can and should explore a variety of possibilities. When we're first exposed to special education, we're often relieved to learn our children are entitled to services to meet their needs. Too many parents, however, learn special ed isn't so special. Why shouldn't we investigate alternatives?

A MODEL OF INCLUSION

Columbine, our neighborhood elementary school, became an inclusive school under the bold leadership of Mike, the principal. (Columbine Elementary is not to be confused with Columbine High School where the tragedy took place in 1999. Because the columbine is Colorado's state flower, many schools have this name.)

Originally, there were no students with "severe" disabilities at Columbine. Some were in the elementary school where the "severe program" was located; others were served by another district. Mike's first step was to bring the Columbine students "home." Next, all students with disabilities were included in regular education classrooms. There was no resource room where students spent the entire day. Special ed teachers, paraprofessionals, and other specialists roamed the school, providing services to various children in their natural classroom settings.

After the first year, educators reviewed their efforts. In general, the specialists were happy, but the classroom teachers weren't. They didn't like so many different people coming and going in their classrooms all day; they felt their classrooms were repeatedly disrupted. In addition, they didn't feel they were able to learn what the specialists were helping specific students with, so they didn't how to help students throughout the day.

After lots of brainstorming, they arrived at a new model to try the next year. The specialists formed a resource team. They cross trained each other: special ed teachers taught gifted and talented teachers and vice versa. Then each member of the resource team was assigned to a specific grade level, with the responsibility of assisting every child in that grade level who was receiving special services of any kind. (Depending on the student population, some grade levels had more than one resource teachers.)

For instance, Mrs. F was assigned to the fourth grade. She assisted all fourth graders who received special ed, gifted and talented, and other academic assistance. She and the three fourth grade teachers collaborated to decide how to best utilize her time.

The classroom teachers and the resource teacher formed cooperative partnerships. In some cases, Mrs. F and a fourth grade teacher would co-teach: each took half the students in the class for a specific lesson. Other times, Mrs. F helped by modifying a student's curriculum, working with small groups of students in the classroom, or providing whatever assistance was needed to meet the needs of the students and their teachers.

Instructional assistants (IAs) assigned to classes that included students with disabilities also provided important supports. Some IAs worked in more than one classroom. For instance, Mrs. P worked in a fourth grade class to help Steve with math and other academics, and she also went to a kindergarten class to help Michelle during writing time.

A trio of educators—classroom teacher, resource teacher, and instructional assistant—collaborated to make inclusion work. They utilized the practice of "role release:" they were not rigidly wedded to their roles—each did whatever was necessary. Often, the resource teacher worked with a student one-on-one. Other times the IA or the classroom teacher provided personal instruction. When the classroom teacher was busy helping one or two students, the IA or resource teacher was in charge of the whole class.

Co-teaching, small group instruction, cooperative learning groups, and a variety of other innovative practices became the norm. Therapists provided services in the classroom setting and worked as consultants. (A few parents still wanted their children pulled out for one-one-one therapies and the school obliged.)

This model of inclusion worked and everyone was happy. The classroom teachers liked the support of the resource teachers and the instructional assistants. Responsibilities were shared, yet the classroom teacher still maintained overall authority. Most importantly, however, was that children with disabilities were seen as "regular kids." They were viewed as competent learners, and educators expected them to participate and be successful.

To stay on top of things, the resource team met for several hours every Friday morning to share and learn from one another, brainstorming ways to support students and classroom teachers. They were no longer known by their labels (special ed teacher, gifted and talented teacher, etc.); they were simply members of the resource team.

The principal took another bold step the following year when he said, "We've taken the labels off the teachers. Let's do the same for the students." Mike called me one day (as he did all other parents) and asked, "Would you like to staff Benjamin out of special ed? If you do, nothing will change. He'll continue to receive the help he's currently receiving. If, for whatever reason, you're ever unhappy and want to staff him back in to have procedural safeguards in place, you can." Obviously, my answer was a resounding "Yes!"

How did this happen? The Colorado Department of Education (CDE) funded grants for innovative and creative projects submitted by schools. Mike submitted a plan in which Columbine would identify the needs of students with disabilities and provide support without labeling and categorizing them per federal and state regulations. Without submitting the labels, however, Columbine would not receive official special ed dollars. The CDE grant replaced the funding the school would normally receive.

As Mike promised, nothing in Benjamin's education changed. But instead of having long, drawn out IEP meetings, Benj, his teachers, and I worked together to figure out what he needed and how to do it. We wrote some goals and objectives but these weren't as important as what went on every day in class. His classroom teachers, resource teachers, and instructional assistants worked diligently to ensure Benjamin's success.

He was expected to participate in and learn from the regular curriculum. If it was too difficult, we worked together on modifications. He used a laptop computer to do his work. When other kids were doing math with pencil and paper, Benj did math on the computer or with a calculator.

The school bought a standing frame and the IA helped Benj into it a couple of times a day. So that Benj didn't feel "different" or left out when he was in it, the standing frame was used when the class was engaged in cooperative learning activities. The kids in Benj's group gathered around him in the standing frame and worked off the large tray that was attached.

Benjamin was provided with many accommodations, modifications, and supports. Even so, he was a "regular kid." He sang in the school choir; created pottery, drawings, and other art work his own way; and had to stay in during lunch when he and some other boys acted up in class!

I never had to argue or fight to get what he needed. His teachers, the principal, and I worked together on a regular basis to make sure things were going well. The educators at Columbine saw parents as experts and respected their wisdom. Most importantly, they saw children with disabilities as children, first.

What worked at Columbine can work at any school if the principal provides the leadership. The inclusion process required a great deal of trust, ongoing communication, collaboration, and a willingness to try new things.

Some educators warm up to inclusion slowly; others experience a revelation after attending an inclusion conference or visiting a school where inclusion is practiced. And others, like Mike, are "just born that way." When Benjamin first started at Columbine, I asked Mike how he came to be a believer in inclusion. His reply reflected an attitude I wish every educator would adopt. He said, "I just thought about what I'd want—and what would be right—if I had a child with a disability." It can and should be that simple.

In classrooms and schools here and there, inclusion is working. Students with disabilities are included, supported, and being educated in regular ed classrooms. Teachers are supported and they're becoming better teachers because of their inclusion experiences. And all students are benefiting from a wide range of new experiences—from innovative educational practices to friendships between students with and without disabilities. For some families, however, there's more to a good education than a child being included in a public school classroom. They're choosing a totally different approach: homeschooling. Check it out, next.

Homeschooling, Unschooling, and Alternative Education
One Family's Experience

NEVER LET SCHOOLING INTERFERE
WITH EDUCATION.
Mark Twain

A quiet revolution is taking place in homes all across the country. For a variety of reasons, parents and children are deciding the public school system isn't the best place for learning.

The earliest proponents of homeschooling were parents who pulled their children out of school for religious or moral reasons. Today, other issues are prompting parents to reexamine the traditional method of American education. Parents are concerned about the social environment, the quality of education, school safety, and more.

When we moved from Texas to Colorado, our children were four and six, and there were lots of things we were looking for in a new community: a cooler climate, a home Benj could get around in, and an inclusive elementary school. We found the school, moved to a one-story house in a beautiful mountain town, and made our dreams come true.

Over the next several years, I was an active school volunteer, working closely with teachers, serving on committees at the building and the district levels, was president of the PTO, and more. I was extremely happy with the education my children were receiving. Like any school, it wasn't perfect. However, I was always able to work out solutions with the caring teachers and staff.

Not only was the school a wonderfully inclusive educational environment, the principal and teachers were creative educators. Multi-age classrooms, cutting-edge reading and writing programs, and other innovations made it the envy of the district and brought educators awards for excellence.

As a big supporter of the public school system, I was shocked when a couple of my PTO cohorts pulled their children out of school and began homeschooling them. My friends and I shook our heads in disbelief. How could these moms possibly think they could educate their children as well as the school could? And what about socialization? Under our breaths, we whispered about their preposterous actions.

When my daughter moved up to the middle school in sixth grade, my faith in the public school system was shaken to the core. This, too, was considered a good school. The sixth, seventh, and eighth graders spent their days at an award-winning campus that was just two years old. But what went on behind the classy facade troubled me.

I was concerned by the lack of real learning. Emily was always on the honor role, but so were lots of students. It wasn't that hard to get good grades, though, with copy-out-of-the-book homework assignments and open book tests. Many parents were thrilled by their children's grades. But I was bothered that Emily's good grades didn't necessarily mean she was learning or understanding the material. When I helped her with her homework, for example, she could answer all the questions on the worksheet. But when I read the chapter in her social studies book and asked her some general questions, she didn't always know what I was talking about.

When I expressed my concern that she didn't understand the material, Emily replied, "I'm doing exactly what the teachers tell me to do." And she was right. Memorization of facts, which were forgotten after the test, passed for learning.

When I expressed my concerns to the teachers, they patiently explained the rationale for their teaching methods: because they had students who came from the three different elementary schools in the district, they had students at all different levels, because none of the teachers at the elementary schools taught the same way. Therefore, the middle school teachers had to find an easy way to teach all the students. Say again? They said their jobs would be much easier, and they could teach to a higher level, if all the elementary teachers taught the same way.

It seems no one in the educational system is willing to take responsibility for the problems in the system. Employers complain college graduates can't read or write. They fault the universities. College professors claim entering freshmen aren't ready for college. They blame the high schools. High school teachers allege students haven't learned anything in middle school. They indict the middle schools. Middle schools say students haven't learned the basics. They criticize the elementary school. Elementary school teachers grumble that children aren't ready to learn and that they can't be babysitters. They blame—you guessed it—parents.

But academics wasn't my only concern. The school used a reward system as a means of social control. If a student came to school every day and did what he he was told, he received "chips" (tokens for good behavior). If, however, he didn't follow the rules, he had to give up one or more chips. For example, if he had to leave class to use the restroom—instead of going between classes—he had to return a chip.

At the end of each academic quarter, every student attended one of the all day "chip parties." The number of chips you "earned" determined which party you went to. Those with the most chips were rewarded with movies and pizza for the whole day. Those with the least amount of chips were entitled to donuts and old movies.

I'm not sure why this was considered such a treat, for more times than I can remember, Emily told me about spending the day in class watching movies (not educational films, but entertainment movies) while the teacher was in a meeting or doing something other than teaching. Movies seemed to be part of the standard curriculum.

The chips were valuable for more than tickets to parties, though. During the school year, students could purchase "Oops Passes," with some of their chips. Late homework assignments were forgiven if the student turned in a such a pass. Some teachers, including my daughter's, often presented students with a variety of goodies during the year for doing something "good." Emily proudly showed me a "ticket" she received one day. If she didn't want to do a homework assignment, she could skip it and just turn in the ticket instead. Emily, along with others, spent more time thinking about chips than learning.

I expressed my concerns to the principal. "Emily's Dad and I don't reward our children for doing what's expected of them," I told him. "If kids do the 'right' thing just to get rewards, what happens when the rewards stop—in high school, in college, or as adults? Will they not do the right thing since there's no reward?" With a deep sigh and some impatience at my apparent ignorance, he explained that the school had to have *some* way to control the students and this is what worked best. (I think prisons use similar methods of control.) He noted that mine was the first and only complaint about the rewards program.

Others in the school had discovered different ways to bribe students. The band teacher occasionally performed with a large musical group in Colorado Springs, twenty miles away. He would guarantee an "A" grade to any band students who attended these concerts on the weekends. A few other parents did complain about this. Our concerns were ignored.

And, finally, I was unhappy with the social environment of the school. When I kissed Emily goodbye every school morning, she was my sweet eleven-year-old. But the kid that got in the car at 2:45 in the afternoon was a different person. This girl looked like Emily, but she was sullen, rude, and had a smart mouth. An attitude adjustment was definitely in order. After about an hour at home, the real Emily finally reemerged.

When she and I talked about this daily problem, Emily found it hard to understand or explain what was happening to her. We finally figured out that she, along with many other students, had to assume a different persona during the school day in order to survive. In a school of 700 students, she didn't share many classes with the girls she had known in elementary school. She made new friends, but the cliques seemed to change daily.

Emily was uncomfortable with some of the more "popular" sixth grade girls because they used foul language, dressed in the wildest possible way, and giggled over things she wasn't ready for. Emily is quiet, a little shy, modest, and a conservative dresser. Tearfully, she said it was hard to find other girls like her.

Middle school is hard for everyone—parents and students. We persevered. I continued talking to teachers and administrators and Emily hung in there. I figured seventh grade would be better. As a supporter of public schools, I would stay active and try to make things better. Imagine my surprise when, at the end of sixth grade, Emily announced she didn't want to go back in the fall. "Homeschool me, Mom," she said. I laughed. Me, I thought? Slap the school in the face by homeschooling my daughter? Me? Give up the solitude of every weekday when I had the house to myself? Me? I don't know how to teach seventh grade. I told Emily we'd think about it. Over the summer I read everything I could find about homeschooling. At the same time, I figured this was a stage that would pass; by the time September rolled around, Emily would have changed her mind. But she didn't.

We did it. Started homeschooling. We're still doing it. And if I had to do it all over again, I would have homeschooled both my kids from kindergarten!

During the first year of homeschooling Emily, Benjamin was in fifth grade at the wonderful elementary school. But while he was home for winter break in December, he participated in our daily activities. I had already decided Benj would join us when he started sixth. If the middle school wasn't good for Emily, I knew it wouldn't be good for Benj. It didn't have a good history of inclusion. During that holiday break, I saw things in Benjamin I had never seen before. He was really excited about what we were studying and he participated in ways he had never done in school. As the two week break wound down, Benjamin wasn't happy about going back to school. He decided he wanted to start his homeschooling right then and not wait until the next September. That's what we did.

Homeschooling, unschooling, and alternative educational opportunities are options for all families today. "Homeschooling" is really a catch-all term that can describe a variety of methods of helping children learn. Some families use a professionally prepared curriculum and replicate a school-like setting in their homes. Others create their own curriculum and things are free and easy. Homeschooling can be as structured or unstructured as a family wants.

"Unschooling" is a term preferred by many, including myself. Unschooling means different things to different people, but generally, it represents a philosophy that children are natural learners who do not need a teacher in order to learn. In our family, it means the kids decide what and how they want to learn. I'm there to help and support them in whatever ways they need.

Alternative education can also mean almost anything, but generally, it refers to using apprentice-like training. Years ago, people learned skills through one-on-one apprenticeships. This is still the best way to learn.

I do not presume to recommend that all parents pull their children out of the public school system and begin homeschooling. Many families are very happy with the current system. Others may not have an adult in the family who can stay home with children, although this isn't always a barrier. Many families choose to join with others, pool their resources, and modify their work schedules to make it work. But if you're the least bit interested or just curious about it, I encourage you to learn more. Contact your state board of education for information about regulations governing homeschooling in your state. In many states, the info is available on state government web sites.

Many, many excellent books about homeschooling and alternative methods of learning can be found at your public library and in bookstores. See the appendix for my favorites. There's no way I could summarize all the information about homeschooling children with disabilities into this one chapter. So I urge you to read every book you can get your hands on to see if homeschooling might be right for you and your family. The Internet is also a good source of information. My purpose in including a chapter on homeschooling is simply to share our family's experiences in the hope that the information will be beneficial to you or someone you know.

When Emily and I first started, I did what many parents do (even though everything I read said *not* to do this): I set up a school-like atmosphere in our den. I realized later that the mechanics of public education are so ingrained in us it's hard to think any other way. Our home was already full of books, but I went out and bought a few more.

In trying to figure out how much time to spend on a subject, we studied Emily's sixth grade day. I was shocked to realize that she spent less than four hours per day on academics. The rest of the seven hour school day was spent in band, art, gym, lunch, and passing periods. We could do better than that! Emily and I designed a schedule that was very similar to a school day schedule: Language Arts from 9:00-10:00, Geography from 10:00-11:00, and so on. We planned a very structured schedule. It looked good on paper. But the reality was something else.

Emily and I took turns reading out loud and we discussed what we read. We worked on math, did science experiments, and in general, mimicked a typical school day. Sometimes she stared out the window, not paying attention, which made me very frustrated. Other times, as we were reading, she interrupted with a question. My answer led her to asking another question and so on and so on. By the time she quit asking me questions, we were on a totally different subject than the one we we started on.

This frustrated me greatly, since the time for that subject was quickly eaten up and we hadn't covered everything I'd planned. For several weeks we continued this way. Emily started being grouchy about things and so did I.

I went back to my homeschooling books to see where I'd gone wrong. After more reading, thoughtful examination of what we'd been doing, and many, many conversations with Emily, we began unschooling. Everything changed overnight. Once she took control of her learning, she was never bored or grouchy.

How ignorant and short-sighted I had been. By replicating the school environment in our home, I had set Emily up for failure. I was basically telling her what to learn and how to learn it. I was dictating what was important for her learn. People don't learn that way! We learn what's interesting and relevant to us, and we learn it in our own way.

When I was able to relax about it all, I learned so much. I began to treasure all the questions Emily asked that took us "off the subject." She was so hungry for information. How could I have gotten frustrated by her curiosity? It was amazing to see where all her questions took us. She taught me how everything's connected.

In public schools—especially in middle and high schools—educators try to teach a "subject." But our brains aren't wired that way. We don't just turn a switch on and off for geography, history, science, and so forth. Things aren't categorized in our brains that way. A question in history might eventually lead us to science and then on to geography. Every question Emily asked was valuable and important. She was learning so much. Because she was asking about what she was interested in, the information stayed with her. We no longer allotted a certain amount of time for something. We kept going until Emily was ready to do something else.

Before we made the switch to unschooling, there were many times when Emily was really engrossed in something. As the "teacher," trying to keep on schedule, I'd look at my watch and say, "Oops, time to stop now and move on to the next subject." What a dumb thing to do! In the unschooling mode, this all changed.

Our experiences helped me realize how the regimentation in schools actually inhibits learning. There's no way, in a class of thirty students, a teacher can allow one student to ask question after question that takes the class away from the lesson plan. It's sad. There's also no way for the class to continue a fascinating discussion once the bell rings. It's not that teachers are bad or uncaring. It's that the structure of public schools, where every child is supposed to learn every thing the teacher says, simply can't allow individual students to be free thinkers.

Once Benjamin started being unschooled, I learned even more. We spend a lot of time reading and doing and talking. I ask the kids lots of open ended questions. "Why do you think that happened?" "What do you think about that?" During the first couple of days after Benjamin joined us, he furiously waved his arm in the air when I asked a question, just the way kids do in public school.

Emily chuckled and said, "Benjamin, we're not in school! You don't have to raise your hand." Several questions later—with Benjamin still raising his hand—he tried to reply to a question, but he couldn't get anything out. "Well, um, um—" he mumbled. Emily and I waited patiently, thinking he was gathering his thoughts. Finally I said, "Benjamin, it's okay to say, 'I don't know'."

Tears welled up in his eyes and he said, "No, Mom. It's not okay to say that." "What do you mean?" I asked. "Of course it's okay to say that when you don't know something."

By now he was sobbing. "No, Mom!" he wailed. "When the teacher calls on you, it is *not* okay to say you don't know." "What are you talking about?" I asked, thoroughly confused.

Through more sobs, he answered, "You can't say 'I don't know' when the teacher calls on you or you'll get in trouble. She'll get mad at you." "What? What do you mean?" I practically screamed.

Emily jumped to Benjamin's defense and said, "He's right, Mom. If the teacher calls on you and you say you don't know, she gets mad and says, 'Well, you must not have been paying attention!' and then you're in trouble."

"But, Emily," I asked, not believing my ears, "what if you just don't understand it? Can't you be honest and say you don't know because you don't understand the material?"

She heaved a big sigh, looking at me as if I didn't know anything. "No, Mom, you just can't do that," she patiently explained. "If you don't know the right answer, it's better to fake it and give any answer. You can't say, 'I don't know.' You just can't." She gave Benjamin a big hug and told him, "Benjamin, you're not in school anymore. It's okay to say you don't know something now. "

During the many years I spent as Mrs. Busy Bee at my children's schools, I learned a great deal about how schools operate, how teachers work together, and more. Many parents looked to me as a resource when they had questions about general and special education. But I've learned more about public schools from my children than I ever did from my own observations and from educators.

My children have never sat me down and given me detailed descriptions. Instead, I've heard comments like, "Boy, I wish we could have done this in school," or "Why don't the teachers let us do this?" or "Now I get it. Why didn't the teacher show me this way?" In turn, I ask them more questions to clarify their statements, and *my* learning continues.

Supporting my children's learning at home is more rewarding and pleasurable than I can describe. I love being with my children. When they were in public school, I dreaded holidays and summer break, just as many parents do. I always wondered what I would do to keep them entertained, how I could keep them from fighting with each other, and all the rest. Now, I can't imagine what it would be like for both of them to be gone all day.

Our days are relatively unstructured. Some days we take "field trips" to museums or other interesting places. Some days, one of the kids goes to work with Dad, where a lot of learning takes place. Some days, we spend almost all day on one thing. Other days, we go shopping, where learning is automatic. You would be amazed at the things kids learn shopping. We have plans for both children to do non-paid internships at local businesses. They'll learn about the world of work and zillions of other things.

Because of her flexible schedule, Emily is a very busy babysitter. Moms in the neighborhood use her during the day and in the evening. She loves little children and once indicated a desire to be a pediatrician. I encouraged her to get some experience in a hospital so she'd know if she would be comfortable in the medical field. She's a junior volunteer at a big hospital in Colorado Springs.

While she still loves little children and babysitting, Emily has now decided she wants to be an interior decorator instead of a pediatrician. At fifteen, she's taken the practice GED test and is ready to take it formally, and she took the PSAT test and did well. (This was an interesting development in light of the fact that she hasn't formally studied some of the things taught in public school.) We recently enrolled her in a two-year correspondence course in interior decorating. She's studying "high school" curriculum, using our home materials, and "college-level" decorating courses using the materials from the correspondence school.

Benjamin wants to be a reporter or a cartoonist when he grows up. He spends a great deal of time writing on the computer. He's writing his life story. He also writes plays and stories. Having his writing critiqued is not one of his favorite things, however.

One day I told him I needed to review his work for correct spelling, punctuation, etc., he refused and told me it was fine the way it was. I explained that when he's a reporter, a copy editor would review his work and make changes, so he better get used to it. He didn't like that idea one bit. He asked me about all the different jobs at newspapers. I reviewed the typical staff hierarchy, staring at the bottom and ending up with the publisher. He wheeled away and returned a while later with this announcement, "Mom, I've changed my mind. I'm not going to be a reporter when I grow up after all. I'm going to be the publisher!" And he probably will.

The burning question most people have about homeschooling is, "What about socialization?" When Emily first proposed the homeschooling idea, my initial reluctance was based on concerns about socialization. But the more I read about homeschooling, I realized there's no basis for concern. Many of the problems in public schools today are probably caused by *too much* socialization with same age peers. Huh? I'll explain.

In my research into homeschooling, I read histories of public education. It's both a fascinating and disturbing story. For most of recorded history, children have been "socialized" in their homes and communities: spending time with people of all ages in their extended families, and with others around the farm and in local communities. It wasn't until the advent of mass public schooling in the 1800s that children in the United States have been with other children all day.

Once children start public school, they're with other children more than they're with their families. Their socialization is actually restricted, since they spend most of their time with kids in their same age group. They have few on-going opportunities to be with people of varying ages. For countless generations, children were nurtured under the watchful eyes of their extended families and friends, which included adults and children of all ages. Once compulsory public school was instituted, however, all that changed.

One book on the history of public education describes how adolescence wasn't even a concept until the advent of public education. Once children were congregated together with same age peers, those between the ages of eleven to thirteen (especially boys) were quickly seen as "troublesome" and the concept of "problems of adolescence" was born.

Authors of many homeschooling books report that children who are homeschooled have excellent manners, are socially competent, are more mature, and so on. This would seem to fly in the face of the obvious. How could they acquire exceptional social skills if they're not with other children all day?

Reverse the question and you have the answer. Children who are homeschooled have exceptional social skills *because* they're not with other children all day. By not spending most of their days with other children their age, they're not exposed to many of the inappropriate behaviors that are prevalent in the congregate settings of public schools. My daughter proved the point. Once she started being homeschooled, the smart mouth and rudeness disappeared. Prior to this, I believed puberty brought out all the ugliness. But now I think it's school that does it.

Parents know, from their own school experiences, as well as from the current experiences of their children, that cruelty, teasing, bullying, cliques, gangs, and other negative influences are common in schools. Few children are able to survive social torment by turning the other cheek. Most choose to defend and protect themselves and their friends by retaliation of some sort.

Soon after Emily began her education at home, she spent one morning describing various events that happened during her sixth grade year at the middle school: someone stole some items from her locker; she was pushed by a girl bully who wanted to fight; and on the last day of school a girl bully got in her face, screaming and cursing and telling Emily she would "get her" if she saw her over the summer. As she told me about these and other occurrences, she was reliving the fear she must have felt.

When I asked why she didn't tell me about these things when they happened, she replied, "I was scared to, Mom. I knew you'd go to the school to talk to the principal and stuff and I thought if you did, things would get worse. When those girls found out, they'd really come after me." Whew. A hug calmed her rapidly beating heart, but the memories still caused fear and pain.

In the big picture of school violence today, these incidents would certainly be considered minor. But I had a better understanding of how difficult it must be for children to be successfully educated in today's schools: it's hard to focus on learning when you're worried about who's out to get you during lunch or on your way home.

During Emily's first year of homeschooling, we ran into a friend while we out walking one day. My friend's daughter was attending the middle school, and Emily and I asked the mom how things were going. She detailed some of the good and some of the bad, and then asked, "Did you know they've started something new since all those shootings at middle schools across the country? Now they're having 'gun drills' as well as fire drills. The kids are taught how to hide under their desks and how to run down the hall in a crouch!" As we walked back home, Emily and I both sighed a big sigh, relieved that Emily didn't have to be afraid of getting shot in school.

In one of the homeschooling books I read, the author noted how most students in middle school develop a generalized aversion to children who are not in their age group. Middle schoolers often think younger children are jerks and at the same time, they're fearful of older students.

I consider Emily a typical child and this was certainly true for her at the time. When she was at the middle school, she and her sixth-grade friends were always talking about the mean seventh and eighth-graders. And they would make fun of their younger brothers and sisters and other younger kids. It's easy to see how this happens. Emily and her classmates went from being the big shot fifth-graders at the elementary school to the lowly sixth-graders at the middle school. Since they were teased and ridiculed by the seventh and eighth-graders, they had to dish it back out to somebody and the easiest targets were younger children.

Children who are homeschooled spend most of their time with their families, where they're exposed to positive behavior and good manners. They're not subjected to the relentless social tension of schools. They get along well with children of various ages—their brothers and sisters and other children who are homeschooled—as well as with adults. Homeschooled children are usually involved in community activities such as church, park and rec activities, volunteering, and the like. Unlike compulsory public education, these activities are voluntary. Parents and children choose to participate and if the social atmosphere is not satisfactory, they move on to one that is.

Some might argue that learning to get along in public school—knowing how to deal with bullies, cliques, and the like—is necessary training for the adult world. I disagree. The only environment in the adult world that's equivalent to the environment in most public schools is prison.

Consider the similarities between public school and prison: you're forced to be there whether you like it or not, you have little or no choice about what happens to you while you're there, a small number of powerful people have authority over many, and you're compelled to be physically close to people you may or may not like.

College isn't like that. You choose what you want to learn and who you want to be with. And you can quit if you don't like it. If you don't like your professor, no one forces you to go to class.

Jobs aren't like that, either. If you don't like your job you can quit. You might have authority figures over you, but you might also be in charge of others. If you don't like your co-workers, you can ask for a transfer or quit.

But in public school, if your daughter doesn't like her teacher, how likely is it the school will let you switch her to another teacher? If your son is having trouble with the school bully, can you get your son (or the bully) transferred to another class or a different school? If you don't like the school your children are attending, can they quit and search for a better one? In almost all cases, the answer is "no."

The analogy of schools being like prisons came out of the mouths of babes: my kids. One day when we were out and about on a field trip, we passed a school bus full of kids. Benjamin said, "Look! It's the prison bus!" "What are you talking about?" I asked. "Well," Emily chimed in, "that's what those kids are like—prisoners. When you're in school, it's like you're in prison. So that's a prison bus. Get it?" I got it.

I asked my children to share their thoughts about homeschooling. Emily wanted you to know:

> I like homeschooling because I can take off during the day and babysit, and I can make up my own schedule and graduate early. I sometimes miss being with some of my friends during the day, but it's much harder to learn at school when you're worrying about other kids. The only reason most kids like going to school is to be with their friends. That's the way I was.
>
> Since we're homeschooled, I can always get the amount of rest I need. It's hard to concentrate at school when you're tired from having to get up so early. I like being able to learn what I'm interested in and not the junk they teach at school.
>
> The most important thing about homeschooling is that I like myself better and I'm in control of my life. That's the best thing.

Benjamin wanted to you know:

> I think homeschooling is fun because I don't have to worry about grades. When you're homeschooled, you don't have to give an answer just to please a teacher.
>
> At first, I missed my friends, but pretty soon I realized it felt good not to have to worry about other kids. With homeschooling you can just be yourself. Some things that happen at school make kids uncomfortable and that doesn't happen at home.
>
> The really big reason why I like homeschooling is because I can spend more time with my family. At home, I can choose what I want to learn. It's fun to make up our own schedule.
>
> We think learning goes on all the time. When you're in public school, you think learning only goes on when you're in class. But that's not true. You can

learn anytime, anywhere. Some of the things they taught at school weren't very interesting. Learning at home is much more interesting.

We enjoy ourselves so much the day goes by very fast. School went by so slowly it seemed to crawl up my arm like an ant.

My greatest fear about homeschooling—that I wouldn't know how to "teach" my children—has never materialized. Emily and Benjamin don't need to be *taught* in order to learn. In fact, I realized that my "teaching" interfered with their learning. They know how to learn. Like all children, they were born to learn. They've taught me how to help them.

Both of my children ask questions all the time. I'm sure your children do, too. At home, their questions are answered. If I don't know the answer, we find it somewhere. Asking questions and receiving answers seems to be one of the most effective ways of learning. I wonder what it feels like for children in public school to be bursting with questions all day long and not be able to have them answered. There are not enough hours in the public school day for teachers to answer all the questions children have.

Again, if you're interested in exploring homeschooling, unschooling, or alternative education, read everything you can get your hands on and talk to families who homeschool. Research your state regulations about children who are homeschooled.

Throughout this book, I've recommended different ways of doing things, and suggested that if the new way doesn't work out, you can always go back to the old way. This is another one of those situations. You can try homeschooling, unschooling, or alternative education for two months, six months, or a year, and if it's not for you, your child, and family, you can go back to the public school system.

In our state, the regulations make homeschooling very easy, and there are no additional requirements for children who were receiving special ed services in public school. I simply had to send a letter to our district stating our intentions. If asked, I must show records (I keep a diary) that my children have spent an average of four hours a day, for 168 days per calendar year, in learning activities.

Per state regulations, my children must be tested in the same time frame children in our district are tested (every two years). I can take them to school for standardized tests at the same time other students in their grade levels are being tested, or I can have them tested using non-standard assessments. I choose the latter. These informal assessments can be of my own design, as long as they're administered by a certified teacher. I "hire" (and pay) my best friend—a teacher—to assess my children. She does this by spending time with them, and talking to them about what they're learning. Then she writes up a report, sends it to the school district, and that's that.

If a child uses a professional curriculum offered by an accredited long-distance school (many of which are very expensive), he'll receive a high school diploma from that school. If a family chooses to create their own curriculum, and does not affiliate with any official program, the children simply take the GED test to get a high school equivalency certificate.

Going on to college is routine for many homeschoolers. They do what other students do: take the SAT, apply for scholarships, and so forth. Some studies have reported that homeschooled students have SAT scores that are higher than the national average.

When my children were in the public school system, we routinely talked about them going on to college. And that's still an option. If that's what they want to do, that's what they'll do.

But my horizons have been broadened by the homeschooling experience. There are many careers that do not require a college education and there are many young people who don't want to go to college. We're helping our children explore self-employment, home-based businesses, and other possibilities. As I mentioned, Emily is studying interior decorating via correspondence classes. She wants to have her own business. Benjamin has decided he wants to go to college via the Internet. Mark and I are 100 percent behind our kids. They have bright futures.

Teenagers and young adults with disabilities can also have bright futures. They can get out of the rut of the service system and into real lives. That's next.

Bright Futures for Teens and Young Adults

IF ONE ADVANCES CONFIDENTLY IN
THE DIRECTIONS OF HIS DREAMS,
AND ENDEAVORS TO LIVE THE LIFE
WHICH HE HAS IMAGINED,
HE WILL MEET WITH A SUCCESS
UNEXPECTED IN COMMON HOURS.
Henry David Thoreau

A brand new world. That's what awaits our sons and daughters as they emerge from childhood and begin to spread their wings as young adults. Before we know it—and before we're ready for it to happen—our children are grown. As they leave the public school system, the signpost shows two paths: one points to The System; the other to A Natural Life.

If our children take the path to The System, they'll become connected to professionals who will write more "I" programs: IHPs (individual habilitation programs), IWRPs (individual work/rehabilitation programs), IPPs (individual program plans), and a host of others. In The System, we should be prepared for delays, as our children are forced to wait weeks, months, or maybe years to get the "help" promised by the adult service system. But if our children take the road to A Natural Life, they can achieve success by using natural supports and generic services. Which path shall your child take?

THE BIG PICTURE

In our society, we expect young people to graduate from high school and then go on to college or some other post-secondary training, join the military, or get a job. At some point, we expect them to move away from their families and begin living on their own.

But society hasn't expected the same from young people with disabilities. We haven't expected them to become independent adults. Instead, they're expected to continue being dependent on the system, as professionals "prepare" them for adulthood.

Many young people with disabilities "graduate" from special education services and enter the adult service system. Because of their disabilities, many are considered "unable to attain gainful employment." This status wins them a lifetime of government assistance (SSI-Supplemental Security Income). They now have the dubious honor of being able to live the rest of their lives below the poverty level.

The infinite wisdom of the system doesn't stop there, however. When young people are considered unemployable, they may be eligible for assistance from vocational-rehabilitation or other employment services. Counselors may attempt to make them "employable" by placing them in a sheltered workshop. There, professionals will "get them ready" for a real job by allowing them to make widgets all day, earning pennies per hour. Many will never leave this place; they'll never be considered ready for a real job.

Others will try to move beyond the spirit-killing environment of a workshop, but find it nearly impossible to escape from the clutches of the disability welfare system. If they *do* find a real job in the community, they can only work part-time: too much income will cause them to lose their government benefits, including Medicaid and food stamps. Some young people give up and give in, choosing to stay in a workshop because the real world is too scary.

In the system, young people with disabilities may also be eligible for habilitation services. When they want to move away from mom and dad, the service system may place them in a group home with other people with disabilities. The few hundred dollars they receive from the government (SSI) is now no longer theirs. They can't be trusted to pay their room and board on their own, so their checks go directly to the operators of the group home. This forced cohabitation with strangers (something people without disabilities would never do) is often considered successful "community inclusion." For many young people with disabilities, this is the end of the road. They will go no further.

Others, though, ever hopeful they'll one day be free, are in perpetual training for independent living. One of the skills they must learn is how to handle money. So, the staff at a group home may dole out a few bucks here and there (funds left over from the their government checks) for spending money.

For some young people with disabilities, living in a group home might be considered paradise compared to their previous existence in an institution, nursing home, or other congregate housing. Others, though, don't even get the chance to try "community living." They're permanent residents of nursing homes, a placement deemed necessary and appropriate because of their significant physical needs. They're not sick, however. They simply need assistance bathing, going to the bathroom, dressing, transferring from the bed to the wheelchair, and help with other daily activities. Government programs will pay the exorbitant costs of nursing home care, but they won't pay for personal care attendants to assist people in their own homes, even though in-home care would cost far less! (Hopefully, pending legislation in the U.S. Congress will address this thorny issue.) In the system, the futures of teenagers and young adults with disabilities are frequently decided by professionals, based on the available services, not on what the young person needs.

BRIANA

Briana, age sixteen, was enrolled as a student receiving special education services, but for the previous year (since she was fifteen) she attended school for only an hour each morning. After that, she went to her part-time job at a fast food restaurant, a job which had been arranged by the special ed teachers. This arrangement was expected to continue until Briana "graduated" at age eighteen.

Everyone seemed happy. Briana liked not having to spend all day in the "yucky" special ed room and her parents were glad they didn't have to fight with the special ed teachers. After dealing with the special ed system for nine years, they were exhausted and ready for a break. They were so relieved, in fact, they didn't think about the ramifications of Briana's placement in a vocational setting.

When they attended a parent workshop about transition services, they were asked what Briana's dream was. "She wants to go on to college as soon as she graduates," they replied. By the end of the workshop, Briana's parents realized their daughter needed to be attending regular classes in order to earn a high school diploma that would get her into the community college. When they discussed this with the special ed teachers at school, Briana's mom and dad were shocked to learn Briana had been placed in the part-time job and excused from attending school because the special ed teachers didn't believe she could learn any more in the public school system.

Educators believed the highest level of employment Briana would ever achieve was an entry level position at a fast food restaurant. Further, educators felt Briana and her parents should be grateful and satisfied by the educators' efforts to place Briana a job that "suited" her. Taking things in their own hands, Briana and her parents began the long and difficult job of getting Briana into regular classes so she could attain her dream of attending college.

MICHAEL

Sixteen-year-old Michael and his parents were also tired of dealing with special educators, so when he was fourteen, they simply bowed out of the process. They let educators write Michael's IEPs and the results were satisfactory. Michael, who had a physical disability and used a wheelchair part time, was included in regular classrooms and needed only minor curriculum modifications.

One day, Michael's mother had a chance encounter with another parent—Jackie—who was well-versed in special education. As they talked about their children, Michael's mother shared her son's dream of becoming a minister. After graduating from high school, he wanted to go to college and divinity school. Jackie then talked about her teenage daughter who also wanted to go to college. She described the courses her daughter was taking on the "academic" track at the high school. Michael's mom didn't know anything about all this, so she decided to do a little investigating. As it turned out, Michael's classes were all on the "vocational" track. If he continued, his high school transcript would get him into a vocational school, but not the college he dreamed of attending.

Educators who devised Michael's IEP knew he was a "bright young man," but they never saw him as "college material." As in the case with Briana, Michael and his family had to hurriedly jump back into the IEP process. The faced a formidable task: trying to fit four years of academic classes into the last two years of Michael's high school career.

REBECCA

Rebecca and her mother visited the vocational-rehabilitation office on the recommendation of the high school special ed teachers. Like most other students with disabilities at her high school, Rebecca—a seventeen-year-old with autism—had spent most of her time in a self-contained classroom where the focus was on life-skills, not academics.

A gifted artist, Rebecca wanted a career that would utilize her natural talent. She didn't want to go to college; she was ready to be through with school, at least for awhile. Several of Rebecca's drawings and paintings adorned the walls of her family's home, as well as the homes of her grandparents and family friends.

At the voc-rehab office, Rebecca and her mother described Rebecca's career goal, pleased and excited Rebecca was confident about what she wanted to do in life, unlike other students her age who needed "career counseling." They were shocked and dismayed when the counselor slowly shook his head and detailed why he wouldn't be able to find Rebecca a job in her chosen field. Instead, he would test her to determine what type of job would be "appropriate." Rebecca declined the offer, and she and her mom made for the door.

On the way home, they decided to use their own resources to find Rebecca a career in art. They knew, unlike the voc-rehab counselor, that artists are needed in a variety of industries: greeting cards, wallpaper, fabric, signs and banners, and many more.

TONY

Tony, age twenty-six, lives in a group home with several other adults with cognitive disabilities, where they're all supervised by resident staff members. Four days a week, for half of each day, Tony's assigned job in the sheltered workshop is stuffing bags for a large hospital. The workshop has a contract with the hospital for this service. Into each bag Tony places a plastic water pitcher, drinking cup, small box of tissues, and other items. The hospital issues these bags to all incoming patients.

For his twenty hours of work each week, Tony earns between $20 and $40, depending on the number of bags he's able to stuff. His average hourly rate of $1.50, far below minimum wage, is legal since most sheltered workshops are exempt from federal minimum wage regulations. Tony works at a job he hates, so he vacillates between angry outbursts and sullen silence. The workshop staff doesn't believe Tony is "ready" for a real job in the community. His "behaviors" prove that on a daily basis.

Unless someone intervenes on Tony's behalf, he'll remain in a house that's not a home and in work that's not a job. Worse, if no one listens to Tony's spoken and unspoken communication, his "behaviors" will continue to deteriorate and he'll probably end up in more restrictive environments.

MARIA

Maria, age thirty-three, begged her case manager to get her a place of her own. She didn't like living in the group home with roommates not of her own choosing, where she was expected to follow the rules set down by staff. A quiet young woman, it took all of Maria's courage to buck the system that focused on getting her "ready" for a real life. Soon, Maria was living in her own place: one side of a small duplex. The case manager was pleased she had been able to fulfill Maria's dream. But all was not as it good as it seemed.

When an uncle visited Maria one day, he expected to find Maria ecstatic in her new home. And she *was* happier than she'd been in the group home. But John knew something wasn't right when Maria asked him to come outside with her so she could smoke a cigarette. John learned the landlord didn't allow smoking in the duplex, and he also wouldn't allow a tenant to have a pet. Maria had wanted her own place for a variety of reasons, including her desire to smoke when she wanted and her dream of having a pet. Neither of these were permitted in her new place.

When John asked Maria why she moved into a place where she couldn't smoke and couldn't have a pet, she just shrugged her shoulders. After gently questioning her some more, Maria began crying and said, "Anything would have been better than the group home." The more John learned about the duplex, the more he knew it wasn't a good place for Maria. It was on the fringe of the neighborhood, facing the back of a liquor store and a lounge, isolated from other houses on the street. Maria needed a home where she could easily meet her neighbors. She had no friends. While the case manager had been successful getting Maria out of the group home, her new place didn't really meet her needs.

John set out to find Maria a better place: he would identify several apartment complexes that were friendly communities, where tenants could smoke and have pets. Then Maria could pick the one that was best. John didn't trust Maria's case manager to help in this effort, but he would need to unravel the system's red tape to make all this happen.

SCOTT

Thirty-four-year-old Scott lives in a group home and the staff is attempting to get him "ready" to live on his own. Twice a week, a support person takes Scott to the grocery store to help him buy groceries. Why does a grown man need help buying a few groceries? Because the staff says he doesn't know how to handle money. Why doesn't he know how to handle money? Because special education didn't provide an education; because his parents never believed he was capable so they didn't give him the opportunities to learn things naturally as he was growing up; and because he's been in congregate settings since he was eighteen, where he's never been expected to take care of himself or be responsible.

Scott's monthly SSI check goes directly to the group home every month, as do his paltry checks from the sheltered workshop where he's employed. The staff then gives Scott a few dollars a week for an "allowance." They shake their heads in dismay when Scott spends his all his allowance on candy and Twinkies on the very day it's given to him. This behavior, they state, is "proof" that Scott is incapable of handling his own money, which is why the majority of his money is handled by staff.

They don't understand that their actions (preventing him from learning how to manage his money) provokes his actions (he's trying to control what money he gets by spending it on what he wants). Under these circumstances, Scott may never learn to control his money because he'll never be given the opportunity to do so!

LINDA

Linda, age twenty-nine, lives in a "family home" (adult foster care). The family has three children, all teenagers, and both parents work.

When she was eighteen, Linda's parents and the case manager decided it was time for Linda to leave home and move into a group home for "habilitation training." Linda has a label of "mental retardation." Her stay in the group home only lasted a year; her behavior got her kicked out. What did she do that was so bad? She acted like a typical nineteen-year-old: she got a boyfriend and they got caught smooching! This was a big no-no at the group home.

Instead of returning to her parents' home, she was sent to live at the state institution. After several years, Linda finally "earned" her way out. But the system didn't think she was ready for a group home again; she needed the supervision of a family (foster) home.

This is where she was living when I met her. When I asked if she was happy, she replied, "Yeah, I guess so. Mary [the mother in the family home] is real nice." But Linda didn't want to talk about herself; she wanted to know about Benjamin. "Do you think he'll grow up and get married and have kids?" she asked. "Yeah, I think he will," I answered, "if that's what he wants to do. What about you? Do you want to get married and have kids?"

Somewhat embarrassed, she bowed her head and then shook it in a "no" answer. "Why not?" I asked. She peered up into my eyes and said, "I can't have any kids. I had my tubes tied when I was twenty-one. I wouldn't ever be a good mother." Anger welled up in me. I had heard this story from other young women with disabilities. "Who told you that, Linda?" I asked, barely controlling my outrage. "Who said you'd never be a good mother? Who told you to get your tubes tied?"

"No one told me," Linda replied nervously. "I just knew I should do it." But I didn't believe her. Her story is too similar to other young women who have been coerced by family members or professionals into "voluntary" sterilization.

Linda told me about her current situation. She worked part-time at a drug store, cleaning and putting up stock. She had been there for a little over a year, and a job coach (a trainer) stayed with her for the three hours she worked each day, Monday through Friday. Why, I wondered, did she still need a job coach after a year on the job? It didn't make any sense. As we talked, I learned she had become close to her coworkers, and they were always ready to help if she had questions. When I asked how much she made per hour, Linda couldn't tell me. "The store pays my case manager, and then my case manager pays me," she said.

As she told me more about her life, I was both sad and angry. In the morning on her way to work, Mary (the foster parent) drops Linda off at the institution where Linda once lived. From eight to nine every weekday morning, Linda waits at the institution (because it happens to be a convenient location) for the job coach to pick her up and take her to work. They spend the next three hours together at the store, then the job coach goes on her way. Linda takes the city bus to the developmental center (a "habilitation training" center) where she "takes classes" with other adults with disabilities. Linda's not sure why she has to take the classes. She's also not sure what she's learning from them. At three in the afternoon, the center's private bus takes Linda and the other "clients" home. Linda's family home is the last stop on the route; after one and a half hours on the bus, she arrives home at 4:30 PM.

She finished telling me about her life by adding the good news. "And now I get to be home alone for fifteen minutes!" she proudly announced. I didn't understand what she meant until she explained. Up until a week or so before our conversation, twenty-nine-year-old Linda was not allowed to be alone in the family home. Someone from the family (one of the foster parents or one of their teenaged children) always had to be there when Linda arrived home. But because Linda had "proven" she was responsible, the case manager and the foster family had agreed Linda could be alone for fifteen minutes after she arrived home from the developmental center. (So now, someone in the family must arrive home no later than 4:45 PM.)

Linda said that during the fifteen minutes, she was required to carry the cordless phone wherever she went in the house, in case anyone needed to call and check up on her. She was anxious to please everyone so she could earn an additional fifteen minutes as soon as possible. She loved being alone in the house. "It's the only time of the day I'm by myself," she added wistfully.

Later, I talked with a couple of people who were familiar with Linda's situation. When I asked why Linda still needed a job coach after being successfully employed in her job for a year, they laughed at my ignorance and explained it all to me.

In the state where Linda lived, the service system contracted with an agency for "employment services" for people with developmental disabilities. In essence, the employment agency billed the state about $35.00 for every hour Linda worked. Out of this $35.00, the job coach probably got paid about $8.00 an hour, Linda probably got paid about $3.00 an hour, and the remainder ($24.00 per hour) went to the employment agency. The drug store may or may not have paid a portion of Linda's salary, via depositing funds with the agency. The "employment" agency netted $18,720 per year for "serving" Linda. (Linda worked three hours a day, five days a week, so 15 hours/week x 52 weeks a year = 780 hours/year x $24.00/hour = $18,720/year.) Linda's gross annual salary was probably about $2,340.

"That's outrageous," I exclaimed. "You're right," the informants agreed, "and it happens all the time, all across the country."

More Horror Stories

In addition to these horror stories are tales of young (and middle-aged) adults with disabilities who are waiting, and waiting, and waiting for vocational rehabilitation counselors to get them jobs. When I present at workshops that include adults with disabilities, I routinely poll the audience: "How many of you are signed up with voc-rehab?" Almost all the hands come up. I follow with, "How many of you are working?" The vast majority of hands come down. Voc-rehab simply isn't working (no pun intended) for most adults with developmental disabilities.

I've met a number of VR counselors. Some are very, very good. Most, however, do a poor job. One of our family's dear friends—Jim—acquired a disability as a teenager and uses a wheelchair. In the twenty years since his college graduation, he's had several different careers, including a stint as a VR counselor. He went into that job with a song in his heart: who better to help people with disabilities find jobs than a person with a disability? He resigned five years later in disgust. He said the bureaucratic red tape inherent in the system got to him, but it was hearing the other counselors gossip and laugh about their "clients" that finally made him turn in his badge.

THE SERVICE SYSTEM

These examples illustrate what happens to millions of young adults with disabilities who exist—not really living, but existing—within the grip of the service system. Many adults with disabilities spend hours of boredom in day programs or adult day care. If staff can keep their charges busy, all is well. Others spend their days making widgets, working for sub-minimum wages, in the unnatural, segregated environments of sheltered workshops. And many are in so-called habilitation centers, state schools, and other residential institutions, where they're surrounded by helping professionals in artificial, soul-numbing environments.

Get in Line and Stay There

When Benjamin was in the third grade, a professional with the school district attempted to help me and several other parents by talking to us about our children's lives when they became adults. He had just returned from a meeting at the agency which serves adults with disabilities in our county. He gravely informed us that even though our children were very young, we needed to go ahead and sign them up for adult services since there was already a long waiting list. He reasoned that if we got our children's names on the list right away, by the time they were adults their names would be up at the top. The services provided by this agency included group homes and sheltered workshops.

I'm sure he expected us to be eternally grateful for his wisdom, but when we responded, en masse, that we would not want these services for our young adult children, his jaw dropped. "What do you mean you don't want adult services? What will your children do if they don't get those services?" he stammered. One mom spoke for us all when she replied, "Our children will do the same things their brothers and sisters and friends do: go to college, get jobs, and live on their own. They'll do what other young people do!" This was a foreign concept to the professional, just as it is to others (both professionals and parents).

There is absolutely no reason why young people with disabilities shouldn't proceed along the same path other young people take. And they can if we believe our children will be successful, self-determined adults, and if we raise them that way! They'll be successful if we presume competence.

Disability Benefits

Children and young adults with developmental disabilities who have no work histories may be eligible for SSI (Supplemental Security Income), depending on the income level of their parents. In most states, receiving SSI automatically entitles the recipient to receive Medicaid health coverage. Currently, the SSI allotment for most individuals is around $400 monthly. However, if the parents' income increases, the monthly allotment is decreased. Income, in this sense, means more than a change in salary. It also means any additional financial assistance the family receives. For instance, if a grandmother or a friend of the family gave the family a load of groceries, bought the child with the disability clothing, or gave the family cash to help pay bills, these could all be considered income and the SSI check could be reduced by the amount of the contribution.

When a young adult with a disability gets a job, *his* income is considered, not his parents'. And this is a major dilemma. When people who receive SSI become employed, they may be in jeopardy of losing their benefits. If they make over a certain amount (and it's not a large amount), their SSI benefits will be reduced or cut all together. This may result in the loss of Medicaid coverage. This creates a *disincentive* to "gainful employment."

A relatively new program enables people to be employed and still retain their SSI and Medicaid benefits. With a PASS program (Plan to Achieve Self-Support), qualified individuals can set aside their employment income in a special bank account. These accumulated funds must be used for work-related expenses (clothing and transportation, for instance, or for expenses of self-employment). In addition to PASS, a variety of waiver programs in many states are helping people with disabilities rise above the poverty level, access community supports, and still retain crucially important benefits.

SSDI (Social Security Disability Insurance) monthly income payments are available to adults with a work history (meaning they've previously paid into Social Security) who acquire a disability after the age of twenty-two. Children with developmental disabilities may be eligible for SSDI if a parent who has paid into Social Security dies. The child then draws on the deceased parent's Social Security account. People who receive SSDI may be eligible for Medicare instead of Medicaid.

Employment Benefits

Another service that may be available to young people with developmental disabilities is vocational-rehabilitation (VR, voc-rehab) services. VR services are eligibility-based. Generally, the eligibility requirements are: the person must have a disability, the disability must be considered an impediment to employment, and the person must demonstrate a need for VR services. For example, a person who was born with three fingers on one hand might be thought of as having a disability, but if the disability is not an impediment to employment and/or if the person doesn't need help finding a job because of the disability, he would not be eligible for VR services.

Voc-rehab services may pay for college or other training programs if the desired employment requires such training. For example, if a person wants to be a lawyer, teacher, or some other position that requires a college degree, he might be eligible for VR services that would pay for college. If a person wants to be a truck driver, however, he would not be eligible for college tuition support since a college degree is not required to be a truck driver. The person may, however, be eligible for tuition assistance for truck driver training.

Language in VR regulations includes a "presumption of consumer choice," meaning the person with a disability (the consumer) should be able to choose what type of career he wants. This presumption, however, is frequently ignored by VR counselors. If a counselor doesn't think a person's employment objective is realistic, he may push the person in a different direction—a more realistic direction (in his opinion). In addition, college tuition assistance may be denied if the employment goal isn't seen as "realistic or achievable."

Employment services for people with disabilities, such as vocational testing, job placement, and job coaching, are also offered by some non-profits and other organizations. But there are inherent flaws in the basic premise of all vocational services.

A Presumption of Incompetence

The primary flaw in employment assistance is the perception that people with disabilities are unable to get their own jobs: they're seen as incompetent. Thus, when an employment counselor places Mary in a job, the employer may have automatically formed a negative opinion (pity, fear, unease, etc.) about her, simply because someone else got the job for her. The employer may assume Mary will fail, but he's willing to "give her a try." This is not a positive beginning.

Another issue that's problematic occurs in the relationship between the employee and the employer: too often, there is none! In Mary's case, for example, the counselor made the initial contact with the employer, set up the interview, met with the employer about Mary's needs, and so forth. The counselor did all the things an employee usually does. The employer and the counselor—not Mary—have established a relationship. As a result, once Mary is employed, the employer may not go to her with concerns about her work; he may go to the counselor, with whom he has a longer or deeper relationship. This situation is not conducive to Mary being perceived as a "real" employee. Mary may have to work very hard to establish an employee/employer relationship with her boss.

The presumption of incompetence is also manifested in the practice of job coaching. This can also get in the way of a person with a disability being seen as a "real" employee. A job coach is a person provided by the employment/vocational agency to assist a person with a disability on the job.

For example, Fletcher has just been placed in a new job and Tim, the job coach, has been assigned to help him. Tim and Fletcher spend time talking about the job and what accommodations Fletcher will need. Tim might visit the job site ahead of time to figure out how Fletcher will perform his job, and how to make the necessary accommodations. Once Fletcher starts his job, Tim will work side-by-side Fletcher to teach him how to do the job. It all sounds hunky-dory so far, but the situation is fraught with negatives.

First, why does Fletcher *need* a job coach? People who don't have disabilities don't have job coaches. Does Fletcher have one just because he has a disability? Is he presumed to be incompetent? How does a typical employee succeed in a new job? Initially, he may trained by a supervisor or a coworker. After the official training is over, he turns to his supervisors and coworkers (natural supports) for help. Why is it presumed Fletcher cannot utilize these same natural supports from coworkers? Or does the employment service presume Fletcher's coworkers and supervisors are incompetent or unwilling to help Fletcher? Is it assumed he will not be accepted unless an intermediary (the job coach) is in place? Some might argue that a job coach is needed to figure out the job accommodations, but, again, we're not giving Fletcher or his coworkers enough credit.

Like a one-on-one aide in school, the job coach often gets in the way of an individual making friends and belonging. Because Tim is always there to help Fletcher, coworkers will most likely stay away from Fletcher; he certainly doesn't need their help when the job coach is there. When it's time for lunch, no one asks Fletcher if he wants to go to a burger joint or sit with others in the lunchroom; he and Tim are a pair. Fletcher is not seen as a real employee; he doesn't really belong.

Fletcher's supervisor regularly checks on how he's doing, but he usually talks to Tim, not Fletcher. When there's a problem, he pulls Tim off to the side to discuss it with him, leaving it up to Tim to explain the situation to Fletcher. This, of course, makes Fletcher uncomfortable around the supervisor. He's beginning to think the man doesn't like him. Every time he comes around, he and Tim leave for awhile, and then Tim comes back to tell him what he's doing wrong. Fletcher figures if the man liked him, he'd talk to him directly.

At some point, Tim may begin to fade the one-on-one assistance. He'll still be in the building with Fletcher, but he'll sit six feet away while Fletcher is working, or he'll move in and out of the room and casually check on Fletcher. He may encourage Fletcher to ask for help from his coworkers. But this is awkward for Fletcher; he's come to depend on Tim. He doesn't really know the other people. He's embarrassed to ask for their help; they might think he's stupid or see that he's making mistakes. Better to keep going to Tim for help. A couple of times, when Fletcher *did* ask for help, his coworkers didn't know what to do. They didn't know if they should help Fletcher; they thought they didn't have the expertise like the job coach had. Instead of helping Fletcher, they ran to find Tim.

The die has been cast. It will be difficult, if not impossible, for Fletcher to ever achieve status as a real employee, one who makes friends with, and depends on, his coworkers. Worse, the employment counselor and Tim may decide Fletcher isn't "ready" for a real job since he's still so dependent on Tim. Perhaps Fletcher ought to go back to the sheltered workshop until he's learned to be more independent.

This isn't rocket science! Fletcher *never had the chance* to be successful because Tim unintentionally created dependence. Tim's help *prevented* Fletcher from achieving success at work. And his presence didn't facilitate friendships for Fletcher, it impeded them.

Would the situation have been different if Fletcher had gotten the job on his own (with informal help from friends or family members, as necessary); if he had been trained the way other employees are trained; and if he, his supervisors, and coworkers had worked together on accommodations and finding the best way for Fletcher to do things? And if all these things had happened, wouldn't Fletcher have enjoyed the wonderful sense of belonging?

Vocational Testing

There's nothing wrong with an individual choosing to be tested, if he thinks the test will help him narrow down the best employment opportunities. A dilemma arises, however, when a professional thinks the *only* way to determine the correct type of employment is through testing. A young adult may tell an employment counselor the type of job he wants, but the counselor doesn't believe he can find a job like that, or he believes the person won't be successful in the chosen field. His solution is to test the person to determine what type of job is suitable. But what happens when the individual isn't interested in pursuing a job that's "appropriate"?

Here's an example. With the common usage of computers, coupled with the ease with which accommodations can be made for their use, employment counselors frequently direct adults with significant physical disabilities into careers that use computers. Jason has indicated he doesn't want to work on a computer. But his counselor thinks this is the only job that's suitable because of Jason's inability to walk and perform other functional skills. If the counselor can get Jason to wear a head stick, he can get him a job doing data entry! When Jason rejects this offer, his name may be dropped to the bottom of the employment counselor's list. The counselor will focus on helping others who are easier to work with, more agreeable, and easier to place.

Be a Good Investigator

Young people with disabilities may be eligible for a variety of different programs. Check with your state Medicaid, Social Security, and vocational-rehabilitation offices or search the Internet. Keep in mind that these programs and services are full of red tape. You may already be aware of the regimentation, regulations, and invasion of privacy that are part and parcel of government assistance. However, there may be some situations in which you're prepared to put up with the red tape in order to get what your child needs.

One of these situations is the need for health care. Some young adults with disabilities end up applying for SSI just so they can get Medicaid. It's not that they need the SSI so badly; it's the Medicaid they really need. If, for example, Roger works at a job where no group health insurance is provided and he's no longer covered by his parents' health coverage, Medicaid may seem to be the only option. In order to qualify for Medicaid, Roger might have to quit the job he has and find a lower paying job to quality for SSI.

If we're creative, we can come up with solutions that won't force our children into the system. For example, if health insurance is not provided as an employee benefit, we might be able to find insurance from other sources instead of resorting to Medicaid. A variety of organizations provide group health insurance for owners and employees of small businesses. If your child becomes self-employed (more about this in the section on employment), he could join the local Chamber of Commerce if it provides group health insurance for member businesses. Other professional organizations also provide group health insurance to their members. Be a good investigator and ask others for help in finding solutions.

Our children will live better lives if we use the service system as a last resort. By using natural supports and generic services (Chapter 15) your child can get what he needs to be successful: a job, a place of his own, friends, transportation, or whatever else he wants or needs. Encourage him to dream big about what he wants to do, and make it happen with the help of folks in your community. Anything is possible: college, vocational school, self-employment, climbing the corporate ladder, marriage and family, and more.

FINISHING HIGH SCHOOL

Will your child receive a high school diploma or a certificate of attendance when he leaves high school? If you don't know the answer, find out. It may make a difference in your child's life, it may not.

Many students with disabilities who receive a segregated special education are given a certificate of attendance instead of a diploma. To receive a real diploma, high school students may be required to successfully complete a specific number of academic courses. And some states may have different types of diplomas, depending on the "track" a high school student pursues: academic, vocational, general, or some other category.

Traditionally, we've believed students who wish to attend college or other post-secondary trainings must have a high school diploma. But with the increased number of students who are homeschooled, this is changing. Many homeschooled students don't receive a high school diploma since they don't attend an accredited high school, and many colleges and universities no longer require a high school transcript. Instead, students present a GED (General Equivalency Diploma) and take a college entrance exam (SAT, ACT, etc.). So your child may or may not need a high school diploma in order to go on to post-secondary education. Research colleges, universities, or other schools to learn about entrance criteria.

Think carefully about what benefits your child is receiving from high school. If your teenager is included in regular education classes and is being successfully educated in the academic subjects he needs for life after high school, if you and your child are happy with the current situation, and if your child will receive a high school diploma or the appropriate credentials for him to continue pursuing his dreams of future employment, then all's well. However, if your teenager is stuck in a segregated classroom, if he's not learning anything that's important or relevant to him, and there's little or no hope that he will (because of the negative atmosphere at school), you might want to consider letting him leave school to pursue additional learning or employment in arenas that are more beneficial than the public school environment.

Prior to our family's decision to homeschool, I would have never made such a recommendation. My ardent belief was that all students need a high school education (and a real diploma) in order to be successful. But our experiences in homeschooling, coupled with the reality of what happens to many high school students with disabilities, have led me to question the benefit of students with disabilities staying in high school just because that's "what's always been done."

Carole: Getting on With Life

Sixteen-year-old Carole was luckier than many high school students with disabilities. Carole, who has a cognitive disability, was included in regular education classes during ninth and tenth grades. But after transition services for students with disabilities were mandated by IDEA in 1990, Carole's high school created new classes for students who received special education services. These focused on the "life skills" students with disabilities would need as adults. All students with disabilities were required to take these classes, and after the first two months of her junior year, Carole was miserable. She had gone from being a typical student to a special ed student. She was still taking some academic classes, but the mandatory special ed classes took the place of others.

In one of the life skills classes, special ed teachers took the class of teenagers with disabilities on field trips "in the community" to help them learn how to shop in a grocery store and become competent in other "activities of daily living." Carole hated these classes immediately. She knew how to shop for groceries since she went with her mom on a regular basis. She didn't like traipsing all over town with a bunch of other students with disabilities she didn't know, and she resented being treated "like a dummy" by the special ed teachers.

Almost overnight, Carole developed what the school called "behavior problems." The well-mannered teenager began rebelling against the special ed teachers. Patty was shocked when, for the first time in her life, her daughter started begging to stay home from school. Carole, the once-happy teenager, was becoming sad, angry, and depressed.

Patty considered fighting the school to try to get Carole out of the special ed classes and back into the academics Carole was missing. But she decided to do a little research first. She discovered that even though Carole had taken regular ed classes in her freshman and sophomore years, and by the time of graduation she would have several more academic classes under her belt, Carole still wouldn't get a high school diploma! She would only receive a certificate of attendance.

Students with disabilities in regular ed classes were graded differently than other students, so even though Carole made good grades, the school didn't consider them "real" grades. Thus, Carole's attendance was considered "participatory;" all of her hard work in the academic classes would not earn Carole a high school diploma. Patty was stymied about what to do, until she began looking at the big picture.

At sixteen, Carole knew what her dream job was. She wanted to be a baker or a chef. Patty and her husband supported Carole's dream. Carole had loved cooking since she was a little girl and as a teenager, she was an expert at making breads and pastries. Patty and Carole had already researched a trade school for bakers and chefs in their community. They had talked about Carole enrolling after she graduated. But with the current situation at the high school, Patty decided to find out what the entrance requirements were for the trade school. An incoming student needed to be at least sixteen and have a high school diploma or a GED.

The family sat down for a very important meeting. After weighing the pros and cons, the decision was unanimous: effective immediately, Carole would no longer attend the high school, she would get her GED, and enroll in the trade school when a new class started in about three months. Legally, everything was fine since students sixteen and older were not required to attend public school in Carole's state. Patty would help Carole prepare for the GED using one of the preparatory manuals available at bookstores.

They would enroll Carole in the two year trade school, paying for the tuition themselves because they didn't want the hassles with voc-rehab. And Carole would maintain her friendships with her typical friends from high school, while making new friends of all ages at the trade school. In addition, Carole would seek a part-time job at one of the many bakeries close by. There were several neighborhood supermarkets with in-store bakeries and a couple of independent bakeries nearby. Classes at the trade school were six hours a day, leaving time for a part-time job during the week and/or on weekends.

Carole's future was much brighter. The trade school guaranteed employment placement after graduation. Carole wouldn't need to put up with the special ed "junk" she hated at the high school, she would be doing what she loved, and she would be treated like the responsible young adult she was. Carole's dream—being a baker or a chef—didn't require her to continue attending public school. Carole and her family didn't view her leaving high school in a negative light. They looked at what was really important in Carole's life, they went for it, and they succeeded!

Think About What's Really Important

Thinking out of the box worked for Carole and her parents. They risked criticism from the school system and even from some close friends and family. But they were willing to take risks in order to meet Carole's needs and help her achieve her dream.

All families need to think out of the box when it comes to the futures of our children. Too many special educators, voc-rehab counselors, and others in the system have low expectations for young people with disabilities. If we don't take responsibility for our children's futures—if we leave their futures in the hands of the system—they'll be shuffled from one program or another based on their disability labels instead of their dreams. Don't depend on experts to steer your child in the right direction and/or make decisions about his future. Talk with your child about the current situation and what he wants to do with his life. Ask yourselves lots of questions and focus on what's really important:

- Is the high school environment beneficial or detrimental to your child?

- Is he learning what's important to him or is he languishing in dead-end special ed classes?

- Will he get a real diploma or a certificate of attendance? Is this an important issue for him?

- If he wants to stay in school, but things aren't satisfactory, what will it take to improve the situation? Can change happen quickly enough to make a difference? Will the changes be worth your efforts?

- If he's ready to leave school early, what will he do? There are a variety of possibilities. He might want to try homeschooling or unschooling in academics and/or other subjects he's interested in. He might be ready to take the GED and head into a job. One or more unpaid internships in businesses in the community might be interesting and beneficial. He might want to study for, and then take, the GED and other tests prior to entering college or a trade school.

If he knows what kind of career he wants and he needs to go to college or a trade school to achieve his dream, waste no time in researching the entrance criteria. Then do what it takes to make it happen.

If your child doesn't have any dreams for his future, get busy on two fronts. First, begin talking to him about his future, letting him know you believe in his ability to do whatever he wants to do. Second, begin exposing him to a variety of potential careers. Take him to work with you and ask friends and neighbors to do the same; when you're at the mall, ask him if he'd enjoy working there; when you watch movies or TV shows, talk about the jobs you see people doing; think about what he enjoys doing for pleasure, and figure out how he could use those interests or skills to earn a living. We're all happier in jobs we love!

VOLUNTEER INTERNSHIPS

Many young people (with and without disabilities) would greatly benefit from learning more about potential employment opportunities by serving in non-paid internships. Traditional volunteer opportunities already exist in hospitals, libraries, museums, zoos, and other non-profit organizations. Volunteer work in any of these places can be very beneficial. Young people mature and learn new things right before our eyes. But we can create non-traditional volunteer opportunities as well. A variety of businesses in your neighborhood can nurture your child's budding employment skills.

Check into small, locally-owned businesses first. They make their own rules and can give you a yes or no without having to check with the corporate office: office supply stores, hair salons, flower shops, dry cleaners, health food stores, pack and ship stores, video stores, music shops, veterinary offices, doctor or dentist offices, insurance agencies, and others. Start with businesses where you already know the employees or the owner and/or network with friends who can get you connected.

Internships are whatever you, your child, and the business manager decide they are. They could be as short as one day or as long as a month; an hour a day three times a week after school or four hours on a Saturday. A business owner might assign your child to shadow one particular employee, or your child might be free to roam the business learning whatever looks interesting from whoever has the time to teach. Your teenager will not only learn what he likes, he'll also learn what he doesn't like! Perhaps most importantly, internships have the potential to become paid employment.

POST-SECONDARY EDUCATION

Traditionally, high school students and young adults with developmental disabilities have not been thought of as "college material" and most professionals have focused on employment in lieu of post-secondary education. But this is a ridiculous practice. There's absolutely no reason young people with disabilities shouldn't further their education in pursuit of their dreams.

Colleges, universities, and other post-secondary training schools including correspondence and Internet courses, whether public or private, may not discriminate against students with disabilities under the Americans with Disabilities Act (ADA). In addition, if the school receives federal funds, Section 504 of the Rehab Act comes into play.

The protections provided by both of these laws mandate that reasonable accommodations be provided to a student with a disability at no additional cost. A qualification to this statement is important, however. The school does not have to provide the *exact* accommodation that's requested. But it must provide an accommodation that accomplishes the same goal. For example, a student who is unable to take notes requests a note taker. The school may elect to provide him with a tape recorder to tape the professor's lectures instead.

In the public school system, the school is required to identify children with disabilities. But in higher education, this responsibility rests with the student. In order to receive the protections of the ADA and Section 504, the student is required to identify himself—as a student with a disability in need of accommodations—to the school's office of disability services or the ADA compliance officer. Additionally, the student will probably be required to show recent (within three years) documentation of the disability from a physician. Schools must be given a reasonable amount of time to provide the accommodations. For example, if a student needs textbooks on audio tape, the school is responsible for ordering them from the publisher. But the publisher may not keep the audio tapes in stock; they're made on demand. Thus, it may take several weeks before the cassettes are ready.

In post-secondary settings, a student with a disability must be specific in identifying what accommodations she needs. She can't expect the school to know, for example, that she needs longer time to take tests. Many schools have excellent counselors (many of whom have disabilities themselves) to assist students in determining what accommodations will be helpful. Professors and instructors are obligated to honor the accommodations.

In some cases, a student may elect to attend college not for the purpose of attaining a degree, but for other reasons: social opportunities, learning about one or two subjects, becoming involved in sports, or for some other reason. I've known students with a variety of disabilities (including Down syndrome and autism) who have enrolled in college to "audit" courses. The student attends classes, but is not graded and receives no college credit. The students I knew took the courses to learn more about the subject, make friends, and experience college life. Research, study, plan, and visit potential colleges, universities, and trade or vocational schools. Check out correspondence courses and distance learning via the Internet.

How will you pay for your child's education? Students with disabilities should look into student loans, just as other students do. Typically, student loans require full time attendance (twelve semester hours). Some students with disabilities may be physically unable to carry a full load each semester, but they can ask for the reasonable accommodation of part-time attendance (six or nine semester hours) and still be eligible for a student loan.

In addition, research the wide variety of scholarships available. The public library is a good place to start. Scholarships come in all shapes and sizes. Most schools offer a variety of scholarships. Professional organizations offer scholarships to students going into their field. For example, accounting organizations provide scholarships for students going into accounting. Some foundations and other organizations specifically target students with disabilities. And don't forget to research voc-rehab. Many adults with disabilities have been terribly unhappy with voc-rehab's efforts to find them jobs, but they were very happy when the agency paid for college!

EMPLOYMENT

Typical high school students often enter the work force as soon as they're legally of age to do so, working at part-time jobs after school or on weekends. As previously discussed, many high school students who receive special education services aren't expected to find their own jobs; they're supposed to go to the special ed teacher and/or voc-rehab employment counselor.

The consensus of adults with disabilities I know is that the best jobs are the ones they got on their own, without help from the system. Whether your child is interested in finding a part-time job or a full-time career position, encourage and help him find employment on his own. When young people with disabilities get their own jobs, their self-esteem and self-determination are greatly enhanced.

Regardless of your child's disability, regardless of what you've been told about your child's potential, and regardless of your own estimation about your child's ability to work, presume he'll be able to get a job and support himself. I know many adults with disabilities who have been considered "unemployable" by their parents or experts in the system, but who are happily and successfully employed. With assistive technology, accommodations, and modifications, they do just fine, thank you. The first step in the ladder is your belief in him. Without that belief, he will surely fail. With it, his potential is unlimited.

Provide help and support the way you would if your child didn't have a disability. Talk to your child about the types of jobs he has expressed an interest in, as well as the ones you think he may be interested in. Many young people (with and without disabilities) haven't had enough life experience to know about the wide variety of occupations. Help your child learn how to find the job he wants: researching jobs through the newspaper want ads, using the Internet, and networking with others.

Role play a job interview: do it yourself or ask the personnel manager where you work to help your child practice. Talk about salary, how to be a good employee, and other important aspects of work. If your child is nervous about asking for an employment application, let her watch you (or someone else) do it. Pretend you're the one looking for a job and take her to businesses around town. Walk in, with her beside you, and ask for an application for yourself, which you'll take home to fill out. Model the behavior and interactions you hope she'll follow. Once you've been to three or four places, ask her if she's ready to do it herself. After you've collected several employment applications, go over them with her at home and help her learn how to complete them.

Under the Americans with Disabilities Act, employment discrimination based on a person's disability is prohibited. But we know discrimination still exists. It often occurs the minute a person with a disability asks for an application and the employer sees the disability. To avoid this situation, many people with visible disabilities find ways to submit an application without being seen. They call employers and ask that an application be sent to them through the mail or by fax, they apply for positions over the Internet, or find other ways (networking, etc.) to make the initial approach. In this way, a person is first judged by his qualifications. When and if he's called in for a personal interview, his credentials, not his disability, will precede him. Help your child learn strategies for coping with these issues.

Seek out employers that promote equal opportunity for people with disabilities. I've seen want ads in local papers from McDonald's, Macintosh Computers, and the Marriott hotel chain that specifically target people with disabilities and other groups.

We need to help our children learn to speak for themselves about the types of job accommodations they may need. For example, an employee might need to have the official employee manual read to him or modified in some way so he understands company policy. A person may need a different type of training than the usual, physical accommodations, or some other modification to enable him to do the job. We need to help our children figure these things out, while at the same time, help them learn to speak up for themselves.

The happiest workers are those who love what they do. To that end, help your child find a job doing something he loves. Keep in mind, however, that just like all of us, he may change his mind (and his jobs) many times before settling into a short or long-term career. Unfortunately, a "change of mind" isn't always welcomed by service providers.

During my tenure as a board member of an agency providing services for people with disabilities, several employment providers described their services at a board meeting. As we listened to representatives from sheltered workshops, Goodwill, and a university-based supported employment project, it was obvious the university project was the best of the lot.

At the end of the formal presentations, we asked the presenters to describe the biggest issues they face. The university professor's answer was the most disturbing. "Well," he replied with a big sigh, "our biggest problem is what happens after we get people jobs. After they've been in a job for a year or so, some of them want to get better jobs, some want to get married and so they want a different job, and some want to go part-time so they can go to college. These people don't know how hard we worked to get them jobs and then they go and want to change things!"

The professor had lost sight of the fact that he was describing what people who don't have disabilities do! His shortsightedness was appalling! I thought it was wonderful that people with disabilities were starting to live real lives: wanting to move up in the world of work, falling in love and getting married, and wanting to go to college. The professor seemed angry that "clients" weren't satisfied with an entry level job for the rest of their lives!

If you and your child are at a loss on which direction to go, or if you just want a little help from your friends, have a Dream Party (Chapter 15). Enrich your child's life by using the natural supports and generic services available in your own community.

Thinking Outside the Box

In our service-based economy, self-employment is becoming a reality for more and more people with and without disabilities. What could your son or daughter do in the way of self-employment? The possibilities are infinite: word processing, lawn care, disability consulting, web site creation, interior design, graphic arts, photography, vending machines, pet walker/sitter, house sitter, professional shopper, house-cleaning services, writer, landscape services, catering, accountant, public relations, mobile car mechanic, doctor, lawyer, and . . . if your child can dream it, he can do it.

Some of these positions require post-secondary education; some don't. Many self-employed individuals work from their homes, making their own schedules, and enjoying the freedom of being their own bosses. In fact, you don't even need to be self-employed to do this: a variety of companies allow employees to work at home. We never know what the future may bring. Many successful businesses, large and small, began with one self-employed entrepreneur!

Job carving—another great option for employment—can be done a variety of ways, but in general, it involves identifying what a person likes to do and does well (or can do well in the right circumstances), and then finding a business where the person's abilities would be valuable even if no job opening currently exists. In essence, you carve a job opportunity.

For example, eighteen-year-old Roni loved to take care of plants, and she had a real green thumb. Roni, her parents, and friends who were helping in her job quest first considered a plant nursery. But after visiting several, Roni realized she didn't like those places: too much dirt, the floors were always wet, and the rows of plants were overwhelming.

Roni's supporters started looking for other places where Roni could take care of plants and make money doing it. They spread the word to everyone they knew about Roni and her love of plants. Through creative networking (a friend of a friend of a friend and so on) they connected with Sandra, the office manager at Delta Graphics.

The company occupied half of one floor in a multi-story office building. The tenants in the building could pay monthly fees to the landlord for nightly office cleaning, weekly window washing, and twice weekly plant maintenance for the many large ornamental plants that adorned every office. If they wished, however, tenants could find their own providers of these services. Like most of the other tenants, Delta found it easier to pay the landlord each month rather than contracting directly with a cleaning service, a window washer, and a plant maintenance service.

When Sandra heard about Roni, she offered to help. She invited Roni for a tour of Delta Graphics. They had a pleasant and informal discussion about the care of the plants. On the spot, Sandra contracted with Roni to come in twice a week and take care of the plants in Delta's offices. She canceled the landlord's plant maintenance service and agreed to pay Roni the amount Delta had been paying the landlord each month ($200.00). Roni would be an independent contractor, not an employee of Delta Graphics.

The professional plant maintenance service had always brought their own equipment. Roni had a few things at home she could bring when she did the plant care, and Sandra agreed to provide a new pair of pruning shears and a supply of plant food. They found a cupboard in the store room to keep these items.

Roni gave the plants more tender loving care than the plant maintenance company ever did. Each Monday and Thursday, Roni spent two or three hours watering, feeding, and pruning the numerous plants in Delta's suite of offices. She took time to polish the leaves on the larger plants. As Roni moved around the different offices, she became acquainted with many Delta employees. Roni's income wasn't much, but she was happy. She was still living at home, she had no expenses of her own yet, she loved what she was doing, and she really liked the people at Delta Graphics.

In her second month of contract work for Delta, Roni unintentionally assumed a few more responsibilities. Everyone at Delta knew Roni's routine: which office she worked in first, where she went next, and which office was her last. Different employees began asking Roni for help. For example, Stan asked, "On your way to Mr. Erickson's office, would you mind giving him this file?" Roni was glad to help. Sandra noticed these little extras Roni was being asked to do. Not only was Roni's green thumb valuable to Delta, but so was her friendly personality and her willingness to help others.

At the next staff meeting, Sandra proposed they expand Roni's responsibilities and hire her as a full-time employee. Sandra's boss, who was often out of town and didn't know Roni very well, asked Sandra what Roni would do forty hours a week. Before Sandra could reply, several employees jumped in: "She could be a runner and help us get files back and forth. It would save us time!" said Stan. "I was hoping she could help us with our filing system," added Laurie. Joe asked, "Could she help with the mail?"

Roni was ecstatic about her new full time position, for which she was paid $6.00 an hour, making her gross monthly income $960.00. She had a variety of duties, including continuing to keep the plants healthy and beautiful. In three months, she would receive a performance review and a possible raise in her hourly wage. Her goal is to save as much money as she can in anticipation of getting her own apartment in six months—an apartment that will also have beautiful potted plants.

Roni could have chosen to offer her plant care services to other businesses in the large office complex where Delta was located. Sandra and others would have given her positive references and Roni's self-employment would have expanded. At some point, she might choose to go back to being her own boss.

Self-employment can take many forms. The possibilities are endless. A couple of years ago I read a newspaper story about a professional who was between jobs. He wasn't having much luck finding a new position in his chosen field. While he was looking for work he needed to have some money coming in, but he didn't want to take an interim full-time job at a convenience store or a fast food place because then he wouldn't have time to look for a job in his field and go on job interviews. He needed something with a flexible schedule.

Many of his friends were working couples with pets. He heard one of them complain about having to take the time to pick up the dog poop in the yard every week. Bingo. The unemployed professional offered to do the dirty work once a week for $7.00. He had his first customer. Soon he had more customers, as other friends asked for his services. Now he had a little money coming in and his schedule allowed him to keep looking for a new job.

But his customer base grew; friends of friends asked for his services and soon he had a full-time job picking up dog poop for $7.00 a yard! Before long, he had to hire others to help. And soon, he began selling poop-picker-upper franchises! He never did go back to his professional career; he was making too much money in the poop business. (I wonder if he tried to sell all the poop to a fertilizer company.) What type of service could your young adult child provide?

In our small town in Colorado, we've used the services of a dog sitter. When we went on a ten-day vacation, we took our dog to the lady's home and paid her $10.00 a day. The rate was a little less than what the dog kennel charged and we liked the fact that our precious pup wouldn't be locked in a cage all day. The dog sitter had two dogs of her own and she was home most of the day. Our pet would be with other dogs in her home and yard. We could have chosen to have the dog sitter come to our house once a day to feed, water, and play with our dog for a few minutes. If a dog sitter took care of five dogs a day, 20 days a month, at $10.00/dog, she could gross $1,000 each month, and if she wished, she could hold down another part time job at the same time to earn even more.

Does your child like to shop? Professional shoppers sell their services to busy executives who are generous givers but have no time to shop for loved ones and business associates.

At one time, only the wealthy paid someone to clean their houses. But today, middle class homeowners have joined the ranks of people who will pay for someone to vacuum, dust, wash windows, and mop. Many women who started out as "the cleaning lady" have acquired so many customers they've had to hire other people to help (like the pooper scooper man). From self-employed cleaning lady to business owner is not a bad way to go!

Earlier, I suggested one good way to get ideas about jobs your child might be interested in was to get in the car and drive around town looking at different business. But this idea won't work when thinking about self-employment ideas since many self-employed people work out of their homes. So take a different approach to get your creative juices flowing. Sit down with the telephone book. Start in the beginning and review every category of listings. With your child, make a list of career ideas that sound interesting. Not only will you see what's already being done, you'll also get ideas for new businesses!

Think about starting your own family business, one your child could help with today, and run himself tomorrow. Look into the vending machine business. Buy a soda machine and put it in a local business. Stock it with sodas and count the quarters all the way to the bank. Then buy another and another and another. It can become your child's business and he'll be successful long after you're gone.

Could your child become a paid consultant, advising businesses on how to become more accessible and user-friendly for people with disabilities? Could your child advise schools how to become more inclusive? Think out of the box. Get creative, be bold, think big. Help your child dream the impossible and watch it come true!

MOVING AWAY FROM MOM AND DAD

Whether your child wants to move into the dorm at school or into his own apartment across town, it can happen. Some parents don't believe this is possible, especially if their young adult children need a lot of assistance. But where there's a will, there's a way.

We can try to work the system to find personal care attendants to help our children dress, cook, go to the bathroom, or provide other daily assistance. This might be a successful endeavor. But it may also be an exercise in futility or a long journey through miles of red tape. The alternative is to look for natural supports.

If dorm life is your child's dream, there are several possibilities. If your child will be attending the same college or university that some of his peers will be attending, recruit one of them to be your child's dorm mate. This must ultimately be your child's decision, of course, but a good friend can be your child's helper. Work out the details so it's a win-win scenario for everyone. You might offer to pay the helper for his time or perhaps your child and his dorm mate help each other. For example, the dorm mate can provide the physical assistance your child needs and your child can provide transportation in his wheelchair accessible van if the dorm mate doesn't have wheels of his own.

You could also ask the office of disability services at the university for ideas. They might have a list of students who are looking for a dorm mate. Students who are studying in a field related to disabilities (medicine, special education, rehab, and so forth) might want to room with a student with a disability as a way of learning more. Who knows what possibilities may exist?

If your young adult child is chomping at the bit to move into her own apartment across town, find ways to make it happen. Slight modifications to the methods described above might help find a roommate to share the rent and provide assistance. A friend or acquaintance from high school might be looking to move into an apartment, and she also needs a roommate. It could be a perfect match. This is where networking is important: spread the word about what your child wants to do.

Young adults with cognitive or behavioral disabilities can successfully move away from mom and dad and they don't have to move into a group home to do it! They can live with a helpful roommate or alone, and in either case, can be supported and helped by friends and neighbors.

Meg uses a power wheelchair, a communication device, and a service animal, but she lives alone in her own apartment. She's become friends with several of the closest neighbors in the apartment complex. Each of these neighbors has a key to her apartment, and each has a particular job. Sheila does Meg's grocery shopping when she shops for herself. When she returns from the store, Sheila unloads Meg's groceries and puts them away. Meg eats things that are easy to fix, so she does her own cooking. Another neighbor picks up Meg's mail everyday, slits the envelopes open, and leaves the mail on Meg's kitchen table.

Four different neighbors take turns helping Meg get ready for work every day: getting her out of bed, helping in the bathroom, and getting her dressed. These four take turns helping her get to bed every night. In addition, a couple of Meg's good friends regularly visit and help, too.

Meg reciprocates by helping her neighbors in various ways. One couple brings their two school-aged children over to Meg's two or three evenings a month when they go out for dinner and a movie. When another neighbor goes on extended business trips, Meg waters his plants and feeds the fish. There are other ways Meg reciprocates, and all the help given and received is done in the spirit of friendship and community. Like Meg, we should expect to be successful. We must consciously make up our minds to succeed. When we believe we'll be successful, we will be.

LEARNING FROM OTHERS

In the chapter on history, you learned about the beginnings of the Independent Living Movement and the Self-Advocacy (People First) Movement. Today, our sons and daughters can benefit from these movements by learning from others with disabilities.

Centers for Independent Living

In cities and towns all across the country, Centers for Independent Living (CILs), also called Independent Living Centers (ILCs), provide assistance to help people with disabilities acquire skills to live independently. These services may range from learning to advocate for oneself, how to find a place to live, or how to cook!

Every local CIL is a little different; what's offered at one may not be offered at another. But what most have in common is that CIL staff members are people with disabilities who can provide peer support to others. CILs originally focused on people with physical disabilities, but their assistance now embraces people with all types of disabilities.

Keep in mind that some CILs have strayed from the original purpose outlined by Ed Roberts when he developed the philosophy of people with disabilities being in control of their own lives. As detailed in Chapter 2, the earliest CILs focused on self-advocacy, systems change advocacy, and learning how to be in control of your own life (independent living).

Today, many CILs offer important skill-building activities, but some have become service providers themselves, which is contrary to the original philosophy. Some CILs provide attendant care for people on Medicaid; others have taken over community paratransit systems. Ed believed CILs should be the watchdog of service providers, to ensure they were doing the right things for people with disabilities. But when CILs move from grass roots organizations focusing on advocacy and self-determination skills to becoming service providers, how can they watchdog themselves?

Even so, a CIL might be a valuable resource, one that can provide peer support and help to your young adult child. If you don't know of a CIL in your area, call the state independent living council for more information (see the appendix). You might be able to find a local center through the telephone book, but some have unique names that may not include "center for independent living" or "independent living center."

One more brief word of warning: be wary of CILs that are run by people *without* disabilities. The philosophy of peer support, and the underlying belief that people with disabilities can and should be in control of their lives, can be easily corrupted if the leadership of a CIL is not in the hands of people who have disabilities.

In addition, there are human service agencies that are not independent living centers at all, but they incorporate "independent living" or similar wording in their business names. I once met an employee of one of these organizations. Based on his business card, I assumed he worked for a CIL. But as we talked, I realized he and I weren't speaking the same language. At one point, he seemed insulted when I asked how many people with disabilities worked at the agency. "We don't hire people with disabilities to work *in our office.* We find jobs that are appropriate for them," he replied. I knew then he didn't work for a CIL.

He knew nothing about the independent living philosophy, Ed Roberts, or self-determination. His company was a non-profit agency that had a state contract to provide employment and vocational counseling to people with disabilities. The words "independence center" were part of the business name. So ask lots of questions, find out who funds the organization, the purpose of the organization, who works there (people with or without disabilities), and more.

Self-Advocacy and People First Organizations

While CILs are actual businesses with "store fronts," Self-Advocacy or People First chapters are organizations of people with disabilities who come together on a regular basis for meetings. And, like CILs, People First chapters may differ from one another. Most are sponsored by local or state disability organizations, such as Arc affiliates.

People First meetings serve several purposes. One objective is social interaction; it's a fun time to meet new people. Members also focus on helping one another learn to speak up for themselves, provide moral support, and teach communication skills. Some People First chapters are very active in legislative advocacy and other areas of systems change, and members teach each other how to work with legislators, how to impact the system, and how to serve on boards and committees.

Self-advocacy groups are autonomous; members create the agenda and run the meetings based on what's important to them. People First chapters were originally focused on people with cognitive disabilities, but like CILs, they now embrace people with all disabilities. The focus of most People First chapters is self-advocacy and self-determination. To that end, they do not want, need, or permit people without disabilities in leadership positions. The only people without disabilities who are involved in self-advocacy chapters are advisors who have been invited to participate. (So don't be offended if you're not allowed to accompany your child to a meeting!) The role of an advisor is to stay in the background until he's needed, and this need is determined by the members, not by the advisor.

People First chapters help make self-advocacy and self-determination a reality for their members. Throughout this book, I've exhorted you to presume competence, and that's exactly what adults with disabilities do for one another in People First chapters. Contacts for People First/Self-Advocacy chapters are listed in the appendix.

Mentors

It's never too late and it's never too early to focus on what our children need to be successful as adults. If you and your child don't know any adults with developmental disabilities, go out and find some today! Benjamin loves to meet adults with disabilities. Even though we always talk to Benj about how successful he'll be as an adult, he needs to see for himself that people who use wheelchairs live what he calls a "regular life." When I return from presenting at workshops around the country, he always asks about people I met who use chairs: "Were they married? Did they have kids? Where did they go to college? What kind of job do they have?"

If possible, try to find a successful adult who has the same or similar disability as your child's. Let that person become a mentor to you and your child. Our family has several adult friends who use wheelchairs. I learn so much from them. When I get stuck on an issue affecting Benj, I go to them with my questions. They have answers based on experience, not hypothetical answers or answers based on professional knowledge. You can meet adults with disabilities at CILs, through People First Chapters, at disability conferences, and other places. Be creative!

For Benj, these friends provide a window to the future. He's not dependent on my belief that he'll be successful; he knows it's a reality when he sees adults with physical disabilities.

I know Benjamin and what his needs are better than anyone else. But I don't know what it's really like to have a physical disability, to use a wheelchair, to need help going to the bathroom or getting dressed, or about anything else that Benjamin experiences on a daily basis. But an adult who uses a wheelchair, who's grown up with a physical disability, does know these things. And I have an obligation to learn from people who are the true experts—people with disabilities—in order to best help my son. I owe him that.

Not only am I obligated to learn from others, I'm also obligated to educate others. And the most important thing you and I can do in this regard is to educate society by promoting positive images of people with disabilities. That's next.

Promoting Positive Images 20

NO WRITTEN LAW HAS EVER BEEN MORE BINDING THAN
UNWRITTEN CUSTOM SUPPORTED BY POPULAR OPINION.
Carrie Chapman Catt

Seventy-five years ago, millions of Americans sat at the breakfast table, sipped their morning coffee and read all about the "menace" of people with disabilities. The daily newspaper detailed the importance of sterilizing men and women in institutions to save the United States from the dangers of "feebleminded idiots."

Today, stories about people with disabilities cover a wide berth, but with few exceptions, the message is still perverse and inaccurate, reflecting popular opinion. At one end are the so-called inspirational stories. Christopher Reeve, the former Superman who has devolved into the "Jerry Lewis of spinal cord injuries," routinely begs for money for spinal cord research to "fix people like me." "Heart-wrenching" tales describe the lives of high school athletes and other young people with "promising" lives who have been "struck down" by injuries "suffered" in accidents, but who "triumph" over their "tragedies," vowing—like Reeve—to walk again. At the other end of the spectrum are chronicles that question the value of saving premature babies and investing in the education of "special needs" students.

Why do we continue to see stories that portray people with disabilities these ways? Maybe the "inspirational" reports are an attempt to make the majority in society feel better: "I guess my life's not so bad after all. I should be thankful I'm not like them." Other stories may be intended to educate the public about the "waste" of tax dollars. In stories about the high cost of children with disabilities, the "menace" message of the 1920s has been repackaged. The threat is no longer to America's moral fiber, but to its fiscal resources. With few exceptions, negative, stereotypical images persist.

If reporters love writing—and the public loves reading—inspirational human interest stories, why don't they visit hospitals to profile babies who are born with disabilities? I think I know the answer. People who acquire disabilities are perceived to have had a "real" life before their injuries. Their lives were valuable because they contributed to—or had the potential to contribute—to society. Babies who are born with disabilities are not perceived as having valuable lives. What, if anything, could *they* contribute to society? How, if at all, could *they* participate in society?

While traveling around the country to do workshops, a seat mate on the airplane will engage me in small talk about where I'm going, the purpose of my trip, and so forth. When I respond that I'm on my way to do a workshop on disability issues, I'm perceived as a professional—a fellow business traveler. The next question, delivered with both respect and curiosity, is usually, "Oh, really, what do you teach?" I give a brief description of the conference or event, along with a few details of the workshop. Invariably, the next question is, "Oh, how did you get into this field?" When I reply, "Well, my son was born with cerebral palsy and—" I'm interrupted with an, "Oh, I'm so sorry."

In the time it took me to say the words, the equality in our short-term relationship evaporated. I'm no longer seen as professional equal, but an "unfortunate mom." The interest my seat mate previously demonstrated is immediately replaced with pity and sadness.

I always respond with, "Why are you sorry? I don't feel sorry for my son and you shouldn't either." I follow with a mini-lecture on how people with disabilities are more like others than they are different. By this time, I'm sure my fellow traveler wishes he had never opened his mouth!

We know that stereotypical perceptions have originated from within the various groups that have been "in charge" of the lives of individuals with disabilities from the beginning of recorded history: religious leaders, social reformers, physicians, educators, government agencies, human services workers, and others. Today, perceptions are spread throughout society by the media and disability agencies and organizations. And, unfortunately in our era, people with disabilities and parents have unintentionally contributed to the myths when they participate in human interest stories that portray people with disabilities as pitiful.

Today, more and more people with disabilities and their families are wresting power from professionals and the system, and they're taking control of their lives. This is a giant leap in the right direction. But there's more we can do. As we go about the business of changing the lives of our families and children, we must also explode the negative disability myths that permeate our culture. We can choose from a variety of formal and informal ways to accomplish this goal.

TEACHING OTHERS

Our efforts must always begin at home, with our families and friends. But our outreach must extend to everyone else we come in contact with, especially those who hold powerful positions. We need to influence those who influence others.

When Benjamin was first diagnosed at the tender age of four months, the pediatric neurologist had these words: "Your son has static encephalopathy. This means he won't walk when other kids do and [yadda, yadda, yadda] . . ." I had no idea what he was talking about, but I knew it wasn't good. Our pediatrician had recommended this doctor, so I assumed I should trust his diagnosis. For ten or twelve days, I stewed and cried and tried to learn what I could from my home medical books, none of which had an entry for "static encephalopathy."

Then I took Benjamin to a pediatric orthopedist—again, as recommended by the pediatrician—who casually announced, "Oh, your son has cerebral palsy." Stunned almost into silence, I squeaked, "But the other doctor said he had 'static encephalopathy'." The orthopedist explained the neurologist's diagnosis was the more accurate medical term for a condition under the umbrella of cerebral palsy. I left the orthopedist's office frustrated that the neurologist didn't tell me the "truth" in words I understood. And I was angry the neurologist didn't put me in touch with other parents whose children had the same disability. That's what I really needed. I didn't need all the medical jargon.

During the next few months, I became better acquainted with the neurologist's nurse and had a number of heart-to-heart conversations with her. I let her know how frustrated I was by the doctor's use of jargon and his failure to give me helpful information. Martha said her boss was like other physicians: he didn't want to be the "bad guy." She added that physicians who make the diagnoses of children with disabilities don't want parents to hate them for giving them the "bad news" about their kids, so they often mince words to soften the blow. In this case, "static encephalopathy" sounded better than "cerebral palsy."

I explained the doctor would have been more helpful if he told me the diagnosis in plain English—cerebral palsy—and if he had put me in touch with other parents. (Years later, the doctor's actions made sense when I looked at reference books for physicians, in which doctors are urged to handle parents with kid gloves at the time of diagnosis, even going so far as to recommend mental health counseling for parents.) Over time, and after many conversations with Martha, she and the doctor made a significant change in how they dealt with parents of kids with disabilities: one of the examining rooms was turned into a parent resource room. They stocked it with pamphlets from disability organizations in our area, acquired a library of videos parents could watch, and began telling parents about support groups and other opportunities to network and learn more. I know this change made a big difference to parents who came after me.

We have countless opportunities to influence the many folks we're in contact with: doctors, nurses, therapists, social workers, service coordinators, grocery store clerks, neighbors, ministers, the friends of our children and their parents, our children's teachers, and others, many others. In casual conversations, you can present new views about your child and others with disabilities, in a kind and helpful manner.

In Chapter 11, you learned about People First Language and how to redefine your child. The simple act of describing our children by their assets instead of perceived deficits is one of the easiest ways to promote positive images of people with disabilities. Talking about your child's interests, talents, and abilities demonstrates the similarities between your child and other children. When people you're in contact with see your child in a different light, they'll begin to see other people with disabilities with new eyes.

Some parents aren't quite sure how to go about doing this, especially if they're not accustomed to talking about their children from an asset-based perspective. If this is you, start by having internal conversations with yourself, practicing what you'll say from now on. If you've enlisted the help of others in identifying your child's assets, they'll know about your new way of thinking and will be there to support you. There's absolutely nothing wrong with announcing, "I've discovered a new way of thinking about my child, and I'd like to share it with you."

This informal strategy will have a ripple effect. By getting other people to talk and think differently about your child, you're providing them with the skills to share this new perspective with others. It grows from there. You have no way of knowing how many individuals you'll end up influencing over time.

INFLUENCING THROUGH PRESENTATIONS

Before I was in the Partners in Policymaking leadership development training in Texas, I was like the majority of Americans who identify public speaking as their "#1 fear"—above snakes and dying. While the training course didn't teach me about public speaking per se, the experience (combined with my determination to change things on behalf of my son and others) propelled me on a path that led first to public speaking and then to my authoring this book.

Never in my wildest dreams did I ever think I could influence others. I had no formal training. But what I did have (and what I hope you have) is passion. By turning our anger and frustration into passion, we can make positive changes. When you have passion—when your heart burns with it—talking about the issues is easy. Don't confuse anger with passion, however. We can feel anger, but we need to channel it into positive actions. Using anger to try to change others usually backfires.

Presentations can be effective means of promoting positive images of people with disabilities. But the *way* the information is presented is critical.

No More Puppets and Simulations

Many disability-related organizations have prepackaged disability awareness presentations which use puppets, videos, and/or storytelling. Other organizations and individuals use simulations: participants without disabilities are asked to sit in wheelchairs, smear petroleum jelly on their glasses, stuff cotton in their ears and the like, all in an effort to simulate having a disability. All of these activities are well-intentioned, but they're fraught with problems.

Puppets might get children's attention, but what ultimate message do they convey? That people with disabilities aren't real? How does a child transfer the image of a cute and cuddly puppet using a wheelchair to the reality of a living, breathing child or adult using a wheelchair who may not look cute and cuddly? Fans of these programs apparently believe children's love of toys (puppets) will open the door to understanding. That's like saying a girl who plays with dolls understands about real babies or a boy who plays with cars knows something about real cars. Puppet shows portray individuals with disabilities as objects.

Would promoters of puppet shows use "black" puppets to teach children what it's like to be African-American? Would the leader of a boys' group use female puppets to teach boys what it's like to be a girl? Both of these proposals are ludicrous, yet for some reason, using puppets is often considered an acceptable method to teach others about disabilities.

Simulations aren't any better. Rather than providing an awareness or understanding of what it's really like to have a disability, simulations often perpetuate and reinforce feelings of pity, and the experience is not realistic. A person who has been blindfolded may laugh when he runs into a wall, but he can't wait to rip the blindfold off and return to "normal." He has no way of knowing or experiencing the reality: that a person who is blind has acquired highly successful skills and strategies for moving around the world. Instead of "understanding" what it's like, he feels pity for blind people because they "can't see."

Simulating wheelchair use is often laughable. Sit a person in a wheelchair and watch him attempt to pop a wheelie. Then watch as he rises from the chair and picks it up to get past an obstacle such as a curb or an incline. Realistic? Hardly.

How, in the course of a workshop, can one simulate cruising for blocks in search of a curb cut to cross the street? Or what it feels like for a waiter to ask your friend what you want to eat instead of speaking to you directly? Or what it's like to go thirsty for hours when you're out because you're never sure if you'll be able to find an accessible restroom in which to empty your full bladder?

Wheelchair-use simulation might teach people what it's like to be unable to walk, but it cannot teach people about the realities of prejudice or the physical restrictions caused by lack of access. And how, within the schemes of puppetry or simulations, can an awareness of hidden disabilities, such as cognitive, behavioral, or learning disabilities be presented?

Puppet shows, simulations, and other methods are both ineffective and demeaning. There is absolutely no method that can enable people to "understand" what it's really like to have a disability, just as there's no method to teach Euro-Americans to "understand" what it's really like to be African-American, men to be women, girls to be boys, and so on.

Disability awareness programs typically focus on the disability, the differences, and/or what people with disabilities can't do. Society is all too aware of these differences, and reinforcing them or trying to explain them does nothing to further equality; it does just the opposite. Perceived differences creates barriers.

Sharing similarities, however, builds bridges. We need to move from disability awareness to *similarity awareness.* The best method to promote positive images is one in which real people with disabilities and their family members teach others about the similarities—not differences—between people with and without disabilities.

Presenting to Your Child's Peers

Parents can wield tremendous influence in their children's lives by presenting information to classmates in inclusive school rooms, teammates in athletics, and peers in any social setting. Again, the way the information is presented is critically important.

The most important component of an awareness presentation is a child's participation. Many well-meaning parents and teachers work diligently to "prepare" students for the arrival of a child with a disability in the classroom. But all too often, the child with the disability isn't included in the preparation. Why not? Because adults think it wouldn't be kind to talk about the student while he's sitting there. This rationale is based in kindness, but this approach can do more harm than good.

Here's what often happens. Let's assume Mrs. Jones is preparing her class for Samuel's arrival on Monday. Her goal is to help the students understand about Samuel and his disability so they won't be frightened by him or cruel to him. Mrs. Jones truly wants her students to welcome Samuel.

Explaining that Samuel has autism, she provides many details about his unusual behavior, his infrequent speech, and other characteristics. She explains that Samuel has never been in a regular classroom, so everyone needs to be patient and help him become familiar with the routine. Her intention is to demystify Samuel, to make him real, to help the students understand his differences. But she's actually painting a picture of a child no one wants to be around.

After Mrs. Jones finishes her talk, the students in her class have a variety of pictures in their heads about Samuel. Few, if any, are flattering. Pretend, for a moment, you're one of the students. What might you be thinking about? Are you hoping Mrs. Jones won't sit

Samuel by you? Are you visualizing some kind of monster? Or maybe you think he's like a baby since he doesn't talk much and he has strange behavior. You probably feel sorry for Samuel, even though you've never seen him. At the same time, you're a little frightened.

This is not a good beginning for Samuel. Most of us are visually-oriented, we form initial impressions about people by what we see. As we get to know a new person, we learn what he's like on the inside. But first impressions stick, and the first visual impression of Samuel—as painted by Mrs. Jones—isn't favorable. Samuel will need to work hard to get his classmates to see beyond their first impressions of him. An unflattering myth surrounds him before any of his classmates have ever laid eyes on him. This is patently unfair.

Presenting information about a child *when the child is not present* is dangerous. Not only is the focus on how different the child is from others, but he's more abstract than real. When the child is present and participating however, other students see a real person and the focus is on how similar he is to the other children. Differences are brought up only after commonalities have been established.

When Benjamin was starting kindergarten, he knew a few classmates from the neighborhood preschool. But the majority of the other students were strangers who had never seen a kid with leg braces, a walker, and a wheelchair. I brought up the need for an awareness presentation at the IEP meeting. The presentation could have been called "Similarities of Kindergartners."

We scheduled it for the first day of school. Yes, that was a hectic day, but there was no time to waste. I didn't want children's attitudes tainted by their parents. Parent: "Hi, honey how was your first day at school?" Kindergartner: "Good, mommy. There's a kid in my class that has a wheelchair." Parent: "What? You mean there's a 'handicapped' kid in your class?" In the blink of an eye, Benjamin would have been defined by that stereotypical word. And who knows what else the child might have learned from his mother?

During the middle of the kindergarten morning, in circle time, I plopped down on the floor facing the group of children. Benjamin sat with his classmates. I began by telling all the children who I was—Benjamin's mom—and asked them how the first day of school was going. After a little chit-chat, I told them Benjamin had a big sister, Emily, who was in second grade, and asked if they had big brothers or sisters. Lots of hands shot up, followed by a chorus of voices shouting out the names of their brothers and sisters.

The kindergartners were an exuberant bunch. Even the shy ones wanted a piece of the action. What an easy bunch to talk to! I then continued asking a variety of questions appropriate for five-year-olds.

When I asked, "Who likes to go to McDonald's?" they all raised their hands. "Yes, Benjamin and Emily both like McDonald's," I added. "Benjamin, what's your favorite food at McDonald's?" When he said, "Hamburger Happy Meal," most of the kids noisily added their agreement. "Wow! You're all alike!" I exclaimed.

"Benjamin, what's your favorite toy?" I asked. "Thomas the Tank Engine," came the reply, followed by a chorus of "Me, too!" from the boys. Most of the girls made faces. "Hmmm," I mused. "So you're all alike because everyone likes McDonald's, but you're different because some of you don't like Thomas the Tank Engine." They nodded in agreement. I continued asking lots of questions like this. Sometimes I directed questions to Benjamin and other individual children, and then followed up by asking the same questions of the whole group.

After each question, I pointed out differences and similarities: "So some of you have blonde hair and blue eyes, but some of you have blonde hair and brown eyes," or "All the girls are like Mary, since they all like dolls. But the boys are different, aren't they?"

Numerous questions and answers established their similarities and differences. Then I eased into disability-related questions. "Does anybody know what a disability is?" was the first. Most kids shook their heads no. Benjamin, of course, raised his hand. Naturally, I called on him for the answer.

"A disability means you have a body part that works differently. Like my legs work differently," came the reply from the young expert. "Do any of you have family members that have a disability?" I asked. Ten or fifteen hands went up! Each of the children took a turn telling the class about a grandmother who used a wheelchair, an uncle who wears a hearing aid, a grandfather who uses a walker, and so on. How proud they were to share!

I pointed out how their relatives were different because they had disabilities, but how they were also the same because they were members of their families. Everyone agreed. I then talked about one of Benjamin's differences: he was the only one in the class who had a disability; but he was similar because he liked the same things (Thomas the Tank Engine, McDonald's, and so on).

From there it was an easy transition to bring Benjamin's walker and wheelchair over to the group. Benj and I explained what each did and why Benj used them. Then he demonstrated by using the walker and wheelchair. "Benjamin, would it be okay for everyone to try out these out?" I asked. He agreed, of course. We had talked about this ahead of time, so he knew this would happen. With great eagerness, many of the kids took a turn with the equipment. When they were seated in a circle again, I passed around two old pairs of Benjamin's leg braces. Many children took their shoes off and tried them on.

Language was the next subject on the agenda. I explained how the word "handicapped" was an old-fashioned word we didn't want to use anymore. I described People First Language (with Benjamin chiming in) and gave examples of labeling by asking the children if they would want to be known by their physical appearance or differences. For example, "Sarah, would you want to be known as the 'glasses girl'?" and "Brandon, should everyone call you 'tall boy'?" The lesson became crystal clear; they all agreed they wouldn't like that.

Before I wrapped up the presentation, I asked if they had questions. Several did, and Benj answered most of them. He and I ended the presentation together by talking about how important it was to ask his permission before pushing his chair or helping in other ways. I gave examples of what it might feel like if someone tried to help them without asking. Everyone understand completely. Success!

Any time your child enters a new classroom, community activity, or other setting where she isn't known to the majority of other children, a similarity awareness presentation is critically important. Your child should do as much of the presentation as she can. One or two of her good friends or a brother or sister could be there to share positive information. But make sure this is agreeable to your child—it's her show!

Tailor the presentation to suit the audience. Focus on similarities first, then gently and positively share information about your child's disability and/or needs. Divulge only what's necessary, keeping your child's dignity in mind at all times. Allow plenty of time for questions. In middle school and high school, awareness presentations need to provided to each class in your child's daily schedule.

Don't Stop With Your Child's Class, Keep Going

In the public school setting, share similarity awareness information to everyone else in the school—staff and students. During Benjamin's kindergarten year, I asked the principal if I could have some time during one of the regular staff meetings early in the school year. Teachers who had children with disabilities in their classes were pretty well up to speed on issues, but other teachers weren't. When their students asked them about "that kid in the wheelchair," they didn't know what to say. Every staff person needed to know how to answer their students' questions in ways that presented positive images of Benjamin and others with disabilities. They needed to know about Benjamin and his walker and wheelchair.

Children who are on the playground during your child's recess need to know. Older and younger students who pass your child in the hall, or see him in the cafeteria or the library need to know. Since people are often fearful of what they don't know, take the fear away by providing knowledge about your child and others with disabilities.

Presentations to other classes will be a little different than the ones to your child's class(es). The main focus will the similarities between people with and without disabilities in general, followed by *some* details about your child. If the talk focuses primarily on your child, the information won't be as relevant to the students since most will probably not have regular, personal contact with your child. To make your presentations relevant, personalize them to your audience.

Following is a description of a presentation I gave to a fifth grade class when my son was in second grade. I began by introducing myself as "Benjamin's mom" and asked if everyone knew who Benjamin was—the kid with blonde hair and glasses who used a wheelchair. They all indicated they had seen him in the hallways, the library, at recess, or somewhere else in school. I spent several minutes talking about different types of disabilities and how people with disabilities are more like others than different.

As I did in Benjamin's class, I asked the students to tell me about any people they knew with disabilities. Many shared stories of family members, friends, and neighbors. We spent some time discussing terminology and I introduced them to People First Language. Next, I discussed the philosophies that disability is a natural part of the human condition and a disability simply means a body part works differently. I talked a little about Benjamin and other students with disabilities in the school.

I asked what they thought about people with disabilities, in general, and Benjamin, specifically. The ones who answered were genuinely kind as they described feeling sorry for Benjamin and others with disabilities. "Why do you feel sorry for them? What makes you feel sorry for Benjamin?" I asked. A typical reply was, "Because he can't walk and he can't run on the playground like the other kids. He can't shoot baskets. You know, it's sad."

"Thanks for sharing," I replied. "Now let's do a little exercise. Close your eyes, and keep them closed, until I tell you to open them. Pretend you're going home from school today and you're involved in a car accident. You wake up in the hospital. You have a closed-head injury, which means your brain will work differently. Also, your spinal cord was injured, so you'll need to use a wheelchair for mobility from now on. Keep your eyes closed. Picture yourself coming home from the hospital. Now picture yourself coming back to school, to this classroom. Remember, your brain works differently, so you might learn differently. It might take you longer to learn some things. Don't forget you'll be using a wheelchair to go to the restroom, the playground, the library, the cafeteria, and everywhere else. Think about this for a moment or two." After about a minute, I asked them to open their eyes.

"Now that you've had time to think about this, how do you want your classmates to feel about you? Do you want them to treat you the same way they treated you before your accident?" I asked. "Yes!" they all answered. "Do you want the teacher and your friends to help you all the time or just when you need it? Since you had a brain injury, what if people think you're stupid, that you don't know anything?" were my next questions. "We should get help just when we need it! Just because we might learn differently doesn't mean we're stupid!" were the indignant replies.

"Do you think you could figure out how to do some of the same things you did before? Would it be possible for you to play basketball from a chair? If you couldn't, would you be able to find something else to do on the playground with your friends?" I inquired. I was barraged with positive replies. Then kids started talking to each other, comparing ideas about all the different ways to do things from a chair.

"You guys are so good!" I exclaimed. "Here's my last question: do you want your friends to feel sorry for you because you have a disability?" "Nooooooo!" they all yelled. "That would be dumb!" several added.

"You're right!" I congratulated them. "Now, let's go back to Benjamin for a minute. Do any of you still feel sorry for Benjamin or other people with disabilities?" Many exchanged glances with each other. Some had sheepish grins on their faces. "No," they all agreed.

At that point, I brought Benjamin and another student with a disability into the classroom. They introduced themselves and asked the fifth-graders if they had any questions. A fascinating interchange began—one that lasted longer than the teacher and I expected, but it was wonderful.

Generally, the length of a presentation to a classroom will be limited to an hour or less. The teacher might impose this time limit, or you might impose it on yourself, knowing the kids will have ants in their pants if you go much longer. To make your presentations effective in a short period of time, tailor your message to the specific audience: a talk to a first grade class will be very different than one to eighth-graders. You can accomplish this very nicely by asking your audience lots of questions. You'll learn what they already know and what they need to know.

In the fifth grade class, for example, it would not have been very effective for me to *assume* the students all felt sorry for people with disabilities and lecture them based on this assumption. I would have spoken very globally about the issue and the kids probably wouldn't relate what I was saying to their own experiences. But by asking them how they felt, then addressing their specific beliefs (feeling sorry for Benj because he couldn't walk, run, or shoot baskets) my message was more relevant and meaningful to them.

Don't ask, "What do you want to know about people with disabilities?" The answer will probably be, "Nothing." Instead, ask specific questions: do you personally know people with disabilities, what do you think about them, what do you feel about them, and so forth.

Before doing any presentation, know what you want the outcome to be. What do you want your audience to know they didn't know before? What do you want them to do with the information? How do you want the audience to be different after your talk? I always tell children to go home and teach their parents!

To reach as many classrooms as possible, write a nice letter offering your presentation and give it to every teacher in school. Some will probably respond right away; others won't show any interest at all. However, once you've done one or two workshops, teachers will spread the good word and you'll get more invitations.

Presentations at Colleges and Universities

Consider giving guest lectures at colleges and universities. Parents are learning about inclusion, about viewing people with disabilities by their assets, and more. Yet college students are still being taught old ways of thinking. If a college or university is in your area, go for it.

Call the school and ask for a catalog to identify what courses are offered. Target general ed and special education departments, first. In addition, contact professors in the fields of health care, sociology, psychology, or any other department that has a disability connection. Introduce yourself, share your qualifications with the professor or the assistant, and ask if you could give a presentation to their classes. Be persistent, determined, and respectful.

Tailor your talk to your audience. Teach education students about inclusive education. Teach medical classes about disability being a natural part of the human condition. Teach sociology and psychology classes about how "normal" our families and children are.

Some parents who started out presenting guest lectures as volunteers are now being paid for their expertise. You may have a new career in the works!

Presentations in the Community

When our children and families are involved in community activities, people around us will receive experiential lessons. Our children's presence will teach them much. But it never hurts to accelerate the learning curve, by you and your child doing a similarity awareness presentation for the karate or ballet class, the softball team, the Sunday school class, and for children and adults in other activities.

If your passion leads you in this direction, take the bull by the horns and offer to give awareness presentations to a variety of groups in your community. The number of potential audiences is unlimited: businesses, PTAs, other schools and school boards, the Better Business Bureau, civic organizations (Rotary, Kiwanis, etc.), state and local government offices, church groups, youth organizations (Scouts, Campfire, etc.), and many, many others.

Rather than making "cold calls" to groups, spread the word that you're available. Ask friends and acquaintances about organizations and groups they're connected with. Use this networking opportunity to get your foot in the door. Your efforts will pay off big dividends in making your community more inclusive. Soon, you won't need to ask if you can speak on the issues, people will be asking you!

WORKING WITH THE MEDIA

Does your blood boil when you read or see a story about people with disabilities that evokes pity or perpetuates negative images? Put your passion to good use and educate those reporters! You're an expert on disability issues, so share your expertise.

Contacting a reporter and blasting her for the stereotypical language she used is not only ineffective, it will probably do more harm than good. We want people in the news business to be our allies, not our enemies. Our ultimate goal is for reporters to see parents and people with disabilities as consultants and advisors. When reporters cover disability-related issues, whether the connection is to education, health care, employment, housing, laws, or any other angle, we want them to come to us for technical advice, to verify facts, or to critique stories.

We want reciprocal relationships with reporters: we can provide them with technical assistance and they can help us (and society) by providing accurate portrayals of people with disabilities. We can also assist by feeding them story ideas about newsworthy people, places, or things in our communities. Imagine how society's attitudes and perceptions might change if reporters replaced pity and prejudice with assets and accuracy in their stories. It's up to us to get the ball rolling.

When you read the newspaper or watch television news, pay close attention to which reporters cover stories that are disability-related or have a potential connection to disability issues. In bigger cities, reporters often have a "beat," an area that's their specialty. In smaller cities, many are "general assignment reporters," covering any and all topics. In either case, become aware of who reports on education, health, children, government, employment, housing, and any other topics that could have a connection to disability issues.

Create a mini-portfolio of these folks. For television reporters, jot down their names, which station they're on, and a brief description of the content of their reports so you won't have to depend on your memory. For newspaper reporters, clip articles, noting the date, and put in a scrapbook. Recruit family members or other parents to help in this effort.

Sometimes the opportunity to initiate relationships with people in the media is dropped in our laps. Other times, we have to create it. Let's look first at creating an opportunity; it can often be the more effective method.

Let's assume you've identified Larry as a newspaper reporter you want to connect with. You haven't seen him do any stories about disability issues, but you *have* noticed he covers both education and health care. When you're ready, call him and introduce yourself over the phone. If possible, call him the day after you've seen one of his stories in the paper. Compliment him on the story and let him know you appreciate his work. Then give a brief description of yourself: a parent of a child with a disability who's very interested in the topics he writes about (education and health care) because these issues affect your child and other children and adults with disabilities.

Say something like, "I just wanted to ask you if it would be okay if I called you every now and then with story ideas that might have a disability angle? And, I wanted to let you know I'm available if you ever have any questions about disability issues." Until you know him a little better, don't unload all your frustrations about how poorly the media covers disability issues. You'll scare him off. Take it slow and easy.

At this point, Larry will begin asking you lots of questions. That's what reporters do. The relationship has begun. Keep it going by following up with a brief note in the mail, letting him know how much you appreciated his time and his interest. Give him your address and phone number again, and send him a brief biography or description of your disability-related activities.

From this point on, send him disability-related information on a regular basis: copies of newsletters or handouts from conferences you attend, newspaper articles that you comment on, story ideas, or other relevant materials. In a letter or in a separate "story" of your own, let him know about People First Language, the idea that disability is natural, the importance of seeing assets instead of deficits, and more. He'll remember you: you're giving him information he's probably never seen before. If you feel really bold, take him to lunch! You're becoming a consultant! Who knows where this could lead?

If it's at all possible, cultivate at least one newspaper reporter and one television reporter. Double your contacts; double your potential for success. These connections will lead to others.

What happens when the opportunity to create relationships is dropped in our laps? This has to be handled a little differently. Let's say you're watching the local news and you see a disability-related story that's just awful. You're so frustrated you're ready to throw your shoe at the TV set. Instead of calling the reporter (Michelle) every name in the book, turn this negative into a positive.

The next day, call Michelle and introduce yourself by telling her your name and that you're the parent of a child with a disability. You're going to thank her—yes, thank her—for doing the story and for bringing disability issues to the public's attention. Pause to let her accept your thanks. Then, in a very positive way, let her know there are alternatives to the way the information was presented. You can say something along the lines of, "Michelle, I wanted to share my perspective about the language in your report. I'm not sure how familiar you might be with People First Language. You know, the public perception of society is to feel sorry for people with disabilities and language certainly reinforces negative stereotypes." Pause to give her time to respond.

Regardless of how she replies, stay positive and helpful. Offer to help her learn. Even if Michelle disagrees with you, stay positive. "Yes, I understand. However, let me point out that . . ." If you become angry and blow it at this point, you've lost the opportunity to make an ally. Persevere. Stay determined. If things get testy, issue another compliment, "Michelle, you're such a good reporter, I was hoping this information would be helpful . . ."

When you're ready to sign off, tell Michelle you'd like to send her information occasionally and ask for her full name and business address (including Email). Let her know you'll be happy to be a "source" for her and that you can put her in contact with others in the disability community when and if she needs this type of assistance. From this point on, keep in regular contact with her. Even if she never initiates a phone call to you, if you're able to influence her attitude and her stories, you've done well.

When Benjamin was three, a local newspaper ran a story that included negative descriptions about people with disabilities. I did just what I'm recommending to you. When I got the reporter on the phone, I told him who I was, including the fact that I was the parent of a young child with a disability. I thanked him for writing the story and bringing disability issues to the public's attention. Then I let him know the importance of using People First Language and offered to send him some information. Before I knew it, he was asking me a ton of questions. His last query was, "I'd like to do a story on you and your son. When can a photographer and I come for a visit?"

I had no idea this would be the outcome of my call. Had I angrily blasted him for the language he used in the story, would he have wanted to do a story about me and Benj? I don't think so. We sometimes have only one chance to kindle the flame, so it's important to make the most of the opportunity. A few days later, the story in the local paper made Benj and I "stars" for a few days. I hoped the positive perceptions presented in that story counteracted the ones readers saw a couple of weeks earlier.

When Benjamin was in kindergarten, I met many parents of his classmates. One of the moms happened to be a feature writer for a Colorado Springs daily newspaper. After we got to know each other a little better, she said she was glad our children were in class together. Kate had never seen a child with a disability in a regular ed classroom; this was something new. She asked lots of questions about Benjamin and about the school being inclusive. The next question was, "I'd like to do a story about children with disabilities and friendships. How would you feel about Benjamin being the focus of the story?"

A half-page spread, complete with color photographs, was on the front page of the "Lifestyle" section a few weeks later. Overall, it was a great story. But there was a downside, one that you might experience in your efforts to influence the media.

While Kate was working on the story, another parent of a child with a disability got wind of it. Helen had a teenage son with autism, she was a well-known advocate in a large school district, and she was well-connected to the media. When she heard what Kate was working on, she demanded that her perspective be included. In the spirit of journalistic fairness, Kate felt she had to honor Helen's "request."

You might have already guessed what Helen's perspective was. She believed children with disabilities should not be educated in inclusive classrooms because of their "special needs," and children with disabilities should "stay with their own kind." To Kate's credit, she minimized Helen's views by burying them towards the end of the story.

Be aware that people who are opposed to inclusion want their views in the public eye as much as we do. As much as I hated seeing Helen's anti-inclusion views in the story, I didn't take it personally. Kate and I have remained friends and I respect her as a journalist. Never blow off reporters if they disagree with you or do something you don't like. You never know when they might change their opinions or want your help in the future.

Who's Who in the Media

When you're thinking about who to make connections with, it's important to know who's who. Years ago, before my children were born, I directed local television newscasts and then became a producer and a writer. My past experience in the media has definitely helped me influence public perceptions disseminated through the media today. I hope it will help you, too. I'll share a basic overview of who's who, but know that you'll be able to learn specific details about the media in your local area from your new reporter friends.

Television

When you watch the local news on television, remember that news anchors and reporters put their pantyhose—or their pants—on the same way we do. They're real people, just like us.

In smaller communities, reporters and anchors may wear many hats, while in larger cities—major television markets—reporters and anchors often have very specific duties.

The anchors in large markets are essentially news readers. Seldom are anchors "in the field" doing reports; they're not reporters. Therefore, anchors aren't always the best targets.

We want to focus on reporters that cover education, employment, housing, legislation, health care, and other topics that could include a disability angle. But in smaller markets, the anchors may also be reporters, and all reporters may be "generalists:" they cover everything. In this case, it's possible your target *could* be the anchor/reporter.

How do reporters find their stories? They get leads (pronounced "leeds") from many sources. If you see a story on the evening news that you also saw in the morning paper that same day, the TV news reporter probably got the idea from reading the paper! When I worked in television, folks in the news department pored over the morning paper to get ideas for stories. On the other hand, when it's "late breaking" news in the afternoon or evening, TV news covers it first because most newspapers don't put out late editions. They can't cover it until the next morning.

Reporters have connections with many "sources"—people who give reporters ideas for stories or tips about newsworthy people, incidents, or events. Your goal is to become a source who can provide leads or technical assistance on disability issues.

Sources from business, government, non-profits, or the general public, provide leads to reporters via written press releases, personal phone calls, e-mail, faxes, and other methods. A little later in this section, I'll give you tips about writing press releases.

Every day, TV news reporters have opportunities to cover dozens of stories. How do they decide which leads to follow up? Sometimes the reporter can make the decision. The majority of time, however, the decision is made by one of the reporter's superiors: the assignment editor, producer, or news director.

In the staff hierarchy, the news director is in charge of the entire news department. Under him are producers, assignment editors, anchors, reporters, photographers, tape editors, and others. Large stations may have people in all these positions, while in smaller stations, one person might wear two or more hats.

The job of an assignment editor is analogous to a traffic cop trying to direct cars and trucks through a six-way intersection when the traffic lights are out of order. In general, he's responsible for knowing what events are happening, deciding which are the most newsworthy, assigning reporters and photographers to cover the events, and so forth. He makes judgment calls on which leads should be pursued. The producer is in charge of deciding which stories actually make it into the newscast. She puts the broadcast together.

If you're successful in getting a TV news reporter to cover your story, there are no guarantees the story will actually air in a newscast. Every day, more stories are covered than can be included in the evening's show. At 4:30 PM, your story may be scheduled to air in the 5:00 PM newscast. But if a reporter is frantically preparing a late breaking story at 4:45 and actually gets it ready by 4:55, your story might get bumped at the last minute. For every newscast, producers make judgment calls on which news stories are actually broadcast.

If your story is time sensitive—if it's about something that happened that day or is going to happen the next day—your story will either air that night or not at all. News departments don't like to air "old" news. If it happens to be a feature story—the "soft" news that's usually positioned right before or after weather or at the end of the newscast—and if it's not time sensitive, it might be broadcast in a later newscast or the next day.

It can be very disappointing if your story doesn't air. And it's also disappointing for the reporter. He worked hard on the piece, but the decision whether to air the story isn't his. It's the producer's (or the news director's). The stories you see in any newscast are the ones a producer or news director decided were the most important. And the scale of importance changes from day to day, depending on what's hot and what's not. Typically, we have a better chance of getting our issues covered on Saturday or Sunday newscasts because those are slower news days. Little, if any, news is generated by government or business during weekends, so there's more air time to fill.

If working more closely with the television news media is something you want to become involved in, try to meet the news director, assignment editors, producers, anchors, photographers, and/or interns, as well as the reporters you single out. In smaller stations, this may be relatively easy since people wear many hats. In metropolitan areas, the task can be harder. But the more people you have a connection to, the better your chances of getting good coverage. If it makes you feel more comfortable, do this with a friend.

News departments aren't our only avenue for getting our issues on television. Check the local TV listings to determine if any stations carry local interview or talk shows. The first place to look in the log is early Sunday mornings. Sometimes it's hard to identify local shows from the abbreviations in TV listings, so call your local stations and ask if they have a public affairs or community program. If so, ask who's in charge of the show. Often, this will be the public affairs (PA) director.

Before calling, watch the show a couple of times to become familiar with it. The PA director may be the host of the show, as well as its producer. Before you call about being on the program, put together two or three ideas that will "fit" on the program. Typically, public affairs programs are videotaped two to four weeks prior to the air date. Keep this in mind if your ideas are tied to an event that's coming up. A program about inclusion, People First Language, or any other "timeless" topic could air at any time.

The host of a non-controversial program typically presents community-oriented information to the audience. On the other hand, some hosts want more of a point-counterpoint program. In this situation, the host may eagerly have you on the show on the condition you appear with someone who has an opposing viewpoint. Even though this can be a bit nerve-wracking, don't turn it down! Just screw up your courage and dive in. Think how many television viewers you'll educate!

Anytime you have a positive interaction (even if it's only a teeny bit positive) with someone in the television industry, write a letter or note of thanks. You'll be remembered!

Newspapers

The structure of a newspaper is a little different than a television station. As with television news, however, reporters may be generalists or specialists.

Editors supervise reporters. At large papers, there may be a news editor in charge of the entire first section, a city editor for the second section (local/state news), a features editors for the "lifestyle" section, and an opinion/editorial (op/ed) editor for the pages which feature columns and letters to the editor. Some newspapers also have people who only write headlines. Newspapers in big cities may have senior or managing editors in supervisory roles. At the top of the hierarchy is the publisher, who owns the paper. The publisher can be an individual or a corporation.

Op/ed pages allow the publisher to express his views (especially political views) and influence public opinion via editorial columns. Some papers are considered conservative, others liberal, and some are in the middle. Syndicated columnists are usually selected because they share similar political philosophies with the publisher.

The quickest and easiest way to get your ideas before the public is with a letter to the editor. Look for guidelines on one of the op/ed pages. Editorial staff members decide which letters to publish. Generally, they select letters that are in response to something that's appeared in the news or op/ed sections of the newspaper. Editors reserve the right to shorten letters. To prevent yours being chopped up, make it brief and to the point.

Writing a guest editorial is an excellent avenue to share your thoughts with a mass audience. Parents all across the country have been successful in having their guest editorials on inclusive education and other topics published in their local papers. Call the op/ed editor and ask what the guidelines are.

In newspapers, there's often a distinct division between reporters who cover hard news and soft news (feature stories in the "lifestyle" section). It's important to contact the appropriate reporter or editor about your story ideas or leads. In a smaller market, there's often a lot of crossover, with reporters writing both news and feature stories.

Newspapers don't have the same constraints as television news: they can print as much news as they want ("all the news that's fit to print"), whereas television news has a finite number of minutes within every broadcast. The odds of getting our stories covered are better with newspapers than television. But every effort will pay off, one way or another. Don't forget to write notes of thanks to newspaper folks.

Radio Talk Shows

If your community has a local radio talk show, make some connections there. Talk show hosts and their producers work together to come up with ideas for shows. In smaller cities, the host might be his own producer. Like reporters for television and newspaper outlets, talk show hosts and producers depend on leads from sources.

Being a guest on a radio talk show not only provides great exposure for disability issues, but it also affords us more time to discus the issues in a live forum as compared to edited thirty-second sound bites in television news. Radio talk shows may interview a a guest for thirty minutes or an hour. That's a lot of time to get your message across.

Because most radio talk shows are live, your message will air unedited. (In a television news story, a fifteen-minute talk with a reporter will be chopped up and the reporter will use only what he thinks is the most important: a thirty-second sound bite.) Similarly, a newspaper reporter may ask you lots of questions, but only use the statements he thinks are important. So radio talk shows can be an important venue for teaching others about disability issues.

If a talk show host/producer is unfamiliar with a topic, he may ask a guest to prepare a list of questions, or provide background information, so he'll know what kind of questions to ask. After all, he doesn't want to appear ignorant. This is great for us! We get to influence the tone and direction for the show.

On the other hand, a talk show host who likes controversy may turn the interview into a debate. Become familiar with the style of a talk show host before approaching him with your ideas. Get a bead on his political leanings: conservative, liberal, middle of the road.

Forewarned is forearmed. If you'll be dealing with a big station, assume the producer has a great deal of power over the content of the show, and approach him instead of the host. If it's a station in a small town, approach the host directly.

In radio, the program manager supervises hosts and producers, and the general manager oversees the entire station. In smaller stations, the talk show host might also be the program manager. Try to make a connection with these folks. And don't forget to write thank you notes.

WRITING PRESS RELEASES

A press release is the most common method of sharing information with the news media. When I was producing local entertainment and general interest programs at a television station in Texas, I received hundreds of press releases each week. There weren't enough hours in the day to thoughtfully and carefully read every word of each press release. Only the most intriguing press releases got my full attention.

If the title and the first paragraph don't jump out and immediately grab the attention of the reader, the press release gets tossed. If it holds the reader's interest to the second paragraph, there's a good chance the whole piece will be read.

A well-written press release follows the formula used in television programs and commercials. Television producers know they must "hook" you in the first few seconds to prevent you from flipping the channel or heading for the bathroom. When you're writing a press release, your headline and first paragraph must compel the reader to want more!

Every press release needs to state the "release date" to indicate the official date the information should be released to the public. Often, the release date is "immediate." Other times, it's a date some time in the future. For example, if a company wants to announce a new product that will be available July 15th, the public relations folks might send a press release to the media on *June 15th*, giving reporters time to interview company executives, consumers who tested the product, or others. But they don't want any news to come out until the official date of July 15th.

Press releases should include the name and phone number of the contact person(s)— one or two individuals who can provide additional information. Usually, the contact is also the individual who is distributing the release. To lend authenticity to your press release, make sure it's on a business letterhead.

The headline should reach out and grab the reader's attention. Take a lesson from the tabloids (but don't make stuff up the way they do!). Who's not intrigued by the headlines that jump out at you while you're waiting in a check-out line? Your headline must make the reader want to know more. It must also make the reader feel something: curiosity, surprise, concern, tenderness, or something else. You want the reader to think, "What?" or "Wow!"

The first paragraph must then deliver the goods. The reader must instantly feel the promise of the headline is genuine. The first paragraph provides more "wow" in greater detail. Subsequent paragraphs provide background, such as additional details about who, what, when, where, and how. To increase the odds your entire press release will be read, it should be no longer than two pages. You can, however, send additional information with the presss release. In media jargon, everything you send is called a "press kit."

If your press release is only one page, at the bottom of the page center the word "End." If it's two pages, put "More" on the bottom of the first page and "End" on the bottom of the second page. Put a header on the top of the second page that states the date of the press release, the headline, and the page number. If the pages become separated, this will enable the recipient to put them back together. Always double space a press release and use a typeface that's easy to read. Stay away from script or unusual typefaces.

Before you send your press release, rewrite it—as many times as it takes—to get the best product. Have other people critique it and accept their criticisms to help you fine tune your wordsmithing.

While most press releases are generated by organizations and businesses, there's no reason you, as an individual, can't send a press release about something you're doing. Create a letterhead and write the best press release ever.

The angle you present in your press release is critically important, as demonstrated in this example. Let's assume Teresa Martin and her second-grade daughter, Becky, are presenting similarity awareness workshops to the classes in Becky's school and Teresa wants press coverage. What angle should she present? That she's taking time out of her busy day to help her daughter teach kids about people with disabilities? No. From a journalist's perspective that's not an exciting, unusual, or newsworthy hook. Remember, the press release will be competing with many others. But consider these angles:

- A second grader is "teaching" at Happy Valley Elementary School; or
- Students at Happy Valley Elementary School are learning more than their ABCs; or
- Kids with disabilities are part of the mainstream at Happy Valley Elementary School.

If Teresa provides the plain facts in her press release, the recipient may not see an angle or understand the importance of what Teresa is doing because (1) he's not familiar with children with disabilities, inclusion, or any other aspect of disability issues, and/or (2) he can't see why his audience would be interested in this. Teresa needs to come up with as many different angles as she can. She can enlist the help of others and get their feedback on the angle that's most provocative. Better yet, she could have a friend or neighbor who knows nothing about disability issues help her decide which angle is the most interesting.

Once Teresa has decided on the best angle, she'll include the other top two or three angles within the body of the press release. This gives the recipient more to chew on when he's considering whether this is a newsworthy item.

While preparing the release, Teresa shared her enthusiasm and her ideas with the school principal. Then she asked for and received permission to use his name as a contact person and to put the release on the school letterhead. This will also garner more attention from the reporter; the school is a known entity, while Teresa is not (yet).

In addition to the press release, Teresa will prepare a cover letter (from the principal on school letterhead). If she really wants to impress someone in the media, she could include an 8x10 photo of Rebecca. She'll put all the information in a large mailing envelope. The cover letter goes on top, followed by the press release, the photo, and any other materials. On the following two pages are Teresa's cover letter and press release.

Apple Valley Elementary School
123 Main Street
Anytown, USA 12345
(555) 555-0000

Date

Mr. Don Hawkins
The Daily-Sun
456 Every Street
Anytown, USA 12346

Dear Mr. Hawkins:

Have you ever seen a seven-year-old teach elementary school classes? It's happening at Apple Valley Elementary School, as described in the attached press release.

I'm sure the readers of *The Daily-Sun* would find the story of Rebecca Martin fascinating. We don't know of another school in Anytown with a second-grader teaching school. The 536 students love Apple Valley's youngest teacher, and many of their parents have shared their approval, too. In addition, our twenty-five member faculty has lauded Miss Martin with kudos.

Rebecca and I, along with the students and faculty at Apple Valley, would be delighted if you could attend one of her lessons so you could share the experience with your readers. The next scheduled workshop is on Wednesday, January 15th from 9:00 to 10:00 AM. If this time or date is inconvenient for you, we could reschedule the lesson to coincide with your availability.

Thanks, so very much, for your time and consideration. Please let me know if you have any questions.

Sincerely yours,

John Doe
Principal

Apple Valley Elementary School
123 Main Street
Anytown, USA 12345
(555) 555-0000

For Immediate Release   Contact: Teresa Martin, 555-5555
                                         John Doe, 555-0000

SECOND-GRADE STUDENT TEACHES CLASSES AT APPLE VALLEY ELEMENTARY

When Rebecca Martin takes her position in front of the class, students at Apple Valley Elementary school pay rapt attention. Unlike other teachers, Ms. Martin is smaller and younger than some of her students, but her message gets through loud and clear. Seven-year-old Rebecca, who has cerebral palsy, is teaching her fellow students about people with disabilities. Boys and girls from kindergarten through fifth grade say the most exciting part of the lesson is when they get to try out Rebecca's wheelchair and walker. But the most important lesson Apple Valley students learn is that children with disabilities are more like other children than they are different.

Apple Valley is among the growing number of schools across the country where children with and without disabilities are successfully educated together. To help open the doors to understanding similarities and differences, Rebecca and her mother, Teresa, are presenting "similarity awareness" workshops in every classroom at Apple Valley, educating over 500 students and their teachers. "Some kids have never seen another kid in a wheelchair and sometimes they're scared of me. I just want to help them learn that I may be different on the outside, but on the inside, I'm just like them," Rebecca stated recently.

Principal John Doe added, "Rebecca and our other students with disabilities are equally participating members of our school community. Rebecca's trainings are educating students in ways no teacher could! We hope other schools can learn from our success." To date, Rebecca has done workshops in fourteen of the seventeen classrooms at Apple Valley. By the end of the year, she will have taught in every class. Next school year, this youngest-ever teacher at Apple Valley will help the incoming kindergartners learn the basics of "similarity awareness" as they're mastering their ABCs.

-End-

Did you notice the cover letter doesn't say anything about disability or what's being taught? This purposeful omission creates an interest that will (hopefully) make the recipient want to read every word of the press release. Use the cover letter to "tease" the reader.

Because this could qualify as a hard news story (time sensitive via the coming presentation), or a feature story (human interest), Teresa will send a press kit to specific reporters at every local media outlet (television, radio, and newspapers). The cover letter to newspaper and television outlets could stress newsworthiness, human interest value, and superb photo opportunities. A letter to a talk radio host would need to be modified slightly to promote that Teresa, Rebecca, and the principal are available to be interviewed on the talk show.

A word or two about the importance of visuals is in order. Television is obviously a visual medium. We "watch" television. Television news people think visually; they want to cover stories that have compelling "moving pictures." When you watch your local newscast tonight, observe how the majority, if not all, of the stories covered has a visual component. If, for whatever reason, there's no video footage to accompany a story, there will at least be a static image over the anchor's shoulder as he reads the story. Newspapers aren't as demanding about visuals as television news, but still, a picture *is* worth a thousand words, and newspaper reporters do like pictures to accompany their stories. So when you're writing a press release, think visually. Propose suggestions about visual aspects of the story.

In addition to visuals, people in the media also like numbers and statistics. In the sample cover letter and press release, the number of students, teachers, and presentations Rebecca did were included. Whenever possible, provide relevant numbers, dates, and other facts.

In your press release, it's fine to boast, as long as you're truthful. When book authors, movie producers, and others are trying to promote their latest product, they flaunt their achievements to snare the interest of the media. You must do the same thing. Remember that your press release is in competition with all the other releases that arrive on a recipient's desk that day. Make yours stand out!

In addition, ensure your press release covers the who, what, why, where, and how of your issue. If you omit critical information, the recipient probably won't call to ask you about the missing data; he doesn't have time. He'll probably just toss your release in the wastebasket and go on to the next one.

Press releases can be sent to people other than media representatives. If a news maker, such as an elected official, is known for having an interest in your issues, send a press release to that person, along with a cover letter inviting him to attend. Many politicians and other news makers will do almost anything to have a forum to espouse their ideas and positions.

In your cover letter to the news maker, indicate you've invited the press to attend. Don't guarantee the press will be there, for you have no control over that. Just state that the news media has been invited.

In your letter to the media, mention that City Councilman Stephens, a well-known supporter of education (or whatever) has been invited. This will spark a greater interest from reporters. News makers and the news media are dependent on one another. Use that to your advantage.

NEWSLETTERS

When you're promoting disability issues, don't forget about the power of newsletters. There are zillions of them, and every newsletter editor is always looking for material for the next issue. On a small scale, you can contact the organizations who publish the newsletters you, your family, or your friends are familiar with. Call local and state-level disability organizations and agencies and ask to be put on their mailing lists.

On a larger scale, contact non-disability organizations and businesses who publish newsletters, locally, statewide, or nationally. Most local libraries have directories of organizations, newsletters, or other listings that will help you in this effort.

FOLLOW THE RULES

During awareness presentations, when working with the media, or in any public relations activities, there are a few hard and fast rules to follow if you want your efforts to be successful.

Never lie. Don't make things up. Don't mislead or exaggerate. And don't guess at an answer to a question. Simply say, "I don't know, but I'll find out and get back to you." A lie, a half-truth, or an exaggeration is almost always discovered—sooner or later—and when it is, *everything* you say or represent will then be suspect. If a reporter has shared your information as truth and then discovers it's false, the reporter is not only embarrassed, but her professionalism has been compromised. She'll probably sever the relationship with you at this point.

Always be courteous and respectful, even when—especially when—you're challenged or insulted. Rise above the ignorance and pettiness of others and maintain your integrity and principles. This is not about you personally, it's about the issues. Don't let your ego get in the way of your mission.

Write thank you notes. This is easy to do when someone has been especially helpful or nice. It's harder when the relationship hasn't produced the results you wanted. Nevertheless, it's important. The potential for change is always there. This person may end up calling you at some point in the future simply because she remembers you as being professional. She may even call for personal reasons if she or someone close to her is touched by disability later on.

SOWING SEEDS OF CHANGE

Many of us keep hoping people in society will change their attitudes and perceptions about our children and others with disabilities. Hope is good, but it's not enough.

Each of us believes our personal attitudes are the "correct" attitudes. When someone tells you she's sorry your child has a disability, she believes pity is the correct attitude. When someone feels your child doesn't belong with "normal" children, he believes the prejudice he learned from his parents. Our job is to expose people in society to new ways of thinking. When we share our perspectives and our expertise with others, we sow the seeds of change.

We can also sow seeds of change by providing leadership to disability and non-disability organizations, and throughout our communities. That's next.

Leadership and Influence

> LEADERSHIP IS THE ABILITY TO GET PEOPLE TO DO
> WHAT THEY DON'T WANT TO DO—AND LIKE IT.
>
> *Harry S. Truman*

Thousands of us are superb activists. We're leaders who are determined to make a difference. We work on the inside and the outside of the system trying to change it. We sit on boards, serve on commissions, create new disability organizations, and volunteer in the old ones. Some of us become employed within the system, hoping to use our influence to make the system work better. We lobby federal and state legislators to enact family support legislation and other laws. Then we lobby some more for increases in funding. Our influence is felt in many places.

Many of our efforts have been very successful. The changes we've helped shape have improved the lives of many children and their families, not just our own. Our work is ongoing, however, for the return on our investment is actually quite small. In the big picture, our achievements often represent token victories for some, instead of wholesale change for all. We get one child included, but others are still left out. We have family support programs, but not enough money to fund them.

We're determined to succeed, however, so we keep going. We're sure our small successes will lead to big ones. Like tireless cheerleaders, we exhort our side to keep the faith, try harder, don't give up, rah, rah, rah!

But many of us are exhausted and discouraged, and we wonder if hoping for change is realistic. Shall we concede defeat or quadruple our labors? No and no. We should do neither. This is no time to surrender to the overwhelming forces we face every day, and we don't need to work harder. We need to work smarter. Our superior efforts haven't yielded superior results because our aim is misdirected.

We want inclusion in regular education, but we target special education.

We want family and community supports, but we lobby the government.

We want changes in society, but we focus on disability organizations.

We're trying to change the great big world around us,
but most of us stay wrapped in the cocoon of Disability World.

We've done excellent work within the disability community. But few of these efforts have penetrated the wall that separates our children and families from the mainstream of society. We may achieve minor victories in the service system, but we haven't changed much in the bigger world of society. We can't keep trying to change Disability World, while ignoring our communities!

Some of us *have* focused on our communities, and we've achieved individual successes. But like changes in the system, our actions haven't always resulted in permanent changes that benefit all people with disabilities or differences in our communities. Far too often, families who come along behind us must battle the same demons.

As long as we hold onto the "entitlement mentality" or believe the system should be supporting us in one way or another, we'll continue to work for improvements in that system. And it does need improving; there's no doubt about that. But even the best system is flawed. Any system of human services is, by its very nature, paternalistic. Regardless of the changes we make to the system, that paternalism will never change. The system doles out services, supports, and even cold hard cash. Systems must operate within well-defined parameters that try to meet the needs of everyone. This, of course, is impossible. No system can provide what everyone needs, for our children and our families are all different.

The human service system does not serve humans. It only gives us what it can, when it can, how it can. We're supposed to be grateful for the goodies doled out to us. We use the system, but we're not part of it (thank goodness!). We're on the outside looking in, hoping to get what our children need. We're little, the system is big. We wait, while the wheels of the system keep turning. We're powerless, the system is powerful. We're anxious, the system is smug. We want change, the system digs in its heels to maintain the status quo.

The power and the paternalism of the system—the bureaucracy, the paperwork, the waiting lists and more—make us feel insignificant. When we feel small, and at the mercy of forces we can't control, we fight to regain our dignity and independence. We fight the system to get what our children need. We fight the system to make it more responsive to our needs. We fight the system to make it treat us like humans and not cattle. And all this fighting takes its toll.

We're angry at a system that doesn't respect us, doesn't serve us, and doesn't respond to our needs. We're frustrated and burned out. We can blame the system for its inadequacies, *but we must no longer blame our problems on the system and see ourselves as victims.* The price is just too high. Our children and families are harmed by the services and programs of the system, as I've outlined in several different chapters.

Alternatives to the system include using natural supports and generic services, as described in Chapter 15. When we see ourselves as citizens of our communities, we recognize no one has control over us but us. In community, we're not small and insignificant, unless we choose to be. There is no formless entity—the system—to fight with. No one doles out what they think we need. No paternalism. No need to feel angry and frustrated. As citizens, we're part of our communities. We're not on the outside looking in. We're on the inside, and we can find what we need for our children and families.

I propose we take the energy we're pouring into changing the system and use it to build capacity in our communities. Let's spend our valuable time creating solutions in our cities and towns instead of begging for services from the system. Isn't it time to live as citizens in community instead of clients in the system? I propose we find creative ways to direct government funding to our communities instead of to the service system—where millions of dollars are siphoned off by every layer of bureaucracy before they finally get to people with disabilities and their families.

Only in our communities—the places where we live and breathe and work and play and make friends—can we effect authentic, long-lasting change that's implemented in ways that are beneficial to all people with disabilities. The system has a life of its own. The system doesn't need us. Our communities do. And we need our communities.

There's a saying in the school inclusion movement: "What's good for kids with disabilities is good for all kids." If you're not familiar with this sentiment, it simply means that any improvements made in schools to benefit students with disabilities ultimately benefits all students. The same could be said for our communities. Anything we do to make our communities better places for children and adults with disabilities will make our communities better for all citizens.

COMMUNITY LEADERSHIP

Many of us never set out to assume leadership roles, we simply saw things that needed changing and took action. Our efforts, even when we fail, are beneficial because they hone our skills. Let's put those skills to work in our communities. Let's blaze some new trails to community, instead of trudging down the pitted pavement of the system. The barriers to inclusion cannot be overcome from within the disability community; they must be addressed from within our communities.

When we become involved in leadership positions in our communities, we need to follow the guideline I mentioned in Chapters 12 and 17: don't initially present yourself as a disability advocate or activist. Establish yourself as an interested community member before bringing disability issues to the table. When you demonstrate caring and commitment to other people's causes, they'll reciprocate by caring about your issues.

There are exceptions to this, however. Some organizations recruit participants to represent specific sectors of the population (women, minorities, disability, and so forth). In this case, you *do* want to advertise your credentials and passion for disability issues.

In all your activities with businesses and organizations in your community, put your thinking cap on and do a lot of wondering: "How can this organization impact people with disabilities? How could this business make our community better for people with disabilities?" Think big. Connect the dots that can unite diverse issues and populations.

When we try to change the system, we identify what needs improvement and that becomes our target. We're going to do the same thing in our communities. As leaders, we can help our communities learn how to embrace all citizens. And then we can spread the good news—that the welcome mat is out—to people with disabilities and others who have been disenfranchised.

Many improvements in our communities will come about unintentionally. Our children's presence and participation in community activities will be living proof that our communities have great capacities. Many organizations will recognize that if they've been successful at including and supporting children with disabilities once, they can do it again.

In our capitalist nation, business and industry—along with government—drive what happens in every day society. To achieve societal change we must impact the movers, shakers, and policy makers in business, industry, non-profit organizations, and government. We can no longer afford to keep preaching to the choir (people in the system and disability-related organizations) trying to effect change. Bursting out of our cocoons and spreading our wings will do more to make our communities inclusive than anything attempted by the system or disability organizations.

What should be changed in your community so people with disabilities and their families are welcomed, supported, and included? What needs to happen so people with disabilities can get what they need from the community instead of the system? What changes can be made in disability organizations and systems that will promote community inclusion for people with disabilities? In this chapter, you'll learn strategies for providing leadership and influence to civic and government entities, business and industry, disability systems, and disability and non-disability organizations. I'll also describe my visions for the future for disability non-profits, disability systems, and family support. First, however, I'll detail how we can effect change within entities that are near and dear to many parents: child care facilities.

TYPICAL DAY CARE CENTERS AND PRESCHOOLS

In spite of the Americans with Disabilities Act which prohibits discrimination based on disability, many day care centers and preschools routinely deny admission to young children with disabilities. Some are blatant about their denials, telling parents, "We don't take kids like that." Others put up smokescreens by saying all classes are full or giving some other legitimate-sounding reason. (Information specific to the ADA and child care facilities is in Chapter 16.)

Proactive leadership can turn this situation around. By using a helpful, friendly, and non-threatening approach, you can gain the trust of people at child care facilities and influence their practices. If you don't want to go it alone, get a little help from your friends. In the following examples, I'll use the term "child care facility" or "center" to collectively refer to day care centers and typical preschools.

When working with child care facilities, try to discover why (or if) the owner or the staff denied admission to kids with disabilities. Are they afraid they won't know what to do? Are they scared of potential lawsuits if they do something "wrong"? Do they think they'll have to hire another person (an aide) before enrolling a child with a disability? Are they afraid a child with a disability will scare off other customers? Or do they just not want to be bothered?

Of course, you don't come out and ask these questions directly. You learn the answers by asking questions like, "Have you ever had kids with disabilities in your center?" or "I know many centers have concerns about children with disabilities. Could you educate me about what these concerns are—in your facility or others?" See the situation from their perspectives. When you discover *why* they don't welcome kids with disabilities, you can allay their fears and help them understand how to successfully include all children.

If a child care facility is already doing a great job including babies and children with disabilities, connect with the owner or director. Make the director your Ally (I'll use this term frequently in this section). Review the suggestions that follow, or come up with your own, and ask your Ally for help in teaching other centers how to do the right thing.

Address the Leadership

If you want to influence a child care facility that's operated by a church or a non-profit organization, approach the committee or board that oversees it. When trying to influence centers that are private businesses, approach the owner or board members (if there is a board). In either case, inquire about attending a committee/board meeting to give a presentation about including young children with disabilities. Ask about serving on the board or committee as a "community representative" and/or find out if you can attend the regular board meetings (are they open to the public?) as a "visitor." If the child care facility is a private business with no board or committee, take the owner or manager to lunch.

You may discover the governing board or the leadership doesn't even *know* children with disabilities are being excluded. Perhaps the director has been acting in ways that go against policies and the leadership is unaware of her actions.

Speak to Their Association

Child care facilities in your community may be members of a formal or informal child care association. Ask around to find out. Offer to address one of the organization's meeting (or conference) about including children with disabilities. If it would make a better impression, co-present with your Ally. She could provide valuable technical assistance to her peers.

Present a Community Workshop

On your own, with your Ally, or with other parents, design and present a community-wide workshop for child care providers. Prepare a two or three hour training program on how to include children with disabilities. Ask a local business to donate money for refreshments; ask a pizza place to donate pizzas. Reserve free meeting space at a community center or ask a hotel or office building to provide a meeting room at no charge.

Publicize the workshop through the media, the Chamber of Commerce, and other outlets. Create a flyer and hand deliver or mail it to all child care facilities. Follow up with personal calls to extend a personal invitation and answer questions. Remind everyone that refreshments or lunch will be served. Ask your Ally if she'll "sponsor" the training, by providing help of any kind or by adding her name to the flyer to give it more authority.

Offer Technical Assistance

On your own, with other parents, and/or your Ally, create and distribute a flyer that advertises free or low cost on-site technical assistance on how to include children with disabilities. Mail or hand deliver it to the centers you want to target. Post your flyer in neighborhood stores. Follow up with personal telephone calls to all child care facilities.

Spread the Good News!

Send out press releases about any of the activities you undertake (described in Chapter 20). Create an angle that will get the attention of the media. Once your activities have been publicized in the media, child care facilities will be calling you!

As soon as you've influenced one or more child care centers to do the right thing, help them write a press release about their terrific center. Ask them to share their "before" and "after" stories with the media. They'll love the publicity and it's a great human interest story. Try to ensure the focus of the story stays on the center and not on one or two individual kids with disabilities. You don't want a reporter writing a "pity" story!

Get the word out to parents of children with disabilities via newsletters from disability organizations and by other means. Many moms and dads use the system and/or special ed preschools because they don't know generic services in the community are available.

Child Care Scholarships

This last idea targets parents and community members, not child care providers. Some parents of children with disabilities want their little ones to use a typical child care center instead of services from the system, but they can't afford the tuition. Work in your community to find businesses who will provide scholarships to families in this situation. Instead of a business donating money to one particular family, set up a scholarship fund through a bank. Ask child care facilities to give a discount to families who access the scholarship funds. You'll be helping families and educating business leaders!

NON-PROFIT COMMUNITY ORGANIZATIONS

Within any community, many non-profit organizations are doing good work. Some provide help and services to individuals and families. Others work on social change. Any and all organizations have the potential to positively impact the lives of people with disabilities. Which organizations in your community would you like to influence?

You could get connected to the YMCA or YWCA—become a board member or sit on a committee—to help make it a more welcoming and inclusive place for people with disabilities. Maybe it needs to be made more accessible. Perhaps the pool needs a lift for people who use wheelchairs. Does the Y actively recruit people with disabilities and their families for membership? Are membership scholarships or reduced membership fees offered to families with low income, including those families that also experience disability?

Check out youth groups in your area, such as Boys' and Girls' Clubs, Scouts, Campfire, summer camps, and similar organizations. Serve as a volunteer or a leader in a group, or seek board membership. Do they have "special" (segregated) programs for children with disabilities or are all children included in the "regular" programs?

Libraries, museums, and other cultural entities are all governed by volunteer boards of citizens, people just like you and me. Become a board or committee member; volunteer as a docent in a museum or a helper in a library. Are these places accessible to people with disabilities? What could these organizations do to reach out to people with disabilities and others who may be invisible in their communities? Do all of these places train their employees to welcome and assist people with disabilities? How can you make a difference?

People with disabilities share many of the same issues that face people of color, women, and older Americans. Get involved in the NAACP, womens' groups, AARP, or other organizations concerned with social change and equal rights. Support their issues and they'll support yours. Disability activists and representatives from other groups can and should collaborate on community issues that affect a diverse constituency.

Join service clubs in your area: Rotary, Civitan, Kiwanis, Lions, etc. The focus of these organizations is community service. But many may have antiquated views about people with disabilities. And, unfortunately for advocates of inclusion, proponents of segregation have reached out to many of these same community groups. Parents of adults with disabilities, who support institutions, congregate living, and other forms of segregation, may have already made allies of these groups. If so, remember these groups have, so far, only heard one side of the story. Our job is to educate them about the other side—the side that promotes community, inclusion, and interdependence.

When you, your spouse, or any other parents become part of a community organization, you can teach people new perspectives. Many members of these groups are active or retired business people who take civic responsibilities seriously. They're often the "movers and shakers" in communities. Make positive connections with them to increase your capacity for networking and influencing. What could these organizations do to make communities more inclusive for people with disabilities. How can you help them?

CIVIC AND GOVERNMENT OPPORTUNITIES

Volunteer at park and rec activities or serve on the board. Are all programs and activities accessible? Do they still provide "special" (segregated) programs and services? Are parks and playgrounds accessible? Inclusive recreational opportunities are rare in many communities. Want your child to play on the city-sponsored soccer team? Volunteer to coach, be the "water-boy," or help find corporate sponsors to buy uniforms and other equipment. Offer to teach a class on awareness, inclusion, access, or some other topic.

Attend city council, county commissioners, and meetings of other government bodies in your area. Cultivate relationships with these policy makers. *Become a policy maker!* Run for public office or serve on a local government committee. What systemic changes can be addressed by these entities to make your community more inclusive? Citizen-run committees are numerous, including those concerned with transportation, human rights, and others that represent components of local governments. Don't wait for a crisis to get involved; your efforts may be too little, too late. When we have relationships with public officials or when we serve on government committees, we can often prevent a crisis from occurring.

Get politically involved. If you don't know the names of your state and federal senators and representatives, call the public library and find out. Make a donation to a candidate. Volunteer in political campaigns. Get to know staff people through phone calls, letters, or in person. Keep them apprised of what's important in your community, in general, and tie those concerns to disability issues. Offer to be a volunteer consultant on disability issues.

Join your community's Chamber of Commerce and/or attend Chamber functions and activities. Find out how individuals can join and what volunteer opportunities exist. Connect with business people and others who can help make your community more inclusive. Offer to give presentations on awareness, the ADA, access, or other relevant topics.

Many people with disabilities would benefit from having service animals. How could the animal shelter help in this area? Some of the national organizations that provide service animals have long waiting lists and specific criteria for eligibility. Furthermore, some are unwilling to share their dog-training expertise with private citizens! But many non-professionals are training their own dogs, and books on the subject are available. Volunteer or get on the board of your local animal shelter and promote the benefits of connecting people with disabilities and pets.

Keep your eyes open for leadership seminars and training programs. If you participate in one you'll be meeting established leaders in the community (the trainers), as well as emerging leaders (the trainees). Look for mentors for yourself, as well as for people with disabilities. There are many people in our communities who are potential allies.

BUSINESS AND INDUSTRY

Banks, grocery stores, shopping malls, gas stations, gift shops, and other types of business in your community have the potential to impact the inclusion of people with disabilities. When you're out and about, move beyond being "just a customer." Introduce yourself to the store manager, the clerk you always see at the grocery store, and so on. When you need to bring up access or other issues affecting people with disabilities, it's much easier to approach the store manager with, "Hi, John. Need to talk to you about something," rather than stiffly requesting, "I want to see the manager." Help businesses become accessible to customers with disabilities. Become a friendly and helpful volunteer consultant.

A local hamburger joint in our small town didn't have any designated accessible parking. The kids and I stopped there regularly for ice cream cones. After the manager began recognizing us as "regulars," I told him Benj and other people with disabilities could get in easier if accessible parking was available by the main entrance. Embarrassed, he said he knew he was supposed to do that, but he just hadn't gotten around to it yet. I asked if he'd like some help: "If you can supply the paint and the stencil, I'll come over and paint the asphalt." He agreed and asked me to check back in a week or so. As it turned out, he sold his building to Taco Bell. When the building was remodeled, accessible parking was included and we got tacos instead of ice cream!

Bone up on the Americans Disabilities Act to know what's covered, but don't use it as a baseball bat. If a business isn't accessible, help the owner or manager find ways to make it accessible in positive, proactive ways. If a building has two steps to the front door—making it inaccessible for a person in a wheelchair or other mobility device—volunteer to help find a solution. If the building owner will supply the lumber, you and some friends or other community members will provide the labor to build the ramp. You'll be loved and respected for your leadership and help. This action could spur other businesses to follow suit. Send out press releases about the great community effort!

In casual conversations, ask business owners and managers about their employment of people with disabilities. Don't make it an adversarial situation; stay in an information-gathering mode. These informal exchanges can get people thinking and help them learn new attitudes. They may come to you for help. If you meet adults with disabilities who are looking for a job, you can connect employers and potential employees.

Do the same thing with local banks, credit unions, and other businesses that are public corporations. Are people with disabilities their customers or employees? Does the bank offer low-interest loans for the purchase of assistive technology, adapted vehicles, homes, or remodeling costs associated with making a home accessible? Get on the board of the local bank or attend the meetings and you'll be making immediate connections with influential citizens. If a public corporation sponsors youth programs or makes large donations to community non-profits, do the recipient organizations include people with disabilities in their services or activities?

Connect and Share

In the connections you make through your volunteer or community activities, share disability issues in the most natural way possible and within the context of the organization's mission or focus. The first step is simply making people aware that individuals with disabilities are members of the community. For so long, people with their disabilities and their families have been invisible. Your presence and informal conversations about your family and your interests will let others know that people with disabilities and their family members are just like everyone else.

CONSULTATION AND TECHNICAL ASSISTANCE

In addition to serving on a board or committee, there are other ways you can provide leadership and influence in your community. Reach out to non-profits, business and industry, and government entities to offer technical assistance and consultation on disability issues. You're already an expert on your child. Become an expert on a variety of disability issues. Talk to other parents about what needs improving in your community. If you don't know any, meet adults with disabilities to find out what they need. Jobs? Independent living? Friends? Recreation?

For example, if you want all park and rec activities to be inclusive, do some homework to discover what the current situation is. Decide what needs to happen to make it better. Think of ways the community can pitch in to help make the changes. Then approach the park and rec folks as a technical consultant with your ideas and solutions.

Never, never, never go in with a problem unless you already have the solution. If you simply go in to complain, you'll probably receive any number of unacceptable responses. You might be ignored. You may be told there's not enough money or that there's no need to do what you're requesting. Or, they might propose a "solution" that's worse than the current situation. Always have solutions before you present a problem.

If you would rather work broadly and informally instead of focusing on a particular issue, start spreading the word that you're available to provide consultation and technical assistance in your areas of expertise. Print business cards or flyers that describe the services you provide. But be careful not to misrepresent yourself or use terms that are confusing. My ears perked up during a recent television commercial when I heard the words, "disability advocacy." "Wow!" I thought, "This guy's advertising he's an advocate. I wonder who he is and what he does." Imagine my dismay when I realized he was an attorney who represents people with disabilities who are denied Social Security disability income. So much for calling ourselves "disability advocates."

Take your wisdom, your leadership, and your vision for an inclusive society and put them to work in your own back yard. Care about others in your community and they'll care about you. In all of your efforts, educate folks about the importance of People First Language and share the philosophy that disability is a natural part of life.

SCHOOL BOARDS AND COMMITTEES

Too often, we advocate on behalf of our own child for inclusion, but we ignore the bigger picture of the entire school or the whole district. In Chapter 12, you learned about redefining yourself—becoming someone other than the "special ed parent"—to improve relationships with educators and others. If you redefine yourself by participating on school committees, you can help change your child's school and the district.

Remember that schools are part of a system, and systemic change doesn't happen overnight. That doesn't mean, however, that all change takes years. Some school buildings have, over one summer, adopted inclusive practices. In some cases, one principal provided the leadership for change; in others, a group of teachers took the lead. Following are some ideas that might work for you.

If your child is under five and the neighborhood elementary school or the district doesn't practice inclusion, don't wait until your little one is ready to enter kindergarten. Even if your child doesn't yet attend public school, you can serve on a school committee or participate in the PTA/PTO as a community member.

If your child is already attending public school, investigate all the different committees in your child's school building, as well as within the district. Offer to volunteer on the one that interests you most. If things are going well in your child's elementary school, but you're concerned about the quality at the middle school or high school, get involved in committee work in those buildings. Become active in the PTA/PTO or other groups.

Attend school board meetings. In most districts, these public meetings are held at least once a month. Before the meeting starts or after it ends, introduce yourself to the board members. Go to every meeting and speak to board members each time. Establish a relationship with them based on your interest in and concern for the school district as a whole. Later on, when you want to discuss specific issues with them—such as inclusion in the entire district—you'll have a connection with them.

Run for the school board. Yes, run for public office in your community! Call your school district's central office to find out how board members are elected. Does each member represent a specific geographic area of the district or do they all represent the community-at-large? How long is the term of office? When is the next election? What's the procedure for placing your name on the ballot? People on school boards are no different than you or me. Most are parents of students in the district. After you get to know one or more of your school board members, ask lots of questions about what it's like to be on the board. Learn as much as you can. Perhaps a school board member will endorse your future candidacy or help you campaign for office.

In every situation, identify yourself as an interested, concerned parent, not a "special ed parent." Many of us assume assertive and aggressive roles in dealing with school personnel. Usually, this is a defensive position we use after we've been unfairly treated. We learn to speak up—loudly and clearly—in our roles as advocates. But when we're moving into new roles in non-disability school settings, we cannot bring those methods with us. Your potential effectiveness will be lost if your "mother from hell" reputation precedes you or if you flex your expert muscles too quickly.

When you attend meetings as a new committee/board member, be humble, listen well, and learn from others. Ask questions. Share your opinions about the topics being discussed. Don't lecture others about your issues—yet. Don't even bring them up until you've established yourself as a valuable, contributing member. This might take two meetings or four or six. Show interest in other people's issues and they'll do the same for you. Your style must be subtle, calm, and persuasive; not angry, frantic, and aggressive.

School committees and groups—from the PTA to the school improvement team and everything in between—all share the same bottom line: they exist to make schools better. Little by little, bring special education, inclusion, or disability issues to the meeting as they relate to your committee's specific purpose. You'll quickly learn that most parents and educators on your committee know little about segregation, resource rooms, inclusion, curriculum modifications, and so forth. Some might not even know that "kids like that" are students in the district!

You want your new associates to see that students with disabilities are part of the whole, not a separate population—even if many *are* currently separated from the mainstream. You'll be enlarging the scope of the committee's work when members realize they've been unknowingly ignoring a large number of students.

Encourage other parents of children with and without disabilities to join you in your efforts. Schools can be resistant to change, but there is power in numbers. Don't, however, make the mistake of identifying yourselves as a "group" representing a particular issue. If school officials or other parents view you as a bunch of rabble-rousers, you become an easy target for them to oppose. Organized groups can be wonderful as long as they share common beliefs, work as a cohesive unit, and practice respect for others. Too often, however, "mob mentality" takes over and chaos results.

Spread Your Wings

Imagine the possibilities if you and other parents of children with disabilities were visible across every school and district committee, the PTA, and other groups. Imagine how things could change when parents and educators who are focused on regular education learn and care about students with disabilities.

When you spread your wings and become involved in non-disability school committees and activities, you'll be pleasantly surprised to learn that parents of typical children have great concerns about their children's education. We're not the only ones who have difficulties with public schools! When we work together on shared concerns, we can create common solutions. And when we serve on committees that make recommendations to the school board, or when we're on the school board, we've *become* policy makers.

For several years, our small, determined special education advisory committee (SEAC) worked tirelessly for change. The school board knew we existed, but out of all the district committees, ours was the least valued. We were perceived as a special interest group that did not contribute to the overall good of district. We finally realized our efforts would be more successful if we spread ourselves out among the various committees in the district. If you're involved in your district's SEAC, would the efforts of each member produce greater long-term results if they were spread across a variety of non-disability committees?

The overall quality of a school can be measured by how it treats students with disabilities and others who are disenfranchised. If the students who are the least valued in society are treated as equals in a public school—if they're valued and included—the school probably does well for all its students. If students with disabilities and differences are relegated to the bottom of the barrel, the school is guilty of promoting a hierarchy where every student is invisibly and arbitrarily ranked in human potential and value.

When we stay in our disability cocoon, it's easy for policy makers, administrators, school board members, and others to dismiss or minimize our concerns. We're perceived as small fish in a big pond. We have, unfortunately, done a great job of segregating ourselves from the mainstream of school issues by focusing only on special ed issues. But when we bring our issues into the overall school culture, we can achieve real change for students with and without disabilities.

NON-PROFIT DISABILITY ORGANIZATIONS

Some non-profit disability organizations are very, very good. Others are very, very bad. Never assume that all disability organizations further the causes of inclusion, equality, and dignity for people with disabilities. Some local chapters still believe people with disabilities are incapable of contributing, participating, or taking care of themselves. Other groups intentionally insulate and separate themselves from their communities, believing only they can support people with disabilities.

If you're currently active in a disability organization, step back and view it from a distance. When we're heavily invested in an organization or if our children have received many benefits from it, we might find it hard to find any fault with its mission or activities. Doing so might make us feel disloyal. Or perhaps we don't know about the entire organization. When I was involved in a group when Benjamin was very young, the activities and services for parents were wonderful, but what was done on behalf of adults with disabilities was not. When looking at the organization as a whole, what needs to be improved?

It may be hard to believe, but influencing disability non-profits can be more difficult than influencing businesses and organizations in our communities. Board members of many disability organizations are often parents of adult children with disabilities who have been involved in disability issues for thirty or forty years. Their children may live in segregated, congregate housing facilities, and attend adult day care or sheltered work programs, existing in isolation and dependence. These parents aren't bad; this is simply what they learned decades ago. Times change, but sometimes people don't.

In some of these organizations, you, as the parent of a child with a disability, are perceived as a newcomer—a novice—in the midst of experienced parents. Yet in the community, you're perceived as a knowledgeable, experienced expert. You can often more easily influence people in the community because their attitudes about disability may not be as entrenched as the attitudes of the older leaders in some disability organizations!

If you're involved in an organization that's ruled by the "old guard," don't give up, but don't expect a rapid or major shift. Sometimes, we just have to be patient and wait for board members to retire. But it's not only board members who hold on to old ways.

Executive directors and employees of disability organizations may also be responsible for antiquated practices. In theory, an executive director of a non-profit works for the board of directors; he is hired and can be fired by the board. The board makes policies; the executive director implements those policies. In practice, however, this isn't always the case. Internal politics, jockeying for position, fighting over turf issues, and other skirmishes are as common in non-profits as they are in the business world (and in IEP meetings).

If the board and the executive director have been together a long time, the board may give the director a great deal of power to *make policy* as well as implement it. As long as the executive director is leading the organization in the way the board likes, everything is hunky-dory. Tensions may arise when a new board member doesn't go along with the status quo.

On the other hand, a board may hire a director for the purpose of taking the organization in a new direction. But the board may not really give the director any power or freedom to implement change. A variety of different situations may exist. It's important to learn as much as you can about the inner workings and the internal politics of the disability organization you want to influence.

Board membership typically includes representatives from the community. Attorneys, accountants, bankers, and other business leaders, as well as family members, are often asked to serve. Organizations should also include people with disabilities as active, participating board members, not as mere tokens. For disability organizations to truly represent the people they profess to serve, the majority of the board members should be people with disabilities and family members. However, this make-up doesn't necessarily ensure it's a good board. The majority might endorse policies that promote segregation and dependency.

The best boards are those that are regularly infused with new blood. For example, parents of younger children with disabilities, as well as people who don't have a connection to disability issues, are often able to contribute new visions and common sense.

I was once a member of a board that routinely ignored its own policies in order to keep certain members on the board. According to the by-laws, a member could only serve two consecutive three-year terms. But one of our board members had been on the board for almost fifteen years! Another was nearing the ten year mark. How could this happen? The chairman of the board made a motion to exempt these two members from the by-laws, the motion was seconded, and the old guard majority outvoted the minority, maintaining its lock on board decisions.

In Chapter 5, I detailed how many disability organizations perpetuate negative, stereotypical attitudes toward people with disabilities. Fund raising efforts that evoke sympathy or pity, along with specialized services and programs that isolate or segregate people with disabilities from the mainstream of their communities, keep old attitudes and myths alive. A fundamental shift in how organizations *perceive* the people they serve is necessary. When this occurs, a change in the purpose and the activities of an organization will follow.

THE DISABILITY ORGANIZATION OF THE FUTURE

I have a vision for disability organizations in the twenty-first century. If enough of us get on the bandwagon, maybe we can make this vision a reality.

What if the mission of disability organizations changed? Instead of focusing on helping people with disabilities, or raising money for prevention or cure, what if they focused on making communities more inclusive? In this capacity, they would no longer provide direct services to people with disabilities and their families. Instead, their funds would be dispersed throughout the community to organizations which would provide services and assistance in inclusive natural settings. In addition, disability organizations would collaborate with each other and with non-disability organizations. Let's look at some possibilities.

Transportation

Let's assume an organization budgets $75,000 per year for operating expenses for its van and the van driver, for transporting "clients" who don't have (1) their own transportation, (2) access to public transportation, or (3) funds to pay for taxis. The disability organization of the future could reallocate these funds in ways that would promote interdependence and community inclusion.

In one method, the organization could provide cash or vouchers to individuals and families to pay for taxis, or to reimburse friends who drive them where they need to go. "Approved" volunteer drivers could drive the accessible vehicle for those who needed it.

In another method, the organization could recruit volunteer drivers from the community and provide a list of these drivers to individuals and families who need help with transportation. This method would enable people with disabilities and their families to make new friends and connections with people in their communities. In addition, this service could be a collaborative effort of organizations who serve diverse populations: people with disabilities, senior citizens, families with low incomes, and others. Instead of the disability organization arranging rides for people (creating dependency), each person needing the service would be responsible for contacting a volunteer driver (promoting interdependency). Volunteer drivers would be reimbursed for mileage.

Employment

Instead of providing sheltered workshops or other segregated or special employment services, disability organizations could collaborate with local businesses to create a "job bank." Businesses could provide opportunities for non-paid internships where high school students and/or adults with disabilities could "try out" a job for a short period of time to learn more about employment in general or specific types of careers. The disability organization could publish a directory of these opportunities. A person with a disability could review the list and contact the employer directly to work out the details. This would lead to increased employment for people with disabilities, increased opportunities to make connections in the community, and an improvement in the business community's awareness of people with disabilities. In turn, this could lead to businesses becoming more accessible and other positive outcomes.

As in the transportation example, people with disabilities would be responsible for initiating calls to businesses. They would be in charge!

Therapy

Instead of providing hand-on therapies for children, disability organizations and their therapists could collaborate with youth activities in the community. If the organization budgets $100,000 per year for therapy services, it could allocate some of those funds to natural settings. The therapist would remain salaried and provide consultative services.

For example, a young girl with a disability could attend ballet classes in the community instead of receiving physical therapy. The dollars normally allocated for this girl's therapy (an estimated $7,000/year) could pay for ballet lessons (an estimated $720/year). The therapist could collaborate with the ballet instructor as needed and/or assist the young ballerina during the ballet classes.

Similarly, other children could receive therapeutic benefits by enrolling in swim, gymnastics, or martial arts classes, or other activities in the community. Again, the therapist would be a consultant to assist the adult leaders of these activities, as well as helping individual children as needed. Using community services would enable children to be included with typical children, and their families would make new connections.

Other Activities

Here are other creative activities the disability organization of the future could engage in to promote inclusion:

- Collaborate with other disability organizations and non-disability organizations to pursue common goals of community inclusion for people with disabilities and differences.

- Provide technical assistance and training to public schools, child care facilities, community organizations, businesses, and other entities, on successful methods of including and supporting individuals with disabilities.

- Teach people with disabilities and family members strategies for using natural supports and generic services.

- Ensure that people with disabilities and family members who support community inclusion constitute the majority on the board of directors.

- Hire people with disabilities and family members for employment within the organization, in both staff and management positions.

Fund Raising: Cash and Other Assets

Fund raising efforts would use "improved communities"—instead of pity, prevention, or cure—as a fund raising theme. They would not beg for money on behalf of people with disabilities. Their operating funds would come from donations made by businesses and individuals who contribute because they want more inclusive communities! And the organization's resources wouldn't be limited to cash donations.

Businesses could contribute by offering non-paid internships to people with disabilities to help them learn about employment, as previously mentioned. Other businesses could donate scholarship funds to pay for community activities for people with low incomes.

Collaborative efforts could help people with disabilities acquire assistive technology. For example, a disability organization could put people with disabilities in touch with companies who are disposing of their old computers when buying new ones.

Instead of giving cash, businesses and people in the community could contribute by offering services, and these services would be compiled into a directory which would be distributed to people with disabilities and their families. For example, a private employment agency (not one that only serves people with disabilities) could donate a certain number of hours of job counseling services. Adults with disabilities could spend time with a professional learning about employment opportunities, interviewing skills, and so forth.

Accountants could donate their time to help people learn about managing money. Child care centers could donate a certain number of hours of child care to a "babysitting bank" which parents could use when they need a babysitter. Businesses and individuals could donate mentorships: people with disabilities could select a mentor to learn more about employment, leadership, or anything else that promotes community inclusion and self-determination.

The opportunities are unlimited. The focus of the disability organization of the future would shift from helping individuals with disabilities to helping communities include and support people with disabilities. And in all cases, the disability organization would work in the background. For example, a staff person would not set up a job internship for an individual with a disability or call the child care facility for parents. Instead, the staff person would give the appropriate information (list of services) to the person with a disability or family members, and allow individuals to set things up for themselves. As necessary, staff members could help make an individual feel confident about making his own contacts by role playing the situation or by other means.

The disability organization of the future would be small and efficient. Because it would essentially be acting as a "broker" of services (the middleman), instead of a provider of services, the staff could be pared down considerably. In addition, because disability organizations would collaborate with each other and with non-disability organizations, employees of all these organizations could "share" employees. All of these changes would reduce the operating costs of each organization!

Collaboration

Why don't today's disability organizations collaborate with one another more? In hundreds of cities and towns across America, seldom do local associations band together to achieve the goals of their constituents: inclusion, independence, community, and more.

In Anytown, for example, why don't the local affiliates of The Arc, United Cerebral Palsy, Spinda Bifida Association, Down Syndrome Association, the Autism Society, and/or other groups work together? This seems so strange. Parents of children who have different disabilities work together all the time, as do adults with disabilities. A few cross-disability coalitions are springing up, but they're generally focused on legislative issues. In general, disability-specific organizations go it alone.

Why isn't collaboration between disability groups happening more? Is it because an organization only cares about one particular disability? Do their mission statements mandate they only work on behalf of people with that particular disability? Do they feel collaboration would jeopardize donations by contributors who only want their money going for one disability? Does competition for donations cloud their vision that much? Are they really working for people with disabilities anymore, or are their efforts actually focused on keeping the organization going? If disability organizations collaborated with each other, as well as with non-disability organizations, they could have a profound influence in making communities more inclusive.

Collaborating with others, working to promote community inclusion, changing fund raising techniques, and seeing people with disabilities in a new light can make the disability organization of the future a reality today. What will it take to move disability organizations in this new direction? What can you do to help make this happen?

DISABILITY SYSTEMS

Billions—yes, billions—of state and federal dollars flow to state and local agencies that serve people with disabilities. Throughout this book, I've repeatedly stated that for many people with disabilities, the system causes more problems than it solves, and it's unresponsive and unchanging. But there are exceptions:

- A regional agency that provides early intervention services scrapped the old way of doing things in favor of a new way. Instead of making very young children come to the center for hands-on therapies, the agency collaborated with the YMCA. Moms and their babies with disabilities joined the Y's baby swim classes, alongside other moms and babies without disabilities. The agency therapist worked side-by-side with the YMCA swim instructors. It was seamless: both professionals helped all participants. The babies with disabilities were not singled out. The moms and babies were included in typical activities, and the babies received the help they needed in a natural environment.

- A school district in a mid-sized city didn't set up its early childhood education program in a public school building. Instead, all children who were eligible for preschool services remained in natural environments (home, day care, neighborhood preschool) and services and supports were provided in those settings.

- An agency providing employment services for adults with developmental disabilities had a long waiting list. The bureaucratic red tape, the rules and regulations imposed by the state, and low funding contributed to the problem. The director of the agency solved the problem overnight when he told his staff, "Go out in the community, use your own connections, and make it happen, one way or another. Don't worry about following all the bureaucratic rules. I'll take responsibility for that. Do whatever it takes to get people jobs." Infused with new energy and the freedom to be creative, the staff members followed the new directive and were successful.

What does it take for agencies serving people with disabilities to change? Leadership by people who have a vision and who are willing to take calculated risks. We can contribute our visions and ideas for change by serving on boards and committees of the agencies dedicated to serving people with disabilities.

University affiliated programs (UAP), protection and advocacy services (P & A), developmental disabilities councils (DDC), interagency coordinating councils (ICC), and other entities operate at the state level. Early intervention, early childhood services, family support, developmental disability services, and other programs are provided by agencies at the local or regional level.

In nooks and crannies here and there, bold individuals and courageous boards and committees are trailblazing new paths within the system. In many cases, their efforts are not highly publicized; doing so might invoke the wrath of the "system police." Drawing attention to their unorthodox methods could bring an end to their progress. Quietly and efficiently, they're bringing common sense into a system that has none. Their efforts begin with new ways of thinking.

New Paradigms

Moving from the antiquated customs of the system to a common sense approach of service delivery is possible when agencies and organizations adopt new paradigms. Concerned citizens, board and committee members, or staff people can introduce a variety of new concepts. The primary paradigm shift requires service providers to redefine their own roles and the roles of the people they serve. The service system can learn many lessons from business.

The traditional paradigm of the service system is based on paternalism: the wise and all-knowing agency benevolently provides for the needs of its clients. And the services provided and the methods used to deliver them have usually been determined by the agency, not by the client. In the real world, businesses design products and services to meet their customers' needs. As these needs change, businesses respond with new products, improvements in services, and more. In the delicate balance of supply and demand, change is the rule, not the exception. Businesses are always in competition. This competition fuels excellence. Customer satisfaction is paramount. Without it, businesses go belly-up.

Unfortunately, there's little, if any, competition in the service system. People with disabilities have few, if any, choices in the selection of service providers. There's no competition to drive excellence and no incentive to constantly improve. Even so, if government-funded disability agencies began seeing themselves as businesses serving customers, instead of providers serving clients, the impact would be phenomenal. But there's more.

Most service providers recognize they're unable to meet the needs of everyone who is eligible for services. They're often as frustrated by this as the people they serve. In almost all cases, their dilemma boils down to money: not enough money to provide services for everyone, not enough money to pay for more staff, and so on. Every agency would like to have more money. However, there are alternatives to the almighty dollar that most agencies have never explored.

In addition, most agencies deliver services in ways that contribute to the continued segregation and isolation of people with disabilities. While this outcome may not be intentional, it is a negative by-product of the way service providers operate. Perhaps we shouldn't be surprised at this since the agencies carry out their functions in isolation and segregation. Think about it. A typical service provider has few, if any, connections to the community-at-large. It's connected only to other bureaucratic agencies. It doesn't operate within its community, but parallel to it. If service providers are invisible in the community—and most are—then so are the people they serve.

THE SERVICE PROVIDER OF THE FUTURE

Service providers can be more successful in meeting the real needs of their constituents and furthering community inclusion when they see themselves as businesses serving customers and engage in creative collaboration with others. Following is a description of what could happen if a hypothetical service provider adopted new ways of thinking. I've named this service provider "Connections."

Connections views its services not as entitlements guaranteed to needy clients but as products offered to customers. It has adopted business practices to ensure customers are treated in ways that promote customer loyalty, just the way real businesses do. They do whatever it takes to make it easy for customers to do business with them. Connections knows that retail providers of goods and services provide a variety of services and accommodations for customers: drive-through windows, toll-free telephone numbers, 24-hour customer service via telephone, opening early and closing late, speedy response, and more. The employees of Connections are learning from successful businesses.

Connections recognizes that employees work to serve the customer, not the organization. In the current service system, employees forget—or are never taught—that without "clients," they'd be out of a job. Millions of Americans earn their livings on the backs of people with disabilities! Connections is working to ensure all employees recognize the roles and relationships inherent in successful customer relations.

To stay focused on its mission to serve the customer, Connections routinely surveys its customers to determine customer needs and customer satisfaction. The results of these surveys, along with customer focus groups and direct customer involvement in decision-making, drives Connections' activities. Continuous quality improvement (CQI) is now a cornerstone of Connections' operations, and the board, committees, and employees are learning how to put CQI strategies to work throughout the organization.

By surveying its customer base, Connections knows what customers really want and need. Because many of these identified needs fall outside the traditional boundaries of Connections' capabilities, responsibilities, or standard operating procedures, the agency is modifying some procedures and working with organizations in the community to meet the needs of its customers.

As an example, Connections collaborates with other entities in the community that already provide a variety of services : child care facilities, community activities, employment services, and others. Instead of trying to *supplant* these generic services with services specifically for people with disabilities, Connections builds capacity in the community by helping typical organizations and businesses meet the unique needs of people with disabilities. The agency is moving toward being a broker and a facilitator of services instead of a direct service provider. By creating a positive presence in the community, Connections is not just impacting the lives of people with disabilities, it's influencing the entire community.

Using non-traditional approaches has become the rule, not the exception. Work shifts have been staggered and office hours have been changed to accommodate the needs of customers. The traditional operating schedule (8:00 AM to 5:00 PM, Monday through Friday) has been changed to 7:00 AM to 8:00 PM, Monday through Friday, and 9:00 AM to 1:00 PM on Saturdays. Following are other examples of Connections' new ways of doing business, based on customer needs.

Services for Young Children

Connections has scrapped its traditional one-size-fits-all early intervention (EI) services. Through collaboration in the community and the use of vouchers, Connections now offers truly individualized assistance. Through a voucher system, parents can choose to stay with the traditional therapeutic interventions or they can design non-traditional methods, such as baby swim classes; baby gym classes; neighborhood child care enrollment for speech and social skills; purchasing items for home use to help with skill development; and other methods that are both natural and unique. All of this is possible because Connections combines its budget with in-kind, financial, and other supports from the community.

Even though the local school district has the legal and financial responsibility of providing early childhood education (ECE) services, Connections is working to influence how schools implement ECE services. During the transition from EI to ECE when children turn three, Connections staff people work closely with parents who want their children to receive preschool services in natural settings in the community.

In addition, Connections staffers are helping build bridges between ECE professionals and typical preschools. First, they invite ECE coordinators and staff members to visit the child care sites in the community where children are receiving EI services in their natural environments. Then they share their methods of collaboration, funding, and other components with ECE personnel in the hopes that the ECE program will begin providing services in inclusive community settings instead of segregated classes in public school settings.

Employment

Staff members at Connections have established relationships with the Chamber of Commerce, the community college, and a variety of businesses and associations. Bypassing the traditional employment approaches through voc-rehab, Goodwill, sheltered workshops, and enclave settings, the Connections staff is forging new paths to real employment for adults with disabilities.

Non-paid internships help many people with disabilities become familiar with a variety of different jobs. In many cases, these internships become full-time, paid positions. Professional employment counselors volunteer their time to help potential new employees determine a career path and learn interviewing skills. These counselors also use their networks to help adults with disabilities find new jobs. Other collaborative efforts with businesses result in on-the-job-training opportunities, peer supported employment, and other options for adults with disabilities.

Housing

With a steady pay check coming in, many adults with disabilities are able to move from group homes and other congregate living arrangements to independent living in the community. Again, the Connections service coordinators look to the community. They ask which neighborhoods their customers prefer, and then fan out to see what's available in apartments and single-family homes. In addition, they encourage individuals with disabilities to spread the word among co-workers that they're looking for a new place. The networking Connections makes with apartment managers pays off with roommate arrangements for some folks. In other cases, co-workers of individuals with disabilities use their own networks to help find independent living solutions for their new friends.

Reciprocity and Flexibility

Connections receives a great deal of help and support from organizations and individuals in the community. In return, Connections provides technical assistance and support to organizations, businesses, and individuals who open the doors to community inclusion.

Being flexible and creative has enabled Connections to meet the needs of its customers through collaboration with community organizations, while meeting government mandates. Connections, its customers, and people in the community work together to achieve successful outcomes; all have an equal role and all share ownership in the process.

Making the Dream a Reality

This idealized scenario doesn't have to remain a dream. Bits and pieces are being done at some agencies and organizations across the country. Because every state is different, changes in human service agencies would originate at different levels. Some changes might require action by state legislatures, some could occur through policy changes, and some could be achieved simply, by the visionary leadership of administrators and boards. *But nothing will change in the system until people in the system choose to make changes.*

What can we do to influence the people in the system to change the status quo? As customers, we can voice our opinions. Collectively, our voices carry more weight. As board or committee members and/or as employees of organizations and agencies, we can talk with others, offer suggestions for change, and share a vision of services that promote dignity, choice, freedom, and contribution and participation in the community. As citizens, we can talk to our legislators and policy makers. We have more power than we know.

GRANT MONEY

Money for good works is out there. Cold, hard cash—in the form of grants—flows from federal and state governments, foundations, and other organizations every day. We can use our leadership and influence to direct these dollars to projects that advance community inclusion for people with disabilities.

Here's a simplified explanation of how the grant process works: an agency has a goal it wants to achieve or an idea it wants to test, or it's looking for innovative solutions to specific issues. It will provide the funding (a grant) to organizations who can fulfill the need.

The agency writes a request for proposals (RFP) which outlines the goal or the idea, the amount of money available, and various details about the who, what, why, where, and how of the project. Organizations who are interested in fulfilling the project then submit their proposals. Funding is awarded to the organization whose proposal best meets the criteria outlined in the RFP.

In many instances, grant money is seed money. When an agency awards a grant, it usually does so in the hope that after the grant recipient completes the project, the activities, practices, or outcomes of the project will continue in one form or another. In some cases, the funder hopes the project can be successfully replicated by other organizations. Alternatively, the funder may hope other organizations will contribute funds to keep the project going after the initial funding is gone. In too many cases, however, these hopes are never realized, and a wonderfully successful demonstration project ends as quickly as it was begun, never having a widespread effect.

Grants come in all shapes and sizes. The amount of the grant can be large or small. The scope can be broad or narrow. We can and should influence how grant money is used and there are many ways to do this.

If you're affiliated with an agency or organization that routinely awards grants, get involved with the grants management process. (If you don't know if the organization awards grants, ask.) Traditionally, grants from government-funded disability agencies are often awarded to non-profit disability organizations simply because these groups respond to the RFPs more than non-disability organizations. Many exemplary outcomes have been posted by these grantees, but the good works don't always result in long-term change. Either the project cannot be (or is not) successfully replicated, or additional funding to continue the activity is not available. To change this, RFPs can be written to encourage non-disability organizations to apply.

For example, let's assume a DD Council wants to fund a demonstration project about increased community inclusion for school-age children. Under usual circumstances, the

RFP would probably be written using parameters and language that target non-profit disability organizations as potential grant recipients, such as The Arc, United Cerebral Palsy, and others. But if the outcome of the project is increased community inclusion, shouldn't community organizations be targeted?

An RFP could describe "Increased community inclusion for school-age children to include participation in community youth programs such as Scouting, Campfire, etc.; park and recreation activities; volunteer opportunities; and other typical community experiences." Such an RFP would stimulate proposals from city park and rec departments, youth groups, YWCAs, and others. If the grant was awarded to one of these groups, the project would ensure community inclusion for children with disabilities during the grant period. More importantly, however, it's highly possible the good works would remain in place permanently and be replicated by others.

Let's assume a coalition of city park and rec departments across the state of Colorado applied for and received the grant. During the term of the grant, each park and rec office identifies effective methods to recruit children with disabilities into inclusive programs, as well as successful ways of supporting and including them. When the official project is over, each park and rec will most likely continue these practices! Further, they could share their methods with other entities in their communities. Taking it even further, they could share the strategies with park and rec folks from all across the United States by doing presentations at park and rec conferences at the regional and national levels.

We need to encourage disability agencies to write RFPs that would entice non-disability organizations to apply. Many positive outcomes can result when we utilize the existing strengths and capacities in our communities. In pockets across the country, this is already happening, as some DD Councils and other agencies award grants to generic community groups instead of disability-related organizations. Is this happening in your state?

The process of community inclusion can work from the other direction, as well. If you're connected to a non-disability organization via board or committee membership, help the organization find grant monies that target people with disabilities. For example, if you're a member of the local park and rec board, keep your eyes open for disability-related grants about community inclusion. If you're on the board at a YMCA that provides child care, be on the alert for grants about babies and young children with disabilities. Many grantors would be delighted to receive proposals from non-disability organizations.

There are so many ways we can use grants to help communities become more inclusive for people with disabilities. If you're not familiar with grant writing techniques and other details about grants, your local library can be a good source of information. In many communities, grant writing courses are offered through libraries, community colleges, and other public service organizations. Seek out others in your community who are familiar with grants and learn from their experiences.

You can discover what grants are available by checking a variety of sources. Federal grants are included in the *Federal Register* which is available from the public library and on the Internet. The *Register* is a newspaper-like booklet that's published every business day. A weekly check of the daily editions will keep you apprised of what's new from the Feds.

For information about grants from state and regional organizations, you might need to make a few phone calls and do a little research. Many state developmental disabilities councils, university affiliated programs, departments of education, and other government-funded agencies maintain a mailing list for its newsletters and other information they disseminate. If you're on the main mailing list, you'll probably also receive notices of grants. A call to the state procurement office would be helpful to find out which state agencies offer grants.

During your research at the library, ask the librarian for directories of foundations. They're another source of funding for non-profit organizations. Some foundations issue RFPs, while others simply respond to requests made by potential grantees. Foundations come in all shapes and sizes. The big national foundation directories are cross-referenced by topic, so it's easy to locate the ones of interest. Don't forget to check out directories of state and local foundations.

FAMILY SUPPORT/RESPITE PROGRAMS

Family support is being touted as an absolute necessity all across the country. In many states, family support programs have already been enacted and funded. In others, the issue is still being debated. This is another hot issue for parents to coalesce around. In Chapter 6, I detailed my concerns about respite/family support.

Family support means different things to different people. In some cases, it's simply another name for respite care services. In others, it's far more. Therapy, equipment, home modifications, and other items needed by a child and his family may be funded by a family support programs. There are so many notions of what family support is or what people want it to be that it's hard to provide a specific definition that's accurate in all cases. But many parents seem to want family support to become a catch-all program to pay for whatever a child and his family need or want, related to the child's disability. If a family is unable to afford a product or service, and if insurance or some other service won't pay for it, many parents are advocating for family support to fill in the gap.

The notion that we should look to the government for entitlements to meet our every need is both demeaning and dangerous. Further, it demonstrates a lack of vision on our part. The unspoken message of family support—like many other unspoken messages of disability services—is clear: our families are so different and so needy that we can't take care of ourselves. We talk about wanting equality, yet we have no problem presenting ourselves as unequal in order to get services or money.

By demanding family support programs and funding, we're sending a dangerous message to our children: the government will provide for you. Do we want our children to grow into dependent adults? Do we want them to turn to the government for help in having their needs met? Or do we want them to be interdependent young men and women who can use the skills of resourcefulness and self-sufficiency they learned from us as they grew?

Family support programs may provide excellent benefits for a large number of families for a relatively short period of time. But the majority of families are still left out of the loop. Family support may provide short term answers for some, but we need long term solutions for many. I have a dream about how to make this happen. It's a new vision for family support. But first, let's look at how things are traditionally done.

A Conventional Approach to Family Support

Let's assume a state has budgeted $250,000 annually for a family support program. Eligible families are entitled to $1,000 each, which can be used for just about anything in support of their children with disabilities: respite, equipment, home modifications, therapy, etc. A total of 250 families will be served by this program each year. The positive impact on these families may be significant. However, in most cases, the benefits will be short-lived.

What will $1,000 really buy? If therapy costs $75 per hour, a family could purchase thirteen hours of therapy. That's one session a month for a year, with one left over. If respite costs $20.00 an hour, a family could purchase fifty hours of respite. That's a little over four hours of respite a month. If a family wants to use its entitlement to purchase equipment or to make accessible home renovations, $1,000 may come in quite handy, or it may barely make a dent in the total expense.

Again, in most cases, the benefits will be of short duration, with little or no long term positive outcomes. In addition, the family support dollars will probably have little, if any, effect on the child's inclusion or success in the community. And thousands of other families of children with disabilities in the state will not benefit from the program at all. But what if the program was funded at a higher level? More money, some think, is always the answer.

Let's say the funding was quadrupled: the state is allocating $1,000,000 for the program, a cool million. Sounds better, doesn't it? Would this increased funding mean the 250 families would each get $4,000 each year? That wouldn't be too bad, would it? It would be great for the 250 families that got the money, but what about the thousands who didn't? Some parents might object to funding the program this way. They might agitate for more families to be served. In that case, 1,000 families would each receive the paltry $1,000. Which way is better?

The real solutions to most of the issues we face are found in our communities. If family support dollars went to communities instead of individual families, we would see widespread, long-term changes that benefit all families with disabilities. Following is an alternative way of operating family support programs that could impact thousands of families, create long-term change, and provide opportunities for community inclusion and participation.

A New Vision for Family Support

In my hypothetical scenario, the state will use the $250,000 to fund grants that provide community support to families of children with disabilities. A total of eleven grants will be awarded, as follows: one grant of $50,000, five grants of $30,000, and five grants of $10,000. Based on the the population density of the state, the largest grant is designated for a metropolitan area, the $30,000 grants will be awarded to mid-sized cities, and the $10,000 grants will go to small towns or rural areas. The state will issue a Request for Proposals (RFP) that focuses on community efforts to support families of children with disabilities, as well as to promote the inclusion of children with disabilities in their communities.

Persons interested in responding to the RFP would form a community team (of 15-20 people) which would include parents of children with disabilities, adults with disabilities, interested citizens, and representatives from local government, public schools, civic organizations, and business and industry. The majority of participants on the committee would be parents of children with disabilities, and they would serve as leaders of the committee. Any number of community teams could form across the state; and more than one team could form in any given community.

Each team would write a proposal detailing what changes in the community would ensure that children with disabilities and their families are supported and included. A team could focus on more than one area of improvement. Teams would survey their communities (formally or informally) and get input from citizens before arriving at consensus about the needs to address. Proposals that include the promise of additional and/or matching funds, in-kind contributions, or collaboration with local governments, businesses, or organizations would receive extra points in the scoring process.

A community group might include one or more of the following activities in its proposal:

- Staff members of all child care facilities and preschools will be trained in successful methods of including young children with disabilities.

- Red Cross babysitting classes will include information and training about caring for babies and children with disabilities.

- Park and rec coaches and instructors will be trained in methods of including children with disabilities and ways to provide accommodation.

- Youth group leaders will be trained in methods to include children with disabilities and provide accommodation.

- An inclusive babysitting/child care co-op will be established to serve the needs of children with and without disabilities and their families.

- Leaders of youth groups (YMCA, boys/girls clubs, scouting, park and rec, etc.) will be trained in positive behavior support strategies.

- Sign language interpreters will be provided at youth activities in the community.

- Parents of children with disabilities will be trained in positive, proactive methods for accessing natural supports and generic services in the community.

- Church leaders and congregations will be trained in ways to support and include children with disabilities and their families.

- A community-funded scholarship fund will be set up to defray the costs of tuition for dance, martial arts, and other classes, for children with disabilities who use these generic services in lieu of medical therapies.

Community teams could focus on these or similar needs, or they could go in a completely different direction. The specifics of how these changes will come about, the collaborative efforts which will be used, and the desired outcomes would all be detailed in a committee's proposal. *The overall goal is to make family support and inclusion a community— not a disability—issue.*

In my list of examples, training and information is a key component in achieving long-term, widespread change. By increasing the capacity in communities, we pave the way for natural family support. When we spend family support dollars on creating capacity in communities, all families of children with disabilities will reap the benefits, not just the few who get the direct benefits of cash in traditional programs. In a metropolitan area, $50,000 would buy a lot of training; $10,000 would do the same in a small town. The actual dollar amounts would be more, since in-kind assistance and matching funds would be added to the grant amount.

Many traditional family support programs provide cash for parents to buy equipment or services their children need. There would be no provisions in community family support to give money directly to families. However, there are many ways to address these types of needs in a grant proposal.

A community team could write a grant that would include the establishment of community "banks" to address home renovation, equipment needs, child care, or other things. For example, a "renovation bank" would include "deposits" of materials and labor by community members that could be accessed by families who need this help. An "equipment bank" could include "deposits" of funds, labor to build products children might need, as well as actual wheelchairs, communication devices, and other items donated by manufacturers or distributors of these products.

In the list of examples on the previous page, the needs described may be related to accommodations that are already mandated by Section 504 or the ADA. For example, the park and rec department may be legally responsible for providing a sign language interpreter or other reasonable accommodation. But we know that many regulations of the ADA are not being followed to the letter. If parents decided to sue over this injustice, there's no way the issue would be settled in time for their child to enjoy equal participation in the park and rec activity. Including this need in community family support is not intended to get the park and rec department "off the hook" for not doing what it's legally responsible for, it's simply a way to ensure inclusion and support for families *now*, not at some distant point in the future.

In the grant proposal scenario I've described, only eleven teams across the state would receive funding in a given year. However, eleven more teams would receive funding the next year, eleven more after that, and so on. In addition, the ripple effect would provide more bang for the buck. For example, the changes that take place in one community could be transplanted in other communities through natural networks. A franchise child care center (Mother Goose Preschool) who learned about community family support in one city could teach Mother Goose locations in other cities. And this would happen even though no money was spent in these other communities!

Can you imagine the possibilities if this scenario unfolded in your community? What would it be like to be able to call on a stable of babysitters—regular babysitters—who knew about kids with disabilities; babysitters who had been trained in how to monitor a trach or feed a child through a G-tube? What would it be like to know every day care and preschool in the community would welcome your child and other children with disabilities? What would it be like to know you could call on expert volunteers to help renovate your home, make equipment for your child, or perform other activities to make your child's life better?

What about families whose children are in out-of-home placements? How could community family support help them? In a myriad of ways that are limited only by the imagination. They could bring their children home, and a variety of groups could be called on to help.

In community, natural supports are the rule, not the exception. Unfortunately, many families of children with disabilities are unaware of this because we're dependent on the system and cut-off from our natural supports. When a church member is ill, for example, congregations pull together and support the person by staying with him, bringing food, providing moral and financial support, and in other ways. When a member of the Rotary club, for example, faces a catastrophic situation, his fellow members provide a variety of natural supports. In these two situations, the individuals needing help turned to their communities before they turned to the system for support. We can do the same thing.

When I was pregnant with Benjamin, I had to go on bed rest in the fourth month of pregnancy. Years before, I had to have surgery on my cervix. Now, a miscarriage seemed imminent and there was no doubt in the doctor's mind that I could lose the baby at any moment. He said I must stay flat on my back until the baby was born. The only time I could move from that position was when I had to use the restroom. At the time, Emily was fourteen months old, we lived in a two-story house, and I had no immediate family nearby. My husband's parents lived in the same city, but my parents, brother, and sister all lived hundreds of miles away.

How could I take care of my little daughter when I had to lie down all day? How would I feed her (and myself), change her diapers, and do everything else I needed to do? The doctor informed me if I was unable to maintain a constant horizontal position at home, he would put me in the hospital for the duration of the pregnancy. That would take care of me—nurses would be there to feed me and make sure my needs were met—but what about my one-year-old daughter and my husband?

The solution was found in our community. My in-laws, people in the neighborhood, and members of our church stepped in to help. We shared our dilemma with neighbors on either side of us and in two of the houses across the street. These were people we knew well enough to chat with while mowing the yard and such, but at the time, we didn't know them intimately. We also shared our situation with our minister and others in our church, some of whom were close friends and some who were only acquaintances from Sunday school.

For the next four months, someone came to our home every single day to bring meals, to provide companionship, and to help me with Emily. Somehow, our neighbors and the people at church worked out a schedule so we always had a delicious dinner. My husband fixed breakfast for us before he went to work. In addition, he prepared sandwiches or other things Emily and I could eat at lunchtime. At some point every day, a kind volunteer knocked on the door and entered, arms laden with our dinner meal. Since I couldn't even get up to answer the door, everyone knew to simply walk in.

Emily and I stayed downstairs all day, with me lying down on the couch or the floor. We made accommodations so she and I could successfully get through each day. Her stack of diapers was stored next to the sofa, along with baby wipes and a trash can. Her toys were close by, too. She and I spent hours playing together on the floor. When it was nap time, I sometimes joined her on our pile of blankets on the floor. Other times I read or watched television as she slept.

On most days, the arrival of the "food-bringer" was the highlight of the day. Some were people I knew well, most were not. But Emily and I got to know them over the months, and they were welcome additions in our lives. In addition to bringing food, they helped with things around the house, played with Emily for a bit, and generally provided us with a sense of well-being. How could I have ever chosen the system's form of support (long-term hospitalization) over the natural supports of people in our community?

My hope is that all families of children with disabilities begin to move from dependence on the system to interdependence in the community. Some parents say they want to, but insist they won't feel comfortable doing it until the community is ready—until the community is more open and welcoming. Some parents wail, "I won't stop using the system until the community has the appropriate supports and services in place!"

But natural supports and generic services *are* in place. People in your own community use these natural supports and generic services every day. It's up to us to identify which are appropriate for our children and families. If they're not a perfect match, we can work with folks in the community to personalize them to our needs.

Traditional family support (assistance to individual families) reinforces the medical model of disability—that the problem is within the child (and, by extension, the family). Community family support is recognition that people with disabilities are more like others than they are different and communities have the capacity to meet the needs of all of its citizens. *The community* is *ready for us; we must believe* we're *ready for community.*

CHANGE IS INEVITABLE

Nothing stays the same; change is inevitable. And, yes, eventually the system will change. But change doesn't always equal forward progress. Change in the system could make things better or worse. Who knows? Is it all right to make our children wait, even one more day, for the system to change? Shall we wait for things to change or shall we assume leadership roles to set change in motion?

Collaboration, networking, creativity, flexibility, using natural supports and generic services, and a determination to put them all together will put us on the path to success. The examples I've outlined in this chapter aren't meant to be prescriptive, definitive one-size-fits-all remedies. Instead, they're dreams, ideas, and models that can fertilize your imagination and the imaginations of those you influence.

NEW FRONTIERS

Parents who came before us were strong and powerful leaders. Without them, we wouldn't be where we are today. We wouldn't have IDEA and other educational protections, or today's wide variety of services for children and families. Because of the efforts of other parents, our children have more services and supports, and are guaranteed more legal protections, than at any other time in history. And speaking on behalf of all parents of children with disabilities today, I am eternally grateful for their efforts.

The trails blazed by these pioneering parents led to rights and equality, because that's what their children didn't have. With IDEA, the ADA, and other laws, our children now have rights and legal equality, but many are still excluded and isolated from the mainstream of their communities.

The frontier facing today's parents is no longer the acquisition of legal rights, but the attainment of social equality and natural lives. It's our turn to blaze new trails—trails that will enable our children to be successful and experience natural lives; to enjoy inclusion in school and in their communities; to have friends; to enjoy typical childhoods; to grow into competent, self-determined adults; and to have the opportunity to define themselves independent of disability labels. For these opportunities to occur, we need to provide leadership and influence in the community, for that's where our children's futures rest and that's where our children belong.

AFTERWORD

I hope the ideas in this book will have a positive influence in the lives of your child and family members. Some suggestions may feel right today; others may feel right in a week, a month, or a year from now. In any case, know that I'm with you in spirit. In your joy and your struggles, you're not alone.

Take the steps—the baby steps or the leaps and bounds—to make your child's dreams come true. If some of the ideas in this book make you say, "Yes, but—" try them anyway. What have you got to lose? You have what it takes to ensure your child lives a natural and successful life. Your common sense, creativity, and dedication will get you there. On the journey, you'll learn so much, just as I hope you've learned from the stories of others in these pages.

See your child's disability as irrelevant, for in the big scheme of things, it is. Look at your child and presume competence. And never, never, never give up. Act as if anything is possible. Your determination and perseverance will make it happen. Remember, failure is not an option!

If this book has helped you and yours, I hope you'll share your experiences with me. (Write to me in care of BraveHeart Press, at the address on the copyright page in the front of the book.) In turn, I can spread the wisdom to other families through my *Disability is Natural* newsletter or in another book. Together, we're better.

My greatest hope is that you, your child, and every member of your family will enjoy natural, happy, and successful lives.

A JOURNEY OF A THOUSAND MILES
BEGINS WITH A SINGLE STEP.
Old Chinese Proverb

References and Bibliography

Abandoned to Their Fate: A History of Social Policy Toward People Labeled Severely Disabled, videocasette recording from the Specialized Training Program, University of Oregon, 1997.

Parallels in Time CD-ROM, from the Minnesota Governor's Council on Developmental Disabilities, 1998.

Willing to Act: Highlights of the 1991 Louis Harris Survey of Amercans' Attitudes Toward People with Disabilities, National Organization on Disability, 1991.

Module 1a: The Activity-Based IEP, manual from The Schools Project, The University of Oregon, 1993.
(Excerpts in "Chapter 17-Inclusive Education," describing activity-based goals and objectives, used with permission.)

Website of Veteran's Department

Lectures of, and personal conversations with, Phil Ferguson, Cary Griffin, Jerry Kiracofe, Herb Lovett, Ed Roberts, Joe Schiappacasse, Ed Skarnulis, Jopie Smith, Tom Tyree, Nancy Ward, and Colleen Wieck.

* * * * *

Atkinson, James. *Martin Luther and the birth of protestantism.* Atlanta: John Knox Press, 1968.

Bar On, Bat-Ami, ed. *Engendering origins: Critical feminist readings in Plato and Aristotle.* New York: State University of New York Press, 1994.

Berkow, Robert, Ed. *The Merck manual, fifteenth edition.* Rahway, NJ: Merck Sharp & Dohme Research Laboratories, 1987.

Blatt, Burton and Frank Garfunkel. *The educability of intelligence: Preschool intervention with disadvantaged children.* Washington, DC: The Council for Exceptional Children, Inc., 1969.

Blatt, Burton Ed. D. *In and out of mental retardation: Essays on educability, disability, and human policy.* Baltimore: University Park Press, 1982.

Blatt, Burton. *Revolt of the idiots: A story.* Glen Ridge, NJ: Exceptional Press, 1976.

Coudroglou, Aliki and Dennis L. Poole. *Disability, work and social policy: Models for social welfare.* New York: Springer Publishing Company, 1984.

Fife, Robert Herndon. *The revolt of Martin Luther.* New York: Columbia University Press, 1957.

Gallagher, Hugh Gregory. *By trust betrayed: Patients, physicians, and the license to kill in the Third Reich.* New York: Henry Holt and Company, 1990.

Gallagher, Hugh Gregory. *FDR's splendid deception: The moving story of Roosevelt's massive disability and the intense efforts to conceal it from the public.* Arlington, VA: Vandamere Press, 1999.

Goffman, Erving. *Asylums: Essays on the social situation of mental patients and other inmates.* Garden City, New York: Anchor Books, Doubleday & Company, Inc., 1961.

Gould, Stephen Jay. *The mismeasure of man.* New York: W.W. Norton & Co., 1996.

Kessler, Ronald. *The sins of the father: Joseph P. Kennedy and the dynasty he founded.* New York: Warner Books, 1996.

Kevles, Daniel J. *In the name of eugenics: Genetics and the uses of human heredity.* New York: Alfred A. Knopf, 1985.

Kronenwetter, Michael. *Welfare state America: Safety net or social contract?* New York: Franklin Watts, 1993.

Kubler-Ross, Elisabeth. *On death and dying.* New York: Macmillan Publishing Co., 1969.

Lenihan, John. *Disabled Americans: A history.* Washington, DC: The President's Committee on Employment of the Handicapped, 1977.

Lifton, Robert Jay. *The Nazi doctors: Medical killing and the psychology of genocide.* New York: BasicBooks, 1986.

Lipsky, Dorothy Kerzner and Alan Gartner. *Beyond separate education: Quality education for all.* Baltimore: Paul H. Brookes Publishing Co., 1989.

Lyon, Jeff. *Playing God in the nursery.* New York: W.W. Norton & Company, 1985.

Malthus, Thomas R. *An essay on the principle of population.* Homewood, IL: Richard D. Irwin, Inc., 1963.

Mensh, Elaine and Harry Mensh. *The IQ mythology: Class, race, gender, and inequality.* Carbondale, Illinois: Southern Illinois University Press, 1991.

Molnar, Gabriella E., ed. *Pediatric rehabilitation.* Baltimore: Williams & Wilkins, 1985.

Neuschutz, Louise M. *Vocational rehabilitation for the physically handicapped.* Springfield, Illinois: Charles C. Thomas Publisher, 1959.

Oliver, Michael. *The politics of disablement.* New York: St. Martin's Press, 1990.

Rothman, David J. *The discovery of the asylum: Social order and disorder in the new republic.* Boston: Little, Brown and Company, 1971.

Smith, J. David. *Minds made feeble: The myth and legacy of the Kallikaks.* Rockville, MD: Aspen Systems Corp., 1975.

Vash, Carolyn L. *The psychology of disability.* New York: Springer Publishing Co., 1981.

Weir, Robert. *Selective nontreatment of handicapped newborns.* New York: Oxford University Press, 1984.

Zwelling, Shomer S. *Quest for a cure: The public hospital in Williamsburg, Virginia, 1773-1885.* Williamsburg, Virginia: The Colonial Williamsburg Foundation, 1985.

The Encyclopedia Americana International Edition. Danbury, CT: Grolier, 2000.

APPENDIX

FEDERAL DEFINITION OF DEVELOPMENTAL DISABILITY

A severe, chronic disability of a person five years of age or older which

(a) is attributable to a mental or physical impairment or combination of mental and physical impairments,

(b) is manifested before the person attains age twenty-two;

(c) is likely to continue indefinitely;

(d) results in substantial functional limitations in three or more of the following areas of major life activities:

(1) self-care,
(2) receptive and expressive language,
(3) learning,
(4) mobility
(5) self-direction,
(6) capacity for independent living,
(7) economic sufficiency; and

(e) reflects the person's need for a combination and sequence of special, interdisciplinary, or generic care, treatment, or other services which are of lifelong or extended duration and are individually planned and coordinated; except that such term when applied to infants and young children means individuals from birth to age five, inclusive, who have substantial developmental delay or specific congenital or acquired conditions with a high probability of resulting in developmental disabilities if services are not provided.

DISABILITY ORGANIZATIONS

When contacting the following organizations, ask to be put on their mailing lists, and check into serving on boards and committees. The following listings were accurate at publication time.

NATIONAL TOLL-FREE NUMBERS

DBTAC: Disability and Business Technical Assistance Centers provide information on the Americans with Disabilities Act. Call 800-949-4232, and you'll be connected directly to your regional office.

PTI: Parent training and information centers provide information about special education law and other topics. Call the Alliance Coordinating Office at the PACER office, at 888-248-0822, to find the PTI for your area.

STATE LISTINGS KEY

AT: Assistive Technology projects provide information on services, including equipment loan, assessments, and more.

DDC: Developmental Disability Councils work toward systems change.

P & A: Protection and Advocacy organizations provide legal services for people with disabilities.

PARTNERS: Partners in Policymaking leadership development programs; some go by different names and use a different curriculum than the original Minnesota model.

SA: Self-Advocacy organizations run by and for people with developmental disabilities. If your state has no listing, contact the DDC or state/local disability groups for additional information.

SILC: State Independent Living Councils, oversees independent living organizations in the state; can provide referral to local CIL in your area.

UAP: University Affiliated Programs, housed within a university, provides training, research, and services.

ALABAMA

AT: STAR Project, 800-STAR656, 334-613-3480
DDC: Devopmental Disabilities Planning Council, 334-242-3973, 800-846-3735
P & A: ADAP, 800-826-1675, 205-348-4928, 205-348-9484 TDD
PARTNERS: Jayne Chase at DDC
SA: People First of Alabama, 205-333-5364
SILC: Kirk Thomas, 334-395-6300; T.M. Jones, 334-281-8780
UAP: Civitan Intl. Research Ctr., University of AL at Birmingham, 205-934-8900,
    800-846-3735

ALASKA

AT: Assistive Technology Project, 907-563-0138 (V/TDD)
DDC: Governor's Council on Disability and Special Education, 907-269-8990
P & A: Disability Law Center, 800-478-1234, 907-565-1002, 907-565-1000 TDD
PARTNERS: No current program, contact DDC for more information.
SA: People First of Alaska, 907-272-8270
SILC: John Woodward, 907-278-5205; Patrick Reinhart, 907-269-3571, 907-269-3635 TTY
UAP: Center for Human Development, University of AK, 907-272-8270

ARIZONA

AT: AZTAP, 800-477-9921, 602-728-9532, 602-728-9536 TDD
DDC: Governor's Council on Developmental Disabilities, 602-542-4049

Arizona (cont.)

P & A: Center for Disability Law, 800-922-1447, 520-327-9547, 520-327-9547 TDD
PARTNERS: Joni Kiser at Pilot Parents, 520-325-3150
SA: Teresa Moore, 602-785-0171
SILC: Dina Konstatos, 602-542-2595, 602-542-6049 TTY
UAP: Institute for Human Development, Northern AZ University, 520-523-4791

Arkansas

AT: ICAN, 800-828-2799 V/TDD, 501-666-8868 V/TDD
DDC: Governor's DD Planning Council, 501-661-2589, 501-661-2763 TDD
P & A: Disability Rights Center, 800-482-1775, 800-482-1775 TDD, 501-296-1775 V/TDD
PARTNERS: Mary Edwards at DDC
SA: No state listing available, contact DDC for information.
SILC: Brenda Tweedle, 501-624-7710, 501-624-7710 TTY
UAP: Center for Research on Teaching and Learning, University of AR at Little Rock,
    501-682-9900

California

AT: Assistive Technology System, 916-263-8687, 916-263-8685 TTY
DDC: State Council on Developmental Disabilities, 916-322-8481, 916-324-8420 TDD
P & A: Protection and Advocacy, Inc., 916-488-9955, 800-776-5746
PARTNERS: No current program, contact DDC for more information.
SA: People First of California, Inc., 916-552-6625
SILC: Mike Collins, 916-445-0142, 916-445-5627 TTY
UAP: UAP/MR Program, UCLA, 310-825-0171; USC-UAP, Children's Hospital of LA,
    323-669-2300

Colorado

AT: Assistive Technology Project, 303-864-5100, 303-864-5110 TDD
DDC: Developmental Disabilities Planning Council, 720-941-0176 V/TDD
P & A: The Legal Center, 800-288-1376, 303-722-0300 V/TDD
PARTNERS: No current program, contact DDC for information.
SA: People First of Denver, 303-831-7733
SILC: Sharon Mikrut, 303-620-4181, 303-620-4152 TTY
UAP: JFK Child Development Center, University of Colorado, 303-864-5261

Connecticut

AT: Assistive Technology Project, 800-537-2549, 860-424-4881, 860-424-4839 and
    860-424-4850 TDD
DDC: Council on Developmental Disabilities, 800-653-1134 , 860-418-6172 TTY
P & A: Office of Protection and Advocacy, 800-842-7303, 860-297-4300, 860-566-2102 TDD
PARTNERS: Molly Cole, 877-743-5516

CONNECTICUT (CONT.)

SA: People First of Connecticut, 203-792-3540
SILC: Dawn Lambert, 203-729-3299, 203-729-1281 TTY
UAP: Pappanikou Center on Special Education and Rehabilitation, University of CT, 860-486-5035

DELAWARE

AT: DATI, 800-870-DATI (3284), 302-651-6793 TDD, 302-651-6790
DDC: Developmental Disabilities Council, 302-739-3333, 800-464-HELP TDD
P & A: Disabilities Law Program, 302-575-0690
PARTNERS: Gail Launay, 302-226-5232
SA: No state listing available, contact DDC for information.
SILC: Griff Campbell, 302-761-8275, 302-761-8336 TTY
UAP: UAP for Families and Developmental Disabilities, 302-831-6974

DISTRICT OF COLUMBIA

AT: University Legal Services, 202-547-0198, 202-547-2657 (TDD)
DDC: Developmental Disabilities Council, 202-279-6085, 202-279-6089 TDD
P & A: University Legal Services, 202-547-0198
PARTNERS: No program.
SA: No state listing available, contact DDC for information.
SILC: Lenora Simpson, 202-442-8663
UAP: Georgetown University Medical Center, 202-687-8635

FLORIDA

AT: Alliance for Assistive Service and Technology, 850-487-3278 V/TDD, 850-487-2805 Fax/TDD
DDC: Developmental Disabilities Council, 800-580-7801, 850-488-4180, 850-488-0956 TDD
P & A: Advocacy Center, 800-342-0823, 800-346-4127 TDD, 850-488-9071
PARTNERS: No current program, contact DDC for information.
SA: No state listing available, contact DDC for information.
SILC: Beth Schultze, 850-487-3431 850-487-3431 TTY
UAP: Mailman Center for Child Development, University of Miami, 305-243-6801

GEORGIA

AT: Tools for Life, 800-479-8665, 404-657-3085 TDD, 404-657-3084
DDC: Council on Developmental Disabilities, 404-657-2126, 404-657-2133 TDD
P & A: Advocacy Office, Inc., 800-537-2329, 404-885-1234 V/TDD
PARTNERS: Dave Blanchard, AADD, 404-881-9777
SA: No state listing available, contact DDC for information.
SILC: Pat Puckett, 770-452-9601, 770-452-7087 TTY
UAP: College of Family & Consumer Sciences, The University of GA, 706-542-3457

HAWAII

AT: ATRC, 800-645-3007 V/TDD, 808-532-7110 V/TDD
DDC: State Planning Council on Developmental Disabilities, 808-586-8100
P & A: Disability Rights Center, 808-959-2922 V/TDD
PARTNERS: Mary Matsukawa, 808-984-8218
SA: No state listing available, contact DDC for information.
SILC: Guy Tagamuri, 808-586-5375
UAP: UAP for Developmental Disabilities, 808-956-5009

IDAHO

AT: Assistive Technology Project, 208-885-3559 V/TDD, 208-885-3639
DDC: Council on Developmental DisABILITIES, 800-544-2433, 208-334-2179 V/TDD
P & A: Co-Ad, Inc., 800-632-5125, 208-336-5353 V/TDD
PARTNERS: Christine Pisani at DDC.
SA: No state listing available, contact DDC for information.
SILC: Kelly Buckland, 208-334-3800 V/TTY
UAP: Center on Developmental Disabilities, 208-885-3559

ILLINOIS

AT: Assistive Technology Project, 217-522-7985, 217-522-9966 TDD
DDC: Planning Council on Developmental Disabilities, 217-782-9696
P & A: Equip for Equality, Inc., 800-537-2632, 312-341-0022 V/TDD
PARTNERS: Ginny Cooke, Phoenix Perth Institute, 773-262-1294
SA: People First of Illinois, 309-820-8844
SILC: John Eckert, 217-744-7777 V/TTY
UAP: Institute on Disability & Human Development, University of IL at Chicago,
    312-413-1647

INDIANA

AT: ATTAIN, 800-528-8246, 800-743-3333 TDD, 317-921-8766
DDC: Governor's Council for People with Disabilities, 317-232-7770
P & A: Protection and Advocacy Services, 800-622-4845, 317-722-5555 V/TDD
PARTNERS: Christine Dahlberg at DDC
SA: People First/Self-Advocacy, 317-352-1930
SILC: Elaine Miller, 317-232-1353, 317-232-1427 TTY
UAP: Institute for the Study of Developmental Diabilities, IN University, 812-855-6508;
    Riley Child Development Center, IN University School of Medicine, 317-274-8167

IOWA

AT: Program for Assistive Technology, 800-331-3027 V/TDD, 319-356-1514
DDC: Governor's Developmental Disabilities Council, 800-452-1936, 515-281-9083

IOWA (CONT.)

P & A: Protection and Advocacy Service, Inc., 800-779-2502, 515-278-2502,
   515-278-0571 TDD
PARTNERS: Contact Partners Coordinator at P & A.
SA: No state listing available, contact DDC for information.
SILC: Norma Boge, 515-255-2850
UAP: Division of Developmental Disabilities, University of Iowa Hospital School, 319-353-1335

KANSAS

AT: Assistive Technology for Kansas Project, 800 KAN DO IT, 316-421-8367,
   316-421-0954 Fax/TDD
DDC: Council on Developmental Disabilities, 785-296-2608
P & A: Advocacy and Protective Services, 785-273-9661
PARTNERS: Josie Torrez at DDC
SA: No state listing available, contact DDC for information.
SILC: Shannon Jones, 785-234-6990 V/TTY
UAP: Institute for Life Span Studies, University of KS, 913-864-4950; Children's Rehab Unit,
   University Medical Center, Smith Mental Retardation Research Ctr., 913-588-5970;
   UAP-Parsons, 316-421-6550

KENTUCKY

AT: Assistive Technology Services Network, 800-327-5287 V/TDD, 502-327-0022,
   502-327-9855 TDD
DDC: Developmental Disabilities Council, 877-367-5332, 502-563-4527
P & A: Office for Public Advocacy, 502-564-2967, 800-372-2988 TDD
PARTNERS: Barbara Wright at DDC
SA: No state listing available, contact DDC for information.
SILC: Sarah Richardson, 502-564-4440, 502-564-6742 TTY
UAP: Human Development Institute, University of Kentucky, 606-257-1714

LOUISIANA

AT: Assistive Technology Access Network, 800-270-6185 V/TDD, 225-925-9500 V/TDD
DDC: State Planning Council on Developmental Disabilities, 225-342-6804
P & A: Advocacy Center, 800-960-7705, 504-522-2337 V/TDD
PARTNERS: Sharyn Scheyd, 504-443-3831
SA: Louisiana Self-Advocacy, 225-927-0855
SILC: Ledidra Carter, 225-922-2000
UAP: Human Development Center, Louisiana State University Medical Center, 504-942-8200

MAINE

AT: CITE, 207-621-3195 V/TDD
DDC: Developmental Disabilities Council, 207-287-4213

MAINE (CONT.)

P & A: Disability Rights Center, 207-626-2774, ext. 104, 800-452-1948 TDD
PARTNERS: No program, contact DDC for more information
SA: Speaking Up For Us of Maine, 207-879-0847, Ext. 15
SILC: Lisa Davis, 207-685-9961
UAP: Center for Community Inclusion, University of Maine, 207-581-1231

MARYLAND

AT: Technology Assistance Program, 800-832-4817, 410-554-9230 V/TDD
DDC: Developmental Disabilities Council, 410-333-3688
P & A: Disability Law Ctr., 800-233-7201, 410-234-2791, 410-727-6387 TDD
PARTNERS: Cheryl Hall , 410-571-9320
SA: Leadership Now, 410-571-9320
SILC: Kimball Gray, 410-319-4455 V/TTY
UAP: The Kennedy Krieger Institute for Handicapped Children, 410-502-9483

MASSACHUSETTS

AT: Assistive Technology Partnership, 800-848-8867 V/TDD, 617-355-7820,
   617-355-7301 TDD
DDC: Developmental Disabilities Council, 617-727-6374, 617-727-1885 TDD
P & A: Disabilities Law Center, Inc., 617-723-8455 V/TDD
PARTNERS: No program, contact DDC for more information.
SA: Massachusetts Advocates Standing Strong, 715-585-2422
SILC: Andrea Schein, 617-695-2622 V/TTY
UAP: Institute for Community Inclusion, Children's Hosp., 617-355-6509;
   Shriver Center, 617-893-0230

MICHIGAN

AT: Michigan Tech 2000, 800-760-4600, 517-333-2477 V/TDD
DDC: Developmental Disabilities Council, 517-334-6769, 517-334-7354 TDD
P & A: Protection and Advocacy Service, 517-487-1755 V/TDD
PARTNERS: Dohn Hoyle, Washtenaw ACA, 734-662-1256
SA: People First of Michigan, 517-487-5426
SILC: 517-371-4872
UAP: Developmental Disabilities Institute, 313-577-2654

MINNESOTA

AT: STAR Program, 800-657-3862, 800-657-3895 TDD, 651-296-2771, 651-296-8478 TDD
DDC: Governor's Council on Dev. Dis., 877-348-0505, 651-296-4018, 651-296-9962 TDD
P & A: Disability Law Center, 800-292-4150, 612-332-1441
PARTNERS: Naomi Beachy, North Central Service Cooperative, 218-894-2600
SA: People First of Minnesota, 651-625-6046

Minnesota (cont.)

SILC: William Bauer, 612-296-5085
UAP: UAP on Developmental Disabilities, University of MN, 612-624-6300

Mississippi

AT: Project START, 800-852-8328 V/TDD, 601-987-4872
DDC: Developmental Disabilities Council, 601-359-1270, 601-359-6230 TDD
P & A: Protection and Advocacy System, 800-772-4057, 601-981-8207 V/TDD
PARTNERS: No program, contact DDC for more information.
SA: No state listing available, contact DDC for information.
SILC: Walter Blalock, 800-443-1000
UAP: UAP at University of Southern Mississippi, 601-266-5163

Missouri

AT: Assistive Technology Project, 800-647-8557, 816-373-5193, 816-373-9315 TDD
DDC: Council for Developmental Disabilities, 800-500-7878, 573-751-8611,
    573-751-8611 TDD
P & A: Protection and Advocacy Services, Inc., 800-392-8667, 573-893-3333
PARTNERS: Vicky Davidson at DDC
SA: People First of Missouri, 816-252-4853
SILC: Karen Benson, 417-466-3711
UAP: UAP for Developmental Disabilities, University of MO at Kansas City, 816-235-1770

Montana

AT: MONTECH, 800-732-0323 TDD, 406-243-5676
DDC: Developmental Disabilities Planning Council, 406-444-1338
P & A: Advocacy Program, 800-245-4743, 406-444-3889 V/TDD
PARTNERS: Deborah Swingley at DDC
SA: People First of Montana, 406-444-3955
SILC: SILC Liaison, 406-444-4175, 406-444-2590 TTY
UAP: Rural Institute on Developmental Disabilities, University of Montana, 406-243-5467

Nebraska

AT: Assistive Technology Partnership, 888-806-6287, 402-471-0734 V/TDD
DDC: Governor's Council on Developmental Disabilities 402-471-2330, 402-471-9570 TDD
P & A: Advocacy Services, Inc., 800-742-7594, 402-474-3183 V/TDD
PARTNERS: No current program, contact DDC for information.
SA: Joe Govier, 308-872-6490
SILC: June Remington, 402-476-3952
UAP: Meyer Rehab Institute, University of NE Medical Center, 402-559-6430

NEVADA

AT: Assistive Technology Collaborative, 775-687-4452, 775-687-3388 TDD
DDC: Governor's Council on Developmental Disabilities 702-687-4452, 702-687-3388 TDD
P & A: Advocacy and Law Center, Inc., 800-992-5715, 702-257-8150, 702-257-8160 TDD
PARTNERS: Cheryl Dinnell, UAP, 775-784-4921, ext. 2352
SA: No state listing available, contact DDC for information.
SILC: Paul Gowan, 775-687-4452 V/TTY
UAP: Research and Educational Planning Center University of NV, 775-784-4921

NEW HAMPSHIRE

AT: Technology Partnership Project, 800-427-3338 V/TDD, 603-224-0630 V/TDD
DDC: Developmental Disabilities Council, 603-271-3236, 800-735-2964 TDD
P & A: Disabilities Rights Center, 800-834-1721, 603-228-0432 V/TDD
PARTNERS: Beth Dixon, UAP, 603-228-2084
SA: People First of New Hampshire, 903-536-9797
SILC: Carol Nadeau, 603-271-2773 V/TTY
UAP: Institute on Disability, University of NH, 603-862-4320

NEW JERSEY

AT: TARP, 800-342-5832, 609-633-7106 TDD, 609-777-0945
DDC: Developmental Disabilities Council, 609-292-3745
P & A: Protection and Advocacy, Inc., 800-922-7233, 609-292-9742
PARTNERS: Jane Dunham, 609-984-3379
SA: New Jersey Self-Advocacy Project, 732-926-8010
SILC: Tim Cronin, 609-292-9339, 609-292-2919 TTY
UAP: The Boggs Center, UMD New Jersey, 732-235-9300, 732-235-9328 TDD

NEW MEXICO

AT: Technology Assistance Program, 800-866-2253, 505-954-8539 TDD
DDC: Developmental Disabilities Council, 505-827-7590
P & A: P & A, Inc., 800-432-4682, 505-256-3100 V/TDD
PARTNERS: No current program, contact DDC for information.
SA: People First of New Mexico, 505-883-4630
SILC: Elizabeth Hutcheson, 505-247-4381
UAP: Developmental Disabilities Division, University of NM, 505-272-3000

NEW YORK

AT: TRAID Project, 800-522-4369 (V/TDD), 518-474-2825
DDC: State Dev. Disabilities Council, 800-395-3372, 518-486-7505 V/TDD
P & A: Commission on Quality of Care, 518-381-7098, 800-624-4143 TDD
PARTNERS: Joyce Steel, The Advocacy Center, 716-546-1700, ext. 234
SA: The Self-Advocacy Association, 518-382-1454

NEW YORK (CONT.)

SILC: Brad Williams, 518-427-1060 V/TTY

UAP: Rose F. Kennedy Center, Albert Einstein College of Medicine, Yeshiva University, 718-430-8522; Westchester Institute for Human Development, 914-493-8204; UAP for Developmental Disabilities, University of Rochester Medical Center, 716-275-2986

NORTH CAROLINA

AT: Assistive Technology Project, 919-850-2787 (V/TDD)

DDC: Council on Developmental Disabilities, 800-357-6916, 919-850-2833

P & A: Advocacy Council, 800-821-6922, 919-733-9250 V/TDD

PARTNERS: Bryant Edgerton, Easter Seals 800-662-7119

SA: Association of Self-Advocates, 919-355-9580

SILC: Donna Holt, 919-733-3364

UAP: Clinical Center for the Study of Development and Learning, University of NC, 919-966-5171

NORTH DAKOTA

AT: IPAT, 701-265-4807 V/TDD

DDC: State Council on Developmental Disabilities, 701-328-8953

P & A: Protection and Advocacy Project, 800-642-6694, 701-328-2950

PARTNERS: Joyce Smith, Dakota CIL, 701-222-3636

SA: People First of North Dakota, 800-472-2670, 701-772-6191

SILC: Pat Danielson, 701-772-5990

UAP: ND Center for Disabilities, Minot State University, 701-858-3580, 701-858-3580 TDD

OHIO

AT: AT of Ohio 800-784-3425 V/TDD, 614-292-2426 V/TDD

DDC: Developmental Disabilities Planning Council, 614-466-5205, 614-644-5530 TDD

P & A: Legal Rights Service, 800-282-9181, 614-466-7264 V/TDD

PARTNERS: Vicky Harman, Arc of Ohio, 614-487-4720

SA: People First of Ohio, 513-871-2181

SILC: Woody Osburn, 800-566-7788, 614-463-1244 TTY

UAP: Center for Developmental Disabilities, 513-636-8383;
   The Nisonger Center, Ohio State University, 614-292-8365

OKLAHOMA

AT: Able Tech, 800-257-1705 V/TDD, 405-744-9864, 405-744-9748

DDC: Developmental Disabilities Council, 800-836-4470, 405-528-4984, 405-428-4984 TDD

P & A: Disability Law Center, Inc., 800-880-7755, 405-525-7755

PARTNERS: Shelley Curtiss, TARC, 918-582-8272

SA: Nancy Ward, TARC, 918-582-8272

SILC: Lew Blockcolski, 580-237-8508 V/TTY

Oklahoma (cont.)

UAP: UAP of University of Oklahoma, 405-271-4500

Oregon

AT: Technology Access for Life Needs Project, 800-677-7512, 503-361-1201 V/TDD
DDC: Developmental Disabilities Council, 800-292-4154, 503-945-9942
P & A: Advocacy Center, 800-452-1694, 503-243-2081, 800-556-5351 TDD
PARTNERS: Michael Bailey, 503-282-6896
SA: People First of Oregon, 503-945-9441
SILC: SILC Director, 503-375-3680 Voice and TTY
UAP: Center on Human Development, University of Oregon, 541-346-3591; Oregon Institute
    on Disabilities and Development, Child Development & Rehabilitation Center, 503-494-8364

Pennsylvania

AT: PIAT, 800-204-PIAT (7428), 800-750-PIAT TTY
DDC: Developmental Disabilities Council, 717-787-6057
P & A: Protection and Advocacy, Inc., 800-692-7443, 717-236-8110 V/TDD
PARTNERS: Kathy Miller, UAP, 215-204-9395.
SA: Speaking for Ourselves, 910-825-4592
SILC: Sandra Weber, 717-236-2400, 717-236-5733 TTY
UAP: Institute on Disabilities, Temple University, 215-204-1356

Rhode Island

AT: Assistive Tech. Access Partnership, 401-421-7005, x 310; 800-752-8088, x 2608;
    401-421-7016 TDD
DDC: Developmental Disabilities Council, 401-462-3191
P & A: Disability Law Center, Inc., 800-733-5332, 401-831-3150, 401-831-5335 TDD
PARTNERS: Deb Kney, 401-785-2028
SA: Deb Kney, 401-785-2028
SILC: Camille Pansa, 401-253-7154
UAP: UAP at Rhode Island College, 401-456-8024

South Carolina

AT: Assistive Technology Program, 803-935-5263 V/TDD, 803-935-5263,
DDC: Developmental Disabilities Council, 803-734-0465, 803-734-1147 TDD
P & A: Protection and Advocacy for People with Disabilities, 800-922-5225,
    803-782-0639 V/TDD
PARTNERS: Redick Loring, The Arc, 803-935-5266
SA: No state listing available, contact DDC for information.
SILC: Maris Parmerter, 803-731-1607, 803-731-1608 TTY
UAP: Center for Developmental Disabilities, University of SC, 803-935-5248

South Dakota

AT: DAKOTALINK, 800-224-5336 V/TDD, 605-224-5336
DDC: Governor's Council on Developmental Disabilities, 605-773-6369, 605-773-5990 TDD
P & A: Advocacy Services, 800-658-4782, 605-224-8294 V/TDD
PARTNERS: Sandy Stocklin at P & A
SA: People First of South Dakota, 605-224-8211
SILC: Shelley Pfaff, 605-945-2207 V/TTY
UAP: Center for the Developmentally Disabled, University of SD, 605-357-1439

Tennessee

AT: Technology Access Project (TTAP), 615-532-9986
DDC: Developmental Disabilities Council, 615-532-6615, 615-741-4562 TDD
P & A: Protection and Advocacy, Inc., 800-342-1660, 615-298-1080 V/TDD
PARTNERS: Partners Coordinator at DDC
SA: People First of Tennessee, 615-898-0075
SILC: Kimberly Hines, 615-297-2666, 615-292-7790 TTY
UAP: Boling Center for Developmental Disabilities, University of Tennessee, 901-448-6511

Texas

AT: Assistive Technology Partnership, 800-828-7839, 512-471-7621, 512-471-1844 TDD
DDC: Planning Council for Developmental Dis., 800-262-0334, 512-424-4080,
    512-424-4099 TDD
P & A: Advocacy, Inc., 800-252-9108, 512-454-4816 V/TDD
PARTNERS: Partners Coordinator at DDC
SA: Texas Advocates, 512-454-8250
SILC: Executive Director, 512-371-7353 V/TTY
UAP: UAP at the University of Texas at Austin, 512-471-7621

Utah

AT: Assistive Technology Program, 435-797-1982, 435-797-1981 V/TDD
DDC: Governor's Council for People with Disabilities, 801-533-4128 V/TDD
P & A: Disability Law Center, 800-662-9080, 801-363-1347 V/TDD
PARTNERS: Nonie Lancaster at DDC
SA: Arc of Utah, 801-364-5060
SILC: Corey Rowley, 801-463-1592 V/TTY
UAP: Center for Persons with Disabilities, Utah State Univ., 801-797-1981

Vermont

AT: Assistive Technology Project, 802-241-2620 V/TDD
DDC: Developmental Disabilities Council, 802-241-2612
P & A: Protection and Advocacy, 802-229-1355
PARTNERS: No program, contact DDC for more information.

Vermont (cont.)

SA: Vermont Peer Support Network, 802-241-2614
SILC: Henrietta Jordan, 802-229-5939
UAP: Center for Developmental Disabilities, University of VT, 802-656-4031

Virginia

AT: Assistive Technology System, 800-435-8490, 804-662-9990 V/TDD
DDC: Board for People with Disabilities, 800-846-4464 V/TDD, 804-786-0016
P & A: Department for Rights of Virginians with Disabilities, 800-522-3962,
    804-225-2042 V/TDD
PARTNERS: Partners Coordinator at DDC
SA: People First of Northern Virginia, 540-364-9540
SILC: Jim Rothrock, 804-673-0119
UAP: Institute for Developmental Disabilities, VCU, 804-828-3908

Washington

AT: Assistive Technology Alliance, 206-685-4181, 206-616-1396 TDD
DDC: State Dev. Disabilities Council, 800-634-4473 TDD, 360-753-3908
P & A: Protection and Advocacy System, 800-562-2702, 425-776-1199,800-905-0209 TDD
PARTNERS: Donna Patrick, 360-725-2870
SA: People First, 800-758-1123; Self-Advocates of Washington, 253-565-3091
SILC: Cathy Baldwin, 360-407-3603 V/TTY
UAP: Center on Human Development and Disability, University of WA, 206-543-2832

West Virginia

AT: Assistive Technology System, 800-841-8435, 304-293-4692 V/TDD
DDC: Developmental Disabilities Council, 304-558-0416, 304-558-2376 TDD
P & A: Advocates, Inc., 800-950-5250, 304-346-0847 V/TDD
PARTNERS: Jan Lilly-Stewart at DDC
SA: No state listing available, contact DDC for information.
SILC: Ann Meadows, 304-766-4624 V/TTY
UAP: UAP at West Virginia University, 304-293-4692

Wisconsin

AT: WISTECH, 608-266-9303
DDC: Council on Developmental Disabilities, 608-266-7826
P & A: Coalition for Advocacy, 800-928-8778, 608-267-0214 V/TDD
PARTNERS: Beth Sweeden, 608-263-6745
SA: No state listing available, contact DDC for information.
SILC: Beryl Gribbon Fago, 608-261-8397, 608-261-8396 TTY
UAP: Waisman Center on MR and Human Dev., Univ. of Wisconsin, 608-263-5776

WYOMING

AT: New Options In Technology (WYNOT), 307-766-2095
DDC: Council on Developmental Disabilities, 800-438-5791, 307-777-7230,
  307-777-7230 TDD
P&A: Protection and Advocacy System, 800-624-7648, 307-632-2496, 800-821-3091 TDD
PARTNERS: No current program, contact DDC for information.
SA: Beverly Stevens, 307-638-8771 (H), 307-777-5675 (W)
SILC: Woody Absher, 307-777-7191 V/TTY
UAP: Wyoming Institute for Disabilities, University of WY, 307-766-2761

CATALOGS OF
HELPFUL, UNUSUAL, OR INNOVATIVE PRODUCTS

Note: Some of the catalogs for special ed products are geared to professionals, but
parents can order from them, as well, in most cases. In any event, you'll find some
interesting (e.g., "not good") reading in those particular catalogs, when you see what's
offered to educators.

AbleNet, Inc.—800-322-0956 ("Solutions for Teaching Students with Severe
  Disabilities")

Access to Recreation—800-634-4351 (neat stuff for people who use chairs)

Adaptability—800-288-9941 (daily living aids)

A.D.D. WareHouse—800-233-9273 (Resources for teachers and parents)

Attainment Company—800-327-4269 (products for special education)

Bright Apple Special Ed Catalog—800-728-9783

Bruce Medical Supplies—800-225-8446 (health care products)

Cambridge Development Laboratory Software Shop—800-637-0047 (computer
  software)

Communication Aids—414-352-5678

Critical Thinking Books & Software—800-458-4849 (great learning stuff for all ages)

D & S Medical—888-SCI-HELP (health care products)

Disability Resource Library—800-686-6049 (disability-related books and products)

Dr. Leonard's—800-785-0880 (health care products)

Edutainment Catalog—800-338-3844 (computer software)

Enabling Devices—800-832-8697 ("Toys for Special Children")

Fas-Track Computer Products-Technology for Teaching—800-927-3936

Feel Good Catalog—800-997-6789 (health care and other interesting products)

Foot Smart—800-870-7149 (shoes, orthotics, inserts)

Free Spirit Publishing—800-735-7323 (great books for kids)

Get Organized—800-803-9400 (products for closets, storage, etc.)

Health Corner—800-460-7282 (health care products)

HearthSong—800-325-2502 (old fashioned and classic toys and crafts)

Heartland America—800-229-2901(unusual general merchandise)

Highlights—800-422-6202 (toys)

Home Again—888-666-0721(books, crafts, and stuff for kids)

HomeTrends—800-810-2340 (neat stuff for the house)

IEP Resources—800-651-0954 (products for special education)

Independent Living Aids 800-537-2118 (wide variety of home health aids)

IntelliHealth Healthy Home—800-988-1127 (high tech and other home health aids)

John Holt Bookstore—617-864-3100 (great homeschooling/unschooling stuff)

Learning Services—800-877-3278 (books, videos, and more for kids)

Library Video Company—800-843-3620 (gobs of videos for home and school)

Lifestyle Fascination—800-669-0987 (interesting high tech devices)

Lighthouse Catalog—800-829-0500 (great low vision products)

MindWare—800-999-0398 ("Brainy Toys for Kids of All Ages")

MOMS (Mail Order Medical Supply)—800-232-7443 (health care products)

Options by Infogrip—800-397-0921(computer keyboards and accessories)

S & S Opportunities—800-266-8856 (adaptive equipment)

Sammons Preston—800-323-5547 (adaptive equipment)

Search Institute—877-240-7251 (asset-based books, posters, etc.)

Sears Home Health Care—800-326-1750, TDD 800-733-7249

SelfCare—800-345-3371 (home health products)

Softspots—800-735-4994 (footwear, orthotics, inserts, etc.)

Source Book for Daily Living—800-454-0755 (daily living aids)

Spilsbury Puzzle Co.—800-772-1760 ("Puzzles, Games, Gifts & Fun")

Student Software Guide—800-874-9001 (discounted computer software for high school students)

Summit Learning—800-777-8817 (math manipulatives)

Textbooks for Home Schools—800-845-5731

TherAdapt—800-261-4919 ("Innovative Therapeutic Equipment")

Therafin Corporation—800-843-7234 (adaptive equipment and more)

Youcan Toocan—888-663-9396 (daily living aids)

Young Explorers—800-239-7577 ("Creative Educational Products")

Zephyr Press—800-232-2187 ("New Ways of Teaching for All Ways of Learning")

OTHER RESOURCES

American Association of People with Disabilities (AAPD), a national organization with a newsletter, membership benefits, and more; 888-712-4672.

Computer Recycling: Computers for Learning, 888-362-7870; National Christina Foundation 800-274-7846

Speech therapy activities are available via a free monthly Email newsletter. Write to: newsletter@speechtx.com and write SUBSCRIBE in the subject line.

SUGGESTED READING

ON PARENTING AND OTHER TOPICS FOR PARENTS

Cline, Foster W. and Jim Fay. *Parenting with love and logic: Teaching children responsibility.* Colorado Springs, CO: Pinon Press, 1990.

Cousins, Norman. *Head first: The biology of hope.* Thorndike, ME: Thorndike Press, 1989.

Fisher, Robert E. *Quick to listen, slow to speak: Living out the language of love in your family relationships.*Wheaton, IL: Tyndale House Publishers, Inc., 1987.

Gordon, Thomas. *Teaching children self-discipline . . . at home and at school.* New York: Random House, 1989. (Read anything by Gordon.)

Hillman, James. *The soul's code: In search of character and calling.* New York: Random House, 1996.

Kushner, Harold S. *How good do we have to be? A new understanding of guilt and forgiveness.* Boston: Little, Brown and Company, 1996.

Latham, Glenn. *The power of positive parenting.* (Can order directly from Mountain Plains Regional Resource Center 1-888-523-5127)

Liedloff, Jean. *The continuum concept: In search of lost happiness.* New York: Addison-Wesley Publishing Company, 1977.

Rich, Dorothy. *Mega Skills: In school and in life—The best gift you can give your child.* Boston: Houghton Mifflin Company, 1992.

Sanders, Pete and Steve Myers. *What do you know about people with disabilities?* Brookfield, CT: Copper Beech Books, 1998.

ON CHILDREN'S LEARNING, PUBLIC EDUCATION, AND HOMESCHOOLING

Ames, Louise Bates. *Questions parent ask.* NY: Dell Publishing, 1988. (Also read the series of excellent books by Ames and Ilg: *Your One-Year-Old, Your Five-Year-Old,* etc. There's one for every age until the preteen years, then the ages are grouped.)

Armstrong, Thomas. *Awakening your child's natural genius: Enhancing curiosity, creativity, and learning ability*. Los Angeles: Jeremy P. Tarcher, Inc., 1991. (Read anything by Armstrong.)

—. *In their own way: Discovering and encouraging your child's personal learning style*. Los Angeles: Jeremy P. Tarcher, Inc., 1987.

—. *The radiant child*. Wheaton, IL: The Theosophical Publishing House, 1985.

Bloom, Jill. *Parenting our schools: A hands-on guide to education reform*. NY: Little, Brown, and Co., 1992.

Cannella, Gaile Sloan. *Deconstructing early childhood education: Social justice and revolution*. NY: Peter Lang, 1997.

de Bono, Edward. *I am right, you are wrong: From this to the new renaissance: from rock logic to water logic*. NY: Penguin Books, 1991. (Read anything by deBono.)

—. *Teach your child how to think*. NY: Penguin Books, 1992.

—. *Teaching thinking*. NY: Penguin Books. 1976.

Dennison, George. *The lives of children: The story of the First Street School*. NY: Addison-Wesley Publishing Company, Inc., 1990.

Dyer, Wayne. *What do you really want for your children?* NY: Wm Morrow and Co., 1985.

Elkind, David. *All grown up and no place to go: Teenagers in crisis*. NY: Addison-Wesley Publishing Co., 1984.

—. *The hurried child: Growing up too fast too soon*. NY: Addison-Wesley Publishing Company, 1981.

—. *Miseducation: Preschoolers at risk*. NY: Alfred A. Knopf, 1988.

Gattegno, Caleb. *What we owe children: The subordination of teaching to learning*. NY: Avon Books, 1970.

Gardner, Howard. *Art, mind, and brain: A cognitive approach to creativity*. New York: BasicBooks, 1982.

—. *Frames of mind: The theory of multiple intelligences*. NY: Basic Books, 1993.

—. *The unschooled mind: How children think and how schools should teach*. NY: BasicBooks, 1991. (Read anything by Gardner.)

Glasser, William. *Schools without failure*. NY: Harper & Row, 1969. (Read anything by Glasser.)

Goleman, Daniel. *Emotional intelligence: Why it can matter more than IQ*. NY: Bantam Books,1996.

Greenspan, Stanley I. *Growth of the mind and the endangered origins of intelligence*. NY: Addison-Wesley, 1997.

Hern, Matt (ed.). *Deschooling our lives*. Philadelphia: New Society Publishers, 1996.

Herndon, James. *How to survive in your native land*. Portsmouth, NH: Boynton/Cook Publishers, 1997.

Holt, John. *Escape from childhood: The needs and rights of children*. Cambridge, MA: Holt Associates, 1995.

—. *Freedom and beyond*. Portsmouth, NH: Boynton/Cook Publishers, 1995.

—. *How children fail*. NY: Addison-Wesley Publishing Co., 1982.

—. *How children learn*. NY: Addison-Wesley Publishing Co., 1997.

—. *Instead of education: Ways to help people do things better*. Boston: Holt Associates, 1976.

—. *Teach your own.* NY: Delacorte Press/Seymour Lawrence, 1981. (Read anything by Holt.)

Kohn, Alfie. *Beyond discipline: From compliance to community.* Alexandria, VA: ASCD, 1996. (Read anything by Kohn.)

—. *No contest: The case against competition, why we lose in our race to win.* Boston: Houghton Mifflin Co., 1992.

—. *Punished by rewards: The trouble with gold stars, incentive plans, A's, praise, and other bribes.* Boston: Houghton Mifflin Company, 1992.

Kotukal, Ronald. *Inside the brain: Revolutionary discoveries of how the mind works.* Kansas City: Andrews and McMeel, Universal Press Syndicate, 1996.

Levinson, Jay Conrad. *Earning money without a job.* NY: Henry Holt and Co., 1991.

Lipsky, Dorothy Kerzner and Alan Gartner. *Beyond separate education: Quality education for all.* Baltimore: Paul H. Brookes Publishing Co., 1989.

Montessori, Maria. *The secret of childhood.* NY: Ballantine Books, 1966.

Nagel, Greta. *The tao of teaching.* NY: Donald I. Fine, Inc., 1994.

Nasaw, David. *Schooled to order: A social history of public schooling in the United States.* NY: Oxford University Press, 1981.

Olson, Lynn. *The school to work revolution: How employers and educators are joining forces to prepare tomorrow's skilled workforce.* Reading, MA: Perseus Books, 1997

Revenson, Tracey A. and Dorothy G. Singer. *A Piaget primer: How a child thinks.* NY: New American Library, 1978.

Wallace, Nancy. *Child's work: Taking children's choices seriously.* Cambridge, MA: Holt Associates, 1990.

Note: A new book, *Designing Classroom Curriculum for Personalized Learning,* will be published in the fall of 2001 by ASCD.

ON BEHAVIOR, RESPONSIBILITY, AND TAKING CONTROL OF OUR LIVES

Beatty, Maura. *Pizza and the art of life management.* Dubuque, IA: Kendall/Hunt Publishing Co., 1996.

Boylan, Michael A. *The power to get in (A step-by-step system to get in anyone's door so you have the chance to make the sale, get the job, present your ideas).* New York: St. Martin's Griffin, 1997.

Covey, Stephen R. *First things first.* NY: Simon and Schuster, 1994.

—. *Principle-centered leadership.* NY: Simon and Schuster, 1991.

—. *The seven habits of highly effective people (Powerful lessons in personal change, restoring the character ethic).* NY: Simon and Schuster, 1989.

Dineen, Tana. *Manufacturing victims: What the psychology industry is doing to people.* Montreal: Robert Davies Publishing, 1996.

Donnellan, Anne M. and Martha R. Leary. *Movement differences and diversity in autism/ mental retardation: Appreciating and accommodating people with communication and behavior challenges.* Madison, WI: DRI Press, 1995.

Glasser, Naomi (ed.). *Control theory in the practice of reality therapy.* NY: Harper & Row, 1989.

Glasser, William. *Control theory: A new explanation of how we control our lives.* NY: Harper and Row, 1985.

—. *Control theory in the classroom.* NY: Harper & Row, 1986.

—. *Reality therapy: A new approach to psychiatry.* NY: Harper & Row, 1990.

Goffman, Erving. *The presentation of self in everyday life.* Woodstock, NY: The Overlook Press, 1973.

Hunt, Morton. *The compassionate beast: What science is discovering about the humane side of humankind.* NY: William Morrow and Company, 1990.

Kaminer, Wendy. *I'm dysfunctional, you're dysfunctional: The recovery movement and other self-help fashions.* NY: Addison-Wesley Publishing Company, 1992.

Lovett, Herbert. *Learning to listen: Positive approaches and people with difficult behavior.* Baltimore: Paul H. Brookes Publishing Company, 1996.

Peck, M. Scott. *Further along the road less traveled: The unending journey toward spiritual growth.* NY:Simon and Schuster, 1993. (Read anything by Peck.)

—. *People of the lie: The hope for healing human evil.* NY: Simon and Schuster, 1983.

—. *The road less traveled: A new psychology of love, traditional values, and spiritual growth.* NY: Simon and Schuster, 1978.

Pine, Arthur Pine. *One door closes, another door opens: Turning your setbacks into comebacks.* NY: Delacorte Press, 1993.

Ryan, Ruth. *Handbook of mental health care for persons with developmental disabilities.* Evergreen, CO: S & B Publishing. [Contact the publisher at 1153 Bergen Park Way #M438, Evergreen, CO 80439, 303-526-5009, 800-856-5007, Fax 303-526-7559, $19.95]

On Community and Leadership

Asante, Shafik. *When spider webs unite: Challenging articles and essays on community, diversity and inclusion.* Toronto: Inclusion Press, 1997.

Berkowitz, Bill. *Community dreams: Ideas for enriching neighborhood and community life.* Impact Publishers, P.O. Box 1094, San Luis Obispo, CA 93406, 1984.

Canfield, Jack and M.V. Hansen. *The aladdin factor.* NY: Berkeley Books, 1995.

Chrislip, David D. and Carl E. Larson. *Collaborative leadership: How citizens and civic leaders can make a difference.* San Francisco: Jossey-Bass Publishers, 1994.

Cohen, Ben and Jerry Greenfield. *Ben & Jerry's double dip: Lead with your values and make money, too.* NY: Simon and Schuster, 1997.

Cowan, John. *The common table: Reflections and meditations on community and spirituality in the workplace.* NY: HarperCollins, 1993.

Etzioni, Amitai. *The spirit of community: The reinvention of American society.* NY: Simon and Schuster, 1993.

Fisher, Roger and William Ury. *Getting to yes: Negotiating agreement without giving in.* NY: Penguin Books, 1981.

Gardner, Howard. *Leading minds: An anatomy of leadership.* NY: BasicBooks, 1995.

Kretzmann, John and John McKnight. *Building communities from the inside out: A path toward finding and mobilizing a community's assets.*Chicago: ACTA Publications, 1993.

McKnight, John. *The careless society: Community and its counterfeits.* New York: BasicBooks, 1996.

McWilliams, John-Roger and Peter McWilliams. *Do it! Let's get off our buts.* Los Angeles: Prelude Press, Inc., 1991.

Oldenburg, Ray. *The great good place (Cafes, coffee shops, community centers, beauty parlors, general stores, bars, hangouts, and how they get you through the day).* NY: Marlowe and Company, 1989.

Peck, M. Scott. *The different drum: Community making and peace.* NY: Simon and Schuster, 1987.

Shafffer, Carolyn R. and Kristin Anundsen. *Creating community anywhere: Finding support and connection in a fragmented world.* NY: Jeremy P. Tarcher, 1993.

Schwartz, David. *Crossing the river: Creating a conceptual revolution in community and disability.* Brookline Books, 1992.

—. *Who cares? Rediscovering community.* NY: Westview Press, 1997.

Wetherow, D. *The whole community catalog.* Manchester, CT: Communitas, Inc., 1992

On Disability and Other Topics

Albrecht, Gary L. *The disability business: Rehabilitation in America.* Newbury Park, CA: Sage Publications, 1992.

Bennett, James T. and Thomas J. DiLorenzo. *Unhealthy charities: Hazardous to your health and wealth.* NY: BasicBooks, 1994.

Callahan, John. *Don't worry, he won't get far on foot: The autobiography of a dangerous man.* NY: Wm. Morrow & Co., 1989.

Charlton, James I. *Nothing about us without us: Disability, oppression, and empowerment.* Berkeley: University of California Press, 1998.

Christensen, Carol and Fazal Rizvi, eds. *Disability and the dilemmas of education and justice.* Buckingham,England: Open University Press, 1996.

Montagu, Ashley. *The elephant man: A study in human dignity.* NY: E. P. Dutton, 1979.

Nolan, Christopher. *Under the eye of the clock: The life story of Christopher Nolan.* NY: St. Martin's Press, 1987.

Percy, Stephen L. *Disability, civil rights, and public policy: The politics of implementation.* Tuscaloosa: The University of Alabama Press, 1989.

Rowan, Carl T. *Dream makers, dream breakers: The world of Justice Thurgood Marshall.* Boston: Little. Brown and Company, 1993.

Shapiro, Joseph P. *No pity: People with disabilities forging a new civil rights movement.* NY: Times Books, 1993.

Shearer, Ann. *Disability: Whose handicap?* Oxford: Basil Blackwell Publishers, Ltd., 1981.

Zola, Irving Kenneth, ed. *Ordinary lives: Voices of disability and disease.* Cambridge: Apple-wood Books, 1982.

INDEX

A

AAMD, AAMR 27, 68, 69
Able-bodied 49, 61
Academics at home 379-388
Accessible
  homes, general 362-371
  mobility at home 356-358
  parking 243
  vans 356-357
ADA 42, 75, 109, 130,
ADD, as label 239
ADHD, as label 239
Adult foster care 535-536
Adults with disabilities 436,
  534-537
Advocacy 271, 273-274
Advocates vs. being parents
  273-274
Alternative education 522
Apology for disability 252
Arc 34
Aristotle 18
Assessments
  assistive technology 320-322
  early childhood 470-472
  IDEA 472
  non-standard 472-482
  special education 468-469
Asset model 256-257, 557
Assistive technology 59-61,
  320-325
  assessments 320-322
  funding for 322-324
  low-tech 325
Augmentative communication
  devices 328-335
Autism
  label 238
  origin of label 66
Awareness presentations
  559-564

B

Barry in blind community
  108-109
Bathroom adaptations 370-372
Bedroom adaptations 367-370
Behavior
  as communication 336-339
  management 341-343
  needs 334-50
Bible 19
Bibs and aprons 365

Bicycle 321
Binet, Alfred 27-28, 29, 30
Birth defect 238
Blatt, Burton 36, 69
Blind community 242
Brain damaged 238
Brown v. Board of Education 39,
  176
Buck v. Bell 31

C

Calvin, John 21
Cardboard bus 112
Castration 19, 21
Centers for Independent Living
  40, 552-553
Cerebral palsy, as label 239
  origin of word 66
Child care facilities
  inclusion in 441-444
  influencing 580-582
Christian influence 19-21, 23
Christianity 19-20, 21-22,
Christmas in Purgatory 36
Chronological age 398-399,
  465
Circle of friends 512-513
Civil Rights Movement 43
Civil War 26-27
Clothing adaptations 376-379
Cognitive disability 238-239
Colonists 22
Communication needs 324-328
  augmentative devices 328-335
  cards 328-332
  facilitated 332-333
  signing 332
Community, defined 391
  everyone is ready 397-400
  inclusion in 391-392, 414-422
  leadership in 579-589
  vs. system 413
Community-based services
  389-390
Community Cafeteria 394
Community teams vs. system
  teams 431-433
Comparisons 226-228
Congenital disability 238
Conventional wisdom 103-132
  of educators 140-41
  of parents in education 142
  questioning 303-304

Cooperation with professionals
  284-288
Court Jesters 19
Crutches 351

D

Day care centers
  inclusion in 441-444
  influencing 580-582
Deaf community 242
Deficit model 47-64, 256-257
Developmental age 29, 226,
  398-399
Developmental delays
  origin of 298-299
Developmental Disabilities Act
  37, 44, 219
Developmental model 211-212,
  398-399
Devil 21, 103
Diapers and toileting 371-376
Dining table adaptations
  364-365
Disability
  body part that works
    differently 59
  invented conditions 69
  irrelevant 394-395
  origin of "problem" 106-107
  social construct 220-221
  tragedy 51
  what it is 49
Disability compensation 23
Disability organizations
  collaboration with others 592
  of the future 589-592
  promoting negative images
    90-100
Disability labels 65-80
  sociopolitical passport 49, 50,
    59
Disability rights movement 35
Disability system
  of the future 593-597
Disabled 236
  defined 234-235
Divine intervention 18
Dix, Dorothea 24
Dobson, James 89
Door adaptations 362-363
Down, John Langdon 66
Down syndrome, as label 239
  origin of label 66

Dream Party 426, 429-431
Dreams 55, 310-313, 427, 429, 438
Dressing skills 377-378
Dwarfism 241

E

Early childhood education 163, 173-192, 438-439, 441-448
  systems change 447-448
  using related services only 445-446
Early intervention 163-173, 192, 438-439, 441
Easel, for reading and writing 386
Eating aids 363-364
  bibs 365
  dining table 364-365
Educable mentally retarded 67
Educating others about disability 259-264, 555-576
Edwards, Bob and sin 97
Electrical adaptations 362
Elizabethan Poor Laws 21
Ellis Island 29
Emotional disorder, as label 239
Employment 547-551
England 21, 23
Environmental adaptations
  bathroom 370-372
  bedroom 367-370
  clothing 376-379
  control units 362
  doors 362-363
  dressing 377-378
  eating aids 363-364
  electrical 362
  kitchen 365-367
Environmental barriers 107-109
Environmental needs
  for behavior 339-341, 342-350
Epilepsy, origin of label 66
Equal Rights Amendment 44
Eugenics 30, 32

F

Facilitated communication 332-333
Family support 599
  vision for the future 600-602
Feeding machine 363
Fighting for rights vs. doing what's right 270
Focus on the Family 89
Foundling hospitals 21
Friendships 423-426

G

Gallaudet, Thomas 25
GED 525, 542
Generic services 413-431
Get-Ready model 110-115
Goddard, H. H. 28-29, 30
Grants 597-599
Greco-Roman societies 18-19, 20, 65, 66
Grief process 47-64
Group homes 532, 534-535

H

Habilitation services 532
Handicapped 236, 264-265
  defined 234
Hawking, Stephen 83
Head Start 174
High expectations 306-307
High school
  certificate of attendance 542
  diploma 533, 542
  finishing 542
Hippocrates 18
Hitler, Adolph 32
Holmes, Oliver Wendell 31
Homeschooling 519-530
Howe, Samuel Gridley 25, 27

I

IDEA 39, 44, 109, 130, 138-139, 163, 453-454
Idiot 27, 28-29, 65, 66
Idiot Cage 20, 103
IEP 173
  Blueprint 482-497, 500, 511
  defined in IDEA 464
  goals and objectives 487-483
  meetings 463
  positive meetings 501-511
  pre-IEP meetings 499-500
  related services 493-496
  team 245, 497
  team per IDEA 497
IFSP 165, 173
Images of people with disabilities 84-91, 555
Imbecile 28-29, 66
Immigration 29
Inclusive education 451-518
  barriers to 142-159
  defined 452
  in IDEA 139, 453-454
  in the system 391
  independent evaluation 480-482
  model of 516-518

Independent living 551-552
Independent living centers 552-553
Independent Living Movement 40-41, 294
Industrial ability 29
Industrial Revolution 23
Infanticide 18, 19, 20, 21, 23, 38
Institutions 24-26, 27, 32, 33, 34, 35, 36, 37, 103
Instructional assistants 148-152, 458-460
Internships 545
Invented conditions 69-70
IPS meetings 513-514
IQ scores 67, 70, 76, 238
  test 27-30, 76
I-Quit role 162
Itard, Jean-Marc Gaspard 24

J

Job carving 540-541, 547-551
Job coaches 535-537
Just-a-Mom role 159-160

K

Kallikak family 28
Kennedy, John F. 36, 37
Kennedy, Robert F. 36
Keyless locks 363
Kindergarten
  entrance criteria 180
Kitchen adaptations 365-367
  eating aids 363-364
Kubler-Ross, Elizabeth 56

L

Labels 65-80
  euphemistic 78-79, 236
  purpose of 49, 71
Learning at home
  history, social studies, geography 387
  reading 380-384
  writing 384-386
Learning disability
  as label 239
Least Restrictive Environment 138-139, 173
Leaving home 551-552
Leprosy 20
Level of disability 66-69, 243
Level of need 68-69
Lewis, Jerry 92, 555
Locke, John 22
Louis-Harris survey 100-101

Low-functioning label 67
Luther, Martin 21

M

Magnifiers 381
Malthus, Thomas 24
Manual wheelchairs 352-355
March of Dimes 33
McServices 394
MDA 92-93
Media 555
  influencing 564-57
  press releases 571-575
Medicaid 59, 323, 538
Medical model 35-36, 47-64,
  317
Mental illness 22, 24
Mental institutions 22, 23, 24
Mental retardation
  environmentally induced 69
  invented condition 69-70
  label 238
Mentors 554
Mobility and positioning needs
  350-362
Montessori, Maria 25
Moral delinquency 22
Moron 28-29, 65
Mother-from-Hell role 161
Motor planning 377
Movies 84-86
Muscular dystrophy, label 239
Myths 81-102

N

National Organization on
  Disability 100
Natural environments 165, 437
Natural lives 393, 400-404,
  414-422, 531
Natural proportions 175, 177
Natural supports 389-390,
  412-413, 427
Nazi Germany 32, 38, 79
Needs
  different perspectives on 315
  using tools for success
    316-320
Negotiation with professionals
  288-292
Neonatalogy 38
Neuro-developmental therapy
  210
Newsletters 575-576
Nightline 87-88
Normal/abnormal 51, 222-225
Normalization 36-37

O

Observation cubicles 20
On Death and Dying 56
Opportunities and experience
  for children 307-308
Oppositional-defiant disorder as
  label 239
Ordinary lives 396
Orthopedic strollers 352
Orthoses 305

P

Paradox 50, 109-110, 130
Paraprofessionals in school
  148-152, 458-460
PARC Case 39
Parent Movement 34, 42
Parent-professional relationships
  268-269, 272
  repairing 276-277
PASS plan 538
PDD, as label 238
Perfection 48
People First Language 233-266,
  557
People First organizations 41,
  553-554
Physical disabilities, label 239
Pilgrims 23
Pinel, Phillippe 22, 24
P.L. 94-142 39, 42, 138-139,
  141, 163
Polio 33
Post-secondary education
  545-547
Power wheelchairs 355-356
Preschool
  church run and ADA 443
  site visits to 443-444
  transition from ECE 442-445
  tuition paid by public school
    446
Press releases 571-575
Prevention 95-97
Privacy, protecting children's
  258-259, 440
Problem of disability
  harmful to children 246
  problem vs. need 250-251,
    255-258
Professional-Parent role
  160-161
Protestants 21
Public education
  crisis in 134, 136
  history of 134-135
Puppet shows 558-559

R

Readiness model 110-115, 180,
  399
Reading, at home   380-384
Reconaissance
  of regular ed classes 463-467
Redefining
  our children 254-255
  ourselves 279-284
Reductionism 51
Reeve, Christopher 555
Reformation, The Protestant 21
Regular ed teachers
  selecting 467-468
Relationships
  with educators 460-462
  repairing 276-277
Renaissance 21
Respite care 120-124, 599
Responsibility (of children)
  308-309, 313-314, 400-403
Retarded, as label 238
Retarding environments 69
Revolutionary War 23, 26
Rivera, Geraldo 37
Roberts, Ed 40-41, 42
Roles, 394
  of children 400, 403-404
  of parents 159-162, 274-275
  of professionals 275-276
Roman Catholic Church 20, 21
Roman Empire 20, 66
Roosevelt, Franklin D. 33
Rousseau, Jean Jacques 22

S

SABE 42
Seating and positioning devices
  359-362
Section 504/Rehab Act 38, 42,
  109
Seguin, Edouard 25, 26
Self-Advocacy Movement 41,
  294
Self-advocacy organizations
  553-554
Self-determination 293-314
  and children 298-314
  and families 295-297
Sensory integration disorder
  as label 239
Sensory training 24
Sequential model 115-118
Service system
  for young adults 537-542
Sheltered workshops 532, 534,
  535
Ship of fools 20

Short stature 241
Sibling associations 297-298
Signing 332
Similarity awareness 559-563
Simulations of disability
    558-559
Singer, Peter 96-97
Sociopolitical passport 48, 50
Special education 104,
        133-162
    alternatives to 515-516
    process 451-452
Special needs 242
    beyond 396
Spina bifida, as label 239
    origin of word 66
Stanford-Binet test 29-30, 76
Sterilization 31, 32, 76,
    95, 536
Straws 408
Strollers, orthopedic 352
Supplemental Security Income
    (SSI) 38, 532, 538
Supreme Court 31, 39
Syracuse University 36
Systems change 267, 589-603

T

Talking vs. communication
    298-301
Teacher's aides 148-152,
    458-460
Teenagers/young adults with
    disabilities 531-554
Telethons 91-93
Terman, Lewis M. 29-30, 76
Therapists
    as consultants 405-406
Therapy 32, 193-216
    alternatives to 407-412
    in public school 455-458
    recreational/hobby 213-214,
        411
    rethinking 404-405
"Tickets" 431
Toileting 371-376
Touched by an Angel 83
Trainable mentally retarded 67
Training schools 25-26,
Truman Show, The 129-130
Tubal ligations 31

U

Unconditional belief 229-230
Unconditional love 309-310
Undesirables 20
Unschooling 519-530
USA Today 87-88

V

Vasectomy 31
Veteran's Administration 22
Veterans with disabilities 23,
    26
Victor, the Wild Boy 24
Virginia 23
Vocational Rehabilitation Act
    31
Vocational rehabilitation
    services 31, 537, 539
Vocational testing 534, 541

W

Walkers, pediatric 351
Walking vs. independent
    mobility 301-303
"What would it take?"
    290-292
Wheelchair accessible
    homes 356-358
    vans 356-357
Wheelchairs 60
    manual 352-355
    power 355-356
When God Doesn't Make Sense
    89
Womens' Movement 43
World War I 30, 31
World War II 33
Wrestling 412
Writing, at home 384-386

Y

Yerkes, Robert M. 30
Young adults/teenagers with
    disabilities 531-544

"Disability is Natural"
The Book, The Video, and More!

Share the philosophy; help others learn a new way of thinking!
Buy for yourself or as gifts for family members, professionals, teachers, and others.

The Book

Disability is Natural:
Revolutionary Common Sense
for Raising Successful
Children with Disabilities

The manual to help children with disabilities lead natural lives! For parents and others who care about kids with disabilities. Item BK-1, $26.95

The Video

Disability is Natural

A five-minute presentation of revolutionary common sense, set to exciting music. Essential viewing for parents, adults and children with disabilities, family members, professionals, educators, and others. Item VT, $19.95

The Newsletter

Disability is Natural

A bi-monthly newsletter featuring creative and practical strategies on inclusion, community, and natural lives for children and adults with disabilities. Timely, important reading for parents, people with disabilities of all ages, and those who care about children or adults with disabilities. Item NL, $16.95/year (six issues)

The T-Shirt

Wear it with pride! The "Disability is Natural" full-color logo is screen printed on the front of a quality 100% pre-shrunk white cotton T-shirt. Adult sizes small, medium, large, and extra-large (order small or medium for children). Item TS, $14.95

The Posters

Two great posters for the home, classroom, or office—for yourself or as gifts for others.

Full-color "Disability is Natural" logo on 16 x 20 inch poster. Item PO-DN, $9.95

"Presume Competence" poster, also 16 x 20 inches, includes the "Disability is Natural" logo. Item PO-PC, $9.95

And more products to come, including books for children and teenagers!

Order Form on Reverse Side

"Disability is Natural" Order Form

Share the philosophy; help others learn a new way of thinking!
Buy for yourself or as gifts for family members, professionals, teachers, and others.
Please inquire about quantity discounts of 20 or more per item.

On the web: www.disabilityisnatural.com   Fax: (719) 687-8114 (credit card orders)
Telephone orders: BraveHeart Press, Toll-free 1-866-948-2222 (credit card orders)
Mail orders: BraveHeart Press, P. O. Box 7245, Woodland Park, CO 80863-7245

Item Code	Item Description (include size for T-shirt)	Price/Each	Quantity	Price

	Sub-Total
Shipping/Handling Charges $5.00 for first item, $2.00 for additional items. Example: one item = $5.00; two or more items $7.00 total. No shipping/handling charges for newsletter. If ordering more than five books, please call for S/H charges. For Canadian orders, add $2.00 to total S/H charges.	**In Colorado add 2.9% tax**
	Shipping and Handling
	TOTAL

____Check or money order enclosed, payable to BraveHeart Press (U.S. funds)

____Charge my   ____Visa   ____MasterCard

   Account #_____ Exp. Date _____

   Name on credit card _____

____Send information about presentations by Kathie Snow.

Name_____

Address_____

   _____

City_____ State _____ Zip _____

Telephone _____ Email _____

"DISABILITY IS NATURAL"
THE BOOK, THE VIDEO, AND MORE!

Share the philosophy; help others learn a new way of thinking!
Buy for yourself or as gifts for family members, professionals, teachers, and others.

The Book

Disability is Natural:
Revolutionary Common Sense
for Raising Successful
Children with Disabilities

The manual to help children with disabilities lead natural lives! For parents and others who care about kids with disabilities. Item BK-1, $26.95

The Video

Disability is Natural

A five-minute presentation of revolutionary common sense, set to exciting music. Essential viewing for parents, adults and children with disabilities, family members, professionals, educators, and others. Item VT, $19.95

The Newsletter

Disability is Natural

A bi-monthly newsletter featuring creative and practical strategies on inclusion, community, and natural lives for children and adults with disabilities. Timely, important reading for parents, people with disabilities of all ages, and those who care about children or adults with disabilities. Item NL, $16.95/year (six issues)

The T-Shirt

Wear it with pride! The "Disability is Natural" full-color logo is screen printed on the front of a quality 100% pre-shrunk white cotton T-shirt. Adult sizes small, medium, large, and extra-large (order small or medium for children). Item TS, $14.95

The Posters

Two great posters for the home, classroom, or office—for yourself or as gifts for others.

Full-color "Disability is Natural" logo on 16 x 20 inch poster. Item PO-DN, $9.95

"Presume Competence" poster, also 16 x 20 inches, includes the "Disability is Natural" logo. Item PO-PC, $9.95

And more products to come,
including books for children and teenagers!

Order Form on Reverse Side

"Disability is Natural" Order Form

Share the philosophy; help others learn a new way of thinking!
Buy for yourself or as gifts for family members, professionals, teachers, and others.
Please inquire about quantity discounts of 20 or more per item.

On the web: www.disabilityisnatural.com   Fax: (719) 687-8114 (credit card orders)
Telephone orders: BraveHeart Press, Toll-free 1-866-948-2222 (credit card orders)
Mail orders: BraveHeart Press, P. O. Box 7245, Woodland Park, CO 80863-7245

Item Code	Item Description (include size for T-shirt)	Price/Each	Quantity	Price

	Sub-Total
Shipping/Handling Charges	**In Colorado add 2.9% tax**
$5.00 for first item, $2.00 for additional items.	
Example: one item = $5.00; two or more items $7.00 total.	**Shipping and Handling**
No shipping/handling charges for newsletter.	
If ordering more than five books, please call for S/H charges.	**TOTAL**
For Canadian orders, add $2.00 to total S/H charges.	

____Check enclosed, payable to BraveHeart Press

____Charge my   ____Visa   ____MasterCard

    Account # _____ Exp. Date _____

    Name on credit card _____

____Send information about presentations by Kathie Snow.

Name _____

Address _____

Address _____

City_____ State_____ Zip_____

Telephone _____ Email _____

"DISABILITY IS NATURAL"
THE BOOK, THE VIDEO, AND MORE!

Share the philosophy; help others learn a new way of thinking!
Buy for yourself or as gifts for family members, professionals, teachers, and others.

The Book

*Disability is Natural:
Revolutionary Common Sense
for Raising Successful
Children with Disabilities*

The manual to help children with disabilities lead natural lives! For parents and others who care about kids with disabilities. Item BK-1, $26.95

The Video

Disability is Natural

A five-minute presentation of revolutionary common sense, set to exciting music. Essential viewing for parents, adults and children with disabilities, family members, professionals, educators, and others. Item VT, $19.95

The Newsletter

Disability is Natural

A bi-monthly newsletter featuring creative and practical strategies on inclusion, community, and natural lives for children and adults with disabilities. Timely, important reading for parents, people with disabilities of all ages, and those who care about children or adults with disabilities. Item NL, $16.95/year (six issues)

The T-Shirt

Wear it with pride! The "Disability is Natural" full-color logo is screen printed on the front of a quality 100% pre-shrunk white cotton T-shirt. Adult sizes small, medium, large, and extra-large (order small or medium for children). Item TS, $14.95

The Posters

Two great posters for the home, classroom, or office—for yourself or as gifts for others.

Full-color "Disability is Natural" logo on 16 x 20 inch poster. Item PO-DN, $9.95

"Presume Competence" poster, also 16 x 20 inches, includes the "Disability is Natural" logo. Item PO-PC, $9.95

And more products to come, including books for children and teenagers!

Order Form on Reverse Side

"Disability is Natural" Order Form

Share the philosophy; help others learn a new way of thinking!
Buy for yourself or as gifts for family members, professionals, teachers, and others.
Please inquire about quantity discounts of 20 or more per item.

On the web: www.disabilityisnatural.com   Fax: (719) 687-8114 (credit card orders)
Telephone orders: BraveHeart Press, Toll-free 1-866-948-2222 (credit card orders)
Mail orders: BraveHeart Press, P. O. Box 7245, Woodland Park, CO 80863-7245

Item Code	Item Description (include size for T-shirt)	Price/Each	Quantity	Price

Shipping/Handling Charges $5.00 for first item, $2.00 for additional items. Example: one item = $5.00; two or more items $7.00 total. No shipping/handling charges for newsletter. If ordering more than five books, please call for S/H charges. For Canadian orders, add $2.00 to total S/H charges.	**Sub-Total**
	In Colorado add 2.9% tax
	Shipping and Handling
	TOTAL

____Check enclosed, payable to BraveHeart Press

____Charge my   ____Visa   ____MasterCard

Account # _____ Exp. Date _____

Name on credit card_____

____Send information about presentations by Kathie Snow.

Name _____

Address _____

Address _____

City_____ State _____ Zip _____

Telephone _____ Email _____